Achieving Supply Chain Excellence Through Technology

volume 2

Achieving Supply Chain Excellence Through Technology

volume 2

The entire contents of this publication are protected by copyright; full details are available from the publisher. All rights reserved. No part of this publication may be reproduced, stored in a retrieval system, or transmitted in any form or by any means – electronic, photocopying, recording or otherwise – without the prior written permission of the copyright holder.

While every effort has been made to ensure the accuracy of the contents of this book, the publisher will accept no responsibility for any errors or omissions, or for any loss or damage, consequential or otherwise, suffered as a result of any material published here.

The publisher assumes no responsibility for statements made by their advertisers in business competition, nor do they assume responsibility for statements/opinions, expressed or implied in the articles of this publication.

The viewpoints expressed in the following articles are those of the authors and do not represent the views of Andersen Consulting or Montgomery Research, Inc. No endorsement, implied or expressed, is made. These articles represent a collection of viewpoints by various parties involved in Supply Chain Management-related activities and are intended to promote discussion in the service of our industry.

This book is available from the publisher at $430.00 per copy plus shipping.

Printed in the U.S.A. ISBN 0-9666413-3-7

Editorial Advisory Board

Dr. David L. Anderson
Dr. Anderson is a managing partner within the Andersen Consulting Supply Chain Practice

Dr. Hau L. Lee
Dr. Lee is the Kleiner Perkins, Mayfield, Sequoia Capital Professor of Management Science and Engineering, and Professor of Operations, Information, and Technology at the Graduate School of Business at Stanford University.

Robert J. Herbold
Mr. Herbold is executive vice president and chief operating officer of Microsoft Corporation

Robert P. Wayman
Mr. Wayman is executive vice president and chief financial officer for Hewlett-Packard Company

George P. Moakley
Mr. Moakley is director, Enterprise Architecture Lab, for Intel Corporation

Andersen Consulting

EDITOR
David L. Anderson

EDITORIAL DIRECTORS
Rachel V. Barere
Mark D. Klinge

Special thanks to Paul A. Basil and Stuart Roach for helping to shape this project.

PUBLISHED BY
Montgomery Research, Inc.
44 Montgomery Street, Suite 3750
San Francisco, CA 94104
Phone 415.397.2400
Fax 415.397.2420
E-mail: ideas@mriresearch.com

©2000 Montgomery Research, Inc.

Montgomery Research, Inc.

CHIEF EXECUTIVE OFFICER
Chris Trayhorn

PUBLISHER
Barry Jacobs

VP BUSINESS DEVELOPMENT
Nick Smith

PUBLISHING DIRECTOR
Anouk Snyder

CONTENT DIRECTOR
Jeff Troiano

PROJECT MANAGER
Melissa Mumbauer

CUSTOMER LIAISON
Christian Muncy

ACCOUNT MANAGERS
Alex Blanchard,
James Cope, Brett Gajda,
Howard Kantor,
Noel Scher

DESIGN CONSULTANTS
Theresa Castro
Frank Doyle

COPY EDITOR
Adam Siegel

PROOFREADER
Judith Carrington

ART DIRECTOR
Sharon Anderson

LAYOUT
Rita Wood

ILLUSTRATOR
Kevin Fox

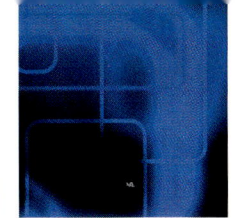

Welcome to ASCET Volume II! We're delighted to offer you a wealth of new information from the leading players shaping the future of the supply chain.

This edition of ASCET is an up-to-the-minute snapshot of the industry, offering troubleshooting, metrics, best practices, and solutions from industry leaders. We're honored to bring together the wisdom and experience of supply chain experts in this virtual seminar; in ASCET Volume II you'll learn about the newest industry trends, as well as how they're being implemented.

When you're done – and admittedly there's a lot to chew on in here – please visit our supply chain portal – www.ASCET.com. The portal offers vertical search and interactive capabilities that pinpoint information critical to business success, strategic partnerships, and collaborative strategies.

We would like to thank Dave Anderson and everyone at Andersen Consulting whose continued guidance and help provide the spark that brings together today's leaders and tomorrow's stars.

We'd also like to thank the editorial panel for their commitment to the project.

We hope to hear from you online, and we invite you to attend our upcoming roundtable forums and interactive channels.

Barry Jacobs
Publisher
Montgomery Research, Inc.

Preface

More than a year ago, Andersen Consulting teamed with Montgomery Research to investigate how companies could achieve supply chain excellence through technology. In capturing the views of the most forward-thinking practitioners, academics, corporations, and system and software companies shaping the future supply chain, we hoped to provide some guidance for those organizations looking not only to raise their supply chain performance levels, but raise the value of their supply chains. We were delighted by the tremendous response we received to the book and Web site ...

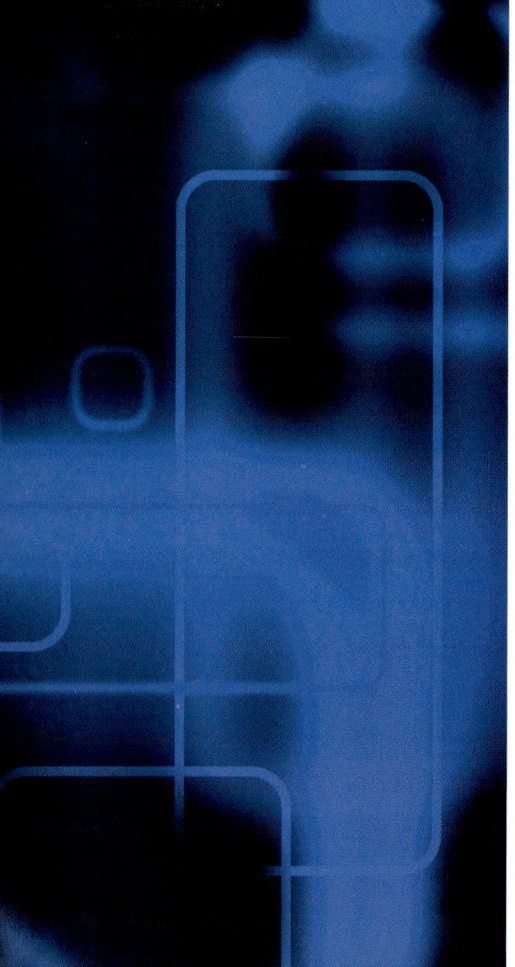

... and as a follow-up, we bring you a more comprehensive book and newly designed Web site. Once again, we investigate the leading innovations in supply chains – from process innovations to enabling technology to tactics for achieving lasting change. We've also added a new section with industry perspectives in which leaders in nearly every industry – including electronics and high tech, entertainment, retail, automotive, natural resources, and consumer products – provide insights and case examples of how technology is enabling breakthrough performance.

From the contributions we received this year, one thing is resoundingly clear: the pace of technological change is tremendous and is being led, of course, by the rapid and continued rise of the Internet. Supply Chain Management is not only a crucial enabler of Internet selling success – cost-effective, higher-service supply chains are the key to competitive advantage for e-tailers and brick and mortar stores alike – but is also being enabled by Internet technology. Companies are getting their first glimpse of the Internet-enabled supply chain and are beginning to see how it will revolutionize supply chain performance. They are finally finding access to the data necessary to better manage the total supply chain from supplier to customer. The Internet provides the common platform on which this data will be shared. More importantly, the Internet-enabled supply chain allows the new levels of collaboration and efficiency that will spell greater performance and value. The new frontier emerging in collaborative processes is in the areas of e-design and e-mediaries. Suppliers and manufacturers are finding new ways to collaborate on the development of new products to shorten the time-to-cash cycle and design supply chain-friendly products. Fewer cross-product components means simpler production and lower costs, and ultimately better service to customers. With the explosion of online

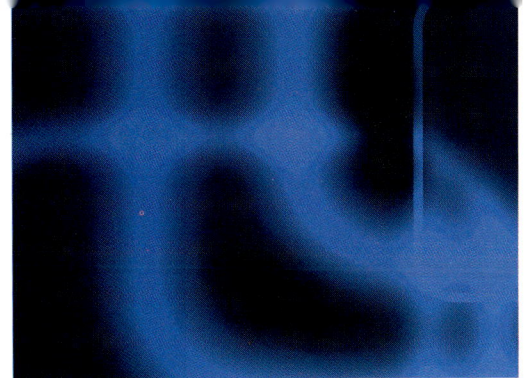

marketplaces, auctions, reverse auctions, and other electronic procurement capabilities, companies are finding new ways not only to cut costs and increase their flexibility, but also new models of collaborating with their trading partners, benefiting all members of the extended supply chain.

The rapidly evolving customer service expectations generated by the e-commerce environment can only be met by superior supply chain performance. To date, there can be little doubt as to the viability of the business-to-consumer e-commerce models. Unfortunately, while companies new and old have made great strides in drawing customers to their online retail Web sites, the fulfillment side has yet to keep pace. In the end, although you can take a "virtual" order over the Internet, you still need to ship physical product. This has placed serious strains on those supply chains that are ill-equipped to meet the response time requirements of near-real-time demand signals. Fortunately, if the access to the customer brought about by the Internet is placing far greater demands on supply chain performance, it is also providing the means to enhance it.

The key success criteria emerging for the Internet-enabled supply chain are centered on acquiring, synthesizing, and communicating supply chain data along the length of the supply chain to achieve synchronization. The articles contained within this book represent the best thinking of academics and business professionals on how this can be achieved – through the careful balance of strategic, technological, and process innovation. On behalf of the partners of the Andersen Consulting Supply Chain Practice, my best wishes for your success in achieving supply chain excellence.

— **David L. Anderson**

The Internet-enabled supply chain allows the new levels of collaboration and efficiency that will spell greater performance and value.

Table of Contents

pg 15 — The Internet-Enabled Supply Chain: From the First Click to the Last Mile
David L. Anderson
Andersen Consulting
Dr. Hau L. Lee
Stanford University

1.0 The Path Forward

pg 21 — Microsoft: Supply Chain and the Automation of Business Process Integration
Bob Herbold
Microsoft Corporation

pg 24 — Peregrine Systems Inc. – The Infrastructure Management Company
Peregrine Systems

pg 27 — Who Will Be the Next Winners in Supply Chain Management?
Bob Wayman
Hewlett-Packard

pg 31 — Retek's retail.com Transforms the Retail Supply Chain by Harnessing the Power of the Internet
Retek Inc.

2.0 Supply Chain Innovations

pg 37 — Supply Chain Synchronizing through Web-Centric Product Content Management
M. Eric Johnson
Dartmouth College, Tuck School of Business

pg 41 — Supply Chain Collaboration: Success in the New Internet Economy
Tom Anthony
PeopleSoft, Inc.

pg 45 — PeopleSoft SCM – Bringing Clarity and E-Business to Complex Supply Chains
PeopleSoft, Inc.

pg 48 — Manugistics – The Intelligent E-Business Decision
Manugistics

pg 51 — Intelligent Commerce and the E-Business Revolution: The Story Continues
Chad Quinn
Manugistics

pg 55 — The Next Generation of B2B E-Commerce: An Interview with Bob Evans
Bob Evans
Aspect Development

pg 57 — Aspect Development – Global Leader in Inbound Supply Chain Management
Aspect Development

pg 58 — viaLink – Optimizing Supply Chain Data Management through Synchronization
viaLink

pg 61 — B2B E-Commerce Comes of Age and Drives Shareholder Value
Christopher Sprague and Bret Kinsella
Andersen Consulting

pg 68 — Walker and Deep E-Business Solutions for the Enterprise
Walker

pg 69 — Dynamic Trading: The Supply Chain Networks that Drive the E-Commerce Revolution
Peter Moore
Andersen Consulting

pg 74 — Teklogix Inc. – Yielding Instant Information from Every Link in the Chain
Teklogix Inc.

pg 76 — TIBCO – The Foundation of the World's E-Business
TIBCO

pg 77	Supply Chain Perspectives from the Business Press *Francis J. Quinn* Supply Chain Management Review *Kevin R. Fitzgerald* Purchasing Magazine *Peter Bradley* Logistics Management & Distribution Report	pg 106	SAP AG – Providing Collaborative Software Solutions for Enterprise Integration SAP AG
		pg 109	Enabling Supply Chain Automation through Information Synchronization *Benjamin Martella* Verano, Inc.
pg 81	ProLogis – The Single Point of Contact for Global Distribution Needs ProLogis	pg 114	Verano – Synchronizing Supply Chain Communications Verano, Inc.
pg 83	The Value Propositions of Business-to-Business Dynamic Commerce *Kyle Appell* Moai *Christopher Brousseau* Andersen Consulting	pg 116	Lawson Software – Self-Evident Applications™ Power E-Procurement Lawson Software
		pg 117	Process-Based Architecture for Back Office: Successful Supply Chain Requires EAI *Dr. Jay Ramanathan* Concentus Technology
pg 92	Moai – Dynamic Commerce Solutions for the New E-conomy Moai		
pg 94	Optum – Supply Chain Execution @ Its Best Optum	pg 119	Concentus Technology Corporation – Process-Driven Software Tools for B2B E-Commerce Concentus Technology
pg 95	Buying and Selling on the Web: Is a Meeting of Technologies Really a Meeting of Minds? *David Dobrin* Benchmarking Partners	pg 121	The Web's Effect on the Service Value Chain *Stephen E. Reiter* ServiceMaster
pg 98	Viewlocity Helps Create Online Trading Communities and Synchronize Supply Chains Viewlocity	pg 128	Commerce One – Leading the World in E-Commerce Solutions Commerce One
		pg 130	Informix Software: Information Infrastructure for Supply Chain Management Informix Software
pg 100	Iron Mountain – Global Leader in Records and Information Management Services Iron Mountain Incorporated	pg 133	TradeMatrix: The New Paradigm of Internet Business *Dave Fischer* i2 Technologies
pg 101	From Supply Chain to Collaborative Commerce Networks: The Next Step in Supply Chain Management *Gordon Anderson* SAP AG		

pg 139	The Promise of Value Chain Optimization *Ted Culotta* Electron Economy		pg 162	Intrepa – The Intelligent Supply Chain Intrepa
pg 143	IMI – Global Fulfillment and Customer Service for E-Commerce Industri-Matematik International		pg 163	E-Commerce: Its Impact on Transportation, Logistics, and Supply Chain Management *Ted Prince* Kleinschmidt Inc.
pg 144	Agile Software – Collaborative Manufacturing Commerce Success Agile Software		pg 167	Channel Strategy as a Value Creator in the Chemical Industry: Shell's Journey *Mark A. Hurley* Shell Chemicals *David S. DuBose* Andersen Consulting
pg 146	Logility – Turning True Collaboration into Business Value Logility			
pg 147	Next Generation Supply Chain: Strategic Planning Technology and Applications *Don Hicks* Llama Soft		pg 170	Calico Commerce – Apply the Art of Selling with the Power of the Web Calico Commerce
pg 151	i2 Technologies – Leading the Way with Intelligent Electronic Business-to-Business Supply Chain Solutions i2 Technologies		pg 171	Europe's 3PL Industry Consolidates on the Road to Pan-European Services *Melvyn Peters* Cranfield School of Management

3.0 Industry Perspectives

			✓ pg 175	Setting New Supply Chain Standards: A Chemicals Industry E-Commerce Case Study *Kenneth M. Smith and Douglass A. Grimm* The Geon Company *Michael S. Sweeney* Andersen Consulting
pg 157	The Future of Automotive Supply Chain: An Interview with Jeff Trimmer *Jeff Trimmer* DaimlerChrysler			
pg 159	Supply Chain Innovation at Harley-Davidson: An Interview with Leroy Zimdars *Leroy Zimdars* Harley Davidson		✓ pg 177	ChemConnect Provides Supply Chain Benefits Today ChemConnect
			✓ pg 178	Categoric Software – Business Alerts System for Event-Driven Supply Chain Categoric Software
pg 161	Fourth Shift – Delivering Complete Care through a Commitment to Success Fourth Shift			

pg 179	**The Race is On for Supply Chain Success** *Jorge Benitez and Bruce Gordon* Andersen Consulting	pg 208	**NONSTOP Solutions – Delivering E-Replenishment to the Pharmaceuticals Industry** NONSTOP Solutions
pg 183	**Making Your Enterprise Internet-Ready: E-Business for the Process Industries** *Fritz Lescher* Aspen Technology, Inc.	pg 209	**Collaborative E-Commerce: Driving E-Commerce in 2000 and Beyond** *Jim Uchneat* Benchmarking Partners
pg 189	**Aspen eSupply Chain Suite Helps Companies Make Faster, Smarter Decisions at all Levels** Aspen Technology, Inc.	pg 213	**Third-Generation E-Business and the Supply Lattice** *George Moakley* Intel Corporation
pg 190	**Essentus – Creating Value at Web Speed for Softgoods Companies** Essentus	pg 216	**Pandesic – Delivering on the Promise of E-Commerce** Pandesic
pg 191	**From Supply Chain to Collaborative Network: Case Studies in the Food Industry** *Bruce Walton and Michael Princi* Andersen Consulting	pg 218	**Compaq's Supply Chain Strategy Weaves a Business Community Fabric** Compaq Computer Corporation
pg 196	**The "e" in Uniteq** Uniteq	pg 221	**Savings Opportunities to the Electronics Industry: An Interview with Derek Lidow** *Derek Lidow* iSuppli
pg 197	**Industry-Wide Internet Initiatives in the Food and Consumer Packaged Goods Industry** *Duane Marvick and Roger Dik* Andersen Consulting	pg 223	**Supply Chain Strategy: Real Options for Doing Business At Internet Speed** *Corey Billington and André Kuper* Hewlett-Packard
pg 203	**Astra Pharmaceuticals and Zeneca: Post-Merger Integration for Procurement** *Min Chang* Andersen Consulting *David Mordia* AstraZeneca	pg 227	**Hewlett-Packard – Enabling Nimble Supply Chains** Hewlett-Packard Company
pg 206	**Sterling Commerce – E-Business Integration Solutions for Supply Chain Management & Optimization** Sterling Commerce	pg 228	**TECSYS – Delivering Software Solutions that Fit. Perfectly. Profitably.** TECSYS Inc.

pg 229	Creating a High-Performance Downstream Petroleum Supply Chain *Don Eichmann* Andersen Consulting	pg 261	The E-Transport Marketplace™ – Logistics Software and Exchange Solutions E-Transport
pg 233	E-Commerce in Energy and Natural Resources: A Dynamic, Challenging Landscape *Barry Jennings* Andersen Consulting	pg 262	Keystone Internet Services – Providing Full-Service E-Commerce Solutions Keystone Internet Services
		pg 263	Evolving E-Business: Not the New Thing, Just the Next Thing *David Cavander* Dechert-Hampe
pg 235	Enabling Technology through Outsourcing *Mark Genereaux* MSAS Supply Chain Solutions Group	pg 268	Datamax – Designing and Manufacturing Thermal Printers for the Bar Code Industry Datamax
pg 237	EMI Music Creates a Hit with Its Supply Chain: An Interview with Mike Frey *Mike Frey* EMI Music	pg 269	Automatic Identification and Data Collection: Scanning into the Future *John M. Hill and Brett Cameron* Datamax
pg 239	Preview Systems Inc. – Enabling Digital Goods E-Commerce Networks Preview Systems, Inc.	pg 273	Fasturn – Transforming Apparel Industry Transactions for Buyers and Sellers Fasturn
pg 241	Streamlining the Printing Supply Chain: A Capabilities-Centric Approach to Technology *Gary Sutula* R.R. Donnelly & Sons *Greg Cudahy* Andersen Consulting	pg 274	A Case Study – VF Corporation Meets IT Integration Needs with NEON's MQSeries Integrator New Era of Networks (NEON)

4.0 Making It Happen

pg 247	Promises Kept – The Challenge of E-Fulfillment *Robert E. Mann* Andersen Consulting
pg 279	Maximizing Supply Chain Value *Kevin Kavanaugh* Ocean Spray Cranberries, Inc. *Paul Matthews* Andersen Consulting
pg 251	Internet Fulfillment: The Next Supply Chain Frontier *Beth Enslow* Descartes Systems Group
pg 258	Descartes Systems Group – A Leader in E-Fulfillment Software Solutions Descartes Systems Group
pg 282	Optimizing the E-Business Supply Chain with Cognos Enterprise Business Intelligence Cognos

pg 283   Leaders of the Web.com: Accelerating the Transition to the Web-Based World
Andrew Berger
Andersen Consulting

pg 287   What About Measuring Supply Chain Performance?
Larry Lapide
AMR Research

pg 298   Robocom's RIMS Warehouse Management System Is an Essential Part of Today's Warehouse
Robocom

pg 299   Business Velocity through E-Supply Chain Excellence
Paul Albright
SeeCommerce

✓ pg 301   Assessing the Value in Your Supply Chain: An Interview with Jeffrey Miller
Jeffrey Miller
Andersen Consulting

pg 303   Are All of Your Trading Partners Worth It to You?
Gary Cokins
ABC Technologies, Inc.

pg 312   webPLAN – E-Business and the CEO's Imperative
webPLAN

pg 313   E-Business and the Supply Chain: Is It Simply supply-chain.com?
John Fontanella
AMR Research

✓ pg 323   The Value of New Planning Systems: An Interview with Narendra Mulani
Narendra Mulani
Andersen Consulting

pg 325   A Quick Start to E-Procurement Savings: An Interview with Charles Findlay
Charles Findlay
Andersen Consulting

pg 327   Increasing Manufacturing Responsiveness in the E-Economy: An Interview with Paul Wimer
Paul Wimer
Andersen Consulting

pg 330   PurchaseSoft E-Procurement Solutions
PurchaseSoft Inc.

pg 331   Performance Simulation: Developing Your People to Build a World-Class Supply Chain
Judith Stimson
Andersen Consulting

pg 335   The E-Supply Chain Reaches Asian Shores
John Gattorna
Andersen Consulting

pg 340   Web-Centric Supply Chain Manufacturing Solutions from Datasweep
Datasweep

pg 341   Netfish Technologies – Orchestrating Business Process Integration
Netfish

pg 342   B2Emarkets – Leading the E-Economy through Strategic E-Sourcing
B2Emarkets

1.0 The Path Forward

Visionary Leaders Discuss the Internet-Enabled Supply Chain

The competitive landscape is ever-changing. In recent years, we have seen the emergence of the Internet and the myriad changes it has generated. The traditional channels used to buy or sell goods and the processes that supported them are being challenged by the new business models leveraging the power of the Internet. Those companies seeking shelter from this whirlwind of change hurry toward certain failure as those that embrace it define new levels of competitive advantage and reap the corresponding rewards.

Speed is the ultimate weapon in the warfare of the e-economy. Speed of getting product to the market, speed to respond to changes in the marketplace and speed of fulfilling customer demand. Speed is invariably linked to the supply chain and the manner in which companies design and execute their supply chains ultimately defines their success. The Internet has provided companies a tremendous new tool with which to enhance the performance of their supply chain and provide a common information platform – whether through collaboration in the design of new product, the planning of material requirements or the rapid shipment in response to an electronic order. Furthermore, it has enabled the creation of Internet marketplaces that bring together a host of customers and suppliers to buy and sell goods far more efficiently than traditional methods would allow.

In this section, three keynote articles explore the emerging Internet-enabled supply chain and how the free flow of information now available through technology is raising the standard of supply chain performance.

> *The Internet has provided companies a tremendous new tool with which to enhance the performance of their supply chain and provide a common information platform – whether through collaboration in the design of new product, the planning of material requirements, or the rapid shipment in response to an electronic order.*

written by:

Dr. David L. Anderson
Andersen Consulting

Dr. Hau L. Lee
Stanford University

http://anderson-d.ASCET.com

The Internet-Enabled Supply Chain: From the "First Click" to the "Last Mile"

How is the supply chain changing amidst the evolution of the information age – or, rather, the revolution in the new economy? The Web offers the supply chain enormous potential and entirely new methods for streamlined coordination between business partners, including third- and fourth-party providers. Companies that want to succeed in the new economy need to enhance communications with their partners and providers. The coming years will see an explosion in e-commerce – with a concomitant need for solutions to satisfy ever more demanding customers.

Supply chains in practically every industry are at the beginning of a startling reinvention triggered by the rise of the Internet. The revolution extends beyond performance improvements and efficiencies gained from automation and communication to include entirely new opportunities to create value. This new value is derived from synchronized supply chains that can reach out to a bigger market, perform mass customization to tailor product and services to meet the individual customers' needs and develop new products and services that adapt to the competitive and environmental needs. The Internet changes the way in which supply chains are managed, planned and controlled. The information, decisions and processes that form Supply Chain Management are moving to the Web, breaking old paradigms of inter-company boundaries. This common ground will be where entire supply chains truly can be synchronized. New upstart specialist providers of both virtual and physical activities will carve out their own unique roles in the new infrastructure. In this churning environment, supply chain capabilities will be crucial. But gaining those vital competitive capabilities will not be through the typical supply chain initiatives of today.

Put simply, the Internet enhances supply chain performance and supply chain is crucial to e-commerce. As the supply chain evolves in the information age, the Web's capability to support tight coordination between business partners means that all the information, transactions, and decisions that are the essence of synchronized supply chains will flow through the Web. Using the Internet to connect the systems of supply chain partners will become the medium through which the essential processes of managing and synchronizing supply chains are carried out. As it does so, it will change the nature of supply chain businesses completely. A company that misses this distinction is in grave danger. It may find itself celebrating the squeezing of supplier margins at auction or the reduction in inbound inventory by sharing forecasts while its competitor builds a tightly linked alliance that shuts it out of the channel to the market completely.

Why is this radical change so certain? It is not that the technology is "cool," nor even that there are efficiencies to be gained. At the heart of the matter are customers' ever increasing demands. Customers – whether they are business customers or individual consumers – are looking beyond cost as the sole arbiter of value. They are demanding innovation and personalization of not only the products but of the associated service and delivery. The increased variety and velocity of business increases the complexity of the supply chain issues exponentially and yet at the same time requires even greater flexibility. The competitive power in this environment will lie with a network of business partners who each bring the specific capabilities to bear. But the supply chain activities of these partners must be tightly synchronized with the demands of the market place. That level of coordination requires not only the ability to com-

Dr. David L. Anderson is a managing partner in the Andersen Consulting Supply Chain Practice. He specializes in supply chain management, logistics strategy, customer service, logistics information systems, and operations outsourcing strategy.

Dr. Hau L. Lee is the Kleiner Perkins, Mayfield, Sequoia Capital Professor of Management Science and Engineering, and Professor of Operations, Information and Technology at the Graduate School of Business at Stanford University. His areas of specialization include Supply Chain Management, global logistics system design, inventory planning, and manufacturing strategy.

More extensive biographies of the authors appear at the completion of this white paper.

http://anderson-d.ASCET.com

municate but also the capability to manage the complexity and immediacy of synchronization.

Supply chains in all industries are encountering new requirements for competition in the e-business environment, characterized by mass customization, massive scalability, faster and more flexible fulfillment and the ability to develop new channels that attract and serve larger customer bases. Traditional supply chain initiatives alone – such as strategic sourcing, contract manufacturing and joint product development – do not sufficiently prepare organizations for eBusiness competition.

How will the Internet-enabled supply chain be different from the traditional supply chain? Many crucial management decisions and processes will take place on the common ground of the Internet rather than within the physical and technical boundaries of a single company. The exact form, role and indeed name of this common ground will vary widely to suit circumstances. A new electronic supply chain information exchange will encompass hubs, auctions and exchanges containing a wealth of not only information but value to customers and suppliers alike. We believe there are four key areas that distinguish the new Internet-enabled supply chain from the traditional supply chain. The first three areas relate to major management processes shifting to or leveraging the Internet. The last area concerns upgrading the performance of physical processes to match the speed and virtual capabilities of the new supply chain.

Weblink

For more on product design, see:
evans.ASCET.com
johnson.ASCET.com

For more on e-mediaries, see:
sprague.ASCET.com
moore.ASCET.com

For more on collaboration, see:
mulani.ASCET.com
anthony.ASCET.com

For more on e-fulfillment, see:
mann.ASCET.com

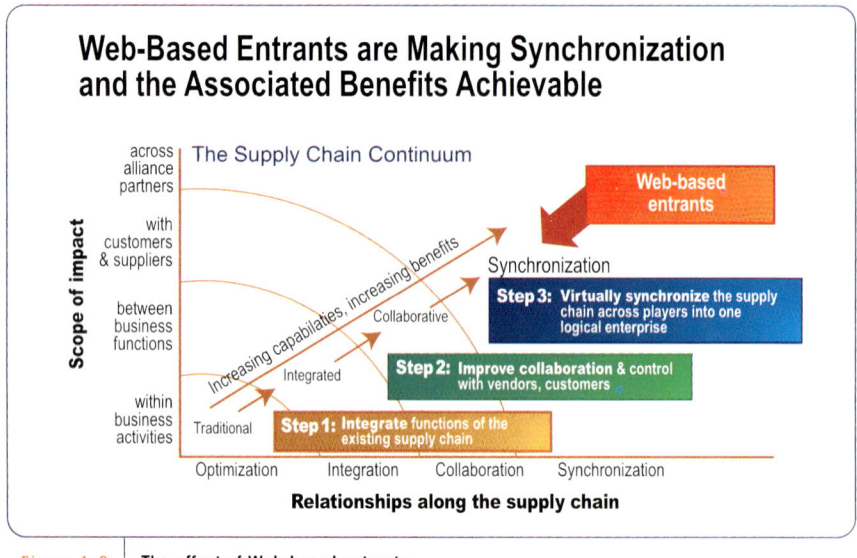

Figure 1.0   The effect of Web-based entrants

eDesign – Product Innovation on the Web

Product technologies are evolving more rapidly than ever, placing substantial pressure on a company's ability to consistently release new innovative products. Traditionally, companies have primarily leveraged internal capabilities and perhaps included a few key suppliers to create new products. But using traditional product data management systems and exchanging engineering data with suppliers during design has been difficult and very limited.

The traditional approach will no longer be enough to continue to compete – shrinking product lifecycles requires that companies partner with customers and a broader range of suppliers to better customize product to customer demands in substantially reduced time-to-market periods. Shorter time-to-market, enabled by collaborative design, is of great value to most companies, since the profit margins in the early part of the product life cycle are greatest and the potential sales gains from being the first to market are tremendous. Internet-enabled technology provides real-time linkages between key suppliers, manufacturers, engineers and marketers. The ability to conduct collaborative design means that companies can iterate many more design alternatives with suppliers. Product upgrades can also be achieved more effortlessly and in a timely manner, enabling companies to stay ahead of their competition. The revenue and profit impacts are thus enormous. Internally, enhanced communication and collaborative processes overcome many of the organization silo issues faced in traditional sequentially oriented design activity. Not only can products be rolled out faster, but the risks of customer needs shifting during development are mitigated. Finally, increased collaboration throughout the design process can minimize product complexities that later drive supply chain inefficiencies and costs in production, logistics and service parts.

Hewlett Packard, for example, is an early example of a company that began using eDesign principles. In the design and production of laser printers, they abandoned the traditional design approach of dedicated teams focused on launch dates, features and functionality. Internal and external design teams collaborated to develop a supply chain friendly product, with modular parts and differentiating components that could be assembled at regional distribution centers rather than multiple dedicated production facilities.

Internet technology is replacing traditional product data management systems as the vehicle to enable collaborative design. National Semiconductor, a leader

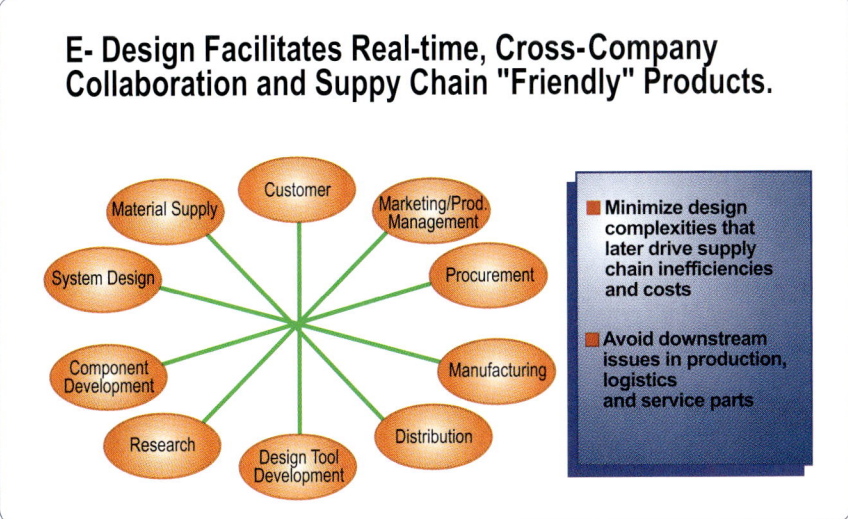

Figure 2.0   E-design facilitates real-time cross-company collaboration.

in the design and manufacture of analog and mixed signal semiconductor products, uses product design portals to allow its customers and supply chain partners to collaborate in the early stages of design for a new circuit. Solectron, a worldwide provider of electronics manufacturing services, uses new Internet technologies to efficiently exchange product information and expedite the engineering change process to reach the market faster. Adaptec, a maker of data transfer/communications hardware and software, has substantially reduced design-to-delivery cycle times and saved $10 million in inventory reductions by using Web-based collaborative design processes with key suppliers in Hong Kong, Japan and Taiwan.

The Internet is also enabling innovative ways to leverage knowledge capital critical to the design process. Yet2.com's Web site brings companies such as Boeing, TRW and Monsanto together to trade intellectual property, saving millions on R & D. For example, DuPont's research and development activities produce 400 patents a year, not all of which are commercially valuable to DuPont. The Yet2.com Web site matches patents to appropriate companies, netting the sellers like DuPont millions in licensing fees and helping the buyers to shortcut unnecessary developments costs and lead-times.

The supply chain can operate more efficiently when producing products designed for cross supply chain disciplines. Collaboration sets this foundation – and reduces the number of potential issues that may arise during the life of the product. Synchronizing product design and supply chain requirements in the early stages of the development process will prepare supply chain partners to efficiently produce and deliver the product in the course of its life cycle.

eMediaries and Exchanges –
Using Online Markets to Revolutionize Buying and Selling

In the traditional supply chain, buying and selling materials means establishing long-term relationships with vendors, distributors and retailers, with multiple inventory sites, long lead-times and fixed margins. Today, the oldest of all business activities – the marketplace – is being reinvented. Companies can now buy and sell across a wide spectrum of emerging Internet-enabled marketplaces.

New examples are being created almost daily, and like traditional marketplaces, trading networks may take many forms. In the supplier-centric model, like W.W. Grainger, sellers provide their catalogs online for all buyers to access. Global companies like BP Amoco are utilizing the buyer-centric model to display their needs online and allow vendors to make bids. The latest development is online marketplaces – the business-to-business equivalent of eBay. These marketplaces are like online bazaars, where anyone can buy or sell all types of goods and services.

Each of these various exchanges provide companies with unique opportunities to tap into performance and cost benefits unavailable prior to the Internet. Regardless of the type of marketplace, the benefits are many: lower product acquisition costs, lower procurement transaction costs, the ability to tap into almost unlimited supply sources to respond to changing market needs, and a means to profitably dispose of unused excess inventory.

The automotive industry is rapidly embracing the value of exchanges. General Motors, a company with an $87 billion annual spend, partnered with CommerceOne to develop TradeXchange. This online marketplace allows suppliers to use custom-designed, Web-enabled applications to conduct real-time transactions with multiple GM organizations including purchasing, finance, engineering, production control, and logistics. GMC expects to save $400 million annually and gain additional revenue from user transaction fees.

Another example is ChemConnect's World Chemical Exchange, which provides a global-neutral market for chemical and plastic manufacturers and buyers. More than 2,500 members, representing 80 percent of the world's top 25 chemical companies, now can conduct round-the-clock trading of chemicals and plastics of all types. This is already a highly competitive field – there are no less than 16 other chemical exchanges.

In each of these cases, technology replaces the middlemen and becomes the mediator between buyers and sellers. These eMediaries can add tremendous value, particularly in the business-to-business marketplace. In fact, BP Amoco Chairman John Browne predicts that 95 percent of BPA's chemical supplies will be purchased online by the end of 2000 leading to a 10-15 percent reduction in over-

http://anderson-d.ASCET.com

all acquisition cost. In some industries – particularly commodity based ones with volatile cost structures or where capacity may go to waste – the advent of an economic method of barter is a great advantage. But the emphasis is less on simply squeezing supplier margins than on providing a free and liquid marketplace.

Solutions from companies like MRO.com, FreeMarkets, Parts.com and PlasticsNet.com provide buyers of all sizes with pricing benefits by employing reverse auction tolls and electronic request-for-quotes. Buyers can access far more suppliers than ever before, and suppliers gain access to new classes of buyers. Clearly, this is an explosive area – this volume of Achieving Supply Chain Excellence Through Technology contains a number of articles exploring the topic. New insights may be gained from articles by Andersen Consulting experts Christopher Sprague and Brett Kinsella, as well as such leading solution providers as Moai Technologies, CommerceOne and PurchaseSoft.

Web-Based Collaborative Planning – the Virtualization of the Supply Chain

Collaborative planning, forecasting and replenishment – a highly visible consumer products industry initiative – has shown the advantages to be gained from business partners who collaborate on planning supply chain activities. This type of development is crushing old paradigms of "ownership" of key strategic, planning and operational information. Traditionally, companies – and departments within companies – keep such crucial information safely in their own databases, on their own servers, and their own staff manipulated it with applications that they themselves owned. This model often results in multiple and competing forecasts and with little use of supplier and customer data, results in a misalignment with demand.

Planning done in collaboration with suppliers, customers and channel partners through open sharing of relevant consumer sales data and material availability focuses on a single forecast shared by all supply chain participants. The significant benefits of sharing information with business part-

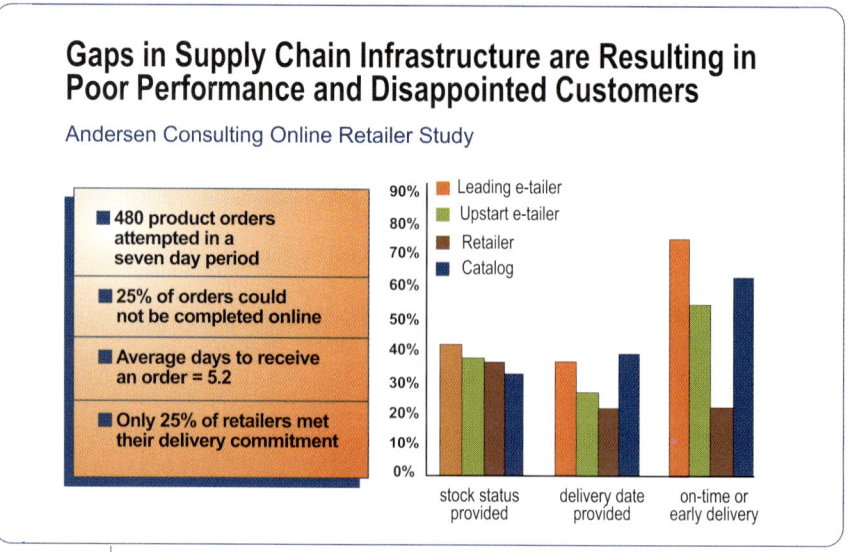

Figure 3.0 The effect of gaps in the supply chain infrastructure

ners are enticing companies to build trust levels and release key information from their direct control. Sun Microsystems is one company that is taking advantage of the collaborative nature of the Internet. They have developed Web-based collaborative planning tools as a way to strengthen strategic relationships with key customers. These tools allow Sun to exchange forecast and product status information with customers on orders, shipments and promotions, and help Sun to manage their products through the entire life cycle. This capability has resulted in substantial reductions in lead times and forecast availability, improved inventory turns, increased customer satisfaction, and more efficient supply chain operations. Sun is just one of many companies in its industry pursuing the benefits of collaborative planning – indeed, the entire industry will make great strides with the RosettaNet initiative to set standards for collaborative planning processes for electronics industry companies.

As companies increasingly collaborate, innovations will move beyond passing information back and forth, and the concept of a shared repository of data will make more sense. The Internet is the logical shared repository. This shift in the sense of ownership drives two other shifts in conventional wisdom. Why should the applications that manipulate the data necessarily be owned by the business partners? Being able to collaborate with business partners across a common technical platform using common applications will alleviate many of the issues of version control, standards and confusion. This will create direct information technology cost savings and build business flexibility into the information technology infrastructure. The final shift will be the consideration that if the data, technical infrastructure and applications do not necessarily have to be owned, why not also have the staff of specialist third-parties assume some of the planning activities?

This sort of Web-based outsourcing is a business model and delivery mechanism for a third-party to provide and manage a common business solution over an electronic network to multiple clients. They would provide entire business processes or application solution sets using the Internet as the medium. A Web host would provide the network services and the hardware and software infrastructure while applications service providers would provide applications and content. Business solution providers will provide the aggregation.

A good example of this model is the partnership between Manugistics Group, Inc. and Freightwise, Inc., a new e-commerce initiative of the Burlington Northern Santa Fe Corporation. Powered by Manugistics' transportation solution, FreightWise offers an online marketplace for buyers and sellers of transportation services and information. FreightWise trading partners will be able to share, view and execute decisions based on real-time information. In effect, the FreightWise Web site will automate transportation and logistics processes by reviewing and selecting the most effective and efficient transportation services across a virtual enterprise. Another example is i2 Technologies' Tradematrix, a dynamic Internet marketplace that provides a one-stop destination for online collaboration and dynamic trading, electronic procurement, spot buying, selling, order fulfillment, logistics services and product design services. TradeMatrix provides an open digital community where customers, partners, suppliers, and service providers gather to conduct business in real-time, enabling companies to make more profitable decisions.

These are just a few examples of an area that is certain to explode with opportunity. Web-based collaborative planning will allow supply chain participants to create a "virtual" store of inventory that each participant can access to satisfy customer needs from any available source. Full knowledge of availability across the supply chain will allow these participants to reduce costs through lower stocks and more efficient shipment planning. By allowing participants to operate supply chains at "eSpeed" through the sharing of production, inventory, product and shipment status, companies can gain competitive advantage by beating others to new customers and markets.

eFulfillment

Matching the Performance of the Physical Activities to the Virtual World

The final capability crucial to success in the Internet-enabled supply chain is not one that will reside on the Web. Rather, the crucial capability is upgrading the physical aspects of the supply chain to match the speed of the virtual world. Demonstrations of the speed and sophistication of the latest technology applications are truly impressive but they paint only half the picture. Will a customer be won through real-time information on product availability be lost when delivery is slow and unreliable? Will a customer be as impressed by the chance to configure their product online if it arrives in a different configuration? Will the online experience be as attractive if the delivery times are no more convenient than travelling to the shops? Will collaborative planning with suppliers make sense absent of confidence in their ability to consistently deliver against fluctuating demand? The primary goal of eFulfillment is the radical reduction of order-to-delivery time to customers.

This reduction requires exceptional supply chain management, not only for new e-commerce ventures, but also for established players who must raise their performance to continue to compete. As evidence, a recent Andersen Consulting study of online holiday purchases highlights some of the issues of operating in the new economy. The study targeted 100 companies that sell products to consumers online. The group included traditional store based retailers with a Web presence, pure online retailers or "eTailers" and catalogers who provided an online order capability. More than one-quarter of Web sites explored could not take orders because they crashed, were blocked or were otherwise inaccessible. Further, traditional retailers with an online presence were only able to give accurate delivery estimates 25 percent of the time. That kind of disappointing performance demonstrates why e-commerce companies are now recognizing the value of the right investments in supply chain capabilities.

The most obvious impact of eCommerce is the heightened requirement to develop a flexible and reliable channel to reach the end consumer – sometimes for deliveries of just a single item. Robert Mann's article addresses some of the challenges of this environment – the next few years will see many companies stretching to create, buy or outsource eFulfillment capabilities.

Theodore Prince, in an article entitled "E-Commerce and Its Impact on Transportation, Logistics and Supply Chain Management," provides an interesting perspective on who among the third-party logistics providers are best positioned to succeed in this environment. And Beth Enslow's article discusses the ways in which companies may turn their logistics operations into high-speed fulfillment networks by leveraging key technologies.

The increasing demands of order-to-delivery are not limited to the business-to-consumer marketplace. As companies collaborate and synchronize their activities more tightly there will be a an ever-increasing value in more flexible and customized distribution channels. For example, Mark Hurley's and David Dubose's article describes how Shell Chemicals reviewed its channel strategy and found many different options to deliver the goods and services to its segmented customer base in a differentiated fashion. And the change does not only apply to logistics. Manufacturing has seen the rise of build-to-order manufacturing as customer demand signals are made more visible by various e-commerce systems. The traditional build-to-stock and build-to-forecast models have become obsolete for some product types because of the massive inventories required to support the ever-constant SKU expansion.

Taking such techniques one step further will lead companies to the assemble-to-order or configure-to-order model where each SKU is produced to the specific configuration of an individual customer. Making this change represents an enormous increase in the complexity of operations, requiring each piece of inventory to be tracked and planned to its eventual customer. But the value proposition to the customer of this mass customization can be significant enough to force this change, especially now that e-commerce can easily capture the customers requirements.

Just as the restructuring of the business models is creating opportunities for new entrants to provide "virtual" services such as marketplaces and exchanges there is also an increased scope for other companies to fulfill new specialized roles in the "physical" execution arena. The advent of the e-economy is pressuring the fulfillment operations of many companies, whether they are shipping small packages to individual consumers or operating tightly synchronized business-to-business transportation. New partnerships are evolving to alleviate these pressures. No matter what industry, or what product, companies will look for innovative ways to continue to reduce order-to-delivery times.

Making it Happen

The message of the Internet-enabled supply chain is that the Internet will not replace Supply Chain Management. Rather, it is an incredible medium that allows supply chain activities to be carried out in a truly synchronized fashion. Internet-enabled tools and solutions will allow development of cost efficient, service effective supply chains. However, speed is the key capability that defines the new supply chain in the Internet age. Speed, cost reductions, and customer service are all impacted by availability. This will be accomplished through better information to manage product flows and reduce inventory. Benefits are further enhanced by greater collaboration between supply chain partners to increase speed and flexibility, and the ability to create entirely new supply chain operations in conjunction with e-mediary deals.

Yet challenges remain. If the new supply chain rule is no longer operating independently, choosing the right partners becomes critical. Integrating supply chain processes and technology across supply chain partners will replace trucks and warehouses as the keys to ongoing competitive advantage. But sharing data and resouces successfully is contingent on trust and openness, issues that still plague many companies. Finally, remember that economics count in overall supply chain design. Electronic commerce will allow competitors to quickly access cheaper products and delivery methods. Consequently, low cost supply chain operations remain critical.

Many companies continue to focus on improving supply chain performance by reducing costs and/or improving customer service. While effective for certain traditional channels and markets, the Internet-enabled supply chain requires a whole new approach to gaining and sustaining competitive advantage. Third-party providers may be used in such areas as call centers, manufacturing, and logistics to set up new channels to reach customers who may disdain traditional channels. Sharing data with supply chain partners provides the information needed to be successful in Supply Chain Management. Without the right data, companies will fail in the new economy. Most importantly, spending time gaining a better understanding of customer needs and focusing on creating experiences that make doing business simpler and easier for them will have tremendous results. The winners in the emerging Internet-enabled supply chain competition will be those companies that discard the traditional rules of doing business while working collaboratively with their customers and supply chain partners to create the future.

About the Authors

Dr. Anderson is a managing partner in the Andersen Consulting Supply Chain Practice. He specializes in Supply Chain Management, logistics strategy, customer service, logistics information systems, and operations outsourcing strategy. Before joining Andersen Consulting, Dr. Anderson was vice president in charge of logistics consulting at Temple, Barker & Sloane, Inc. and a vice president of Data Resources, Inc. where he founded the firm's transportation and logistics consulting practice.

Dr. Anderson is a member of the Institute of Logistics, the Council of Logistics Management, and the Canadian Association of Logistics Management. He is currently serving on the National Science Foundation committee on Surface Freight Transport Regulation and has published numerous articles on supply chain compression, global logistics trends, outsourcing and operations management. He is a member of the Board of Directors of the Northwestern University Center for Transportation Studies and of the Stanford University Supply Chain Forum.

Dr. Hau L. Lee is the Kleiner Perkins, Mayfield, Sequoia Capital Professor of Management Science and Engineering, and Professor of Operations, Information and Technology at the Graduate School of Business at Stanford University. His areas of specialization include Supply Chain Management, global logistics system design, inventory planning, and manufacturing strategy. He is the founding and current Director of the Stanford Global Supply Chain Management Forum, an industry-academic consortium to advance the theory and practice of global supply chain management.

Dr. Lee has published widely in journals such as Management Science, Operations Research, Harvard Business Review, Sloan Management Review, Supply Chain Management Review, IIE Transactions, Interfaces, European J. of Operational Research, and Naval Research Logistics, etc. He has served on the editorial boards of many international journals, and is the current Editor-in-Chief of Management Science.

Dr. Lee has consulted extensively for companies such as Hewlett-Packard Company, BayNetworks, SUN Microsystems, Apple Computer, IBM, General Motors, Xilinx Corp., Andersen Consulting, Eli Lilly and Company, Booz-Allen and Hamilton, Raychem Corp., McKesson, Motorola, and NON-STOP Logistics Company. He has also given executive training workshops on Supply Chain Management and global logistics in Asia, Europe and America. Professor Lee obtained his B.S. degree in Economics and Statistics from the University of Hong Kong, his M.S. degree in Operational Research from the London School of Economics, and his M.S. and Ph.D. degrees in Operations Research from the Wharton School of the University of Pennsylvania.

Microsoft: Supply Chain and the Automation of Business Process Integration

written by:

Bob Herbold
Microsoft
http://herbold.ASCET.com

Integration is crucial in effective Supply Chain Management business applications, and, even more importantly, business processes. The Internet revolution of the past decade has brought real-time integrated business processes within reach of forward-thinking organizations. To this end, streamlining and simplifying the supply chain must occur. Businesses now have fundamentally new computing demands, such as the need to maintain systems (or more systems than before) that are designed from the beginning to run non-stop – 24 hours a day, 365 days a year. One such solution is Microsoft's "BizTalk" XML-enabled business integration process.

Effective Supply Chain Management requires integrated processes. The last 10 years have seen a technological revolution that has offered automated solutions that make Supply Chain Management even more streamlined and efficient than it has ever been. And one key component of Supply Chain Management is integrated business applications.

The integration of applications is extremely difficult. It always has been. But integrating applications is just a means to an end – the real end is integrating business processes. Organizations that wish to thrive in the twenty-first century must do a better job of integrating their processes, not only within their organization, but also between themselves, their partners, and their key customers.

In this new century, the race will go to the swiftest and most efficient. Businesses who have not effectively integrated their processes with applications will find themselves losing competitive steam. The supply chain – including businesses, partners, and customers – must be streamlined.

And it's still not that simple. Business processes need to be automated and integrated more effectively, but that must be within the context of other more tangible business objectives. Organizations must embrace the global marketplace in order to expand the market for their goods and services. While that indeed expands their possible reach, it also introduces fundamentally new computing demands for many – the need to maintain systems (or more systems than before) that are designed from the beginning to run non-stop – 24 hours a day, 365 days a year.

Furthermore, organizations need to reduce cycle times across the board, for physical as well as virtual processes, in order to reduce time to market and deliver against higher customer and partner expectations. Organizations need to make better decisions – and make them faster than before – to outsmart their competitors. They need to create, maintain, and share knowledge more effectively, to identify and capitalize on new business opportunities as well as simply avoid making mistakes that might be avoided. They need to establish and maintain "dynamic business relationships" to streamline producing and providing goods and services to customers.

All of these challenges are about integration and interoperability, making different entities work together.

But guess what? All of your competitors are trying to achieve these same objectives. The distributed computing platform and associated integration services you choose therefore become critical. The goal then is to realize these objectives as cost effectively as possible in the short and long term, with the fastest time to market, because the new market is all about speed. If you don't adapt your business to meet

Robert J. (Bob) Herbold is executive vice president and chief operating officer of Microsoft Corporation, the leading worldwide provider of software for personal computers. He is responsible for worldwide operations at Microsoft, including finance, manufacturing and distribution, information systems, human resources, corporate services, and Microsoft Press. He also oversees Corporate Communications and Corporate Brand and Research, which includes public relations, corporate advertising, market research and marketing issues that cut across the product divisions.

| 1.0 The Path Forward | 2.0 Supply Chain Innovations | 3.0 Industry Perspectives | 4.0 Making It Happen |

The BizTalk Framework

Microsoft has developed and sponsored BizTalk, an industry initiative supported by a wide range of organizations, from technology vendors like SAP and CommerceOne, to technology users like Boeing and BP/Amoco. BizTalk is not a standards body. Instead, it is a community of standards users, with the goal of driving the rapid, consistent adoption of XML to enable e-commerce and application integration.

The BizTalk Framework™, is a set of guidelines for how to publish schemas in XML and how to use XML messages to easily integrate software programs to build rich new solutions. Its design emphasis is to leverage what you have today – existing data models, solutions, and application infrastructure – and adapt it for e-commerce through the use of XML.

Enabled B2B and e-commerce process automation businesses can use BizTalk-Server as a platform on which to build their Business-to-Business e-commerce solutions for:

- Trading partner integration: Web-based or traditional Internet-based electronic data interchange (EDI), supply chain integration, order management, invoicing, and shipping coordination
- Automated procurement: maintenance repair and operations (MRO) pricing and purchasing, order tracking, and government procurement
- Business-to-business portals: trading communities, electronic catalog management, content syndication, post-sale customer management
- Business process integration or exchanges: commerce site-to-enterprise resource planning (ERP), commerce site to legacy, and ERP to ERP integration

For any company engaged in any level of business-to-business integration,

these challenges "on Internet time," you will see yourself lose your customers and key partners to those that do.

What Will It Take?

To make it fundamentally easier to integrate business processes within and between organizations, and to do so in a manner that allows you to accomplish your business objectives at the lowest cost and with the fastest time to market, a number of challenging issues need to be addressed:

- Open standards must exist for business document formats as well as the means for routing these documents between disparate systems.
- Automated and standard transformation and routing services must be available to convert and route data in varying formats.
- A business-oriented tool is needed for creating and managing distributed business processes, as well as specifying business document exchange within them.
- Security must be built-in, allowing communication to be encrypted and digitally signed.
- Simple mechanisms must exist for existing applications as well as new applications to take advantage of these integration services.
- The services must leverage standard Internet transport protocols as well as open data formats in order to work easily between organizations as well as within them.
- The services must be cost effective and accessible to small and medium organizations, as well as large organizations, in order to effectively enable mass market B2B interaction and trading.
- The services must work with the operating systems, transports, and business document formats that you already have in place, in order to minimize the time to market and maximize ROI.

BizTalk Framework

The BizTalk Framework is a set of implementation guidelines that anyone can use, from governments, industry groups, and large international corporations to the smallest of businesses, to define business

data using XML. XML allows the creation of arbitrarily complex tag sets representing any object or idea imaginable. Some very basic conventions are needed in order to promote the use of Extensible Markup Language (XML) in a consistent, interoperable way.

The BizTalk Framework implementation guidelines are documented and available for anyone to use at www.biztalk.org. Since the BizTalk Framework is 100% compliant with the World Wide Web Consortium (W3C) XML 1.0 recommendation, it is operating system, programming model, and programming language-independent; many different applications and platforms are generating and consuming BizTalk documents.

The BizTalk Steering Committee (composed of industry standards organizations, software companies, and multinational corporations) drives the BizTalk Framework; committee members share the collective interest of promoting the open use of XML to provide better interoperability between applications and business processes.

Microsoft also employs industry experts to work closely with relevant standards groups across various industries in order to promote this framework. They work with these industry organizations in order to provide them the tools and framework that allow them to move into the XML world more quickly to the benefit of their constituents. The overall goal of this effort is simply to promote the adoption of XML in various industries for intra-organization and inter-organization application and process integration.

Cross-Industry Investments

The second set of investments represent cross-industry efforts in the form of a community, a globally accessible document library, and many third party products, tools, portals, and services that will support BizTalk.

First, www.BizTalk.org provides a community that allows organizations to learn about XML, access pointers to training, as well as collaborate through newsgroups and other public forums.

> The BizTalk Framework is a set of implementation guidelines that anyone can use, from governments, industry groups, and large international corporations to the smallest of businesses, to define business data using XML.

The second tangible investment is for public libraries to store BizTalk document schemas, allowing organizations to find and reuse these valuable schemas; they may also register themselves as interested parties or users of those schemas so that they may be automatically notified when an update occurs. Furthermore, organizations can also upload their own schemas for use across a set of partners or trading community, or in order to promote a given XML grammar as a tool for solving a specific business challenge.

The third cross-industry effort is to work with partners so that organizations have many choices for products, tools, services, and portals that use BizTalk technology. Many sites promote goods and services online and participate in collaborative or trading communities. For example, there are standard schemas associated with the http://eShop.msn.com shopping portal that allows manufacturers to upload product information in various product categories for consumer comparison and research. In addition, there is a standard schema that merchants can use to represent an offer they wish to extend online for a good or service that they sell. This allows open automation of the promotion efforts by these global merchants by providing a mechanism to promote their goods and services online using open, standard data formats and transports.

Tangible Products

The third set of investments is in tangible products: XML-enabled platforms, development tools, and industrial-strength server applications.

All of the versions of Windows 2000 have full XML support built in. Not only does Windows 2000 support the core XML standard, but it also supports other key XML technologies, such as XML Namespaces, the XML Document Object Model (DOM), XSL, and XML Schema. Internet Explorer 5.0 provides XML support as well.

Development tools build new applications, and adapt existing ones, to provide and consume XML. Tools create valid schemas for use internally or between you and your trading partners. Tools map between various data formats, whether between two XML document formats, or between an XML and non-XML document format, such as EDI or a flat file.

In addition, Microsoft also provides a server product called BizTalk Server 2000. BizTalk Server 2000 will provide the industrial-strength, reliable environment for document transformation and routing in order to facilitate trading partner integration, electronic procurement, B2B portals and extranets, as well as automating value chain processes.

Summary

Integrating distributed business processes is hard work within an organization, and integration is often prohibitively expensive. There are many things that need to be done in order to deliver on the goal of making it fundamentally easier to integrate business processes within and between companies. The BizTalk Initiative is a collective set of investments that Microsoft is making in order to achieve the goal of business process automation independent of operating system, programming model, or programming language.

BizTalk Server provides the right combination of document interchange and transformation capabilities coupled with enhanced trading partner management tools.

Product Features

Microsoft BizTalk Server enables companies to integrate and manage business processes by providing the following infrastructure features:

- Support of complex business process definition, automation, and integration
- Document interchange, business rules-based routing and reliable delivery services
- Application integration adapters for major ERP applications
- Security by means of digital signature and encryption
- Support for existing industry data formats (including XML, HTML, Flat Files, EDI X12, EDIFACT).
- Support for existing industry transport protocols (including HTTP, SMTP, SMIME, FTP, DCOM, MSMQ, SNA, EDI-INT)

The future belongs to organizations that can reach the farthest. Globalization and improved communications have reduced barriers to communication to almost nil. However, only the adoption of common and uniform standards will provide businesses with the cutting edge they need to surpass their competition. BizTalk, and cross-platform standards such as XML, will help make this possible.

http://peregrine.ASCET.com

Peregrine Systems, Inc. – The Infrastructure Management Company

Contact Information

**Peregrine Systems, Inc.
Worldwide Headquarters**

12670 High Bluff Drive
San Diego, CA 92130
Toll Free 800.638.5231
Phone 858.481.5000
Fax: 858.481.1751
www.peregrine.com

For sales information contact:
sales@peregrine.com

John J. Moores
Chairman

Stephen P. Gardner
President and CEO

Douglas S. Powanda
EVP, Worldwide Operations

David A. Farley
SVP, Finance and CFO

William G. Holsten
SVP, Worldwide Professional Services

Frederic B. Luddy
VP, North America R&D, and CTO

Since its founding in 1981, Peregrine Systems, Inc.™ has consistently been a market leader, growing from a solutions-based consulting and customization company to the leader in the Enterprise Service Desk arena in the mid-1990s, to the world's leader in providing Infrastructure Management software and e-infrastructure solutions today.

Our strategy has evolved as the business environment and the needs of our customers have changed. From the mid-1980s to the mid-1990s, our customers were concerned only with computers and IT assets, and operated virtually in a reactive or fire-fighting mode – they were simply solving problems as they occurred. Tool providers dominated the market because there were no established "best practices."

With over 1,100 employees and over $138 million in worldwide revenue as of the end of fiscal 1999, Peregrine Systems is the acknowledged leader in the global Infrastructure Management marketplace.

The Importance of Infrastructure

Organizations use their infrastructure every minute of the day. They use infrastructure to build products, to sell and deliver goods and services, to support their employees, supplies and distributors in the fulfillment of their core business mission. They are changing the way they do business and investing heavily in their infrastructure in order to improve competitive position. All organizations, whether they are a Global 2000 financial services firm, a government agency, or a telecommunications firm, are increasingly dependent on their infrastructure. Whether they are creating new sales channels through the Internet or e-commerce or reorganizing in an effort to maximize the efficiency of their organization, the health of their infrastructure – its computers, networks, telephone systems, buildings, real estate, transportation fleets – can define the organization's success or failure.

New ways of doing business also drive the need for new ways of measuring success. Many organizations have begun evaluating their managers based on Return On Assets (ROA), not just Return On Investment (ROI). But in order for any ROA goal to be meaningful to the business, organizations must know what they own, where it is, how much it costs, how well it is working, and if it is fulfilling their business mission. The growth of Infrastructure Management is being fueled by the promise of greater operational productivity and increased financial asset performance by answering these simple questions.

Peregrine Systems Infrastructure Management solutions address all aspects of an organization's infrastructure – information technology, buildings and real estate assets that house it, transportation fleets that support it, and the people that run it.

True Infrastructure Management provides a discipline that unites these unique aspects to simultaneously achieve two critical goals:

- Maximize the usefulness and availability of the infrastructure to serve the needs of an organization.
- Minimize the investment and expense required to acquire and maintain that infrastructure.

Peregrine Systems Solutions

Peregrine Systems was the first to recognize the importance of providing complete solutions to help organizations proactively manage all aspects of their infrastructure. Peregrine Systems offers a suite of products that allow companies to take control of all aspects of their infrastructure, maximize effectiveness, and ultimately reduce total cost of ownership.

AssetCenter™
AssetCenter is the leading Asset Management solution that dynamically and proactively manages an organization's assets through the entire life cycle from cradle to grave, including procurement, leasing, tracking, and cost-management. AssetCenter helps corporations increase productivity, improve quality of service, and as a result lower total cost of ownership.

FacilityCenter™
FacilityCenter provides tightly integrated solutions for Operations and Maintenance Management, Facility Management, Real Estate Management, and Technology Management.

FleetAnywhere™
FleetAnywhere is a three-tiered, client/server, Windows-based, fleet management software that will help you track your fleet of vehicles and equipment.

Get.It!™
Peregrine Systems Get.It! employee self-service solution for company intranets offers next generation employee self-service applications designed to improve productivity and lower costs.

InfraCenter™ for Workgroups
InfraCenter for Workgroups is a complete Infrastructure Management solution that manages IT assets through their entire lifecycle, from procurement through help desk support to retirement. InfraCenter for Workgroups enables mid-range companies and departments of larger organizations to make informed business decisions to optimize their ROI, increase organizational productivity, and lower the cost of their IT infrastructure.

InfraTools™
InfraTools delivers enterprise level management tools to corporations of all sizes to help manage their IT infrastructure, including service and asset management. InfraTools Remote Control, InfraTools Desktop Discovery, and InfraTools Network Discovery provide the most flexible and robust solutions on the market for graphical remote control, desktop inventory scanning, and network discovery and mapping.

Knowlix™ for Workgroups
If you manage volumes of rapidly changing information to deliver quality support, then you need Peregrine Systems knowledge management solutions. Peregrine Systems Knowlix for Workgroups integrates your workflow and accesses multiple "knowledgebases" at the same time, builds new knowledge real-time, distributes knowledge in many different formats, and measures knowledge usage.

ServiceCenter™
ServiceCenter is an integrated suite of applications designed to help enterprise organizations effectively manage the complex IT environment and reduce the Total Cost of Ownership (TCO). ServiceCenter allows organizations' personnel to be more effective at diagnosing and solving infrastructure problems, effectively managing change, and better manage the costs associated with these activities all while improving the level of service provided.

Worldwide Professional Services
Peregrine Systems provides Professional Services to assist our clients and partners in shortening the time between the purchase of our applications and the realization of business value. We sell applications, but those applications also come with powerful tools that permit them to be tailored to the precise business process or workflow our customers wish to implement. Professional Services offers training, on-site and remote implementation services, and ongoing project management to ensure delivery of complete, fully-adapted, and immediately useful solutions to a trained and prepared customer organization.

Worldwide Customer Support
One of the key metrics monitored by Peregrine Systems is our maintenance contract renewal rate. This metric provides a report card on the value customers derive from our software. For many years, we have enjoyed a remarkably high rate of customer retention versus software industry norms. Our customer support staff, now expanding to an integrated worldwide team, is the primary reason for this successful performance.

Peregrine Systems offers a range of customer support service plans, from the basic Bronze plan to the deluxe Platinum plan, that incorporates components of Professional Services such as training and periodic on-site system analysis all within a single, convenient annual fee. We work with every customer to define the plan and support processes that best meet their needs. Customer Satisfaction is among our highest priorities, and we use our own ServiceCenter products to create a solution that monitors and manages the issues of each of our customers around the globe.

Peregrine Systems Research and Development
Behind all Peregrine Systems products is a world-class Research and Development team. With major locations in San Diego and Paris, the Research and Development team numbers more than 50 full-time staff. The team has energy and enthusiasm to take on major new projects, as well as the experience to understand that our applications are used in business-critical settings and must contribute to our customers' success.

Peregrine Systems uses a mix of proven and advanced technology, from C and relational databases, to C++, Java, and the incorporation of reusable objects. Our products operate on a remarkable assortment of clients, from Web browsers, to Windows, IBM 3270, and many more. The server breadth stretches from Windows NT to all of the major versions of UNIX, to OS/390(MVS) on the mainframe. The scope of our technology reflects the varying computing environments used by our enterprise clients. We always strive to develop products to match our customers' needs, not to suit our preconceptions.

http://peregrine.ASCET.com

Partnerships and Alliances

Providing a complete solution to Infrastructure Management requires integration with many other technologies, applications, and existing databases. To provide both technology and integration skills, Peregrine Systems has formed the Connections Partner Alliance and the Workgroup Connections Partner Alliance.

The Connections Partner Alliance program is specifically designed to provide the most comprehensive set of customer solutions for Infrastructure Management and maximizing IT resources. Connections Partners are classified into two categories – Technology Connections for complementary product vendors, and Solutions Connections for resellers, consultants, outsourcers, and systems integrators.

The Technology Connections program addresses the needs of customers for flexible solutions by providing an opportunity for integrating other leading software products with Peregrine Systems products. The Solution Connections program extends the network of leading integration and consulting partners who provide comprehensive services to Peregrine Systems customers.

The Workgroup Connections Alliance program is specifically designed for Value Added Resellers (VARs) with superior industry knowledge and unrelenting commitment to total customer satisfaction in the middle-market businesses. Workgroup Connections Partners are classified into two categories – Regional VARs with dedicated sales and support teams located in their assigned regions, and National VARs designed to market their product solutions through their nationwide direct sales forces.

Who Will Be the Next Winners in Supply Chain Management?

E-services, trading communities, portals, and value collaboration networks (which we foresee as the next evolutionary step) are changing our view of the business world. This world features a more functional, capable, and vastly extended supply chain. Users within it have convenient access to the information they need to make optimal supply chain decisions, and transactions are transparent to all players trading goods and services. The end result could well be a global, supremely efficient market with as yet unthought-of measures of supply chain and operational excellence.

In the 1980s, the single most important mark of operational excellence for a company, it could be argued, was a healthy bottom line. Finance executives used massive enterprise resource planning systems to achieve the efficiency needed to wring costs and inefficiencies from their companies' business processes and systems. Since the latter part of the 1990s, top-line growth has assumed new status, with competitive advantage won through vision, innovation, and mind share. Increasingly, however, companies are judged heavily on both top and bottom lines. We live in a world of "ands." We need to wring out all the inefficiencies from business processes and systems inside our companies and cut costs, and we have to generate new revenue. We have to show both quarter-over-quarter growth in profits and long-term growth potential. We have to demonstrate operational efficiency and innovation. Investor confidence is very much about whether people believe a company can innovate, make smart decisions, and then capitalize on those decisions to reduce expenses and increase profits.

The next decade, heavily sculpted by the Internet, will redefine what we mean by operational excellence. And one of the key drivers of achieving that excellence will be a company's supply chain. Supply Chain Management – of strategic importance because it reaches into virtually all aspects of a business and because it has profound implications for customer relationship management – will separate the winners from the losers in the years ahead.

Learning from a Major-League Supply Chain Challenge

Customers no longer buy just products. In some sense, they also buy the whole supply chain, basing their purchase decisions on such things as which company is the easiest to do business with, which will ship fastest, and which is the least expensive.

HP, a global company with a diverse product line and more than 110,000 suppliers around the world, may be one of the most complicated supply chains in the world. The company maintains the largest parts database in the world, with 205,565 part numbers across 258 categories of products. Some products are sold exclusively through channels, including computer resellers, retailers, wholesalers, and OEMs. Others are sold direct to both consumers and businesses via HP Shopping Village and HP Business Store, respectively. Managing the channel component alone requires skillful planning.

Manufacturing aspects are equally challenging. HP printers – produced at the rate of one every second – are manufactured through contractors in 13 separate locations worldwide. Cartridges, on the other hand, are manufactured in-house. Managing several outbound distribution flows is made even more difficult by the need to move the final options and choices as close to printer customers as possible.

As for HP's personal computers (PCs), the company has more than 100 separate suppliers and three methods of manufacture. HP uses 11 primary manufacturing sites worldwide, complemented by four secondary sites dedicated to

---

Robert P. Wayman is Executive Vice President of Finance and Administration, and Chief Financial Officer of Hewlett-Packard Company. He is responsible for HP's overall financial activities and for multiple corporate departments, including Corporate Services, Controller, Treasury, Tax, Licensing and Customs, Information Systems, and Real Estate. In addition, Wayman is a member of HP's Executive Council. With a 30-year career beginning in 1969 as a cost accountant, to his 1993 election to the HP Board of Directors, to the present day, he has served HP in many responsible posts. Wayman holds a bachelor's degree in science engineering and a master's degree in business administration from Northwestern University in Evanston, Illinois.

configuring systems to order. Additionally, channel partners at 18 channel assembly sites complete final product configuration. Again, the goal is to move final PC assembly as close to the customer as possible.

Market and competitive pressures also play into supply chain complexity. In the PC business, HP deals with expected seasonal events, such as year-end or holiday shopping and back-to-school. For example, demand for post Thanksgiving Day shopping – one of the busiest, if not the busiest, shopping days of the year – can be unpredictable. For each of the last two years, HP has participated in a sales blitz with Wal-Mart on the day after Thanksgiving. Last year, HP delivered a record number of PC and printer bundles to Wal-Mart for this promotion and sold out in just five hours. HP also deals with unexpected events precipitated by competitors and suppliers. It is not uncommon for competitors to start price wars, for example. Overnight, cost structures can topple. Meanwhile, suppliers can shift to a next-generation microprocessor without warning, immediately rendering a current product obsolete.

Paths to Progress

Considering all the complexities involved, how can any company achieve operational excellence through supply chain? HP uses a two-pronged approach to Supply Chain Management: technology and processes. Each has a key role in optimizing supply chain and customer relationship management systems, allowing the company to work more efficiently, generate new business, and, most of all, help build customer loyalty. Neither part, no matter how well developed or fine-tuned, is useful without the other.

On the technology side, the good news is that, thanks to the Internet, there are now platforms, tools, and solutions that allow partners across an entire supply chain to share information. Rather than having to make totally independent decisions on critical issues such as forecasting, production schedules, inventory levels, and distribution plans, companies can now share information with partners and make the best choices for everyone involved. The tighter the integration of information among the companies, the greater the benefits to all.

As a result of its many supply chain initiatives in demand planning, demand and supply matching, and in distribution and logistics, HP has compressed its supply chain processes from months to just hours, with substantial improvement in reducing inventory and inventory-driven costs. In fact, HP's channel inventory is the lowest in its history, with inventory-driven costs declining by more than 20% each quarter last year.

The second area of supply chain focus at HP comprises the processes that will enable HP to adapt supply to meet demand on a real-time basis around the world. To achieve that, a fast-reaction supply chain is a must.

Success at HP

HP's printer supply chain is just such a chain. HP's manufacturing process combines steady manufacturing in low-tax markets with flexible, local-market manufacturing that allows HP to respond quickly to market demands. For example, HP's Asian factory manufactures products primarily for customers in North America and Europe, more than 80% of HP's worldwide sales. These markets are very dynamic; the product life cycles are very short; and product pricing declines very rapidly. So the company uses the factory in Asia to build products that it knows will sell. This keeps the factory very focused. Meanwhile, the factories in North America and Europe are tuned repeatedly to respond quickly to market changes. This local presence is used as a sort of shock absorber in the event of sudden market shifts. HP attributes much of its success in the printer business to this dual-response manufacturing approach.

In its computer products business, HP assesses daily the supply and demand for parts. The process requires that demand patterns be synchronized to the flow of parts and that parts be moved around the world daily to meet demand. To accomplish this, HP built an organization that monitors the supply chain as a continuum from the customer to the supplier. Within that context, focused teams monitor and manage various aspects of the chain so that sub-parts of the chain can be managed while optimizing the whole.

In both the printer and computer businesses, critical processes are required to create fast-reaction supply chains.

How Does the Internet Strengthen Supply Chain Management?

The Internet has provided a way to connect businesses to one another, thus making supply chains more efficient, but HP sees a world emerging beyond e-business and e-commerce as we know it today. The Internet has fostered rapid advances that will prove essential to the future of supply chains:

- Money can be exchanged
- Information can be shared
- Key business processes are on the Internet

The next step, HP believes, is to catalyze this whole infrastructure so that it can support billions of new devices and trillions of new transactions, and become fundamental to the fabric and economics of business and society. This will be achieved by the mass proliferation of Internet-based services that HP calls e-services.

Think of e-services as assets made available on the Internet. Assets can be applications, computing resources, services, processes, or information. They can

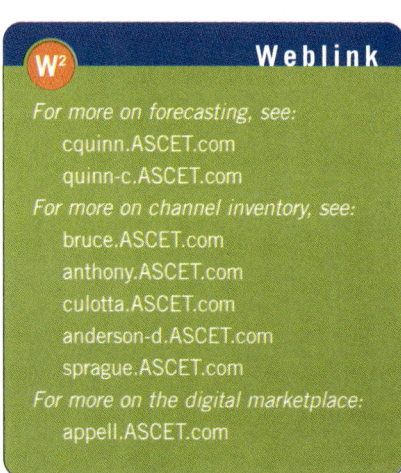

Weblink

For more on forecasting, see:
cquinn.ASCET.com
quinn-c.ASCET.com

For more on channel inventory, see:
bruce.ASCET.com
anthony.ASCET.com
culotta.ASCET.com
anderson-d.ASCET.com
sprague.ASCET.com

For more on the digital marketplace:
appell.ASCET.com

be dynamic and automate transactions without human intervention, complete tasks, or solve problems. As such, e-services can be used by people, applications, businesses, cars, cell phones, equipment, or machinery on the factory floor.

The proliferation of e-services is expected to span all industries. Whole sets of business-to-business e-services are already on the rise, driving new revenue streams and creating new efficiencies in the supply chain. Possibilities already within reach for corporate use include automated billing, automated Supply Chain Management, procurement, and even modular enterprise resource planning. All are expected to be available on the Internet as services that can be subscribed to.

Computing e-services will give companies much more flexibility in the way they manage their Information Technology (IT) infrastructures. These e-services, all available via the Internet, will include such things as MIPS on demand, outsourced storage, directory services, and data mining services.

Consumer e-services – still in their infancy – will, over time, offer the public streamlined financial or vacation planning, home relocation, or traffic routing (many of these services may be available on a pay-as-you-go basis). In the business supply chain realm, users will use services with "utility-like" infrastructures to access information and data resources anywhere on corporate networks. Unlike current corporate intranets and large proprietary e-business and e-commerce systems (to say nothing of their EDI predecessors), these new e-services will be modular and highly accessible to a larger number of users.

Today's Internet typically requires user-initiated transactions; Web sites are accessed from a user's PC. We expect that in the near future e-services will handle entire transactions over an Internet that will be accessible from a variety of devices (some already in existence). The new e-service paradigm is devoted to driving transactions and capturing new revenue streams as opportunities arise.

Many forward-looking companies will also provide a variety of means for their users both to interface with modular e-services and to pay for them. IT infrastructures and e-services may be paid for on a per-usage basis. When will this become reality? Many indicators imply that this revolution has already arrived and will influence how companies will manage IT and business processes, including Supply Chain Management, in the future.

This means that traditional software companies are already beginning to offer their products as a pay-as-you-go service on the Internet. The results promise that companies will be able to lease or rent e-services that do the same job as a large in-house system, including e-mail, procurement, human resources, or enterprise resource planning applications and customer relationship management. Application service providers (ASPs) are at the center of the new enterprise IT architecture. Companies will install these applications on a rental, subscription, or pay-as-you-go basis. By outsourcing as much as possible, companies will be able to free on-staff IT resources and capital to apply to strategic initiatives

Optimizing Supply Chain Management Systems

E-services would also help optimize Supply Chain Management systems to better meet business needs. For example, instead of building expensive in-house systems, businesses would pay for the infrastructure and application e-services they needed over the Internet when they needed them. Businesses could realize an almost instant return on investment because systems would scale quickly by adding capacity on demand, and new functionality could be added on a modular basis.

Dynamically brokered e-services could help businesses meet thousands, if not millions, of new customers or trading partners. In addition, business intelligence e-services, such as data mining, can provide the real-time information needed to help meet customer and partner needs better than the competition.

Intelligent e-services can integrate systems dynamically and make business operations more efficient – no more isolated islands of data.

Here's an example of how e-services can optimize supply chain interactions: If one of a manufacturer's distribution points is short of inventory, an intelligent e-service can select another ship-from location. But it can go even further than that. It can consider not only the location, but also the current weather conditions. If the closest alternative is snowed in, for example, it can order from a more distant shipping point with good weather. This e-service considers both structured data, such as distances, and unstructured data, such as weather maps.

E-services can also benefit the supply chains that nonprofit organizations use. For example, HP has sponsored an innovative way to distribute surplus food to charities. ResourceLink is an Internet-based collection of e-services that connects companies that have food to donate with the homeless shelters and disaster-response centers that need it. One of ResourceLink's e-services even lines up transportation companies that have extra cargo space so they speed delivery of donated items.

The Rise of Next-Generation Trading Communities

The next major evolution of business-to-business e-commerce is a new digital marketplace – portals, which can be catego-

> *E-services are assets made available on the Internet. Assets can be applications, computing resources, services, processes, or information.*

http://wayman.ASCET.com 29

rized as either horizontal or vertical. Horizontal portals, or functional hubs, automate business processes like human resources, accounting or procurement across different industries. Vertical portals or hubs are designed to serve as trading communities for buyers and sellers in specific industries.

For example, PlasticsNet is billed as the trading post for the 5,000 suppliers and 18,000 buyers that make up the $370 billion plastics industry. e-Steel specializes in matching buyers and sellers of steel.

VerticalNet is helping nearly 50 different vertical industries create their own content-driven communities, with a goal of moving toward facilitating trading in those communities.

According to a recent cover story in *Business* 2.0 magazine, these new digital marketplaces create value by aggregating buyers and sellers, creating marketplace liquidity, providing a critical mass of buyers and sellers, and reducing transaction costs. By 2002, online exchanges are expected to account for 29% or $129 billion of the $446 billion Internet economy. Business-to-business exchanges are expected to account for $88 billion of the proceeds.

HP is helping to fuel the creation of a number of these new trading communities, many of which are optimized around supply chain integration.

Trading community participants gain valuable information and capabilities that enhance their planning and execution activities, including the following:

- Forecasting of customer demand through complex, multi-tier channels
- Real-time collaboration with trading partners and their customers
- Fulfillment and delivery of complex, multi-vendor orders
- Ability to comparison-shop across vendors
- Complete visibility into order status

These trading communities are beginning to use a variety of transaction models or brokering mechanisms to mediate transactions between participants. These models range from fixed-price mechanisms, typical of catalog purchasing, to dynamic pricing mechanisms such as auctions, exchanges, or barter.

The online listing or catalogue model simply creates value by aggregating buyers and suppliers in one place. It's ideal in situations where demand is predictable and prices don't fluctuate much or very often.

The auction or bid model works best for industries where non-standard or perishable products or services are bought or sold. For example, iMark.com uses an auction model to sell used capital equipment, and AdAuction.com auctions perishable goods online and print advertising inventory.

The auction model also works well in industries where demand and prices are volatile and businesses are looking for ways to manage excess supply and peak-load demand. PaperDeals.com is a marketplace where paper mills can unload excess inventory or slow-moving paper stock to commercial printers.

One of the biggest benefits of these dynamic marketplaces, or online auctions, is that they allow businesses to sell excess inventory to their distributors, resellers, or corporate accounts. Companies can choose to participate in auctions only occasionally, or they can work with market-makers and brokers to actively manage all aspects of their supply chain. The implications of this are many. Buying and selling would not be based solely on price, but also on the basis of terms and conditions, warranties, or any number of business factors.

Real Options Theory

E-business exchanges facilitate the real-life manifestation of a revolutionary concept: real options theory. In a recent *Business Week* story, the reporter wrote that real options theory essentially boils down to this: When the future is highly uncertain, it pays to have a broad range of options.

HP experimented with applied real options theory in the early 1990s; this was a response to the 1980s process of customizing inkjet printers for foreign markets at the factory, then shipping them in finished form to warehouses. While customizing at the factory was cheaper than doing it in the field, demand forecasts often prompted the production of too many printers for France and not enough for Germany, or vice versa.

The solution was to ship partially assembled printers to the warehouse and have them customized there. While customization costs for HP have risen, matching supply and demand still saves $3 million a month. HP has carried out other real options theory applications in excess inventory management, channel management, logistics, and the buying and selling of components. In some cases, dynamic pricing models have enabled HP to trim total inventory costs by as much as 20 to 30%.

Over time, these dynamic trading marketplaces will add e-services such as payment processing, receivables management, credit analysis, shipping, logistics tracking, fulfillment services, warehousing, inspection, and risk mitigation services such as escrow and warranties. They will essentially help to manage all of the critical components of the supply chain.

E-services, trading communities, portals, and value collaboration networks (which we foresee as the next evolutionary step) are changing our view of the business world. This world features a more functional, capable, and vastly extended supply chain. Users within it have convenient access to the information they need to make optimal supply chain decisions, and transactions are transparent to all players trading goods and services. The end result could well be a global, supremely efficient market with as yet unthought-of measures of supply chain and operational excellence.

Retek's retail.com Transforms the Supply Chain by Harnessing the Power of the Internet

It's 9 a.m., August 23rd. The GMM wants to review the buy, the design team needs feedback on a new concept, the CFO has asked for revised sales projections, quality control needs to have new goods inspected in the warehouse, the customs broker still can't release those goods for the back-to-school promotion, and you have two vendors waiting to see you and POs to approve. And on top of it all, you're supposed to be in touch with what's happening in the rest of the retail world.

Just another typical day in the life of a retailer. The challenges retailers face have always been complex. The industry, by definition, is defined by constant change and multi-faceted processes. In order to get the right product in the right place at the right time for the right price, retailers must rely on clear communication and the collaboration of others through a fully integrated global supply chain.

The goal of effective Supply Chain Management is efficiency – a simple concept, yet amazingly difficult to actualize. When it comes to the retail supply chain, logistic providers and software vendors alike have long promised to help their clients realize this goal. Ultimately, their efforts have been stymied by an inability to remove complications inherent in the supply chain. The end result of their endeavors, while a measured improvement over past techniques, was not the quantum leap retailers and their suppliers needed to remain competitive.

The Quantum Leap: A Real-Time, Collaborative Culture Created by retail.com

If there were some way to increase communication, visibility, and accountability between all members of the supply chain – some means to create a "single version of the truth" – the impact could be immediate and staggering. Such a solution once seemed lost in the complex nature of the supply chain; however, recent innovations have redefined how retail business will be conducted in the future.

By harnessing the power of the Internet to seamlessly connect retailers with their trading partners in the supply chain, retail.com – powered by Retek – creates that quantum leap retailers have been waiting for. With one simple click, retail.com bridges the divide between vision and results. Retailers can now get the information they need to make critical decisions and take actions quickly, securely, and affordably. As the premier business-to-business retail Web source, retail.com transforms the supply chain from a complicated series of phone calls, faxes, post-its, and plane trips to a dynamic, transparent, and highly collaborative network.

Retek's retail.com is the new infrastructure for the retail supply chain, helping the retail community achieve higher standards of timeliness, accuracy, and productivity.

Retail.com: The New Infrastructure for the Retail Supply Chain

Retail.com solutions are designed to improve core retail processes – from assortment development and merchandise planning to sourcing, purchasing, P.O. tracking, store openings, and promotions – by linking retailers and trading partners together through the Web. As the retail supply chain is complex, retail.com groups its online services (called "e-services") into six categories of solutions.

Buying Solutions

With retail.com, retailers can now source production in a revolutionary new way that produces immediate cost savings through improved control and access to the world's best resources. By taking

Contact Information

John Buchanan
Chairman and CEO

Gordon Masson
President

John L. Goedert
SVP, Research and Development

Gregory A. Effertz
VP, Finance and Administration, CFO, Treasurer, and Secretary

David A. J. Bagley
VP, Product Strategy and Marketing

Retek Headquarters
Midwest Plaza
801 Nicollet Mall, 11th Floor
Minneapolis, MN 55402
Phone 612.630.5700
Fax 612.630.5710
www.retek.com

http://retek.ASCET.com

full advantage of the Internet, retail.com's Buying Solutions help merchants move faster while bringing suppliers and business partners closer through a collaborative and dynamic exchange. For example, retail.com Private Label Exchange (one of our Buying Solutions) enables retailers to make direct purchases from suppliers, seek competitive bids for desired products, and participate in online solutions.

Production and Design Solutions
Retailers can also reduce the time it takes to produce designs, deliver products, and coordinate events through retail.com's Production and Design Solutions. By linking retailers and partners via the Web, these solutions dramatically improve collaboration throughout the entire design and production lifecyle. One e-service, retail.com Design, makes it possible for entire product ranges to be conceived, developed, and finalized online in a highly visual environment. Once product designs have been finalized and orders are placed, retail.com WebTrack (another e-service; see case study) can be coupled with monitor purchase orders. This particular e-service helps retailers and partners keep events on track, avoid delays, and accelerate the movement of merchandise throughout the supply chain.

Logistics Solutions
With retail.com Logistics Solutions, retailers can control costs, optimize the flow of goods, and monitor every aspect of domestic and international logistics. As with all retail.com solutions, Logistics Solutions are Web-based and allow for instant communication throughout the supply chain so retailers can receive up-to-the minute availability of cargo and space worldwide – while also negotiating directly in a real-time market. Additionally, due to our alliance with Celarix™, retailers can determine the actual landed cost of merchandise, coordinate freight payments, and perform detailed logistics analyses with the Celarix™ Transportation Exchange.

Selling Solutions
With retail.com Selling Solutions, the focus is on selling. Retailers can increase inventory turn and free up open-to-buy (OTB) quicker by marketing to the specific needs of customers. Web-based Selling Solutions allow retailers to continually analyze the competitive landscape so as to maintain margins and brand equity. One of our solutions, retail.com Surplus Auction, allows retailers to eliminate excess merchandise. By providing consolidated merchandising lists, "smart" notification of relevant auctions, and access to going market rates for applicable goods, retail.com Surplus Auction offers retailers complete visibility to demand, pricing, and availability. As an added benefit, retail.com also acts as a neutral partner, ensuring auctions are truly competitive.

Support Solutions
In addition to supporting the flow of merchandise through the retail supply chain, retail.com offers Support Services that aggressively address a variety of other vital retail functions. One such function? Data integration. To securely synchronize a retailer's in-office data (from existing software) with retail.com e-services, retail.com offers retail.com Integrator. Easy to install, this e-service helps reduce maintenance, eliminates double entry, and increases overall efficiency.

Planning Solutions
Retail.com Planning Solutions help retailers maintain and increase gross margins, predict and react more quickly to changing customer needs, and make better buying decisions – all through better planning.

These solutions give retailers and their trading partners the collaborative tools needed to plan at all levels – from high-level plans to lower level assortment and key item plans. Through better planning, an optimal mix of merchandise for customers can be achieved. Within this solution category, watch for our next e-service, retail.com TopPlan.

Retail.com: e-Services
As indicated, each retail.com solution offers a myriad of e-services. The following describes in more detail three specific e-services. For an in-depth description, log on to our Web site: www.retail.com.

Figure 1.0 retail.com – The place to do business on the Internet

Retail.com WebTrack
Retail.com WebTrack is an event management tool brings transparency and utility to an otherwise obscure and cumbersome process. By creating a collaborative "event track," WebTrack simplifies and illuminates the supply chain – facilitating real-time information exchange and complete visibility to all pertinent activity within the supply chain. WebTrack essentially shortens the supply chain, allowing retailers to cut lead times and be more responsive to their customers.

With a library of pre-constructed templates, retail.com WebTrack assists retailers and their partners by tying together multiple events, times, and people into a more manageable – linear, yet dynamic – process. With intelligent alert management features, WebTrack also ensures that deadlines are met and exceptions are recognized before problems arise.

Retail.com Design
While much is made of the physical supply chain, today's retailers understand that the information supply chain is just as critical to their business. Like its corporeal counterpart, the information supply chain relies on effective collaboration to drive true value from its processes. retail.com

Figure 2.0 — retail.com's highly visual design

database and accessed via the Web by everyone in the supply chain.

Retail.com Assort

Developing the optimal mix of merchandise for customers – buying the right product in the right quantity for the right space constraints – is the focus of retail.com Assort. A living and breathing tool that becomes more refined as decisions are finalized, retail.com Assort helps retailers establish the breadth and depth of their product assortment while collaborating with others via the Web.

Retail.com: News and Resources

In addition to providing retailers with a variety of e-services for improving their retail infrastructure, retail.com also recognizes a retailer's need to obtain the latest retail news and trends for timely decision-making. Through our News and Resources, retail.com provides a central database of up-to-date, retail-specific content. From designer interviews and analysts' predictions to daily news feeds and trade show calendars, retail.com News and Resources provides retailers with all the retail buzz – from what's hip and new to what's selling and where.

In order to present this content in an easily accessible manner, retail.com also offers what's called an Intelligence Center. This Center acts as a customizable home page. Alerts or analyses from the various e-services can all be directed to this page, which can then be linked to a retailer's pager, cell phone, fax, PDA, or e-mail for easy access. Specific retail news and trends can also be screened and funneled to the Intelligence Center so that information is pertinent to a retailer's particular needs and requirements.

Retail.com: Powered by Retek

Retek is the leading provider of Web-architected software for the global retail industry. The applications provided by Retek support key retail operations and business intelligence requirements for fashion, specialty, department store, mass merchant, grocery, convenience store, drugstore, and electronic retailers throughout the world. By providing retailers with proven multi-channel retailing solutions, Retek has become the standard for success in the retail industry.

Design brings an unparalleled level of collaboration to product conception, design and development.

With our highly visual Design Development Area, retail.com design allows retailers to get early feedback on design, color, labeling, packaging, or costing. Images, spreadsheets, text, and other product information can be placed in a central

---

Storehouse and retail.com: One of Many Client Success Stories

Storehouse, a leading retail chain with revenues of more than £1.3 billion ($2.134 billion) generated though 494 stores in the UK and 248 overseas, is one of retail.com's client success stories.

In 1997, this clothing and homeware giant wanted to improve their on-time product availability. Basically, they wanted to take a hard look at their own internal processes (including their network of international suppliers) and figure out why deliveries had been late. So they hooked up with retail.com and subscribed to our first e-service, WebTrack. WebTrack uses the Internet to track critical paths (multiple events, people, places, and times) through the retail supply chain and provide a common basis for evaluating and managing availability levels.

During the planning period, the user team recognized that every Storehouse buyer for every department had a different spread sheet or paper-based system for tracking the development of critical paths. Without a common method, it was difficult to know what products were late and why.

WebTrack brought these decentralized processes together, creating a common database for order tracking. By sharing information in real-time, buyers and suppliers could create realistic critical paths using common electronic templates. WebTrack's alert system also kept everyone updated, so that problems were quickly detected and resolved. And, over time, greater understanding of lead times was developed, thus creating an easier, smoother supply chain operation.

As for hard, measurable results? With retail.com WebTrack, Storehouse slashed lead times within its supply chain by up to 50%. This, in turn, helped Storehouse reduce lost sales and stock outs, increase buyer productivity, enhance vendor relationships, provide for rapid ROI, and improve customer relationships.

http://retek.ASCET.com

2.0 Supply Chain Innovations

Changing the Rules: Collaborative Supply Chains in the E-Econony

Innovation is the cornerstone to progress. The innovative technologies employed on many fronts of the supply chain represent an unprecedented opportunity for executives to reap greater efficiencies and competitive advantage. These advancements include: the Internet as a channel for global and instantaneous communication, the continued development of evermore powerful optimization and planning software and innovations in tracking technologies that lay the foundation for real-time management of supply chain activities. In addition, the technology has created an environment in which new business models such as electronic trading networks can grow.

While the advances in technology have certainly had a profound impact on the ability to better execute supply chain processes, innovation can also be found in the processes themselves. Whether making enhancements to existing processes or designing new processes supporting entirely new business models, new ways of executing supply chain activities continue to abound. In fact, it is easy to lose sight of the opportunities for process improvements when executives are confronted with an increasingly dazzling array of technology. It is the marriage of collaborative processes with enabling technology that drives greater capability and increased benefits.

The insights and creative energies of academics and business professionals are shared in the following section, which discusses a wide spectrum of supply chain innovations available to practitioners today.

> **Whether making enhancements to existing processes or designing new processes supporting entirely new business models, new ways of executing supply chain activities continue to abound.**

Supply Chain Synchronizing Through Web-Centric Product Content Management

In the drive to improve supply chain performance, managers in diverse industries have achieved substantial gains by sharing information. Much of the excitement has focused on making inventory and product movement data transparent throughout the supply chain. More recently, companies have also found that sharing information related to market intelligence and promotional plans can dramatically improve forecasting, smoothing the replenishment process. Yet with so much energy focused on inventory and sales data, relatively little attention has been given to sharing information about the product itself. This is about to change! What started as a move by manufacturers to automate the engineering change process is now being fueled by initiatives throughout the supply chain, from trading exchanges to third-party logistics providers.

Introduction

Over the past two years, manufacturing firms in many high-paced industries like computers and electronics have begun to realize that synchronizing material flow and demand signals alone will not eliminate bullwhip inefficiencies. To tame the bullwhip, they also need product content synchronization. To understand why, imagine a tightly coupled supply chain where inventory and sales data traveled instantly to all partners, allowing material to be quickly pulled from suppliers and manufacturers through distribution and to the final customer. Orders arrived on time and in the correct quantities, but the products were assembled to specification from an obsolete revision, or worse yet, they contained components from inferior vendors causing system conflicts or quality defects. Scrambling to rework defective products, other orders fell behind and delivery performance suffered while millions of dollars of supply chain losses were incurred through write-offs of obsolete products and components. While synchronizing material flow and demand is a key element in effective Supply Chain Management, maintaining up-to-date product content information across the supply chain is equally important.

Managing Product Content

Product content information is all the data needed to manufacture a product to the correct specifications and at the most recent release. This includes such details as the bill of materials, drawings, lists of approved manufacturers for each component, and process information needed by manufacturing to build and test a quality product. Typically, bills of materials (BOM), which are lists of parts and sub-assemblies that make up a product, are arranged in a hierarchical format. For example, at the highest level is the final product. The next level of the BOM consists of major sub-assemblies followed by the smaller assemblies and components that make up each sub-assembly. Accuracy of this information is critical for procurement to buy the correct parts and manufacturing to assemble the right product.

The need for product content synchronization has exploded as industry after industry disintegrates into a string of outsourced services coordinated by virtual manufacturers. In firms where marketing, R&D, procurement, manufacturing, and distribution are co-located on a single site, synchronization (and collaboration) can occur without good information management. In

---

written by:

M. Eric Johnson
Tuck School of Business
Dartmouth College
http://johnson.ASCET.com

From 1991 through 1999, M. Eric Johnson was Associate Professor of Operations Management at the Graduate School of Management at Vanderbilt University. His expertise is in Supply Chain Management, manufacturing logistics, and high-tech industries and toys.

He has consulted with Pepsi-Cola Co., Fleetguard, Andersen Consulting, Service Merchandise, Ford, and others.

He has been at Tuck since 1999.

the early idea stages of a product, designers can propose ideas over coffee with colleagues in marketing and manufacturing. During a new product introduction, manufacturing engineers can stroll down to R&D whenever questions arise. When changes occur in the design or sourcing of material, development and procurement specialists can run downstairs to the shop floor to be sure the changes are understood and will not create production conflicts.

However, today few companies have such control over their products. More likely, designers are in Boston, assembly is outsourced to Southeast Asia, components are procured from an array of global firms, and distribution is handled by third-party providers who not only fulfill orders but also customize the products for unique customer needs. For OEM manufacturers, product licensees each have their own unique design needs, marketing issues, and distribution requirements. Each partner in the chain must, at a minimum, have accurate, current product content information. Yet in many supply chains, critical product content information is often transferred in a hodgepodge of drawings, CAD files, spreadsheets, and text documents. Poorly managed product content information is a key source of supply chain headaches.

For example, consider WebTV, who designs, manufactures, and distributes TV set-top boxes that allow customers to use their televisions to surf the Web. Throughout the life of the product, speed

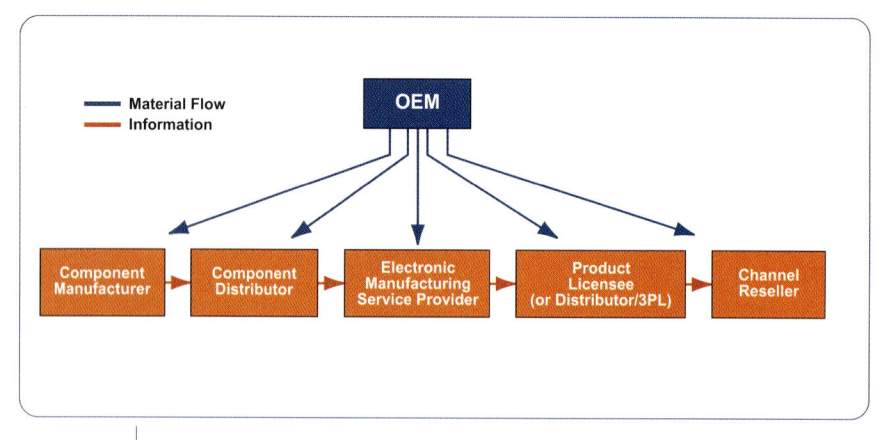

Weblink

For more on product management and development, see:
uchneat.ASCET.com
zimdars.ASCET.com
wayman.ASCET.com

For more on synchronization, see:
martella.ASCET.com

For more on collaboration, see:
prince.ASCET.com
ramanathan.ASCET.com
wayman.ASCET.com

Figure 1.0 — A typical virtual supply chain in the computer and electronics industry.

is critical — both in bringing the product to market and in responsively changing and customizing the product for customers needs. For these supply chains, everyone from R&D through distribution requires immediate access to accurate, up-to-date product content information. And, like many high-tech companies, WebTV manages a complex supply chain without ever physically touching the materials or product. Starting with component manufacturers like Toshiba, to component suppliers like Marshall, then to a electronic manufacturing service (EMS) provider such as Flextronics for assembly, and through licensees like Sony out to the retail channel, WebTV coordinates material and information flows (see Figure 1.0).

For virtual firms, managing the information needed by each player in the supply chain is by far the biggest challenge. One slip in the information relay race and products are assembled with the wrong parts or orders pile up waiting for components. For example, consider a typical blunder made by an OEM who designed and marketed an electronic product. In a move to improve the functionality of the product, designers at the OEM made a routine change in one key specialized component that was supplied from their component distributor. The procurement managers at both the OEM and the manufacturing partner made the change and started ordering small quantities of the new component from the distributor. However, because the product content data was not integrated with the procurement systems, no one updated the forecast for the new component to reflect the ramping volumes that were planned. Since the distributor and manufacturing service provider did not realize the oversight, no plans were made with the component manufacturer to ensure the needed quantities would be in place. The component distributor had a small number of the components in inventory and quickly delivered initial orders, giving the manufacturing service provider the feeling that the part was readily available. Finally when a large order for the component was placed, the distributor realized the mistake, but it was too late. The component manufacturer could not deliver the component in time for the pending ramp-up. For the OEM, this meant having to go to the licensee and explain why the new product would have to be delayed for several weeks. The licensee had already planned a major product rollout supported by advertising and had made many promises to its retail channel partners. After tense negotiations, the component manufacturer offered to switch production at one of its plants to expedite the chip, but at a cost of $3 million. In the end, rather than delay the product introduction, the three partners, the OEM, EMS, and distributor, split the cost and expedited the chip.

While not all coordination mistakes are as costly as this one, the cumulative cost of many smaller mistakes is significant. Even managing simple tasks, like the approval process for engineering changes, is a nightmare in many organizations.

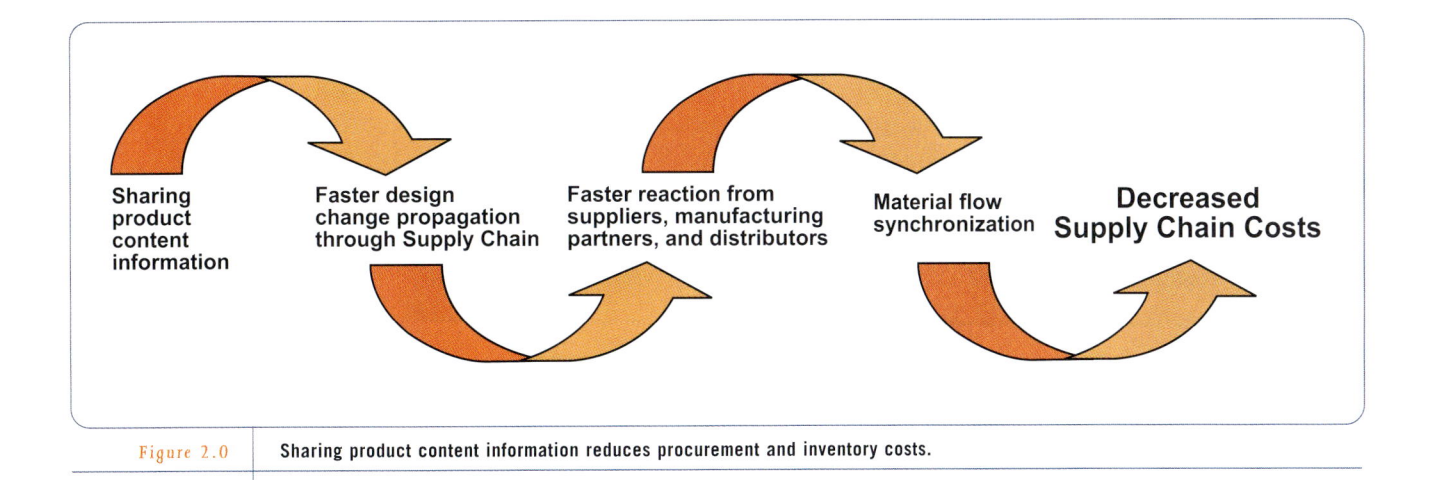

Figure 2.0 — Sharing product content information reduces procurement and inventory costs.

Proposed changes are often routed by fax, phone, e-mails, and meetings to capture the necessary signatures to be released to manufacturing. Once released, changes often come as a surprise to manufacturing and sourcing partners, adding cost and time. On a routine basis, mistakes that create short delays in component deliveries to the EMS mean that reserved capacity at the EMS will go idle waiting for the part. In cases where the delay is clearly related to stumbles in the OEM product change process, the EMS may ask the OEM to help pay for the cost of the disruptions, typically $5,000 to $10,000 per day. Of course, these costs are peanuts when compared to the substantial effect on total supply chain cost and potential lost revenues from delayed products.

Product Data Synchronization

Tortured by supply chain costs related to product content, manufacturers in many industries have worked to improve their data management practices. Some firms like Hewlett-Packard and General Motors created their own homegrown design tools to help better coordinate designers and manufacturers. Many third-party companies including CAD and workflow software vendors also jumped into product data management market. Yet maintaining up-to-date product content is not enough. The information must be shared with supply chain partners. A myriad of proprietary systems, while improving data quality, often hinders coordination between supply chain partners. The Web is quickly changing that.

Product collaboration software vendors such as PTC and Agile Software are rapidly evolving into Web-based services that dramatically improve the ability of the supply chain members to communicate and collaborate with one another about new or changing product content. By bringing together all product content including drawings, bills of materials, approved vendors, process instructions, and a complete product history into a single portal, Web-centric systems automate many painful tasks. For example, using a system like Agile, a designer making an engineering change can work through a Web browser to create the proposal. For each change, comments and product history is included so anyone examining the product can see why changes were made. When the proposal is complete, the software simply tosses an e-mail containing a hyperlink to the proposed change to all of the people on the product team. By clicking on the hyperlink (with appropriate security), those who need to approve the proposal can see the changes, including drawings and product history. If the approvers agree with the change, they simply click an acceptance button and their response and comments are recorded with the proposal. After that, anyone who looks at the proposal can see who has accepted it thus far and who has not yet registered an acceptance or rejection. When all the required team members have approved the change, the Agile system will automatically notify everyone related to the product that the change has been approved and release it to manufacturing and procurement.

Many of the early adopters of product management systems were primarily interested in automating the engineering change process. However, they quickly learned that product content synchronization would lead to material flow synchronization with big supply chain dividends. An early adopter of Web-centric product management was PairGain Technologies, who designs, manufactures, and markets DSL (Digital Subscriber Line) networking systems. Service providers and private network operators worldwide used PairGain's products to deploy DSL-based services, such as high-speed Internet, remote LAN access, and enterprise LAN extensions over the existing infrastructure of copper telephone lines. In the past, the process for releasing new products and product changes was manual and time-consuming. It required many meetings and extensive travel between PairGain and its manufacturing partner SCI. The labor-intensive activities slowed product development and caused many expensive mistakes. After using Agile's Web-centric product, the need for frequent design meetings evaporated. Both within PairGain and at SCI's manufacturing plant in Brazil, engineers could interact daily with an ongoing dialog about product content.

Along with the improved product content collaboration, PairGain also restructured its supply chain to synchro-

http://johnson.ASCET.com

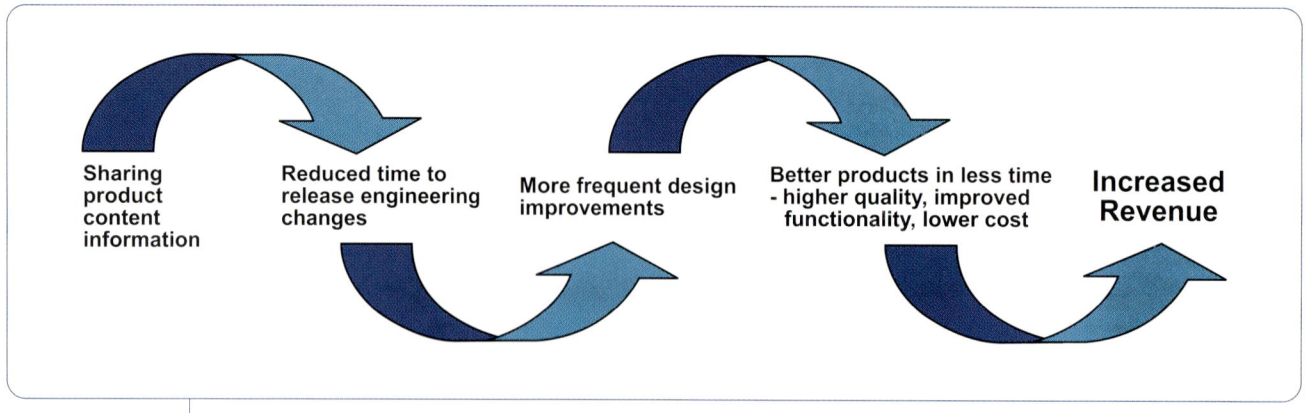

Figure 2.0 — Sharing product content information enables supply chain partners to develop better products, enhancing revenue.

Sharing product content information → Reduced time to release engineering changes → More frequent design improvements → Better products in less time - higher quality, improved functionality, lower cost → Increased Revenue

nize the flow of information, material, and cash, reducing inventory and slashing costs. In the past, the supply chain often held up to six months of component inventory, making changes to the product very slowly. By 1999, with only a few days of inventory in the pipeline, product changes could be made within one week. Since component prices were constantly dropping, PairGain was able to reduce its purchasing costs by not making procurement decisions months in advance. In fact, on many standard components, payment was made electronically upon consumption. Its component supplier, Arrow Co., held inventory at the SCI plant in Brazil and delivered just in time to the production line. For PairGain, re-engineering the management of product content was a critical step in synchronizing the entire supply chain (see Figure 2.0).

Web-Centric Product Collaboration

As with many Web-based technologies, the initial changes aimed at automating cumbersome coordination processes led to far larger opportunities. As we have seen, synchronizing product data management translates into many cost savings. However, a far more interesting impact of a Web-centric approach is how it changes the process of content management. Traditionally, distribution of product content follows a push process with the design engineers making product design decisions and sending those decisions to others in the supply chain. In disconnected push systems, changes are expensive and thus are discouraged. Without instant access to content information, others within the supply chain operate with old information. More importantly, communication about product content is slow, hindering feedback from supply chain partners.

For example, if a designer specifies a new component or product change that makes the manufacturing process more difficult or affects the end quality of the product, it may take days or weeks for the supply chain partners to discover the issue and provide appropriate feedback. Automating the change process reduces the time and cost of engineering changes, making it possible to turn out frequent design improvements. Allowing supply chain partners to see the most recent information and suggest changes enables true collaboration and concurrent engineering where all supply chain partners participate in the design process. For example, a firm selling products worldwide could get feedback from regional partners, ensuring that the product would conform to local tastes and regulations well before the design is finalized. This leads to better products with fewer defects, improved functionality, and lower cost. The result is increased revenue (see Figure 3.0).

But why stop with product development process? By integrating product content management systems with B2B exchanges, designers and buyers could work together to rapidly develop new products. Neutral portals, such as those under development by Agile and PTC, that provide secure product management services could become gathering points for supply chain partners. Within the portal, partners could collaborate on the design process while being supported with a host of other services from procurement to contract manufacturing. From a proposed BOM linked to the exchange, component costs could be quickly established and procured using relevant trading technologies (request for quotes, reverse auctions, etc). Manufacturing and logistics services could also be evaluated and procured. Even after sales service such as spare parts and repair services could be outsourced and managed through such an exchange. Then we will have true supply chain synchronization!

Supply Chain Collaboration: Success in the New Internet Economy

written by:

Tom Anthony
PeopleSoft
http://anthony.ASCET.com

Supply chain collaboration is continuing to emerge as a fundamental change toward new methods of conducting business. Closely united partnerships with emphasis on greater supply chain visibility and proactive response to changing market conditions are going to be the requirements rather than the goals placed on businesses. Today's technologies are accelerating the race toward the development of new business models and collaborative solutions. This trend is encouraging heavy investments in technology infrastructure as businesses prepare to be part of this new business environment.

Companies preparing for this new economic model are faced with several key challenges:

- Support of multiple technologies
- Support of multiple collaborative business models
- Scalability of collaborative solutions

Disparate systems and processes present challenges to businesses looking to execute on the supply chain collaboration vision. As business transactions that have historically been internally focused now need to become external to the organization, your ability to succeed will be based on your ability to provide an integrated view across your business processes. Organizations that rely on human intervention or lack integrated systems will run into scalability issues as the business world begins to transact at an accelerated pace. Response times expressed in days will no longer be an acceptable measure as the business world continues to move towards the real-time exchange of information.

The emergence of trading exchanges for specific business transactions such as procurement and transportation adds additional complexity to the underlying infrastructure challenges. Very few companies will have the luxury of dealing with a single exchange. Most businesses will need to comply with the specific business process and data requirements of multiple trading exchanges. This will again force issues of infrastructure flexibility to the forefront in order to support multiple business channels and trading partner relationships.

Internet-based communications technologies surrounding the transfer of XML-formatted data will continue to evolve. Many existing trading partners will require support of EDI-based transactions for years to come while more forward-looking companies will require conformance to XML-based standards. The proliferation of multiple XML-based standards will fuel the requirements for flexibility at a trading partner level. Businesses will be forced to support multiple communication technologies and partner-specific communication standards well into the future.

A seamless 360-degree customer and partner view of your business is critical to your continued success. All outward-facing systems must be integrated across your internal organization. Throughout the process of customer contact, order placement, procurement, production, and fulfillment your outward communications must be consistent, timely, and accurate. As you prepare your business for collaborative commerce, you must ensure that your systems are tightly coupled, flexible, and allow you to extend your reach outside the walls of your business.

Challenges of Supply Chain Collaboration

Supply chain collaboration occurs when two or more companies share the responsibility of exchanging common planning, management, execution, and performance measurement information. Collaborative relationships transform

Tom Anthony is the Supply Chain Collaboration Strategy Manager for PeopleSoft, Inc. Tom has been with PeopleSoft's product strategy organization since 1998. Working with world class manufacturing and distribution operations for the past 10 years, he has worked to build unique supply chain solutions for the consumer packaged goods, high-tech, and wholesale distribution markets. Tom serves on the U.S. Chamber of Commerce Logistics Council and is committed to the development and support of next-generation supply chain solutions.

how information is shared between companies and drive change to the underlying business processes. Businesses are looking toward collaboration as an opportunity to optimize their supply chain and relationships with their trading partners. Supply chain collaboration poses complex challenges to supply chain partners in that there is a broad spectrum of collaborative initiatives, disparate standards for communication, and various levels of trading partner competencies and business processes. Collaborative relationships will require suppliers and consumers to support multiple simultaneous business models and communication media in order to fully realize the benefits of collaborative business. Your business systems must be flexible enough to support the variances in technologies and business models that can be as unique as the trading partnerships themselves. Collaborative business stands to reap the benefits of a highly effective supply chain when systems are able to support the broad spectrum of trading relationships across the end-to-end business process.

The term collaboration is used broadly in today's market and encompasses multiple functional areas. It is important to recognize the functional areas of collaboration as well as the initiatives that are taking place within each area. The figures within this article illustrate several of the collaboration initiatives that are currently underway and then describe the processes involved.

Cost has historically been a barrier to the technological implementation of col-

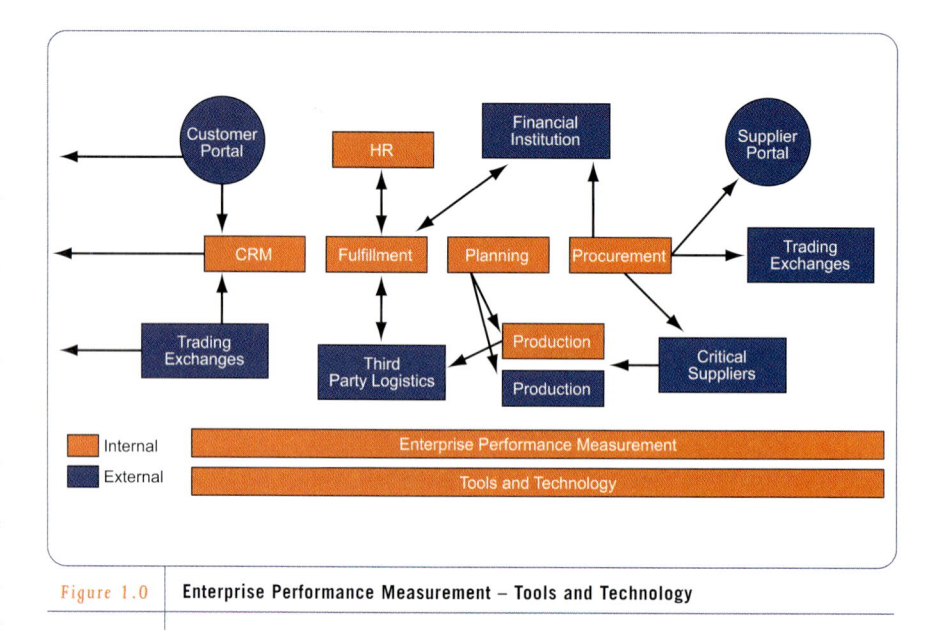

Weblink

For more on supply chain initiatives:
uchneat.ASCET.com
srivastava.ASCET.com
For more on standards, see:
uchneat.ASCET.com
For more on partnerships, see:
ramanathan.ASCET.com
For more on competencies, see:
prince.ASCET.com

Figure 1.0 Enterprise Performance Measurement – Tools and Technology

laboration initiatives; however the Internet and XML-based messaging has emerged as a medium for low-cost information exchange between business partners. These technologies are acting as a catalyst for change in the development of new standards to support collaborative business models. Pilot programs have already shown that collaborative solutions can provide significant strategic direction in the areas of reduced inventories, reduced stock outs, improved customer service, and improved supply chain process efficiency.

The consumer packaged goods (CPG) sector has historically been a leader in developing and implementing collaborative initiatives. Consumer products companies started building EDI-based collaborative solutions through the development of the UCS standards. The Efficient Consumer Response (ECR) initiative focused on solutions for VMI and customer replenishment. Today, the Voluntary Interindustry Commerce Standard (VICS) organization is supporting the development of the CPFR standards for the CPG industry. Notables such as Kimberly-Clark, Sara Lee, Procter & Gamble, and Hewlett Packard are piloting CPFR initiatives with leading retailers like Wegmans and Wal-Mart and achieving the benefits of collaborative commerce.

The collaborative business model that is used between trading partners is based on the depth of their trading relationship. For example, within inventory replenishment there are multiple models for how the customer orders and item quantities are determined. The simplest trading relationship for replenishment is based on a pull model where the customer determines the appropriate item balances and places an order with the supplier when the goods drop below minimum inventory levels. As the trading relationship matures, the supplier may agree to manage the replenishment of inventory through a VMI model. In this model, the supplier will maintain visibility of current customer inventory balances and create customer orders for replenishment based upon the customer's sales forecast. For more strategic relationships, CPFR could be used to further strengthen the overall supply chain visibility and management. In a CPFR model, the supplier and customer work together to develop a joint sales forecast and agree to parameters of acceptable variances. Customer point of sales information is tracked against the joint forecast and when variances are not within the agreed upon tolerance levels, both the supplier and customer are notified so that the appropriate action can be taken. This proactive approach to the inventory replenishment process requires close interaction between the trading partners

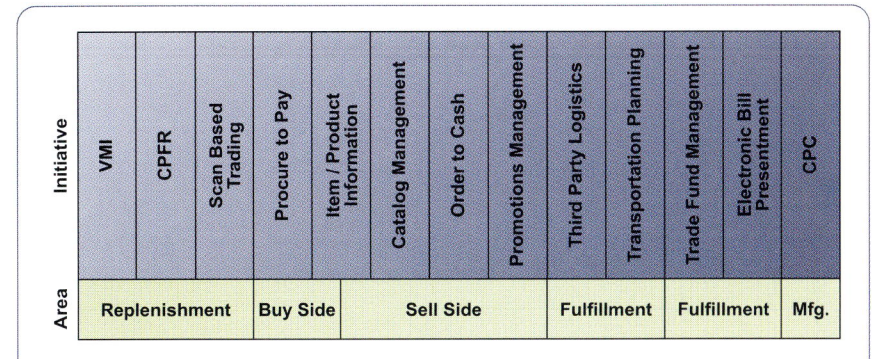

Initiative	VMI	CPFR	Scan Based Trading	Procure to Pay	Item / Product Information	Catalog Management	Order to Cash	Promotions Management	Third Party Logistics	Transportation Planning	Trade Fund Management	Electronic Bill Presentment	CPC
Area	Replenishment			Buy Side		Sell Side			Fulfillment		Fulfillment		Mfg.

Collaboration Initiatives	Description
Vendor Managed Inventory (VMI)	Supplier manages a customer's inventory levels using either traditional Min/Max/EOQ or forecasting replenishment models.
Collaborative Planing Forecasting and Replenishment (CPFR)	Supplier works with the customer to develop a joint sales forecast that is used as the basis for replenishment. Actual sales vs. forecast are compared to alert parties of variances so that proactive action can be taken.
Scan Based Trading	Suppliers provide manage customer inventory levels and provide goods on consignment. Customers exchange point of sale information with suppliers to drive both replenishment and billing activities from actual sales activities.
Procure to Pay Transactions	Traditional transactions that are used for placing a purchase order, communicating changes, and acknowledging receipt with a supplier.
Item / Product Information	Suppliers and customers share information related to items that they purchase/sell. This initiative is focused on keeping the information in synch across multiple suppliers and customers.
Catalog Management	Customer centric exchange of supplier catalog information with facility for customers to place orders against new products/items with minimal data entry.
Order to Cash Transactions	Traditional transactions that are used receiving sales orders, communicating changes, sending an advanced ship notification, and invoicing a customer.
Promotions Management	Suppliers provide notification to customers for planned promotions, exchange activity information against a promotion
Third Party Logistics	Suppliers can outsource the fulfillment of goods to a third party logistics (3PL) provider to service smaller regions, or to handle excess inventory. The 3PL must receive sales order information and send back shipment details.

Figure 2.0 Different varieties of Supply Chain Collaboration Initiatives

and helps reduce inventory levels through the supply chain.

Across the overall supply chain, a supplier must manage multiple distribution channels with multiple levels of relationships from casual buyers to strategic partners. As the strategic level of partnership matures between the supplier and a customer, the collaborative business model used to support the relationship will likely change as well. In addition, distribution channels may be limited in their ability to supply detailed and accurate information used to drive the replenishment process. This will result in suppliers needing to support multiple collaborative business models to support the broad spectrum of trading relationships.

In many cases, the requirements of multiple collaborative business models equate to multiple systems to support the business processes. Many collaboration initiatives in place today heavily leverage human intervention or utilize point solutions that are not fully integrated across the multiple business processes. There are also multiple technology alternatives that can be used to facilitate the collaborative process. The reduced cost of transferring information utilizing XML-based technology has in some ways added complexity to collaboration in that there is a proliferation of communication standards. A supplier will likely need to communicate via EDI, and multiple customer specific XML data formats for the same set of business transactions. The result is that suppliers not only need to manage multiple collaborative models, but must also manage multiple communication methods within each model.

The same statements can be made for both the supply side and the demand side of collaborative relationships. Customers must manage multiple supplier relationships in much the same way the suppliers must manage multiple customer relationships. Material can be forecasted and procured directly with the supplier and can also be directed through the use of a trading exchange. The additional business models associated with using a trading exchange increase the overall complexity of the supply chain.

In the end both suppliers and their customers must provide a seamless end-to-end process that can meet the business and technological requirements of their respective trading relationships. They will need a flexible solution that can support multiple business models and work seamlessly across their execution systems. Seamless execution will reduce the amount of manual intervention that is

http://anthony.ASCET.com

often required in maintaining the trading relationships and will allow the process to flow through a common process stream.

Conclusion

For companies seeking to effectively develop and manage business-to-business and business-to-consumer commerce with customers and suppliers, you must utilize collaborative commerce solutions that enable comprehensive business process interaction for selling, buying, and developing products and services over the Internet. For example, PeopleSoft users enable their customers and suppliers to become part of the extended collaborative community exchanging business documents and information throughout the product, customer order, and purchase order lifecycle. They are leveraging Internet-enabled solutions that offer modular, best-of-breed functionality for back-end and front-end processes including: procurement, forecasting, advanced planning, customer order fulfillment, and customer relationship management. These solutions provide secure, direct interaction with customers and suppliers through the Internet that leverage leading-edge collaborative commerce techniques.

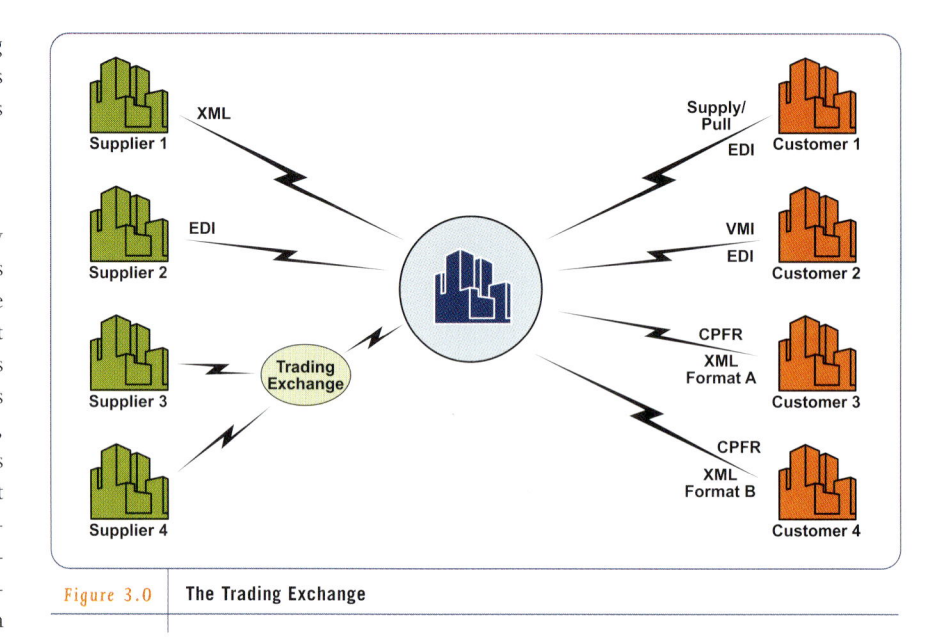

Figure 3.0 | The Trading Exchange

PeopleSoft SCM – Bringing Clarity and E-Business to Complex Supply Chains

An enterprise's supply chain is an intricate collaboration among producers, suppliers, distributors, and customers – and it moves at the speed of electronic business. Mastery over this nexus requires a far-reaching and flexible set of Internet-enabled management, transaction, production, and strategic decision support tools. The integrated PeopleSoft Supply Chain Management solution includes:

- Supply Chain Planning
- Manufacturing
- Sales and Logistics
- Materials Management
- E-Procurement and E-Store
- 100% Internet PeopleTools technology

PeopleSoft Supply Chain Management brings an innovative approach to resource optimization and a global perspective across the enterprise, yet enables disparate operations to be managed locally. A single, integrated system balances inventories, schedules production for peak efficiency, captures and administers a high volume of orders, and helps companies produce and deliver products to exact specifications.

Organizations unite their front and back offices, streamline their vendor relationships, conduct business-to-business buying and selling, and collaborate among customers and suppliers with the agility of an Internet browser. And PeopleSoft solutions include features, functions, and best practices that answer the specific needs of varying vertical sectors.

Reduced inventory, lower costs, reliable promise dates, faster delivery schedules, and high customer satisfaction result – along with a quick time-to-benefit for an enterprise information technology investment.

Customer Insight

Hewlett-Packard Network Server Division on ROI of PeopleSoft SCM solutions:

"We need to achieve a strategic level of inventory worldwide – our inventory devalues at 2.5% monthly, and worldwide inventory rebalancing is vital. Since switching to weekly planning with PeopleSoft, inventory levels at our distribution centers have decreased by 40%. I estimate that we're saving as much as one million dollars a month through these efficiencies. That's a return on investment of roughly eight times." - Roger Smith, Planning Projects Manager, Hewlett-Packard Network Server Division

The Enterprise eBusiness Management Backbone

PeopleSoft Supply Chain Management solutions work in close integration with PeopleSoft business management solutions. This ebusiness foundation enables global access to timely and accurate information and strategic decision support on people, money, customers, supply, and demand – a complete end-to-end integrated solution for manufacturers and distributors. PeopleSoft business management solutions include:

- Customer Relationship Management
- Enterprise Performance Management
- Financial Management
- Human Resources Management

PeopleSoft solutions meet worldwide business needs with multicurrency and multilingual capabilities, tax and tariff support, and many other global requirements.

Contact Information

Craig Conway
President

Michael Frandsen
General Manager, SCM Division

Michael Goija
Products and Technology

Peoplesoft Inc.
Corporate Headquarters
4460 Hacienda Drive
Pleasanton, CA 94588
Toll Free 888.773.8277
Phone 925.694.3000
www.peoplesoft.com

Net Revenue
$1.4 billion

Nasdaq
PSFT

Number of Employees
7,000

Figure 2.0 PeopleSoft's eProcurement Application: Officeplace.com

Meeting Industry Needs Top to Bottom

PeopleSoft Supply Chain Management addresses the varying challenges of specific industry verticals, supporting mixed-mode manufacturing, product configuration, and complex channels of distribution. These major industry sectors include:

- Wholesale Distribution
- Industrial Products
- High Technology
- Consumer Goods

We've worked with advisory groups from these industries to identify the winning strategies and best business practices for these sectors. Adaptable design, open-integration architecture, and our modular framework enable customers to choose precisely the functionality that they need and to tailor applications to their own requirements without adopting rigid business models.

The Wholesale Distribution Challenge

Many wholesale distributors are reeling from the effects of changing business factors that have threatened the conventional, intermediary role of the distributor with obsolescence. E-commerce, time-certain logistics providers like UPS, and supply chain strategies that limit stock on hand are challenging the traditional roles and services of the industry. To compensate, distributors are seeking new ways to add value and services to their products. They are embracing the Internet and forging new business models and partnerships.

The PeopleSoft enterprise solution addresses supply chain management, e-commerce, and enterprise business management to offer wholesale distributors flexible support for both emerging and traditional business models. Collaboration with business partners yields better pricing and a smoother supply chain. A comprehensive, integrated planning and business operations backbone promotes cost-containing efficiency for a better bottom line.

Customer Insight

The Fastenal Company on PeopleSoft Demand and Inventory Planning:

"We're improving our company's supply chain by using Demand and Inventory Planning. The system excels at all of our requirements. We find it very flexible, easy to work with, and intuitive, and we plan to expand because, through this exception-based paradigm, we can handle a much greater number of items.

"We like the direction PeopleSoft is going with supply chain planning, business analytics, and the Web – it's a forward-looking company. We'll get our core systems in place and then look at where we'll go next with PeopleSoft." – Dr. Peter Guidinger, Operations Research Manager, Fastenal

The Industrial Products Challenge

Mixed-mode manufacturing is critical to the broad industrial sector. Companies must be able to handle make-to-order private label, custom, and original equipment manufacturer (OEM) components right alongside catalog standard components and finished goods – accommodating products that have short life cycles and high variation as well as those that are manufactured to a forecast.

The PeopleSoft solution meets these needs through its combination of "low touch" execution systems (easy to prototype, learn and use) and advanced planning plus Flow Production System techniques. For mixed-mode manufacturers who must manage a hybrid of low-volume-high-changeover and volume production in the supply chain – or even in the same bill of material – the PeopleSoft solution for the industrial sector is ideal.

Customer Insight

Toyota Motor Manufacturing North America on PeopleSoft Manufacturing:

"Flexibility was key to our decision to go with PeopleSoft. Toyota was able to effectively implement solutions that are flexible enough to support Toyota's production principles of a flow manufacturing system and continuous improvement. Because Toyota can now more effectively track and monitor its parts order process from order through shipment, service levels are improved, which ultimately benefits the Toyota owner." – Jim Bolte, General Manager of Information Systems, Toyota Motor Manufacturing North America

The High-Tech Challenge

The high-tech industry faces particular challenges posed by complex product configurations, dramatically shortened product life cycles, and convoluted networks of suppliers and subcontractors.

PeopleSoft answers these needs with support for multiple modes of manufacturing and product configuration, global supply chain visibility, enhanced communication and collaboration among trading partners, and advanced planning and optimization. Product lifecycle management requires "use up" logic to reduce inventory and integrated change control to manage development and release of new products.

Customer Insight

Hewlett-Packard Network Server Division on planning cycles and supply chain visibility:

"Prior to switching to the PeopleSoft system, we created a monthly enterprise plan for our distribution centers. But our resellers need faster turnaround times, and our demand changes too quickly to rely on a monthly plan. We moved to a weekly planning cycle, which we could not have done using the lengthy sequential planning steps we had before. With PeopleSoft, our entire planning process is 60% faster than it used to be."

– Roger Smith, Planning Projects Manager, Hewlett-Packard Network Server Division

The Consumer Goods Challenge

Time and cost pressures from powerful, consolidated retailers. Increasingly complex distribution channels and promotional efforts. The demand and distribution sides of the consumer goods industry pose particularly complex quandaries, while companies must also grapple with a steady stream of changes in manufacturing and supply due to acquisitions, new product proliferation and time-to-market urgency.

PeopleSoft's Demand Planning addresses one of the most important and difficult factors in a successful consumer goods strategy. The demand plan drives enterprise planning and ensures that resources and schedules are targeted towards a well-defined market strategy. It draws on market intelligence from events, promotions, seasonality profiles, and campaigns, and uses a multi-user, collaborative approach to forecasting. Promotions management, customer relationship management, and supply-chain optimization also speak directly to CG exigencies.

Customer Insight
**Eagle Family Foods
on PeopleSoft adaptability:**

"Our primary objective was to have powerful information for decision-making. Secondary to that was efficient processing of transactions. We wanted a focused, one-data source for our information, and we wanted flexibility and expandability. Our future growth plans include acquisitions. If we move into different categories, different sectors, is the system we select flexible enough to go there with us?

'We looked at the major ERP vendors, and it was a relatively easy choice to go with PeopleSoft. First, it was less expensive to purchase and maintain than some of the others, and it equaled or bettered them in functionality. PeopleSoft was very expandable and very flexible, able to do what we needed to do for our business."
– Harold Strunk, Vice President, Sales Support, Eagle Family Foods

Supply Chain Business on the Internet

Our 360-degree view of customers, suppliers, employees, and performance is powered by advanced PeopleTools technology and executed with 100% Internet capability. PeopleSoft Applications for eBusiness are Internet-ready with scalable transaction and analytic processing capabilities, open integration, and 100% Internet browser-based deployment.

PeopleSoft eStore

PeopleSoft eStore delivers a comprehensive online sales and customer service solution. It combines best-of-breed online selling functionality with integration into Order Management and other back-office systems to support business-to-business and direct-to-consumer sales. This online commerce promotes enhanced customer relationships, personalized services and pricing, and the capture and analysis of purchasing trends.

PeopleSoft eStore is designed for established enterprises looking to create new sales channels and supplement existing channels – as well as for rapidly developing companies reliant on the Internet for success.

Customer Insight
**Cybex International Inc.
on PeopleSoft eStore**

"We have to have our e-commerce completely integrated into our business system. It was very fast and straightforward to add eStore to our PeopleSoft backbone." –
Thor Wallace, vice president and CIO, Cybex International

Customer Insight
**Green Mountain Coffee Roasters
on PeopleSoft eStore:**

"The beauty is that we'll be able to take orders on the Web site and have them flow directly to the PeopleSoft back end, and those orders will get fulfilled through the same efficient distribution system. We have only one set of business processes that go on behind the scenes." - Jim Prevo, CIO, Green Mountain Coffee Roasters

PeopleSoft eProcurement

To some, the Internet is a mixed blessing. To purchasing departments, it's just a blessing. Integrated into the PeopleSoft eBusiness Backbone and developed with Commerce One, PeopleSoft eProcurement is a Web-based electronic procurement application providing a single interface for thousands of users across the enterprise to manage all types of maintenance, repairs and operations (MRO) goods and services activity.

PeopleTools and the Internet

The foundation for all PeopleSoft applications is PeopleTools – our toolset and development environment. Packaged with our solutions, PeopleTools enables the rapid development, deployment, and cost-effective management of PeopleSoft eBusiness applications – providing the business rules and metadata for rapid business collaboration on the Internet.

With the PeopleTools Internet architecture, PeopleSoft applications can be deployed from a server-centric development platform over the Internet and accessed through a browser – greatly reducing the cost of deployment, expanding the user base, and connecting the extended enterprise.

New Sales Channels, New Customer Expectations

Today, manufacturers and distributors are competing to meet the increasing time, price, and service demands of multiple sales channels. The requisites: know the customer, anticipate demand, understand product and customer profitability, and quickly exploit new revenue opportunities.

"Customer" can mean everything from a huge manufacturer subcontracting components to an individual end consumer ordering from a Web site catalog. What they have in common is greater-than-ever expectations requiring responsiveness in kind. PeopleSoft systems integrate to provide effective execution and comprehensive business intelligence about customers and revenues.

http://peoplesoft.ASCET.com

Manugistics – The Intelligent E-Business Decision

Contact Information

Gregory J. Owens
*president and
chief executive officer*

Terrence A. Austin
*executive vice president
electronics & high technology*

Richard F. Bergmann
*executive vice president,
global sales & services*

**Manugistics, Inc.,
Corporate Headquarters**
2115 East Jefferson Street
Rockville, MD 20852-4999
Phone 301.984.5000
Fax 301.984.5370
www.manugistics.com

Manugistics Group, Inc. (Nasdaq: MANU) is the leading provider of e-business solutions that enable intelligent decisions across trading networks.

Anticipating the needs of business in the Internet economy, our solutions empower network trading partners to make the right decisions for profitable growth. Powered by our Manugistics NetWORKS™ family of products, these solutions ensure real-time decision-making at eSpeed.

With over 20 years of experience in helping companies make better decisions, we are driven to provide solutions that are reliable and quick to implement. Tailored for each customer, these solutions deliver competitive advantage by translating strategy to action. Manugistics is known as the solutions company that delivers results.

This success is echoed by our over 900 strategic clients including companies such as Avnet, Compaq, Dayton Hudson, Exel Logistics, Nokia, Timberland, The Limited, Unilever, and Wal-Mart.

The company's solutions are the preferred choice by companies with dynamic requirements across trading networks. These companies include those with any of the following characteristics: eBusiness initiatives, large volume, multiple channels, short product life cycles, complex distribution networks, a variety of customers seeking new ways of doing business, and third parties such as contract manufacturers and logistics providers. Examples of these consumer-driven industries include: agricultural products, apparel/footwear/textiles, automotive, consumer products, consumer durables, electronics and high technology, food & beverage, process industries, and over-the-counter pharmaceuticals. For example:

- Warner Lambert, a leading pharmaceutical manufacturer, received significant benefits within 12 months of implementation, increasing order fill rate to 99% and reducing supply chain costs by $2.2 million.
- Tenneco Automotive increased order fill rates to 96%, improved inventory turns by 25 percent and reduced inventory levels by 50% at both its own facilities and at its customer sites.
- Alcatel, one of the world's largest telecommunication component manufacturing companies, obtained ROI in less than 12 weeks and posted a 25% reduction in past due orders.
- Payless Cashways, a full-line building materials and lumberyard retailer, saved "hundreds of thousands" of dollars in shipping costs just 4 months after implementing the first phase of Manugistics NetWORKS Transport™ solution.

Profitable Growth @ E-Speed

Through helping some of the world's most recognized companies make profitable business decisions, Manugistics has emerged as the leader in its field. Manugistics has been able to help clients increase revenues and reduce the

profitable growth @ eSpeed

time and expense necessary to manufacture and distribute products for their customers – often achieving substantial results in a very short period of time.

Manugistics' industry-leading clients include:

- Ten out of the top 15 Fortune 500 manufacturing companies
- Eight out of the top 10 consumer product companies
- Four out of the top five apparel companies
- Eight out of the top 10 largest pharmaceutical companies
- Two out of the top five auto parts suppliers
- The largest motor vehicle company

Leading organizations can no longer operate as

separate entities. Global manufacturers have working partnerships with their customers, suppliers and worldwide subsidiaries. This environment demands intelligence for real-time decision making and access to information – both of which are delivered by Manugistics' NetWORKS™ solutions. These solutions powered by a new architecture – Manugistics WebWORKS™ – provide application portability and intelligence to transform the traditional supply chain into a trading community.

Now businesses and their trading partners have the technology to share, view and execute decisions based on real-time information. This increased visibility of critical information across trading networks translates strategy into action, delivering profitable growth at e-speed.

E-Business Today

Manugistics is dedicated to integrating its solutions with other leading companies in related fields to provide comprehensive solutions to its customers.

Through these partnerships and Manugistics WebWORKS Open Application Integration™, Manugistics can easily be integrated with a variety of critical applications including enterprise resource planning (ERP), transaction systems, execution systems, legacy systems, warehouse management systems and point-of-sale data that affect or complement the supply chain.

Manugistics' solutions are further strengthened by its strategic partnerships with ERP organizations, including Baan, SSA, J.D. Edwards, Marcam, Oracle, and SAP.

Manugistics also has strategic alliances with world-class consulting partners such as Andersen Consulting, CSC, Deloitte & Touche, Ernst & Young, KPMG Peat Marwick, Kurt Salmon Associates, IBM Consulting, and PricewaterhouseCoopers to provide implementation and consulting assistance to Manugistics' clients.

Manugistics' Customers Achieve Profitable Growth

Manugistics' mission is to deliver profitable growth for its customers across all industries. Representative clients around the world include: Alcatel, Allied Domecq Plc., BASF, Bristol-Myers Squibb, Dana Corporation, Deere & Co., DuPont, Glaxo Wellcome, GoodYear, Harley-Davidson, Hewlett-Packard, Hormel, Lucent, Mitsubishi Motors, Nabisco, Nokia, Paccar, Sony, Starbucks, Tenneco Automotive, United Distillers Nestle, Vintners (UDV), and Wal-Mart.

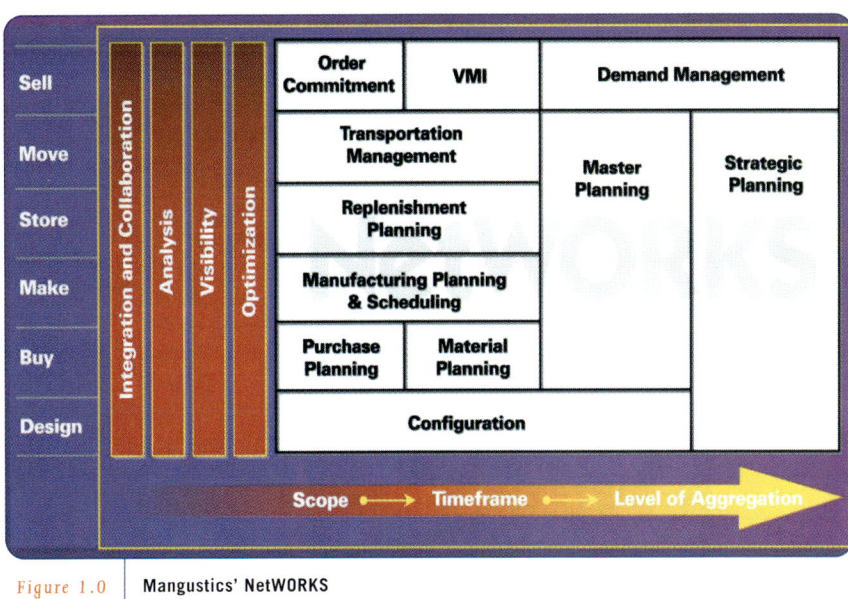

Manugistics Drives Financial Results

Manugistics became a publicly held company in 1993 and is traded on NASDAQ under the symbol MANU. Manugistics generated total revenues of $177.6 million for the year ended February 28, 1999. Manugistics currently has more than 800 employees.

A Leading Global Provider

Headquartered in Rockville, MD, Manugistics has global offices in Australia, Brazil, Belgium, Canada, France, Germany, Ireland, Italy, Japan, The Netherlands, New Zealand, Taiwan, Spain, and the United Kingdom. The Company also operates North American offices in Atlanta, Chicago, Denver, Irving, Philadelphia, and San Mateo.

Manugistics, the Manugistics logo, and working as one are registered trademarks and Manugistics NetWORKS, Manugistics WebWORKS and VIEWpoint are trademarks of Manugistics, Inc. All other product or company names mentioned are used for identification purposes only, and may be trademarks of their respective owners. Additional information about Manugistics can be found at the company's site on the World Wide Web, at http://www.manugistics.com.

Manugistics and Gordon Food Services: Driving Profit through Leading Edge Technology and Supply Chain Best Practices

The Challenge
- Goal: To continuously improve excellent customer service levels and product quality in the face of rapid growth.
- Strategy: Keep supply chain systems on the leading edge of technology and best practices by completely re-engineering procurement and inbound logistics processes
- Solution: Manugistics

Results
- Ahead of schedule on expected 5-year ROI
- 3 months prior to planned rollout, used

Figure 1.0 Mangustics' NetWORKS

http://manugistics.ASCET.com

Manugistics Demand to help plan, manage, and rebalance inventory levels in response to addition of new DC
- Maintained 98.7% service level througout rollout of new solution
- Significant improvements in seasonal inventory planning

Number 97 on Forbes Private 500 list, Gordon Food Service (GFS) distributes more than 14,000 items and plans approximately 45,000 Demand Forecasting Units (DFUs). To meet the needs of its fast-growing business, GFS worked with GartnerGroup, AMR, and other independent consultants to evaluate its best practices in supply chain, and identify a plan that would enable the company to continue to provide excellent service and quality products to its customers throughout the midwestern U.S. and Canada.

"Manugistics is an integral part of our growth and logistics strategy. Manugistics helped us to improve our distribution and logistics processes to best practice allowing us to be more responsive to Customer demands in very competitive food service channels." – Greg Van Drie, Gordon Food Service

Once Manugistics was selected, team members from GFS's logistics and information systems staff were tasked with creating a new logistics process and implement the new solution. During the next 15 months, the team defined, prototyped, and piloted a repeatable, horizontal (cross-functional) logistics process that leveraged Manugistics Demand. The process integrated various functional areas, including sales, marketing, DC operations, marketplace, procurement, and GFS vendors. Then, three months prior to the planned rollout of the new processes, a major new DC was opened. Despite being in the pilot stage at the time, the new solution was used to help, plan, manage, and rebalance inventory levels between all existing distribution centers based on the redistributed order demand.

When Manugistics Demand went into production in August, 1998, GFS achieved a number of significant benefits. First, during the rollout, GFS was able to maintain its historically high (98.7%) customer service levels. Second, the solution provided the ability to recognize the seasonal patterns of customer demand. As a result, GFS is able to achieve better inventory planning both before and after each season, providing improved service levels and more efficient inventory planning at the DCs.

The final phases of the project are planned for the end of 1999, and are expected to deliver additional savings through improvements in safety stock strategies, inventory turns, mix planning, exception management, and DC-to-vendor communication of replenishment plans.

About Gordon Food Service

Gordon Food Service helps satisfy the appetites of Midwesterners and Canadians. A broad line food distributor serving schools, restaurants, and other institutions, the company's products range from fresh produce to sanitation systems. Not merely a food distributor, the company also sells food in bulk through its 70 GFS Marketplace retail stores across four states. The late Isaac VanWestenbrugge (an ancestor of the Gordon family) founded the company as a butter and egg distributor in 1897. GFS is still owned by the Gordon family.

Intelligent Commerce and the E-Business Revolution: The Story Continues

written by:

Chad Quinn
Manugistics
http://quinn-c.ASCET.com

Y2K definitely ended with a fizzle. Not one of the predictions for major technological disasters was realized. Yet despite the capabilities of systems around the world to sidestep the millenium bug, the holiday season saw its fair share of perilous technology-related activity. While retailing on the Internet shot up from about $8 billion last year to an estimated $20 billion this year – and Forrester Research estimates that "e-tail" spending will hit $184 billion by 2004 – news and water-cooler conversations were filled with stories of e-tail misses.

Dot.com

Toysrus.com disappointed shoppers by failing to keep its site up and running. The company also neglected to list some items as out of stock. Then, as Christmas neared and it became evident that the items clearly would not be found in Santa's sleigh, the company desperately attempted to appease its frustrated – and giftless – customers by offering $100 gift certificates as consolation prizes. Despite the difficulties, this dot-com indicated that it understands how critical the success of its online business will be in the future.

Disney.com was not so forward thinking. In a similar scenario, no out-of-stock notice was received. When customers phoned to inquire about an order that never arrived, they were told that the company didn't even stock the item – and then were directed to a major retailer. Disney may be the master of merchandising, but they clearly don't have their dot-com ducks in a row.

Buy.com made some customers happy – but it won't be reaping any rewards. When purchasing videos from the site, not only did customers find it impossible to order multiple quantities of an item via the Web, and had to phone in their order, once the orders were placed the items were often shipped twice. For some happy but confused consumers, Santa's sleigh overflowed with extra videos this season.

Amazon.com's Jeff Bezos was named Time magazine's "Person of the Year," but this distinction didn't change the company's bottom line. One call to Seattle-based Amazon.com's service center generally resulted in 30 minutes of on-hold time before it was disconnected, an outcome that apparently surprised even the e-tail giant. Despite record sales in 1999, the world's most well known dot.com continues to lose money.

Despite these mishaps, dot-com companies are thriving; stock prices are continuing to rise and remain the darlings of Wall Street. But there is a clear need to address the issues faced by even the best of the dot-coms. Profitability is a necessity.

Many companies appreciated the importance and potential dollar value of the Internet in 1999 – and knew that they had no choice but to be an Internet player. But many still do not have the processes and technology to support this real-time order and intelligent fulfillment environment. Assuming that, despite their mistakes, they are still in business in Y2K, the imminent challenge is to turn dot-com ventures into clear profit centers.

A handful of companies have already taken the plunge and proven that e-business means more than just e-tail – and that it can lead to considerable profit. Mitsubishi Motor Sales of America, for example, has slashed vehicle lead times in half by leveraging the Internet to create a true e-business trading network. As a result, customer satisfaction and operational efficiency have improved significantly.

How did this move to e-business come about? And how will it continue to change tomorrow's business models? Answering these questions provides some important insight into how the shift to e-business is changing how we

Chad Quinn, Vice President of E-Business Solutions for Manugistics, is responsible for helping build a group within the company that strategically works with e-commerce providers and third-party logistics providers to create new revenue streams for Manugistics.

http://quinn-c.ASCET.com 51

perceive technology, and how technology will drive the success of tomorrow's e-business trading networks.

The Internet and E-Information

You remember the days. They weren't very long ago. The Internet was a novelty. Techies surfed, posted, chatted. Serious business stayed away.

Slowly, respect for the Internet grew. Most businesses set up WANs and gave at least some of their workers access. Even small business – a traditional technology laggard – got involved. According to IDC/LINK, in 1997 Internet penetration stood at 50% of all businesses with fewer than 100 employees. This access was used for two things:

- E-mail: Again and again, studies showed that e-mail topped the list of Internet uses in the workplace. Indeed, the Internet revolutionized business-to-business communication, packing mailboxes with mission-critical statistics, urgent documents, and bad jokes.
- Home pages: Want the world to know about your business? Create a home page. At first, home pages contained limited real value – amounting to little more than online advertisements and "brochures." Then they expanded to include additional information, like product descriptions and catalogue information. However, home pages did not allow online ordering. They had to

retreat to the analog world – the phone or fax – to place an order. The result: "commerce interruptus."

In both cases, the Internet held little usefulness for businesses. Sure, messages could be sent a bit faster. That helped employees communicate. Maybe customers would call after seeing your Web site – if they could find it. But the technology did not change the process of business: how businesses related to one another, how goods were ordered, shipped, and paid for.

The Internet and E-Commerce

Today, the situation has changed a little. Web sites now house a mountain of company information, and documents zip around the globe at a furious pace.

The biggest recent development? E-commerce hit primetime, and businesses are busy polishing their Web sites to accept secure credit card transactions. This trend has not gone unnoticed in analyst circles. Forrester Research predicts that global online business will explode to $3.2 trillion in 2003. Meanwhile, stocks of many e-tailers shot skyward toward the end of 1999, with names like Amazon.com, eBay.com and etoys.com reaching unimagined valuations. For a while, any IPO with an Internet angle was sure to triple in price during its first trading day.

But is this it? Has the Internet reached its zenith with the advent of e-commerce? Is there no more territory to conquer?

Some companies seem to think so. Giddy with success from their e-commerce ventures, they seem to believe that the Internet can take them no farther. This ailment afflicts even companies known for their technological innovation.

But how technically revolutionary are they really? Many e-tailers use the Internet to sell their products. Essentially, their Web sites act like virtual store clerks, recommending products, locating ordered items, and cashing the customer out. But other than their high technology faces, many dot-coms operate much like their brick-and-mortar brethren.

For a moment, let's look at what con-

% OF BUYERS USING THE INTERNET IN THEIR JOB

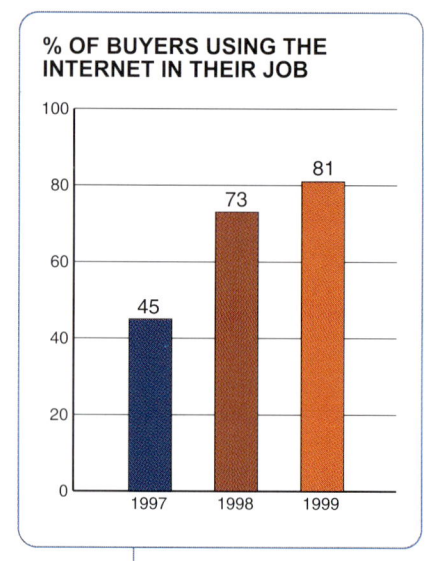

Year	%
1997	45
1998	73
1999	81

Figure 1.0 | Growth of the Internet

sumers – sitting at their PCs – never see. First of all, they never see that most e-tailers really function like traditional retailers. They buy products en masse, keep huge inventories, and fill orders one-by-one. Therefore, these companies face the same operational problems as traditional sellers, which often are stuck with too much product and must severely discount inventory to move it out of the warehouse.

And consumers never see the tremendous brick-and-mortar that supports the operation. So, don't believe the fallacy that e-tailers are bound, someday, to make money because of their low-cost business models.

The problem is simple. The Internet has opened a new channel for selling, and therefore changed the way e-tailers sell to their customer – both the public and their business trading partners. But, for the most part, they have not used the Internet to change the way they buy from their suppliers. With little integration of their trading networks, e-tailers must guess what consumers want, and order accordingly. Those guesses then sit in mammoth storehouses until they are moved – often at a loss.

The Internet and Intelligent Commerce

Can e-tailers become profitable? Certainly. But to do so, they must conduct "intelli-

---

Weblink

For on global issues, see:
hicks.ASCET.com
manheim.ASCET.com
ramanathan.ASCET.com
peters.ASCET.com

For more on forecasting, see:
uchneat.ASCET.com
wayman.ASCET.com

For more on back office, see:
ramanathan.ASCET.com

gent commerce." They need to work together with partners throughout their e-business trading networks to leverage the Internet, closely integrating with their suppliers, distributors, and customers. Of course, integration within their own enterprises is a prerequisite.

In doing so, today's e-tailers could immediately fix their most glaring operational deficiencies. They would be able to halt the red ink, increase shareholder value, and vastly accelerate an otherwise plodding march to profitability. Now, let's consider some specific ways that companies in all industries could leverage intelligent commerce to cut costs, boost productivity, and improve efficiencies.

Fix #1: Availability to Promise

The primary purpose of online selling is convenience and speed. Unfortunately, many existing online processes are not conducive to either. In many cases, consumers place orders quickly using the Internet, but filling the orders is a time-consuming process that does not leverage the capabilities of today's advanced technology. When faced with orders for out-of-stock items, many e-tailers operate exactly like a brick-and-mortar stores, special-ordering items, waiting for them to arrive at the distribution center, then shipping the order to the consumer – a costly process that wastes time and undermines the value of e-tail as a whole. Furthermore, because many frustrated customers will simply leave the site, look for the title elsewhere, and possibly never return, it's a process that will ultimately undermine e-tailers' revenues as well.

If e-tailers practiced intelligent commerce, consumers would know immediately which items were available to promise. This knowledge would be related quickly to the consumer, leading to a much more satisfying shopping experience. Indeed, order fulfillment times on promised items also would be slashed – as would the cost of fulfilling the special order – since orders could flow rapidly to the appropriate supplier. The result: greater sales and more satisfied consumers.

In addition, with intelligent commerce, e-tailers and their customers would have much greater insight into shipping costs. Currently, most U.S.-based e-tailers suffer from an inability to accurately forecast the full cost of shipping products internationally, limiting their appeal to a global audience. When these companies do ship abroad, their margins often plunge even further. With intelligent commerce, e-tailers would be able to more accurately forecast the cost of international shipping and accurately pass those costs along to the purchaser. With closer ties with suppliers, they also would be able to cut the costs of doing business with customers around the world.

Fix #2: Intelligent Forecasting

Intelligent commerce permits companies to engage in accurate forecasting. Currently, most e-tailers lack the ability to accurately predict customer demand. Because they are forced to rely on their best guess at what consumers want, inventory often sits in a vast warehouse until it is moved out – often through deep discounting. With intelligent commerce, e-tailers would be able to predict demand based on past order histories, ensuring that they don't get caught with too much or too little capacity.

Fix #3: Inventory Reduction and Transportation

As stated above, most e-tailers maintain huge inventories. Because many items aren't ordered in large quantities, they waste valuable warehouse space and create a growing need for bricks and mortar warehouses – the precise thing that the e-tail revolution is expected to eliminate. Alternatively, as too many consumers experienced during the 1999 holiday season, the latest 'hot' items are often not in stock at all, leading to unhappy, dissatisfied consumers.

With an integrated e-business trading network, e-tailers would be able to ramp up or down on specific items quickly. Suppliers would know in real-time the status of an e-tailer's supply. They would know which items were moving and not moving – and would increase or decrease incoming supply accordingly. As a result, the e-tailer would have more of its most popular items in stock, and fewer of less popular items. Back orders would be less common, and customers would be happier. In addition, the cost of processing orders and restocking inventory would be reduced.

Fix #4: Integration of Back Office Operations

Finally, e-tailers must revamp their back office operations. Unfortunately, many companies' inefficiencies don't stop with their suppliers. They also suffer from weak back office integration – integration between order-taking and order fulfillment. Orders may proceed efficiently to the warehouse floor. But there is little intelligence built into the system. In most instances, each order is handled as a separate entity. Orders cannot be consolidated – even if multiple orders, placed minutes apart, are going to same address. The result: higher transportation costs and lower customer satisfaction. With tighter integration on the back end, e-tailers would gain greater intelligence within their own organizations, yielding even more efficiencies in getting products to consumers.

From Business-to Consumer to Intelligent E-Business Trading Networks

Few would question that companies like Amazon.com, Buy.com, and eToys.com have mastered the business-to-consumer part of their Internet strategies. However, many of these companies have largely ignored the business-to-business potential of the Internet. According to industry analysts, that is a huge oversight.

Forrester Research predicts that business-to-business e-commerce will explode – fast – from $43 billion in 1998 to $1.3 trillion in 2003. In fact, some analysts believe that within five years, 90 percent of all business transactions conducted over the Internet will be business-to-business transactions.

Looking ahead, Mitsubushi Motors has jumped into the future by creating an e-business trading network that tightly integrates its supply chain with its e-commerce initiative to conduct intelligent commerce. Unlike many of today's e-tailers, it has used the Internet to create seamless connections among its stakeholders: dealers, suppliers, and corporate offices. The result: outstanding operational efficiencies and happy customers.

How did Mitsubishi do it? The company developed an e-business trading network that allows it to collaborate closely with its 500 North American dealers. At headquarters, a "profile" is developed of each dealership. This profile is based on factors such as dealer geography, customer buying patterns, promotions, seasonality, etc. Dealers help refine these profiles. Using the Internet, this information is sent directly to the shop floor, ensuring that the appropriate mix of automobiles are manufactured and shipped to each dealership. Dealers can even place special orders into the plant schedule with no middleman.

Mitsubishi's own vehicle lead times have been cut by more than 50 percent – dramatically reducing port and distribution center inventories. And, of course, less inventory means lower carrying costs, reduced cycle times, fewer unwanted vehicles, and higher profits.

Even more importantly: customers quickly get the cars they want. They don't have to compromise in any way, a huge competitive edge in an industry where more than 40 percent of customers must compromise when purchasing their vehicles. And, of course, happy customers equal return business.

Can Mitsubishi's success be duplicated – or exceeded? Of course. Using the Internet, businesses in nearly any industry can optimize their supply chain with their e-commerce strategy to create an e-business trading network of manufacturers, suppliers, and distributors that communicate and execute in real time. In turn, even a company's internal operations will improve significantly. The end result: a move from 'electronic commerce' to 'intelligent commerce.' It just takes a little foresight, and the knowledge that, over the next few years, the Internet will dramatically transform business-to-business relationships.

The Next Generation of B2B E-Commerce: An Interview with Bob Evans

q&a with

Bob Evans
Aspect Development
http://evans.ASCET.com

Aspect is a leading global provider of collaborative solutions for business-to-business e-commerce and inbound supply management. The company has seen its business take off in recent months as companies are looking for B2B e-commerce solutions. We talked with Bob Evans, Aspect's President and COO, about the impact of e-commerce on upstream supply chain collaboration.

We've seen explosive growth in B2B e-commerce. What's going on?
No question, this whole market of enabling businesses to effectively buy and sell with one another over the Web has just taken off, surprising a lot of folks. It has quickly moved beyond the experimental phase, where companies were installing transaction automation systems to automate the purchase of office supplies – what's referred to as "first generation" systems. Companies are now racing to include their high-value direct spend on things like the parts, components, and materials that go into their products and mission-critical MRO (maintenance, repair and operations) items.

Even more exciting is the fact that practically every industry is moving forward with an Internet exchange initiative. These exchanges have the potential to significantly change the way companies do business with one another at a very fundamental level.

Companies rarely jump at the chance to fundamentally change things. Why the sudden interest in all this?
It's about benefits. There are big benefits for the companies that do it right.

Let's start inside the enterprise. Consider the benefits that a large company can achieve if it can really leverage its full buying power and get all its divisions to work together to share design and operations information. By linking together a company's product development, sourcing and procurement, and operations organizations with collaborative processes and information, product engineers and operations personnel can choose which items to use from the same databases that the purchasing people use to determine which suppliers to buy them from. By making these choices in a collaborative way, the customer's whole organization benefits greatly – reducing spend, increasing re-use, and getting better products to market faster.

Now, B2B e-commerce opens up another layer of benefits in that it is now possible to extend these collaborative processes and information "outside" the enterprise, across multiple companies in a B2B exchange. Engineers in one company can collaborate on a new product design with the engineers at their suppliers. Similarly, purchasing organizations in multiple companies will soon have the ability to compare their spend patterns, aggregate their demand, and negotiate better pricing with suppliers; this benefits all participants in the exchange. That's the business that Aspect is in. Our solutions for B2B e-commerce enable collaboration inside our customers' businesses and with their trading partners. GartnerGroup has started calling it "Collaborative Commerce."

Give us an example of the kind of benefits a company can expect.
Working "inside" an enterprise, these new Collaborative Commerce solutions can help customers increase Earnings Per Share (EPS) by 15 to 20%. Our 180 customers have already documented almost $3 billion in benefits realized by these enterprise inbound supply management programs. But we think that another 10 to 15% EPS improvement is possible by extending these collaborative processes and information "out-

Since joining Aspect in April 1999, Bob Evans has helped lead the company's aggressive move into the eMarkets space, dramatically increase its market presence, and preside over the company's largest sales growth in its history. Prior to joining Aspect, Mr. Evans held a position as managing partner, Industry Programs, for Andersen Consulting's global Supply Chain Practice.

side" the enterprise and across the B2B exchange.

How can companies like Aspect already be developing solutions for the "next generation of B2B e-commerce"? What happened to the "first generation"?
Here's what's happened. The first generation of B2B e-commerce was focused on transaction automation. That makes sense, since until companies can exchange purchase requisitions, price quotes, orders, invoices, and even payments electronically, you really can't get much else done. But you have to ask a simple question: Why will buyers and sellers agree to participate in a B2B e-commerce exchange? No participants; no exchange.

The obvious answer: because exchange participants expect to realize substantial value. In our view, creating such value depends on having three things at the B2B exchange. First, you have to have the ability to automate transactions. Next, you need content – that is, detailed information about products and suppliers. Furthermore, this content has to be "buyer-friendly," meaning that it has to be well organized and easily accessible; it has to be standardized so buyers can compare alternatives; and it has to be manageable in the sense that any one buyer can indicate which items and suppliers are "preferred" so that all the people in their company buy the right things from the best supplier.

Weblink

For more on product development:
johnson.ASCET.com
ramanathan.ASCET.com
srivastava.ASCET.com

For more on transactions, see:
wayman.ASCET.com
manheim.ASCET.com
uchneat.ASCET.com
srivastava.ASCET.com

Finally, you need to be able to link the participants in a B2B exchange in such a way that they can collaborate with each other on product design, sourcing, and demand planning decisions. We call that decision support.

The next generation B2B exchange will have transaction automation, content and content management, and decision support capabilities. That's why participants will join an exchange.

Tell us more about decision support.
Let's go back inside the enterprise. The inbound supply chain is where companies design the products they will sell, source the components and materials needed to make those products, and procure and manage the plant, office equipment and supplies needed to conduct business. By way of contrast, the outbound supply chain is where companies make, move, and deliver the products that they sell. Companies like i2 Technologies and Manugistics have focused on decision support for the outbound supply chain. Aspect is focused on the inbound side where we help companies optimize design, procurement, and operations by enabling them to collaborate. The way we do that is to provide the information systems for executives to make decisions about what they should be buying, who they should be buying from, at what price, and how they can share design information with other design teams in the company.

And how about these new exchanges?
The emergence of B2B e-commerce exchanges is rapidly altering the way people think about supply chains. B2B exchanges are vastly different. Think about it. Chains are linear: each link connected to, at most, two other links. Relationships between companies, like a chain, are "hard-wired" and difficult to change. They are about integrating and optimizing operations within a single business enterprise. B2B exchanges, on the other hand, are networked, with everyone connected to everyone else. Relationships between companies are dynamic, constantly changing. And the focus is on aggregation and collaboration.

Earlier this year I did a presentation at Stanford University titled "The End of Supply Chains." We're in a new world of collaborative e-commerce.

Can you give an example of how Aspect is actually helping a customer in this collaborative e-commerce area?
Sure, take Celestica. Celestica is a $5-billion contract manufacturer of electronic products for companies like IBM, Hewlett-Packard, and Sun Microsystems. They have 19,000 employees at 30 manufacturing plants worldwide.

They are using Aspect's solutions to let their engineers work directly with their customers' engineers to select the best components and create the optimum design of products that Celestica will ultimately build for them. And if they select from Celestica's preferred parts list, Celestica passes on the additional savings they get from buying in massive volume.

The stock market has been going crazy over everything in this new B2B e-commerce space. Just how big will this market be – or is it a passing fad?
Nobody knows for sure, but some industry experts have predicted that over 100,000 B2B exchanges will be created worldwide over the next several years. We've also seen estimates that the cost of creating an exchange can range from $10-80 million. Even if only one-fourth to one-half of that is spent on software, the market is huge, in the billions.

As a reality check, consider that it's also been predicted that as much as $1.3 trillion dollars of business will be flowing through these B2B exchanges by 2003. If the exchange operators can collect fees in the range of one to two percent, we're talking billions in revenue for them.

The numbers work. Of course, it all depends on one thing. Can the B2B exchange create massive value for the participants? Fortunately, this is exactly what Aspect's solutions do.

http://aspect.ASCET.com — web link

Aspect Development – Global Leader in Inbound Supply Chain Management

aspect DEVELOPMENT

Aspect Development was founded in 1990 to develop and market an information management solution for companies that would enable them to manage their inbound supply chain – all the parts, materials, and supplies that companies buy to make, manage, or distribute their products. Aspect's solution offers an entirely new approach to organizing information and making it readily and intuitively accessible to end-users. Headquartered in Mountain View, Calif., with sales, marketing, content development, and support offices worldwide, Aspect's 800+ employees constitute the world's largest organization dedicated to developing solutions for Inbound Supply Chain Management. More than 20 sales and support offices worldwide serve the North American, European, and Asian markets.

The company has built a successful business selling solutions for Component & Supplier Management and e-procurement to the world's largest companies based on its unique content management, search, and information retrieval software, and e-content databases that contain information on millions of parts and supplies from hundreds of suppliers. Aspect established and continues to lead the Inbound Supply Chain Management industry, selling decision support and content solutions into three major business units, e-CSM (Component and Supplier Management), e-procurement, and e-market. E-CSM solutions optimize product development processes, by providing decision support and collaboration for design and procurement. E-Procurement solutions optimize non-production/MRO spend, by providing decision support and collaboration for operations and procurement. E-Market solutions provide the content and decision support infrastructure for Business-to-Business e-commerce portals and marketplaces.

Customer Profile

Aspect's customers include over 170 of the world's leading manufacturers of high-tech, Aerospace & Defense, Automotive, Industrial Equipment, Process, and Consumer Processed Goods. Companies such as: 3COM, Cooper Industries, GEC Marconi, Ford Motor Company, Emerson, Rockwell Automation, Compaq, Lucent, Boeing, Hughes Space, Motorola, Newport News Shipbuilding, Gates Rubber, General Instrument, Samsung, Honeywell, IBM, Lockheed Martin Vought, Motorola, Occidental Chemical, Shell Oil, and Sun Microsystems are just a sampling of Aspect's extensive customer list.

Market Leadership

Over the past several years, Aspect has helped create one of the most important markets for the new millennium – enterprise solutions for inbound supply chain management. For the first time, manufacturers are becoming aware that this critical front-end portion of their supply chain actually determines 75% of product cost, and that streamlining this process creates enormous cost savings. Aspect's solutions help companies streamline their inbound supply chains by optimizing the suppliers, components, and materials used to create and process products, and by enabling strategic collaboration between product development, procurement, and the supply base. Companies that have fully implemented the Aspect solution have saved more than $2 billion in hard dollar savings.

Aspect Services

Using Aspect's unique Rapid Deployment Methodology, Aspect's Professional Services organization delivers the following service solutions: Process Consulting Services, Data Content Services, Implementation Services, Educational Services. Aspect CSM solutions are designed and delivered through a combination of these services, together with Explore software and Aspect's Reference data content to optimally solve the customer's business issues.

Contact Information

Romesh Wadhwani Founder
Chairman and Chief Executive Officer

North America Headquarters
1395 Charleston Road
Mountain View, CA 94043
Phone 650.428.2700
Fax 650.968.4335
Info@aspectdv.com
www.aspectdv.com

Solution Inquiries: info@aspectdv.com
Investor Relations: lclerkin@aspectdv.com
Public Relations: mprocter@aspectdv.com

Branch Offices
Atlanta, GA
Boston, MA
Chicago, IL
Orlando, FL
Cleveland, OH
Boulder, CO
Dallas, TX
Detroit, MI
Los Angeles, CA
Montreal, Quebec
Nashua, NH
New York, NY
Toronto, ONT

viaLink – Optimizing Supply Chain Data Management Through Synchronization

Lack of Synchronization is Hindering Industries' Transition to E-Commerce

E-commerce works. Recent studies have shown that forward-thinking companies who have adopted new business processes and technologies tend to have margins that are .5% to 1% higher and turns that are 2- to 3-times higher than companies who have not (Dechert-Hampe & Co. "Strategic Research on B2B Readiness in the Food Industry", © 2000.)

The grocery industry has long recognized the need for e-commerce. Realizing that supply chain innovations depend on speedy exchange of key information between trading partners, some companies have already invested in EDI data transfer capability. However, many grocery retailers have hundreds, if not thousands, of suppliers. To implement EDI, trading partners were required to attempt to create hundreds of point-to-point electronic connections – a "haystack" approach.

Many of the companies who invested in EDI have been disappointed that only a small percentage of their trading partners have made similar commitments. Furthermore, even where EDI is implemented successfully, many times one or more of the trading partners eventually handle these electronic messages manually. Usually, only a few types of business documents (Purchase Orders and Invoices) are exchanged electronically. The result of this is that only a tiny fraction of the core business interactions in the supply chain are conducted electronically, and virtually all advanced supply chain applications have been inaccessible to this industry.

viaLink Achieves Synchronization With Shared Database

viaLink Offers The Food Industry Single-Point Synchronization, based on The "Hub And Spoke" Model of E-Commerce

Several industries have already successfully used the hub concept. The travel industry applied the idea in its SABRE®, system, built by American Airlines and maintained in Tulsa, OK. Thirty thousand travel agents and three million consumers have decided it's easier to make travel plans by connecting one time, to one hub, than it is to call 600 airlines, 50 car-rental companies, 35,000 hotels, and dozens of railways and cruise lines individually. FedEx has successfully applied the hub-and-spoke model, too; their hub is in Memphis. The telephone company applied hub and spoke over a hundred years ago – one wire from each telephone into a central solution.

It's about time we applied hub and spoke to solve our industry's e-commerce bottleneck. The good news is that it's already happening. The viaLink services provide a secure, low-cost, consistent way for participants in the retail supply chain to communicate about items and costs.

Instead of making many connections to reach many trading partners, each participant only makes one electronic connection to the viaLink services, in UCS EDI or some other convenient format. With viaLink, each retailer and supplier works out the electronic interface only once. Online data translations allow seam-

Contact Information

Lewis "Bucky" Kilbourne
Chairman and CEO
405.936.2473

Bob Baker
President
405.936.2310

Bob Noe
Executive Vice President
972.934.5501

Pat Fitzgerald
Senior Vice President
972.934.5515

The viaLink Company
13800 Benson Road
Edmond, OK 73013-6417
Toll Free 888.viaLink (842.5465)
Fax   405.936.2599
www.viaLink.com

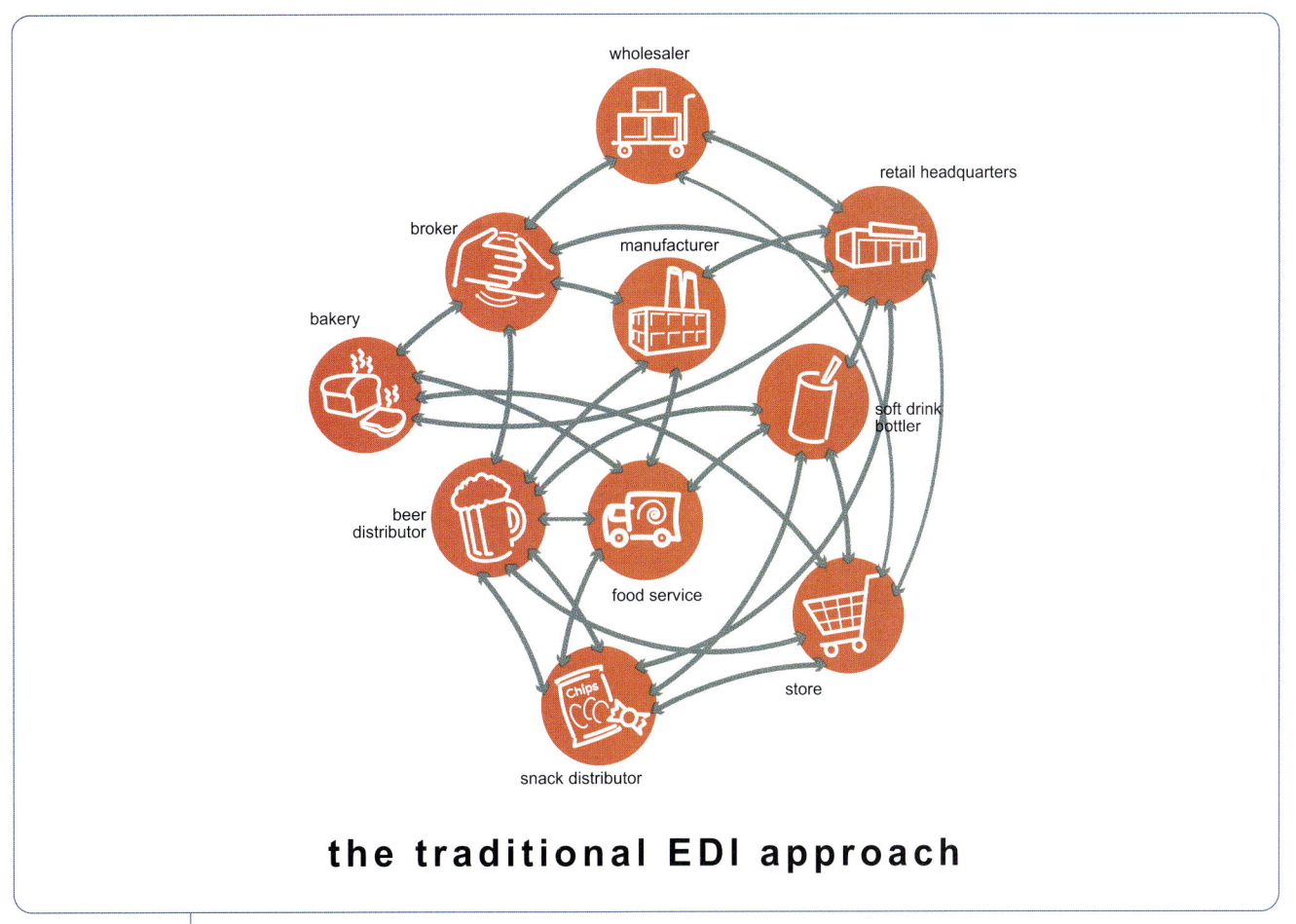

the traditional EDI approach

Figure 1.0 — The Traditional EDI Approach

less electronic connections directly into the subscribers' systems.

The result is an astonishing new level of supply chain visibility, with benefits for manufacturers, distributors, and retailers.

viaLink's Synchronization is Achieved through syncLink Service
syncLink℠ Item Catalog service is the foundation of all the viaLink services. It is a single database of item information for the industry. SyncLink Item Catalog database contains information about trading partners, and the items, prices, and promotions that constitute the trading relationship between the partners. This data becomes the data-of-record for the trading relationship, and forms the trusted foundation for e-business between the partners.

Three additional viaLink subscription-based services make e-commerce accessible and easily implemented.

1. Chain Pricing Service allows a brand or manufacturer true visibility to the supply channel that is delivering its products to the retailer. For example, a headquarters' brand representative can print a report that details the pricing offered to a specific retailer from all the distributors who sell to that retailer, provided that these distributors report merchandise to the retailer on viaLink and have granted reporting permission to the brand representative.

2. Item Movement Service allows manufacturers, retailers and distributors to share actual item performance information on a daily basis. This new level of business information enables simplified business processes for each of the trading partners. For example, performance-based programs are now easily accessible to the supply chain. A manufacturer and retailer can engage in scan-based promotions with access to single, trusted, and secure repository of actual performance data. Distributors have daily access to retail sales, to improve service levels.

3. Scan Based Trading Service allows a retailer to engage its suppliers on a new level of e-business, increasing sales and productivity for both the retailer and the supplier. As the trusted third-party in a trading relationship, this viaLink service builds on the information provided through Item Movement, then adds daily inventory activity such as counts and

http://vialink.ASCET.com   59

solution provider

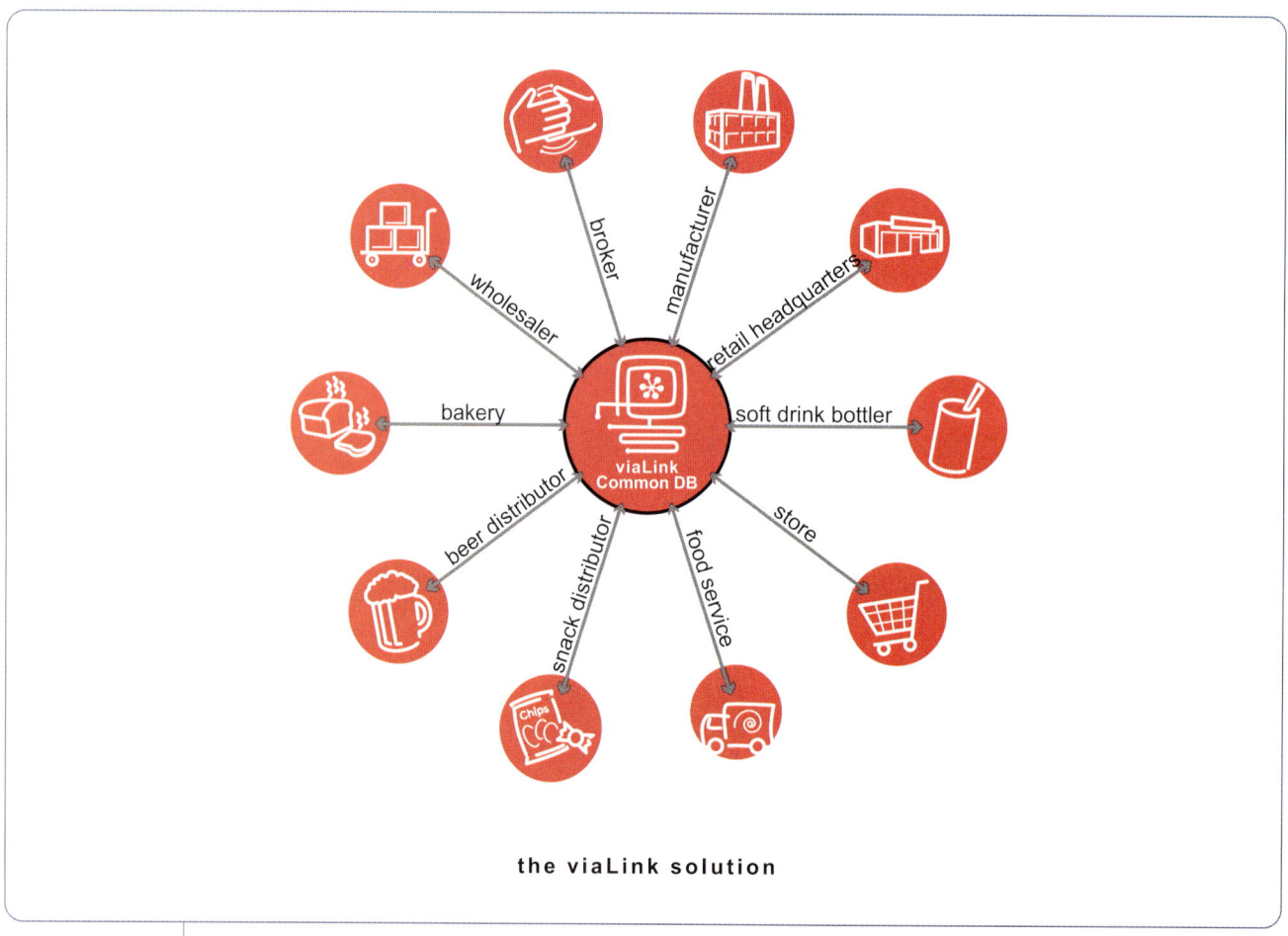

web link — http://vialink.ASCET.com

Figure 1.0   **The viaLink Solution**

adjustments. This comprehensive view of trusted and secure account-quality information allows the trading relationship to be based on actual retail sales, rather than on purchases by the retailer.

The viaLink services are revolutionizing the way manufacturers, distributors, and retailers exchange critical information in the food industry.

The viaLink services operate over the Internet, providing the widest range of connectivity options, making e-business easier and more effective for all trading partners, from the largest national brands to the smallest local operators.

At viaLink, CPG meets Technology

The viaLink Company was formed by food industry experts – people who have learned the complexities of the industry from the inside out. Based on solid business experience, the viaLink services offer methods for handling such problems as item maintenance, store-level pricing, promotions, authorization, pricing zone mapping, standardized EDI data structures, and the intricacies of communications, security and confidentiality. viaLink has successfully helped more than 250 customers in more than 40,000 store locations make the transition to e-business.

viaLink Products and Services

Instead of making many connections to reach many trading partners, each viaLink customer makes only one electronic connection to the viaLink services, in UCS, EDI, or some other convenient format.

Only a tiny fraction of the core business interactions in the supply chain are conducted electronically, and virtually all advanced supply chain applications have been inaccessible to this industry until viaLink introduced its synchronized electronic pricebook.

The viaLink Services are revolutionizing the way manufacturers, distributors, and retailers exchange critical information in the food industry.

The viaLink Services operate over the Internet, providing the widest range of connectivity options, making e-business easier and more effective for all trading partners, from the largest national brands, to the smallest local operators.

B2B E-Commerce Comes of Age and Drives Shareholder Value

written by:
Christopher Sprague
Bret Kinsella
Andersen Consulting
http://sprague.ASCET.com

The refrain is now common. Business-to-business (B2B) e-commerce is exploding. Trillion-dollar market estimates by 2003 and 90% compound annual growth rates are causing the bright spotlight that used to shine on business-to-consumer (B2C) companies to shift to B2B opportunities. Three years ago the story was AOL and Yahoo. Two years ago, it was Amazon. Last year it was eToys and eBay. This year it is Ariba, Chemdex, Commerce One, and VerticalNet that have broken through the mindshare clutter. While the B2C milestones have helped define technology standards, transaction capabilities, buying experiences and business models, we believe that B2B e-commerce will be the vehicle that truly delivers on the promise of the Internet.

Awakening of the B2B Slumbering Giant?

The emergence of B2B e-commerce is similar in magnitude to the industrial revolution that spawned new manufacturing methods, distribution channels, and buyer-supplier relationships. Similarly, B2B e-commerce represents another revolution that is fundamentally reshaping business relationships and is causing dramatic shifts in channel power as information and communication imbalances disappear. Moreover, just as B2C e-commerce empowered consumers and several nimble retailers with more commerce options and lower costs, B2B e-commerce is presenting buyers and suppliers with compelling value propositions to both lower transaction costs and increase the value captured in business relationships. These value propositions are opening the door to a new set of players that focus on facilitating buyer and supplier adoption of e-commerce capabilities.

To be clear, businesses are in the very early stages of e-commerce adoption. The underlying technology is still being refined. Businesses predicated on new models are being introduced daily, hoping to deliver innovative value propositions. Companies such as Celarix and Electron Economy, which are focused on solving supply chain and fulfillment complexity, are only now emerging.

So what? What's in it for me? Plenty. Electronic commerce presents opportunities to increase revenues and decrease supply chain and customer relationship costs, translating into higher margins that deliver higher shareholder value – key drivers of the CEO agenda. For visionary entrepreneurs, e-commerce presents an opportunity to create new businesses, new industries, and enormous value for their investors and customers.

In our conversations with executives and entrepreneurs we cover a common set of questions. What does the e-commerce solution and competitive landscape look like today? What trends are driving e-commerce adoption and marketplace evolution? How can I leverage the Internet and e-commerce opportunities to create value? This article explains how the diverse, competitive, and complex landscape is being driven by the rate of buyer and supplier adoption of e-commerce practices in different sectors. Moreover, we discuss the paths, pitfalls, and benefits associated with embracing e-commerce opportunities.

Christopher Sprague is an associate partner in the Andersen Consulting Supply Chain Practice. He is a leader in the development of e-commerce strategies that focus on using procurement to deliver operational and strategic benefits. He has recently assumed leadership responsibility for Andersen Consulting's e-procurement market offering.

Bret Kinsella is a manager in the Andersen Consulting strategy competency. His work focuses on strategiesy for building new e-commerce marketplaces. Mr. Kinsella's professional experience includes e-commerce strategy, business plan development, market and customer segmentation, alliance building, procurement solutions, and project management.

Section I – A Snapshot of B2B E-Commerce in the New Millennium

B2B E-Commerce Today – New Economics and New Channel Powers

Since the advent of the Industrial Revolution, one paradigm has reigned supreme in business-to-business commerce – supplier power. In recent years, some very large corporate buyers such as AT&T, Compaq, and General Motors recognized that their buying volume granted them certain channel powers that allowed them to dictate pricing and service levels for some commodities. However, strategic sourcing luxuries are reserved for only the largest buyers and only for a limited number of commodities. The time and expense associated with gathering expenditure data, negotiating new pricing with suppliers, and then managing contracts have been undertaken by many large corporations only to find that the benefits don't stick. Although they may have negotiated lower prices, the true benefits can be elusive if they are unable to deliver the enterprise's demand.

The Internet is inverting the economics of procurement. Electronic commerce technologies are not only extending traditional value propositions to new classes of buyers and suppliers, they are also presenting entirely new value propositions. Buyers have access to more information, buying tools, and electronic access to suppliers. This translates directly into better commodity pricing and lower transaction costs. Additionally, new channel intermediaries are providing buyers large and small with access to these value propositions as well as providing significant value to suppliers such as increased access to qualified customers, lower transaction, and customer service costs. The result of these changes? Channel power is shifting to Internet-enabled buyers and the new intermediaries, B2B marketplaces.

E-Commerce Value Propositions Are Spreading Rapidly – First Suppliers, then Buyers, then B2B Marketplaces

Supplier-Centric Developments

First suppliers published information on the Web. A simple value proposition: publish brochure-ware on the Internet and make it easier for customers and potential customers to access and less expensive to update. Then suppliers such as W.W. Grainger, the nation's leading business-to-business distributor of maintenance, repair, and operating supplies and related information, recognized an opportunity to expand sales volume by providing transaction capabilities on their Web site. About the same time, companies such as Dell and Cisco turned to e-commerce to reduce sales and service support costs by transferring sales to the Web and away from costly call centers and field sales representatives. Other suppliers, such as Ingram Micro, a wholesale distributor of computer-based technology products and services, adopted electronic auctions to achieve better excess inventory disposition pricing. As in the past, benefits accrued to the suppliers. However, as more suppliers came online, pricing differences became easier for buyers to access due to lower search costs. With this buying came the often tedious need to surf multiple supplier Web sites to compare pricing, service level, and quality, and it presented new challenges in controlling off-contract buying. Could there be a better way?

Buyer-Centric Developments

These activities were closely followed by the availability of Web-enabled tools designed to meet buyer needs. Electronic procurement software packages were developed by companies such as Ariba and Commerce One to create process, demand management, information, and transaction efficiencies for large buying organizations. British Telecom, CIBC, Citigroup, Chevron, Eastman Chemical, FedEx, and Transamerica are a few of the Fortune 500 companies with the resources and buying power to deploy enterprise-level e-procurement systems. While implementation of these systems combined with the required process and organizational changes can often cost millions of dollars, these changes can translate into considerable benefits. And despite initial concerns, suppliers found that they to were able to achieve broad benefits as well by conducting business online. These benefits included: lowers sales costs combined with broader reach, accurate electronic orders, better customer service, the potential to plan production around demand, and more.

B2B Marketplace Developments

B2B marketplaces are the frontier that promises to extend buyer benefits beyond the Fortune 500 and offer new value propositions to Fortune 500 buyers. These new supply chain or channel intermediaries are also positioned to provide benefits to suppliers, large and small. Smaller buyers benefit from lower published pricing and product search costs. Buyers of all sizes are benefiting from better pricing by employing reverse auction tools and electronic requests-for-quotes facilitated by such companies as BizBuyer, Commerce One, and Moai. These solutions allow buyers to access far more suppliers than ever before and use e-commerce tools, data, and strategic sourcing to rationalize their supplier base. Suppliers win also by gaining access to new classes of buyers and are experiencing lower transaction costs through intermediaries such as Chemconnect and PlasticsNet.

With that said, B2B e-commerce is in its infancy. Channel power struggles are uncertain. Will buyers win? Will new intermediaries dominate or fail? Will sup-

---

Weblink

For more on channel inventory, see:
wayman.ASCET.com
bruce.ASCET.com
anthony.ASCET.com

For more on revenues, see:
peters.ASCET.com

For more on customer relationships:
srivastava.ASCET.com

For more on shareholder value, see:
srivastava.ASCET.com

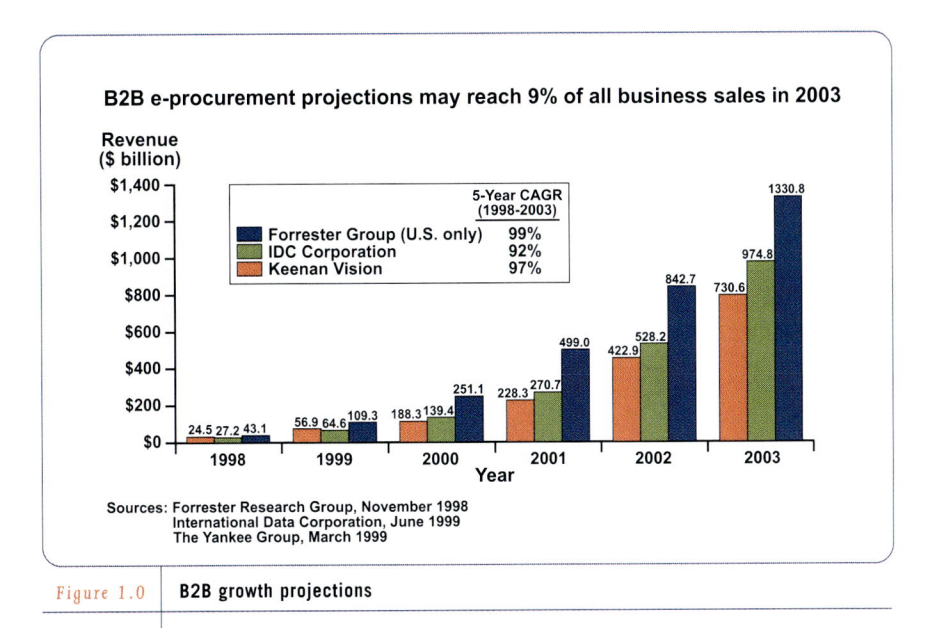

B2B e-procurement projections may reach 9% of all business sales in 2003

Year	Forrester Group (U.S. only)	IDC Corporation	Keenan Vision
1998	24.5	27.2	43.1
1999	56.9	64.6	109.3
2000	188.3	139.4	251.1
2001	228.3	270.7	499.0
2002	422.9	528.2	842.7
2003	730.6	974.8	1330.8

5-Year CAGR (1998-2003): Forrester Group (U.S. only) 99%; IDC Corporation 92%; Keenan Vision 97%.

Sources: Forrester Research Group, November 1998; International Data Corporation, June 1999; The Yankee Group, March 1999

Figure 1.0 — B2B growth projections

pliers reassert their power? Moreover, the ability to scale buying activity and supplier connectivity, and navigate the myriad fulfillment challenges is still unproven. Where will buyers congregate? Will integration with suppliers ever allow widespread or true real-time price, inventory, and order-tracking capabilities? Will B2B companies succeed in fulfillment where B2C companies to date have come up short?

Section II – B2B E-Commerce Moving Forward

Which Catalysts are Defining the Evolution of E-Commerce?

Executives, entrepreneurs, and venture capitalists are all placing bets on how the market will evolve and who will be on the winning end of the channel struggles. To answer these questions and others, Andersen Consulting has developed a scenario planning framework around traditional purchasing practices, three new marketplaces listed above (supplier-centric, buyer-centric, B2B marketplaces) and the catalysts driving e-commerce today: buyer and supplier adoption rates. With each scenario comes different business and operating models, value propositions, and vendor solutions.

The two factors that Andersen Consulting believes will determine the rate at which we arrive at the trillion-dollar e-commerce world are:

- Buyer B2B adoption rate: the extent to which buying organizations are able to migrate from paper-based or EDI platforms to automate B2B transactions using e-commerce enablers and new market mechanisms.
- Supplier B2B adoption rate: the extent to which manufacturers, distributors, and other intermediaries are able to use enabling technologies and new business models to deliver new value to their customers and themselves.

Taken together, these two factors identify the four market scenarios in which organizations currently are transacting and could transact. Four marketplace scenarios define how buying and selling organizations will transact in B2B e-commerce: traditional, supplier-centric, buyer-centric, and B2B marketplaces (see Figure 2.0).

Today each of these worlds exists in varying stages of development. Market leaders and innovators are aggressively in "land grab" mode trying to execute new business models and lock in major customer segments. For instance, Ariba, Commerce One, and Oracle are battling for Fortune 500 clients for their procurement application software. Ford's AutoXchange is competing head-on with General Motor's TradeXchange to create electronic trading markets in the automotive industry. Chemdex and SciQuest are battling to attract a critical mass of researchers in the life sciences arena. Metalsite and eSteel are battling in the metals segment. And while this is going on in the United States, similar competition is emerging in other parts of the world, such as Ariba and Telefonica teaming up against Commerce One and Banacci to create Latin American e-commerce marketplaces.

Traditional Scenario – Suppliers and Large Buyers Win

The lower left quadrant represents everything that you would expect of the pre-Internet and pre-e-commerce era. It is a world of paper-based solutions and supplier-dictated pricing. Because of their cost and complexity, EDI connections that rely on proprietary networks are suitable for only the largest corporations and generally are reserved for key production resources. Relationships here are fragmented, and there is considerable informational disparity between buyers and suppliers. In general, suppliers have an information advantage and, therefore, channel power. Only very large buyers such as Fortune 500 companies can set their own prices and then only for a small subset of commodities. For the balance of commodities, Fortune 500 and most other buyers are price takers – that is, suppliers control the price and service umbrellas for products and services.

Supplier-Centric Scenario: Early Inroads in B2B E-Commerce

As the Internet became commercially viable, the first B2B e-commerce wins came from seller-centric offerings in the upper left quadrant. Suppliers recognized opportunities to make old practices more efficient and maintain their one-to-many relationships that they had cultivated. Buyers in turn were forced to access multiple Web sites to conduct buying. Going forward, this quadrant will continue to provide suitable solutions for small and

http://sprague.ASCET.com 63

mid-sized businesses, but will only serve large buyers on rare occasion. Companies such as Dell, W.W. Grainger, and Works.com are well positioned to succeed in this space. Moreover, most suppliers will reap benefits from additional spot-buy sales and lower transaction and customer service costs as a result of having a presence of this sort.

Buyer-Centric Scenario: Introducing the "Electronic Avon Lady"

While some suppliers were investing to publish electronic catalogs, early adopters of intranet buying solutions were forcing other suppliers down this same path. Ariba and Commerce One have defined the buyer-centric world in the lower right quadrant by developing applications to streamline many-to-one buying for Fortune 500 companies. They provide strong buyer value propositions in demand management and process savings. Buyers in this category are large enough to negotiate terms that even the largest commodity suppliers are willing to concede. As a result, large volume buyers have become price makers. With that said, the suppliers learned that being price-takers was not all bad. Not only do they gain greater market share within these corporations, but they also are able to reduce sales costs, reduce order entry errors, receive faster payment, and optimize production based on real-time market demand.

Buyer-centric solutions, however, are designed for large enterprises. In fact, the original solutions were available only in enterprise editions with price tags in the seven digits. Buyer-centric solutions focus on aggregating large catalogs of commodities from existing suppliers and placing them in searchable databases where buyers can easily access items and create purchase orders. The considerable effort involved in establishing these systems, reliance on process and demand management savings, and their high cost make buyer-centric solutions inappropriate for most small or mid-sized businesses. But what about organizations that lack the procurement volume to invest in e-procurement? What about organizations unwilling or unable to spend millions to make procurement more efficient? Is there anyway they can access e-commerce value?

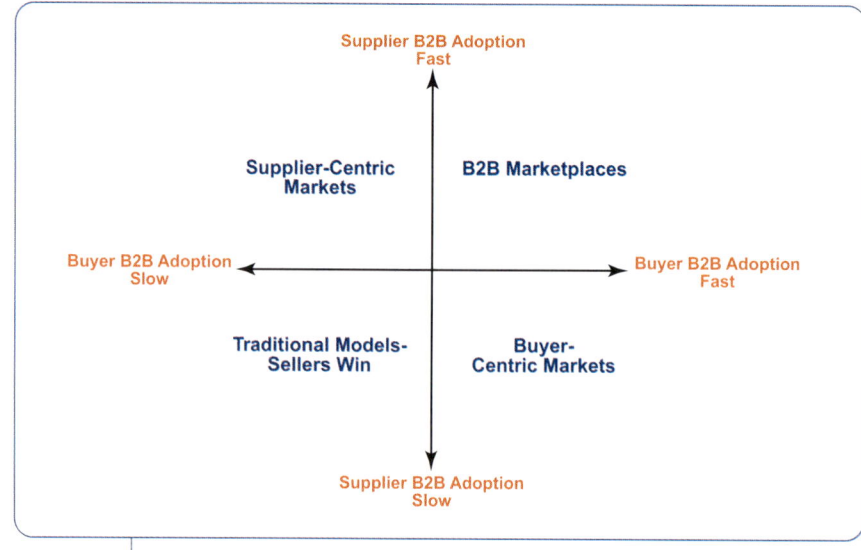

Figure 2.0 | B2B marketplace scenarios

B2B Marketplaces Scenario: Creating Entirely New Buying Alternatives

The upper right quadrant consists of entirely new business models and new businesses. Some have a bias in favor of suppliers. Some have a bias in favor of buyers. Some claim neutrality. What they intend to do well is bring together previously fragmented communities of buyers and suppliers through many-to-many platforms. These communities can be designed for large or small companies and potentially for both. Unlike the buyer-centric scenario that requires large capital investments for "inside the firewall" solutions, we are now seeing a variety of hosted services and procurement portals targeting both horizontal and vertical markets with transaction-based pricing instead of the seven digit up-front costs.

Winners in this space will organize communities in industries with thousands of buyers and suppliers to facilitate trade. They will provide tools to manage information, suppliers, and customer relationship management activities, to buy and sell more efficiently as well as publish industry-oriented content. Moreover, they will provide multiple value propositions to both suppliers and buyers.

B2B Evolution – Favoring Buyers or Suppliers or Both

Three strategies are emerging as viable options for businesses in each of the quadrants:

- Focused entrenchment
- Migration
- Multiple markets

Focused entrenchment: A focused entrenchment strategy involves making a decision to either help buyers or suppliers, and requires a company to be dedicated to one quadrant. Companies such as Harbinger, a worldwide provider of business-to-business e-commerce software, services, and solutions, are committed to helping suppliers navigate e-commerce complexity by deploying, maintaining, and even hosting electronic catalogs. Moreover, marketplaces such as ChemConnect have no intention of committing solely to supplier-centric or buyer-centric solutions, but are committed to developing many-to-many trading communities.

Migration

Migration strategies are being employed by companies that are either not succeeding in the quadrant they originally entered or are seeking greater opportunities in an adjacent quadrant. For example, Elcom, a company that develops, licenses, and uses Internet-based e-procurement systems, has not achieved broad recognition or critical mass in the buyer-centric market. However, they have recognized an opportunity to use their buying platform as a hosted solution that could be offered to large or mid-sized companies. Moreover, they took the additional step of developing StarBuyer, an online catalog with public pricing where customers can buy goods and services through a single interface. These actions are moving Elcom away from the buyer-centric to the B2B marketplace arena.

Multiple Markets

At this point, however, many companies are not willing to commit to one quadrant because of the tremendous opportunities available and the usefulness of their technologies in multiple markets. From the onset, Commerce One developed a platform that was suitable for buyer-centric solutions or B2B marketplaces and have customers in both quadrants. Ariba, the early leader in buyer-centric e-procurement solutions, recently acquired Tradex to give itself more functionality and a greater presence in the B2B marketplace arena. Aspect Development, whose solutions provide digital catalog content management and decision-support tools for high-tech industries, not only deploys and maintains catalog content for suppliers, but also is spawning vertical marketplaces for many-to-many communities. Moai Technologies is providing auction software for large suppliers and for B2B marketplaces. Straddling multiple markets is attractive, but it carries inherent risks for those companies with limited time and resources. The largest, most aggressive businesses employing this strategy will succeed while others will be forced to adopt an entrenchment strategy as competition and resource constraints begin to take a toll.

Section III: Opportunities for Delivering Shareholder Value

So where is the value and what should I do to capture it? The first place to start is procurement of indirect goods. This section describes the types of benefits organizations can achieve, likely migration options for capturing value, a number of enablers required for success and several barriers that will threaten the process.

Early adopters that have combined strategic sourcing with e-procurement have been able to achieve savings of 10 to 30% per billion of indirect goods and services purchases by changing the way they buy. Benefits from transforming procurement fall into the following categories:

• Reducing price paid by consolidating

PROCUREMENT COST LEVERS

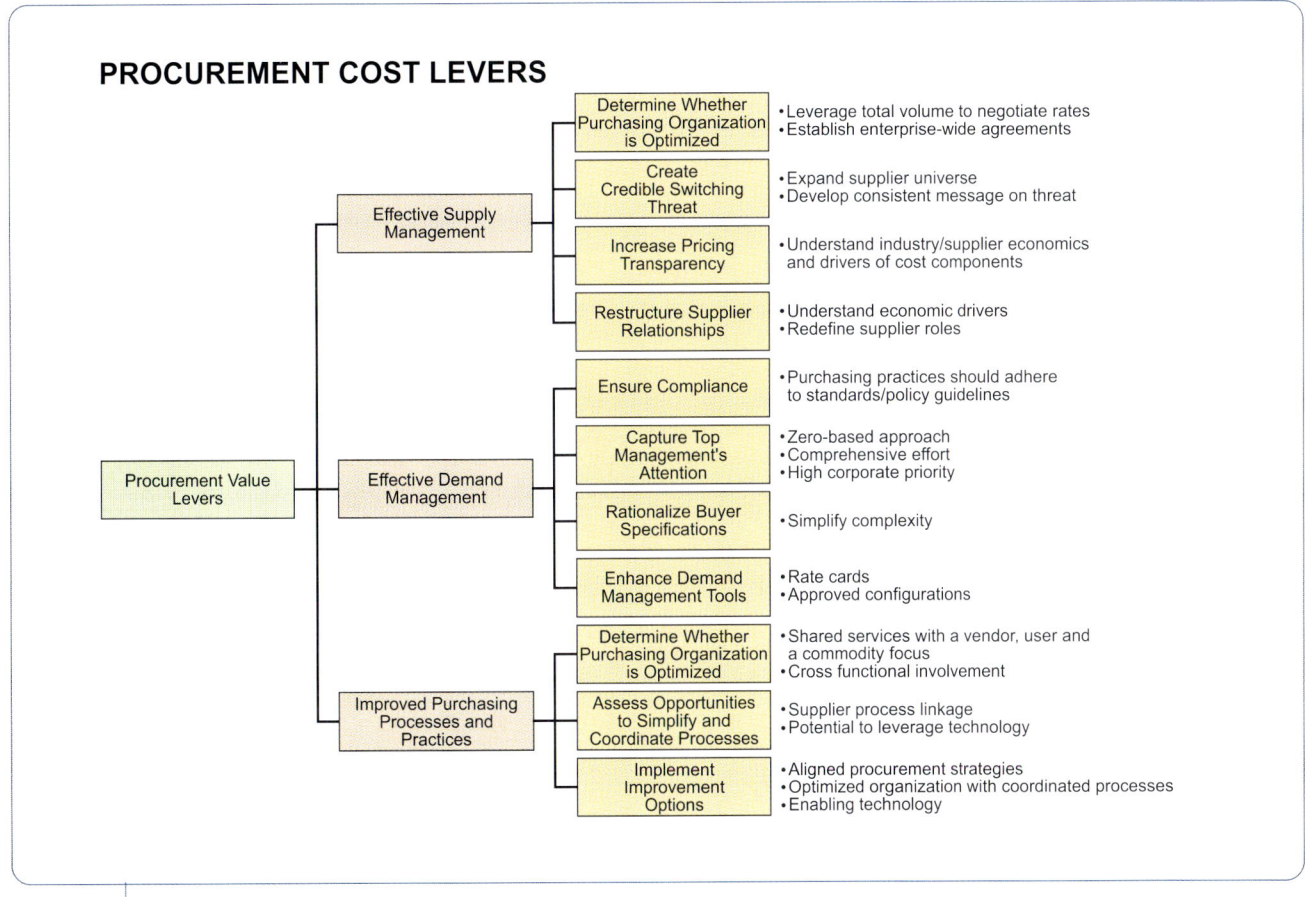

Procurement Value Levers
- Effective Supply Management
  - Determine Whether Purchasing Organization is Optimized
    - Leverage total volume to negotiate rates
    - Establish enterprise-wide agreements
  - Create Credible Switching Threat
    - Expand supplier universe
    - Develop consistent message on threat
  - Increase Pricing Transparency
    - Understand industry/supplier economics and drivers of cost components
  - Restructure Supplier Relationships
    - Understand economic drivers
    - Redefine supplier roles
- Effective Demand Management
  - Ensure Compliance
    - Purchasing practices should adhere to standards/policy guidelines
  - Capture Top Management's Attention
    - Zero-based approach
    - Comprehensive effort
    - High corporate priority
  - Rationalize Buyer Specifications
    - Simplify complexity
  - Enhance Demand Management Tools
    - Rate cards
    - Approved configurations
- Improved Purchasing Processes and Practices
  - Determine Whether Purchasing Organization is Optimized
    - Shared services with a vendor, user and a commodity focus
    - Cross functional involvement
  - Assess Opportunities to Simplify and Coordinate Processes
    - Supplier process linkage
    - Potential to leverage technology
  - Implement Improvement Options
    - Aligned procurement strategies
    - Optimized organization with coordinated processes
    - Enabling technology

Figure 3.0 Procurement Cost Levers highlight the different ways in which organization can track the benefits that come from transforming procurement.

purchases enterprise-wide with suppliers who can deliver with the lowest total cost of ownership
- Reducing the cost of buying by centralizing and streamlining processes while providing business users the ability to self-service their own demand
- Buying less and better (managing demand) by proactively influencing business buyers to buy what they need from the preferred suppliers
- Managing suppliers by proactively generating information automatically as a by-product of day-to-day transactions that provides real-time knowledge and feedback
- Growing revenue by extending complementary procurement service offerings that increase your customer's or supply chain partner's profitability and effectiveness

Migration Options for Buying Organizations

Most large organizations are starting in the lower left (traditional) quadrant when it comes to indirect procurement. There are several migration paths organizations are taking in search of procurement related savings. While some give the appearance of savings, they may in fact drive costs and overall spending up.

Option #1- Seller-Centric Panacea (Buyer Beware)

Devoid of an overall procurement strategy, decentralized buying organizations are likely to take advantage of supplier-centric Web sites to order directly. While this gives the appearance of effective procurement, there are a number of drawbacks to this strategy:

- Fragmented buying across multiple suppliers – failing to have enterprise-wide sourcing – suppliers now proliferate as buying divisions go online with their favorite suppliers.
- Perception of decentralized control – decentralized organizations further strengthen their claim on procurement and likely develop redundant, non-standard purchasing systems and drive up costs.

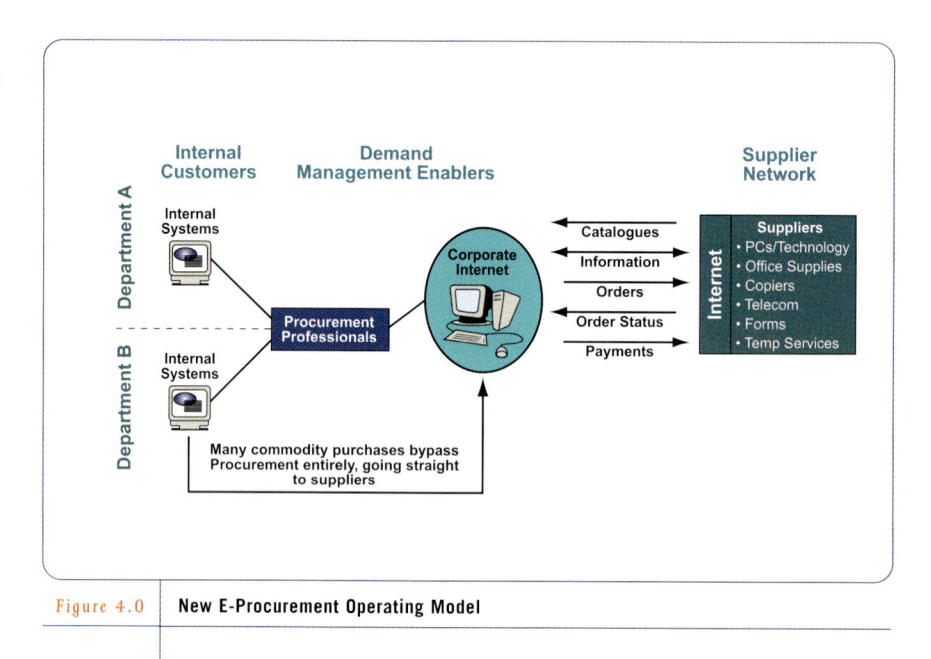

Figure 4.0 | New E-Procurement Operating Model

- Potentially increased spending – with this access, it is likely that spending will increase, due to a lack of an overall approach to proactively manage demand.
- Minimal buying information – suppliers now control spending data leaving clients with the only option of "reading the accounts payable tea leaves" to try to understand where and with whom they are spending.
- Lost control – left decentralized, the corporate CFO has little power and finds the organization cannot manage procurement effectively.

Decentralized buying is the CFO nightmare that is now being addressed by many large organizations. Given the need for bottom-line profits, many CFOs find it unacceptable not to be able to answer easily the questions "What are you spending? With whom? For what?" Increased financial pressure will mean more organizations will find this situation untenable. Some may resort to strategic sourcing to rationalize suppliers and negotiate lower prices, which may be a good short-term strategy, though experience shows that savings are rarely sustained without launching similar initiatives every three years. So what options do they have for more fundamental change and recurring savings?

Option #2- Buyer-Centric E-Procurement Solutions (Transform Thyself)

Many organizations will decide to adopt buyer-centric solutions found in the lower right quadrant. This is typically driven by corporate and divisional CFOs in industries that are under pressure to deliver increases in the bottom line. Ideally, many of these organizations have engaged in strategic sourcing but find that they cannot make the benefits last without e-procurement. With these solutions, they can now publish catalogs with preferred supplier deals on desktops enterprise-wide, allowing commodity users to interact and transact with the assistance of automated approval workflow.

Andersen Consulting can help these organizations to develop new e-procurement operating models (see Figure 4.0) which transform procurement end to end. Such models combine "inside the firewall" infrastructure with Internet communications directly to suppliers. More specifically, they rely on:

- The application to gain access to customized catalogs with pre-negotiated items and prices from preferred suppliers
- The intranet to consolidate the organization's buying with electronic desktop catalogs, automated approval routing, and integration with financial systems

- The Internet to check availability electronically, place orders, track order status, and make payments

Underlying this new business model are a series of key enablers:

- Intranet-enabled processes to reduce the cost of buying and selling through the use of automated workflow, electronic catalog access, ordering, and more
- Enterprise resource planning systems integration to provide critical information, enable workflow, capture critical information, link with general ledger and financial systems, and generate management information
- Technology infrastructure to provide the networks and connections to allow information to flow seamlessly within and outside the enterprise
- Change management to initiate fundamental behavioral and organizational change required to realize and sustain benefits

While this is a logical migration path taken by many of the early adopters, it requires organizations to commit millions of dollars to roll out these solutions enterprise-wide. Moreover, a number of barriers and "disablers" typically stand in the way of successfully implementing these programs:

- Financial commitment: Organizations are challenged to fund the initiative, given the large up-front license, customization, installation, and integration costs.
- Politics of procurement: Even with a go-ahead, organizations implementing shared services procurement are challenged to wrestle control away from decentralized buying organizations.
- Market confusion: Given the variety of solutions and alternative business models, organizations can spend months in the request-for-proposal or request-for-information vendor churn, often with little to show for their efforts.
- Implementation complexity: Simply put, it's hard to integrate disparate solutions while transforming processes and the organization.
- Supplier adoption: Realizing benefits requires suppliers to deliver electronic content and e-commerce-enabled processes and interfaces, which in many cases simply do not exist today.

Despite these barriers, an increasing number of organizations are able to build the procurement strategies and migration plans to deliver badly needed bottom-line relief.

Option #3: Transformed B2B Markets – Best Practices Procurement

Many organizations want to move to buyer-centric solutions, but they find themselves in "e-procurement gridlock," stuck with traditional procurement inefficiencies due to "disablers." Perhaps by waiting, some buying organizations believe that alternative solutions will come along that may cost less to implement and deliver benefits sooner, and they may be right.

A number of solutions now are being introduced that allow organizations to outsource technology and process management. Requiring buyers to have a browser and Internet access, these sites provide access to approved commodities and suppliers at contracted prices or an efficient channel for the inevitable spot buys. In addition to these services, a number of industry-specific catalog hosting sites, auctions, exchanges, and bartering systems are beginning to take hold. All of this presents new opportunities to reduce prices and process costs by paying for the service per transaction instead of large up-front subscription or software licensing fees.

Final Thoughts and Recommendations

Andersen Consulting believes that businesses will rapidly see the promise of the Internet being delivered through B2B e-commerce and will adopt indirect goods – and eventually direct goods – procurement via the Web. Finally, we believe that history is making a comeback with a "return to timesharing." Where companies used to share time on mainframes due to cost, they will now adopt outsourced procurement enablement to reduce cost and complexity. A variety of outsourcing alternatives will allow organizations to buy services that will facilitate management of supplier relationships, buyer relationships, information, and transaction services.

So what should you do? If you are reading this white paper, you are likely to be interested in what one of our clients refers to as "figuring out how you can take the dollars off the table and put them in the pocket." While this can be done, one cannot underestimate the challenges associated with enterprise-wide change. Our strong recommendation is that organizations diligently try to understand which of the scenarios can deliver the most value and do so the fastest. Based on this effort, they can put in place a B2B procurement strategy focused on answering where, when, and how the benefits can be realized. For new businesses, the decision is which benefits do you want to deliver to buyers or suppliers. Those answers will determine marketplace strategies and allow them to effectively facilitate e-commerce adoption and benefits realization for buyers and suppliers of all sizes.

Acknowledgement

Special thanks to a great core team including Mark Basile, Margaret Bawden, Christopher Brousseau, Jay Holata, Mike Princi, and Ed Starr whose contributions have made this white paper possible.

Copyright© 2000 Andersen Consulting LLP

solution provider
weblink — http://walker.ASCET.com

Walker and Deep E-Business Solutions for the Enterprise

WALKER

Walker (NASDAQ: WALK) is a leading, global provider of e-business solutions for the enterprise and has been a supplier of enterprise software for over 25 years.

Walker's answer to surviving in the e-business world is to implement Deep e-business which goes far beyond simply offering transaction-based capabilities that enable self service on the Web. Deep e-business includes collaborating with partners, process integration across the entire value chain, and complex security structures. The following Walker guidelines help you manage the complex processes and drive your Deep e-business decisions:

Define a Web-based Business Strategy

Decide what you want your e-business to accomplish and create new web-based processes to support it. Let your e-business strategy drive the technology architecture decisions, not the reverse. Deep e-business is an evolutionary process, not a revolutionary one. Start by putting a Web browser interface onto existing applications, but don't stop there.

Build Integration in from the Start

Use only platforms that are built to standards which offer the dexterity and interoperability necessary to streamline communication between partners and vendors. Use an open, server-centric architecture running proven e-business software solutions that have integration capabilities built in. Centralized processes are easy to deploy and create consistency across your organization.

Build on a Robust Platform

The necessity for platform robustness cannot be overstated. Centralized e-business architectures require enormous power to handle transaction surges and intense throughput demands. Scalability provides the flexibility required of an e-business. Reliability to "five nines" is essential when you have the global reach of an e-business. e-business systems require sophisticated security that permits virtual views of corporate data without threatening its integrity.

E-Procurement, E-Revenue, and E-Insight Solutions

Walker applications contain all the elements of Deep e-business. With Deep e-business solutions in three areas — e-procurement, e-revenue, and e-insight — Walker offers specific Web-based solutions for use in your e-business.

One of Walker's customers, a large, US-based manufacturing company recently implemented Walker's Deep e-procurement solution. The customer's scalability requirements were enormous and since Walker's Deep e-procurement solution is the most scalable electronic procurement application available on the market, they are now able to handle high volume transactions. Their suppliers also have an easy-to-use interface for Web-based inquiries, all invoices come in electronically, and inventories are automatically updated. The customer has automated their entire supply chain, from requisition to payment, eliminating task intensive purchasing activities, and saving time and money.

Contact Information

Frank Richardson
CEO

Stan Vogler
CFO

Paul Lord
President

Walker Headquarters
303 Second Street, 3N
San Francisco, CA 94107
Phone 800.742.5925
info@walker.com
www.walker.com

Dynamic Trading: Supply Chain Networks Driving the E-Commerce Revolution

The impact of e-commerce on Supply Chain Management goes beyond providing an effective communication medium. A powerful tool for collaboration, e-commerce in effect helps the supply chain coordinate itself; this can open up a wealth of opportunities to create "Dynamic Trading Networks" by shifting the responsibility for certain activities to the right business partner.

Supply Chain Evolution

Many early Internet success stories build on the medium's highly effective communication capabilities to enhance current ways of interacting and doing business. Consumers now have the capability to research, browse, and order a wide range of products and services. Businesses can now simply and economically share all kinds of information, ranging from employee benefits to material requirement forecasts, and annual reports with their suppliers, customers, employees, and shareholders.

However, beyond those capabilities, something more fundamental is happening. Businesses are discovering that the ease of communication inherent in e-commerce can change the nature of business relationships. New specialist companies or departments can undertake specific logistics activities that were previously integrated into a company's core operations. The impact on the way the supply chain operates is far-reaching: the supply chain as it is known today will effectively disintegrate; the management of supply chain activities will become far more dynamic and decision-making will occur faster and will be based on real-time information.

This disintegration and the increased speed of decision-making create the opportunity for dynamic trading. The disintegration effect will often include the separation of the logistics information from the physical flows. Specialist logistics groups will not own any traditional logistics assets, but rather will manage the systems and make the decisions related to the supply chain network. The existing distribution companies will own the assets and execute the plans.

This disintegration comes at a time when most logistics professionals are focusing their time and their investment dollars on integrating the different components in their supply chain – internally, across functions within their companies, and externally with their trading partners, including both suppliers and customers. As companies will need to rely on the ready access to information contained in their transactions systems, this effort is a prerequisite to the emergence of dynamic trading.

In the longer term, specialist logistics companies may not remain independent operations, but could be bought and folded back into the operations of leading companies. If the new logistics companies can position themselves to generate premium profits and gain the power in the supply chain, then larger organizations will seek to take them over. Looking past the disintegration, the next stage in the evolution of the supply chain will more than likely be the reintegration of power and ownership of the supply chain. The current phase of disintegration represents the start of that process.

Dynamic Trading Networks

Understanding the impact of disintegration and reintegration of the supply chain in an individual company can be difficult because there are so many variables generated by other players. For one particular company, linking up with an industry-based service organization may be the best choice; for another, focusing on interaction with selected customers might provide the greatest source of value; while for a third, taking the bold step of creating an industry-level supply chain solution to generate a new revenue stream might offer the most attractive business outcome.

The initial consideration for most compa-

Peter Moore is an associate partner in the Andersen Consulting Strategy Practice. He has experience in logistics, supply chain and manufacturing strategy, business process re-engineering, and productivity improvement. He has worked with companies in the food, beverage, confectionery, pharmaceutical, industrial products, and process industries.

nies is to determine which trading partners provide the best opportunity (or greatest real threat) for changing how business is conducted. From a supply chain perspective, there are two groups of trading partners: upstream partners such as suppliers, or downstream partners such as customers and consumers. Other partners operate in a parallel sense in the supply chain, such as third-party logistics providers or competitors. These partners tend to focus either on supplier-related or customer-related activities and therefore fall into either the upstream or downstream relationships described above.

The second consideration is the nature of the changing relationship. Will the e-commerce opportunities be used just to impact the way information is exchanged or will there be a fundamental change in the delivery mechanism as well? Information exchange alone can be as simple as automating current paperwork, such as Internet-based ordering and invoicing, but most companies take the opportunity to provide new services that are not possible in the old world. Examples of these services are collaborative planning, provision of supply and forecast information, and vendor-managed inventory.

In the examples above, the delivery activity has not significantly changed. The same truck leaves the supplier's warehouse and delivers product to the customer even if the delivery frequency and reliability has improved. More ambitious companies are pushing the possibilities further and are

	Information	Information and Delivery
Customer	Dynamic Service Network	Dynamic Delivery Network
Supplier	Dynamic Purchase Network	Dynamic Supply Network

Figure 1.0 — Four supply chain models

considering what new delivery mechanisms are possible. What about consolidating all deliveries for the industry by dealing with multiple suppliers or goods produced by other companies? Why not find alternative delivery networks that cut out intermediaries and deliver directly to the end customer or use third parties (for example franchisees or even customers) to act as stocking and delivery agents on behalf of the company?

Taking into account these two dimensions of the type of relationship (supplier or customer) and the nature of the relationship (changes in information or in information plus delivery), four supply chain models emerge from the use of e-commerce technology: purchase, service, supply, and delivery.

One feature of dynamic trading networks will be an increased focus on the function of logistics. In fact, a lack of logistics skills may be the limiting factor to the development of e-commerce rather than any paucity of technology skills. All types of networks have a large impact on supply chain processes, and companies will need managers with experience in supply chain planning, distribution, customer service, or procurement - the core skills of logistics – if they wish to implement successfully.

Let's look at each of the four dynamic supply chain networks in more detail.

Dynamic Purchase Networks

Dynamic purchase networks initially will be the most common form of supply chain e-commerce. Today, the technologies and processes that form these networks are known as e-procurement. E-commerce technologies and new-generation software packages used to redefine communication occur with suppliers. Typically, catalogues are made available online for an organization's employees to select items and make purchases with fully automated purchasing transactions and supplier communications. Central databases and effective control and approval processes provide improved coordination throughout the business. The unparalleled access to information given to purchasing departments enables them to select and manage suppliers in line with the objectives of their business.

The critical success factor for dynamic purchase networks is to ensure that the procurement strategy and the new e-commerce-enabled approach to purchasing are synchronized. The most common mistake is to apply a one-size-fits-all approach – to implement an online catalogue and put everything in that catalogue. Purchasing professionals in the company must reconsider the existing purchase strategies for each commodity group and supplier in the light of new technology and develop the new approaches to purchasing that best serve the objectives of the company.

Purchasing may be conducted through the enterprise resource planning system, with transactions communicated through the Internet rather than with paper or electronic data interchange. Alternatively, users may be provided with purchasing cards to order through the Internet, by telephone, in person, or by automated transaction. Another solution might use a browser-based catalogue from which users select items. The order transactions can be automated by the system with external communication being conducted over the Internet. The catalogue can

---

Weblink

For more on logistics, see:
  peters.ASCET.com
  prince.ASCET.com
  hicks.ASCET.com

For more on upstream chains, see:
  evans.ASCET.com

For more on collaborative planning:
  uchneat.ASCET.com

For more on VMI, see:
  anthony.ASCET.com

be maintained either by the supplier or by the company making the purchase.

Supplier networks typically demonstrate a particularly quick payback of benefits. The required automation and simplification of processes reduce both labor and transaction costs. Collation and greater visibility of purchasing information improves decision-making and negotiation. Clearer information reduces cost by enabling the consolidation of orders and transportation activities. And finally, the inherently tighter purchasing controls maintain compliance with negotiated contracts.

Dynamic Service Networks

Dynamic service networks leverage the ability to easily communicate with customers through e-commerce to offer (and often charge for) value-added services. The ability to process and communicate information readily with customers enables companies to link themselves into their customers' systems and processes and start to undertake services that were once thought of as in-house activities. The services then provide a differentiating factor when the customer assesses alternative suppliers when the contract is up for renewal. The customer's decision about best supplier becomes determined less by product price and more by service capability.

The most important elements for developing dynamic service networks are deep understanding of the customer's business and the capability to develop advanced logistics services. Companies typically miss this opportunity because they only understand their customers' businesses through the eyes of the purchasing officer they deal with, and rarely get the chance to interact with senior operational or logistics managers. This leads to the self-reinforcing view that only price is important in the relationship, and the supplier quickly puts itself in the position of lowest-cost provider, which usually means razor-thin margins.

Most companies deal with a large number of customers, but often these multitudes can be grouped into a few customer segments, each of which has different service needs. Successful service providers recognize these different needs and tailor service offerings to each segment. The services typically reduce cost or add value to the customer's supply chain - for example, by reducing transaction costs, reducing stockouts and production downtime, or freeing up the customer's management time.

Companies often dedicate resources to managing inbound supply and often have mixed results. Suppliers, therefore, have the opportunity to offer to conduct the inbound logistics activities on behalf of their customers. This might mean undertaking or supporting the planning function for the customers' inbound logistics. It might mean executing transactions such as inventory management, purchasing, reporting, or replenishment activities. There is potential to provide support information on costing, product performance, or manufacturing process advice.

For the supplier who has relatively sophisticated customers who value logistics and business services, there is an opportunity to gain efficiencies in inter-company transactions as well as to lock the company into the customer's business.

Dynamic Supply Networks

Dynamic supply networks change the nature of the supply model covering several companies or even an entire industry. These networks tackle the inefficiencies that build up when no one company has visibility to the potential synergies in supply. For an example, consider two companies with operations in the same region that are ordering items from overseas. Each will be placing orders with similar logistics requirements (similar pick-up point, similar destination, similar timeframe) but no one has the network visibility to see the logic of bundling the products together to reduce transport costs and provide an improved service.

The critical aspect of creating dynamic supply networks is to recognize the industries in which supply inefficiencies have built up and then establish the capability to manage a more effective network. Trucks, ships, and planes are being underused by companies that manage their supply chains as two-dimensional logistics

Case Study: L-trans

Natural resource companies, such as oil and mining companies, have complex inbound logistics operations that bring thousands of maintenance and engineering items from international suppliers. Freight forwarders undertake the transportation activity from supplier to the companies' facilities, and the transport costs typically are borne by the customer.

L-trans, an Internet-based system developed by BHP, an Australian natural resources company, extracts purchase orders from a company's transaction system and provides the transportation companies with forward visibility of items to be shipped. All transactions between the resource and freight companies are conducted over the Internet so that paperwork is eliminated.

The benefits of the system are substantial both to the resource company and the logistics provider. Transactions costs are reduced by up to 60 percent and transportation costs can be reduced by as much as 20 percent as shipments are consolidated.

Case Study: Cisco

Cisco is famous for its Web page where companies can order items directly over the Internet. This service goes beyond just simple ordering. You can configure your own items, get up-to-date pricing and delivery information, and also review your order history and current deliveries. This is a great example of a service network.

Less well known is that 65 percent of items ordered from Cisco are not made or even handled by Cisco – turning Cisco into an example of a delivery network. Cisco accepts orders through its Web page and immediately transmits them to the appropriate supplier. The supplier has the capability to accept the order, arrange delivery, and even brand the activities. Each supply replenishment transaction is treated as an independent order generated deep within an ERP system. The purchasing department then acts on the order with limited consideration of consolidation opportunities.

Dynamic supply networks operate on the basis that there are multiple points of supply and multiple points of delivery that must be actively managed as a network. The network managers create value by gaining complete visibility across the network, and, therefore, can make decisions to maximize the efficiency of the total network. Once established, dynamic supply networks are often popular with all participants. The customers of the network see the reduced costs and better service of the system. They tend to be comfortable participating with their competitors as inbound logistics is rarely seen as a point of differentiation.

The capabilities needed to manage dynamic supply networks are deep logistics skills with a particular focus on systems development, planning and customer service. The first challenge is to create and maintain the network through the effective use of systems. Internet-based systems are critical for capturing the transactions and communicating with transport providers and suppliers. The transactions are then summarized into databases supported by decision support systems. The managers of dynamic supply networks conduct the planning activities based on the output from the decision support systems, coordinating with transport providers and suppliers to deal with any exceptions. The supply network will continually evolve as customers, suppliers, and products change. Therefore, a strong focus on customer service is needed to innovate and continuously improve the service, ensuring that the network continues to add value to the participants.

The benefits from dynamic supply networks come from the combination of greater automation of processes and the ability to consolidate purchase orders across supplier and transport providers. An early benefit is the reduction of administrative costs for each transaction. The major cost reduction target is transportation – by consolidating loads and reducing unplanned shipments. However, improved visibility of demand across several companies creates the opportunity to drive down procurement costs through not only volume price breaks with customers, but also a more powerful negotiation position. Further, tighter control of the supply side allows managers to gain other efficiencies elsewhere in the supply chain. Lower inventories, fewer stock outs that lead to lower production losses, and better customer service are some of the secondary benefits that may be achieved.

Dynamic Delivery Networks

Dynamic delivery networks redefine how a group of related products are delivered to the marketplace. Like supply networks, there are multiple sources and multiple delivery points so that the benefit is in the effective management of the total network. Unlike supply networks, strong competitive pressures are often at work as companies compete for access to the marketplace.

Within dynamic delivery networks, customers order a wide range of products from a single organization, which then coordinates delivery from a variety of supply sources. Customers place orders to a central point either across the Internet or to a call center that then routes the order to be fulfilled from the most economical supply point. Electronic commerce is critical to provide connectivity across the network and to allow players to join without great expense.

Creating a delivery network is perhaps the most challenging of all the dynamic trading networks, but also perhaps the most rewarding. The opportunity to take on the role of network manager undoubtedly will attract interest from companies that either hold or have an ambition to hold the balance of power in the market. The key to becoming a network manager and achieving competitive advantage will lie in creating a recognized brand and achieving excellent execution.

Logistics will be the core capability of the network manager. The ability to set up, operate and develop a complex multi-company network requires deep skills across the full suite of logistics functions.

---

product a Cisco product. Guess who gets the greatest margin?

Case Study: Descartes

One reason that dynamic trading networks are about to take off is that the core functionality is now available in software packages. The early pioneers had to custom-build their own information technology systems, but today vendors have created systems that can be the starting point for companies operating as network managers. One network management software provider is Descartes, whose Deliverynet.com tool provides visibility of supply chain activities and information to support key network decisions. It has the capability to monitor supply chain activities and signal if checkpoints are not met. It also can translate terms between companies limiting the amount of standardization that needs to be achieved before the network is operational.

Case Study: Ryder – Andersen Consulting – IBM alliance

There are a few logistics companies that are taking a proactive approach to developing dynamic networks, recognizing that they need to supplement their transport and warehousing skills with information technology and service definition skills. One example of this is the partnership between Ryder – the world's largest third-party logistics provider - and Andersen Consulting and IBM. Ryder has partnered with these two players, recognizing that despite its huge resources it could not hope to build the service definition and information technology capabilities required to take on network manager roles. Andersen Consulting's experience in developing solutions for businesses based on leading-edge information technology coupled with IBM's deep technical and information technology

Strategic skills are required to develop the optimum network configuration, alliance management is needed to marshal a large number of companies around a common economic imperative, and planning skills are needed to ensure that inventory and supply arrangements are in place to meet demand. Many of the operational activities may be outsourced to third-party providers, but the network manager will still need a strong capability in distribution and transportation management.

Success in creating a delivery network will have significant economic benefits. The network manager will hold the balance of power in the industry and over time will be able to generate premium profits from its operations.

The New Players in the Network

The new supply chain networks will play out quite differently in various industries, depending on the current logistics inefficiencies and areas of supply chain complexity. For consumer companies, delivery networks will be a major strategic consideration. For resources companies, supply networks will provide early benefits. For industrial suppliers, service networks will apply. Most companies will benefit from purchasing networks.

The critical role in the new supply chain networks will be that of the network manager. In most cases, this is the position that will hold the power in the network and will extract a premium profit. The network manager initiates the network relationships, controls admission, and manages the information that makes the network function. The key success factors for becoming a network manager are being the first to build critical mass operations in the network or having some of the capabilities to effectively manage and develop the operations. These capabilities include:

- Service management culture
- Strong business and logistics management skills
- Systems development capabilities
- Working in partnerships or alliances
- Speed of change delivery

In theory, third-party logistics providers should be steaming into the new world based on their expertise in transportation and distribution. But, with a few exceptions, this is not proving to be the case. The logistics companies seem to be the laggards in developing the capabilities to manage dynamic networks - it might be a case of the people closest to the action being among the last to see it coming.

Many of third-party logistics companies are traditional companies with a deeply ingrained view of logistics based on their transportation and warehousing past. Managing contracts, managing assets, and managing industrial relations have been the traditional competencies for many of the industry leaders. The required information technology, planning, and service development competencies are harder to come by. In fact, many logistics providers are well behind in the information technology race, still lacking the generation of client/server business systems that are common in most of their customers' systems.

Capturing the Value from a Dynamic Trading Network

The development of a dynamic trading network should be thought of as a new business venture run by entrepreneurs rather than as a traditional change project. This creates a more iterative and practical approach that can achieve earlier results. Particularly valuable is early feedback from the market to start-up activities so that adjustments to the business model can be made. Andrew Berger's article "Leaders of the Web.com – Accelerating the Transition to the Web-based World" discusses how this might be achieved.

The combination of e-commerce and logistics is driving the next stage of supply chain evolution. Fast, secure and seamless transmission of information between groups of suppliers and groups of customers is reshaping the business landscape by creating dynamic trading networks. These networks enable companies to offer superior customer service, reduce costs, and better manage their operations. Ultimately, the network manager will occupy the leading profit position in supply chain networks — that role will go to the organization that combines the business, logistics, service, and information technology skills needed to effectively manage the complex interplay of a trading network. Companies that can understand the extent of change underway in the supply chain and quickly reposition their organizations for network trading will be those that capture the value from dynamic trading networks.

Copyright© 2000 Andersen Consulting LLP

---

operations skills enables the partnership to offer services that each could not offer on its own. A recent success has been the $100 million contract to run Ford's North American inbound logistics service – a great example of a dynamic supply network linking thousands of suppliers to several of Ford's plants using information to ensure smooth and efficient running of the supply chain.

The network manager role is expected to be filled from one of three sources. It could be an innovative industry participant that will use its capabilities in both logistics and information technology to establish itself in the role of network manager. The company is likely to be a leader in its industry with a track record of successful strategic initiatives; it will seek to develop and manage a network for its industry sector. Or, it could be filled by new entrants starting from scratch and leapfrogging the existing players that are constrained by existing investments and traditional mindsets. The new entrants are likely to have strong entrepreneurial management teams targeting specific industry sectors and will partner with other groups to provide funding, infrastructure and systems. As a third alternative, a third-party logistics provider could make the strategic changes to its management capabilities and step into the role.

http://moore.ASCET.com

Teklogix Inc. – Yielding Instant Information from Every Link in the Chain

Contact Information

Ian D. McElroy
President and Chief Executive Officer

Gordon A. Wilde
Vice President of Finance
and Chief Financial Officer

Michael A. Rose
President, Americas

Bruce Brown
Vice President of Marketing

Teklogix Inc. Headquarters
2100 Meadowvale Blvd.
Mississauga, Ontario L5N 7J9
Canada
Phone 905.813.9900
Fax 905.812.6300
www.teklogix.com

The supply chain is growing – both in scope, as it expands to include more and more activities, and in its increasing impact on the bottom line. Timely delivery of information is a critical aspect of efficient Supply Chain Management. An efficient logistics system must therefore not only handle physical processes, such as purchasing, manufacturing, transport, warehousing, and delivery, but also track the information associated with these activities as they occur.

In short, regardless of the unique activities that make up your supply chain, finding ways to deliver and receive information – instant, useable, and accurate – from every link in the chain has become a competitive must.

Teklogix is a global provider of real-time data collection and communications solutions that facilitate the flow of critical, real-time information. We enhance our clients' supply chain operations by designing, installing and supporting total wireless solutions for the mobile workforce — effectively extending the interactive communication power of your wired business to your mobile workers through an easy-to-implement, easy-to-operate wireless system. The benefits include improved productivity, accuracy, timeliness, efficiency and, ultimately, competitiveness.

Our innovative wireless local- and wide-area solutions are specifically designed to optimize supply chain operations in such areas as manufacturing, warehousing, distribution, transportation, and logistics management for single or multi-site facilities.

Sharp Insight

While our core business is designing wireless solutions that bring mission critical information down to business in real time, we accomplish this by first understanding the unique supply chain challenges of many vertical markets. These include:
- Food and Cold Storage
- Transportation and Logistics
- Automotive
- Textile and Apparel
- Pharmaceutical
- Electronics
- Chemical

Comprehensive Solutions

Regardless of the application, Teklogix provides comprehensive supply chain solutions that encompass:
- Pre-installation consulting and services
- Detailed site surveys
- System recommendations and design
- Equipment and accessories
- Government licensing
- Technical reviews
- Coverage guarantees
- User training
- A wide range of service plans

Unchaining the Power of the Supply Chain

Along the supply chain, manufacturing, warehousing, and logistics companies move product from location to location via various modes of transport. Teklogix specializes in developing supply chain solutions for organizations with complex logistics activities, high inventory levels and/or high transaction rates. Organizations that have implemented Teklogix' systems routinely confirm the benefits of enhanced productivity, increased operating efficiencies, and accelerated customer response.

Teklogix' wireless local area network (LAN) and wide area networks (WAN) solutions provide total portability of information in real-time. Wireless systems link host computers with remote points across the supply chain, allowing mobile workers to collect and send secure data, access corporate databases, and receive prioritized work instructions instantaneously. By collecting data at the source and placing computer power at the point of transaction, Teklogix solutions provide more accurate, actionable information to businesses, with immediate feedback capabilities that boost productivity and, ultimately, competitiveness.

Technology that's Built to Measure

Teklogix is the only company to offer customers a choice – or a combination – of radio technologies: 2.4GHz (IEEE 802.11) spread spectrum, 902 spread spectrum, optimized narrowband and Mobitex for wide area coverage. Our highly experienced technical and sales representatives are well-versed in the unique advantages of each of these, and can guide our customers in making the right decisions about which technology (or which combination) will best serve their specific business needs and perform optimally given the size and shape of their site. Teklogix solutions are also built with the future in mind: flexible and expandable to meet new business needs, a Teklogix system can also be counted on to integrate effectively with emerging wireless technologies.

Fast and Flexible

Today, as more and more companies are seeking interoperability options, Teklogix demonstrates our innovation with the unique 802.IQ protocol: this new standards-based high performance protocol offers the flexibility of an open system plus the peak performance of a Teklogix' optimized wireless protocol. Flexibility such as this allows customers to select a high-performance system that is uniquely suited to their current and future requirements.

Teklogix offers a wide range of extremely rugged, hand-held, and vehicle-mount wireless data computers that can perform in the harsh conditions that often characterize our markets. Our complete portfolio of equipment for wireless LANs and WANs includes Radio Frequency network controllers and wireless gateways that allow seamless data capture, transfer, and access. All Teklogix equipment is specifically designed to support the high transaction rates typically found in manufacturing, warehousing, distribution, and logistics applications.

Teklogix' solutions feature the industry's fastest response times and broadest coverage areas, as well as the widest range of connectivity options to all major computer platforms, and seamless integration with virtually all warehouse management software. They are also backed by the most comprehensive selection of service plans in the wireless data communications industry.

Wireless Frontiers

Since Teklogix began laying the groundwork for real-time wireless communications more than 30 years ago, we've played a pioneering role in the industry. This track record continues today with the addition of the Integration Services Group and Teklink, Teklogix' wide area wireless solution.

The Integration Services Group (ISG)

Teklogix' software integration solution, which enables customers to seamlessly extend the capabilities of SAP R/3™ to mobile workers.

Teklink

Teklogix' wide area wireless solution, which allows mobile workers – vehicle-borne and in remote locations – that work across large area logistics facilities to communicate in real-time with multiple host platforms. Teklink extends real-time capabilities beyond the warehouse and across the supply chain, integrating easily and seamlessly with wireless LAN systems.

Competitive Advantage

Teklogix' high performance wireless supply chain solutions help large-scale, high-value organizations reduce product distribution costs, increase efficiencies in their operations, optimize asset utilization and enhance customer responsiveness. Teklogix customers include many Fortune 1000 companies and other major organizations around the world that have implemented automation technologies to compete in today's global markets.

Teklogix' solutions deliver customers a competitive edge: employee productivity is increased, distribution costs are reduced, paperwork is eliminated, operational efficiencies are increased and customer orders are processed in minutes instead of days. Faster and more accurate information processing also increases stock turns, reducing inventory levels and floor space.

Building a competitive advantage is a strategic necessity in today's global market. With a payback on investment in as little as four months, a Teklogix solution unchains the power of the supply chain.

A Word about Teklogix

Currently, there are more than 6,000 Teklogix systems installed in 50 countries. The Company has 38 sales and support offices and 26 independent distributors throughout North America, Europe, Asia, Australia, the Middle East, and South and Latin America.

Teklogix' world headquarters, which encompasses manufacturing, is located in Mississauga, Ontario, Canada. It is here, and in Vancouver, Canada, that Teklogix fulfills its major commitment to research and development in wireless data communications. Teklogix' Advanced Technology Group is central to the Company's R&D activities, anticipating and researching the technologies and trends that will give way to innovative new wireless data communications solutions for customers.
Teklogix is ISO 9001 registered.

The Company is publicly traded and is listed on the Toronto Stock Exchange under the symbol TKX.

http://teklogix.ASCET.com

TIBCO – The Foundation of the World's E-Business

Contact Information

Vivek Y. Ranadive
Chairman, President, and CEO

Paul G. Hansen
EVP, Finance and CFO

Rajesh U. Mashruwala
EVP, Sales and Marketing

TIBCO World headquarters
3165 Porter Drive,
Palo Alto, CA 94304
Phone 650.846.1000
Fax 650.846.1005
www.tibco.com

The Internet is driving exciting new business models, which allow companies to interact in a more streamlined fashion and save time and money. The new economy offers more lucrative ways to increase revenues, grow marketshare, and get new services to market faster. All while reducing overall operating costs.

Benefiting from this exciting new Internet economy, however, requires that businesses streamline operations, automate business processes, and squeeze the inefficiencies out of the supply chain. And to do that your systems all need to be integrated into a single, synchronized flow of information. You also need to develop secure, personalized portals to extend business processes out over the Internet to connect with customers, partners, and suppliers.

TIBCO has the Solution

TIBCO Software is a leading provider of real-time infrastructure software for e-business. Recently ranked by IDC as the number one provider in the Businessware category, TIBCO's products and services enable computer applications and platforms to communicate efficiently across networks, including the Internet. With TIBCO, you can connect and automate all your internal business processes, from order entry to fulfillment. You can also extend your business processes over the Internet for Business-to-Business (B2B) and Business-to-Consumer e-commerce seamlessly and reliably.

Portals

Successful Internet portals are personalized, aggregate content and transactions, and provide single sign-one security. Through a portal your customers and partners can connect with you for e-commerce and services. TIBCO provides portal construction tools, infrastructure, and hosting services to allow you to get your portal up and running quickly.

B2B Connectivity

Seamless connectivity with your trading partners extends your business process beyond the enterprise. Real-time, secure B2B connectivity lets you reduce costs and increase the efficiency of your business. TIBCO offers market leading B2B integration to help you make all the right connections.

Business Process Automation

Automating your business processes saves you save time and money. TIBCO's work flow and integration management solutions help you synchronize the flow of information with the flow of work.

Supply Chain Integration

Integrating your legacy systems in your business processes is key to succeeding in the Internet economy. You have to have all your systems tied together and communicating in real-time in order to do business over the Internet. TIBCO offers hundreds of adapters for connecting your ERP, billing, and customer care applications into TIBCO's core e-business integration infrastructure so that you can fully integrate your enterprise into a seamless flow of information and do business in real-time with your customers.

TIB technology was first used to "digitize" Wall Street and has been adopted in diverse industries, including manufacturing, energy, telecommunications, and e-commerce. TIBCO Software's global client base includes Cisco Systems, Yahoo!, Sun Microsystems, NEC, 3Com, AT&T, Philips, Bechtel, Seagate, and Netscape.

For more information about TIBCO's e-business solutions, contact one of our worldwide offices today.

| 1.0 The Path Forward | 2.0 Supply Chain Innovations | 3.0 Industry Perspectives | 4.0 Making It Happen |

written by:

Francis J. Quinn
Supply Chain
Management Review

Kevin R. Fitzgerald
Purchasing Magazine

Peter Bradley
Logistics Management
& Distribution Report
http://quinn-f.ASCET.com

Supply Chain Perspectives from the Business Press

Supply Chain Management and the Internet revolution are changing – permanently – how companies manage their supply chains and their business. The Cahners Supply Chain/OEM group of magazines has been covering the explosive growth of both modern Supply Chain Management and the Internet since their emergence almost a decade ago. The editors of Supply Chain Management Review, Purchasing, and Logistics Management & Distribution Report discuss where the supply chain is headed and what impact it has on profits, inventories, and other performance metrics.

Introduction

The business technique known as Supply Chain Management has forever changed the way in which companies move their goods to market. It has impacted every stage of the supply chain process – from the initial sourcing of raw materials to the final point of sale. And as the potential of the Internet and other advanced technologies expands, the advantages of integrated supply chain management promise only to intensify.

The evolution of this management concept has been rapid and remarkable. From virtual anonymity a scant decade ago, supply chain management has soared into prominence today as a core competitive differentiator. Few observers have had a better vantage point to view its ascent than the business journalists who cover the subject every day.

This article brings together three of those journalists from the Cahners Supply Chain/OEM Group of magazines. They are the chief editors of Supply Chain Management Review, Purchasing, and Logistics Management & Distribution Report.

In separate articles below, these veteran industry observers offer their perspectives on what the future holds for supply chain management overall and for the key functional areas within an organization that make SCM an operating reality.

Collaborating in an E-Enabled Future
By Francis J. Quinn,
Supply Chain Management Review

At its very essence, Supply Chain Management is as much about collaboration as it is about the physical movement of goods. How effectively you move product from the raw materials stage to final point-of-sale really depends on how well you work with others. These include the various functional entities within your organization as well as your key customers and suppliers. They also include the providers of logistics services who help create a seamless distribution network. (The accompanying graphic, developed by AMR Research, shows the scope of collaborative opportunities within the supply chain.)

Collaboration entails sharing of data, operating plans, and even certain financial information. For many, particularly those that have usually treated suppliers like indentured servants and customers as merely necessary evils, this notion of collaboration represents radical change. Yet change is no longer an option. It's a competitive necessity.

Supply chain collaboration today is being enabled and facilitated by information technology. The Internet, for example, is allowing supply chain partners to communicate information instantly and accurately to take excess inventory,

Francis J. Quinn, Kevin R. Fitzgerald, and Peter Bradley are the chief editors respectively of Supply Chain Management Review, Purchasing, and Logistics Management & Distribution Report. These publications are part of the Supply Chain/OEM Group of Magazines, published by Cahners Business Information, 275 Washington Street, Newton, MA 02458.

The authors can be contacted at fquinn@cahners.com, k.fitzgerald@cahners.com, and pbradley@cahners.com.

http://quinn-f.ASCET.com   77

activity, and cost out of the pipeline. Innovations like hub-based trading communities, Internet-enabled purchasing webs, and collaborative business communities are leading to efficiencies never before imagined.

Supply-chain related technology is creating a powerful impact, too. There is Transportation Management Systems (TMS) software for streamlining and integrating your transportation operations. Warehouse Management Systems (WMS) let you run your distribution centers and warehouses more efficiently and profitably. And Advanced Planning and Scheduling (APS) technology helps you match procurement and production activities more closely to actual customer demand. Advanced software now lets companies share this critical data with their supply chain partners – regardless of the information systems in place.

The industry pacesetters are aggressively applying advanced technologies like CPFR (Collaborative Planning, Forecasting, and Replenishment) to build mutually beneficial alliances with their supply chain partners. The advantages of close collaboration have been demonstrated convincingly by leaders like Dell Computer, Procter & Gamble, and Wal-Mart. A recent study by Andersen Consulting only underscores the point. The firm's in-depth survey of the food and consumer products industry found that the retailers with the highest profit margins were far more likely to collaborate on new products and services than the lower profitability retailers.

Weblink

For more on warehousing, see:
peters.ASCET.com

For more on global supply, see:
hicks.ASCET.com

For more on movement, see:
johnson.ASCET.com

For more on CPFR, see:
anthony.ASCET.com
uchneat.ASCET.com

If the technology is in place and the benefits so evident, why have so few companies aggressively developed their extended supply chain capabilities? The leading consulting firms and business gurus like Michael Hammer suggest that only a small fraction of the Fortune 1000 fully understand the power of supply chain management – and have implemented programs that reflect that understanding. The percentage of believers among mid-size and smaller companies is even less.

Part of the problem centers on an inability to get people to work toward common objectives. At first glance, persuading the internal functional areas to cooperate in moving product to market might seem a fairly straightforward exercise. After all, we're part of the same organization, right? But, remember, that Purchasing, Production Planning, Inventory Management, Transportation, Warehousing, and Customer Service historically have sought to optimize the performance of their particular area – as often as not, at the expense of some other. Exacerbating the problem is the fact that the managers in these departments continue to be compensated on that basis.

The supply chain partners, both internal and external, need to be convinced of the real benefits of collaboration. Traditionally, quantifying those benefits has not been an easy proposition. But increasingly, the bottom-line case for supply chain efficiency is being made – both in industry-wide studies and within individual organizations.

The most recent research documenting the supply chain-profitability connection comes from the Performance Measurement Group, a subsidiary of PRTM consulting. The firm's Supply Chain Benchmarking Survey examined best practices across a range of high-tech and consumer-packaged goods companies in North America, Europe, and Asia.

The survey established a clear relationship between supply chain performance and profitability. It found that the market leaders have reduced their supply chain costs to 4-5 percent of sales. Overall, they spend 5 to 6 percent less on supply chain management as a percent of sales than the average performers. Is this cost advantage a big deal? As the study authors point out, for a company with $500 million in sales, it translates to a $25-30 million cost advantage every year.

Studies like this paint a broad picture of SCM's quantitative benefits. More specific examples of individual company initiatives are instructive as well. A recent Supply Chain Management Review article described a series of collaborative supply chain initiatives at Procter & Gamble designed to integrate and simplify the interfaces along P&G's extensive supply chain. The results of this ongoing effort have been nothing short of remarkable. Finished product inventory has been cut by 10 percent over the last three years; average return on equity has risen dramatically; and net profit has increased from 6.4% to close to 10%.

The broad industry research and company case studies underscore a message that bears repeating: the benefits of effective supply chain management are quantifiable. SCM does exert a powerful, positive impact on key performance metrics like profitability. Collaboration is the key to realizing those benefits, and technology is the key to successful collaboration.

A Lead Role for the Purchasing Professional
By Kevin R. Fitzgerald,
Purchasing Magazine

Twenty years ago the job responsibilities of a purchasing professional were clear and basic: Get quotes from suppliers of the products and services, accept the lowest bid, and process purchasing orders until the next contract is due. Purchasing departments were largely isolated from engineering and other technical functions. In fact, the purchasing department was often the place that corporate management would put deserving veteran employees "out to pasture" until they reached retirement.

A dynamic new business environment – constantly being energized by advances in information technology – has radically altered that picture. Today, purchasing is integrated into virtually all aspects of cor-

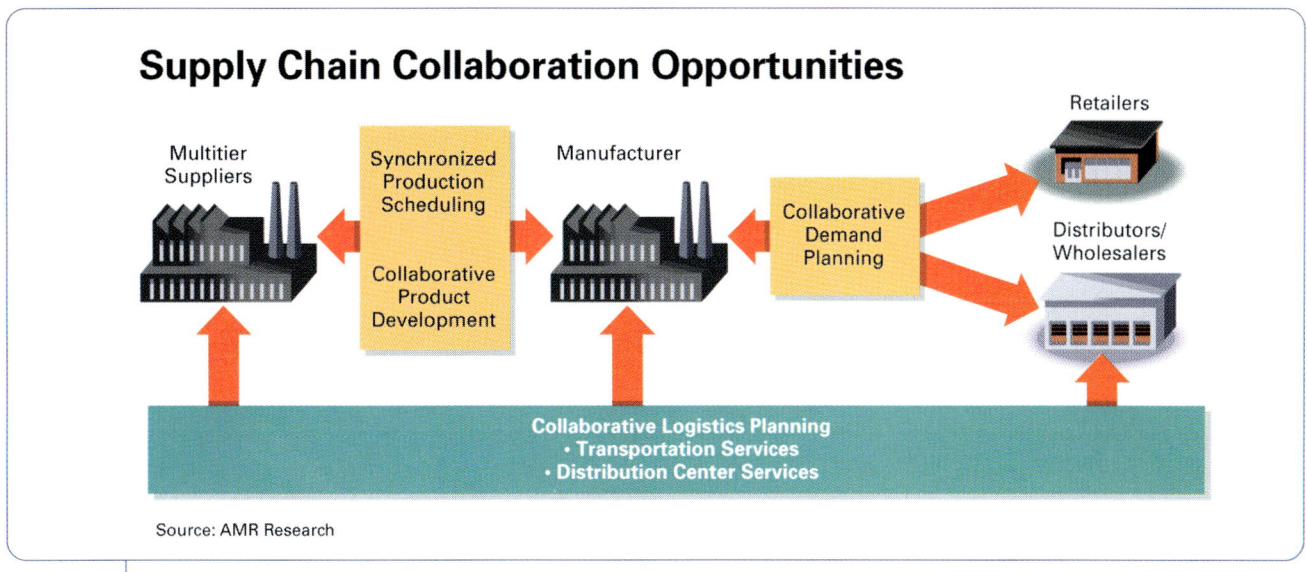

Figure 1.0 Supply chain collaboration opportunities

porate business, whether it be product design, inventory management, global supply negotiations, and even creation of long-term business strategies. Purchasing no longer is bound by the walls of the "functional silos" that existed for decades in corporate America. The managers working in this discipline now routinely make decisions that directly affect market competitiveness and the company's technological direction. In short, purchasing professionals no longer are focused solely on the "tactical" aspects of business. Their work is highly strategic as well. The decisions they make are critical to the profitability and future success of their organizations.

The strategic nature of their work promises only to intensify as supply chains become more global and as technology – particularly e-procurement – becomes more pervasive.

Specifically, purchasing professionals of the future will be deeply involved in implementing supply strategies, not with processing reams of transaction-based paperwork. Figure 1.0 shows, the trend toward widespread Internet use among purchasing professionals already is well under way. Purchasing executives will be held responsible for linking sourcing, purchasing, and the supply chain to the financial plan of their companies' businesses. They also will be responsible for staying on top of global supply issues that can affect sourcing and profitability.

A major challenge for tomorrow's purchasers will be how to best implement new technologies, especially Web-based e-procurement, so that it helps achieve strategic supply and business goals. E-procurement is the most powerful tool ever made available to purchasers. But every effort must be made to ensure that e-procurement systems actually increase value across the supply chain. Toward this end, purchasers must be very careful to re-engineer business processes to their most efficient before e-procurement systems are implemented. Otherwise, they'll simply be automating inefficient business processes.

Going forward into this new century, successful purchasing professionals increasingly will adapt a global perspective around supply. Trade barriers continue will continue to fall, and business growth will be strongest in markets that are still developing. Those organizations – and those purchasing professionals within the organization – that recognize the new global realities will prosper in the future; those that do not will be left behind.

Purchasing professionals of tomorrow will be faced with other supply chain challenges as well. They will be tasked with measuring costs through all links in the supply chain; developing and executing outsourcing strategies; managing onsite supplier representatives; and interacting more closely with the technical functions, both inside their own companies and with suppliers.

Ironically, there will be fewer purchasing professionals in the future, but they will be much more important to the success of their companies. Tomorrow's purchasing professionals will be multi-skilled, with strong backgrounds not only in purchasing, but also in technology, finance, and management. They will, in essence, function more like executive-level business people than purchasing agents of old.

In reality, the purchasing agent of decades past is gone forever. And the purchasing manager who has a limited range of tactical responsibilities is fast disappearing. A new purchasing professional for a new century has emerged. This individual recognizes his or her strategic role in a global supply chain and stands ready to leverage new technologies in performing that role.

It's All About Logistics Execution

By Peter Bradley

Logistics Management & Distribution Report

In the supply chain, execution is what really counts. Back when I was in the

http://quinn-f.ASCET.com   79

newspaper business, we used to joke that we had available to us incredible resources: reporters around the world, million dollar presses, sophisticated advertising programs, and more. Yet at the end of the day, we counted on a core of 12-year old boys and girls on bicycles to reach our customers. I didn't know it at the time, but that was a crucial lesson in the role of logistics in supply chain success.

Among the reason businesses have focused on supply chain strategies is the imperative to compress the whole business cycle. Managers are under pressure to accelerate turn times and thus deliver more inventory turns, to reduce order-to-delivery times, to shrink the time it takes to turn a concept into a product, and to speed up the cash cycle and reduce working capital.

At the same time, businesses are becoming increasingly international in their sourcing, production, and distribution. SKUs are proliferating to meet the demands of customers that have more power than ever before. New channels are developing — electronic commerce is at the head of the list — and old channels are undergoing change. Product life cycles, particularly in the high-tech sector, grow shorter by the day, adding to the requirement for speed to market. Even in a robust and healthy economy, pricing flexibility is constrained. Thus costs, too, must be held in check, and profitability gains realized either by improved productivity and gains in market share.

All this has forced businesses to take what might be called a holistic look at their enterprises, including upstream suppliers and downstream customers. They need to carefully consider how all the parts contribute or detract from the entire supply chain process. Information technology has been a crucial enabler to allowing that process to occur. The idea that information can replace inventory has become almost a cliché. Inventory, warehouse, and transportation management systems have been key enablers of more efficient processes. What is sometimes overlooked in discussions of supply chain efficiency, however, is the crucial role of physical execution to supply chain success. From a supply chain perspective, this means effectively managing the movement and storage of goods from the beginning of the manufacturing process through final consumer fulfillment. A longtime manager for one of the world's largest transportation company put it succinctly when he said, "After you move the bytes, you have to move the boxes."

As many Internet retailers have quickly learned, sometimes to their chagrin, it is much easier to set up a Web page and offer products for sale on line than it is to fulfill those orders with the same efficiency and still make a profit. Some of the biggest Internet businesses — Amazon.com most notably — are investing millions of dollars to improve their distribution networks. That's a clear acknowledgement that logistics execution is imperative to their business success.

Providers of logistics services have made remarkable strides over the last 20 years to improve and enhance the services they provide. Carriers can provide information and flexibility considered impossible only a short time ago. They are critical partners in any supply chain execution strategy. The development of third-party logistics offers managers additional resources for managing the flow of goods.

The concept of a supply chain suggests a fairly linear process. Yet as any supply chain manager knows, the reality is far more complex — more like an intricate and ever-shifting web. At each intersection in any such web lies an interchange that demands a logistics solution. Perhaps it's overstating the case a bit to say that logistics, as much as information, holds the supply chain together. But it's not much of an overstatement. The critical importance of logistics to supply chain success is undeniable. Think about that when you head outside and pick up the morning paper.

ProLogis – The Single Point of Contact for Global Distribution Needs

You don't have to be an avid reader of the *Wall Street Journal* to realize that business as we know it has changed. In what's being called the "New Economy," you're reminded of it every day, whether you're shipping products to customers halfway around the world or producing a spot for your latest Internet start-up.

At ProLogis, we're reacting to the New Economy by helping our customers meet new challenges. From solidifying our North American operations to expanding our growing presence in Europe, and beyond. From new advances in our refrigerated group to the launching of our Customer Services group. We believe that we are now uniquely positioned to offer our current – and future – customers whatever kind of distribution services the New Economy demands.

With more than 1,600 distribution facilities owned and operating throughout North America and Europe, ProLogis is recognized as the world's leading provider of integrated distribution facilities and services. As pioneers in the distribution industry, we're committed to our "Global Distribution Solution" of providing our customers with exceptional corporate distribution services and facilities to meet their expansion and reconfiguration needs worldwide.

Our ProLogis Operating System™

At ProLogis, our expertise goes beyond the actual distribution facility. We offer customers a complete supply chain package, consisting of site selection, acquisition, development, marketing, leasing, operation and long-term management of distribution, light manufacturing, and temperature-controlled facilities.

Our service offerings are built around the ProLogis Operating System™. This unique approach to our business is based on the seamless integration of four indispensable groups of talented, experienced individuals, all working toward the same goal of maximizing customer satisfaction. The ProLogis Operating System™ is made up of four groups: the Market Services Group, the Global Services Group, the Global Development Group, and the Customer Services Group.

The Market Services Group

The dedicated professionals in this group are based in our local markets and provide in-depth expertise in these metropolitan areas. Their familiarity with local real estate market conditions, business environments, and available resources is critical to helping our customers meet their objectives. This group helps build strong relationships by delivering quality facilities and providing the important day-in/day-out property management and leasing services that keep our customers satisfied.

The Global Services Group

As the single point of contact for our multi-market customers, the professionals in this group work closely with local project teams to ensure that facilities in every location meet specific customer needs. The Global Services Group is dedicated to developing strategic partnerships and long-term relationships that start with a thorough understanding of each customer's business and distribution facility needs.

The Global Development Group

Our Global Development Group focuses on creating master-planned distribution parks with both inventory and build-to-suit facilities. The Global Development Group has already developed more than 40 million square feet of state-of-the-art facilities for our customers around the world.

Contact Information

Insight Management Support Systems
Richard F. Powers
dpowers@insight-mss.com
19820 Village Office Court
Bend, OR 97702
(541) 388-6998 Office
(541) 388-9884 Fax
Temperature Controlled Facilities

CS Intergrated LLC
Cyriel L. Godderie
cgodderi@csicold.com
701 Martinsville Road
P.O. Box 840
Liberty Corner, NJ 07938
(908) 542-2000 Office
(908) 604-2558 Fax

Frigoscandia AB
Thomas B. Svensk
thomas.svensk@frigoscandia.co.uk
Box 912, S-251 09
Helsingborg, Sweden
+46 (0) 4217-80-00 Office
+46 (0) 4217-81-90 Fax

Paul Congleton
14100 East 35th Place
Auroura, CO 80011
Phone: 303.375.9292
Fax: 303.375.8581
www.prologis.com

The Customer Services Group

Core to our business is identifying a customer need and bringing all of our operating groups together to reach an optimal solution. This philosophy requires that we deliver outstanding customer service in a growing number of value-added areas. These include analyzing and re-configuring distribution networks, tax incentive analysis and negotiation consulting, site selection and design/build services, and materials and equipment leasing, as well as other value-added customer services.

Our Partners

Logistics Network Optimization

INSIGHT is one of ProLogis' partners, and the world's leading provider of fully integrated logistics network optimization software. This technologically advanced software offers manufacturers and distributors who operate worldwide the ability to achieve a wide range of logistics network solutions.

INSIGHT's logistics network optimization software offers ProLogis customers many benefits, such as comprehensive consultation on optimization and reconfiguration of manufacturing and distribution networks. This includes guidance on selecting optimal facility locations, counseling on the appropriate number of plants and distribution centers, Supply Chain Management, and transportation planning. Use of INSIGHT software has provided customers with annual logistics costs reduction of up to 15%.

Temperature Controlled Logistics

Since 1840, CS Integrated LLC (CSI) has been at the forefront of temperature-controlled logistics. In fact, CSI pioneered the "consolidation" concept that enables customers to save money by combining shipments. Today, CSI provides customers with consistent, high-quality logistics services through temperature-controlled facilities in strategic markets located across the United States.

In January 1998, ProLogis acquired Frigoscandia AB, Europe's largest refrigerated distribution company. Combined with CSI, these two companies make ProLogis the largest temperature-controlled logistics company in the world. Together they offer customers a flexible range of value-added supply chain logistics services and expertise. This includes facility development and management, multi-temperature storage technology, blast-freezing, inventory control, order selection, productivity and measurement standards, cross-docking operations, EDI information applications, and both common carrier and in-house transportation.

Figure 1.0 Customers drive growth

Our Customers

ProLogis has been providing distribution solutions to customers around the world since 1994. In that time, our client list has grown to include Nike, PepsiCo, FedEx, The Home Depot, The United States Postal Service, and UPS Worldwide Logistics.

Our Vision

With e-commerce and globalization driving the New Economy, we know that it's crucial for our customers to look at distribution in a new way. They must not consider distribution a necessary expense, but a way to gain a competitive advantage.

As we chart our way through the new millennium, the ProLogis mission is to provide all the distribution services necessary to help our customers transform their supply chain into a powerful tool for the New Economy.

For more information about how ProLogis can help your business, contact us at 303.375.9292.

Our Shared Success: ProLogis & Colrane

The Colrane Company is a distributor of high quality paper products for the printing industry. ProLogis and Colrane have been doing business together since 1996, with ProLogis providing distribution facilities in four markets nationwide: Atlanta, Denver, Los Angeles, and San Francisco (East Bay). Just like the New Economy, things can change fast in the paper business. In 1998, Colrane had to realign its distribution locations due to a major change in its customer base. It needed a facility to meet the new paper distribution requirements of customers in Manhattan and New Jersey, while its Denver facility had become less viable in its operations. However, several years remained on its Denver lease with ProLogis. Meanwhile, ProLogis had purchased a 40,000-square-foot facility in the Meadowlands, across the Hudson River from Manhattan.

ProLogis invited Colrane to inspect the newly acquired property in New Jersey. The facility was perfect for Colrane. Since the Meadowlands facility was larger than Colrane's space in Denver, the two companies worked on a lease trade. Colrane signed a new lease on the New Jersey facility and ProLogis cancelled the old lease in Denver. Colrane was able to realign its distribution operations and ProLogis was able to provide flexibility and creativity in meeting a customer's needs.

The Value Propositions of Business-to-Business Dynamic Commerce

written by:

Kyle Appell
Moai

Christopher Brousseau
Andersen Consulting
http://appell.ASCET.com

This work builds on a previous paper, "The Value Propositions of Dynamic Pricing in Business-to-Business E-Commerce," which explored the impact of dynamic pricing at two critical touchpoints in the enterprise value chain: sourcing and selling. We extend the definition of dynamic "pricing" to dynamic "commerce" and discover the important role online exchanges play in this emerging space. Our objective is to understand how dynamic commerce drives bottom-line results for innovative businesses through increased revenues, lower costs, and improved processes.

Introduction

With the advent of e-commerce, businesses now have low-cost, global access to a highly focused and greatly expanded network of stakeholders in their enterprise value chain. One of the most promising opportunities to improve this network is the application of dynamic commerce to an organization's sourcing and selling activities. Innovators in this space are demonstrating that dynamic commerce is a critical component of business-to-business (B2B) trading relationships, driving significant bottom-line results through increased revenues, lower costs, and improved processes. Furthermore, analysts project that up to one-third of B2B e-commerce in the next several years will be conducted dynamically.

A formal discussion about dynamic commerce would be incomplete without first examining how the concept of dynamic "commerce" differs from that of dynamic "pricing." The latter describes a process in which goods and services are traded in markets where price adjusts freely to supply and demand. However, pricing is just one of the data points used during the valuation of an offer. Other components of the transaction process include, but are not limited to, searching for and qualifying vendors, comparing offerings, negotiating business terms (price, shipping, packaging), conducting the transaction, fulfilling the purchase, and collecting payment. Since the exchange of goods and services often entails valuation of many variables beyond price, the notion of "commerce" best captures the breadth and complexity of real-world business requirements.

The decision to purchase a new home, for example, requires consideration of a wide range of variables in which price is one factor among many. Other negotiable variables might include condition of the property, move-in dates, mortgage terms, and conditions or inspections. Complicating the process is the fact that many of these variables are negotiable, and vary depending on how they are packaged in the final offer. By providing a centralized, real-time mechanism for negotiating each of these variables, online dynamic commerce improves the ease and efficiency of the entire transaction. Thus, "dynamic commerce" can be defined as the exchange of goods and services in electronic markets where not only price, but also other factors, fluctuate freely while all participants enjoy significantly lower interaction costs.

Dynamic commerce is reshaping existing business practices and simultaneously fueling the growth of entirely new companies, such as marketplace-focused exchanges. The emergence of new interactive networks and the ever-increasing acceptance of e-commerce tools and capabilities are only two of the many factors driving the dramatic growth in this arena. While companies continue to discover innovative ways to apply dynamic commerce technology, it remains the most beneficial mechanism to sell excess, obsolete, or slow-moving inventory as well as time-sensitive, limited, or scarce products. Even more significantly, dynamic commerce is quickly becoming the dominant forum for procuring goods and services.

Our objective is to define the value proposition of dynamic commerce in B2B

Kyle Appell is Manager of Opportunity Assessment for Moai in San Francisco. Christopher Brousseau is a manager with Andersen Consulting's Palo Alto Center for Strategic Technology.

online transactions at two critical touchpoints in the enterprise value chain: sourcing and selling (see Figure 1.0). This paper focuses on the transactional component of dynamic commerce and the emergence of online exchanges. It provides background on the emergence of online dynamic commerce solutions, explains the business benefits of these solutions, and describes specific business applications for dynamic commerce.

Business Benefits Overview

As we have stated, the Internet is a powerful means to connect buyers and sellers quickly, efficiently, and at a very low cost, whether there are just a few trading partners or thousands. Improvements in the speed and efficiency of conducting commerce have driven several waves of innovation. Sharing product information and enabling online ordering were just the beginning. The new trend involves the integration of dynamic commerce functionality as a critical means for businesses to build a more tightly aligned value chain that also extends across an even broader network of trade and service partners. The benefits of this transformation are significant and immediate as evidenced by the impact on the way innovative businesses source and sell today (see Figure 2.0).

To illustrate the benefits of dynamic commerce, it is useful to first examine the sell-side advantages. Leading U.S. businesses, on average, generate annual

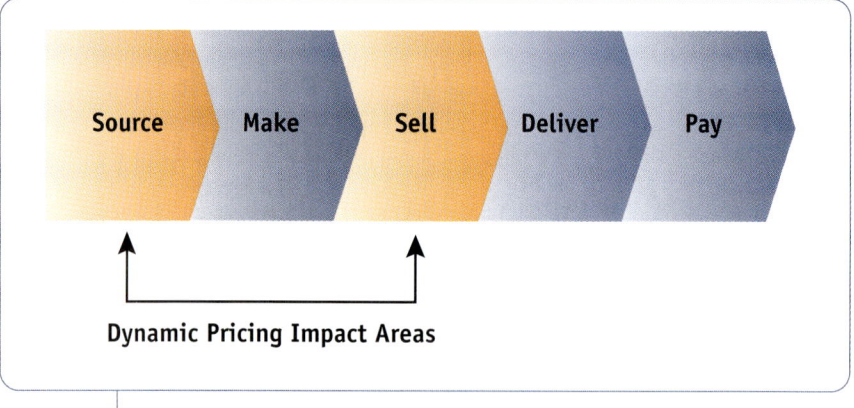

Figure 1.0 | Critical touchpoints in the enterprise value chain: sourcing and selling

Dynamic Pricing Impact Areas: Source → Make → Sell → Deliver → Pay

Weblink

For more on dynamic pricing, see:
wayman.ASCET.com
moai.ASCET.com

For more on enterprise value chain:
culotta.ASCET.com

For more on B2B e-commerce, see:
evans.ASCET.com
sprague.ASCET.com

For more on customer-facing activities:
bruce.ASCET.com

For more on MROs, see:
evans.ASCET.com

revenues of $11 million each from investment recovery activities[1] (investment recovery is revenue from the sale of assets no longer needed by the enterprise). These revenues represent net recoveries from selling surplus and/or excess inventory to third party intermediaries at a significant discount (roughly 20% to 30% of their original market value). The significance of this problem becomes clearer when you analyze in detail the costs that businesses incur in managing and liquidating this inventory. Along with the cost of carrying aged and obsolete inventory, U.S. businesses are required to write down the value of these assets to their true market value. These charges, which can amount to nearly 80% of the original value of the surplus merchandise, are applied against earnings, and thus directly impact the bottom line. The net result is that old and inefficient inventory liquidation practices cause companies either to tie up or consume a tremendous amount of valuable capital, and simultaneously impair their earnings. Early adopters of dynamic commerce applications have taken advantage of the opportunity to reduce the gap between surplus inventory and net recoveries dramatically (see Figure 3.0). In fact, some companies have more than doubled their investment recovery dollars in the course of just a few months (or in some cases, weeks).

Dynamic commerce also offers tremendous benefits for procurement of both direct and indirect goods in the context of short-term (spot) buys and, more importantly, long-term contracts. To gauge the size of this opportunity, large companies spend an average of 36% of sales for indirect goods alone.[2] Given such a sizeable base, even a two percent decrease in purchasing costs quickly improves an organization's margins. Dynamic commerce positively impacts procurement costs in two ways. First, competitive bidding reduces contract costs. Second, it simplifies the RFQ process. Even with e-mail and fax, the labor-intensive process is ripe for significant cost savings and cycle time reduction. By automating this process and implementing dynamic commerce capabilities, companies have managed to cut approximately 15% from the cost of vendor contracts and reduce purchase cycle times by two-thirds.[3,4] With these savings, purchasing teams have more time to focus on critical tasks, such as evaluating vendors and managing the larger, more complex supplier relationships.

Online exchanges are also emerging as a highly effective and, in many ways, a uniquely beneficial model for dynamic commerce. Since they are essentially electronic trading hubs where businesses come together to conduct transactions, exchanges combine the benefits referenced above pertaining to selling and buying applications. Exchanges also alleviate market inefficiencies caused by decentralization of information and fragmentation of buyers and sellers. By providing a centralized conduit for conducting business

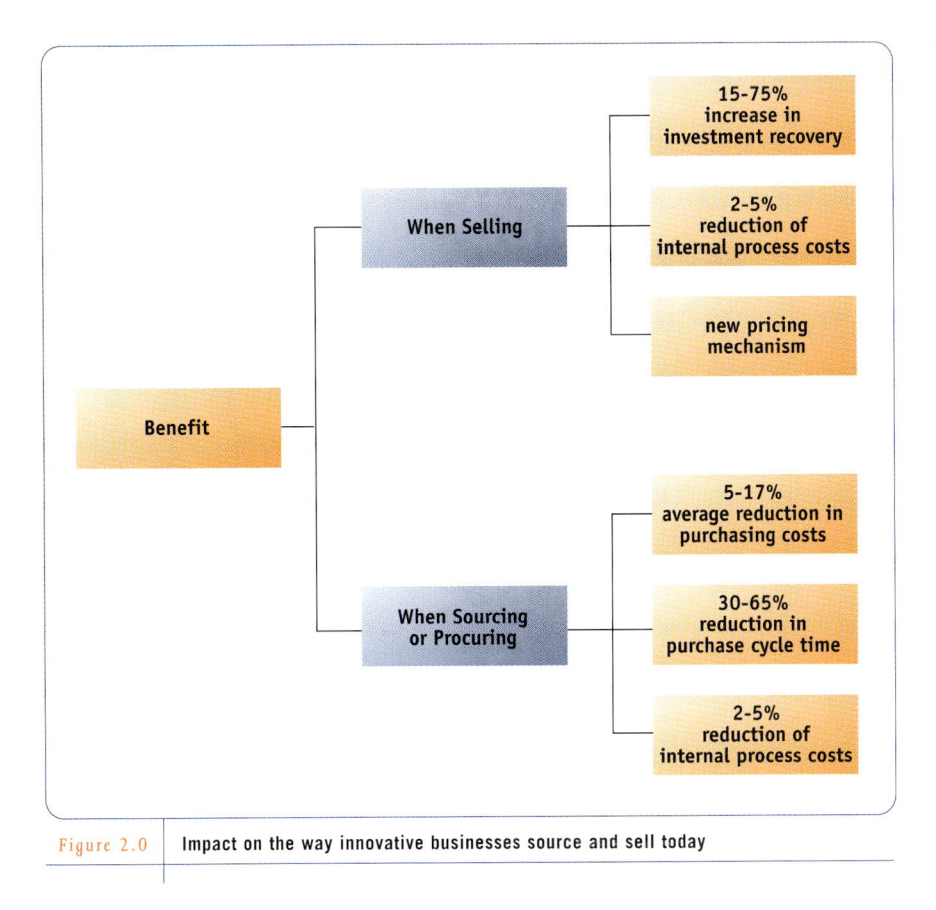

Figure 2.0 — Impact on the way innovative businesses source and sell today

Benefit:
- When Selling
  - 15-75% increase in investment recovery
  - 2-5% reduction of internal process costs
  - new pricing mechanism
- When Sourcing or Procuring
  - 5-17% average reduction in purchasing costs
  - 30-65% reduction in purchase cycle time
  - 2-5% reduction of internal process costs

online, electronic marketplaces pull together many participants with similar and complimentary interests, creating an online trading community. These communities serve to minimize search and transaction costs inherent in many existing physical markets in which the sheer number of players, as well as the magnitude of geographic and time constraints, act as impediments to commerce. Therefore, participants in exchanges benefit from more efficient communication, greater ease of interaction, better access to market information, and standardized operating procedures. Finally, when they are successful, exchanges create a significant amount of liquidity in the markets they serve, which fuels greater participation.

An Overview of Dynamic Commerce

Throughout the course of history, changes in the business world have tended to occur in evolutionary patterns sparked by revolutionary ideas. Today, this change occurs at a much faster pace. As e-commerce achieves critical mass in the business and consumer communities, the "first mover" is no longer guaranteed a competitive advantage. Forward thinking and critical insight into how technology will impact business, and moving to facilitate those changes, will increasingly become the marks of true strategic advantage.

Shortcomings of Static Pricing

To appreciate the value propositions that dynamic commerce offers B2B e-commerce, one must first understand the shortcomings of static pricing models as well as business trends and changes in technology that are driving this evolution.

For centuries, businesses conducted transactions by bartering (a precursor to dynamic commerce). In the Industrial Age, however, mass production and extended distribution chains encouraged large economies of scale and made face-to-face customer contact impractical. As a result, static (or menu-driven) prices became necessary to manage the sale of the enormous increase in both volume and variety of products over far larger geographic regions. Many businesses realized huge gains, but they lost the ability to interact with customers individually.

Today, menu-driven pricing is the de facto standard for business, and, as a result, people tend to overlook its shortcomings. Static prices are often referred to as "sticky" because they are typically slow to adjust to market conditions, thereby causing a gap between the price that is charged for a good and its actual market value. In light of the proliferation of different product Stock Keeping Units (SKUs), the use of static pricing is not surprising because a tremendous amount of effort is required to determine how to price each item and how to keep pricing catalogs current. But static prices provide only a glimpse of the overall market demand, conveying only whether or not there was a buyer at a given price. As a result, businesses spend a substantial amount of money on market research to help them understand and forecast demand. Enabled by the Internet, dynamic commerce solves the dilemma of "sticky" prices by providing virtually instantaneous knowledge about market demand, such as how many bidders exist, who they are, how motivated they are, and the prices and quantities they desire.[5]

E-Commerce Trends

The Internet is ushering in a new era of B2B commerce, which has already proven itself a viable channel for marketing and selling to consumers (see Figure 4.0). Widespread Internet access means that consumers possess better market information and greater buying power. With low-cost access to the global marketplace, it is no longer necessary to buy from only local vendors.

The focus of most e-commerce strategies today is twofold. "Customer-facing" e-commerce applications provide better customer service, order processing, and direct access to accurate marketing information. "Vendor-facing" e-commerce applications result in backward integration of the enterprise supply chain and create

http://appell.ASCET.com

efficiencies within the market. Not surprisingly, initial e-commerce strategies like translating printed catalogs online, automating customer service, and order processing were natural extensions of traditional business practices that were rooted in static pricing models.[6]

The ubiquity and ease of Internet access, and the tremendous power to exchange large amounts of information in real-time, is changing the traditional model of static pricing. Dynamic commerce models are themselves rapidly stratifying into distinct strategic business formats. Figure 5.0 illustrates how various market interactions between buyers and sellers shape the way companies integrate dynamic commerce technology into their Internet strategy.

Presently, the most common forms of dynamic commerce are auctions and exchanges. A supplier interested in selling off surplus inventory, for example, will benefit from a traditional ascending (English or forward) auction where the highest bidder wins. A simple variation of the auction mechanism (which has acquired the popular name "reverse auction"), where sellers compete for the allocation of business from a buyer and the lowest bidder wins, can be used for sourcing activities. For example, a manufacturer seeking an efficient means to source lower-cost raw materials and services can utilize reverse auctions to bid out procurement contracts. Finally, businesses looking for additional market liquidity or access to new trade and service partners have the option of participating in or creating market-making exchanges.

Role of Exchanges in Dynamic Commerce

Exchanges solve fundamental and pervasive inefficiencies that hinder trade, such as the fragmentation of buyers and sellers, high search and transaction costs, and limited market information or highly variable demand. Traditional exchanges (e.g., stock or commodity exchanges) also provide liquidity and a standardized process for trading commodity-type goods where long-term, highly integrated relationships are not necessary. One prevailing exchange format in B2B e-commerce today is the bid/ask exchange model.

The bid/ask exchange is well known because this format has been used in the financial and commodity markets for decades. Bid/ask exchanges are simply "double-sided" auctions, which can be described as markets where multiple buyers post offers to purchase (commonly known as "bids"), and multiple sellers post offers to sell (often at a given price, known as the "ask" or "offer") for identical goods. Essentially, each buyer is hosting a

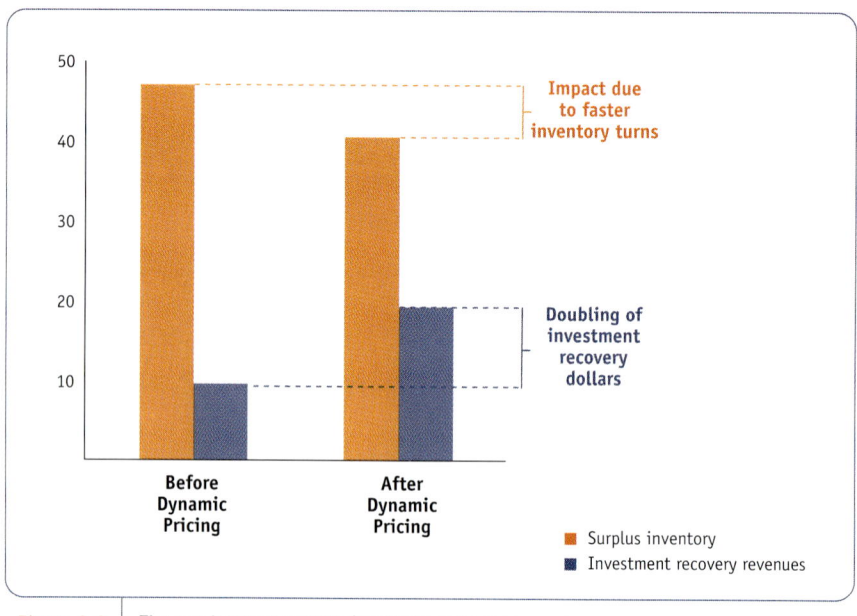

Figure 3.0 | The gap between surplus inventory and net recoveries

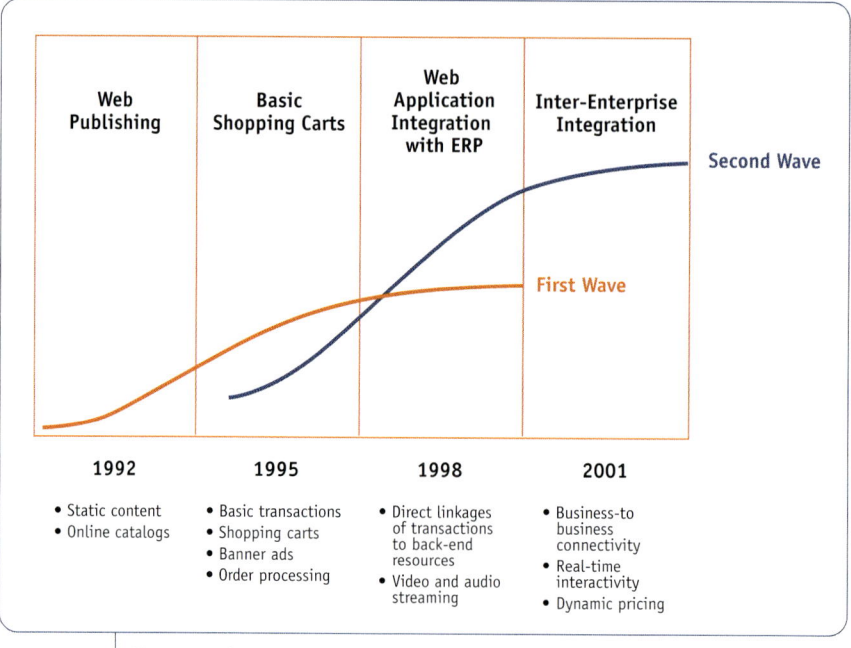

Figure 4.0 | The Internet is ushering in a new era of B2B commerce

86   Achieving Supply Chain Excellence Through Technology

Figure 5.0 Market interactions between buyers and sellers

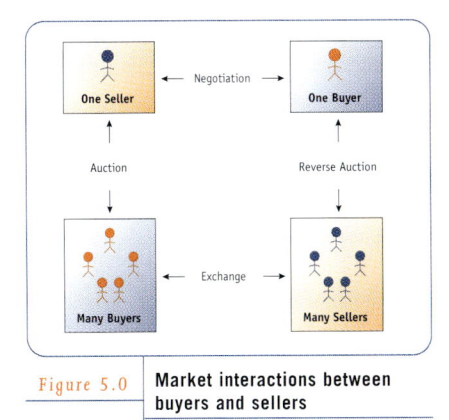

reverse auction in which sellers compete, and each seller is hosting a forward auction in which buyers compete. In an exchange, all of these events are blended into a single forum; transactions result from the process of matching bids and offers. Time is a key differentiator between exchanges and auctions, as the interactions between participants in exchanges are continuous (e.g., the NASDAQ) while auctions are discrete events.

Variations of the bid/ask exchange model will quickly evolve to include complex, multi-attribute bidding as well as online negotiation formats that enable participants to match terms beyond price and other standardized valuation factors. The buyer often has special considerations such as where and when delivery must occur, but the seller may also require special handling instructions that limit shipping options. At this point, the buyer and seller must arrive at an agreement in order to complete the transaction. In a dynamic environment, they can negotiate these complex terms online either synchronously or asynchronously and arrive at mutually agreeable terms in addition to price.

Role of Dynamic Commerce in E-Marketplaces

Auctions and exchanges have unique strengths for matching business needs. Exchanges are good forums for trading where the goods are relatively standardized and sufficient market mass and trade volume exists for a continuous trading environment. Auctions are well suited for selling and sourcing when the market characteristics of that good or service preclude the creation of an exchange of the product qualities of the good or service favor an auction (i.e., an extremely complex sourcing requirement). In either event, dynamic commerce is an important component of electronic marketplaces that seeks to facilitate the full slate of transaction activiites from requisition-to-pay, sourcing, and selling processes. These electronic marketplaces are being created to address cross-industry needs (horizontal marketplaces) as well as needs of specific industries (vertical marketplaces) that have unique business requirements.

Market Requirements for Dynamic Commerce

Dynamic commerce is best suited to certain types of products, services, or markets. There are several unique characteristics that identify when dynamic commerce can occur (see Figure 7.0).

First, the products or services being traded should have one or more of the following qualities:

- Well-defined (clearly specified or widely understood)
- Relatively standardized (e.g., commodities or near commodities)
- Perishable (e.g., foodstuffs) or time-sensitive (e.g., airline seats)
- Depreciating value (e.g., computer components, automotive parts)
- Scarce (e.g., limited resources, art auctions)

Second, the marketplace will most likely have at least one of the following attributes:

- Uncertainty about the price exists due to imperfect information about the marketplace. This may occur in cases where the product is new, the level of supply and/or demand is unclear, or the market is highly fragmented.
- Sufficient competition exists among bidders or can be created with the introduction of new bidders. In some markets, a critical mass can be achieved with as few as five to seven bidders. It is becoming much easier to overcome the hurdle of insufficient competition with the globalization of trade and the widespread use of the Internet.
- A buyer or seller exists with sufficient market clout to make and stimulate competition.
- Geographical or physical constraints between buyers and suppliers create a high cost to participate in, or expand, markets through traditional means.
- Value chains exist in which middlemen create pricing or information inefficiencies.
- A significant variance exists between supply and demand, perhaps because of long production lead times after an order is made or large fluctuations in demand.

Finally, online exchanges are most likely to form in markets that are characterized by one or more of the following:

- Fragmented markets with sufficient numbers of both buyers and suppliers
- Large trading volumes
- Goods or services with well understood valuation standards (i.e., Arbinet's line quality), or those which can be evaluated on price alone (i.e., commodities)
- High search and transaction costs associated with traditional trading mechanisms
- Multiple stages of negotiation
- Markets that require frequent spot purchases

Not all products are suited for dynamic commerce; some specialized products require relationship-specific investments between buyers and suppliers in order to bring the product to market successfully. A complex electronic component that is specifically designed in conjunction with a key supplier to meet strict performance and quality requirements is one kind of example.

Other market situations where dynamic commerce may not be appropriate include:

- Small markets without sufficient breadth and volume of market demand
- Markets where the price of a commodity is well understood

http://appell.ASCET.com

- Monopoly situations where buyers negotiate directly with the supplier

Future Vision

The future of e-commerce will bring a proliferation of digital marketplaces (both horizontal and vertical) in conjunction with new technologies that will further leverage dynamic commerce. Electronic agents will first scour the Web for buyers and suppliers, searching for goods on sale, or purchasing demand. More sophisticated agents may eventually compete in dynamic commerce markets on behalf of companies or individuals. Nevertheless, as prices approach their "true" market value, trade partners will increasingly compete on factors such as reliability, quality, and value-added services, and not just price.

The consensus among industry analysts is that the rapid growth of B2B e-commerce will be driven, to a large extent, by the adoption of trading exchanges and dynamic commerce. The early adopters of B2B dynamic commerce were mainly corporations that used auctions to improve the process for selling surplus inventory. Enterprises will continue to find new applications for online commerce solutions that match supply and demand such as reverse auctions for procurement. The real growth in dynamic commerce is expected to take place in emerging online marketplaces (see Figure 6.0). These marketplaces will be in a high-growth phase over the next several years as they try to build market share. By 2004, online marketplace revenues will reach $1.5 trillion, over half of all B2B commerce. The challenge will be to attract and retain a critical mass of buyers and seller by creating value through content, commerce, and services. Dynamic commerce solutions will be critical to the success of online marketplaces because they allow transactions to be conducted according to market factors, can be tailored to specific industry needs, and can be packaged according to buyer preference. In fact, dynamic commerce is projected to grow at an average annual rate of 133%, to $750 billion over the next five years.

Dynamic commerce engines will grow to support even more complex

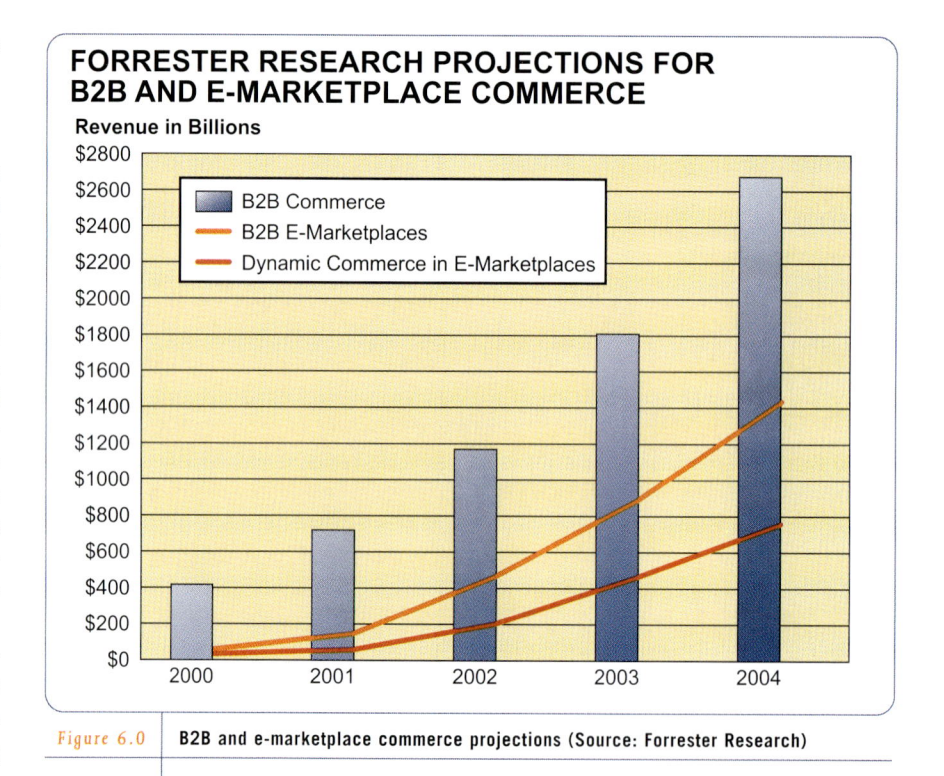

FORRESTER RESEARCH PROJECTIONS FOR B2B AND E-MARKETPLACE COMMERCE

Figure 6.0 | B2B and e-marketplace commerce projections (Source: Forrester Research)

transaction formats, such as:

- Multi-attribute auction formats that use criteria in addition to price, quantity, and time (such as "condition of goods," "delivery-time," and "supplier performance history")
- Complex multi-line RFQs and bid schedules
- Formats that allow a higher level of negotiation between buyers and sellers
- Continuous-matching formats where automated agents, comparable to current computerized stock-trading systems, perform the matching in real time

Business Applications for Dynamic Commerce

Dynamic commerce is changing the very nature of how goods and services are traded along the enterprise value chain. At each step, businesses have direct and low-cost access to an extended network of trade partners. Figure 8.0 illustrates the market space and demonstrates how businesses that use dynamic commerce have positioned themselves within the enterprise value chain.

This section explores the specific applications of dynamic commerce that enhance selling and sourcing activities, specifically in the context of e-commerce applications. First, it explores the seller-centric capabilities of dynamic commerce as a new pricing mechanism and channel for liquidating excess inventory. Next, it examines buyer-centric applications of dynamic commerce for the selection of long-term contracts and spot buys. Finally, it outlines potential benefits and risks to both the buyer and seller.

Seller-Centric Application: Liquidation of Surplus Inventory

Major businesses have learned a difficult lesson about the cost of carrying excess inventory. Aggressive international competition and faster product life cycles have forced companies to rethink manufacturing processes, inventory management, and supply chain activities in an effort to adopt continuously leaner practices. Despite their successes, it remains impossible, if not economically impractical, to reduce surplus inventory levels to zero. This issue is not a small one. On average, businesses

Attributes	Suitability	Example
Commodities and Near Commodities	High	Raw materials (coal, precious metals; food airline seats, services, transportation, equipment)
Standard components & materials	High	Valves, pipe, electronic components
Custom products requiring low or common tooling	Medium	Stamped metal parts, machined metal parts, chemicals
Complex/specialized tooling	Low	Specialized electronic components requiring close collaboration during design and production

Figure 7.0 Attributess that identify when dynamic commerce can occur

Seller-Centric Dynamic Commerce Applications: Benefits & Risks

Seller-centric dynamic commerce applications carry risks and benefits to both buyer and seller.

Benefits to Seller (company):
- Enhanced revenues
- Lowered costs and improved efficiency
- Access to a larger and more diverse group of buyers
- Real-time access to market demand information
- Stronger relationships with trading partners
- New channel to dispose of aged, unused, or idle assets

Benefits To Buyer (Trade Partner):
- Opportunity to lower price
- Lowered cost and improved efficiency
- Access to a larger and more diverse group of suppliers
- Better information about the market conditions
- Ability to participate in multiple auctions concurrently
- Means to smooth out supply and demand shocks

Risks To Seller (Company):
- Yield control over pricing to market mechanisms
- Exposure to new competition
- More complex logistics

Risks To Buyer (Trade Partner):
- Pay more than market value
- Credibility of product and/or supplier
- Access to customer service

Note
A more detailed description of the benefits and risks of seller-centric dynamic commerce applications is available at http://appell.CRMproject.com.

Buyer-Centric Application: Use of Dynamic Commerce for E-Sourcing

A potentially more significant application of dynamic commerce lies in the field of

in the United States carry approximately $18 billion in surplus inventory annually, an amount equivalent to about one-tenth of all finished goods[7].

While it is easy to think of surplus inventory in the narrow context of unsold, obsolete, or refurbished goods, this categorization actually encompasses a broader range of goods. For discussion purposes, surplus inventory can be divided into two basic product categories. The first category consists of those goods or services that are perishable – items whose usefulness and functionality last for a finite amount of time. In the event they are not used prior to their expiration, their value diminishes to zero. These types of products include chemicals, pharmaceuticals, airline seats, or advertising space. If a company holds these products for too long, the products will expire before being sold, resulting in lost revenues and, potentially, disposal costs.

The second class of surplus inventory includes goods whose value depreciates with time yet maintain some salvage value. Computers, electronic devices, and stamped metal parts are prime examples. As more powerful and improved devices are introduced to the market, older models become less desirable and potentially obsolete. The challenge to the selling company then becomes to accurately predict the rate of technological change and forecast the impact this change will have on product demand – an extremely difficult task.

The process for selling surplus inventory is also inefficient. Many companies still trade orders by phone and fax, a slow and labor-intensive process. In addition, when companies yield control of inventory to third party intermediaries, they lose their influence over where and at what price the merchandise is sold. Although some businesses need inventory to protect effectively against variability in demand, a more efficient way to manage excess inventory does exist.

Dynamic commerce offers a more effective solution to this problem. Rather than selling off surplus inventory to third party intermediaries, companies are now using the Web to auction surplus goods directly to customers. Figure 9.0 illustrates the kinds of participants who are buying through this channel. By leveraging the inherent flexibility of the Web to target a select group of highly motivated buyers or extend the reach of businesses across a maximum number of participants, dynamic commerce has a distinct advantage in generating competition and market liquidity. In addition to realizing improved returns and more efficient processes, companies are retaining greater control over their brand, extending a valuable service to their customers, gaining more valuable market insight, and reducing costs.

sourcing and procurement; it applies to both long-term supplier contracts and unpredictable spot buys. Several businesses have used dynamic commerce solutions in common procurement activities such as supplier consolidation, annual negotiations, and corporate-wide projects to gain savings through purchasing activities. These solutions can be applied both to strategic (or direct) goods and services related to a buyer's manufacturing operations, as well as to indirect purchases (commonly called Maintenance Repair and Operating resources, or MRO). Although there are clear differences concerning financial details and procurement methods, the fundamental value proposition is identical for all of these purchasing methods.

Many companies already use simple forms of competitive pricing for sourcing or supplying goods. Typically, the process requires sealed bids from prospective suppliers that are evaluated by the buyer. The buyer then selects one or more suppliers and negotiates detailed terms for specific contracts. This process can be labor-intensive for both parties and may result in contract terms that vary from supplier to supplier based on the market position of the supplier and the negotiating skills of both the trading partners.

Such varied contract terms may result from incomplete market information. Buyers often rely on suppliers for detailed product information. Since many supply industries are fragmented, buyers primarily look to suppliers with whom they have worked, or discovered in targeted advertising, trade journals, or aggregated catalogues. But supplier productivity can vary widely and is continually changing, making it very difficult for buyers to gather, organize, and evaluate vendor performance on an ongoing basis. As a result, buyers come to rely on outsourced strategic sourcing initiatives, where third parties periodically visit an organization, dig through vast amounts of transactional information, re-check the supplier landscape, and re-source long-term contracts with suppliers for key commodities.

By using dynamic commerce solutions, a buyer can automate the RFQ tender and bid processes. The Internet gives buyers the ability to eliminate geographic and cost barriers to potential suppliers, and to include additional suppliers into the bidding process at a very low cost. A real-time auction greatly increases competition in the marketplace by giving suppliers instant feedback on where they stand along with the opportunity to submit new bids and win the contract.

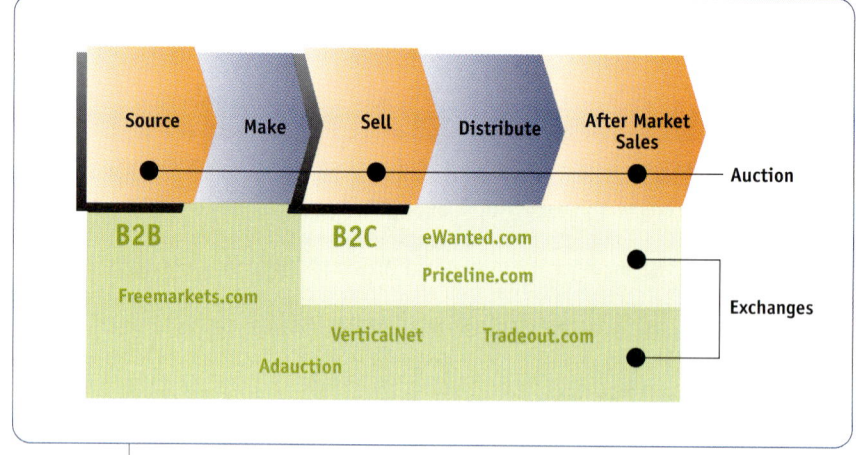

Historically, the economic leverage provided by competition has been most beneficial in markets where the products or services are commodities or near commodities, which means that the goods are well standardized or consistently specified. Coal and printed circuit boards are good examples. Between 1995 and 1998, companies that implemented reverse auctions for sourcing realized an average cost reduction of 17% as compared to previous contracts for similar goods[11]. Sprint used reverse auction services to source long-term contracts, which cut proposal cycle times by 70% and led to significant cost savings on $75 million worth of telecommunications services contracts. Visteon Automotive Systems achieved "multi-million dollar savings" on contracts for printed circuit boards by hosting the bidding process in a reverse auction format.

Buyer-Centric Dynamic Commerce Applications: Benefits and Risks

Buyer-centric dynamic commerce applications also carry benefit and risk to buyer and seller.

Figure 8.0 — How businesses that use dynamic commerce have positioned themselves

Benefits To Buyer:
- Opportunity to create or increase competition for buying dollars
- Better information about the marketplace
- Enhance the RFQ process and compress cycle time
- New supply management capability

Benefits To Seller:
- Access to new customers
- New and timely information on state of the market
- Automated RFQ process
- New demand management capability

Risks To Buyer:
- In the event that sufficient competition does not materialize, the price could be higher than the buyer expected
- Risks of taking on new suppliers
- Potential effects on decision-making and relationships

Risks To Seller:
- In the event that sufficient competition exists to ignite a bidding frenzy, the price may fall below that desired by the vendor
- Risks of taking on new buyers
- Potential effects on decision-making and relationships

Note
A more detailed description of the benefits and risks of buyer-centric dynamic com-

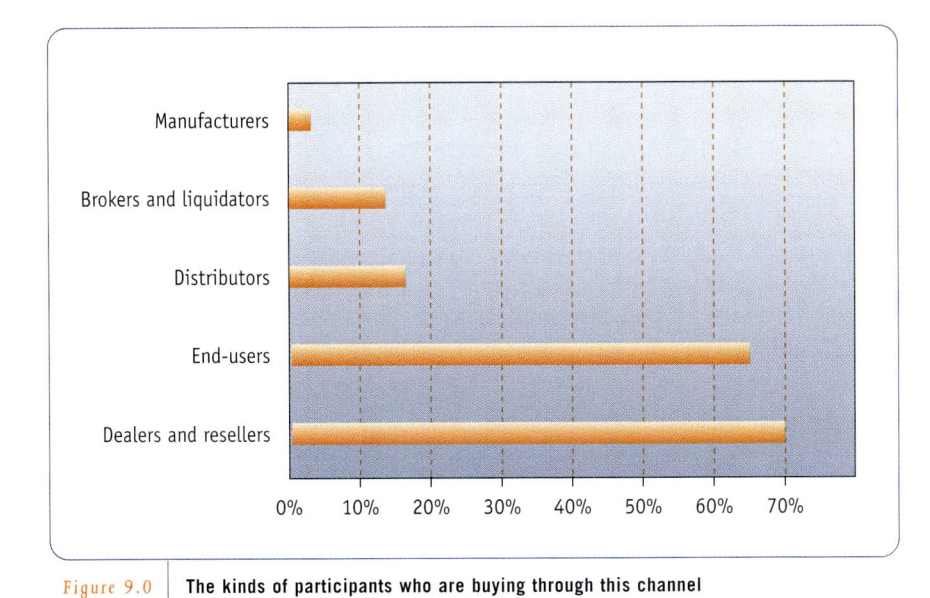

Figure 9.0 — The kinds of participants who are buying through this channel

Conclusion

As businesses engage in the "e-economy," they face significant challenges and opportunities. Widespread, low-cost access to trade and service partners allows businesses to create a vast, yet tightly integrated, supply chain network and realize tremendous value.

To thrive in the e-economy, businesses must capitalize on the strategic advantages that come from speed and information. Businesses must embrace capabilities that allow them to optimize all aspects of their expanding reach to customers and business partners. Sourcing and selling are two key elements of this network. In each of these activities, dynamic commerce clearly creates significant value for both buyers and suppliers.

The current wave of e-commerce is dynamic commerce, which delivers advantages of speed and information to innovative businesses. Fast-moving enterprises are proving that dynamic commerce, in the form of auctions or exchanges, can be a valuable piece of a company's overall e-commerce strategy — a strategy that can result in increased revenues, lower costs, and improved processes.

A glossary of the terms discussed in this paper is available at http://appell.CRMproject.com. Andersen Consulting and Moai engaged in joint research and development of this report. The data on which this report is based were not independently verified. Accordingly, the results may reflect inaccuracies in the underlying data. Other methods or approaches to the study may have yielded different results. Copyright ©1999 by Andersen Consulting and Moai. All rights reserved.

Footnotes

1 Center for Advanced Purchasing Studies, "Purchasing Performance Benchmarks for Investment Recovery," 1999, ISSN# 1078-1234.

2 Killen and Associates, 1997.

3 Harvard Business School White Paper # 9-598-109, "FreeMarkets Online," February 26, 1998, page 20.

4 NewsEdge Corporation, "A.T. Kearney Employs Internet Technology in Business-to-Business Competitive Auctions," September 3, 1999.

5 The Economist, "The Heyday of the Auction," July 24, 1999.

6 Forrester Research, "Anatomy of New Market Models," February 1999.

7 Businessweek, "Goodbye to Fixed Pricing?" May 4, 1998.

8 NewsEdge Corporation, ibid.

9 Information Week, "Going, Going, Gone!" October 4, 1999.

10 CIO Web Business Magazine, "How Bazaar," August 1998.

11 These savings are averaged over nine different commodity types including: plastic molded parts, metal stampings, metal castings, metal machinings, chemicals, pole line hardware, commercial valves, corn sweetener, and printed circuit boards.

http://appell.ASCET.com

Moai's LiveExchange Solutions

Contact Information

Anne Perlman
CEO

Deva Hazarika
Founder

Frank Kang
Founder

Date Founded
1996

Headquarters
San Francisco, CA

Number of Employees
100+

Net Revenue
N/A

Moai
25 Lusk Street
San Francisco, CA 94107
Phone 415.625.0601
Toll Free 888.244.Moai
Fax 415.625.1200
www.moai.com
info@moai.com

Solutions

LiveExchange full-service solutions focus on dynamic commerce needs. These best of breed solutions are LiveExchange Enterprise, LiveExchange Marketplace, and LiveExchange ASP. A full spectrum of services are offered by Moai's Professional Services Organization and world-class partners. A partial list includes technical account management, training, customization, and installation.

Moai is the leader in dynamic commerce solutions for a wide range of applications including trading exchanges, online auctions, and reverse auctions for procurement of goods and services. With the advent of e-commerce, businesses have low-cost, global access to a greatly expanded network of stakeholders in the enterprise value chain. One of the most promising opportunities for improving this network is the application of dynamic commerce to an organization's sourcing and selling activities. Innovators in this space are demonstrating that this is a critical component of e-commerce, resulting in increased revenues and profitability, improved control of their sales channels, and reduced inventory overhead.

Moai has established world-class partnerships to ensure customers are offered a comprehensive dynamic commerce portfolio. Moai partners with the leading technology companies to develop integration modules for their Internet applications and services. Premier consulting and system integration firms deliver technical account management to ensure that the business objectives of Moai's customers are consistently met before, during, and after implementation. Moai also partners with the leading e-commerce platform companies to ensure total customer satisfaction.

Moai identifies and implements the ideal combination of technology and services to meet an individual company's business requirements. This provides customers with incredible time-to-market advantages and the opportunity to stay focused on their core business. Moai's industry expertise ensures customers' success in dynamic commerce. Best practices consulting is offered for customers interested in leveraging Moai's experience in dynamic commerce. The Professional Services team at Moai and its partners are available to install the Moai Dynamic Commerce solutions and provide site customization, branding, and integration. Customers can also attend in-depth training sessions on all aspects of the technology. Moai helps companies create customized exchange sites that will easily adapt and grow with changing business needs over time. Moai's goal is to ensure that customers are successful in online dynamic commerce today and in the future.

Moai's LiveExchange Solutions

Moai offers three best-of-breed LiveExchange full-service solutions focused on meeting specific dynamic commerce needs. LiveExchange Enterprise is ideal for creating enterprise-driven, dynamic commerce markets run by a single company that want to sell or procure products and services online. LiveExchange Marketplace is designed for industry-specific or marketplace-focused exchanges that bring together multiple buyers and sellers. LiveExchange ASP is ideal for broad-based portals and service providers supporting a full range of turnkey e-commerce capabilities.

On average, Moai customers enjoy a significant return on investment through revenue enhancements, cost reductions, and efficiency gains within the first year. Moai's LiveExchange solutions help businesses with procurement by simplifying and accelerating the Request for Proposals/Request for Quotes process, vendor selection, and negotiations. By implementing dynamic pricing and automating the procurement process, companies have demonstrated saving up to 15% on contracts and can potentially realize a 70% improvement in procurement cycle times. Moai assists companies in every facet of dynamic commerce, providing innovative technology, hosting services, and technical and industry expertise.

Turnkey Solutions for Hosting

Moai offers hosting services as a cost-effective, full-service, turnkey solution for companies that must meet dynamic commerce needs immediately. The hosting option is ideal for companies that want to outsource IT functions and accelerate their time to market. Moai provides functional customization, including integration with existing back-end processes and logistics functions that are critical to making a commerce site successful. Along with its partners, Moai manages everything from integration to auction administration, eliminating the need to invest in hardware, additional bandwidth, and IT personnel.

GoCargo.com Chooses Moai to power its Online Shipping Exchange

The shipping industry faces many challenges. First, the variability and economics of international trade makes optimizing cargo loads from port-to-port a very complex task. Unbalanced trade economies mean that service providers face returning containers to their home-port at half their capacity. This represents a significant lost opportunity. Yields could be improved by optimizing container loads and streamlining procedures to fill them. Since the marginal cost of filling even one additional container on a freighter is far outweighed by the fixed cost of actually sailing across the ocean, incentive to maximizing loads exists.

Aside from the economic and political complexities of international trade, the shipping industry is also very competitive. It is highly fragmented as evidenced by over 500 carriers, 2,500 vessels and 350 ports. Furthermore, no single carrier maintains more than a six percent share of the world vessel capacity. This intense competition between the shipping service providers has depleted margins and is forcing the industry to find effective cost saving measures.

GoCargo.com has introduced an online shipping exchange to help achieve cost savings in the industry. The company has capitalized on recent deregulation within the shipping industry by creating an exchange that allows importers and exporters to publicize the parameters of their payloads. Shipping service providers then have the opportunity to bid on this cargo competitively. The exchange allows shippers to optimize their rates and, at the same time, carriers and intermediaries are able to bid for shipments that best match their services based on commodity, trade route, or volume. Ships that are near capacity mean dramatically improved returns for service providers.

The introduction of the GoCargo.com exchange has decreased the time shippers take to find a carrier, negotiate terms, and close a deal. Traditionally, this process could take several days and was labor intensive. Now the process can be completed, in many cases, within one hour. Shippers increase their purchasing power by gaining access to more information and service providers worldwide. In turn, service providers have expanded their customer base, included value-added services such as liquidation of excess capacity, increased revenues, and reduced sales costs by automating many business practices online. These benefits are the result of removing some on the barriers faced by the shipping industry that kept shippers and service providers from maximizing profits.

LiveExchange Enterprise Designed for businesses that want to use auctions for asset management, procurement, or new revenue streams

LiveExchange Marketplace Designed for entrepreneurial "dot-coms" that want to create marketplaces for buyers and sellers.

LiveExchange ASP Designed for companies that want to create trade communities and aggregate numerous Web sites.

Dynamic Commerce Engine All solutions are built upon Moai's industry-leading dynamic commerce technical architecture.

Hosting Services Moai provides turnkey LiveExchange solutions, which include administration and hosting.

Industry Expertise Moai Professional Services provides dynamic pricing business expertise, technical implementation, integration and customization.

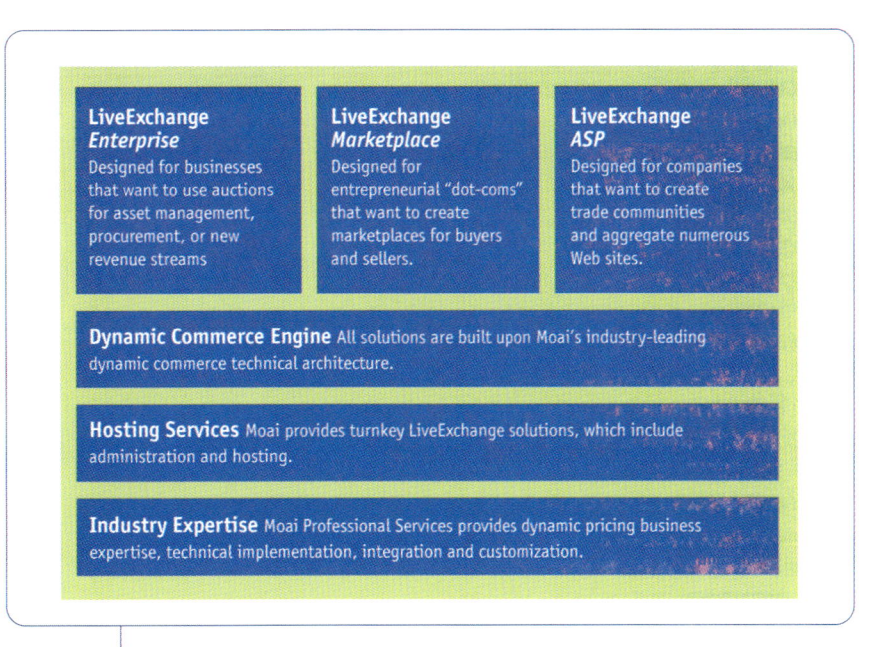

Figure 1.0   LiveExchange Solutions

http://moai.ASCET.com

Optum, Inc. – End-to-End Fulfillment @ Its Best

Contact Information
Dave Simbari
President and CEO

Optum, Inc. Headquarters
*11 Martine Avenue
White Plains, NY 10606
Phone 800.561.0462*

Primary Locations
*Costa Mesa, CA
Charlotte, NC
Tongeren, Belgium
Melbourne, Australia*

www.optum.com

Optum is a leading provider of configurable end-to-end fulfillment solutions for e-commerce and traditional businesses. We combine robust products with consulting services to bring clients the comprehensive fulfillment solutions they need. Our solutions target fast-moving, high-volume, piece-pick distribution operations, which are characteristic of today's e-commerce environment. The Optum solution is architected to enable a high degree of inter- and intra-enterprise connectivity and is distinguished by its configurability and ability to scale to any type or size of distribution network.

Our products and services provide comprehensive end-to-end fulfillment solutions by addressing key business processes including:
- Outbound Logistics, which encompasses the entire order-to-delivery fulfillment cycle
- Inbound Logistics, which manages incoming products, components, and related materials into a company's supply chain network
- Inventory Visibility and Decision Support, which optimizes the execution of all inbound and outbound logistics by providing enterprise-wide order visibility and related product availability.

We have implemented over 750 client sites to date, with over 250 sites completed in 1999 alone. Some of the leading companies in order fulfillment are Optum clients, including Anixter, Invacare, Merisel, NCR, Reichhold Chemicals, Solectron, Systemax, W.W. Grainger, and Webvan.

Why Fulfillment is Strategic

The rapidly rising importance of the Internet as a medium for business-to-business and business-to-consumer commerce is increasing customer expectations and triggering dramatic growth in small-parcel deliveries to homes and businesses. Customers are demanding rapid delivery of the products they order and instant access to accurate information regarding product delivery status.

Businesses are being forced to adopt a new fulfillment model that operates with a high degree of velocity, flexibility and customer-responsiveness. Many current fulfillment systems have been built according to a traditional business model that places a premium on efficiency, focusing on the principles of mass production and economies of scale. These current fulfillment systems often have an inadequate architecture for scalability and configurability and cannot handle dynamic order volumes and enterprise connectivity.

Our Proven Solution

We meet the demands of this new fulfillment model. We provide the configurable fulfillment solutions needed to manage a company's complete fulfillment needs. Our solutions consists of software products, professional services, and third-party software and hardware that enable comprehensive inbound and outbound logistics processing, as well as inventory visibility and decision support. Our solutions offers the following key benefits:
- Configurability: Flexibility and agility to manage an evolving logistics organization with applications that can be continuously re-configured to accommodate our clients' changing needs.
- Scalability: Scalable logistics infrastructure that can accommodate a wide range of operational complexity and transaction volumes.
- Visibility: End-to-end, real-time visibility enabling our clients to make decisions quickly to reduce errors and ensure on-time delivery.
- Connectivity: Inter- and intra-enterprise system connectivity to allow companies to effectively collaborate with their customers and trading partners.

Buying and Selling on the Web: Is a Meeting of Technologies Really a Meeting of Minds?

Sellers want to get closer to customers, manage the full relationship lifecycle, and increase margin by selling value-added services. They're using the Web for this. Buyers want to automate the buying process, drop or add suppliers in seconds, and negotiate discounts on commoditized products. The Web is being used for this. Is there something wrong with this picture?

On Internet Time

This paper was completed on January 30, 2000, at 7:45 p.m. We're on Internet time now. By 8:15 p.m., some of what drives these comments will be out of date, and by the time you read it, the world in which it was written will be the stuff of nostalgia.

Still, isn't there something to be said now, on January 30, which will be true in future times, like in February?

I think there is, if you step back from the technology and start looking at what you might call "the struggle." The struggle is the struggle to make money, to get people to buy, to get a good price, to make a deal, to deliver on a deal. The struggle is older than the Internet – at least that's what they say – and the struggle on Internet time retains at least some of the features of that older struggle.

Let's express it in simple Internet terms. For all businesses, the ratio of e-selling activity to e-buying seems to be roughly 4:1. And I'm just talking about activity. If you start looking at corporate focus or C-level energy, it's 97% on the sell-side, and if you look at valuations – well, nobody ever doubled their stock price by spinning off a buy-side dot-com.

But looking at the economy as a whole, shouldn't the amount of buy-side activity roughly match the amount of sell-side?

Here's another way of looking at things:

For any two companies that are buying products through most of the commercial marketplace products (e.g., Ariba, CommerceOne, Intellisys), the large company shoulders the lion's share of the fees. This is in keeping with the famous "wallet" principle of software pricing, for example "charge what's in the wallet." But again, it doesn't make much macroeconomic sense. The fees should be roughly similar.

And one more angle to consider:

Sellers think that the Internet brings them closer to buyers, whereas buyers think the Internet makes it easier to buy automatically or else to hold auctions, where all suppliers are held at arm's length.

The struggle is a bit out of whack, here on Internet time. But if we can figure out how the "whack" is going to get back in, maybe we can actually see farther ahead than February.

Let's look first at the situation from the buyer's point of view, then from the supplier's and then from the trading communities (see Figure 1.0).

Contradictions on the Buy Side

Let's make a distinction between ordering and buying. Buying is figuring out what you want, finding it at a good price, ordering it, getting it, and paying for it. Ordering is sending in the order.

Why doesn't buying and selling activity match up? Partly because buying companies are just trying to improve ordering. They want to order over the Internet instead of faxing in the order, phoning in the order, or sending it EDI.

Boy, is that boring. No CEO is going to transform his/her company and triple valuation by Internetting orders. It's boring, too, because the technology is stupefying: bits and bytes, messaging and publish/subscribe, XML.

Notice that the prospect of providing your customers with operational efficiencies should

---

David N. Dobrin, Ph.D., partner, leads Benchmarking Partners' analysis of enterprise applications and consults on Electronic Business Information Architecture Strategy (E-BIAS), focusing on integrating demand/supply chains and e-business to ERP.

He has helped lead supply chain implementations at a variety of multinationals including Raychem, Schlumberger, Johnson & Johnson, Unilever, and AT&T.

Dobrin is part of a team of practitioners who teach an MIT course for executives and graduate students entitled, "Developing the CEO Team's Value Chain Network Strategy."

not keep sellers all agog. A lot of these buy-side technologies are just null from the seller's point of view. The Internet buy is just the same buy. No new channels, no new revenues — just fewer fax machines and fewer telephones ringing.

Of course, partly because it's not exciting, you might think that stuff would get done. But, oddly enough, here's what seems to be happening.

To take the same order, there are now three ways of transmitting it. Buyers set up a way of creating an order and transmitting it over the Web, possibly with some kind of Web page in the DMZ on their site, but very often expecting an EDI back end. (Let's call this a buyer-based order.) An intermediary sets up connections on both ends with a catalog in the middle. (Call this a trading community order.) The seller sets up a way of using the Web directly; just log in and place an order on their Web store. (Call this a "seller-based order.")

"If only everyone did it my way!" Buyers want sellers to use buyer-based orders. But those stubborn sellers would have to log into the Web sites of all their customers, and they find that burdensome. Sellers want buyers to use their store. To satisfy them, all the buyers would have to log into the Web sites for everything they buy — no way! Intermediaries tell everybody to quit wasting time and just log in to their portal. And confusion reigns.

When you extend the discussion beyond ordering to the full buying process, you see the same tensions. Buyers and sellers aren't getting together because each has different goals and different expectations of benefit. Viewed from their point of view, the behavior makes sense, but from a macro view, it can sometimes verge on the silly.

Take, for instance, the one benefit on the buy side that really does make CEOs wake up and take notice: sourcing. The logic goes something like this. "You're spending $2.5 billion a year. If you could consolidate your spend and get a 10% discount with the selected suppliers, you could save $250 million a year, and it all flows to the bottom line."

Never mind that this sourcing argu-

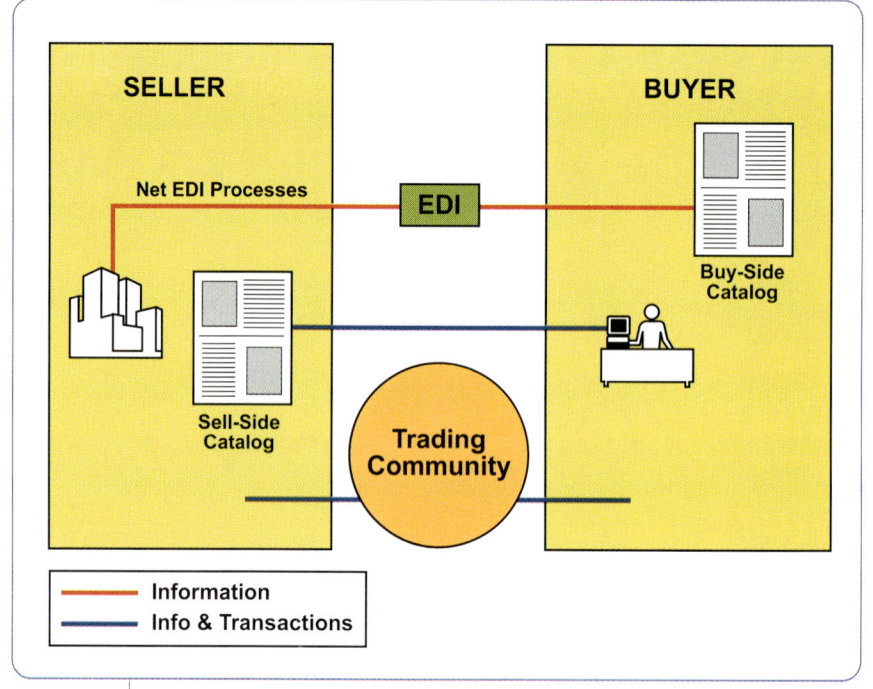

Figure 1.0 — The buyer's point of view, the supplier's point of view, and then that of the trading communities.

ment long predates the Internet and, technically, has nothing to do with the Internet. (You could have consolidated suppliers and negotiated discounts long before the Internet.) And set aside the fact that macro-economically, this can't work. (If everybody could negotiate a 10% discount, the economy would deflate by 10%.) What are the real problems?

The first is that "getting control" can impose new costs on the company even as the price of purchased goods goes down. There is a reason why purchasing has always had a hard time enforcing its rules: employees find it more efficient for them to go around the system. If they can't go around the system any more, they'll pay the costs of lost time, failed deliveries, getting the wrong product, etc. Like any other new requisition system, an Internet requisition system can slow the company down and cost it money. There is also a cost that is specific to Internet requisitioning — internal and external logistics costs can go way up, because orders are smaller.

The same set of effects can also be seen at the supplier. Once they get over the chagrin attendant on realizing that an Internet hookup means lower margins, they react in the natural way — by lowering service levels. They shift the cost back onto the customer in less visible ways.

Both internally and externally, unless sourcing over the Internet provides benefit to all the parties involved — actual buyer, supplier, etc. — it is unlikely that the sheer exertion of power will accomplish very much.

Everywhere else in purchasing the same contradictions emerge. The Internet systems designed to enable purchasing haven't yet evolved to the point where they enable the buyer and seller to cooperate. Without that cooperation, you're off Internet time; benefits will be slow, painful, and expensive (relative to our ambitions for the Internet). Not only will we not be in a new age come March, the struggle will probably be pretty much the same.

Why is it that the companies that have the money are paying the money to set up buy-side solutions? It's simple. The marketplace actually perceives the risks of setting up these buying solutions, and they are insisting that the companies that are setting them up shoulder the risk.

Contradictions on the Sell Side

The essential contradiction on the sell side, of course, is the mirror of the contradiction on the buy side. Buyers are out for discounts and operational efficiencies; they want to commoditize their suppliers. Suppliers are out to sell more services and more highly differentiated products. They want to create a new relationship with the customer and exploit it.

Internet technology, on the one hand, seems to be on the seller's side. It lets you track relationships; it makes it easier for your customer to place orders, track orders and get information; it makes it easier for the sales force to communicate.

Wait a minute – the technology also makes it easier for buyers to seek out all of your competitors and get information from them, too. The technology makes it tempting for buyers to work on an exception basis, where servers are actually placing the orders and tracking all normal orders, so you, the seller, have no control over the order placement and timing. The technology makes it harder for salespeople to work in the normal way, because so much of setting up a trading relationship now involves managing the bits and bytes.

Dig in and you get even more contradictions. Take the desire to sell services and products more suited to individual customers (mass customization). The more complex the product and the more service attached to it, the harder it is to buy over the Internet. It's hard to set up systems to take in more and more variations in product. It's hard to assess or compare highly differentiated products. It's hard to measure delivery of services and often hard to value them.

These same companies are also investing on the sell side in two competing Internet technologies, often without realizing that the competition is occurring. On the one hand, they are putting serious money into sales force automation tools. These have the aim, in the short term, of making the sales force more efficient and freeing them up for more face time with the customer. Eventually, they will be the tools for managing the complex relationship with the customer that they plan on setting up. On the other hand, they are putting up e-stores and – very slowly – putting up catalog content on trading communities or participating in auctions.

Typically, they are worried that an e-store might create channel conflict with their distributors. But their biggest channel conflict is with the sales force that they're empowering. If people want to do buying over the Internet (as opposed to just ordering), and if they want to put more and more of their spend into disengaging buying processes, like auctions or empowering the requisitioner, what is the salesperson going to be doing with all that face time? Shouldn't they be putting the money into people who know how to behave at a reverse auction? (A reverse auction is a situation where the buyer puts out a proposal and asks the sellers to name an ever-lower price.) What happens when actual buyers are spread throughout the company? This isn't a relationship sell any more.

Contradictions at Trading Communities

A fair number of companies have already seen how they can step into the middle and resolve these contradictions – and maybe make a little money for themselves in the process. They are setting up trading communities.

Trading communities are good for buyers because they allow companies to leverage the cost of managing the buy. If buyers are smart, they can also combine their total spend and get discount based on the total volume.

Trading communities are good for sellers because they give you low-cost access to new customers, and they take some of the trouble and expense out of selling. They're doing the distribution for you.

Of course, trading communities are bad for buyers, because they create the illusion of a free market, when in fact the number of sellers is limited, and the trading community itself (typically) depends for its income on the sellers. The trading communities, moreover, are offering market-making services (guaranteed delivery, payment and billing, and financing) without either the regulation or the capitalization to back them up.

And trading communities are bad for sellers because each community has multiple barriers to entry, which are expensive, and it's unclear whether the community is doing anything more than cannibalizing existing customers. With trading communities, too, you lose control of the relationship with your customers and the sales process, and you invite head-to-head competition on price with other factors – like quality and reliability, which are more difficult to bring into the process.

Trading communities are good for the people who run trading communities, at least today, because of the stock valuations, but the business model is difficult to work out. Do you charge the buyers or the sellers? Plus, it is difficult to recruit participants, the technologies are in their infancy, and if the communities do succeed, the barriers to entry are much smaller than they were for the original player. To differentiate oneself, one must provide content and an easy buying experience to the buyer, but the former is difficult to get, and the latter is difficult to build.

Eventually, all this will shake out, but probably in a very messy way. There won't be just one trading community; there will be many. People will end up deploying resources just to deal with all the trading communities. Some people will learn how to exploit the systems; some will not.

The people who are paying for trading communities right now are the people who have the most money – usually the buyers. This means a) that trading communities are tilted in favor of the buyers; and b) that the marketplace makers can't yet make enough money by setting up a marketplace where everybody pays a (relatively) equal amount. If you join in a marketplace quickly, because this is Internet time, you may get burned. Maybe you should look at working with it on regular time.

Viewlocity Helps Create Online Trading Communities and Synchronize Supply Chains

Contact Information

Greg Cronin
CEO

Moe Trebuchon
COO

Stan Stoudenmire
CFO

Jeff Cashman
SVP, Global Marketing
and Business Development

**Viewlocity
World Headquarters**

3475 Piedmont Road
Suite 1700
Atlanta, Georgia 30305
Phone 877.512.8900
Fax 770.512.7113
info@viewlocity.com
www.viewlocity.com

Products
Viewlocity provides the e-infrastructure for business-to-business online trading communities and traditional supply chains, connecting you with your trading partners.

Services
Our people offer situation assessment, consulting, training, implementation, strong customer support, and detailed follow-through on every project.

Client List
Korea Trade Network, Kraft, Jacob Suchard, Nestle, New Zealand Dairy, Perrier Group, Pfizer, Philips, Quantum, Schenker SE Banken, Siemens, Sony Marketing Asia-Pacific, Swedish Pharmacy, Sykes, Syntegra, Telia AB, TNT, tradehub, UK Electricity, Unilever, Volvo, Wallenius Wilhelmsen AS, Warner-Lambert, Wyle Electronics.

Viewlocity is a global provider of the e-infrastructure for Business-to-Business (B2B) online trading communities and traditional supply chains. With more than 3,200 installations worldwide, AMTrix®, Viewlocity's flagship product, empowers organizations and their business partners to connect, communicate, and collaborate throughout the extended supply chain.

Viewlocity has 12 offices worldwide, with its global headquarters in Atlanta, GA, European headquarters in London, and its Asia-Pacific headquarters in Singapore. Focused on the high-tech, consumer products, retail/e-tail, and logistics service provider industries, Viewlocity markets its products and services in more than 50 countries through its direct sales organization and through a global network of integration partners.

What Can Viewlocity Do for You?

Viewlocity helps you leverage your current IT investments and can guide your journey to participating in online trading communities. With Viewlocity, you will be able to better:

- **Connect** – We offer the integration infrastructure that is the foundation of any B2B project. We can integrate disparate applications within your enterprise using real-time data conversion, intelligent messaging, and graphical business workflow modeling.
- **Communicate** – Once connected internally, you can begin integrating externally with your trading partners, no matter what systems you or your partners have.
- **Collaborate** – Viewlocity will help you collaborate better with your trading partners by starting your own private online trading community or joining a public exchange.
- **Synchronize** – By providing increased visibility of your supply chain and solutions for specific logistics problems, our synchronization applets ultimately create more value for your customers.

Why Viewlocity?

- Viewlocity empowers more online supply chain trading communities worldwide than any other provider. And we can do it faster and remotely.
- Our software fills the gaps no matter what systems you have today or plan to have in the future.
- We can connect you to your trading partners, no matter what software they use.
- We can help you collaborate with your trading partners in a many-to-many, multi-threaded information hub, where you have "event-based" messaging versus a point-to-point message in batch mode.
- We're truly global with a vast knowledge of the technical and service requirements for different cultures, infrastructures, and regulatory environments.
- Our management team has vast B2B and supply chain expertise, while nearly a third of our employees have over 10 years of supply chain experience.
- We are committed to leveraging strong relationships worldwide with leading consulting and systems integration partners to drive high-impact, high-value solutions.

Viewlocity sets the standard in e-infrastructure for online trading communities and traditional supply chains. Our solutions break down the technology barriers so you can work closely with your trading partners and manage the flow of goods no matter how different your systems are from those of your partners.

We have a global presence that is larger than any comparable vendor. Our name may be new to you, but you probably know our more than

750 customers. Viewlocity was launched in 1999 from one of Europe's leading IT firms, Frontec. We have plenty of experience, with over 3,200 installations worldwide in more than 50 countries.

Not only are we seasoned in implementing quality e-infrastructure solutions, but we also have an exceptionally well-experienced executive team that comes from leading firms like i2, Booz Allen & Hamilton, Andersen Consulting, Manhattan Associates, Manugistics, and PricewaterhouseCoopers.

Viewlocity has formed strong partnerships with respected firms like SAP, Oracle, J.D. Edwards, and IBM as well as hundreds of systems integration firms. Nurturing these relationships and building a strong, global team has been Viewlocity's focus since its inception.

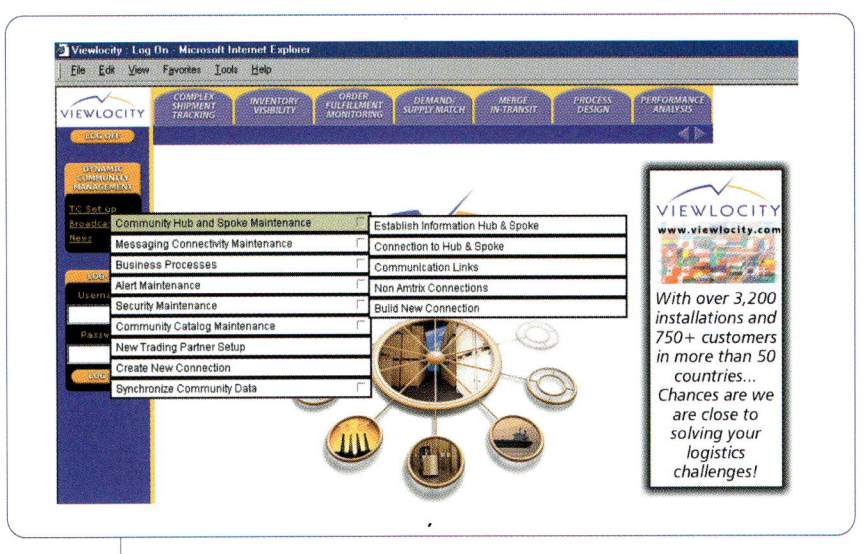

Connect: Quickly Building your E-Business from the Inside Out

Viewlocity can help you in your first step toward B2B commerce, by helping you integrate all the systems within your enterprise and give you visibility over vital information. The connections transcend all levels, bridging the gaps between business processes, databases, technologies, communication layers, and software systems. Being fully integrated and connected internally allows you to begin to use that information to make better decisions, faster.

Our infrastructure integration offerings include:

Viewlocity's Message Integration Engine, SmartSync™, delivers a distinct blend of heterogeneous messaging across countless formats and protocols using a message broker foundation and broad connectivity to leading supply chain, ERP, and logistics solutions.

Our SmartSync Process Manager is tightly integrated with Viewlocity's message integration engine. Users can graphically model trading community-based workflows and rapidly drive understanding of the re-designed business processes.

Viewlocity's SmartSync Matching Engine supports transaction exchanges and bid-and-ask auctioning as well as advanced optimization techniques – proven with installations across the globe.

SmartSync Connectors offer predefined integration with leading ERP and supply chain planning and execution systems including Baan, IMI, JD Edwards, Manugistics, Oracle Applications, PeopleSoft, and SAP. The SmartSync™ Connector Development Platform empowers your organization to quickly develop integration connectors for other applications, including legacy systems that exist within today's enterprise environment.

Communicate: Breaking Down the Barriers

Once you have connected your systems internally, you are ready to begin to integrate externally with your trading partners. Viewlocity's SmartSync products provide the ability to integrate with your trading partners through remote connection capabilities. In other words, you don't have to send a technician to your trading partner's site, which will save you and your partner time and resources. In addition, because Viewlocity offers an extensive library of pre-built connectors that leverage formats from XML to EDI, you reduce your implementation timeline dramatically.

Collaborate: The Online Trading Community is Here

The promise of e-business is the synchronization of value and the creation of wealth by linking virtual enterprises and supply chains. Much of the focus today is on simple buying and selling of products over the Internet, but this is just the beginning. Industry leaders in the future will participate in collaborative business communities, where companies can truly leverage their key suppliers and their customers as part of a virtual enterprise.

Synchronize: Finally the Complete E-Business Vision

Once you are well connected externally and you are communicating better with your trading partners, you'll find that your supply chain operations are synchronized, which will ultimately create happier customers. Viewlocity's solutions allow extreme flexibility for your company, because it allows you to translate information from your trading partners, no matter what communication standards they use.

Partial Client List

ABB, ECnet, Alcatel, American Standard, Asia Business Venture Holdings, Asia Pacific Breweries, Bancnet, boo.com, British Gas Trading, British Telecom, Brown & Williamson, Carlton United Breweries, Carrefour SA, China Customs, China Telecom, Danish Post, DuPont, Electrolux, Ericsson, Exel, Gerber, and Integral Energy.

Figure 1.0 Viewlocity's SmartSync Solutions

http://viewlocity.ASCET.com

Iron Mountain – Global Leader in Records and Information Management Services

Contact Information

Richard Reese –
Chairman of the Board,
Iron Mountain

Peter Pierce –
President, Iron Mountain

Joe Nezi –
Executive Vice President,
Sales & Marketing,
Iron Mountain

Ralph Selle
Vice President, Marketing
Arcus Data Security

Ken Rubin
Managing Director
Iron Mountain Consulting Services
(IMCS)

Iron Mountain
745 Atlantic Avenue,
Boston, MA 02111
800.883.8000,
fax 617.535.4766
www.IronMountain.com

Products/Services
Business and Healthcare Records
Storage and Management
Records Management Consulting
Vital Records Protection
Data Security Services
Disaster Recovery Support
Facilities Management
Imaging Services
Destruction Services
Storage Cartons and Supplies

The so-called "paperless office" has become nothing more than a myth as computing and communications devices generate increasingly higher volumes of paper records and the volume of information doubles every three to four years. Sensitive issues such as the control and proper retention of paper and electronic records such as e-mail add another measure of concern.

Records management represents a unique opportunity for senior-level executives to reduce costs while managing risk and information assets more efficiently. Yet all too often, companies maintain ineffective in-house records storage and management programs draining valuable resources and increasing risk.

Iron Mountain Inc. includes three primary operating companies: Iron Mountain Records Management, Arcus Data Security, and Iron Mountain Consulting Services. Iron Mountain provides secure, cost-effective hardcopy storage throughout its record centers worldwide. Through Arcus, Iron Mountain offers data protection and disaster recovery services to support companies' critical business continuity efforts. And Iron Mountain Consulting Services brings these and other elements together to enable organizations to develop, implement, and support company-wide records management programs.

Iron Mountain Records Management

Established in 1951, Iron Mountain is the world's largest records management company. Iron Mountain partners with organizations to outsource the costly and cumbersome function of records storage. Clients receive the advantages of secure storage with easy access. Iron Mountain helps clients save money, reduce liability, and improve control over records. Clients also receive the benefits of a records management system – SafeKeeperPlus. Through SafeKeeperPlus, clients can track, access and control records, and ensure consistency throughout their organizations.

Iron Mountain's services include storage, retrieval, delivery, and destruction of hardcopy business records. More than 120,000 companies trust Iron Mountain to store their records. Iron Mountain's Healthcare Information Services caters to the specific requirements of the medical community. Unique vital records facilities protect irreplaceable information assets.

Iron Mountain Consulting Services (IMCS)

IMCS helps leading corporations better manage the litigation, compliance, and risk exposures related to their records management practices. Clients gain better access to information and lower records-related costs. IMCS works with clients to develop company-wide records management and retention programs that standardize the treatment of paper records, electronic documents, and e-mail. Based on an analysis of a client's situation, IMCS designs customized, comprehensive records management solutions and tools.

Arcus Data Security

Arcus Data Security is the world's leader in off-site data security and disaster recovery services.

Its network of over 75 worldwide facilities provides customers with a wide array of business continuity services. Services include off-site data security and vaulting, secure media library moves, disaster recovery testing and support services, electronic vaulting, disaster recovery consulting, and a broad range of high quality media products.

Arcus has performed successfully in more than 125 actual disasters, 1,000+ media library moves, and over 10,000 disaster recovery tests. Arcus also offers software escrow and intellectual property protection through DSI Technology Escrow Services.

white paper

written by:
Gordon Anderson
SAP AG
http://anderson-g.ASCET.com

From Supply Chain to Collaborative Commerce Networks: The Next Step in Supply Chain Management

Traditional ERP systems improve efficiency within the four walls of an enterprise by integrating and streamlining internal processes. Companies have been able to reduce cost and increase customer service due to the integrated processes enabled by systems such as SAP R/3. But on its own, an enterprise generates only a portion of the value-add created in a supply chain. Hence, a paradigm shift is taking place as companies realize that the next great leap in Supply Chain Management depends on streamlining and collaborating on inter-enterprise business processes with partners.

There are many ways in which business partners can collaborate, and exchanging information to improve the planning process is nothing new. Normally, the exchange takes place by phone, fax, mail, or e-mail. However, the unstructured nature of the process limits the potential collaboration activities. In some cases, EDI is being used to transfer data, but the high cost and rigidity of EDI technologies limits both the number of partners one can deal with and the types of collaborative activities.

Enter the Internet

Internet and associated technologies such as XML promise to revolutionize inter-enterprise business processes by enabling seamless information exchange between business partners. High volumes of data can be transferred at low cost, and even minor business partners can exchange information in an economical manner. Interactive online access to each other's systems can be achieved easily via a conventional Internet browser.

Internet technologies enable enterprises to establish secure, scalable, and dynamic collaborative commerce networks with their business partners at a low cost. These networks allow enterprises to carry out collaborative activities ranging from product design to order execution with chosen partners.

As in any networking environment, the network itself provides the means by which information moves from one place to another. As companies approach inter-enterprise planning and execution, they realize that it is not enough to have an infrastucture to move information around. For real collaborative commerce, a solid backbone of the right information is paramount for success.

Business Value

The goal of Supply Chain Management has always been to increase customer service and simultaneously reduce costs. Supply chain costs are driven by inventory along the chain (finished goods, work-in-process, etc.) and the capital investment required to meet expected demand. Factors like functional silos within companies and weak hand-off participation among supply chain partners have been the main reason for supply chain inefficiency. The task of reducing supply chain costs is expected to become even more difficult due to increasing mass customization of products, a rise in outsourcing, and the globalization of markets.

ERP systems such as SAP R/3 streamline internal processes so that companies can work with "one number" within the enterprise. Advanced Supply Chain Management solutions greatly improve internal planning processes. Internal collaboration, concurrent real-time planning, and optimization have resulted in

http://anderson-g.ASCET.com 101

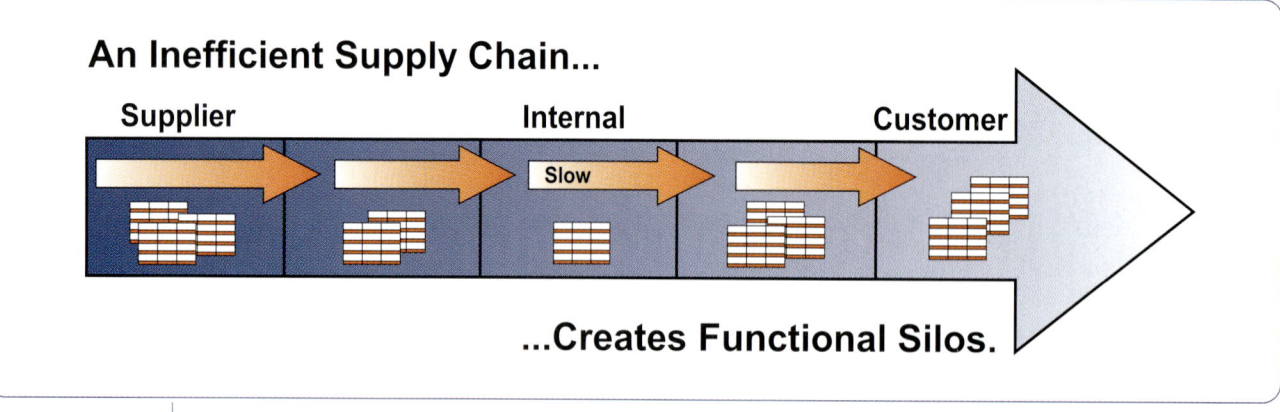

An Inefficient Supply Chain...

Supplier → Internal (Slow) → Customer

...Creates Functional Silos.

Figure 1.0 An inefficient supply chain creates functional silos.

increased ROA, reduced inventory, and compression of cycle times.

Collaborative planning will now extend the boundaries of supply chain management to include all relevant business partners and enable collaborative business processes across the network. The distinct entities in the network such as suppliers, manufacturers, and retailers will be able to cooperate and act as a single entity focused on delivering enhanced customer value while reducing costs throughout the entire chain. The net result: "one number" across the supply networks.

The direct fiscal benefits include lower inventory levels, higher inventory returns, improved cash flow, and reduced capital investment. Enterprises can increase their profitability and their market share at the same time. The indirect benefits include tighter relationships with customers leading to higher customer satisfaction. Leading-edge companies perceive collaborative abilities as a significant competitive advantage that will help them retain existing customers and acquire new ones.

Advanced supply chain management greatly improves the picture. Internal collaboration, concurrent, real-time planning, information sharing, and value-added service are all key factors in speeding up the process. The results include increased ROA, reduction of variability and inventory, and a considerable compression of cycle times.

Ultimate efficiency, however, is achieved through collaboration. Collaboration removes the divisive barriers that formerly separated the distinct links in the chain: procurement companies, production companies, and so on. Though the supply chain partners still consist of distinct entities, they cooperate at an unprecedented level because they realize the mutual benefits. The results of real-time collaboration and true partnership include low inventory levels, high inventory returns, an improved cash flow, and a drastic reduction of the dreaded bullwhip effect.

Supply Chain Collaborative Planning Enables Dynamic Collaborative Networks

Best in class, collaborative planning
The goal of collaborative planning, as the name suggests, is to help enterprises carry out collaborative supply chain planning activities with their business partners. Thus, relevant input from business partners can be taken into account to synchronize planning across the network and leverage advanced supply chain management systems to generate optimized plans based on data from the supply network. Enterprises can now focus on enhancing customer value by enabling true business collaboration across business partners in their networks.

Collaborative planning solutions should be designed to:
- Enable exchange of required planning information with business partners
- Allow the use of browser to read and change data
- Restrict user access to authorized data and activities
- Support consensus planning process
- Support exception-based management
- Generate "one number" for supply chain planning across networks
- Be used with an integrated enterprise solution or as a stand alone collaboration server

It is imperative that your advanced Supply Chain Management system leverage Internet technology to enable collaborative planning across business partner networks. The salient features include:

- Browse and update data via a browser
- Multiple partner access

W² Weblink

For more on collaborative commerce:
evans.ASCET.com

For more on inter-enterprise planning:
reiter.ASCET.com
culotta.ASCET.com

For more on functional silos, see:
quinn-f.ASCET.com

For more on forecasting, see:
lapide.ASCET.com
uchneat.ASCET.com
wayman.ASCET.com

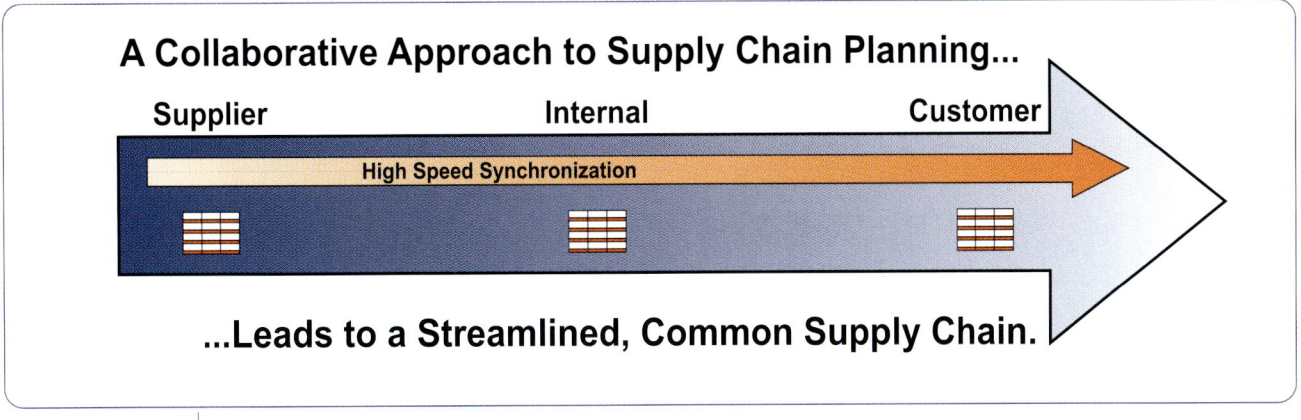

A Collaborative Approach to Supply Chain Planning...

Supplier → Internal → Customer

High Speed Synchronization

...Leads to a Streamlined, Common Supply Chain.

Figure 2.0 — A collaborative approach to supply chain planning leads to a streamlined, common supply chain.

- User configuration of negotiation process as a series of activities
- User configurable screens and workplaces
- Authorization to restrict partner/user access to selected data and activities
- Easy selection of products and data to be used for collaboration
- Alerts business partners to exceptions via Internet e-mail with relevant data
- Connect to multiple systems (e.g., R/3 and non-R/3)
- Link to partner systems using XML technology over the Internet
- State-of-the-art Internet security technology

Visibility

Advanced supply chain management solutions must enable visibility across the collaborative networks by enabling planners to view logistics plans of their business partners. POS data, promotion data, inventory data, production plans, distribution plans, shipment plans, and more can be shared across the network.

Responsiveness

Advanced Supply Chain Management solutions must enable companies to plan collaboratively and reduce order cycles. Planners are alerted to exceptions in the network enabling them to react in real time.

Exception-based management allows planners to focus on critical activities without being deluged by data.

Synchronization

Advanced Supply Chain Management solutions must enable enterprises to plan concurrently across the commerce network. Procurement, production, and distribution can be planned by taking constraints such as capacities and materials across the entire supply network into account. This leads to tighter synchronization between business partners, enabling the network to act as a single company.

Collaborative Commerce

Advanced Supply Chain Management solutions must enable enterprises to form dynamic collaborative networks by using the Internet browser as the collaboration medium. Given the global ubiquity of the Internet, enterprises can form dynamic collaboration communities on the fly.

Internet technology to enable collaborative planning:
- Consensus-based forecasting
- CPFR compliant collaborative forecasting
- VMI
- Supplier collaboration

Each of these processes is described in more detail in the next segment of this white paper, but it is important to note that these are only examples that illustrate the variety of ways in which enterprises can collaborate with their partners.

Internet-Enabled Consensus-Based Forecasting

Collaboration is based on consensus

Consensus-based forecasting allows you to create plans for different business goals (strategic business plan, tactical sales plan, operational supply chain plan, etc.) and integrates them into one consensus plan that drives your business. In advanced Supply Chain Management solutions, you take this process a step further and create a joint business plan together with your supply chain partners that drives your business as well as theirs.

Several parties are usually involved in creating a consensus-based forecast, among them the central planning department that creates a consolidated forecast for all products, the key account manager who creates a forecast for a specific retailer or wholesaler, and the sales department, which forecasts its own demand. Each of these parties bases its forecast on specific information. The goal of consensus-based forecasting is to consolidate the various forecasts into a common time series to be used for further planning.

A typical consensus-based process, using forecast data from different sources, is described below:

1. Department-specific forecasts are made. Departments involved:

   - Sales (created for a combination of

product and customer, goals are tactical: maximize sales, focus on promotions, orders, POS data, competitive info, customer information)
- Logistics (created for combination of product/item and location, goals are operational: minimize costs, fulfill orders, focus on shipments, material and capacity constraints)
- Marketing (combination of product family/market zone, focus on promotions and events, causal relationships, and syndicated POS data, goals are strategic: increase demand, reduce stock)
2. Team meeting is held to reach consensus. A special planning book is used for this purpose. Time specifications include a planning horizon (short to medium term), buckets in days, and a specified frequency (once weekly)
3. Manual adjustments can be made
4. Accuracy of forecast is checked against actual sales data

What is CPFR?

Collaborative Planning, Forecasting and Replenishment (CPFR) is one of the fastest growing technologies for both retail and consumer goods firms; it is hailed as the next great advance in inventory and customer relationships. CPFR is a cross between continuous replenishment programs (CRP) and vendor-managed inventory (VMI). Analysts agree that VMI has been successful in many cases, but inaccurate forecasts and undependable shipments have been major obstacles to higher performance.

Collaboration requires redefinition of a company's goals and direction. It requires trust between partners. For it to succeed, partners must be willing to share their promotion schedules, POS data, and inventory data. While redefining a company's direction is no easy task, the benefits can be great for those companies that do manage the leap across traditional barriers. Consumer goods companies can expect major sales gains and a reduction in inventory, while retailers can count on increased in-stock customer service leading to higher sales and optimized promotional costs.

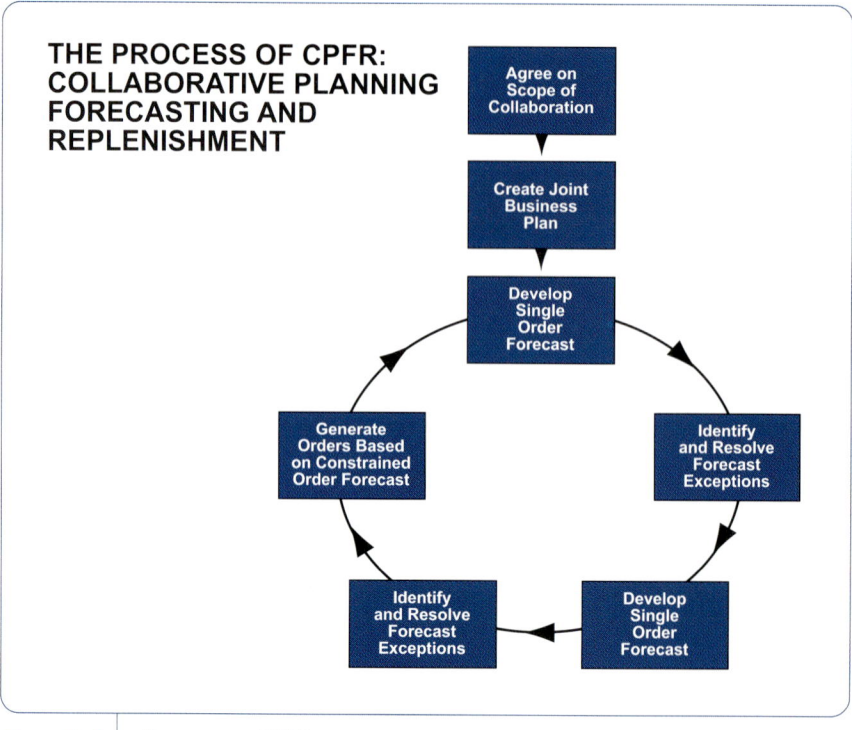

THE PROCESS OF CPFR: COLLABORATIVE PLANNING FORECASTING AND REPLENISHMENT

- Agree on Scope of Collaboration
- Create Joint Business Plan
- Develop Single Order Forecast
- Identify and Resolve Forecast Exceptions
- Develop Single Order Forecast
- Identify and Resolve Forecast Exceptions
- Generate Orders Based on Constrained Order Forecast

Figure 3.0 The process of CPFR

The Collaborative Planning FR Process

Buyer and seller develop a single forecast and update it regularly based on information shared over the Internet. It is a business-to-business workflow, with data exchanged dynamically, designed to increase in-stock customer stock while cutting inventory. The basic process consists of seven steps:

- Agree on the process: define role of each partner, establish confidentiality of shared information, commit resources, agree on exception handling and performance measurement.
- Create a joint business plan and establish products to be jointly managed including category role, strategy, and tactics.
- Develop a single forecast of consumer demand based on combined promotion calendars and analysis of POS data and causal data.
- Identify and resolve forecast exceptions. This is achieved by comparing current measured values such as stock levels in each store adjusted for changes such as promotions against the agreed-upon exception criteria (in-stock level, forecast accuracy targets).
- Develop a single order forecast that time-phases the sales forecast while meeting the business plan's inventory and service objectives, and accommodating capacity constraints for manufacturing, shipping, and more.
- Identify and resolve exceptions to the forecast, particularly those involving the manufacturer's constraints in delivering specified volumes, creating an interactive loop for revising orders.
- Generate orders based on the constrained order forecast. The near-term orders are fixed while the long-term ones are used for planning.

How to Make It Work

Mutual trust and open communication are key to CPFR success. Ingrained fears and the tendency to maintain secrecy and promote aggressive competition must be overcome. Many companies are loath to share planning data for fear that competitors will somehow gain access to confi-

Step 1	Each partner can make only one proposal for the consensual time series. All the propositions for a consensual time series are used as the basis for negotiations. At the end of this process (step 4) a single consensual time series will have been agreed upon. The proposed time series are generated either in SAP APO, for example in Demand Planning, or are transferred into SAP APO from outside via an interface. The data transfer could occur automatically through a standard interface or manually via an Internet browser.
Step 2	Once all partners have proposed a time series, the first consensual time series proposal is calculated. The rules for generating the time series are implemented as a macro in a planning book.
Step 3	Analogous to step 2, the macros for alert generation are started. Alerts refer to individual planning folders.
Step 4	Branching into a planning book is possible from the Alert Monitor. All relevant data (planning folder, aggregation level) is stored in the alert. Partners can suggest alternatives solutions in the planning book. When the planning book is saved, new alerts are generated through macros. The end of this step occurs either when the dominant partner declares it to be over or when all partners have reached an agreement.

Figure 3.0 The process of CPFR

dential information. In fact, security is a major concern.

Questions like "who gets what portion of the generated savings" must be answered before the collaborative process begins. An understanding of each other's data, tribal knowledge, and performance measurement is needed. Management must take the lead in creating working alliances and combating adversarial relationships. New systems and methods must be learned, and last but not least, one trading partner alone will not bring in big benefits. The key is to involve large numbers of partners.

Internet Enabled VMI

Vendor Managed Inventory (VMI) is a service provided by a supplier for its customers whereby the supplier takes on the task of requirements planning for its own products within the retail company. For VMI to work, the supplier not only must be able to track the amount of its products stocked at the customer site, it must also take into account the customer's sales forecasts.

Making VMI possible via Internet provides small retailers with an economical alternative to participating in supply chain planning. It also allows the retailer to maintain control over the data it is sending to the supplier and change it if necessary. To achieve their goals, participants will be able to access the Supply Network Planning data through Internet planning books.

Supplier Collaboration

Just as the exchange of forecast and sales data between retailers has mutual benefits, the planning process can be improved even more if suppliers and customers engage in an early exchange of planned dependent requirements and production quantities. In the automotive industry, strong integration between supplier and customer is already widely accepted. Suppliers are connected to their customers, in this case, auto manufacturers, by EDI. That solution, however, requires large investments on the side of the supplier. The World Wide Web offers an economical alternative to traditional EDI, making it an especially interesting option for smaller companies that deal with more limited amounts of data.

A supply planner can have access to those aspects of the planning situation that affect him. Users can have access to production plans as well as dependent requirements. Internet-enabled planning books allow users to have an interactive role; for example, if the delivery of the dependent requirements can't be made in time, an alternative date can be suggested.

Process flow and status management

Both process flow definition and status management support the consensus reaching process. The following process is a typical example:

1. Create a variety of time series per partner
2. Create a proposal for a consensual time series
3. Generate alerts
4. Agree upon consensual time series

Depending on the scenario, the consensus-reaching process is repeated several times. For example, according to the Collaborative Planning standards, a consensus should first be reached on the sales forecast and then on the production order forecast.

Conclusion

Advanced Supply Chain Management solutions must enable the creation of dynamic collaborative networks. Enterprises can implement a streamlined supply network resulting in better customer service and lower supply chain costs. In essence, CPFR ushers in the brave new world of collaborative commerce networks.

SAP AG – Providing Collaborative Software Solutions for Enterprise Integration

About SAP™

Based in Walldorf, Germany, SAP AG is the leading provider of collaborative business software solutions that integrate the processes within and among enterprises and business communities. Since the introduction of Web interfaces and a scalable, Internet-ready architecture in 1996, SAP has been working with companies making the transition to the Internet business model.

The ability of SAP to deliver customer-centric, personalized, and collaborative inter-enterprise solutions on demand is one of the foundations of mySAP.com™. mySAP.com provides an open, collaborative business environment enabling companies of all sizes and industries to fully engage their employees, customers, and partners to capitalize upon the new Internet economy.

mySAP.com reflects the SAP commitment to e-business – a significant step beyond e-commerce – as companies seek to extend their investment in technology to adapt to the modern Internet business landscape, in which each customer's needs must be met immediately. Delivering such optimal service requires an integrated, open marketplace on the Internet, with companies leveraging suppliers, partners, and customers. With an ecosystem that includes more than 900 partners, industry-specific functionality for 19 industries, and the experience gained by working with a customer base exceeding 12,000 companies and more than 10 million licensed users around the world, SAP is in a unique position to help businesses gain competitive advantages in the Internet economy. The flexible mySAP.com offering can be implemented to fully integrate an organization's operational business processes from finance, human resources, and manufacturing, to sales and distribution while at the same time enabling the company to reach out to its customers and business partners along the supply or value chain.

SAP Solutions and Internet Technologies

The technological foundation for SAP collaborative business solutions is the Internet-Business Framework that supports a company's ability to create an agile business software environment enabling fast responses to new business demands. It provides a comprehensive, scalable platform with which companies can conduct e-business. Strengths in SAP technology that facilitate inter-enterprise collaboration and inter-operability include an inherently thin-client three-tier Internet architecture, more than 1,500 open interface definitions openly published on the Web, and an open and flexible component-based architecture. Platform support for parallel application and database servers provides for high scalability. At the same time, the SAP architecture offers customers world-class reliability and security as well as the reassurance of accepted industry standards such as XML.

SAP Software: Reflecting the Modern Enterprise

All software developed and marketed by SAP is delivered to customers through mySAP.com. mySAP.com offers companies seamless end-to-end integration of SAP and non-SAP solutions, originating at the point of customer contact and extending throughout the business operation to provide the total e-business environment.

mySAP.com is comprised of four key elements:

- The mySAP.com Marketplace, an open electronic business-to-business hub that enables inter-company relationships for buying, selling, and communicating.

- The mySAP.com Workplace, an enterprise portal that provides users with a personalized, Web-browser-based work environment that offers everything they need to do their jobs.

- mySAP.com business scenarios, which enable collaborative, role-based, business-to-business (B2B) and business-to-consumer (B2C) solutions through SAP™ and third party software applications.

- Web-based application hosting, which provides a quick, cost-effective delivery mechanism for companies to adopt parts or the full range of mySAP.com solutions.

The mySAP.com e-business environment has gained major global momentum since its availability in the fourth quarter of 1999. Today, there are over 500 business partners worldwide and 3,000 business directory participants in the Marketplace with over 38,400 users registered resulting in more then 6000 hits per day. The mySAP.com Business Scenarios have been adopted in more than 400 installations of Customer Relationship Management (CRM), 390 installations of e-commerce, 1180 installations of Business Intelligence, and 350 installations of Supply Chain Management solutions. In North America, over 9000 users are accessing SAP solution in a hosted applications environment.

Components available through mySAP.com

- Comprehensive B2B and B2C components for e-commerce (selling and procurement) improve the flow of information between key suppliers.

- The SAP CRM components support business scenarios enabling greater customer participation in the continuum of market intelligence, cross-selling, business planning, production execution, product maintenance, and customer support with industry-specific Internet functionality.

- Business intelligence components provide a holistic, closed-loop solution that offers the most current, nearly real-time information encompassing operational data, analytical intelligence, and contextual knowledge. Using these tools, decision-makers can make informed business decisions, drive the decisions to operational systems, and monitor the results. Specific business intelligence components from SAP are as follows:

- The SAP Business Information Warehouse™ (SAP BW™) component converts internal and external business data into business intelligence for decision-support needs. Including a broad range of predefined reporting templates with industry-specific and user role-based functionality, SAP BW has been one of the top selling data warehousing solutions since its introduction in 1998.

- The SAP Strategic Enterprise Management™ (SAP SEM™) component vertically extends integrated data to support business managers and senior executives in making key business decisions with new value-based management processes such as strategic planning, risk management, and value communication. It includes a corporate performance monitor complemented by rich scenario planning and is designed to provide a sophisticated dashboard for management that can enhance the long-term value of a company by providing the right information at the right time for making management decisions.

Components for Supply Chain Management

- The SAP Advanced Planner and Optimizer™ (SAP APO™) component improves demand-forecasting and increases production efficiency.

- The SAP Logistics Execution System component enables the efficient flow of goods along the supply chain with greater speed and accuracy.

- The core enterprise application components for financial accounting, logistics, and human resources, originally

---

From Supply Chain to Collaborative Commerce Networks: The Next Step

Gordon G. Anderson – SAP

Traditional ERP systems improve efficiency within the four walls of an enterprise by integrating and streamlining internal processes. Companies have been able to reduce cost and increase customer service due to the integrated processes enabled by systems such as SAP R/3. But on its own, an enterprise generates only a portion of the value-add created in a supply chain. Hence, a paradigm shift is taking place as companies realize that the next great leap in Supply Chain Management (SCM) depends on streamlining and collaborating on inter-enterprise business processes with partners.

There are many ways in which business partners can collaborate, and exchanging information to improve the planning process is nothing new. Collaborative Planning now extends the boundaries of SCM to include all relevant business partners and enable collaborative business processes across the network. The distinct entities in the network such as suppliers, manufacturers, and retailers are able to cooperate and act as a single entity focused on delivering enhanced customer value while reducing costs throughout the entire chain. The net result: "one number" across the supply networks.

In advanced SCM solutions, you take this process a step further and create a joint business plan together with your supply chain partners that drives your business as well as theirs. Enterprises can implement a streamlined and agile supply network resulting in better customer service and lower supply chain costs – and thus dynamic collaborative networks are enabled.

To read this paper in its entirety, go to http://anderson-g.ASCET.com.

launched in 1992 as SAP R/3®, help companies link their business processes, tying together disparate business functions to synchronize an entire enterprise to run more smoothly. SAP R/3 is the most widely accepted enterprise application product on the market today. With more than 22,000 installations worldwide, it has become a de facto standard platform for enterprise application software.

Industry-Specific Functionality

Aligned with customers and their needs, SAP software offers solutions specific to 19 different industries with functionality designed to address requirements unique to each of those industries' business objectives: aerospace and defense, automotive, banking, chemicals, consumer products, engineering and construction, healthcare, higher education, high technology, insurance, media, mill products, oil and gas, pharmaceuticals, public sector, retail, telecommunications, transportation, and utilities.

For each of the above industries, SAP has created a solution map, laying out the breadth and depth of each industry's specific business process requirements and best practices, and has mapped them to SAP as well as complementary partner solutions to complete the end-to-end business process, including Web-enabled processes. Accessible through the Internet, each solution map gives customers a powerful planning tool for continuing to enhance and refine their business processes for greater efficiency and investment return.

SAP Service and Support

The worldwide SAP service and support organization is available to customers 24 hours a day, 365 days a year. SAP supports the entire customer life cycle, including evaluation, implementation, and continuous business improvement of SAP software. ValueSAP™ is a comprehensive offering designed to optimize the economic value of customers' investments in SAP software.

With its TeamSAP™ approach as an inherent part of ValueSAP, SAP demonstrates its commitment to the SAP partner ecosystem for successful implementations. With roughly 45,000 consultants around the world trained in SAP software, SAP and its partners team up using defined processes and tools for the fastest and most cost-effective implementation possible, as well as products designed to optimize businesses with the latest Internet functionality. Analogous to the SAP Solution Maps, the SAP Services Map provides customers of all sizes with a clear view of services, illustrating how SAP and partner services effectively and comprehensively support a business's life cycle with SAP products and services.

Additional information about SAP can be found at www.sap.com.

SAP, mySAP.com, R/3, SAP Business Information Warehouse, SAP BW, SAP Strategic Enterprise Management, SAP SEM, SAP Advanced Planner and Optimizer, SAP APO, ValueSAP, TeamSAP, and all other SAP product and service names referenced herein are trademarks or registered trademarks of SAP AG. Other product and company names herein may be trademarks of their respective owners.

© Copyright 2000, SAP AG

Note: *Any statements contained in this document that are not historical facts are forward-looking statements as defined in the Private Securities Litigation Reform Act of 1995. Words such as "expect" and "project" as they relate to the company are intended to identify such forward-looking statements. The company undertakes no obligation publicly to update or revise any forward-looking statements. All forward-looking statements are subject to various risks and uncertainties that could cause actual results to differ materially from expectations. The factors that could affect the company's future financial results are discussed more fully in the company's most recently filed Form 20-F and Form F-1 as filed with the Securities and Exchange Commission on June 24, 1998.*

Enabling Supply Chain Automation through Information Synchronization

written by:
Ben Martella
Verano
http://martella.ASCET.com

The Internet has solved the problem of global communication and information access. Now, as enterprises become increasingly "virtual" and "extended," the basic business processes that support a synchronized supply chain become more information-intensive. Synchronizing the information essential to supply chain operations will be the new e-business challenge. The next iteration of supply chain technology, then, must provide a process-based infrastructure for management of information that drives the virtual enterprise.

Introduction

In the e-business model, where enterprises become more virtual and distributed, the basic business processes linking them to their suppliers and trading partners become more information-intensive. As a result, companies increasingly turn to industry organizations to provide information and process models to normalize communications in the inter-enterprise space. Through specialization and segmentation, virtual enterprises are able to focus their efforts on core competencies, but are still left with the task of adapting to new industry standards for exchanging information throughout the supply chain.

A key component of supply chain automation (SCA), "information synchronization" refers to the ongoing technical and business processes that convert data into useful information. These include analyzing, publishing, collecting, controlling, and monitoring. Supply chain participants, whether doers or decision-makers, must be able to dynamically invoke these basic information management processes if they are to remain synchronized around a common set of business objectives. Strategic advantage will flow to those companies that implement this kind of flexible, process-oriented infrastructure – an underlying "information supply chain" – for managing the flow of information throughout the supply chain.

Shifting from Enterprise to Supply Chain Perspective

The new e-business paradigm brings with it a rate of change and span of control that no longer accommodate the 12- to 24-month technology implementation cycles of the previous economic model. Centralized, transaction-based applications do not provide the scalability and flexibility needed for supply chain automation in a demand-driven, e-business environment.

Virtual enterprises striving to achieve competitive advantage through supply chain automation face a number of challenges in a global marketplace where change is constant and is often out of their control. Even components most fundamental to supply chain automation – the partners themselves, the technology systems those partners use, and the information partners need to perform effectively – are in a continuous state of flux. These components are respondents to, not drivers of, forces at work in their respective competitive markets.

While implementing an enterprise resource planning (ERP) or other enterprise application is entirely within the control of the corporation, implementing a supply chain automation infrastructure requires the cooperation of many different entities – all of which have information systems, requirements, and processes particular to their own business. They are limited in their ability to handle IT demands, and have multiple customers of their own who also have their own processes, and so on. This presents a challenge unique to all business-to-business (B2B) integration efforts – especially supply chain automation.

E-businesses attempting to automate their supply chain by implementing a single information technology solution will find it a very

Ben Martella leads the sales and professional services teams at Verano in delivering Web-based supply chain automation solutions.

He has more than 16 years of sales, sales management, distributed application, network implementation, and Supply Chain Management experience. Most recently, Ben has held senior sales management positions in high technology companies, namely Neuron Data and OpenConnect. Ben spent eight years in the manufacturing industry, where he was the director of MD-11 Management Systems for Douglas Aircraft.

He is now responsible for defining Verano's strategic direction in the supply chain automation market.

expensive and time-consuming endeavor – one that results in an inflexible, proprietary solution. During the yearlong implementation cycle, changes in the marketplace, corporation, or supply chain will have occurred that make the solution part of the problem. These rigid architectures of classic enterprise systems are incapable of synchronizing the ever-broadening range of information available in new applications, environments, and formats.

Focusing on Information

Whether a product manager in Dallas sends customer feedback to software engineers in Boston, or a car manufacturer in Asia utilizes U.S. survey results to define the shape of a new family car, it is the timely processing of business-critical information that ensures survival in demand-driven, e-business environments. Without it, opportunities are lost, inefficiencies abound, and customer satisfaction dwindles. Concepts like "just-in-time inventory" and "made-to-order" have arisen out of competitive necessity, and so too has the notion of "information synchronization."

In a product supply chain, consumer demand is but one kind of information. Other essential information exists in unstructured formats, like CAD drawings, schematics, engineering change orders (ECOs), and technical specifications. In addition, corporations have current investments in ERP, customer relationship management (CRM), or other internal systems that contain vast amounts of information

Weblink

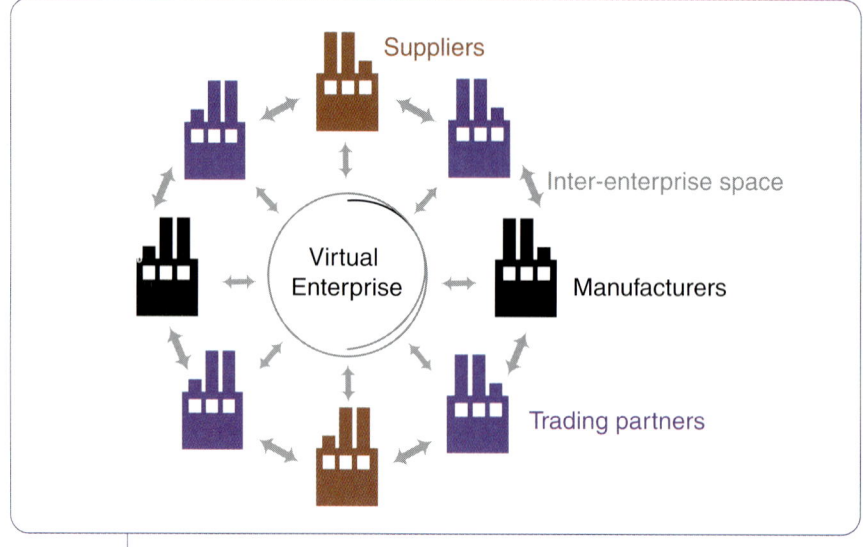

For more on ERP, see:
  ramanathan.ASCET.com
  hicks.ASCET.com
  anthony.ASCET.com
  sprague.ASCET.com
  culotta.ASCET.com
  uchneat.ASCET.com
For more on management, see:
  johnson.ASCET.com
  peters.ASCET.com

Figure 1.0 — The virtual enterprise environment

useful in supply chain planning and decision-making. In fact, it is not uncommon for businesses to use several distinct systems to manage their supply chain, further compounding the synchronization challenge. Finally, the Internet holds a wealth of knowledge, readily available to decision-makers but dispersed throughout an intricate network of millions of HTML pages and PDF documents.

Clearly, to achieve optimal financial and strategic results, decision-makers in a virtual enterprise must draw upon the information contained in Internet, enterprise, and supply chain systems – so business decisions are based on a complete view of the value chain, from corporation to consumer. The challenge is to create an efficient, comprehensive flow of information across the supply chain to enable this kind of decision-making. With the multitude of technologies, platforms, and applications in use at organizations worldwide, it becomes even more important to focus on a process-based approach to synchronizing the information supply chain.

Managing E-Business Relationships

The diversity of information types, sources, and technology systems begets the Internet as a fundamental building block in communications infrastructures. Companies must work at "Internet speed" to keep pace with the needs of consumers that are far more educated and demanding precisely because the Internet offers such quick and easy access to information. Web browsers and e-mail programs are the essential tools for today's savvy consumer. Convenience and speed are the norm – and not only in the business-to-consumer (B2C) marketplace.

As companies are realizing the substantial return on investment (ROI) that can be gained through business-to-business (B2B) integration efforts like supply chain automation, suppliers, and trading partners are demanding the same fast, easy access to information that is afforded to end consumers. In order to achieve the high levels of collaboration required to synchronize the supply chain, companies must balance the needs of customers with those of suppliers and partners.

This includes offering suppliers and partners the same communication vehicles as consumers, namely the Internet and e-mail. But whether B2C or B2B, the access and transfer of information over the Internet raises issues of security. A high value is placed on intellectual property – it is often the very basis for the existence of a business. And while a synchronized supply chain requires trust and collaboration, it also demands proper access control and security measures to safeguard proprietary

110 Achieving Supply Chain Excellence Through Technology

information. This is particularly critical in supply chain communications, where the content may pertain to planning, transactions, or other strategic business activities. In addition to balancing the needs of customers and suppliers, businesses must maintain equilibrium between open communication and responsible information exchange.

Achieving Synchronization

A synchronized supply chain can bring about many advantages, including operational efficiencies, reduced costs, and increased customer satisfaction. The challenges to achieving synchronization through technology, however, are also many. Constant change, diverse information requirements, disparate information systems, and the safeguarding of valuable intellectual property present a few of the major barriers to implementation and adoption.

In a business environment where outsourcing is common, competition is global, and products are becoming increasingly complex, companies should approach supply chain automation through the fundamental perspective of information synchronization. Information synchronization is both an objective and a feature of successful supply chain automation projects. Rather than introducing new technology or applications, information synchronization focuses on providing the key information management processes required for continuous collection, communication, and management of information throughout the supply chain. Achieving the fastest, most cost-efficient means of communicating the most comprehensive set of information can translate into supply chain excellence. But no matter how many applications are involved, a process-oriented infrastructure is needed for synchronizing information.

Key Attributes of Information Synchronization

The following highlights key attributes of the technology infrastructure underlying successful supply chain automation pro-

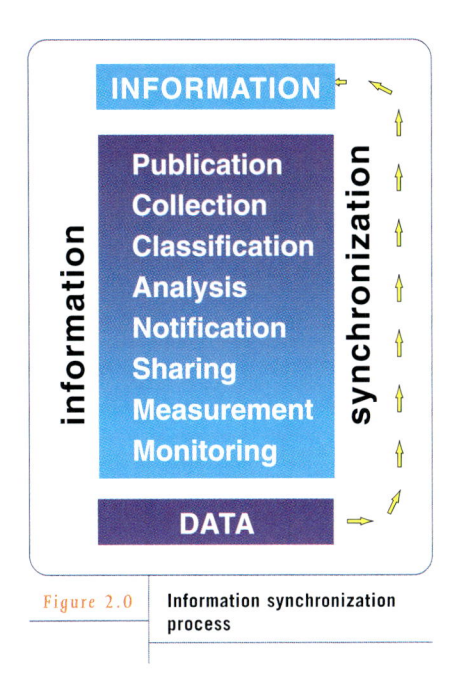

Figure 2.0 Information synchronization process

jects:
- Integration with existing systems and processes
- Information synchronization technology should support a fundamentally incremental and iterative implementation process. This will enable companies to dynamically address the many opportunities and forces shaping their supply chain management and automation objectives.

Broad, expanded view of content

The information exchanged throughout a supply chain may exist as CAD drawings, ECOs, graphical images, or in some other business-specific format. Enterprise systems contain other types of useful information, such as ERP reports, customer profiles, text documents, financial spreadsheets, as well as Internet and intranet content. To facilitate the exchange of this wide array of information formats, the technology infrastructure that supply chains use to communicate and share information must be open and flexible enough to support any type of information, derived from any source.

Typically this takes form as an Internet-based and standards-based vehicle that is able to collect, access, and present information in a way that is useful to decision-makers. Leveraging the Internet, the technology should integrate with existing corporate information systems by consolidating enterprise and supply chain information in a single, searchable repository. This synchronization of all information relevant to supply chain decision-making – regardless of data type, format, or location – is the foundation of a supply chain automation infrastructure.

Safeguard of intellectual property

Once the foundation is set to support the various types of information involved in supply chain communications, appropriate measures must be established in order to ensure the safety of intellectual property and other digital assets. This requires the technology solution to provide solid content management functionality in the form of access control, encryption, and audit trails.

Access Control

For maximum flexibility with the highest degree of security, the technology should enable access control be set for distinct pieces of information at the individual or group level. This provides a flexible, user-driven approach to granting controlled access to information – regardless of where the information is physically stored.

Encryption

As a second line of defense in safeguarding intellectual property, valuable supply chain information should be encrypted to further prevent unauthorized use. When coupled with access control, encryption ensures that only "authorized users" would be able to view the contents of an information packet traversing the Web.

Audit Trail

To aid in the ongoing monitoring of supply chain information and processes, the technology should generate a secure, authenticated audit trail with usage and activity reports. Audit logs must be maintained to record the publication, notification, acknowledgement, and downloading of content, along with other updates, accesses, or connections to the informa-

http://martella.ASCET.com

tion. This provides managers the real-time feedback essential to closed-loop supply chain operations.

Robust information management and processing

After the information is synchronized and secured, automation and resultant benefits begin to take shape. The communications infrastructure is in place to enable the timely and continuous exchange of information in a rapid and effortless way. The most valuable information is the most current information. Thus, the technology should feature efficient information management and processing facilities that automate the publishing, organization, collection, and notification of supply chain information.

Publication

Supply chain participants must be provided with an intuitive, drag-and-drop interface for real-time content publication if continuous information sharing is to occur. Information should be uploaded easily through the use of automated profiles and interactive wizards. The new information must be automatically published for immediate discovery and reuse throughout the supply chain. Once published, supply chain managers must be able to add, delete, or modify information to maintain operational objectives amidst constantly changing variables.

Collection

It is neither economically nor technically viable to approach supply chain automation by simply providing online access to information. A single point of access in conjunction with a Web-based repository offers a much more attractive platform from which to implement the many new information synchronization processes that were not a primary objective of the previous enterprise systems. The technology solution should provide intelligent agents to automatically harvest enterprise and Internet content. Suppliers should be able to specify the content to be collected and delivered – from any source – on scheduled, event-driven, or dynamic inter-

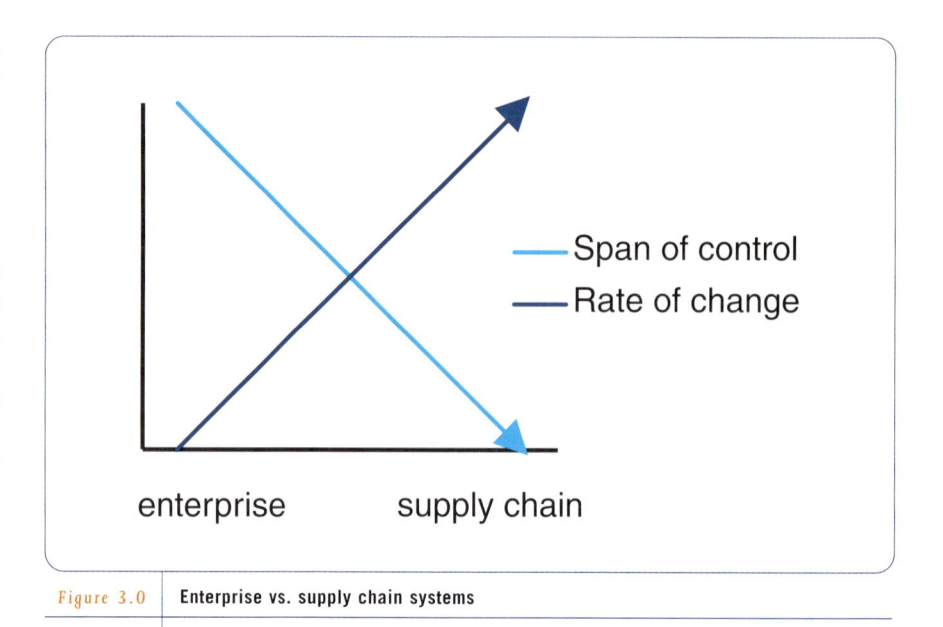

Figure 3.0 **Enterprise vs. supply chain systems**

vals. Database connectivity and XML conversion are key requirements in this area.

Classification

To enable efficient reuse of information, the technology solution must be able to classify information by extracting key concepts based upon a flexible set of business rules. This information is key to all of the subsequent processes outlined here.

Analysis

Once data is published, collected, and classified, there should be flexible, business-rule driven facilities to analyze the information to determine subsequent workflow and notification processes.

Notification

In an Internet-based infrastructure, e-mail is a principal method of communication. But in successful supply chain automation, the technology solution must automate that process for maximum efficiency. When new information has been made available or changed, automatic e-mail notifications must be sent in a timely and reliable manner to a configurable list of supply chain participants.

Sharing

The technology solution should offer supply chain participants a mechanism for searching based on relevant supply chain information – such as project name, supplier name, or part number. This kind of advanced context-sensitive searching assures highly accurate query results.

Measurement

Continuous improvement demands key business processes be measured for compliance to some standard of operation. Information synchronization will not be consistently sustained in an environment that does not provide built-in mechanisms for business process measurement.

Monitoring

Management by exception is impossible without closed-loop monitoring. Technology solutions should provide a clear and extensible framework for monitoring business process compliance to a flexibly defined set of business rules. Information synchronization involves too many individual processes to conform to other management paradigms.

Conclusion

The new, virtual enterprises will operate in an environment where the rate of change is inversely related to a constantly diminishing span of control. This will bring about a new generation of technology that is necessarily more information- and process-based than the traditional systems and technologies of the last economic model. The companies that thrive as e-businesses are those that rethink their approach to process management and communication in terms of information synchronization.

Information synchronization and, consequently, supply chain automation demand an underlying technology infrastructure that:

- enables implementation of key information synchronization processes
- utilizes the Internet as a common communications medium
- secures sensitive information from unauthorized use
- augments and integrates existing technology solutions

While there are countless software applications available for managing supply chains, it is a major challenge to bring enterprise information into the supply chain decision-making process – or vice-versa – by implementing a single technology solution. However, if companies utilize technology to implement a process-based means of synchronizing information, they are more likely to succeed as virtual enterprises than those attempting to synchronize the technology itself.

Verano – Synchronizing Supply Chain Communications

Contact Information

Sonia Bhanot
CEO

Ben Martella
VP Sales

Verano Headquartes
411 Clyde Avenue
Mountain View, CA 94043
Phone 650.237.0200
Fax 650.237.0211
info@verano.com
www.verano.com

The forces at work in today's economy demand dramatic changes in the way companies design, manufacture, sell, and support their products and services. The very same technology that opened global markets enables global communication – and competition.

Synchronized supply chains are key to competitive advantage in this new field of competition, yet most companies are still not able to share the full spectrum of information essential to their customers, suppliers, and partners. Unstructured information such as engineering change orders, design specifications, schematics, and Internet-based content comprises more than 85% of the corporate information pool, yet there has never been a way to effectively manage this information and incorporate it with traditional supply chain content from ERP, Customer Relationship Management (CRM) and other enterprise systems.

Verano Supply Chain Portal Solution

Verano brings this essential content into the extended enterprise with a Web-based means to access, search, measure, and control corporate and supply chain information. Verano's Supply Chain Portal automatically captures information from enterprise and Internet sources and then secures it, manages it, and publishes it to a portal environment, and then notifies all affected parties – on a 24x7 basis.

Automated Supply Chain Communications

Successful supply chain synchronization demands the timely and continuous exchange of information. When the right supplier has the right information at the right time, business decisions can be made that add value for everyone in the chain – especially the end consumer. Verano's Supply Chain Portal brings Supply Chain Management to the Internet, with a common, automated platform for communicating and leveraging any type of information.

Optimized Business-to-Business Integration

Today's extended enterprises find themselves competing supply chain to supply chain – not company to company – yet they must perform with the same flexibility and speed of a single entity. Information sharing is critical to this close business process integration, so Verano's Supply Chain Portal complements existing technology solutions by extending their reach to the entire supply chain with an open, systematic, and secure means for business-to-business communication over the Internet.

Integrated View of the Extended Enterprise

With many businesses using three or more different software applications to manage their supply chain, creating a seamless, end-to-end flow of information across the entire supply chain can be challenging. Verano's Supply Chain Portal consolidates content from different systems, organizes it to maximize productivity, and instantly publishes it to an always-available information source. The result is a single point of access to both enterprise and supply chain information – so business decisions are based on a complete view of the value chain, from corporation to consumer.

Targeted Search Results

Verano's Supply Chain Portal employs advanced context-sensitive searching that assures highly accurate query results. Unlike search engines that can generate thousands of hits with a single search, Verano's Supply Chain Portal will

Information Synchronization: A New Perspective on Supply Chain Automation
by Ben Martella, Verano

Companies striving to achieve competitive advantage through supply chain synchronization face a number of challenges in the global marketplace where change is constant and often out of their control. Even the most critical elements – the partners themselves, the technology systems those partners use, and especially the information the partners require to perform most effectively – are in a continuous state of flux. Those attempting to automate their supply chain by synchronizing the information systems used by supply chain participants will find it an expensive, time-consuming process with major barriers to adoption.

Information synchronization is both an objective and a feature of successful supply chain automation projects. Rather than introducing new applications, information synchronization focuses on providing the key information management processes required to collect, communicate, and manage the flow of information throughout the supply chain. Information synchronization must accept many different types and sources of data – such as engineering change orders (ECOs), drawings, enterprise resource planning (ERP) reports, and technical specifications.

This white paper will describe how companies that utilize technology to synchronize supply chain information achieve far greater success as "virtual enterprises" than those that attempt to synchronize the technology itself and highlight the key attributes of a supply chain automation solution.

To read Ben Martella's white paper in its entirety, please go to http://martella.ASCET.com.

---

search using metadata as the query criteria. Searching on elements such as project name, supplier name, or part number returns fewer and more relevant hits.

Drag-and-Drop Publishing
Supply chain portals are only as valuable as their information is current. Verano combines drag-and-drop desktop publishing with automated profiles and interactive wizards to ensure that valuable information is uploaded easily and consistently. Powerful global editing features enable supply chain managers to add, delete, or modify metadata to maintain critical operational objectives in an ever-changing supply chain environment.

Notification
When new information has been made available, Verano's Supply Chain Portal sends e-mail notifications to a configurable list of users. The e-mail has a configurable subject heading and includes a URL link to the document. E-mail notifications can be conditionally activated based upon content values.

Access-Controlled Content
Verano's Supply Chain Portal provides access control at the user, group, or document level. This flexible, user-driven process alleviates the need for separate databases, transactions, HTML forms, and all the other failed means of trying to ensure that critical supply chain information won't inadvertently end up in the wrong hands.

Audit, Measure, and Improve
Verano's Supply Chain Portal generates a secure, authenticated audit trail that provides the information required for continuous monitoring and improvement of supply chain processes. This information provides supply chain managers with the real-time feedback and control mechanisms essential to closed-loop supply chain operations.

Information is Key to Strategic Advantage
Information sharing plays a critical role in achieving supply chain synchronization. Verano's Supply Chain Portal technology helps companies collect, communicate, and manage the flow of information throughout the supply chain. It supports any type of information, from ERP, CRM, or other enterprise reports to ECOs, CAD drawings, and technical specifications. It complements existing technology investments in supply chain automation, and extends their reach into the entire supply chain. By combining supply chain information with information from traditional enterprise systems, Verano's Supply Chain Portal ensures that trading partners have online access to all the information necessary to perform as effective, value-adding participants in the supply chain.

Lawson Software – Self-Evident Applications™ Power E-Procurement

Contact Information

William Lawson, Sr.
Chairman and CEO

Richard Lawson
President and COO

John Cerullo
Co-Founder and Chief Technologist

US Headquarters
Lawson Software
380 St. Peter Street
St. Paul, MN 55102
651.767.7000

Revenues 1999
$270M

Founded
1975

The rapidly emerging field of e-procurement uses high-performance PCs, visually dynamic product catalogues, plus Web and Internet technologies to automate and streamline the purchasing process. E-procurement allows companies to integrate and automate the processes of item selection, approvals, order placement, receiving, and payment generation, creating a "Reqs-to-Checks" (Requisitions to Accounts Payable) process.

Lawson's e-procurement creates this electronic "Req-to-Checks" process by providing integrated purchasing solutions and strategies, with leading-edge Self-Evident Applications for e-services to automate, streamline, and enhance administrative and operational processes. Lawson's e-commerce-ready application services will include electronic catalogues, trading communities, application service providers, integration tools, and system integration services, leading the way in transforming business processes to e-business processes faster and more flexibly than any other solutions provider.

E-Requisitions

E-requisitions allow clients to extend the requisitioning process to all users who have access to Internet-capable computers without having to be connected to the local- or wide-area network. Requesters using a desktop browser to access the company's intranet can choose items they need from online catalogs showing approved items. In some cases, users may view product catalogues at a supplier's Web site. Countless hours are saved by creating online requisitions, plus many more are saved by eliminating paper requisitions that must be converted into electronic form. Accuracy and timeliness skyrocket, while redundancy declines drastically. Users have full access to inquiries, product information, and historical data.

E-Purchasing

E-purchasing provides the core of information necessary to manage one's replenishment business as information exchange accelerates exponentially causing data overload and communication errors. Integrated with Accounts Payable and Invoice Match, Purchase Order acts as the foundation for a high-volume business environment.

Through electronic bids buyers submit bid requests to selected vendors via e-mail. Buyers then review and analyze bids by items or vendor, accepting and finally creating the Vendor Quote.

E-Warehouse

E-Warehouse allows users with access to the Internet to enter e-receipts directly into the system, eliminating the need to send hard copy through the mail for later translation and entry. Distance is no longer a consideration as receipts can be entered from across the street or across the country. In many cases, items received remotely were previously not entered into the system, and were invisible to the system when invoice matching and payment processes began, creating severe bottlenecks, as well as impacting timely processing and the accuracy of historical data files.

E-Payables

E-payables allow suppliers to electronically receive information on the status of their invoices that was previously a tedious, time-consuming task, eliminating hours of telephone contact, holding time, and waiting for return calls from already burdened Accounts Payable staff. No longer subject to standard office hours and time zone restrictions, vendors have 24-hour instant access to payment information.

E-Expenses

E-expenses, when used within the e-payables service, becomes a comprehensive tool to help users process, review, and reconcile employee advances and expenses, anytime, anywhere, via the Web.

written by:

Dr. Jay Ramanathan
Concentus Technology Corporation
http://ramanathan.ASCET.com

Process-Based Architecture for Back Office: Successful Supply Chain Requires EAI

Data-bound organizations will simply no longer be able to handle the volume of transactions, nor achieve the required flexibility, to successfully prepare their back-office operations to adequately support e-commerce requirements of value chains in business-to-business markets. This paper discusses the new requirement: process-centric architecture. It is a kind of "meta-system" built on a CORBA and COM-based framework strategy that goes beyond traditional data-centric approaches offered by the enterprise application integration (EAI), middleware, or message broker framework.

Competitive Advantage Via IT Architectures

Today there are only two types of enterprises: those that change and those that disappear. New value chain or supply chain requirements have seriously raised the bar. Survival now requires quantum improvements in speed, flexibility, and customer responsiveness, along with a totally open view of the back-office process. These attributes can no longer be achieved by adding or even better integrating applications. The survivors must dig deeper to reshape their IT architectures to preserve the important processes driving their business. The demands for global collaboration, partnerships, virtual manufacturing, and unlimited flexibility require it. Otherwise, the very applications designed to "save" them will actually force these companies to alter the processes that have made them successful.

Thus, as companies try to leverage their internal capabilities toward the Internet via e-commerce and Web-based customer portals (front office), the CIO may well hold the company's future in her/his hands as corporate architecture and enterprise systems support the business strategy, especially process re-engineering. Why? Because the essential architecture of traditional application integration strategies is built around the manipulation of data rather than the business processes. The result: data-bound business organizations that cannot effectively compete because they are handcuffed by the massive volumes of data, transactions, etc., required by e-business – and by the difficulty of separating that data from supported applications.

Enterprise Integration and Evolution

Before a company can hope to take advantage of supply chain management or Web-based front office automation, it must address the back office issues. Currently, Enterprise Resource Planning (ERP) captures the lion's share of the CIO's attention as companies attempt to restructure their business around these massive data-centric back office systems. While ERP commands this attention, it cannot hope to cover all back office issues where legacy systems and many other domain specific applications must be orchestrated.

The ERP Shock Wave

As a kind of shock wave of ERP expansion moves through the back office, Product Data Management (PDM), Virtual Product Development (VPD) environments, and Manufacturing Execution Systems (MES) are not yet easily included. Workflow management of core business processes, enterprise application integration (EAI), and the growing shift toward Web integration are all adding to the swirl of confusion. Legacy systems must be considered as well, for they will not be replaced quickly enough to ensure the success of most ERP implementations, which assume replacement strategies or massive coding rewrites.

Dr. Jay Ramanathan, Chief Technology Officer of Concentus Technology Corporation, has over 20 years of experience in computer science research, technological transition, and product development.

She is responsible for the establishment and operations of the organization, including the funding and research development of the company's powerful Process-Centric Work Management software. Concentus was founded as a commercialization "spin-off" of a software research project that she managed at Ohio State University.

The company's technological lineage descends directly from that early research in object technology and concurrent engineering that represents the core intellectual property of Concentus products and is recognized in many industries as visionary.

http://ramanathan.ASCET.com

Collaboration ad hoc is Good – and Bad

Additionally, the present state of the art does not easily support the collaboration required for supply chain success. Loose integration of applications with the underlying business processes results in collaboration that is mostly ad hoc and devoid of any formal business and workflow logic. Ad hoc collaboration is not in itself a problem. In fact, it's the way people naturally work with each other and in this sense it actually facilitates the functioning of supply chains.

Problems arise not from the ad hoc nature of work, but from the inability of data-bound IT architectures to support ad hoc collaboration within the company's natural workflow logic – how the company actually works. The problem worsens when the organization spans a heterogeneous set of companies, geographies, and environments. Add to this the numerous applications within a company or supply chain, and the traditional integration strategies rapidly fail. The enterprise becomes unresponsive and collaboration is limited to point-to-point mechanisms such as fax transmissions or e-mail, or perhaps some sort of access to data repositories. System integration takes on too many direct interfaces and too much "glue-code," and thus does not demonstrate the flexibility required for successful ad hoc interactions.

Change Is Imminent

In a world of change, these massive implementations will often require a significant change in scope before they are ever fully deployed. Change must be planned for and, in fact, the ability to change is the real differentiating core competency in the market place. Best-of-breed "super systems" must be configured, executed, delivered, and managed in an environment that welcomes and supports significant, ad hoc changes to the sets of tools, data vaults, organizations, and core business processes. These "super systems," or "meta-systems," provide a framework for integration, collaboration, change, and business competitiveness.

Success in e-business can only occur when you see your business as a rational set of processes, rather than a conglomeration of data to be manipulated. While monolithic "stovepipe" approaches to application coverage are giving way to best-of-breed strategies, a process view, supported by a "meta"-level architecture, is still required for full supply chain success. That's because traditional, data-centric solutions provided by legacy systems, ERP backbones, vertical applications, stovepipes, and even middleware will either slow the company down or cause it to change its processes in order to accommodate the limitations of the solutions themselves.

The Object Management Group (OMG) is a prime example of how industry, both customers and vendors alike, has recognized the need for a standards-based framework to support the plug-and-play integration of many software applications. CORBA (Common Object Request Broker Architecture) is framework architecture that can provide any company with the basic roadmap for creating an effective process-centric "meta-system."

OMG and CORBA, until recently, have lacked the availability of tools that can support the enterprise-scale approaches that are desired. Proprietary approaches are available, yet they may not yield the same market acceptance (COM/DCOM, OAG, proprietary EAI applications). While CORBA-based frameworks are more desirable, Java-based-frameworks, proprietary frameworks (IBM), and EAI application vendors all are projecting their views into the market.

A Liberated Enterprise is a Process-Driven Enterprise

A robust CORBA-based "meta-system" must be process-based, i.e., founded on a flexible framework for the configuration, execution, delivery, and management of core business processes across Virtual Private Networks (VPNs) and the Internet. A framework is more than a collection of object classes; it includes rich functionality and strong interconnections that provide an efficient infrastructure for the "meta-system" builder. In the process-driven environment, supported by process-centric architecture, front office, back office, and supply chain business processes can now be configured for optimal and ad hoc management and execution.

The process-centric framework can easily configure and manage any set of enterprise applications, any set of data sources, and any set of participants inside and outside the enterprise…in other words, across the supply chain. That includes the company's and their partners' front and back offices. How? By decoupling applications and data from business process, the "meta-level" process-centric framework allows just the right combination of data and applications to be delivered, in context, to the person who needs it at any given moment or point in the process. Thus, liberation is possible when any combination of data, applications, and even EAI frameworks can be served on a totally ad hoc, totally flexible basis. This can only happen when the applications and the data that support them no longer have to travel together. We call this "process mail."

A Process-Centric Enterprise is a Successful Enterprise

Thus, the process-centric IT framework not only is required for back office performance in the supply chain environment, but it supports all of the critical success metrics of the traditional data-centric strategy.

Finally, and most importantly, the enterprise can become vastly more competitive in direct proportion to its liberation from the bounds and limitations of traditional data-centric IT architecture.

Concentus Technology Corporation – Process-Driven Software Tools for B2B E-Commerce

Contact Information

Jeff A. Burke
Vice President
Sales and Marketing

Concentus Technology Corporation
5115 Parkcenter Ave. Suite 150
Dublin, OH 43017-7623
Phone 877.638.2397
Fax 614.792.0998
sales@concentus-tech.com
www.concentus-tech.com

Success in e-business can only occur when you see your business as a rational set of processes, rather than data to be manipulated or applications to be integrated. Never has this been truer than in the current Business-to-Business (B2B) arena where value and supply chains are requiring quantum improvements in speed, flexibility, and responsiveness. The challenge faced by business organizations is this: How to enable e-business performance while preserving the valuable business processes that drive the company, and how to be able to reconfigure those processes on the fly without disrupting the business.

It's about Enabling Business Process...

Thus, e-business success in the B2B arena will rely on the organization's ability to manage its key processes with speed and agility. This process-centric strategy cannot be achieved by traditional IT approaches that rely on manipulating large volumes of data. The sheer volume of transactions required for B2B commerce will simply outstrip the ability of these traditional data-driven approaches to respond with the necessary speed and flexibility. Acceptable solutions must go beyond buying new applications, major data integration programs, or simply attaching a Web front-end to a suite of legacy applications. The solution will require these companies to look at the very IT architecture supporting the enterprise.

The business process represents the company's core competency in action. It is currently supported by enterprise applications and legacy systems, corporate and commercial data, and people who must interact, such as customers, employees, partners, and suppliers.

The EAI Solution and More, Much More...

While current process-enabled solutions, such as workflow, Enterprise Application Integration software and emerging Best Practice Management solutions can handle simple processes, most cannot address the increasingly complex processes that must be deployed for successful e-commerce participation. That is because they are still essentially driven by data. The technology tools necessary for true competitive success will not only go beyond current solutions, but they must be quickly and economically deployable.

The Uniquely Powerful Concentus Solution

The Concentus Solution is a process-centered IT architecture that supports literally any process, regardless of complexity. It is an e-commerce process platform that integrates and manages any combination of people, tools, and data as well as corporate portals, offering role-based access through a Java-based desktop and virtually unlimited off-the-shelf e-business applications that can be quickly configured and launched to meet the changing dynamics of e-business.

The Concentus three-level solution set consists of:

1. MetaExpress™ Process Engine™. It sits at the heart of the Concentus solution. Capitalizing on the strength of its open, object-oriented architecture, MetaExpress offers a unique work management framework built around a process engine that serves configurable, role-based work processes (combination of data and applications). It was the first commercially available CORBA-compliant workflow

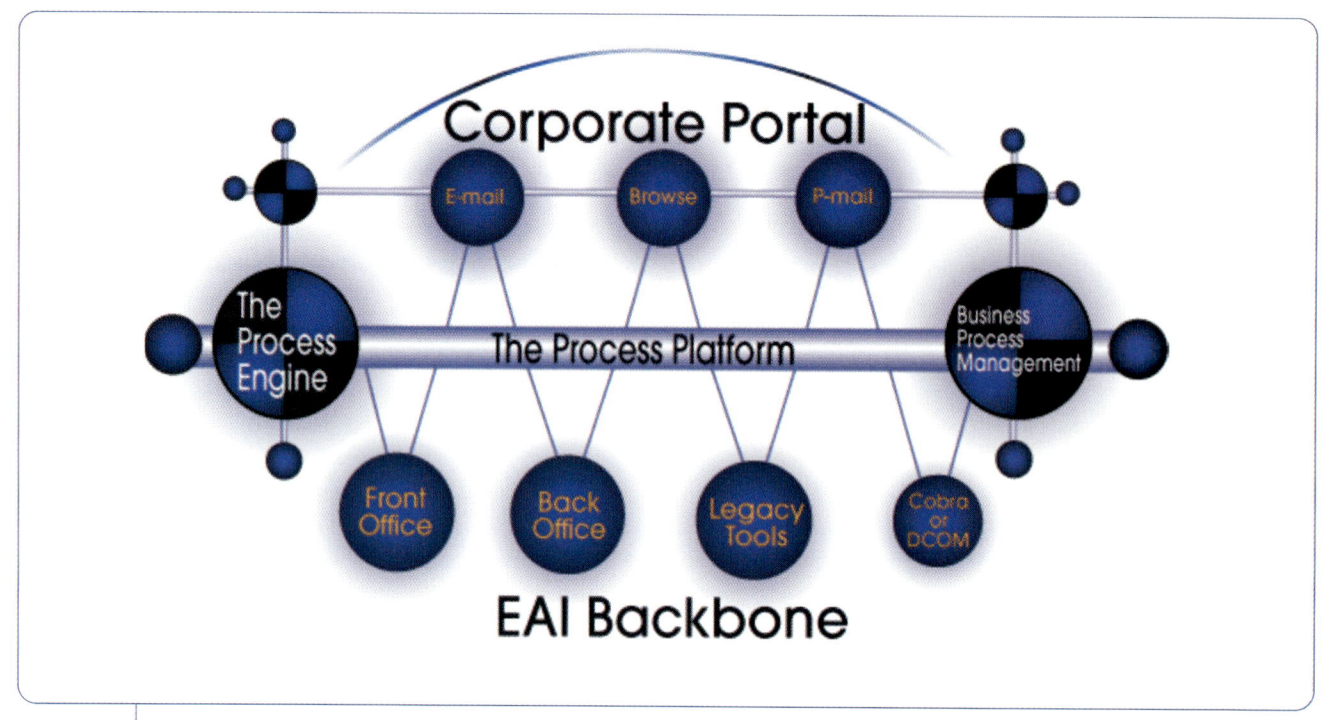

Figure 1.0 The Concentus Workbridge Solution

engine. It offers hundreds of APIs (application programming interfaces) and also meets interface standards developed by the NIIPP (National Information Infrastructure Protocol Program) Consortium and the WFMC (Workflow Management Coalition).

MetaExpress can define and execute virtually any business process through a graphical user interface. It defines new processes or modifies existing ones without requiring programming. It can drive highly complex internal processes, by providing virtually unlimited single points of access across the entire enterprise. And it can support myriad transactions and processes required by e-commerce.

2. WorkBridge, an e-commerce process platform that offers a process-based solution for rapid deployment of Internet applications with a browser-based corporate portal and seamless, totally open links to virtually any front office, back office, or value chain application. Applications can be docked in hours.

Because it is powered by Concentus' MetaExpress Process Engine technology the WorkBridge process platform offers totally open application integration services and allows access to all corporate data. This capability alone, means that any user on the corporate information system can access, use and even change just the data required for the job they are doing.

3. A set of configurable vertical applications that are built on the process engine and can be deployed fully throughout the supply chain or e-commerce framework through WorkBridge. Initial vertical applications are: WorkBridge Change Manager to handle complex engineering changes and WorkBridge Procurement Manager, offering bid, proposal and contract management services.

The Bottom Line: You'll Get There Faster and at a Fraction of the Cost

Concentus delivers process-driven software solutions that enable unprecedented speed to market for any company's B2B e-business strategy. By focusing on the company's business process, the process-driven software allows deployment of any B2B e-business solution in days, versus the months required for traditional integration approaches. What's more, it's graphically configurable, thus drastically reducing the cost of change and maintenance. That's a necessity for any company requiring the agility and competitive edge produced by faster deployment of e-business solutions.

The Web's Effect on the Service Value Chain

written by:
Stephen E. Reiter
Service Master
http://reiter.ASCET.com

From plaything of the academic and military communities to a revolutionary platform for business, wealth generation, and information exchange, the Internet is changing the way we do everything – and opportunities abound for the quick and resourceful. The supply chain is no exception to this transformation: the extension of Internet technology to the service value chain will increase geometrically over the next several years. Expectations for total revenue over the Web for B2B service sector alone are estimated to be between $300 billion to $400 billion dollars by the year 2002. The looming question: what piece of that market will your organization capture?

As we enter the new millennium, we are faced with a worldwide revolution of a proportion and rapidity that mankind has never witnessed before. The decades-old World Wide Web or Internet that was created by the National Science Foundation was a network point of contact for various defense and governmental agencies, with a smattering of technical wizards. Over the past couple years the net transformed itself, setting the entire globe in a spin within a twinkling of an eye. Imagine going from an academic curiosity into a major platform for enterprise, an immense wealth-creator and a tool for a free exchange of ideas. Because of this transformation occurring, no person, business enterprise or nation will ever be the same.

An eternity ago – in 1997 – I co-authored a book entitled *Supply Chain Optimization* with Chuck Poirier, a notable expert on management practices and Supply Chain Management. As we performed our research, at over 100 of the best and most astute corporations in the world, we barely encountered any mention of the Web. We identified through our interviews the need and benefits to provide linkage between the four levels of a consumer supply chain – from the suppliers to the manufacturers (plants), to the distributors and finally, the retailers. This model became known as the Inter-Enterprise Solution (IES). It was developed to enhance the profitability of all major corporations in the hard goods industries. In the retail/consumer products industry alone we identified that there was potential savings in the $80 billion to $100 billion range. Our desire was to change the way management treated Supply Chain Management as a strategic tool to harness waste in their operations and to enhance value through the various levels of the value chain.

Yet, we had to utilize tools such as EDI and other expensive, sophisticated and difficult-to-use communications enablers to link the various levels of the model. If that book were being written today, the Web would have been core to the model and deemed a requirement to successfully link disparate organizations.

What Does This Mean?

From its humble and technical beginnings, the Internet has created nothing less than a revolution in the history of the human race. Arnold B. Baker, head economist at Sandia National Laboratories, stated that "there's going to be a fundamental change in the global economy unlike anything we've had since cavemen began bartering." If you read the print or listen to the broadcast media, there are many that have proclaimed a statement of this ilk, but what does that mean? If we examine the real impact of this phenomenon to date and what will most likely occur over the next three to five years, there are five major categories of disruption that become obvious:

- Death of traditional time and distance
- The introduction of ubiquitous and virtually free telecommunications
- The advent of a truly global market
- We are (like it or not) all connected
- Access to the best training and education

Stephen E. Reiter is ServiceMaster's Senior Vice President and Chief Information Officer. In 1997, Reiter co-authored "Supply Chain Optimization" with Chuck Poirier, a notable expert on management practices and Supply Chain Management.

http://reiter.ASCET.com

Death of Traditional Time and Distance

Back in ancient times (pre-Web), transactions between people, organizations and nations would require days or months to execute. The use of electronics solutions such as Electronic Data Interchange (EDI), which had its origin in the rail transportation industry, was expensive and required significant investments of time and money to comply. Although there were and are still standards, they were co-opted most often with special custom modifications that made the standards virtually useless. At a division of $17 billion Tenneco (called Packaging Corporation of America) in 1991, there were hundreds of custom EDI modifications required to meet customer demands. Each of these required many weeks or man-months of efforts to implement, with even more time and cost to maintain these modifications. Today, many of those traditional borders no longer exist as the Web consolidates, within a 15-inch screen, the world of commerce and enables technology to break down pre-existing barriers.

With the advent of the Web, we have realized an ANY5 environment – that is, the access and availability of information and voice communications can now be 24x7 – providing: any information, at any time, any where, in any form, to any one.

Business and personal time can now have the advantage of dealing with a truly global set of needs or desires without concern about wall clock time. When I managed a staff of thousands of professionals who were domiciled in 14 different time zones, I could manage them closely, even though they rarely saw each other face to face for at times up to a year or more. This was accomplished through the use of Web-based tools and developing a set of standards that provided a basis for understanding. We established a set of 60 basic pieces of information (key performance indicators or KPIs) on a company intranet with a daily or weekly frequency. Complementing these were another 18 pieces of information that were reported every 30 days. We were then able to maintain local autonomy in meeting our customers needs, yet satisfy management's understanding of whether the managers in remote locations were hitting targets. If targets were not met, there was a set of diagnostics that flagged danger points.

For the last couple of decades the U.S. metals industry has suffered through a period of major changes. The results were a highly fragmented industry, with major global players affecting profitability through actions such as having the old Iron Curtain countries dumping aluminum and steel at prices that U.S. metals manufacturers could not even buy as raw material. This practice and other constraints help national metals companies face staggering losses and negative shifts in the market. Like so many other core industries, metals also faced numerous other fears, such as a set of larger consolidated buyers who perceived metals as a commodity, as well as the improvements in alternatives such as plastics that caused margins to fall precipitously during the late 1980s and the 1990s. Many of these competing products responded by developing highly efficient supply chains. Inventory levels at the metals companies grew 8-10 times during the period, with turns averaging 1.5–2.5, along with poor cycle times throughout the industry.

A start-up venture called MetalSite.com came along and elected to transform its selected industry. Metal products industry has been under substantial pressures since the early 1970s. Funded by a collaboration of venture capitalists and industry players (25% of domestic industry invested, 40% signed up as of 4Q 99), MetalSite covers each step in the business process for each participant in the industry.

The founders and partners created an entirely new paradigm based on the speed and accuracy of Web-based transactions to link the various levels of the value chain. Two of the U.S. companies as well as seven other global metals companies have claimed to have already returned the cost of their investments through the improvements offered by MetalSite.

MetalSite operates a deep vertical market focusing solely on utilizing an e-commerce solution to manage the process of sourcing – or the buying and selling of metals and related products. Customers opening the MetalSite Web site can not only buy and sell product; they can review news within their industry and connect with other professionals in the metals industry around the world. MetalSite was launched in 1998 to conduct online sales of steel products in the United States. Today customers can engage in the commerce of other metal products such as copper, aluminum and other metals from a wide range of suppliers. The company provides a buyer-driven auction forum for metal products that enables sellers to post their products up to five times daily. Bidders submit their offers in a secure environment to the sellers responsible for fulfillment, with a set of capabilities that track the customer's history of past transactions, usage and bids.

MetalSite sets up a set of standard processes and Web-based transactions that strongly encourage the buyers and sellers to go through a set of involved transactions. Buyers of steel and other metals must specify such information as type and grade of product they wish to buy. Through this process, MetalSite assigns a knowledgeable engineer to work with a set of expert buyers to create product specifications that drive the Request for Quote (RFQ). Acting as an agent, MetalSite researches availability globally and screens for those qualified to meet these well-defined specifications.

Adopting a similar model to MetalSite in a different industry has led

---

W² Weblink

For more on optimization, see:
prince.ASCET.com
hicks.ASCET.com

For more on the value chain, see:
uchneat.ASCET.com

For more on distribution, see:
anthony.ASCET.com

For more on bulletin boards, see:
prince.ASCET.com

For more on auctions, see:
appell.ASCET.com

THE INTER-ENTERPRISE SOLUTION

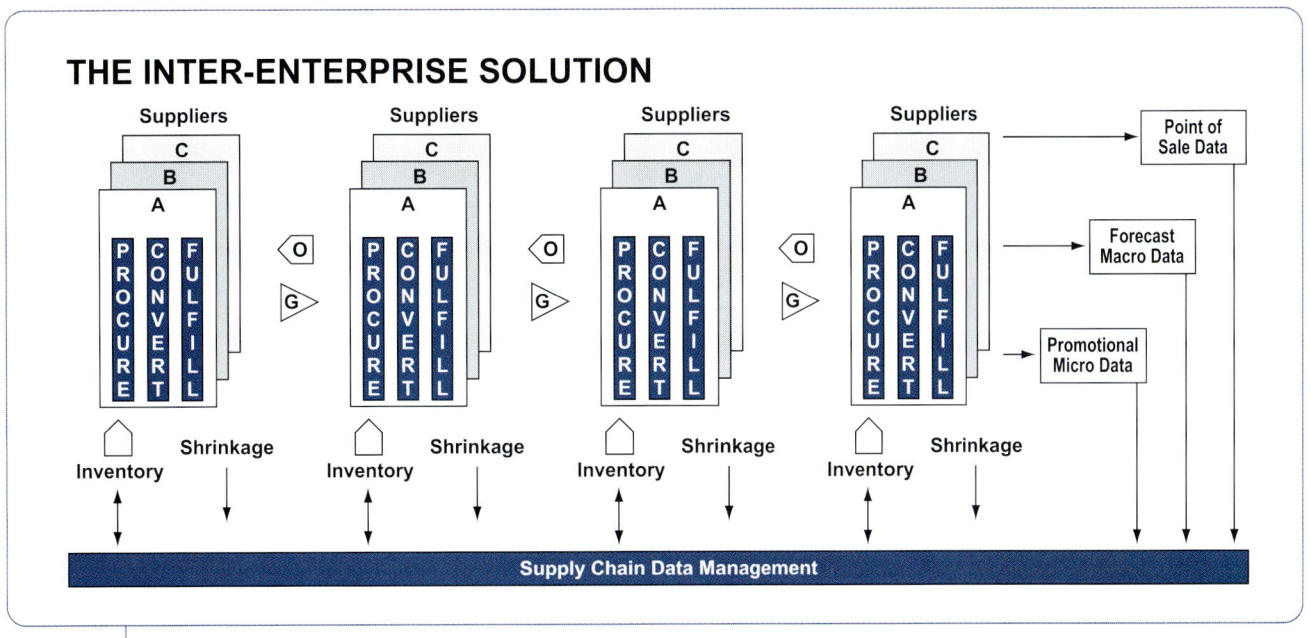

Figure 1.0 — The Inter-Enterprise Solution

to multiple competing e-commerce providers in the pulp and paper industry. This industry is almost as large globally as the automobile industry. In the past there have been multiple point solutions developed to provide e-commerce for this industry. Offerings include selling specialty rolls of paper, used equipment for paper mills and converting operations, or even the acquisition of off-grade board and trim as a raw material to be included in new containerboard rolls. Today, there are two primary sites that post various forms of paper rollstock for sale. These companies are Paperexchange.com and Paperdeals.com.

Each company has adopted different processes for the buyer and seller to interact with their site. One such example is the commission structure. Paperdeals offers a sliding scale that drops to as low as 1% for sales over $25,000. Paperexchange commissions is fixed at 3% regardless of the dollar value of the transaction. Paperexchange maintains the anonymity of the buyer and seller until after the deal has concluded with the Web company acting as the intermediary, and does not reveal this information until the end of the bidding process. In contrast, Paperdeals has an entirely different process. The site posts the paper for sale along with the name of the party who wishes to sell, then it acts as a bulletin board or consumer auction site. The parties engage in a rather conventional type of auction until the deal is agreed to. There are a number of different bidding processes that are allowed within Paperdeal's site. The basic contractual agreement between the two sites is very different. Paperdeals is simple and straightforward, since they act only as a bulletin board.

Paperexchange is more complex and detailed since they act as more of an intermediary than as a posting site. An example of this complexity is, after a credit-approved transaction is filed, payments are governed by credit-approved purchase terms. This is handled as a separate document, with itemized credit-approved transactions. When this occurs, Paperexchange acts as a purchaser on behalf of a credit-approved member. Payment terms are a minimum of 45 days. In the event Paperexchange does not collect the payment, they cover the transaction fee to the seller within 90 days from the date of the invoice.

Paperdeals is simpler. Participants can either create an auction anonymously, or it is also possible to simply post your name and that products you have for sale. Financially, Paperdeals requires that each party that have sufficient funds to pay the action fees for each sale when an account is opened during registration. Paperdeals immediately debits your account upon the closing of a transaction, compared with Paperexchange, which allows payment up to 30 days after invoicing.

Both believe that they can reduce time and cost of the transactions between buyers and sellers; yet neither one been embraced by the industry as a whole. Barriers, which are largely culturally based on a "we've always done it that way" mentality have not yet been overcome. When they are, estimates of cost reductions exceeding $30 per ton (or $450 million) are considered by experts to be very conservative. Reductions will come through such areas as yield management, reduced inventories, better use of working capital, as well as the advantage of a much greater access to the overall market. Another area of reduction not addressed in the $30 per ton will be the administrative and selling costs. Estimates are reductions in cost exceeding 50% – today it represents 4 to 4.5% of the total cost.

http://reiter.ASCET.com

Ubiquitous Telecommunications – Virtually Free

Few industries have witnessed such disruption as telecommunications since the breakup of AT&T or Ma Bell in 1984. Over the past 15 years the entire complexion of this industry has changed. The cost of long-distance calls plummeting from $.25+ per minute of service to rates at sub-$.03 per minute on large corporate deals and even sub-$.02 rates for VoIP or Voice over Internet Protocol rates. In pre-divestiture days, the AT&T monopoly was forced by the government to subsidize rural and local telephone service with fees garnished from business clients. Today we have realized a shift to a rate structure much more consistent with market forces. As many of us recall back in 1984 most television services were brought into the house using wireless devices called antenna and were essentially free. Phone service was always brought into the home via copper cables. That market has changed dramatically with the difference much more pronounced now that television is delivered by cable with a bill coming monthly and with telephone service going wireless.

For the first time, in the year 2000, local and long-distance companies will compete outside their respective markets. In late December of 1999, the Federal Communications Commission (FCC) granted Bell Atlantic permission to enter the long-distance market in the state of New York. In response to this action, AT&T, MCI/WorldCom and Sprint elected to begin offering their own form of local telephone service. Almost immediately the cost of local services dropped 20% for those within NY. Many others across the country can expect a similar drop in costs as these competitive environments are duplicated in other markets. Two of the largest mergers in history – MCI/WorldCom's offer of $116 billion for Sprint, and Vodafone AirTouch's $148 billion offer for German wireless carrier Mannesmann are, according to Wall Street analysts, only the beginning.

Surge of demand in the industry is being driven by a rash of new commercial and consumer-based services for voice, data, video and image transmissions, global universal access (wired and wireless), multiple services per customer including high-speed internet access, as well as a growing base of new and innovative services. The growth in the U.S. market is anticipated to exceed 9% in the year 2000 alone to over $250 billion. The boundaries between wired and wireless services will begin to blur rapidly as we step through the year 2000. The battle lines have been formed, with victory defined as nothing less than ownership of the access to your household or business.

Due to the expanding use of web-based technologies, the growth curve of data traffic in the U.S. during 2000 will cause the volume of data related traffic in the U.S. to surpass voice related traffic. This will happen even though voice services will still grow at over 5%. All this is possible because of the monumental capacity of optical fiber that has been installed in the ground. These slivers of glass know no current limitations as a medium, and the current limitation of electronics placed on each end of the strands of fiber are growing capacity at geometric orders of magnitude offering ubiquitous service. This is all happening while the price of access and use is being driven down to be virtually free by the competition. Isn't it a wonderful world!

You Can't Hide in a Truly Global Market

Many companies have learned the hard way that in a global economy, you can no longer prevent the world from seeing your "dirty laundry." The competition now has a real time view into your strategy. In it's infancy the use of the web was left to people who did not understand the implications of the first two Ws in "www" or World Wide Web. Often the organizations did not control what was placed on the Web. Business Units, remote locations and/or functional departments would develop and post their own web presence. For that matter they did not understand that the audience could virtually include anyone from customers, to competitors, even terrorists. Company secrets that were treated with a great deal of security were transmitted for the world to see without realizing what had occurred.

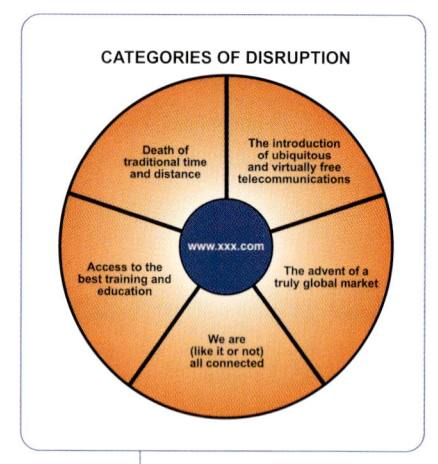

Also, there were many times when corporations did not understand that the entire world could view what was posted, not just their intended audience. A prime example of this happened about four years ago when the marketing group of a major food product corporation posted some recipes on the web using one of their core products as an ingredient. Their recipe was for a cream cheese cake. If you followed the ingredients and instructions for mixing and baking the cake in the United States it turned out as intended. Unfortunately, the basic ingredients of the U.S. market for cream cheese are different then that produced in England. Additionally, the English often use cream cheese as a topping for such items as baked potatoes. Needless to say the taste of the baked cake produced in the U.K. produced significantly poorer results than in the U.S.

On a much more positive note, the advent of the web has developed some wonderful new opportunities for meeting the needs of commercial and consumer markets. ServiceMaster, a $6 billion corporation, recognized these needs and has begun to offer to other corporations, as well as consumers, an opportunity to outsource their tasks. Many of these tasks offered are those many of us hate to do. In the consumer segment the tasks that

Figure 2.0 Categories of disruption

ServiceMaster offers to help with include maintenance of both the interior and exterior of the home. They cover activities such as lawn care, painting, repairs or remedial and preventative-maintenance of the major appliances (from hot water heater and furnace to refrigerator), furniture repair, clearing clogged drainpipes or even cleaning the house. Given a common problem within Western society, the lack of personal time, along with an increasing amount of disposable income, ServiceMaster has taken the opportunity to offer an option to select any or all the services offered, as well as be a link to those they don't. Access to all these services will be made through a local branch as well as through the Web or via phone to a national call center.

As in other Web-based systems, while the ease of use and functional richness of the technology is critical, the key (supply chain) issue is fulfillment. These lessons were learned by analyzing mistakes and later corrections made by the early adopters of Web-based business, such as Amazon.com in the consumer segment and Cisco in commercial. These offerings typically used a package delivery service to bring their product to the buyer who ordered via the Web. ServiceMaster was faced with the dilemma of having a service worker show up at a predefined destination (your home) at a specified time, to deliver a service of sufficient quality to satisfy the customer. ServiceMaster was faced with the challenge that although many of the services were offered by internal business units, a number of the customers either had needs that could not be fulfilled by these units or had needs that had to be fulfilled by a third party because of customer preference. The solution to this problem was one learned through things learned from their American Home Shield (AHS) unit. AHS sells home warrantees and has designed a business model that requires them to use over ten thousand third-party fulfillment agents such as dishwasher/refrigerator repairmen, as well as heating/ventilation/air conditioning (HVAC) and drain cleaning personnel, rather then hire and employ the service worker directly. As the need to provide more refined scheduling and efficient use of the service workers time becomes more essential, ServiceMaster is beginning to use some sophisticated scheduling techniques which come from software and expertise obtained from extensive experience by manufacturing supply chain experts.

We're All Connected

On May 12, 1999, Lou Gerstner Jr., Chairman and CEO of the $90 billion IBM, met with industry analysts and issued the following statement: "The storm that's arriving – the real disturbance in the force is when the thousands and thousands of institutions that exist today seize the power of the global computing and communications infrastructure and use it to transform themselves. That's the real revolution."

During the week of January 11, 2000, proof that we are all connected came in the form of a merger, or more appropriately an acquisition, by AOL of the communications giant Time Warner. In terms of time and net income, AOL is an upstart. Yet this megamerger is highly ironic – it is the first time in history that an Internet-related corporation, barely a blip on the horizon only a handful of years ago, has taken over an industrial-age corporate giant. David has once again met up with Goliath and won a major victory. AOL has been able to leverage its extraordinary stock valuation to obtain access to the content it wants to distribute.

This is not only Supply Chain Management, this is providing integration of the entire value chain virtually in the hands of a single entity. Let's take a peek at what the combined company looks like as a supply chain. First we address the distribution of the product or control of the channel of access to the consumer market, or what we refer to as channel management. AOL Time Warner will have:

Cable:
Time Warner Cable
Internet Services:
America Online, Roadrunner, CompuServe
Telephone:
Multiple alliances with Bells for DSL (high-speed service)

Satellite:
Stake in DirecTV

Then let's look at the content or media assets:
Print:
Time, People, Sports Illustrated, Entertainment Weekly, Money, Fortune and 27 other titles
Film:
Warner Brothers Studios, New Line Cinema, Turner Classic Movies
Music:
Warner Music, EMI (to be approved)
Television:
CNN, TNT, TBS, HBO, WB Networks
Web Content:
AOL, CNN, Magazine Web sites, MapQuest, Moviefone

What does this portend for the future? Well, first let's ask the question, can it work? Almost immediately, many of the shareholders of AOL swung the emotional curve from enthusiasm to depression as the stock rode the roller coaster. There were even comments about filing legal motions to prevent this transaction from being finalized. Another issue will rise: the ability to merge two very different cultures, one a century-old conservative conglomerate, the other a fast-moving Web-economy firm. What comes to mind is the acquisition of Rolm by IBM in the mid-1980s and how terrible the results were.

Yet, almost immediately after the initial announcement of the transaction, AT&T and other carriers began to look at other options such as Disney. Is there a possibility that a MCI/Sprint could buy or merge with a Viacom or with the News Corp. (owned by Rupert Murdoch)? We also should look at the consolidating RBOCs and the huge appetite they have to enhance their presence. Since Mike Armstrong was announced as the Chief of AT&T, he has been on the acquisition trail to obtain cable companies. When they complete the takeover of the Media One Group, AT&T will be the largest cable operator in the U.S. with connections to more than 25% of the nations' cable customers. One thing is for sure, as the thirst of the world for Info-tainment grows, so will the willingness for the chairmen of major corporations, to provide them more and more at a price.

The extent of the connection does not stop at the back door either. When in San Francisco the week before Christmas, I had the occasion to meet with Vincent Barabba, Chief Strategist for GM. This Fortune 1, and its competitors, intends to capture a larger portion of your time, attention and pocketbook. By this time next year, GM and Ford will provide owners of their vehicles the opportunity to spend some of that 80 minutes a day the average car owner spends driving. This daily ride will be spent sending or receiving e-mail, stock quotes, planning for watching a movie or buying tickets for theatrical event, making dinner reservations, taking courses online or, of course, making or taking phone calls. Ford's CEO, Jacques A. Nasser, on April 9, 1999, told reporters at the North American International Trade Show "we will do nothing short of transforming our cars into portals to the Internet." There will no longer be any need to worry about steering and using keyboards; these vehicles will be equipped with hands-free voice-activated technologies. People will talk to their dashboards rather than using one of the many dangerous devices such as the current array of car phones or even portable units such as Palm Pilots or PCs. Therefore using mobile devices in automobiles will be no more dangerous or destructive than conversing with a passenger.

As of yet, many of the other car companies are unwilling to stake their future profits on what they have termed Net-Cars. Executives at DaimlerChrysler, Toyota and Honda have publically stated that they will not pin their hopes on this strategy. In fact, Richard Colliver, sales chief at American Honda Motor Company stated that they prefer to focus on their core competency – building and selling vehicles.

Of course the car companies will be able to obtain access to a new source of recurring revenue, as the seller or channel manager to car-based communications services. Either by buying up the source or developing alliance programs, the major automobile "manufacturers" will make billions in profits by providing wireless capacity to the motorist. Estimates by leading industry analysts add about $10 billion in revenue for these services by the end of the decade. All this is possible through very affordable hardware and access. The devices necessary will add minimal cost to the acquisition price of the vehicle (in the lower hundred-dollar range) while subscribers will be charged about $10 per month for basic services. The GM strategist detailed the technologies already on board today such as its OnStar navigation and safety systems that use wireless and satellite communications. You see you can run or ride, but you can't hide!

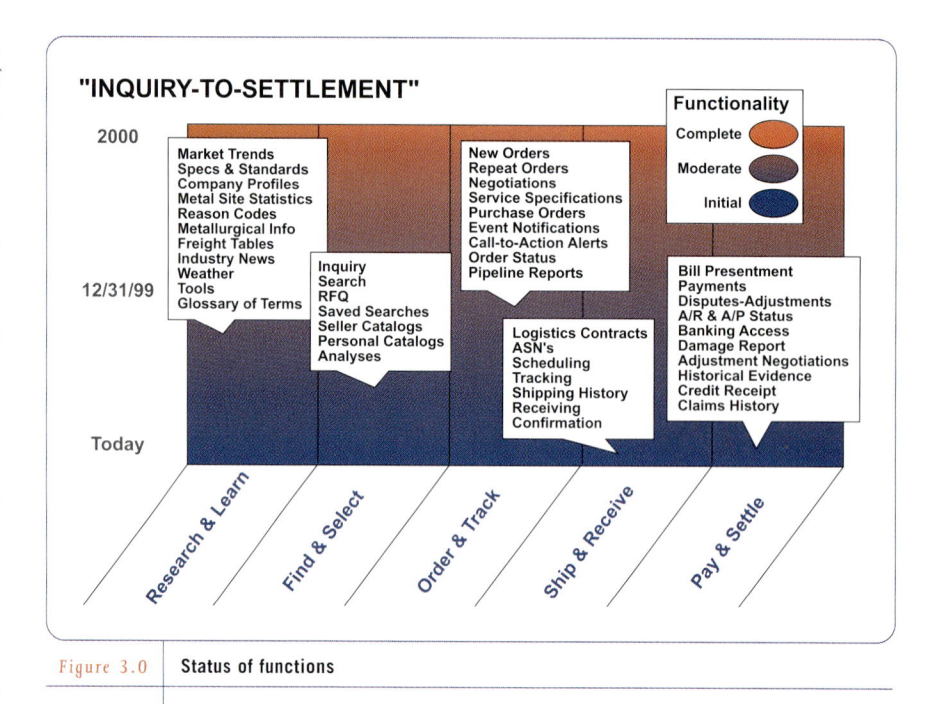

The biggest question on Wall Street is, will the car companies be able to capture the consumer base, or will a much more fleet of foot set of providers get there first? The answer to that question will become clear over the next couple years. Just hold onto your hat (and steering wheel) we are in for one heck of a ride.

Access to the Best!

I have had the honor of teaching students at a graduate degree program in a midwest graduate school of business, and received strong and positive feedback from my students in their evaluations at the end of the term. Yet, I realize that if my students were ever given a choice to attend my course, or one taught by such a notable as Peter Drucker or Henry Kissinger, there would not be a choice. Most students in their right mind would strongly prefer access to the quality, experience and knowledge transfer that arises from learning from one of the masters of our time. The opportunity is becoming available through the web, to provide "distance learning" to the ANY5 community.

The concept of distance learning is not new. During the mid-1980s, before the web became a household name, states such as Indiana offered via cable and telephone services, education to remote areas not anywhere near a major institution. In 1986 I lived in a town of 4,000 residents, Batesville, Indiana, home of a multi-billion dollar corporation. Yet we were over an hour away from any major population center, and even further from the state's centers of higher education, one could learn without driving so far out of town. Through an arrangement with the local telecommunication's provider (Contel), a student could register for a 2-year degree program from a community college, or a

Figure 3.0 — Status of functions

program from such great schools as Purdue, Ball State, or Indiana University. Of course, if you wanted to attend the basketball games and witness Bobby Knight throwing a chair across the floor, you'd have to drive two hours to Bloomington.

Education is a huge part of the nation's economy, with a total spent last year of $780 billion. Yet only a small portion - ten percent - is spent on for-profit education with the amount of venture capital spent totaling only $3.3 billion. This represents a 4X increase over the year before. With venture moneys available at an ever-expanding rate, hundreds of entrepreneurial efforts will come forward. According to Michael Moe, an analyst with Merrill Lynch, the year "2000 will be the year when the revolution will become very visible."

Today, there is already in place a $63 billion corporate training market that will embrace the use of the net for content and delivery. In 1998, only $550 million was spent in "e-learning." That number is projected to grow to $7.1 billion by the end of year 2002, according to IDC. Companies such as Teach.com, Knowledge Universe and Digital Think have redefined the state of teaching. Many of the hardware and software companies have captured significant revenue in this market (i.e., Sun has already captured over a billion dollars per year in the education segment). Although much of the work to date has been done by internal operations, there are numerous firms that have elected to outsource that effort.

Thought of as a supply chain, the provider can and will often be different than those that developed the content or those who marketed the product. Enthusiasm is growing in the Web-based education market. Howard Bloch, an analyst with Bank of America Securities, suggested, "there will be a tremendous migration away from classroom training to online learning." Others have gone so far as to classify distance learning as the next "killer application." Whether attacking the needs of industry or replacing government-sponsored education in the classrooms and homes of our children, many firms see huge electronic commerce opportunities, if they can capture a small part of the 53 million K-12 students in the U.S. alone. A leader in this area is Family Education Networks, which offers a series of education Web sites, including one that allows parents to connect with their children's school. Last year, over 2.5 million hits were counted from 9,000 schools that already participate in this exercise. Another fact that does not get lost on entrepreneurs, high school teenagers spend about $100 billion in disposable income.

Conclusion

There is good and bad news as we see the revolution rushing to the streets. Opportunities abound for those who are swift of foot and have the wherewithal to create fortunes beyond their wildest imagination. Some will succeed and many will either fail or not attempt to venture out at all.

The effect of the Internet on the supply chain has already hit many of our existing organizations whether we sell goods or services. Without a doubt, the extension of this technology on the service value chain will increase geometrically over the next several years. Expectations for total revenue over the Web for the B2B service sector alone are estimated to be between $300 billion to 400 billion dollars by the year 2002. The looming question is what piece of that market will your organization capture?

Commerce One – Leading the World in E-Commerce Solutions

Commerce One is the leader in global e-commerce solutions for business. Through its products, portals, and services, Commerce One creates access to worldwide markets, allowing anyone to buy from anyone, anytime, anywhere.

Commerce One offers solutions for companies that want to establish an e-commerce portal, and those looking for a comprehensive e-procurement solution and robust return on investment. These solutions enable buyers and sellers around the world to trade in a barrier-free environment and create new business opportunities for all trading partners.

Commerce One has established the Global Trading Web™, which is the world's largest business-to-business(B2B) trading community. Comprised of many open e-marketplaces, the Global Trading Web provides unprecedented economies of scale for buying organizations, suppliers, and service providers worldwide. Through the Global Trading Web, trade is accelerated, technology barriers are eliminated, and costs are reduced for all trading partners.

Commerce One Solution

Commerce One offers solutions for businesses that are looking to capitalize on the strategic and competitive advantages that e-commerce has to offer.

For enterprise buying organizations we offer the most comprehensive e-procurement solution in the market that will streamline your procurement operations to deliver a robust ROI.

For suppliers, we offer a way to streamline your selling and order entry process while providing you access to the tremendous buying power of the trading community on the Global Trading Web, which provides cost savings and additional revenue potential.

For Internet Market Makers who want to establish an e-marketplace on the Global Trading Web we offer solutions to help you set up a B2B portal that you can offer as a service to your customers and partners and will create new revenue opportunities for your business.

Commerce One also provides a full range of services to help your organization with the planning, implementation, training, and support of the solution you choose.

Commerce One Products

Commerce One offers the following e-commerce products and services that work together to deliver value to all trading partners within the supply chain.

Commerce One BuySite

Commerce One BuySite is an electronic procurement application for all purchasing, everywhere in the organization, everywhere in the world.

The only completely interactive e-procurement application, Commerce One BuySite provides direct, real-time access to suppliers and instant access to the Global Trading Web.

Commerce One MarketSite

Commerce One MarketSite' is offered in two forms:

- As a service through the MarketSite global trading portal (operated by Commerce One)
- Or as a technology solution with the MarketSite Portal Solution for businesses who wish to build their own e-marketplace

Contact Information

Mark Hoffman
President, CEO
and Chairman of the Board

Robert Kimmitt
Chief Operating Officer

Peter Pervere
Vice President and
Chief Financial Officer

Chuck Donchess
Executive Vice President
Corporate Strategy

Commerce One, Inc.
1600 Riviera Avenue
Suite 200
Walnut Creek, CA 94596
Toll Free 800.308.3838
Phone 925.941.6000
Fax 925.941.6060

Employees
Commerce One has over 700 full-time employees as of February 2000.

Founded
January, 1994 as DistriVision Development Corporation. Renamed to Commerce One in April of 1997.

www.commerceone.com
Email: info@commerceone.com

Through MarketSite, whether you access it as a service or build your own service, trade is accelerated, technology barriers are eliminated, and costs are reduced for all trading partners.

Commerce One MarketSite
Global Trading Portal
Commerce One MarketSite is the U.S. portal for exchanging goods and services among businesses worldwide. Buyers and suppliers can access the MarketSite portal for comprehensive e-commerce transactions and value-added services that streamline the buying and selling process to save time and reduce costs.

Commerce One MarketSite Portal Solution
The Commerce One MarketSite Portal Solution allows Internet market makers to build open marketplaces and link them to the Commerce One Global Trading Web. Included in the solution are all the products, components, and services necessary to create and deploy an open, business-to-business trading portal. The solution offers Internet market makers the opportunity to offer new services to their customers and partners while creating new revenue opportunities for their business.

About Commerce One
Commerce One is the leader in global e-commerce solutions for business. Through its products, portals, and services, Commerce One creates access to worldwide markets, allowing anyone to buy from anyone, anytime, anywhere.

The company has over 700 full-time employees, as of February 2000.

Commerce One was founded in January of 1994 as DistriVision Development Corporation. The company was renamed Commerce One in April of 1997.

Commerce One is publicly held and is traded on NASDAQ under the symbol CMRC.

Informix Software – Information Infrastructure for Supply Chain Management

Based in Menlo Park, CA, Informix Software specializes in advanced information management technologies that help enterprises in the i-economy get to market quickly, generate new revenue, build a unique strategic advantage, and solve their most complex business problems. Informix offers customers a complete software infrastructure that delivers highly scalable transaction processing, integrated business intelligence and complete e-commerce solutions.

Challenges of Supply Chain today

From supplier to customer delivery, logistics to order processing, design to finished product, intra-enterprise and inter-enterprise, businesses must make intelligent, informed decisions – and deliver on them accordingly – in real time.

Information is the essence of the modern enterprise. With customers, suppliers, shippers, and even their own internal corporate divisions globally dispersed, success hinges upon effective sharing of information.

Today's supply chain must work symbiotically, delivering products on time, with a consistently high level of service, anywhere in the world. Integrated order entry applications need real-time transportation schedules, inventory data, and order acceptance criteria. Sales flow through data must automatically trigger shipping of replacement stock. And getting the information where it needs to be in real time knowing what your suppliers and customers need when they need it translates into competitive advantage.

Enabling technologies such as cross-functional business applications, event-based workflow systems, real-time information systems, and process-based applications thus become essential competitive weapons as enterprises move into the 21st century.

Real-Time Execution Meets Real-Time Decision Support

Integrating the supply chain requires that the entire enterprise work interactively, concurrently amassing, processing, analyzing, and responding to customer needs.

For the modern enterprise, the information system collecting real-time information from throughout the supply chain becomes an empowering tool, enabling delivery of accurate, time-critical decisions.

Businesses today require an integrated solution that allows them to track, manage, and share mission-critical information consistently across the enterprise. At the heart of their solution, they need a high-performance, scalable, easy-to-manage, flexible information infrastructure and a true partner that will support them every step of the way to be the supply chain backbone.

The Informix Solution: The Supply Chain Backbone

Performance and scalability are at the heart of an Informix-based information technology solution for Supply Chain Management.

Today's complex, mission-critical supply chain management solutions require a combination of Online Transaction Processing (OLTP), e-commerce, and decision support. To meet

Contact Information

Jean-Yves Dexmier
CEO

Phil Rugani
Vice President of
Americas Operations

Jim Marshall
Vice President of
Corporate Marketing

Informix Software Inc.
4100 Bohannon Drive,
Menlo Park, CA 94025
For your local office in
the US and internationally
Phone 650.926.6300

please visit
www.informix.com/retail/

Products
Informix Internet Foundation.2000,
Cloudscape, XPS, Red Brick, i.Sell,
Visionary, Media360

Services
Informix Consulting offers
systems integration services
to customers

these needs, you need a scalable database that can be dynamically adjusted to accommodate larger amounts of data and more concurrent users – across the enterprise, across the country, around the globe.

When it comes to selecting the most appropriate information technology to meet your objectives, you want to be sure that you choose best-in-class tools and solutions. Informix's database and solutions for OLTP, distributed e-business, e-commerce, and decision support environments scale from hundreds of gigabytes to multiple terabytes.

Your Supply Chain Choice

Informix has demonstrated leadership in providing information technology across the supply chain, with leading international customers and partners. They choose Informix because we understand the business fundamentals, technical challenges, and support requirements that are changing the industry. And we have key partners who leverage our technology. Our partnerships result in business solutions and third-party products that are completely integrated with our technology, including emerging technology such as the World Wide Web, workflow automation, document management, imaging, and multimedia.

Solutions offered for SCM

Online Transaction Processing (OLTP)

Foundation.2000, Informix's flagship database server, is designed for the high volume transaction demand of supply chain. Foundation.2000 combines high performance transaction processing with Object Relational Database technology, all with a smaller memory footprint than previous versions of the Informix server. Informix's OLTP offering provides businesses and software developers the platform to support mission critical supply chain environments.

Distributed E-Business

Cloudscape database provides retailers and retail software developers a robust, lightweight, and admin-free database system designed to run on all Java platforms. Cloudscape is a 100% Pure Java Object Relational DBMS and supports any certified Java Virtual Machine (JVM). Businesses looking to deploy applications to suppliers or customers for SCM will find Cloudscape the perfect platform to develop solutions that are scalable, yet easy to administer and manage remotely.

Online E-Commerce

Informix i.Sell is Informix's value-priced, end-to-end e-commerce solution. i.Sell integrates Informix's powerful database and application server technology with an e-commerce application suite, tools, enterprise consulting, and global services and support to provide complete, rapidly deployable e-commerce solutions. i.Sell is designed for businesses looking to create business portals where suppliers and customers can interact and exchange information.

Business Intelligence

The difference between winning and losing markets is understanding customers' needs. Increasingly, enterprises are choosing to implement data warehouses with vast stores of historical data consolidated from diverse sources into one easy-to-use reference database for time-critical decision support.

The advantages are clear:
- Profile customer buying patterns and histories in moments
- Analyze your market as it changes, enabling rapid product and service customization and response
- Track and respond to business trends
- Analyze data according to business dimensions
- Monitor and control operation support systems
- Focus customer acquisition and retention on the most profitable customers
- Insulate operational systems from ad hoc queries, thereby improving performance
- Integrate data from mainframes and open systems, maximizing use of resources.

For more information on Informix Solutions for Supply Chain, please visit www.informix.com.

Informix Software – The Technology Platform at Peapod

Peapod, Inc. is the leading Internet grocer in the U.S., and hosts the country's fifth-largest e-commerce site. Peapod depends on Informix® Dynamic Server™ to manage the over 30 million database calls generated by the site daily, and to provide a customized shopping experience for each of the company's over 100,000 members.

"The whole concept of grocery delivery and errand services has been around since the beginning of time," noted John Furton, chief information officer at Peapod. "Peapod was able to leverage a technological infrastructure into what had been a pretty labor-intensive activity, to make it efficient, and ensure a high level of quality. Informix has been very much a part of that technology platform since the beginning. In fact, I would say Informix is the technology platform at Peapod."

A New Shopping Paradigm

In the summer of 1990, Peapod first began testing the waters for what was then a radical concept: convincing the American public to do its grocery shopping online. "Our biggest challenge was to prove that consumers would shop this way," Furton remembered. "Then we also had to demonstrate that we delivered satisfactory service, so that people would be compelled to use us again."

The fledgling Skokie, Illinois-based company initially convinced Chicago's Jewell/Osco Foods chain to take a chance on a co-venture. The resulting agreement enabled area residents to log onto Peapod's site and select from a full range of Jewell/Osco's canned, packaged, and produce items, then Peapod employees delivered the orders to customers' doors. So new was the concept, Furton recalls, that Peapod sold modems to its first customers as part of their service, as few home PC-users had such devices at the time.

As word of Peapod's convenience and quality of service spread throughout the Chicago area, the company quickly found that its technological infrastructure was poorly suited for rapid growth. The small, PC-based RDBMS system that housed Peapod's grocery inventory was barely able to support the transaction loads that increased daily.

"When we started seeing bigger transactional volumes, we migrated to a UNIX environment," Furton said. "We knew we'd need a 'real' database engine to power the back end. Informix Dynamic Server and Informix 4GL were ideal for our needs."

Powering a Growing Business

Peapod's IT team eventually selected Informix Dynamic Server as the database engine for its e-commerce site. With Peapod's burgeoning popularity, the database's ability to scale was a key consideration. The flexible development and production environment of Informix 4GL was also a perfect complement to Peapod's new system, enabling the company to quickly develop and deploy the applications needed to gain a strong competitive advantage.

"Informix Dynamic Server has always scaled to meet our growing needs," said Jon Wilson, Peapod's director of database and application development. "The throughput is also exceptional – we're highly transactional, versus being a 'read-only' site, and it handles the transaction loads quite well. In addition, we used the 4GL tools from day one. They were a quick and easy way to get our business systems up and running."

Customizing the Shopping Experience

Since Peapod's official debut in 1995, the company's reach has expanded into seven major U.S. markets. Informix Dynamic Server generates 800,000 dynamic pages and logs 32 million database calls daily. But with the robust performance of the database enabling a 1.1 second response time, each customer can enjoy a customized, hassle-free shopping experience from the comfort of home or office.

For example, the Informix database enables Peapod to store specific shopping preferences for each member. Selections based on desired caloric or fat content, vegetarian or kosher preference, etc. are archived for each customer, then presented on appropriate "aisles" as customers navigate through their own customized "store." Grocery items are further grouped in accordance with customers' historical preferences in sorting through items on each "shelf."

One of the most powerful functions Informix Dynamic Server and Informix 4GL have enabled Peapod to develop is what the company calls its Universal Event Processor (UEP). This personalization tool presents shoppers, who may be visiting the site simultaneously, with completely different marketing promotions and advertisements, based on who the shopper is, what he/she has bought in the past, and how the shopper chooses to navigate through the store. A mother who frequently purchases diapers, for example, may be presented with a coupon offering savings on baby food; regular buyers of snack foods may be offered a coupon good for 50 cents off of a new type of potato chip.

"For every session, Informix Dynamic Server is firing off hundreds of requests to see what we should display, based on customer criteria," Wilson said. "The database easily manages all of this dynamic content, including customer criteria, demographics, and so on. Then, depending on what a shopper does in the application with the ads that come up, we write electronic coupons that take that amount of money out of the customer's order."

Sorting and Reporting Customer Data

Such robust transaction management also enables Peapod to maintain and instantly update behavior data as customers navigate through the site. Consequently, the company can track and report customers' buying habits back to suppliers, providing reports in any way preferred.

"Procter and Gamble might want to know what their category share is in the e-commerce space, versus the in-store environment," Furton said. "They can easily see that in the regular grocery world, Tide might have 45% of the laundry powder aisle. At Peapod, Tide might have that same 45%, but it could also be responsible for 80% of laundry powder sales to college-educated women with more than two children, who work outside the home. Our Informix database enables us to provide our suppliers with very comprehensive information they can't get in the 'outside' world."

TradeMatrix: The New Paradigm of Internet Business

written by:
Dave Fischer
i2
http://fischer.ASCET.com

The Internet is dramatically changing the way business is being conducted today. Web sites that initially provided only company information are becoming more sophisticated and complex. The Internet facilitates delivering solutions that provide collaboration, procurement, product ordering, and other inter-company processes. Companies are looking for ways to take advantage of leading-edge solutions and services that leverage the power of the Internet. With a plethora of Internet-enabling software companies offering solutions, businesses must choose carefully when deciding who offers them the best competitive advantage.

Today, companies are faced with a myriad of solutions that address some of these issues, including indirect procurement, collaboration, marketplaces or trading communities, and cataloging (for selling). Each solution is unique and lacks a consistent approach in solving a set of business problems. While point solutions, like indirect e-procurement, have generated significant savings for users, a holistic view of business-to-business e-commerce solutions has not been embraced. For example, direct material procurement, which represents a much larger portion of purchasing expenditures than indirect material procurement, is not being addressed by today's Internet commerce companies.

A number of other issues exist alongside these solutions including:

- Each solution is independent of the others, so there is no leveraging of information from one source to another, such as a consistent marketing message to the user.
- There is no cohesive information technology strategy. Each solution has its own architecture and standards.
- Typical e-procurement products only address a very small portion of the goods being bought by companies and are limited to office supplies and other simple items. The limited collaboration processes provided are not integrated with planning and forecasting systems.
- Digital marketplaces are transaction-oriented, supporting only spot buying and selling. Trading community participants are limited in their ability to access other marketplaces.
- Customer-facing solutions are not linked to fulfillment processes. This leads to reduced customer service and profitability.

In general, most e-commerce solutions focus on streamlining existing processes within a single company, rather than reinventing and linking processes across multiple companies.

To solve these problems, companies must have on-demand access to intelligent, role-based solutions that help them effectively plan and execute their business strategy. These services must provide:

- Buyers with intelligent, direct, and indirect procurement processes, along with planning and search tools that span multiple trading sites and portals. Buyers benefit from increased service levels, while reducing costs.
- Sellers with the ability to present not only their own goods and services, but also those of their partners, while portraying a unified brand to their buyers. Sellers must also provide their customers with value-added services and content, leading to increased service levels, revenues, and profits.
- Designers with access to product design and development collaboration. Design collaboration and workload planning assist with opti-

Dave Fischer is a vice president at i2 Technologies.

mally deploying scarce resources to bring new products to market more rapidly.
- Service providers, including logistics providers, outsourced manufacturers and warehousers, with the ability to understand and be linked with the physical movement of goods. With this capability, service providers provide maximum customer service at minimum cost.

TradeMatrix is the only electronic marketplace that can bring all of these elements together as an integrated, holistic set of services. TradeMatrix is uniquely able to bring these services together through a consortium of best-in-class partners who have a common interest in bringing game-changing value to customers. Available with a common, personalized, thin client user interface, TradeMatrix quickly delivers a new paradigm to business. TradeMatrix's design is based on i2's secure and robust DecisionFlows and workflows, incorporating intelligent planning algorithms. The net result is sustainable, maximized profitability levels for TradeMatrix participants.

The Evolution of E-Commerce

The single largest driver behind the explosive growth in e-commerce has been the Internet, which has emerged as the fastest-growing communication medium in history. International Data Corporation (IDC) estimated that there were 142 million Internet users in 1998 and anticipates 500 million by 2003. Business must react quickly to the Internet. The ability to dynamically and ubiquitously share information in real time, as well as buy and sell goods via a standard Web browser, provides corporations with a compelling competitive advantage.

Electronic commerce transactions will explode. IDC estimates that business-to-business transaction volume will increase to $1.3 trillion by 2003. Fear is also a significant motivator. CEOs are afraid of being "Amazoned." For every eBay, Amazon, and Yahoo!, there is another dot-com emerging on the horizon. Traditional companies are changing old models and thinking in new ways. In the digital economy, the competition is only a click away.

Companies have struggled with how best to use the Internet to achieve high-impact business results. Selling over the Internet can be classified into the following four categories:

- Company Presence – Basic company information
- Product Ordering – Purchase products online from one vendor
- Collaboration – The ability for companies to share information in a one-to-many scenario for mutual benefit of all parties
- Marketplaces – The public or private exchange of information in a many-to-many environment

The cost, sophistication, and business value of enterprise Web sites have increased dramatically across all industries (particularly in the consumer-oriented sites) since 1996. As referenced in Figure 1.0, GartnerGroup forecasts that an even greater growth in value and cost is anticipated.

In the late 1990s, e-commerce companies and dot-com Web sites focused on developing store fronts to stimulate sales. These predominantly B2C solutions included personalized Web front ends appealing to consumers and enabling sellers to increase up-selling and cross-selling opportunities. More recently, development work has concentrated on providing the dual back-end processes of fulfillment and, separately, customer care. Many of the newer applications include the returned goods process, required to accommodate unsatisfied shoppers.

Even though the B2B market is much bigger in terms of trade revenue than the B2C market, it has matured much more slowly. Only within the past two years have companies started to address B2B issues. Specifically, there has been the emergence of e-procurement solutions that help buyers manage and control purchasing processes. Separately, a few collaboration software vendors have been building simple, communication-based solutions relying on industry data standards such as RosettaNet, VICS, Opening Buying on the Internet (OBI), and others.

In the B2B world, marketplaces have experienced rapid growth and proliferation. Offering to bring buyers and sellers together, marketplaces or trading communities provide participants with the ability to post requirements and bid on goods and services. Marketplaces have typically evolved to meet the needs of a specific industry, such as eSTEEL (metals) or Chemdex (life sciences). C2C sites, such as eBay and Yahoo!, offer this same functionality enabling consumers to sell to one another directly.

These segments are beginning to converge. For example, more auctioning is taking place in the B2B world; at the same time, a growing number of companies are selling through direct and indirect channels. The result – a single multi-faceted virtual trading community – is emerging.

Improving on Current E-Commerce Solutions

Hardly a day goes by without news of an Internet-focused company reporting huge sales gains and negative profits. The profitability paradox results from:

A firm must spend a significant percentage of its revenue on advertising to attract new customers and gain market share.

Customer loyalty is virtually non-existent. To keep customers, a company must have a high order-fulfillment rate, which translates into high inventories and reduced profitability.

Fulfillment processes are de-coupled from the customer-facing solutions lead-

---

Weblink

For more on collaboration, see:
anderson-g.ASCET.com
walton.ASCET.com
moore.ASCET.com
johnson.ASCET.com

For more on business models, see:
benitez.ASCET.com
fontanella.ASCET.com

For more on auctions, see:
appell.ASCET.com
dobrin.ASCET.com

PHASES OF INTERNET-ENABLED EBUSINESS

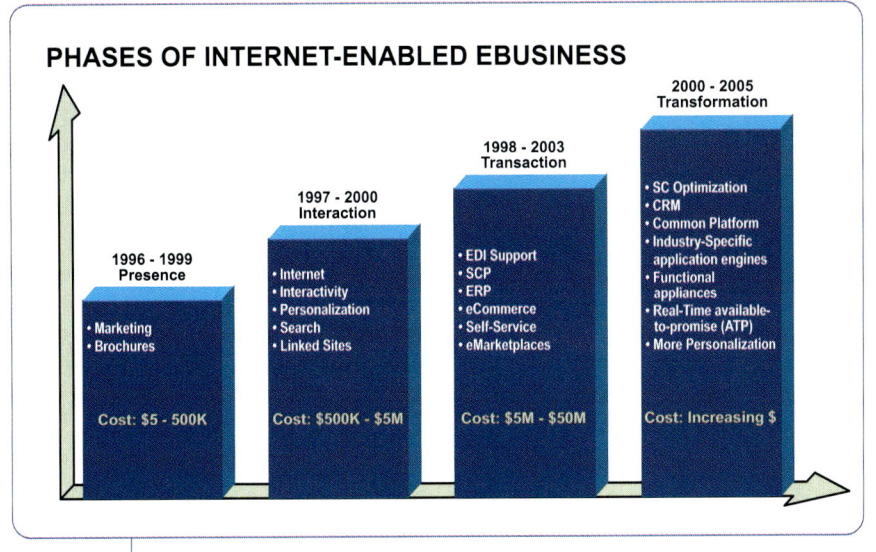

1996 - 1999 Presence
- Marketing
- Brochures

Cost: $5 - 500K

1997 - 2000 Interaction
- Internet
- Interactivity
- Personalization
- Search
- Linked Sites

Cost: $500K - $5M

1998 - 2003 Transaction
- EDI Support
- SCP
- ERP
- eCommerce
- Self-Service
- eMarketplaces

Cost: $5M - $50M

2000 - 2005 Transformation
- SC Optimization
- CRM
- Common Platform
- Industry-Specific application engines
- Functional appliances
- Real-Time available-to-promise (ATP)
- More Personalization

Cost: Increasing $

Figure 1.0 Transformation Yields Value, Source: Gartner Group

---

ing to overall increased operating costs.

The marketplaces for goods and services are limited to vertical industry segments. Greater corporate profitability could be achieved with more customers, content, services and sellers.

Processes or solutions currently provided by software companies do not leverage the transaction and collaborative powers of the Internet. Instead, they simply automate existing business processes at a lower cost.

Solutions offered are point solutions only – there is not a complete set of processes that span a company's extended enterprise.

Auctioning is used to drive to pricing for all goods.

The implication of each of these factors is discussed in detail below.

Market Share

Market share and industry leadership means that a company must attract and retain a larger percentage of customers than its competitors. In the traditional world of one-to-one sales, it takes a great degree of effort for a sales representative to convert a competitor's customer. With the Internet, customers are equally as hard to attract, especially with the huge number of options "just a click away." Even with marketing on the Web, including banner advertising and special offers, conversion rates are typically in the low single digits, hovering just above one percent. Companies are forced to spend millions of dollars attracting customers. This is the single largest reason why e-commerce companies suffer negative profitability.

Customer Loyalty

Once a company has attracted customers, another vendor or competitor is just a click away. How does an Internet-based company keep its customers? Customer retention, also referred to as "stickiness", is related to the value the customer gets from the site. In both the B2B and B2C worlds, this means that the customers must get high-quality products and services at a competitive price, delivered on time. Customer satisfaction is vital for an electronic commerce site to be successful.

Since online customers demand immediate gratification, this means promising products and services immediately, even if the date is estimated. When more than one item is ordered, this becomes especially difficult. How does a company accurately inform buyers when the products and services will be delivered, and at what price? Existing Internet commerce solutions are unable to satisfactorily service multiple product shipments and often do not comprehend true transportation time and costs.

De-coupled Fulfillment

Typical e-commerce sites have the ability to take an order, but do not have the ability to see if fulfillment is possible, except at very basic levels. As most tend to have already promised delivery, fulfillment is executed at any cost. It becomes even more complex when considering multiple line items for an order. Does a company have to ship them all together? If a seller ships the products when they are available, who absorbs the extra shipping costs? Does a seller understand customer preferences? The procurement process is also impacted. One vendor may be able to ship all the items for a total lower delivery cost than multiple vendors.

Vertically Focused Marketplaces

Marketplaces focus on a specific type of product or service such as plastics, steel or travel. This clearly defines the participants, but it also excludes potential customers. For example, if a buyer is looking for a specialized machine tool, there are multiple marketplaces where he may be able to purchase the tool. Further compounding the problem, he may have to pay an access fee to search each site.

Existing Business Processes

Many Internet commerce solution providers simply automate existing processes. Electronic procurement is a good example of where this has occurred. In the previous example, when buying multiple line items, the procurement process should include the total delivered cost – not just the cost of each single line item. In another procurement example, maintenance and repair parts are usually handled as indirect goods. What is missing? The interdependency of parts usage and the integration with a company's planning applications. By not linking these processes together, excess inventory is carried and service levels suffer.

Point Solutions

In the long list of solutions on the Internet, there are no products or offerings

http://fischer.ASCET.com

that cover more than one or two processes. The result is companies are forced to link disparate vendor solutions, including their own legacy systems. This not only increases information technology costs and time-to-value, but also reduces the payback that can be obtained from a fully integrated solution. For example, if a company uses two different customer-facing solutions, can the solutions share personalization data? If not, this means that the firm does not have the ability to take "lesson learned" about a particular customer and apply it to some other process, where the same customer may be impacted. Additionally, this means that a company is asking the same customer for identical data, multiple times.

Auctioning Goods

Auctioning and reverse auctioning are important to electronic commerce. For the spot market, it is a mechanism for both buyers and sellers to maximize their value. Auctioning also assists with the vendor selection process of some indirect goods. However, for procurement of direct goods, auctioning is a poor solution as it assumes that all parts and components are commodities. Additionally, as Dr. Hau Lee wrote in his paper, "The Bullwhip Effect," companies need visibility to reduce costs. Auctioning completely removes visibility, driving up costs, rather than down.

Change the Business Model

To efficiently leverage the vast of amounts of data generated on the Internet, solutions need to fundamentally change the way business is conducted. Instead of automating existing legacy processes, which are based on decades-old, manual execution workflows, solutions need to provide companies with processes that support strategic decision-making processes. Workflows also need to drive decision execution. Additionally, solutions must cross multiple marketplaces so that buyers can find all possible goods and services, while sellers need only participate in one place to gain worldwide exposure.

The value of any marketplace is dependent on the services provided. A world-class marketplace solution must support not only supply chain excellence, but also product life cycle and customer intimacy services. The marketplace solution must also be able to resolve conflict among any of these variables to achieve superior customer satisfaction. A technology framework that allows applications and services to be easily added, monitored, and removed is also a critical success factor.

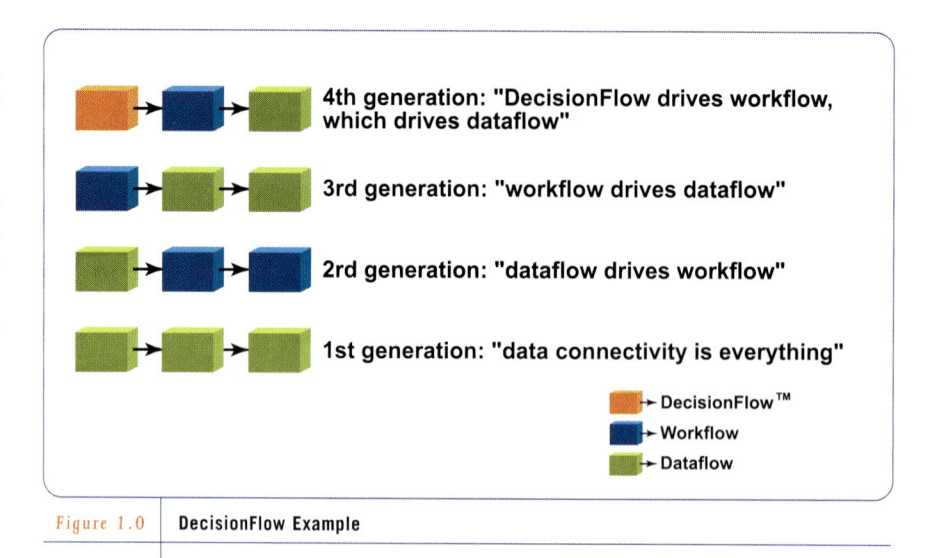

DecisionFlows

A DecisionFlow is a decision-support process that evaluates multiple courses of action, and then helps arrive at an optimal decision before committing to a specific course of action. Successful collaboration between members of an e-business trading community begins with interaction at the planning level in order to make optimal decisions. In a simple example, if a buyer orders two books from an electronic retailer, wouldn't it make sense to find out when the vendor can deliver the books before the buyer places his order? Correspondingly, the electronic retailer or seller should determine if it is going to make a reasonable profit on this order before it quotes the price. Both of these questions can be answered in a DecisionFlow.

By focusing on decision-making first and transactions second, a DecisionFlow integrates the decision and execution processes. This capability represents the next generation of thinking in e-business workflow management.

Figure 1.0 **DecisionFlow Example**

- 4th generation: "DecisionFlow drives workflow, which drives dataflow"
- 3rd generation: "workflow drives dataflow"
- 2rd generation: "dataflow drives workflow"
- 1st generation: "data connectivity is everything"

- DecisionFlow™
- Workflow
- Dataflow

"Portal-of-Portals"

Electronic commerce buyers are demanding access to worldwide Web sites. They are also requesting single-portal entry that allows them to use or view the content of other portals and marketplaces. Using the technology described above, users can seamlessly access and use data from other sites, while leveraging services in both their single-entry portal and other marketplaces.

For sellers, the "portal-of-portals" concept is even more important because it allows them to market and sell their products and services to multiple customers and prospects. This capability enables sellers to market and brand goods of other suppliers in a virtual organization. For example, a company may want to sell additional up-scale products to "wine connoisseurs" with the knowledge that the wine-consuming segment has a propensity to buy expensive consumables. With the "portal-of-portals" concept, this company can sell cars, computers, books, and even tailored vacations, in addition to providing content about vintages, wineries, and other information that appeals to the wine drinker.

In a business-to-business example, a commercial carpet manufacturer may want to position the company as a new office fulfillment company. In this scenario, the carpet maker not only provides the carpet and its installation services, but also the decoration, furniture, electrical services, and security services. Virtually any business can re-invent itself emphasizing its core competencies.

Process Excellence
To succeed in today's increasingly competitive global market, world-class companies are concentrating on achieving process excellence. At a high level, companies focus on three main processes:

- Supply Chain Excellence
- Customer Intimacy
- Product Life Cycle Excellence

Top companies are striving to excel in two or more of the process classifications. To achieve top performance levels, the companies need advanced solutions that manage not only each set of processes, but also any combination, in an integrated approach. Winning companies will benefit from revenue and profit growth, high customer service levels, and increased agility.

Supply Chain Excellence
The processes of buying, making, moving and selling products and services comprise supply chain planning. For this set of processes, companies need superior DecisionFlows and workflows that can leverage the available data, and in real time, maximize performance. These processes need to support:

- Collaborative Forecasting and Planning
- Supply Planning
- Distribution Planning
- Master Planning – including Profitability Planning
- Procurement
- Detailed Factory Planning
- Transportation Planning
- Demand-Supply Matching

The net benefits of Supply Chain Excellence have been well documented and include:

- Improved customer service
- Increased revenues
- Decreased inventories
- Decreased logistics costs
- Decreased manufacturing costs

Customer Intimacy
In order to achieve best-in-class customer intimacy, businesses need to support the four core processes:

- Attracting customer
- Matching customer needs
- Fulfilling customer needs
- Servicing customer needs

Advanced Customer Management (ACM) planning systems are used to evaluate customer buying trends. The findings are then used to develop targeted marketing programs aimed at attracting a particular customer set. Once customer relationships are established, CM helps tailor the products and services offered – increasing the probability of a sale, or potentially, an up-sale.

For all customers, and particularly those purchasing products from the Internet, fulfillment is vitally important to maintaining customer loyalty. CM solutions must provide real-time fulfillment planning, comprehending any constraints in a seller's supply chain. Finally, self-service and other customer care processes must be supported, ensuring customer loyalty and add-on sales. Who needs a CM solution? Certainly any company that wants to sell on the Internet, plus those firms with complex and dynamic sales and marketing channels.

Product Life Cycle Excellence
Product Life Cycle Management (PLM) solutions work by managing four basic processes:

- Strategic Product Management
- Resource Planning and Scheduling
- Design Optimization
- Product Transition Planning

PLM solutions direct the efforts of the Research and Development function to ensure that scarce resources are focused on efficiently producing new and innovative products. The first step is to match new ideas and projects to long-term, strategic business goals. Second, once projects are launched, it is essential that people and resources are coordinated with project requirements, including both design and trading partners. The third step includes providing designers with access to component design specifications and design part-

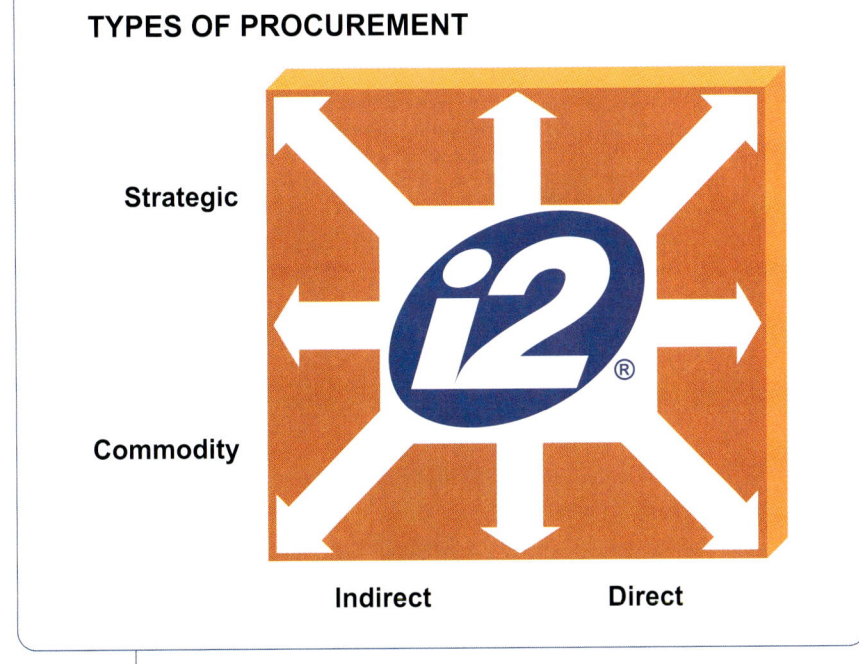

Figure 3.0 i2's procurement options

ners' resources. Next, product introduction planning takes place. This activity involves new product planning, along with the replacement of older products. The product life cycle process must be tightly integrated with the Supply Chain Management planning (SCM) processes. Finally, there is product phase-out period. During this time, the demand for any of the remaining product inventory may be significantly impacted.

What makes these PLM solutions unique? Like SCM and CM solutions, they are built with algorithms embedded into their DecisionFlows that help plan tasks and activities more effectively. Additionally, the collaborative planning flows, within the PLM solution, address needs across multiple organizations and companies.

Benefits of PLM solutions are:

- Reduced time-to-market for new products
- Unprofitable product development activities stopped earlier in the development cycle
- Better coordination between design partners resulting in higher quality
- Reduced design costs

Open Technology Framework

Technology, along with the companies developing and using new technologies, is changing at an ever-increasing pace. With this climate of constant change, information technology departments are looking for solutions that can be quickly implemented, provide on-going support, and link disparate vendor software in an open architecture, based on industry standards.

Summary

Some companies are finding ways of leveraging the Internet to speed up business processes. They are challenging their competition by inventing and executing new business paradigms. Based on the vast number of Internet-enabling software companies, how does a company find and integrate the right set of products to achieve competitive advantage? Additionally, how can a firm use these tools to make a profit, which is virtually unheard of in the Internet world?

The Promise of Value Chain Optimization

written by:
Ted Culotta
Electron Economy,
http://culotta.ASCET.com

There has been a tremendous amount of information disseminated within the past six months regarding how the Internet will change everything you do, if it has not done so already. The reality is that while the change effected by the Internet has been in the form of a truly enabling technology, it is still incredibly difficult for the average business executive to discern what all this change really means and how best to leverage it. There are a few basic tenets that all business executives must grasp or risk being overrun by better-adapted competitors.

Seller Beware

The first tenet is clearly the shift in the balance of power in the buyer-seller equation. Historically, large marketing organizations thought they knew better than the customer what the customer wanted – or at least that is the premise upon which they operated. Companies manufactured new items (or new and improved items) and pushed them through the channel, sometimes rather forcefully, to buyers who had little choice, but to buy them. What consumers desired was not the most important factor to the majority of these companies. What was important was what you were selling to those buyers. However, any marketing student can tell you, if you do not listen to your customers and sell what they want, you will be out of business very quickly. In a few years, buyers will hold all the cards (those that they do not already hold). Customers have little tolerance for problems and if problems do occur, they expect prompt and thorough resolution. Customers also expect choices in product categories. This has led to customization efforts on the part of those companies that are listening to their customers. The bar has been raised in every facet of customer expectations. Companies that do not realize this now are already on their way to extinction.

The central theme surrounding the buyer-seller shift in power is that buyers and sellers now have a tremendous amount of information at their disposal. Buyers use this information to find the products that they want, or, put another way, to bypass organizations who do not provide the exact products that they want. Effective selling organizations use it to provide the right products to their customers at the right time (remember this concept, as it will be revisited). The selling organizations that will survive are those who leverage the power of the Information Age to learn exactly what it is that their customers do want.

The good news is that the tools to accomplish this customer intimacy are available. There are a multitude of applications and services on the market today to assist companies in managing customer interactions, recording and accessing buying histories, and targeting customer needs based upon these interactions and buying histories. Companies can leverage technologies such as personalization, collaborative filtering, sales configuration, voiceover IP, and real-time support to serve their customers. Effective Customer Relationship Management (CRM) is no longer just a tool to enhance sales and marketing efforts; it is an absolute must for the continued success of any organization. Not knowing your customers is a guaranteed recipe for failure.

The shift in power to the customer has exposed one glaring problem in most business organizations: they are incapable of handling the demands placed upon them by a value chain driven by customers as opposed to the traditional marketing-driven chain. In the immediate future, this shift will be the major point of differentiation between those organizations that will thrive and add value to their customers and shareholders and those that will falter. Companies that are able to leverage the power of the Internet across their value chains will become the leaders within their industry cate-

Ted Culotta is a senior manager in product development at Electron Economy. Prior to joining Electron Economy, he worked in transportation and operations management at Ryder Integrated Logistics where he implemented and managed operations for such clients as Pacific Bell, Apple Computer, Hewlett-Packard, Acer, and Komag. He has also held positions at United Parcel Service and Airborne Express, and he is currently working on a book about railroad freight equipment constructed during WWII.

gories. The importance of good customer information provides companies with some of the raw materials for effective value chain management, but the actual work lies in other parts of the chain.

XML: Putting Everybody on the Same Web Page

One of the most important developments in the Internet era is the adoption of XML (Extensible Markup Language). XML promises to do for business communications all the things that EDI (Electronic Data Interchange) could do – plus many things it could not. EDI's deficiencies were many, but two key shortcomings led to its failure to be universally adopted. Its transaction-set standards were very rigid, requiring much customization by nearly each and every trading partner. This customization eliminated the benefits associated with a common communications tool. Customization made the exact transaction-set different among trading partners so that even the common denominators in EDI were "uncommon." The other major drawback was cost. Transactions had to be routed through Value Added Networks (VANs) before being sent on to the recipient of the message. VANs resulted in EDI being costly for all except the largest users. Due to the complexity of custom mapping for transaction sets and the high cost of sending messages, EDI was doomed from the outset to be a niche solution. However, the groundwork laid by EDI is what has enabled the "XML Revolution."

XML has conquered the drawbacks of EDI. In contrast to EDI's rigid transaction formats, the XML standard is extremely flexible in terms of formatting, which has made it infinitely easier for trading partners to adopt it for information exchange. Small trading partners without large IT departments can use XML as easily as Fortune 500 companies because of XML's flexibility. In addition, the cost of communication when using XML is markedly lower due to usage of the Internet as the communications vehicle, as opposed to VANs. XML's appearance on the business communications stage and its inherent advantages over EDI have fostered the ability for all trading partners to communicate across a value chain, not just those with large IT staffs and budgets.

The widespread adoption of XML has led to the most important change in the evolution of the value chain: integration, integration, and yet more integration. Integration is the first key to creating inter-enterprise value chains. Many of the software advancements made throughout the last decade have been enterprise-centric in their scope. They have helped companies manage their internal operations across multiple disciplines, such as human resources, finance, and manufacturing. The giant ERP implementations of the 1990s, such as SAP, Oracle, and PeopleSoft, have clearly revolutionized the way companies manage their internal operations. ERP packages assisted companies in taking the first steps toward value chain integration. Through EDI communications, firms were able to crudely link their systems with those of their largest and closest trading partners. Unfortunately, due to the constraints of EDI, companies that had invested in ERP solutions could not completely disseminate information to trading partners.

Enter XML. Within the past couple of years, an entire industry subset has developed around the need to integrate disparate systems, both internal and external. There has been a wave of new Enterprise Application Integration (EAI) providers to assist companies with the XML-based integration of their own internal ERP systems, as well as integration with trading partners' systems. XML is proving to be the perfect medium for these integration efforts.

To Get the Big Picture, You Need to See Every Detail

Companies are gaining an all-encompassing view of their operations. With the integration of ERP systems, sales and marketing information can be automatically transferred directly to the back-end systems that manage the operations of a company, such as manufacturing and procurement. Difficult tasks such as demand planning have been dramatically eased as an enterprise-wide view of all corporate functions is constructed.

While this enterprise-wide view has provided business executives with previously unavailable information for decision support, it remains an evolutionary, rather than revolutionary, step in the advancement of the concept of an inter-enterprise value chain. To ensure success, companies will need to create an integrated view of all the constituents that comprise their value chain, from the smallest raw materials suppliers to the point at which goods arrive at the end consumer, be it business or retail. The enablers for this inter-enterprise wide view are already in place and currently executing this task. They are many of the same EAI providers that integrated internal ERP systems.

The integration of an entire value chain represents the foundation for the revolution taking place in value chain management. Once all the partners in a value chain are integrated, the participants in the value chain have all the integral information they need for effective business decision-making. It may appear that companies have acquired all the necessary tools for decision-making capabilities across their value chains. However, simple integration is merely the enabler, not the solution.

Integration of all the partners in a value chain is not the silver bullet to all the objectives of today's business executives, such as higher inventory turns, build-to-order (BTO) or configure-to-order (CTO) sales channels, automatic procurement and replenishment, inventory-less manu-

---

Weblink

For more on decision support, see:
evans.ASCET.com
manheim.ASCET.com

For more on procurement, see:
evans.ASCET.com
fischer.ASCET.com

For more on the value chain, see:
uchneat.ASCET.com
reiter.ASCET.com

For more on value-added, see
prince.ASCET.com

facturing, and supply chain optimization, just to name a few. While all of these functions, and more, are improved by integration, they are not revolutionized. Essentially, integration alone represents the same state of affairs, just at a faster pace. There needs to be something else to drive true value into the value chain.

Value Chain Management: An Intelligent Framework Open to Everyone's Input

The revolution in Value Chain Management (VCM) will come not from integration, but intelligent execution based upon the enabling capabilities that integration provides. The giant leap forward will occur when firms take all the data available throughout a value chain and execute business processes using an intelligent system. Put differently, integration is really a messaging architecture to relay data about disparate trading partners in a value chain. The leap will come when intelligent business systems outside the value chain constituents' internal systems, but connected to the value chain, make decisions that optimize the entire value chain. This leap can be thought of as systems that optimize not the discrete enterprises or units within a value chain, but the entire value chain. Value Chain Optimization (VCO) enables dynamic, real-time execution across all participants to continually "tune" all operations.

The drivers of VCO will be the customers at the head of the chain. It will also be the goal of VCO to ensure that every customer demand is met. Each player in the value chain will be concerned with the happiness of the end customer. All players in the value chain will know who their real customers are, not just the next company in the chain to whom they ship their products. Only in this way can a truly customer-centric, responsive enterprise be constructed.

This new paradigm will require many companies to retool their thinking about their partners. Issues of trust will be important, but the consequences of isolationism are too great to prevent intimate value chain relationships. All sales information must be shared among all constituents in the value chain. This "perfect" visibility will elevate demand planning to previously unseen levels. Imagine how efficiently chains will operate when every supplier sees in real time how effectively the products to which they supplied components or materials are selling. Marketing, manufacturing, distribution, procurement, and a host of other functional areas will all operate in a dynamic environment of "perpetual optimization."

Perpetual Optimization

To enable this value chain optimized world, new applications will need to be deployed to handle these new tasks. At the highest level, an intelligent system must be in place to monitor all facets and functions of the value chain. New information from the sales end of the chain needs to be captured at point of sale and quickly integrated into the system and disseminated to all partners. Updates from all the trading partners about their operations must also be disseminated to the chain in real time. All of this information must be screened against the business rules for each partner, as well as for the business rules of the chain as a whole. These business rules will act as intelligent decision support mechanisms for the entire value chain. These rules will be applied and the value chain "re-calibrated" and re-optimized. This optimization will be occurring continuously, thereby ensuring that each participant in the chain is being directed to perform business tasks that optimize the entire value chain.

This intelligent system to manage the operations network will function like an enterprise-wide Decision Support System (DSS). Laid across the entire value chain is an intelligent business rules-based operations network, capable of fine-tuning and optimizing the entire chain, "on-the-fly" in real time. Each time a change is made to the network (for example, an order of components is complete or a shipment is delayed due to bad weather), that new status is communicated to the intelligent system which then adjusts operations to react to the change and notifies the affected parties' systems and the affected parties themselves, if necessary. As conditions change, business rules are modified in real time, either through the intelligent capabilities of the system or manually by a value chain partner, to reflect changes to operational processes. The result is a system that leverages the visibility provided by integration of partners, but layers it with capabilities to optimize all of the partners' activities to the benefit of the entire value chain and ultimately, to the value chain's end customers.

The Components of Collaboration

Below this inter-enterprise wide intelligent system, there will be systems to manage functions arising from the availability of data enabled by integration. Perhaps the greatest effect will be felt in the area of Collaborative Planning, Forecasting and Replenishment (CPFR). CPFR applications help to manage the integrated demand functions enabled by inter-enterprise integration. Broken down into its three core components, CPFR provides the following to a value chain: Collaborative Planning whereby the partners in a value chain combine their resources to map the future needs of the chain; Collaborative Forecasting where the partners in the chain forecast collectively to ensure that all constituents can be planning against the same targets, thereby dramatically improving the efficiency of the entire value chain; and Collaborative Replenishment, which takes the shared knowledge of the value chain to enable partners to replenish against more accurate forecasts and real-time consumption data. CPFR provides a means to integrate all partners in a value chain for the goal of a cooperative approach to forecasting business and keeping value chain operations lean. CPFR will eliminate the problems we have all witnessed where a poor marketing/demand projection is sent to partners, resulting in inefficiencies throughout the chain, such as too much or too little inventory. With the integration of effective real-time sales data throughout the value chain, CPFR leverages that sales data to continually help value chain partners refine business plans and operations. CPFR trims a tremendous amount of fat out of the supply chain by ensuring that all parties are operating to the same plan.

CPFR, in conjunction with the intelligent DSS capabilities of the network, will provide a new level of efficient resource allocation. Value chain partners can expect better information to furnish a host of benefits. Human resources can be more effectively scheduled and managed through far-improved information about manufacturing and operating schedules. Procurement can be effectively automated, both on an existing contract basis and through such enhancements as dynamic procurement using connections throughout the partners' own value chain and other connected value chains. Partners will also enjoy the ability to procure dynamically from the multitude of existing and future horizontal and vertical business-to-business (B2B) marketplaces. Use of transportation resources can be improved in several ways. Capacity can be scheduled more accurately in advance of its actual usage. Optimization can occur among many trading partners to collectively use resources and drive down unit transportation costs. The onerous task of managing carriers and paying bills can be automated throughout the network. Transportation moves will be visible to all partners, removing uncertainty. Financial transactions surrounding value chain activities can be conducted directly with partners, including financial services providers who will be a part of the network. These are a few examples of how VCO promises to deliver the dream of a truly collaborative network.

One question many business executives will face is what to do with their considerable investments in the previously mentioned ERP systems. Continue to leverage them. Much of the information delivered to the intelligent network will be enhanced by existing ERP systems before being disseminated to the value chain. The value of these ERP systems will not be diminished in any way. In fact, it will be enhanced by its inclusion in the value chain.

It's Not What the Technology Does – It's What It Does for You

How does a business executive begin to leverage the exciting opportunities that Value Chain Optimization affords? The first step is to conduct research. There are many, many solutions available in the marketplace today. However, the marketplace is in a true state of genesis. Analysts and the media often lump many companies into categories that misrepresent the true capabilities of a solution or provider. Due diligence is a must. It is of paramount importance to understand truly the business need that a solution or provider addresses (not necessarily what the technology will do). To identify business needs, a great deal of introspection is important for a company before any steps are taken to find a solution that addresses the business need(s). A company's understanding of its own business requirements should always be the precursor to any assessment of technology solutions. Technology enables business process management; business should not enable technology. Additionally, the solution itself must be examined, not the marketing message of the provider. The solutions are very complex technologies designed for very complex problems. The weight given to their research should be just as complex. The best advice is simple: research before executing.

Value Chain Optimization, when practiced effectively, will do what every company has been attempting to do since businesses were first invented: Deliver the right products, to the right place (or customer) at the right time at the right cost. Collaboration across an entire value chain, with an intelligent system to manage the constant flux of inter-enterprise operations, will deliver on this goal.

Copyright ® 2000 Electron Economy, Inc.

IMI – Global Fulfillment and Customer Service for E-Commerce

Industri-Matematik International

Industri-Matematik International (NASDQ: IMIC) is the leading provider of advanced Supply Chain Management solutions. The company specializes in pull-driven supply chain environments with complex logistics, information-rich, high-transaction volumes, and rigorous demands for customer responsiveness. This includes consumer goods, business equipment, and high-tech manufacturing, as well as large retail, wholesale distribution, and third party logistics providers.

Industri-Matematik has implemented applications worldwide at market-leading organizations such as British Airways, Campbell Soup, Canon, Carlton & United Breweries, Ericsson, Hartz Mountain, Kellogg's, Skyway Systems, Starbucks, and Warner/Electra/Atlantic.

Supply Chain Management in an E-Commerce World

E-commerce is setting higher standards for supply chain performance. Market leadership requires new levels of supply chain speed, collaboration, and customer responsiveness. Today, the Web front end alone is not enough. Fulfillment and customer service are now the defining factors in this new environment and they are differentiating those companies that win customers and profits and those that lose.

Vivaldi™ – Global Fulfillment and Customer Service for E-Commerce

Industri-Matematik's new VIVALDI™ suite of fulfillment and customer service applications provide the most advanced supply chain solutions available. Vivaldi combines best-of-class capabilities in advanced order management, supply chain execution, and customer relationship management to give organizations the unique ability to manage customers from the time they are acquired, through fulfillment, and into service and support. The result is truly sustainable competitive differentiation through increased supply chain speed, scalability, efficiency, customer responsiveness, and collaboration.

Zero Inventory and 100% Visibility

Vivaldi enables businesses to realize a vision of zero inventory and 100% visibility. Its applications bring inventories to their lowest possible levels by moving goods through the supply chain as quickly as possible, and provide maximum visibility with total, real-time information about the supply chain and customer needs. Vivaldi enables companies to deliver the right products to the right customers at the right time.

Strategic Alliances

Industri-Matematik's alliance partners provide complementary hardware, software, and implementation skills to maximize Vivaldi application performance and speed time to benefit. All partnerships are developed with the focus of providing superior business solutions for our clients. Recently, Industri-Matematik's global fulfillment and advanced order management capabilities were chosen by IBM for its Global Supply Chain Management initiative. This alliance will help companies increase the speed, service, and profitability of their supply chains as they move to e-business.

Additional information about Industri-Matematik can be found at the company Web site, www.im.se, or by calling 856.793.4400.

Contact Information

Stig Durlow
Chairman of the Board,
President, & Chief Executive Officer

Karl Asp
Treasurer and Chief Financial Officer

John P. Geraci Jr.
Senior Vice President,
Worldwide Sales & Marketing
and President Americas

Mats Lillienberg
Senior Vice President,
Product Development

Industri-Matematik
Corporate Headquarters
Box 15044
S-104 65 Stockholm, Sweden
Phone +46.8.676.5000
Fax +46.8.676.5010

Industri-Matematik
US Operational Headquarters
305 Fellowship Road
Suite #200
Mount Laurel, NJ 08054
Phone 856.793.4400
Fax 856.793.4401

http://www.im.se

Agile Software – Collaborative Manufacturing Commerce Success

Superior technology and good marketing will not rescue a product that arrives late in the high-stakes broadband marketplace, and Redback Networks has figured that out.

Introduction

Speed. Agility. Knowledge. These are the watchwords for success in today's intensely competitive business environment. Those who possess these attributes are re-writing the rules for doing business in the Internet Age. Those that do not are at increasing risk of watching their market share and margins plummet.

How are the winners succeeding? Companies like Redback Networks are embracing business processes and systems that directly connect them to their customers (demand chains) and their suppliers (supply chains) – facing outward, not inward. They are leveraging the skills, knowledge, and speed of their supply chain partners to:

- Bring products to market faster
- Respond faster to customers
- Avoid production problems related to inventory and materials
- Reduce inventory and production costs

Successful companies today work together with their supply chain partners, using their combined knowledge, to do things smarter and faster. To tie it all together, these companies are using the Internet to link their web of suppliers into a horizontally integrated manufacturing network that operates smarter and faster than the old vertically integrated manufacturers of the past.

The Impact on New Product Introduction

Nowhere is the trend to increase competitiveness through speed more apparent than the increasing pressures on the new product introduction (NPI) process, and time-to-market. Speed-based competition is driving shorter product life cycles as competitors strive to out-do each other and deliver the latest and greatest to the customer. It is driving an explosion of product variants and options in order to offer customers more configurability and choices than the competition. This quickly translates into intense pressure on the new product introduction process, the transition to volume production, and on product life cycle management. In short, get it done fast, but quality must not suffer, and keep costs under control.

Redback Networks is a case in point. Redback leveraged a virtual manufacturing model to take on industry giants like Nortel and Cisco Systems – and win!

0 to 60 in No Time: Redback Uses Agile Anywhere™

If you've ever fumed at delays while logging onto the Internet, or tapped your fingers while waiting for a multimedia message to download, you know about the urgent need for broadband access. Carriers, Multiple Service Operators (cable MSOs), Network Service Providers (NSPs) and Internet Service Providers (ISPs) are all scrambling to meet this demand from users large and small, in corporations and at home. The challenge for service providers is to prevent surging demand for broadband offerings from overloading their current backbone infrastructure, causing system-wide performance problems.

Redback Networks, Inc. (Nasdaq: RDBK) is an extraordinarily successful entrant into this market that has developed hardware/software solutions that quickly and economically expand broadband access. The company's Subscriber Management System™ (SMS) enables Carriers, MSOs, and NSPs to rapidly deploy broadband services to thousands of corporations, medium-

Contact Information

Bryan Stolle
CEO

Tom Shanahan
CFO

Carol Schrader
Vice President of Marketing

Ken Coulter
Senior Vice President of Worldwide Field Operations

Agile Software Corporation
One Almaden Blvd.
San Jose, CA 95113
Phone 408.975.3900
Fax 408.271.4862
Info@agilesoft.com
www.agilesoft.com

Products

Agile Anywhere™ product suite allows supply chains partners to form virtual manufacturing networks for product introduction, manufacture, and change.

Agile Buyer™ enables online procurement of direct materials, demand aggregation, and automated Web-based RFQ processes.

and small-sized businesses, home workers, and residential subscribers. Redback gives service providers a competitive edge by allowing them to be first with high-speed-access offerings. Arriving first is critical because it locks in subscribers, opens revenue streams, and paves the way for introduction of more lucrative, value-added services down the road. And arriving first in this market has fueled Redback's successful 1999 IPO, and its subsequent merger with Siara Systems.

A High-Stakes Race – To Be First

Like its major customers, Redback Networks is also involved in a high-stakes race. By being the first-to-market with top quality solutions, Redback can lock in market share, create loyalty and open huge opportunities for growth. Unfortunately, the equation also works in reverse. Superior technology and good marketing will not rescue a product that arrives late due to production delays or quality concerns.

"As the vice president of operations here at Redback," said Sean Laskey, "I needed to bring extremely high quality product to market extremely quickly. To compete with people already established in the industry, I needed to come right out of the gate looking like a big company. I chose Agile Software as one of my primary partners because it allows me to run my outsourcing operations seamlessly; to change products very quickly, or on the fly; to communicate those changes to my suppliers via the Web; and ultimately to ship high quality product to our installed customer base in a short period of time."

Scalability was another important reason for choosing Agile. Redback execs knew that proper execution of their strategy could lead to explosive growth and did not want to put themselves in the straightjacket of an inflexible business system.

"I have a comfort level that Agile can scale with me as I grow," said Laskey. "I can get into it as a five-person company and have essentially the same product that a 1000-person company would use, at a price that scales to the startup and works its way up to the larger users. You can have Agile up and running within a couple of days at the startup stage. Then, as you grow from small to medium to very large, you add users and complexity but you never have to uproot your operations. That's a huge advantage because when an operations group has to stop and uproot a software system, you lose months of efficiency."

Tight communication and collaboration with outsourced suppliers and independent distributors is essential to Redback's success. Feedback from these sources has enthusiastically validated the decision to use Agile Anywhere. "There's been a lot of excitement, both internally

For outsourced manufacturing operations to succeed, supply chain partners must collaborate on product content management.

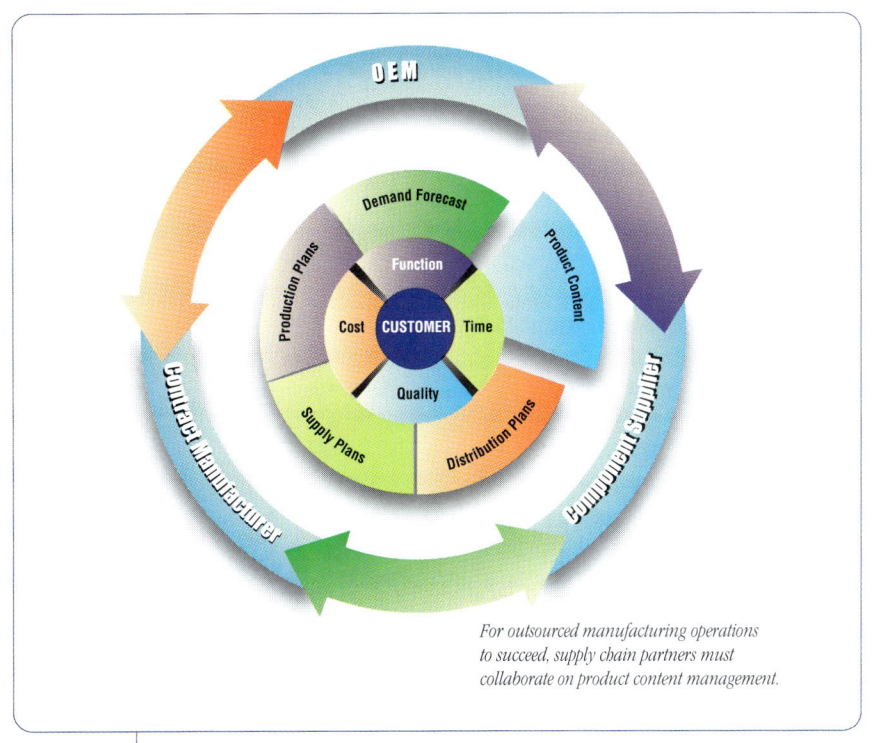

Figure 1.0   **Supply chain collaboration requires product content management**

and externally," said Laskey. "We're hearing extreme satisfaction on the part of our outsourced suppliers. When they need a product specification through a Bill Of Materials (BOM) or an Approved Vendor List (AVL), or just about any other Redback-related data, they can grab it off the Internet in an incredibly short time, and have precisely the same data that we're using within our four walls. It really cuts down on the faxes and phone calls and helps our suppliers feel that they're actually a part of Redback."

And has Redback come "right out of the gate looking like a big company," as Laskey put it? Stock prices aside (Redback has sustained terrific market confidence since its IPO), it would seem so. *Fortune Magazine* (July 19, 1999) wrote: "Redback beat Cisco to market by almost a year, and Nortel Networks' product is still not out." Not bad company to keep – or beat.

http://agile.ASCET.com   145

solution provider

web link — http://logility.ASCET.com

Logility – Turning True Collaboration into Business Value

To ensure competitive advantage, organizations must find more advanced ways to communicate and streamline business processes over the Internet. Logility has long recognized the revolutionary value of the Internet and has quickly emerged as an innovator in Web-based products to create greater efficiencies throughout the value chain. In 1996, Logility introduced the first Web-based value chain product, the award-winning Demand Chain Voyager, in tandem with Heineken USA.

The leading supplier of business-to-business (B2B) collaborative value chain solutions via the Internet, Logility is a driving force in transforming the way companies conduct business.

Logility's comprehensive B2B solutions provide easy-to-use, end-to-end, Internet-based Value Chain Management (VCM) solutions to conduct a broad range of business processes.

Logility Voyager Solutions™

Logility Voyager Solutions are integrated, Internet-based VCM solutions that help manufacturers, distributors, and retailers synchronize demand with supply.

i-Commerce Collaboration Solutions

Logility Voyager XPS™ and other Internet-based solutions enable our customers to collaborate with trading partners. Voyager XPS is designed to facilitate Collaborative Planning, Forecasting and Replenishment (CPFR) via the Internet. There is clearly tremendous opportunity for generating value through CPFR for Logility customers; in fact, many early adopters of CPFR concepts are already reaping benefits such as:

- Reduced cycle time
- Decrease in forecast error
- Inventory reduction
- Increase in fill rates
- Increased revenue

i-Community

i-Community is a Logility-hosted Web-based collaborative network of trading partners established to offer a more effective means for seamless exchange of information utilizing Voyager XPS. The Logility i-Community allows organizations to collaborate regarding forecasts and replenishment plans with trading partners over the Internet.

i-Connection℠

i-Connection is an integrated application hosting services and applications management to provide an alternative solution for companies that prefer to have Logility host their VCM applications.

Express ROI™

Express ROI is our strategy for ensuring our customer's complete satisfaction – and continued success – also includes a commitment to responsive, total support. This proven program maximizes the value of their Logility solution in the shortest time possible by capitalizing on the industry's fastest return on investment. We also provide 24-hour response line assistance and Web-based support as well as industry and product specific education.

Logility Clients

Logility's customers include ConAgra, Eastman Chemical Company, Heineken USA, Pharmacia & Upjohn, Reynolds Metals, Sony Electronics, Timex, and VF Corp.

Contact Information

J. Michael Edenfield
Chief Executive Officer, President and Director

Larry R. Olin
Vice President – Sales

Donald L. Thomas
Vice President – Customer Service

Andrew G. White
Vice President – Product Strategy

Logility
470 East Paces Ferry Road, NE
Atlanta, GA 30305
Phone 800.762.5207
Fax 404.264.5206
ask@logility.com
www.logility.com

Next Generation Supply Chain Strategic Planning Technology and Applications

What is supply chain strategic planning? It's not execution, and it's not re-engineering. It is strategic decision-making and business-planning by forward-thinking companies. Operational supply chain strategy remains the weak link in the market, mainly due to the degree of difficulty involved in using sophisticated models and complicated algorithms. In the future, we will see the application and integration of powerful new models to produce a whole new class of supply chain strategic planning suites. All the while, supply chain planning will grow and merge with the IT-based, demand planning-focused solutions.

Introduction

Nearly two years after the publication of my series, "The Manager's Guide to Supply Chain Planning Tools and Techniques," things are as confusing as ever. If my stated goal was to help people understand how the different supply chain planning tools and techniques fit together, to contribute in some small measure to the overall level and quality of supply chain knowledge and competency, then I failed miserably. It remains a challenge for even the supply chain planning gurus themselves to sort through all the breathtakingly ambiguous pronouncements about "we can optimize your supply chain" and "your passport to world class supply chains" that are trumpeted without embarrassment across hundreds of Web sites and thousands of sales brochures.

Since neurotic obsession is an integral cycling phase of every aspiring software developer's psychological Carnot cycle, I must refuse to give up. This white paper will attempt to make some small progress in seeing both the "forest for the trees" and the real business issues for the software tools. What's more, we must identify what part of the forest we are going to be operating in, as it's a wide world of simulated firs and optimized evergreens out there. Our approach, therefore, must be to identify the parts of the forest in which we will *not* be camping, before setting out on our orientation hike in our own neck of the woods.

Our neck of the woods happens to be supply chain strategic planning. It is not "execution" or planning in general, and definitely not "supply chain reengineering," but instead, decision-making and business-planning problems considered strategic by the companies that deal with them.

Objectives and Agenda

We will begin by exploring the current state of supply chain planning and improvement thinking. What are the "strategic" supply chain planning questions? What are the main approaches used by consultants to answer these questions? How are process-based and operational-based approaches different?

Next we will discuss a methodology for integrating the use of the most advanced problem solving tools for our neck of the woods: strategic decision making. Supply chain strategic planning questions often require multiple techniques to get at the best answer. We will dive into some good detail about how these tools work, what they do, and what they don't do.

Finally, we will highlight examples from several companies, to show you how the thought leaders in this area are putting these technologies into practice. We have a lot of ground to cover, but it will be worth the journey!

Here's a disclosure note: You need to know that the company I work for, LLama-Soft, is one of the vendors with tools cited in this article.

Donald A. Hicks is President and Chief Executive Officer of Provo, Utah based LLama-Soft, Inc..

http://hicks.ASCET.com

Hopefully, it will become apparent that this report has not been written as a sales-oriented or promotional article, but rather as an educational piece that attempts to clarify and elucidate, rather than to color and obfuscate. Obviously, we believe we provide an important missing piece in the supply chain strategic planning market. However we are kept honest by the fact that LLama-Soft is not the only answer, and indeed, can't provide the answer to every single problem in this extremely important and diverse area.

What are Supply Chain Strategic Planning Problems?

Every company that manufactures, distributes, transports, or stores inventory to sell to customers has to make many, many decisions about how its operations will run. An office products company, assuming that it is already currently in business, must decide each day what will be produced on Line 2, Plant 1. It must decide how much of each product, and in what sequence. Another company is grappling every day with how many widgets to pull out of inventory and put on the truck to Cleveland. Companies make millions of these decisions every day. They are important, but they assume that very little in the overall situation can change. This makes them "operational" decisions.

Other, higher-level decisions, don't make the same kind of assumptions. If you free up the decisions, if you let the inventory target for SKU AG001011 target change, or if you can select to ship from one of several warehouses by different modes of shipment, then you are dealing with tactical decisions. Tactical decisions assume that core structural components of the network, such as products and sites, are fixed, but how the components interact, and the rules for interaction that the sites follow, are allowed to change.

Finally, for strategic planning decisions, anything can change – except, of course, the external demand market. The goal of strategic planning is to arrive at the most efficient, highly profitable supply chain system that serves customers in a market.

Of the three types of decisions (all of which overlap with the other two), supply chain strategic decisions involve the largest capital expenditures, the biggest risks, and, if made poorly, the most dire results. Strategic supply chain decisions often pose such significant questions as:

- How many plants and warehouses should I own?
- Should I close any of them?
- Should I stock inventory? For which products? In which locations?
- Should I outsource the task of transporting goods throughout my network?
- Should I make the key subassemblies, or purchase them? From where?

As you can see, from strategic decisions all else flows. Can you truly optimize the production schedule at the Detroit plant if you don't even know whether you should manufacture products in the U.S.? Can you seek optimal safety stock levels while deciding whether inventory should exist?

It's a little – no, it's a lot – like making sure your boat crew is moving your craft as fast as possible, without bothering to check which direction you are pointed in.

Two Paradigms to Supply Chain Strategy

Technology vendors are making the situation worse. Promises to optimize and improve your supply chain without analyzing and understanding the supply chain's complexities and dynamics at best rely on chance, and at worst border perilously on fraud.

I dare you to do a Web search on supply chain optimization. You will find IBM promising "Supply Chain Optimization" by Web-enabling your enterprise, a book from CSC Consulting on supply chain optimization, and i2 and Manugistics offering "solutions" that optimize your supply chain. Are these guys speaking the same language?

Actually, they're not! All of these companies, and the many others you will find, all do something different. Most of them do what they do extremely well. Most of them truly can help improve various aspects of supply chain performance. None of them do everything, and if they tell you they do and you believe them, call me immediately – I've got some beautiful beachfront Utah property to sell you.

To understand where all of these companies are coming from, you must understand where they have been. Over the last few years, supply chain vendors and supply chain ideas have evolved into two camps, or tribes: the IT Tribe and the Logistics Tribe.

The IT Tribe

The larger tribe is the IT Tribe. Members of this tribe believe that information is the key to supply chain improvement. They focus on collaborative planning, sharing information, and getting companies synchronized with their suppliers and their customers. They also focus on getting internal departments and divisions synchronized so that they can be centrally controlled and coordinated. This tribe is incredibly good at marketing.

The Logistics Tribe

The smaller, more ancient tribe, is the Logistics Tribe. The Logistics Tribe focuses on applying high-powered numerical analysis to large data sets to solve huge planning problems through analysis and optimization. The Logistics Tribe has been around for several decades, and knows a lot about things like industrial engineering, logistics, and operations research. This tribe is incredibly bad at marketing.

Weblink

For more strategic planning, see:
manheim.ASCET.com
sprague.ASCET.com
appell.ASCET.com
anderson-d.ASCET.com

For more on Optimization, see:
reiter.ASCET.com
culotta.ASCET.com
enslow.ASCET.com
prince.ASCET.com

Perhaps surprisingly, both tribes are right in their core theses. Both tribes have a lot to offer the modern enterprise. I find it useful to differentiate between the two tribes by how they orient their focus on the enterprise: the IT Tribe has an external focus, keying in on interactions with other enterprises, while the Logistics Tribe has an internal focus, and hones in on operations within the enterprise itself.

You can also differentiate the two Tribes by skin color, if you wish. The typical Logistics Tribe member looks a little pale and is comfortable with 1950s fluorescent industrial lighting technology. He or she rarely leaves the building. The typical IT Tribe member just got back from vacationing on St. Thomas before leaving for training in Germany or the Netherlands.

The point here, and there is one, is that the two tribes of supply chain improvement are both essential and complementary. A company that is looking for improvement dollars by coordinating their production schedules with their customers will likely find dollars. The company that is seeking to trim yen outlays by increasing manufacturing flexibility and optimizing their distribution network cost structure will probably be able to do so. The most powerful approach, and the approach that will be the standard in the future, is to leverage the external and the internal focused efforts, to make the two tribes work together.

Strategic Decision-Making: Qualitative vs. Quantitative Orientations

Now that we understand the lay of the land, and the strange native peoples that inhabit that land, let's start to focus back in on the strategic planning issues.

We have already talked about supply chain strategic planning problems, and pointed out that they were the most important, biggest dollar (and hence highest risk) problems facing companies. We also discussed the two tribes' approaches to solving them. An important implication, which I want to state explicitly, is that strategic planning problems are also the most difficult to analyze and solve rationally.

It is often the case that high-level discussions of supply chain strategy are completely devoid of facts. High-level decisions about how to organize company operations and logistics end up being a forum for political gaming and salesmanship, with outcomes decided by personal charisma and volume, rather than rationality and science.

It's no wonder that supply chain strategy often boils down to who has the biggest gun. Supply chain strategic problems have been nearly impossible to model and analyze rationally. The problems involve huge data sets, with complex data interrelationships and a great deal of uncertainty. There is no single computational approach simply to "solve" a strategic planning problem, which leaves a void. Non-quantitative or "soft" arguments can win on the gray battlefield of murky logic and guesswork.

Imagine that instead of discussing how to improve global supply chain strategy, company executives were discussing, say, global weather patterns. The engineering-minded folks would bring up their computer models, talk about butterflies over the Sea of Japan, and the need to model individual air molecules. The non-technical folks would argue that the weather has "always worked this way" and that "I've been in the weather business for 20 years, and I know how the weather operates." Let's face it, when fact vacates the discussion, everyone left arguing sounds like a yapping poodle or a silly clown.

The Next Generation: Operational Strategy

This problem is common to many companies across many industries. The need is present for tools and technologies that can help move the discussion into a fact-based approach. The tools and techniques that perform this function are, in fact, the next generation of supply chain software applications. These tools will leverage the data provided by IT, but will use powerful engineering and operations research algorithms to move supply chain strategic planning decisions into an orientation I call Operational Supply Chain Strategy.

Increasingly, the IT Tribe will pose supply chain strategy questions that must be answered using Operational Strategy approaches. Take the case of a global merger between two large companies. The wizards in the CFO's office determine that the merger is good business and makes sense financially. IT is brought in to "integrate the supply chains."

Historically, the result would be a fixation on linking ERP systems, a project that aligns and combines corporate databases with little or no thought to how the actual supply chain operations of the new combined company can be improved. Simply linking IT systems will not provide the cost-cutting measures or efficiency improvements that the CFO is looking for. The architects of the merger must analyze and arrive at an operational strategy for the new company, based on the physical reality of the business.

There are many reasons why Operational Strategy and real operational improvement are not part of the typical IT reengineering effort or ERP implementation today. One is the issue of tribal affiliation raised earlier. Another is the fact that these IT-based projects are so complex and sweeping, an attitude gets promoted that "we should just get the system in place, then figure what to do with it." While this attitude is understandable, the problem is that it is the operational changes that will provide the ROI promised by the IT project in the first place! This is why many companies implement ERP or supply chain planning software packages looking for an ROI that doesn't materialize. Automating a process doesn't improve it, but just makes it automated.

Real improvement comes from making a change to the way business gets done, both from a process standpoint and from an operational standpoint.

Introduction to Operational Strategy

The operational strategy to supply chain strategic planning can, from a macro-level, be thought as a four-step process. Remember that in strategic planning

http://hicks.ASCET.com

almost anything goes; therefore, we have to start from the few things that can't be changed, the most important thing being, of course, customer demand.

From customer demand, we need to go through four different steps or phases to analyze and make the big decisions. The four phases are network optimization, network simulation, policy optimization, and design for robustness.

Network Optimization

From customer demands, we need to decide on the basic structure of the network. Which sites will be included (out of the hundred of candidate site locations) and who will supply whom? What is the fundamental network configuration that will best minimize the total cost of servicing the demands (which we can't really control, but which we can better manage through our external collaboration improvement efforts)? The task of structural design means being able to evaluate millions and millions of potential structures, and selecting the single least cost network.

This is exactly what "network optimization models" do very well. Utilizing huge math models and highly advanced solution-finding technologies, network optimization tools have been widely used for strategic planning. The leading vendors are companies such as INSIGHT, Intertrans (now part of i2), and CAPS Logistics (now part of Baan).

Network Simulation

The problem with network optimization is that in order to evaluate millions of models the models are greatly simplified to basically cost-focused math models. When it comes to finalizing the proposed design, or selecting which network design is best out of the three or four alternative designs, we need to better predict how each design will really operate in the real world. For this we use "network simulation." Network simulation uses a very detailed and complicated model which will tell you how well a proposed supply chain will run, but will not tell you how to change it to make it better.

There are many vendors who provide "general discrete event simulation" modeling tools that can be used to build these complicated models. Additionally, a new class of "supply chain simulator" tools is emerging. These supply chain simulators are specific to supply chain problems and are usually based on an existing modeling platform. LLama-Soft, Inc., with through its tool "Supply Chain Guru," provides, at this time, the only fully "off-the-shelf" application of this kind, but there are several others tools likely to be released and marketed in the next few years.

Policy Optimization

Once a network design is finalized, and the sites and products are set in place, the task is to come up with the best "operating rules" or policies for the supply chain structural objects to follow. Policies include rules about whether inventory should be kept for various products, whether full truckload shipments suffice, or whether LTL shipments are needed to achieve the necessary customer service; should we make or should we buy for each of our products and main sub-assemblies?

Policy optimization is a very difficult task, and there are currently no tools that are both detailed enough to predict network performance and intelligent enough to prescribe what policies to use. There are really two main technologies available that come close. First, there are network optimization models that apply multi-time period analysis or more detailed production planning constraints. Second, and more promising, are those tools that apply optimization or goal-seeking methods to simulation models, to attempt to prescribe how the simulation model can best be improved. Eventually, even higher level intelligent design tools will apply combinations of simulation and optimization models in tandem to truly design how networks should be designed and how they should operate.

Design for Robustness

The fourth phase of supply chain strategic planning is the geekily named "Design for Robustness." Basically, for the first three phases of operational strategic planning, we have focused our efforts on designing the best supply chain based on what we expected to happen. In design for robustness, we attempt to evaluate if there are things that might happen, to ensure that our network doesn't perform poorly under "other than expected" conditions.

This is a difficult concept for most people to grasp. Think of it this way: the goal of supply chain management is not just to be profitable — there is an implicit goal to avoid extremely bad performance even under conditions that are unlikely but possible. Optimal supply chain designs, arrived at through the first three phases, often tell us to close warehouses, or move plants, or to make other "big ticket item" changes. What if we were wrong about demand? What if the cost of supply doubles? What seemed like a good idea given our forecasted conditions may kill us under other conditions.

It leads us to the paradox: optimal answers are not necessary the best answers. Our job is not only to succeed, but also to avoid failure. This fourth step is the most difficult to grasp because it forces us to consider unpleasant possibilities and unplanned events. However, it is exactly a "robustly designed" supply chain that will ensure your company's survival under nearly any circumstance.

One Final Note on the Four-Step Methodology

Rarely will a company go from phase to phase completely. Rather, most companies already have a network structure they wish to modify, as opposed to starting with a complete "blank sheet of paper." Sometimes many of the policies are fixed, but we want to do contingency planning. Perhaps we need to identify whether our current structure can handle what we expect to happen, but if "that other thing" happens, what will the new optimal structure be? Strategic planning, at its core, cannot simply be "automated." Since the context and the problem are so completely intertwined, you can never take the man out of the loop — and that is exactly what makes strategic decisions so difficult to make properly.

i2 Technologies – Leading the Way with Intelligent B2B Supply Chain Solutions

i2 Technologies is the world's leading Marketplace Service Provider (MSP). As such, i2 develops, sells, deploys, runs, and maintains electronic marketplaces for the Business-to-Business (B2B) and Business-to-Consumer (B2C) environments. i2's MSP offering is based on its TradeMatrix technology which provides the necessary services, content, infrastructure, and operational partners required to implement an efficient eMarketplace. i2 is clearly differentiated for the following reasons:

- Breadth of services – i2 offers a complete set of services including direct and indirect procurement that allows clients to create a complete eMarketplace solution.
- Marketplace-to-Marketplace Capability (M2M) – i2 allows clients to utilize the offerings of multiple marketplaces
- Physical execution capability
- i2's rich heritage in supply chain - the core of any marketplace is the optimization of the supply chain. i2 is the leader in this space having produced $7.5 billion worth of value for its clients in 1999. i2's products are used to plan, manage, and optimize $3 trillion worth of goods worldwide.

i2 Technologies is the leading provider of B2B intelligent business solutions based on its TradeMatrix electronic marketplace solutions and electronic Business Process Optimization (e-BPO) solutions, including software for global supply chain management. i2's RHYTHM family of products provides comprehensive, intelligent support for planning and scheduling functions across both inter-enterprise and intra-enterprise supply chains. Based on intelligent concepts such as constraint management and concurrent planning, the RHYTHM solution essentially provides a framework that allows truly integrated, near real-time Supply Chain Management by ensuring that all functions work together simultaneously rather than in a sequential, iterative manner.

i2's solutions encompass the total supply chain and are fully integrated. They provide plans that span the entire scope of planning from strategic plans through tactical and operational plans to execution scheduling. As the planning horizon gets shorter, the granularity of data and the number of constraints to be managed increase, while the plans created become more and more detailed. The i2 Planning Funnel (below) is a representation of planning levels and activities mapped over time, ranging from strategic decisions that encompass a longer time horizon, to scheduling and execution decisions that are considered near-term.

TradeMatrix

TradeMatrix is the only electronic marketplace that can bring all elements of indirect and direct procurement and collaboration together as an integrated, holistic set of services. TradeMatrix is uniquely able to bring these services together through a consortium of best-in-class partners who have a common interest in bringing game-changing value to customers. Available with a common, personalized, thin client user interface, TradeMatrix quickly delivers a new paradigm to business. TradeMatrix's design is based on i2's secure and robust DecisionFlows and workflows, incorporating intelligent planning algorithms. The net result is sustainable, maximized profitability levels for TradeMatrix participants.

TradeMatrix is an electronic marketplace that can offer a community of vertical and horizontal services that enable effective and efficient trading. These services would include services for buyers, sellers, and third party providers. Core capabilities enable e-procurement, collabo-

Contact Information

Supply Chain Planning and Optimization Officers

Sanjiv S. Sidhu
Chairman of the Board
Chief Executive Officer

Gregory A. Brady
President, Worldwide Operations

Pallab Chaterjee
COO

Bill Beecher
Vice President and Chief Financial Officer

For more information, contact
Paul O'Brien
Director, Global Alliances
Phone 781.329.3416
paul_obrien@i2.com

i2 Technologies, Inc.
One i2 Place
11701 Luna Road
Irving, TX 75234
Phone 469.357.1000
Toll Free 800.800.3288

info@i2.com
www.i2.com

Case Study: Improved Visibility at Toshiba Corporation

Company Background
Toshiba Corporation produces portable computers, semiconductors, and computer peripherals such as CD-ROM drives and hard-disk drives. In fiscal year 1996, ended March 31, 1997, Toshiba Corporation posted sales of $43,979 billion. The company employs 186,000 worldwide.

Production Characteristics
Toshiba experiences highly volatile market demand, limiting the company's ability to effectively rely on forecasts. In addition, competitive pressures were forcing Toshiba to establish a strategic initiative to plan its sales operations using a supply chain management approach.

Toshiba's Challenges
Toshiba's market conditions required the company to quickly recognize how changes in supply affect existing product allocations and customer order commitments. The balance of supply and demand must be continually monitored to ensure that the manufacturing facilities are producing the right product in the right quantities at the right time to meet commitments.

Why i2?
Based on the company's challenges and an intense review of supply chain management solutions, Toshiba chose i2's RHYTHM® supply chain management solution because of its ability to quickly determine how a change in supply affects existing supply allocations and customer orders. i2's intelligent allocation and Available-to-Promise delivery date calculation capabilities were also important factors in Toshiba's decision to implement

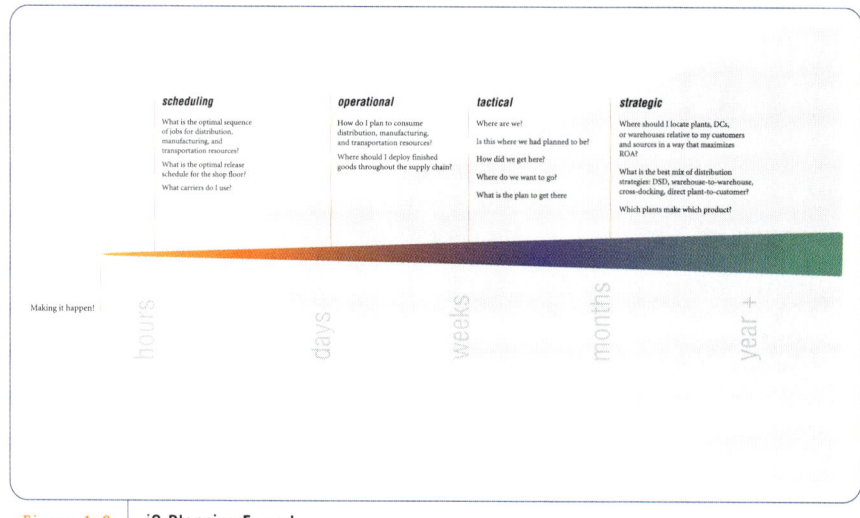

Figure 1.0   i2 Planning Funnel

ration, fulfillment, customer care, retail, planning, product development, and content.

TradeMatrix marketplaces already launched are:

- Hightechmatrix
- Myaircraft.com
- Softgoods.com
- Frieghtmatrix.com

e-BPO
i2 is the recognized leader in supply chain planning and optimization, with more than 10 years of experience in optimizing business processes. i2's RHYTHM solution for e-BPO, which focuses on optimizing and integrating business processes across the enterprise while driving intelligent collaboration with trading partners, builds on i2's proven capabilities.

E-BPO offers the forward visibility, intelligence, and rapid execution required for high-velocity business. Velocity in business means combining intelligence and rapid execution to outpace the competition. To achieve high-velocity business, companies must address some critical questions including:
- How can I increase the velocity in my supply chain to achieve industry-leading cycle times and customer service levels?
- Can I make, deliver, and service the product I'm about to launch better than anyone else in my industry?
- Are my sales, marketing, and customer service organizations optimized to achieve maximum marketing presence and customer satisfaction levels?
- How can I balance resource requirements across my core business processes to maximize company-wide profitability?
- What long-term human, financial, and physical resources are required for me to dominate a new market?

The high-velocity enterprise delivers the right product or service at the right time, while making rapid course corrections as needed, thereby achieving maximum market share and profitability.

The e-BPO solution is distinctly different from transaction systems. e-BPO is a new category of software that enables multi-enterprise optimization, while powering e-business initiatives such as collaboration with suppliers, partners, and customers.

E-BPO maximizes a company's operational velocity by integrating and optimizing the five key business processes: Supply Chain Management, Product Lifecycle Management, Customer Management, InterProcess Planning, and Strategic Planning. In addition, e-BPO features a unique architecture that helps an enterprise interact with its suppliers and customers with more efficiency and

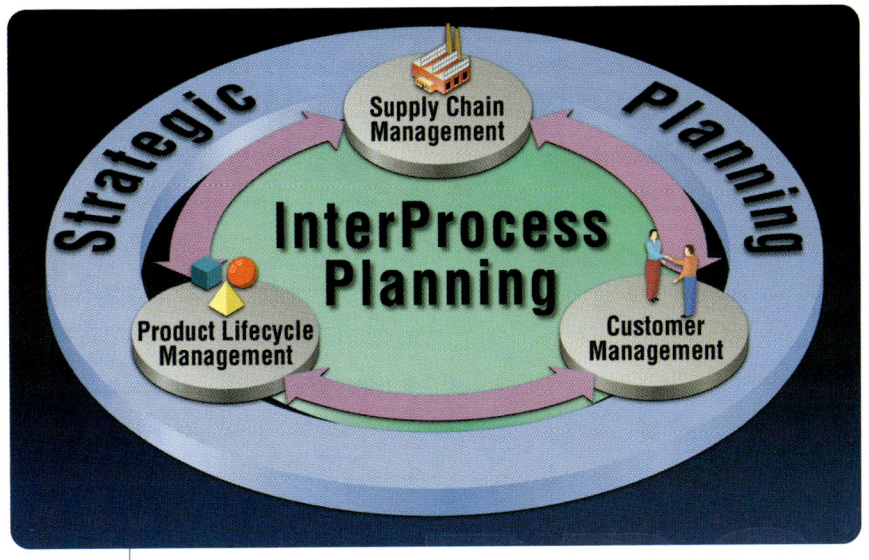

Figure 2.0 — Forward visiblity, complete integration, and high-performance Supply Chain colutions from i2

responsiveness than ever before, connecting them to the business planning and execution processes.

E-BPO represents next-generation e-business through the integration of Web front-end applications with back-end business optimization. e-BPO is the only solution that leverages the power of advanced planning engines and the Internet to optimize and integrate all core processes across the enterprise.

Industry Focused Solutions

i2 offers extensive industry experience developing and implementing e-BPO solutions. We have put our comprehensive domain experience to use developing industry-specific solutions that focus on the key business drivers that determine success in a particular industry. By knowing which performance metrics each customer must improve to achieve "best-in-industry" results, we can deliver a highly focused solution set to give our customer maximum competitive advantage – quickly.

i2 is organized into industry groups that are responsible for the development and delivery of focused e-BPO solutions for specific industries. Some of our target markets include high-tech/electronics, semiconductors, consumer durables, retail, industrial products, metals/paper, textiles/apparel, automotive, chemical, oil/gas, and pharmaceuticals.

Strategic Alliances

At i2, we believe that successful customers and successful partners make a great company. i2's Alliance Program exists to enable the success of our customers by facilitating the implementation of high value solutions, and the integration of i2 software with other key strategic solutions. The alliance program accrues significant benefits to our customers by facilitating mutually beneficial relationships. i2's alliance partners include ERP vendors, consulting companies and system integrators, platform providers, and complementary software providers.

RHYTHM.

RHYTHM's Contributions

With RHYTHM, Toshiba made several important changes in its demand management process, including a flattening of the allocation process to eliminate intermediate service organizations. Now, orders from dealers, overseas subsidiaries, and customers come directly into Toshiba's headquarters for fulfillment – thus reducing the order's planning cycle time. Toshiba is working to reduce its monthly planning cycle time from 27 days for domestic production and 18 days for overseas producion.

Toshiba's Results

RHYTHM enables Toshiba to provide an accurate delivery date for every purchase order, so dealers can provide more reliable customer service. Toshiba's planning cycle time has been reduced by 66%. And RHYTHM's ability to provide immediate visibility into the impact of changes in supply on Toshiba's entire operations has greatly improved the company's ability to capitalize on changing market conditions.

http://i2technologies.ASCET.com

3.0 Industry Perspectives

Gaining Insight From Industry Leaders

Increasing shareholder value defines success. Finding and creating opportunities that accomplish this is the pursuit of every executive, and the supply chain offers fertile ground in which to harvest such prospects. Reinvention of the supply chain is often a necessary step in reaching the promise of reduced cost, increased asset productivity, and competitive advantage. Fortunately, this is a journey that can be successfully navigated through numerous paths, and the specific business models, processes, and tools available to stay the course vary from industry to industry.

All vertical markets are focused on integrating, extending, and enhancing their supply chains. In recognition of this fact, the following section considers the Internet-enabled supply chain from the perspective of a number of industries – automotive and transportation, chemicals, consumer goods, electronics and high tech, energy, media and entertainment, and retail – each highlighting the subtleties of Supply Chain Management unique to their business environment. From online trading networks in the electronics industry to strategies for online retail fulfillment to the impact of e-commerce on the chemicals industry, the articles that follow represent the experience and focused consideration of industry experts on the strategies and actions necessary to thrive in a particular market setting.

> *All vertical markets are focused on integrating, extending, and enhancing their supply chains. The following section considers the Internet-enabled supply chain from the perspective of a number of industries . . . highlighting the subtleties of Supply Chain Management unique to their business environment.*

# The Future of Automotive Supply Chain: An Interview with Jeff Trimmer

DaimlerChrysler is taking advantage of its recent merger to improve its supply chain, even as globalization and a marriage of resources on two continents push the envelope of traditional Supply Chain Management. DaimlerChrysler and its suppliers are relying on new technologies, such as EasyMap, a mapping tool, to work through the supply chain. In this interview, DaimlerChrysler executive Jeff Trimmer discusses recent innovations, such as Extended Enterprise, corporate supply chain integration of Daimler-Benz and Chrysler, the role of the Internet, and the challenges presented by competitors.

What are the greatest opportunities for improving the automotive supply chain?

The question itself contains the answer. The answer lies in the supply chain. Over the last 10 to 20 years, OEMS, and more recently the Tier One suppliers, have "leaned" themselves out, and actually are working quite well together. The opportunity now lies in the Tier Two and below suppliers. There are enormous opportunities to eliminate waste, improve quality, and reduce cycle time if we can connect and manage multiple tiers of the supply chain. There are really two problems here. The first is identifying and connecting the chain. The Internet provides this opportunity. Before the Internet we could talk about managing the supply chain, but we had no way of hooking the multiple tiers together. The second problem is the type of suppliers in the lower tiers. Typically, these are smaller suppliers with limited resources. Helping smaller suppliers upgrade their capabilities and participate constructively in the supply chain will be a major challenge.

What are latest and greatest tools used at DaimlerChrysler for its supply chains?

Well, we can't give away all our secrets, but we're excited about a couple of projects we're working on. One is called EasyMap. It's a supply chain mapping tool that both our internal people and suppliers can use to lay out the various levels of the supply chain. We've already had some exciting examples of suppliers using this tool to identify opportunities to eliminate waste from the supply chain. Some other projects include our new Balanced Scorecard for suppliers that allows us to tailor rating criteria for different commodities, a new systems cost model we're developing called Total Cost of Ownership. The field is moving ahead quickly.

Which innovations in the supply chain have long-term value?

I think the Internet and the techniques of business-to-business e-commerce are very exciting right now. The problem, I think, is that many analysts and not a few companies are focusing on the wrong things. There is too much focus on using the Internet for auctions and catalogue buying. Clearly, there is some value in reducing transaction and purchase costs using Internet purchasing for auctions and catalogue buying, but if that's all you're focusing on, I believe you're missing the major opportunity of the Internet. It is very difficult to have a long-term strategic relationship with a supplier if all you're doing is buying his products at auction. The real opportunity in the Internet, I believe, is to manage those long-term strategic supplier relationships more effectively. For the first time, we have a tool in the Internet that potentially allows us to manage the complexity of our supply chains through multiple tiers. Companies that use this tool to eliminate waste, reduce cycle time, and improve quality throughout their supply chains will not only satisfy their customers better and earn greater profits for themselves, but will also see their supply chains earn greater profits as well.

Jeffrey Trimmer is Director of Operations & Strategy, Procurement & Supply for DaimlerChrysler Corporation. Prior to the merger, he held the same position for Chrysler Corportion. He is responsible for continuous improvement activities, administrative support, intranet activities, strategic studies, and systems developments in Daimler Chrysler's Procurement & Supply organization. He also acts as the Automotive Industry Action Group (AIAG) liasion for the company.

Automotive & Transportation

How does DaimlerChrysler plan to meet the challenge of AutoXChange?

This touches on some ongoing projects at DCX, but let me just say that the Ford/Oracle JV is an interesting concept, and at its heart is the concept of using the Internet to manage the supply chain. I'm not just sure how quickly they'll be able to realize the benefits of this venture beyond some initial purchases of MRO items, etc. As far as DCX' plans, we have been active in the use of the Internet with our suppliers for a number of years. In fact, if you really looked at operational applications that use the Internet, I believe DaimlerChrysler is the leader in installed applications. We already are 100% electronically connected with our production suppliers; all our production schedules, supplier releases, purchase orders, and supplier payments are handled online. The challenge for us is to take this leadership to the next level. We are actively working on a number of projects which will be announced at the appropriate time.

Can you discuss supply chain practices of German automotive manufacturers and their integration at DaimlerChrysler?

I really can comment only on the former DaimlerBenz programs. DaimlerBenz had a very active and well-supported supplier relations program called Tandem. It was a strong program for communication, joint work on costs and waste elimination, and technology identification and management. It was limited in that it concentrated solely on first-tier supplier relationships. As you are aware, the Chrysler program was called the Extended Enterprise, which is now a trademarked name for DCX. Over the last year and a half, we have worked together with our German colleagues to pull together a new integrated supplier program which we call the new Extended Enterprise. This program was introduced to our suppliers in our First Global Supplier Plenum in Frankfurt last September. The key to the new Extended Enterprise was to tap the best aspects of both prior programs – the technology management and communication aspects of Tandem, and the multiple-tier management and benefit-sharing aspects of Extended Enterprise. To these best practices we've added two new concepts. First, we now offer suppliers the opportunity to take advantage of multiple market and brand opportunities. We can now offer our suppliers the chance to become true global suppliers by supplying both Chrysler and Daimler operations. Second, we believe the opportunities to use advanced electronic communication and management techniques will be key. The new Extended Enterprise was conceived to use the best of both prior companies and to add new flavors to our global supplier relations efforts. We're working now to flesh these general concepts out into specific global programs including global commodity strategies, a new global Total Cost of Ownership cost management program, a global e-extended enterprise electronic strategy, and so on.

Supply Chain Innovation at Harley-Davidson: An Interview with Leroy Zimdars

Harley-Davidson is well known for its high-quality products – it should be equally well known for its streamlined supply chain, which is characterized by quality, cost, timing, technology, supplier responsiveness, and capacity planning. In this interview, Leroy Zimdars, director of Supply Chain Management at Harley-Davidson, discusses Harley's supply chain process: the process involves working closely with suppliers to streamline production. The company is moving toward a Web-based approach for accessing information, and trigger inventory replenishment systems represent the future of the supply chain. Rather than "push," Harley "pulls" inventory into the plant. Harley also utilizes composite supplier performance ratings, tool management tracking, CAD technologies, and Web-based collaboration.

Harley-Davidson is known for delivering a consistently high quality product. How does process drive quality?

There are a number of different areas in the process that affect our quality, starting with product design. We work to design quality into the products we develop, and we do this through a concurrent product methodology, which is very specific for both product development and the input that we get on design from our engineers, our manufacturing people, and our suppliers. We involve everyone in the early stages, and everyone effectively designs products together.

We use electronic processes such as EDI and bar coding; we use bar codes and electronic trigger systems for replenishing materials. In many cases our suppliers get a planning schedule, but we actually pull materials from their facilities into ours by means of the trigger system. We have a whole range of electronic resources: funds transfers, POs, and scheduling.

What types of training do you think hold the most promise for extending and enhancing your enterprise?

We offer a large variety of training types for our suppliers. In order to meet our requirements, we have a Continuous Improvement Team that reports to the Materials Group and works both with our suppliers and the Continuous Improvement Programs in our facilities. We have a highly formalized methodology for instructing suppliers that can last up to three months; then we can work with them to drive improvements in their facilities, and we can share the benefits with them. We do P-Pap training and SPC training; we also have training on our materials management strategy as well as master supply agreements that we've developed with our suppliers. We have training for the Master Supply Agreements as well.

Which bar coding system do you use?

We have our suppliers conform to the EAGE standard; there are a number of different companies where they can buy software, bar code printers, and so on. We try to stay standardized because we have a number of suppliers that do business with automotive suppliers – they all follow the EAGE format, so we do the same.

What types of software and technologies do you think hold the most promise for extending and enhancing your enterprise?

We're moving toward a Web-based approach for accessing information. We're currently developing software that will allow suppliers

Leroy Zimdars is director of Supply Chain Management at Harley-Davidson Motor Company.

access to daily production schedules and production status via our Web site. We feel that using trigger inventory replenishment systems represents the future: rather than *push*, we *pull* inventory into the plant, where items are actually re-ordered at the point of use on the shop floor based on a signal sent from our computer to the supplier.

We're moving toward composite supplier performance ratings; we have a number of plants that will be linked in the near future to measure quality, cost, timing, technology, supplier responsiveness to corrective action, and capacity planning capabilities.

We're developing tool management tracking: we use a wide range of steel-die processes for everything from high-pressure die-casting to permanent molds and stampings, and we need to know where tools are and how to replenish them.

We're using CAD technologies, where our suppliers have compatible CAD systems and can effectively transfer data through these systems.

We're piloting Web-based collaboration; we've established a Web site to bring people together with Netmeeting. We currently rely on Netmeeting and the telephone for conferencing, but we're going to expand to video; it's going to allow us to communicate, collaborate, make commitments, and offer store metrics and performance of chain metrics all on one Web site.

Weblink

For more on EDI, see:
srivastava.ASCET.com
prince.ASCET.com
herbold.ASCET.com

For more on replenishment, see:
anthony.ASCET.com
culotta.ASCET.com
cavender.ASCET.com
uchneat.ASCET.com

For more on bar codes, see:
hill.ASCET.com

You'll enter into that with all your strategic partners, I assume.
Exactly. And we can expand this to a great number of chains to be able to collaborate. With this we can cover everything from working through problems to actually driving continuous improvement down to the second or third tier of the chain by working together and driving them through a common interest.

What's the biggest challenge you see in the collaboration effort underway between industry leaders?
I think that there are a couple of ways of looking at it. There is, first of all, the issue of communication: the Web provides for really effective communication, but whenever you rely on electronic communication and you're not face-to-face there's always the issue of "Is the message being transferred correctly?" The other, larger issue is trust. If you look at company-to-company or company-to-supplier, it's important to understand the motives behind wanting some sort of information, or collaboration. We have a long way to go in getting companies to be willing to be open with one another or trust one another.

We've been able to develop the Master Supply Agreement with our suppliers, and we've established a clear understanding of the lines of responsibility and expectations. So when we begin moving down a path with our suppliers there's a clear understanding over our joint development of a product – what happens if that product is patented? Who has responsibility for it? – and we don't get into an argument after we've begun designing something. The same is the case if there's a product liability or warranty-related issue. We try to be very clear up-front; once you've established that clarity and established trust, there's a lot more openness. Two words: Be clear.

How does commodity strategy development relate to the supply chain?
In a number of different ways. When we develop a commodity strategy, our intent is to create a clear understanding with our supply base and our internal stakeholders of the expectations we have of a given commodity, beginning with what the customer wants and expects. We document both customer and stakeholder expectations, and try to look five years or more into the future.

Then we establish what the product looks like. We want to know what the customer is looking for. We want to know what are the style-related issues. We look at design from a process standpoint that relies on core competency. We focus on internal versus external issues. We look at the product from a commercial standpoint that concentrates on financial issues and cost implications. We look at it from a performance understanding standpoint that focuses on quality management and product delivery requirements, and we look at it from a technology and R&D standpoint that tracks the capabilities that we expect our suppliers to be working on.

This brings us back to trust, in a way. In order for you to really be able to get a partner, either a supplier or another company, to share with you – especially very confidential information – you need to have a clear understanding of trust. This only happens when you clearly explain to your partners what their role is going to be – and what benefits they're going to derive by working with you.

That's what we do. And that's how we believe we can get suppliers to be open with technology. Once we do that, our strategy is to identify what the gaps are within our supply base and what the supplier needs to do to close those gaps. All of this helps us better to understand future needs. How can we improve things? It could involve rationalization of suppliers, from 300 or less. We could create chains and tiers where one of our suppliers manages the others. We can plan for new source development if there's a new technology that we're looking for based on customer requirements that our supply base can't produce today. We're driven by a clear-cut strategy.

http://fourthshift.ASCET.com — web link

Fourth Shift – Delivering Complete Care through a Commitment to Success

FOURTH SHIFT
When you're ready for *change*™

What do you and NBA champion coach Phil Jackson have in common? As leaders of major corporations, you need to get very different entities to collaborate to produce a winner. Chances are one enterprise system won't fit all your operations. What's good for corporate may not be right for a remote manufacturing facility. Yet, these entities all need to work as one.

Fourth Shift continues to its tradition of contributing to winning corporations with its new initiative called Complete Care. It puts the power of "e" to work for you with seamless, real-time information flow to the critical points inside your business and to outside trading partners.

The Elements of Complete Care

Complete Care by Fourth Shift is organized around four functional areas critical to the success of your enterprise.

The e-ERP Backbone is the core that supports all of your critical business systems. Our function-rich e-ERP Backbone incorporates the latest 32-bit Microsoft® technologies, allowing seamless connectivity between all areas of your business including manufacturing, order-entry, product configuration, and financials.

Fourth Shift Customer Care means extending your front office to the virtual enterprise and beyond. Build enduring relationships with your customers via the Internet by enabling interactive collaboration and contact between your employees, your business partners, and your customers.

Customer satisfaction is critical. But you can't satisfy customers without a solid supply chain. In today's increasingly complex business environment, the supply chain is getting longer and involves more players. Fourth Shift Supplier Care means involving and monitoring all key points along your supply chain.

Employees are among your most vital assets. Today's competitive labor market and more mobile workforce means that attracting, hiring, and training new employees is more expensive than ever. Fourth Shift Employee Care means taking control and simplifying human resource and payroll functions to provide employees with tools and services they need and appreciate.

Fourth Shift Leads with "e"

Fourth Shift services have expertise in every form of "e." Whether it's XML or EDI, at Fourth Shift "e" means getting your information to where it can make your organization more competitive than the competition.

Fourth Shift has helped organizations strengthen every link in the supply chain. From connecting multiple facilities in multiple countries for Emerson Electric, to building an integrated EDI/barcode solution that helped CME corporation meet Honda America's EDI demands.

Customer service at Fourth Shift means providing a full range of business services to help our customers stay on the leading edge in every area of their operations.

Get More with Fourth Shift

Complete Care is a company-wide commitment to our customers' success. Fourth Shift Complete Care is much more than creating a seamless flow of information at critical points in your business. It's your team player that can cover the entire court or play a role within the greater enterprise. The advantage is yours with a system that can be quickly implemented in remote manufacturing plants and rollup to corporate or be the foundation for your entire supply chain. Sophisticated functionality, easy implementation, single source for enterprise applications, service, and support, and decades of experience equal the Complete Care roster.

Contact Information

M.M. Stuckey
CEO

Jim Caldwell
President

Dave Latzke
CFO

Randy Tofteland
VP *Sales*

Fourth Shift Corporation
Two Meridian Crossings
Minneapolis, MN 55423
Toll Free 800-342-5675
Phone 612.851.1500
Fax 612.851.1560
info@fs.com
www.fs.com

Intrepa – The Intelligent Supply Chain

Contact Information

Tim Conroy
Chief Executive Officer

Bruce Eicher
Chief Operating Officer

John Stitz
VP, Marketing & Strategic Alliances

Intrepa
4215 Edison Lakes Parkway
Suite 100
Mishawaka, IN 46545
Phone 219.247.1570
Fax 219.247.1575
www.intrepa.com

Regional Offices
Atlanta
Charlotte
New York Metro
Indianapolis
San Jose
Orange County, CA

Products
Logistics PRO for Transportation
Logistics PRO for Warehousing
Logistics PRO for Asset Management
Logistics PRO for Supply Chain Collaboration

Intrepa is the leading provider of integrated Supply Chain Management (SCM) solutions for traditional and e-business environments. With over 10 years of experience in developing and implementing world-class software solutions for warehouse, transportation, asset management, and supply chain collaboration, Intrepa has delivered over 300 successful installations of SCM.

Solution Suite

The Logistics PRO suite of products expands "beyond the four walls" and includes scalable solutions for transportation, warehousing, asset management, and supply chain collaboration. Logistics PRO supports transportation functionality for carrier assignment, modeling, order consolidation, and shipment processing. Warehouse functionality includes traditional Warehouse Management System functions, as well as dynamic slotting of inventory, Web-enabled activities, productivity tracking, full vendor compliance labeling support, and executive information retrieval. The asset management module provides tools for labor planning, activity-based management, and radio frequency (RF)-directed processing for "Best Path" and interleaving of tasks. With the supply chain collaboration module users have Web access to critical information, business-to-business and business-to consumer collaboration, and trade exchange integration.

Industry Expertise

Intrepa participates in industry specific initiatives to provide solutions incorporating industry best practices for a variety of business sectors, including publishing and media, automotive and service parts distribution, consumer products and retail, food and beverage, healthcare, and third-party logistics.

Supply Chain Collaboration

Companies looking to survive in the 21st century must embrace supply chain collaboration tools. If a company is smart about it, they can gain the ever-elusive competitive edge. Collaboration is about expanding and focusing, outside the four walls, on relationships with external customers/suppliers, external customers' customers, and external suppliers' suppliers. Efficient Healthcare Consumer Response and Collaborative Planning, Forecasting and Replenishment are examples of industry initiatives leading the way in establishing objectives and guidelines to accomplish undeniable benefits.

Advanced Technology

Intrepa's industry-leading research and development team utilizes the most advanced technology available today. Intrepa's vast research team is constantly working with the industry's most innovative technologies of today for product releases well into the future.

Current advanced technologies include mobile computing devices (such as Windows CE for RF devices), smart phones, pagers, and all devices supporting online Internet browsers, integration with advanced material handling equipment such as automated carousels, high-speed sortation equipment, in-line weigh-n-motion scales, pick-to-light, and automated picking devices.

Ability to Execute

Logistics PRO's component based n-tier architecture allows for ease of integration with host applications, phased implementation of functionality for quicker return on investment, and allows for ease of application upgrades as new functionality is developed. In addition, Logistics PRO's technology backbone allows Logistics PRO functionality to be executed over an internal intranet or via one of Intrepa's Internet software hosting providers.

Like your business, Logistics PRO is driven by the demands of the marketplace. With dedicated development and support resources, significant R & D investments and an unparalleled commitment to be the leader in SCM, Logistics PRO is the right solution for the future. Get Logistics PRO and get going.

E-Commerce: Its Impact on Transportation, Logistics, and Supply Chain Management

The transportation and logistics industries have only intermittently applied B2B e-commerce to their practices. Transportation carriers have had a great deal of trouble utilizing e-commerce solutions to fulfill customer supply chain expectations, primarily with tracking and tracing. Customers want to know the exact location of their shipment and to be alerted when its time-definite delivery is threatened. Although Internet technology is present, old business models prevail and customers are trapped in information silos. Logistics intermediaries arose to manage the functions of transportation carriers. Those intermediaries are now attempting to manage the information flow for customers. E-commerce is now transforming the role of the intermediary.

Around 1990, a confluence of factors began to change the role of logistics in major corporations. Quality initiatives and re-engineering were forcing companies to evaluate entire processes, rather than individual components. Supply Chain Management, the integrated control over goods, information, and money, followed.

Supply Chain Management represented an attempt to develop a unified process by which goods and services would be produced for customer sale and consumption. Logistics was now being considered as more than simply an opportunity to minimize cost – it was developing into a core component of corporate profitability.

More recently, the Internet has become part of our daily lives, and during that time we have watched a progression of Internet innovations. Internet browsers and the development of the World Wide Web made the Internet available. Search engines were developed in response to the proliferation of Web sites. Commercialization of the Internet, initially business-to-consumer, spawned online shopping. Search engines morphed into portals, adding content, shopping, and other items.

Finally, e-commerce came into full flower with the online auction leading the way. E-commerce exists along two dimensions. The first dimension defines the parties: B2B (business-to-business), or B2C (business-to-consumer).

The second dimension defines the transactional nature. Here there exist several categories of service types. Sell-side servers are electronic storefronts and catalogues that manage the purchase process from the selection of items through payment. Buy-side servers provide the capabilities for purchase orders to be entered and fulfilled. Usually there are well-established business rules that are incorporated into the e-commerce application. Marketplace applications establish electronic communities which both buyers and sellers can access.

Sell-Side E-Commerce

The use of the Internet to provide sell-side e-commerce has been widely adopted in the transportation and logistics industries – primarily as a means to provide customer service and to "sell" its product. Almost every transportation company offers its customers the ability to log onto its Web site to make bookings, or to track and trace shipments.

Many of these initiatives were developed for fairly simple reasons. When a customer opts to visit a Web site instead of calling the service center, the company usually benefits, as the transaction requires no paid employee. This not only represents a cost savings, but also eliminates the risk of any unfavorable customer/employee exchange. Such a risk is a constant worry in a full-employment society

white paper

written by:

Theodore Prince
Kleinschmidt Inc.
http://prince.ASCET.com

Theodore Prince, as Senior Vice President Sales and Marketing, is responsible for all commercial activities of Kleinschmidt Inc., a value-added network providing electronic data interchange and other technological solutions to corporations throughout North America.

He has spent his career in the transportation industry, including 20 years working for a variety of surface transportation carriers.

Mr. Prince has a B.S. in Economics from the Wharton School of the University of Pennsylvania and a Master's degree in Transportation from the University of Pennsylvania Graduate School of Engineering and Applied Sciences.

Automotive & Transportation

http://prince.ASCET.com

where companies are unable to attract and retain qualified employees. The danger increases when the company competes in a global market where calls can be coming throughout a 24-hour day.

The range of these solutions has varied. Some companies have tried to create a competitive advantage with their Web pages by developing signature options unique to their brands. They have developed a customized portal for each customer with sophisticated support capabilities that can also be customized – including offering languages other than English.

Sell-Side E-Commerce Obstacles

Despite the promise, transportation carriers have had trouble utilizing e-commerce solutions to fulfill customer supply chain expectations. The primary problem involves tracking and tracing. Customers want to know the location of their shipment and to be alerted if its time-definite delivery is threatened. This problem can manifest itself in two forms: the shippers and the intermediate carriers.

If a shipper wishes to track an individual shipment, he must go to a Web page for each carrier or logistics provider. Multiple shipments therefore require constant movements between Web pages. Three problems result from this type of setup. First, the shipper must match carriers to shipments prior to tracking, which is sometimes complex and difficult for the customer. Second, carriers usually allow tracking from either the equipment ID or their shipment ID. Carriers do not always retain the unique shipment ID that the customer utilizes (i.e., purchase order, lot number, customs file, Renban number, etc.). In some cases, this makes it almost impossible for a customer to locate the shipment for tracking. Third, and perhaps most important, the customer lacks a single point of focus. All of this leads to sub-optimization for customers. E-commerce has not delivered value to them and, as a result, their supply chain suffers.

Some transportation movements are intermodal – they involve more than one carrier and different modes. Often an intermediate, intermodal trucker is involved. Truckers, usually the last link in the intermodal chain, must know when equipment is ready for movement. But they too suffer from disaggregation of information.

For example, a Chicago trucker must browse eight separate railroad Web pages to keep current. This is laborious, as the trucker must inquire about one piece of equipment at a time. Although the railroad may have generated an e-commerce cost savings, there is none for the trucker. Most railroads have not developed sites where truckers may view all their moves at one time. (Some carriers provide such capability to customers.)

Major port areas experience the same problem. Truckers are forced to browse numerous Web pages for different steamship lines and marine terminals. But without complete information, these truckers are unable to optimize their movements. For example, they may depart a terminal empty without realizing a return move will be available. Additionally, a concentration of moves during daylight, which could effectively be spread out over more hours, continues to plague the business.

So there is a real cost to this peak demand. Better information could lead to more level utilization, which would allow truckers to be more profitable without raising rates. Carriers would benefit while terminal assets would become more productive. Customer service would improve without any additional infrastructure capacity.

Shippers have also been reluctant to complete the supply chain loop. Although information about goods may be exchanged, integration of financial transfers has lagged behind. Although electronic funds transfer has become routine, it is often a standalone application. Funds are transmitted separately from remittance advises instructing the recipient on application of funds.

In many cases, such transfers increase the very workload they were meant to alleviate. The recipient may just deposit the cash to a customer clearing account. They may find themselves with large unapplied balances at the same time they have apparently overdue invoices.

The Rise of Intermediaries

At much the same time companies came to recognize the need for logistics' awareness, an increased awareness of core competencies developed. As more sophisticated financial tools, such as activity-based costing (ABC) and economic value-added (EVA), entered the corporate mainstream, management became focused on the return of assets. Outsourcing allowed an organization to concentrate on its core competencies and customers, and to take advantage of greater operational flexibility.

The quest for supply chain improvements that could support overall corporate performance inspired many companies to seek help achieving these results. As the scope of operations grew to be global, outsourcing became more common. It has been estimated that more than 60% of Fortune 500 manufacturers used some form of third-party logistics services (3PLs). And many use more than one.

Using 3PLs enabled businesses to improve their financial positions by reducing operating and capital expenses. It also simplified transportation purchasing decisions by providing scope and scale unavailable from individual carriers. Successful 3PLs boast service throughout the world and can do so across various modes: surface, ocean, and air. Scale provides the volume to handle business in a very cost-effective manner.

Information technology allows 3PLs to manage the business and take full advantage of scope and scale. Some customers believe that 3PLs can provide better service than can the underlying carriers because they have the systems advantage, including customer service operations. Often, the merger of systems and scope enables the 3PL to perform helpful functions such as regulatory compliance and determining the total delivered cost of goods for sale.

Some recent surveys suggest that the rush to employ 3PLs has subsided. The current trend is to develop a lead logistics provider (LLP) or Fourth-Party Logistics Provider™ (4PL)*. A 4PL is treated as a strategic partner, rather than a tactical one (such as the 3PL) A 4PL is a supply chain integrator that synthesizes and manages the resources, capabilities, and technology of its own organization with those of complementary service providers to deliver a comprehensive supply chain solution.

The skill sets necessary for a 4PL are unique and differ significantly from the operating expertise needed for logistics outsourcing. Strategy consulting, business process review and redesign, technology integration, and savvy people management are some frequently cited prerequisites for 4PLs, as are global capabilities and the organization to manage multiple service providers. A 4PL that can also provide 3PL services has become known as an "infomediary."

Not by coincidence, 4PL/infomediary growth accompanies the explosion of e-commerce. Customers are being forced to develop solutions in Internet time. There is a dawning recognition that the first mover accrues most financial benefits from innovation and that the benefits of simply catching up are even smaller than they used to be.

Buy-Side E-Commerce

Although sell-side e-commerce may define the manner in which services are provided, buy-side e-commerce will determine the ultimate configuration of the market and industry survivors. Forrester Research estimates that e-commerce transactions will double every year, reaching $1.3 trillion by 2003. (This sum increases tenfold if traditional electronic data interchange transactions are included. While most new transactions are Internet-based, the embedded base of EDI over private networks is expected to remain in place for many years.)

Most industry focus has been on the business-to-consumer (B2C) market in the form of initial public offerings and market valuations. There has been great interest in which portions of the transportation and logistics industry will benefit from this new form of distribution. Despite all this publicity, 90% of this market is business-to-business (B2B).

Buy-side e-commerce is compelling to businesses for the economies that seem apparent. It offers a convenience, timeliness, and choice that may not always be available. In many cases, multiple vendors offer sales to multiple customers. Although e-commerce is still in its infancy, some companies have already generated significant savings by moving their purchasing to the Internet. This can also be a means by which 3PLs can assure themselves an adequate, cost-effective supply of underlying carrier transportation capacity.

While they show promise, buy-side transactions are not largely employed amongst transportation carriers. Many carriers seem to think they are engaging in e-commerce if they have a Web page showcasing their newest equipment. This is not the case, and they are overlooking a multitude of opportunities.

Marketplace E-Commerce

The growth of buy-side e-commerce in the transportation industry is similar to – but more accelerated than – the development of other areas of the industry. Early on, logistical operations involved a complex chain of transportation transactions, a large number of participants and hand-offs, and a multitude of redundancies and reworking.

The transportation world was easily broken down to three groups. At the basic level an asset-based carrier provided services directly to a customer. Here, one saw a series of many one-to-one relationships. Customers had numerous bilateral contracts with carriers, and carriers had many one-to-one contracts with customers. Contracts involving multiple carriers and multiple customers were almost non-existent.

Beyond this basic arrangement two other marketplace solutions formed. Bulletin boards developed on which truckers posted notes at truck stops offering capacity and responding to notes seeking capacity. This method required an actual presence at the truck stop. Over time, truck brokerages performed load matching by improved communications (i.e., phone, fax, e-mail). Truck brokerage evolved into 3PL.

The e-commerce methods available through the Internet built upon the former methodologies. The bulletin board is the simplest. Here, the provider gathers and posts information about available loads (from carriers) and desired loads (by customers). When customers or carriers see an item, they can contact the other party.

The business model is fairly simple. The bulletin board provider charges a monthly subscription fee and offers levels of service, remaining mindful of the goal of offering the preeminent bulletin board. Users will rarely look at more than one or two sites. A first mover advantage exists for the provider who quickly becomes the largest.

To grow revenue the provider has two options. It can either expand into other modes of transportation, which may not be easy, or it can offer additional value-added services. One bulletin board for motor carriers provides credit checks, handles fuel purchases, and obtains group discounts. Often these are services rendered by a third party who offers access to their services through the bulletin board, and pays a fee to the bulletin board.

Another type of marketplace e-commerce is the auction. These sites perform a freight rate auction marketplace. Shippers either place their desired bids on the site (for carriers to view and offer bids) or they may just request the carriers' best rates. Some carriers might advertise capacity and seek bids for it. The process is blind. At a predetermined date and time, the winning parties are advised of the "winning bid."

Although this system sounds straightforward, it carries numerous potential problems. Customers may wish to limit the bidders. For example, the customer loses out if the winning bidder is a company with which he does not necessarily conduct business. Carriers have similar concerns. More sophisticated auctions offer filters for bid specifications.

Here, the business model is a combination of subscriptions and transaction fees. A big problem, however, is that there is no guarantee of a final bid which will move freight (and generate a fee). Some auction sites attempt to solve this by requiring freight payment through them.

The e-commerce marketplace also offers the exchange method, a process similar to that of an auction, but with several distinguishing features. For example, one can see the moving rate as the market moves to a price. It is like a commodities exchange. Currently, however, only providers offer capacity, and speculators will be kept out by preliminary screening of participants by the exchange operators.

The exchange system also is flawed for the following reasons. It can be used unlawfully, or as a means for participants to send pricing signals to each other. (There are such precedents in the airline pricing systems.) Additionally, an exchange could find itself possessing sensitive anti-trust data that could incriminate its customers.

And ever more problematic is the amount of information that the exchange will possess. Although it sanitizes the data of individual parties, it could potentially sell information about market and pricing trends to both customers and carriers.

As with auctions, the business model compensates the site by a combination of subscriptions and transaction fees.

What Will the Future Bring?

Many wonder what the advent of the Internet and e-commerce will mean to the transportation and logistics industry.

A large number of carriers fear that the technology will cause further depression of rate levels. This is a valid concern. Internet auction sites have usually yielded two types of results. For products, the price can sometimes rise, but for services, the price frequently has been driven down (perhaps reflecting the "perishable" nature of services).

In today's transportation market, the cause is not so much e-commerce, but basic microeconomics. If supply exceeds demand, the price will fall. E-commerce sites will not cause rates to fall further than they would – but they may cause rates to fall faster. Better communication and information in the marketplace will allow prices to achieve market equilibrium more quickly.

E-commerce penetration can be determined by supply and demand in addition to market aggregation and intermediation. A market with a few major carriers (e.g., six major railroads) will be harder to penetrate than one with numerous carriers (e.g., 50,000 interstate truckers). Transportation markets with well-established (transportation) intermediaries (i.e., consumer products) will be easier to introduce to e-commerce solutions than markets that do not traditionally rely on intermediaries (e.g., domestic bulk commodities).

Shippers will be forced to consider their options carefully. If they suspect that demand is close to, or exceeds supply, they will want contracts for most of their expected traffic. But if they suspect that supply will exceed demand, they will want to buy most of their capacity on the spot market. A bad forecast for market conditions could have catastrophic results.

3PLs and other intermediaries must make these purchased transportation decisions on two levels because they both buy and sell transportation. For the intermediaries, the possibility always exists for bankruptcy, due to unwise choices made in an attempt to garner arbitrage profits (i.e., sign contracts with carriers and float rates with customers).

The advent of e-commerce suggests a range of possible outcomes. Carriers may find pricing on the spot market unappealing because they lack the necessary information systems and personnel to handle such market dynamics. In such cases, dealing with 3PLs may be the easier option.

Rather than getting caught with capacity that must be sold at a steep discount, carriers may seek contracts with 3PLs for large cargo commitments. These rates may be lower than those for some cargo, but such action also requires less employees, less time and less information technology. Overall, the economic result may be more sensible. Customers have often proven themselves ingenious at using spot market pricing tricks to establish a basis for ongoing rate levels. Carriers may just wish to avoid subjecting themselves to this rate whipsawing.

Some 3PLs may feel large enough to move from e-commerce marketplaces to buy-side solutions. This would offer them the benefit of auction-type economics, without requiring them to share the economic benefit with other parties, some of whom may be industry competitors.

The long-term possibilities of developing a true transportation commodity exchange are intriguing, and we could see further movement in that direction in the future. The natural gas and electricity industries (which, like transportation carriers, are also asset-based, network-operating companies) are seeing the development of commodity exchanges as the industry divides between providers and marketers. There have been some efforts to provide transportation futures, but they have never operated through a formal exchange. Naturally, a fair number of regulatory issues must be resolved for this development to take a serious turn.

Information is a critical component of the supply chain and will continue to drive change in the transportation and logistics markets. E-commerce will be a major component of this transition.

Due to e-commerce, an inevitable market shakeout awaits the transportation industry. The number of transportation and logistics e-commerce products proliferates daily. Despite their success in attracting venture capital, most will succumb to the handful of survivors, who will, in turn, be absorbed through mergers and acquisitions. And while many B2B sites claim to eliminate the need for intermediaries, many are becoming intermediaries in their own right. Sites that claim to embrace intermediaries risk becoming trivial as the intermediary, with its existing customer base, lowers the site's price by leveraging it against other sites.

The e-commerce business models will prevail, and, like Internet time, the shakeout will be brief – but memorable.

Note

* Fourth-Party Logistics™ is a registered trademark of Andersen Consulting.

written by:

Mark A. Hurley
Shell Chemicals

David S. DuBose
Andersen Consulting

http://hurley.ASCET.com

Channel Strategy as a Value Creator in the Chemical Industry: Shell's Journey

A shifting business landscape – introduced by the Internet – puts the chemical industry in a position to leave "boom and bust" cycles behind. This new landscape means new opportunities for Shell Chemicals; Shell has determined that there are two ways to achieve market leadership: restructuring portfolios and lowering costs, and creating operating discipline. By implementing more streamlined channel strategies along its supply chain, Shell has been able to reduce the number of business units and garner significant improvements in its ROI, while refusing to myopically cut costs at the customer's expense.

The Business Situation

"How can we increase our competitiveness in an industry that is experiencing a shifting landscape?" This is the question that challenged Shell Chemicals executives in the late 1990s. In addition to significant consolidation, the chemical industry is "poised to be able to break free from the cycle of 'boom and bust' and move into a new era," according to the September 1999 *Financial Times Management Report* on the changing structure of the global chemicals industry.

What did moving into a new era mean for this $16 billion global manufacturer of petrochemicals? Shell Chemicals is one of four major Royal Dutch/Shell companies and comprises 21 business units that produce chemicals ranging from ethylene to high-performance polymers. Executives leading this enterprise once believed that its fragmented business approach, due to a large number of business units and country-based organizations, inhibited its ability to reap the benefits of global reach and scale. Through a peer benchmarking report, Shell determined that its operating cost structure was fairly high relative to that of the competition.

In response to the competitive challenge, Shell Chemicals set forth a bold course of action – to become the leader in the global petrochemicals industry, significantly increase value to shareholders, and achieve a 50% improvement in return on average capital employed (ROACE) in the near term. Shell determined that there were two ways to achieve the goal of market leadership: 1) restructure the portfolio and lower costs, and 2) create operating discipline. Restructuring meant more sharply focusing Shell's operations and shedding the number of business units by 40%, from 21 to 13. This reduction would enable the organization to concentrate on producing chemicals that are "close to the cracker," that is, more fundamental and basic, and realize $300 million in near-term cost reductions.

The second response – the creation of operational discipline – meant the globalization of business operations and the development of significant competence in procurement, manufacturing, and demand chain. Shell had largely run its chemical operations on a regional basis; the European sales and operations group had its own set of policies and procedures, as did the United States, Canada, and others. The globalization effort would establish consistency across regions and enable Shell to leverage its scale on a worldwide basis. To create operational competence in distinct areas, Shell assigned an executive with global responsibility to each of these three areas. The purpose of these new groups is to build leading-edge practices through centers of excellence. The processes are implemented and executed by the business units, manufacturing, sales, and fulfillment organizations. Supply Chain Management was to become a focal point.

Mr. Hurley is Vice President of Customer Fulfillment, Americas, for Shell Chemicals. Mark focuses much of his time on creatively leveraging demand chain management against customer needs. He has been with Shell for 19 years and is based in Houston.

Mr. DuBose is a senior manager in Andersen Consulting's Strategy Competency. Mr. DuBose is an expert advisor in the development and application of channel strategy in concert with effective Supply Chain Management. He consults heavily in the chemical industry market space.

Chemicals

Focus on Demand Chain and Channel Management

One of the key changes involved in migrating from a "supply/push" operating discipline to a "demand/pull" customer strategy. With a mandate to dramatically improve operations and become more market-focused, Shell began to explore an approach to increase its effectiveness with its customers by understanding their needs, their "buyer values." Buyer values include items such as delivery accuracy/speed, technical service expertise, research and development, quality specifications, order management, and more. Historically, Shell had not developed a clear perspective on the differentiated needs of its customer base; instead it focused only on volume and profitability. While customer contribution (volume, profit, strategic importance) are certainly important components of value to Shell Chemicals, these items must be evaluated against the lens of customer needs to be interpreted correctly. Put another way, Shell determined that it was critical to look simultaneously at overall customer value as well as customer needs. The central idea is to match the products and service offerings desired to Shell's offering to each customer segment.

To better understand its customers' buyer values, Shell conducted numerous customer satisfaction surveys and other instruments aimed at obtaining a measure of customer feedback/opinion. Through a workshop-driven process of discovery, the Channel Strategy team determined the relative importance of different buyer values

Weblink

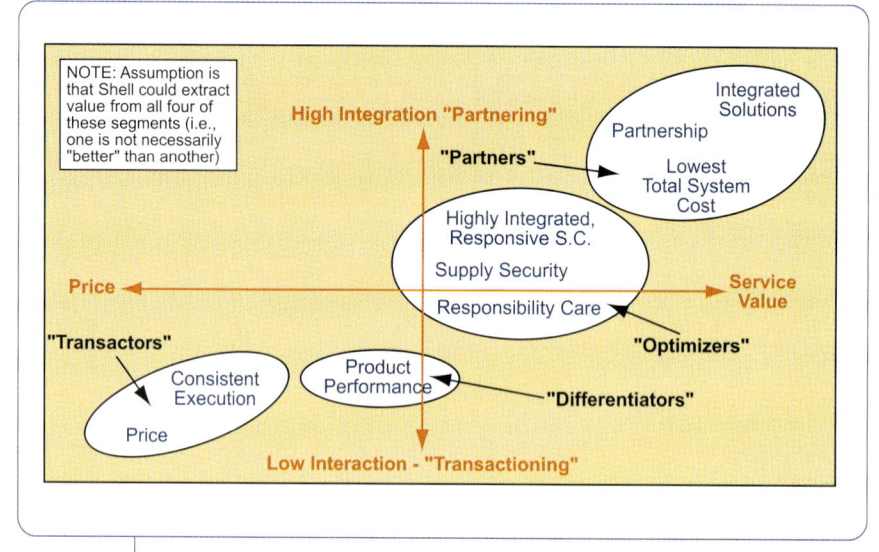

More on customer-centric practices:
 enslow.ASCET.com
More on customer segmentation, see:
 srivastava.ASCET.com
 billington.ASCET.com
 fischer.ASCET.com
 benitez.ASCET.com
For more on optimization, see
 reiter.ASCET.com
 culotta.ASCET.com
 prince.ASCET.com

Figure 1.0 | Partnering versus transactioning

to Shell's customer base across all business units. Then, the team mapped representative customers on two continuums: perceived level of integration desired by the customer versus value to Shell (strategic, financial). Four fairly distinct clusters, or "segments," emerged: partners, optimizers, differentiators, and transactors.

With customer segments defined at the "80/20" level, the next step was to understand how best to serve customers according to their needs as well as understand Shell Chemicals' ability to deliver products and services. Several of Shell's businesses traditionally have approached the market via two distinct channels: direct to the customer and indirect to the customer, through a distributor. The former channel typically is used for higher volume customers for whom there is significant economy of scale. The distributor channel generally is used for customers who are specialty chemical users or who simply have a lower usage rate that necessitates the use of expensive less-than truckload freight. A distributor often is able to service these customers more cost-effectively by being able to deliver a full truckload of product to multiple customers, similar to the way soft drink manufacturers deliver soft drinks on a dedicated route.

The team worked to change its model of sales channels from the two-prong concept to something that is more focused on how best to reach the different customer segments. In this new model, instead of thinking of a distributor as a channel, a distributor is now considered a trading partner that can add value through delivering the product/service bundle in the most effective and efficient manner to the end customer.

Similarly, other customer-centric activities – from making the purchase decision through placing the order to settlement and technical support – might all be better handled by different "channel partners." These channel partners could be supply chain specialists, such as third-party logistics providers that arrange freight and own storage terminals; back-end operations specialists, such as outside payment processors; virtual, such as an Internet chemical broker/sales agent, or even an insourced function or service like electronic marketing. By exploring various options, the Channel Strategy team became aware that there were many different options to deliver goods and services to its segmented customer base in a differentiated fashion.

Making Channel Strategy Happen

The challenge for Shell was to translate the implications of channel strategy into

Figure 2.0 **Customer Segments**

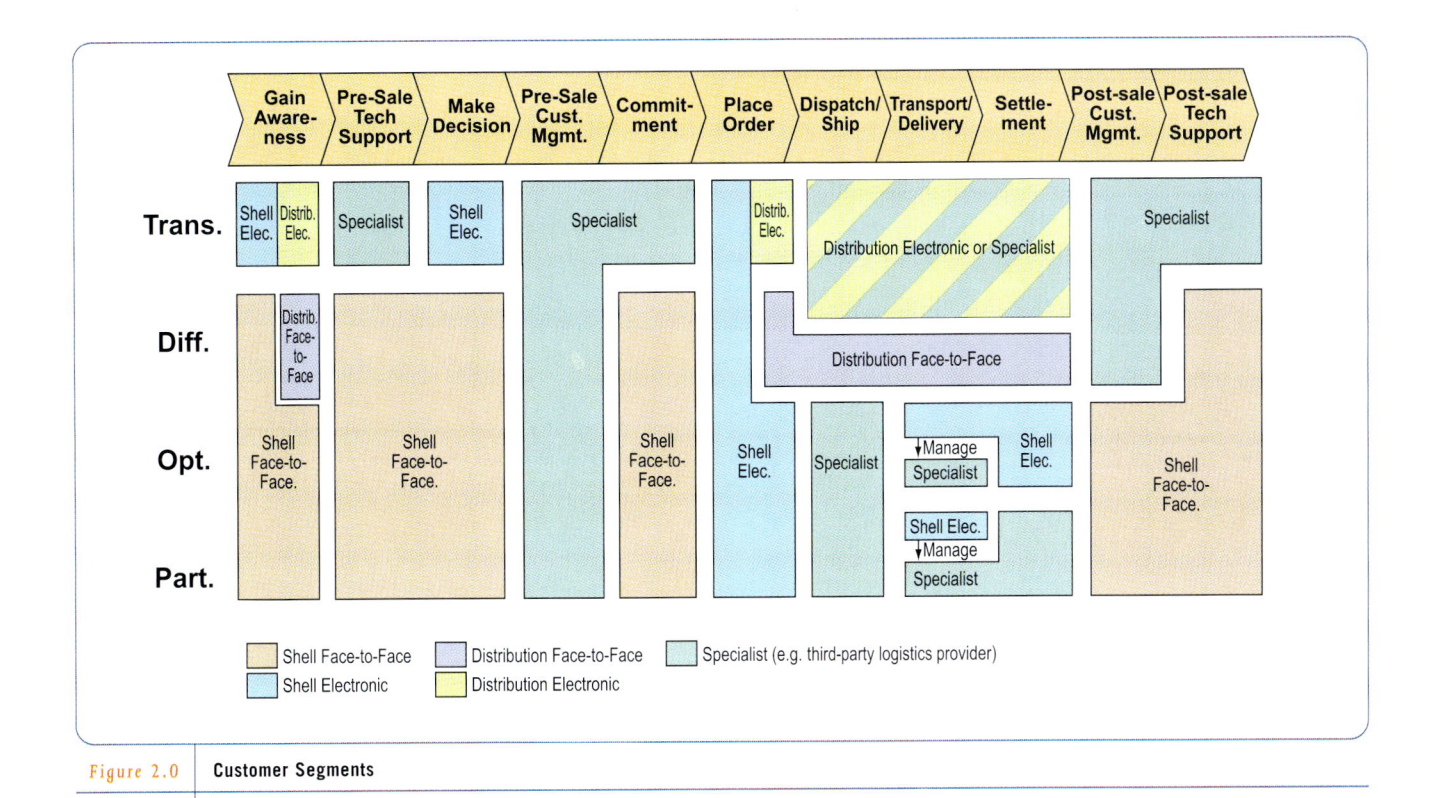

a specific set of initiatives that was actionable and clear in terms of scope. The Demand Chain Management group maintained ownership of the project and determined that it would focus on a single business unit to begin the process of change. The Base Chemicals business unit, which had been very involved with the Channel Strategy effort, volunteered to participate as the "lead project" business unit.

The next question was to determine the appropriate scope. The project team quickly decided that it was crucial to focus on a limited set of key areas to get the maximum benefit with as little complexity as possible. The Channel Strategy team determined the following fundamental workstreams:
- Determine the best logistics network to serve the customer base
- Create specific service packages for the different customer segments
- Segment the distributor base and recast the distributor as a channel partner

Each of the workstreams is connected to the other two. For instance, the service level (that is, delivery time requirements) has a direct impact on the design of the logistics network in terms of where to deploy product relative to the customers. Or, for example, shifting certain customers to distributors affects choices around the core distributor group as well as the volumes and flows through the supply network. While the channel strategy "problem" had been simplified at Shell, balancing customer service, growth, and cost remained a complex proposition.

The Shell Chemicals/Andersen Consulting team used sophisticated supply chain optimization software. The tools enabled the team to perform analysis that captured the critical trade-offs, quantifying the impact of different network and service scenarios on a case-by-case basis. Through the optimization technology and the art of supply chain modeling, the Channel Strategy group contemplated various what-if scenarios, including different sourcing strategies, delivery service changes, and transportation mode changes – all in the context of delivering the products and services to different customer segments with unique needs.

Going Forward at Shell Chemicals

Shell reasoned that there existed a multi-million-dollar value proposition associated with implementing channel strategy at one business unit, and, while channel strategy is not right for all business units, there is significant additional value to be gained from this approach with other business units. Currently, Shell is looking at other dimensions of the channel strategy proposition, like developing a Web site to sell chemicals to certain customers. The key learning at Shell was to break the strategy into digestible units and execute in a manner that makes sense and creates value at a reasonable rate, while being extremely sensitive to the customers' ability to deal with change. Tying into the overall business strategy is absolutely essential. The supply/demand chain organization plays a pivotal role in making it come to life.

Far from being a myopic cost-cutting exercise, channel strategy at Shell Chemicals is all about adopting the customer's vantagepoint and looking back toward its operations to guide strategic decisions to build value.

http://hurley.ASCET.com

web link — http://calico.ASCET.com

Calico – Apply the Art of Selling with the Power of the Web

Contact Information

Alan Naumann
President & CEO

Dave Barrett
Chief Operating Officer, Executive Vice President

Matt DiMaria
Vice President, Marketing

Beverly Powell
Vice President,
Business Development

Calico Commerce, Inc
333 West San Carlos Street, Suite 300
San Jose, CA 95110
Phone 408.975.7400
Toll-Free 800.372.5371
Fax 408.975.7410
info@calico.com
www.calico.com

Field Offices:
Atlanta, Boston, Chicago, New York, Germany, Sweden, and London

Products:
The Calico eSales Suite includes:
Calico eSales Configurator
Enables customers to interactively drive the purchase process

Calico eSales Loyalty Builder
Makes it easier for customers to buy online by customizing the buying experience.

Calico eSales InfoGuide
Automatically delivers critical information during the buying process.

Calico eSales Quote
Provides customers with an accurate, easily understood list of con

Calico Technology, Inc., headquartered in San Jose, CA., is a leading provider of e-commerce software and professional services that enable the interactive buying and selling of complex products and services across all sales channels. Calico™ eSales® Suite is a Web-based, guided selling solution for business-to-business and business-to-consumer e-commerce environments. By interactively guiding customers through a personalized buying process, the Calico eSales Suite helps corporations build stronger customer relationships that result in increased revenue and reduced sales costs.

Calico eSales Suite goes beyond simple online order taking by guiding customers through complex or considered purchase decisions. The Calico eSales Suite thin-client architecture is unique in its ability to scale up to the needs of high-volume e-commerce environments and span multiple sales channels. Calico eSales Suite delivers guided selling power over the Web, as well as through stand-alone kiosks, field sales personnel, resellers, and telesales environment. With Calico eSales, users can analyze requirements, access marketing data, configure solutions, develop quotations, and generate proposals over the Internet or intranet, using desktop or laptop computers. Calico eSales allows customers to increase their competitive advantage by expanding channels of distribution, reducing costs, boosting revenues, increasing customer satisfaction, and building brands.

Calico Industry Solutions

Calico's customers have demonstrated that a huge opportunity exists to revolutionize the way they interact with their customers. The Calico eSales Suite has been deployed by computer, networking, telecommunications, retail, and manufacturing industry leaders such as Dell, Gateway, Cabletron, and Nortel. By using Calico's Web-based guided selling solutions, these companies have increased revenues and customer satisfaction while reducing their cost of sales. Calico has built a solutions approach that takes advantage of a substantial knowledge base of industry-specific configuration and business challenges such as knowing how to discover customer requirement, model customer behavior, and integrate with supply chain systems. The industry solutions approach allows Calico to quickly deliver customer-tailored solutions that drive sales effectiveness, enhance the buying experience, and reduce costs.

Calico eSales Professional Services

Since every business is different, no two eSales systems are alike. That's why Calico's products are adaptable to meet each company's individual needs. Calico offers full professional services and support, ranging from pre-development design and customization to implementation, post-deployment maintenance, and consultation. Our staff of highly trained professionals works with each customer to develop a solution that is right for them. By capturing the business logic that reflects the art of selling for each company and then creating models that support it, Calico's professionals provide a uniquely tailored solution.

Strategic Alliances

Partnering is fundamental to Calico's business model. The Calico eSales Suite provides even greater benefits when integrated with front and back office systems. Calico provides state-of-the-art technology that complements partners' offerings. Calico's key partners specialize in the following areas: front office, back office, supply chain, e-commerce, and systems integration. A current list of partners is included in Calico's Web site.

Europe's 3PL Industry Consolidates on the Road to Pan-European Services

The growth of the European freight industry in the 1990s has offered a lesson that the country-by-country model for logistics is no longer valid; companies have begun to reorganize themselves into continental operations based on integration and rationalization. The pace of change, however, has been slow. The introduction of the Euro as common European currency has made the need to restructure logistics systems greater than ever. The years to come will bring about a rationalization and consolidation of European third-party logistics systems, followed by globalization.

In 1991, my colleagues and I expressed the following view:

"Several key developments provide the foundation for the proposition that the 1990s will be the era of the freight mega-carrier, with the future European freight industry coming to be dominated by a few, very large, companies."

Perhaps we were presumptuous. The proposition was, and still is, based on two key developments. First, activity within the logistics services market has been stimulated by events outside it. The globalization of business, coupled with increasing competitive pressures, has led many manufacturers and retailers to assess their core competencies and as a consequence has provided new opportunities for third party logistics (3PL) service companies. In some cases, this has led to the demand for one single pan-European 3PL service provider, yet this remains very much the exception at present. Exploiting this latent demand will necessitate an increasing concentration in the industry, either through acquisitions, mergers, or alliances. Second, the deregulation of the freight markets in Europe coupled with the completion of the single European market has released new logistics operators into the field.

By 1993 our enthusiasm had heightened. Work on "Reconfiguring European Logistics Systems" in conjunction with Andersen Consulting confirmed our view that the country-by-country model was no longer valid and companies had set about reorganizing themselves into regional (European) operations. The emphasis was very much on integration and rationalization. The motivation was clear: to cut out layers of cost resulting from excessive levels of administrative and inventory duplication, none of which was providing appropriate customer service levels. Critically, companies recognized the need to separate their sales function from that of physical fulfillment.

Yet the pace of change in Europe has been slow. While companies are aware of the logistics opportunities presented by a single European market, many struggle to implement their strategies effectively. Translating vision into reality presents major challenges in which the management of people and information are paramount. With the introduction of the Euro in January 1999, the need to restructure has never been greater:

"Simplification and standardization are having a profound effect on our business – we still have miles to go in realizing this, but the Euro will accelerate it – and will bring increasing transparency in pricing across the continent – but any price reductions triggered by an increase in transparency could be offset in part by lower distribution costs and greater operational efficiencies."
– John Pepper, Chairman, Procter & Gamble, June 1998 in *The Financial Times*

Additionally, the dearth of pan-European logistics service providers has been a significant barrier to European restructuring. So what has hap-

---

Melvyn Peters is Senior Lecturer in Logistics and Transportation at Cranfield Centre for Logistics and Transportation at Cranfield School of Management in the UK. His areas of specialization include European Supply Chain Management, physical networks, logistics in Eastern and Central Europe, and logistics outsourcing.

Previously, Mr. Peters worked with Christian Salvesen, Securicor, and DRG Sellotapes. He spent several years involved in logistics-related research at the University of Westminster, London. His consultancy experience includes work with Argos, NatWest Bank, Emhart, Exel Logistics, and DHL.

pened to our proposition that "mega-freight" carriers will emerge in Europe? And what are the trends in Europe's 3PL market?

3PL European Market Size

Total logistics expenditures in Europe amounts to approximately $129 billion, of which $31.6 billion (24%) is contracted out. The 3PL industry is set for continued levels of growth with one forecast indicating that total European logistics expenditures will reach $155 billion in 2002, and that 3PL will increase its share of this expenditure to 28%, representing revenues of $44 billion. Despite this, the 3PL market in Europe is characterized by a fragmented set of players, although there are signs of consolidation. An example from Germany is Deutsche Post's unprecedented acquisition spree to consolidate its position in the express parcels market and to develop wider logistics service skills.

Europe's Leading 3PL Companies

The financial figures in Figure 1.0 inflate somewhat the market share of the leading 3PL players as they include incomes generated outside of Europe and some non-logistics-related income. Europe's leading 3PL companies achieve logistics revenues that equate with a market share ranging between 0.5% and 6.0 %.

Cranfield Survey Work

To monitor the development of 3PL outsourcing, Cranfield has been involved in a number of studies. Most recently this has involved collaborative work with Northeastern University, and Mercer Management Consulting, Inc. The Mercer surveys are designed to gauge the current status and future prospects of 3PL services in Europe and North America as perceived by their CEOs. The survey covers issues related to geographical scope, alliance building, industry service offerings, selling of third-party services, and the dynamics impacting on the 3PL industry. In all, 18 European CEOs, representing the largest European 3PL companies, responded to the latest survey in 1998.

EUROPE'S LEADING 3PL COMPANIES

Company	Country	Revenue (Millions)
Deutshe Post	D	15,840 - 98
TPGroup (TNT only)	NL	1,103 - 98
Stinnes Logistics	D	7,700 (Schenker + BTL) 98
Gefco KN	F/D	5,800 (1.5 + 4.3) 98
GEODIS	F	2,952 - 98
NFC (Exel)	UK	2,584 - 98
Panalpina	CH	2,946 - 97
Ocean Group	UK	1,908 - 97
Thyssen Haniel Log	D	1,744 - 97
Tibbett & Britten	UK	1,500 - 97
POTE	UK	1,421 - 98
Hays plc	UK	1,360 - 97
Fiege Logistik	D	1,300 - 96

Figure 1.0   Europe's leading 3PL companies

Those CEOs predict a stable growth rate of between 10% and 15 % per annum over the next three years. However, this growth rate hides the continuing decline in basic service margins and is one of the underlying causes leading to the industry consolidation we are witnessing. Some of the main findings are:

- Although the market for contract logistics will continue to grow, the loss of control and service quality issues are the primary constraints to increased 3PL usage.
- The emphasis on Europeanization picked up in earlier surveys has been replaced by a drive towards globalization.
- The offering of Value-Added Services and Information Management may be the keys to differentiation, but 3PL revenues continue to be largely generated by basic services.
- The price of services offered is an important issue in the choice of 3PL providers; lower cost is still the main driver for outsourcing.
- As users retain fewer 3PL providers, 3PL service offerings will need to expand – either directly or through alliances.
- Supply chain integration, globalization, and logistics information systems represent the biggest opportunities for growth as users focus more and more on core business processes.

The Key Revenue Generators

The top two revenue generators for 3PL providers, though not necessarily profits, remain basic services: warehouse management/services and transport services. Revenues from value-added services seem to be stable at around 30% in both Europe and North America, but growth seems illusory.

While it is possible to identify examples of successful value-added services for almost all of the survey respondents, these are often customized solutions, and as such the providers find it difficult to replicate easily the service with other customers.

Some shippers use an increasing scope strategy explicitly to test and develop 3PL relationships with providers. The relationship starts with letting the provider manage transportation, progresses to minor warehousing activities, and is followed by all warehousing (inventory management not included). The next step is to

DEUTSCHE POST'S - ACQUISITION SPREE

Courier/Express	Transport/Logistics
1998 GP Paket Logistik (D) Serviso (Pl) DHL (25%) Ducros (F - 87.9) Global Mail (US)	**1998** Securicor Distribution (UK- 50%) Danzas Holdings (CH)
1999 MIT (It)	**1999** Trans-o-flex (D 75.2%) Nedlloyd Log Div (NL) ASG (Sw)

Figure 2.0   Deutsche-Post's acquisition spree

add different value-adding services, e.g., packaging and light assembly. This approach to outsourcing enables the shipper to evaluate the provider on different levels of complexity, and ultimately whether to continue or terminate the relationship, through a phased introduction. Such an approach is an alternative to the full-scale evaluation of multiple providers for complex multiple activities. This phased approach is attractive to companies who lack the resources to evaluate and implement 3PL solutions and who feel no need to outsource immediately all 3PL activities. At a European level, however, it does rely on the selected 3PL provider having adequate Pan-European capability.

American CEOs appear to attach greater importance to value added services than their European counterparts, perhaps hoping that value-added services will enhance the complexity of their service offerings and in so doing improve the margin they are able to achieve. However, basic service provision remains critical in Europe and North America. 3PL providers must provide high-quality and cost-competitive basic services if they are to retain customers. Providers who demonstrate an ability to drive down user-basic logistics costs will be rewarded with additional business.

Growing service complexity will encourage some 3PL companies to move away from an asset-based to a more management/information-based service portfolio, acting as first tier service providers.

Opportunities for 3PLs

The outsourcing market remains strong. This is reflected in CEO comments about new markets emerging in Eastern Europe and Asia. The emphasis is shifting to globalization, as 80% of the European 3PL companies are already present in eight or more Western European countries. At the global level, the opportunities for 3PL companies stem from global sourcing and the rise of consumerism in Eastern Europe and Asia. Fears surrounding the impact of the Asian crisis appear to have been tempered by the realization that economic recessions often have a positive effect on the outsourcing market.

The pace of change associated with globalization and Europeanization forces companies to concentrate on their core competencies; geographical separation places new strains on supply chain activities with the need for integration. This provides new opportunities for 3PL companies. However, 3PL companies are themselves finding it difficult to integrate their activities across borders. 3PL CEOs have indicated that there are opportunities to increase operational efficiency. In part this will need to come not only from a more realistic approach to contract development more in line with true geographical capabilities and a greater use of alliances to provide wider service offerings but also from better asset utilization of shared resources through operational networks.

In a follow up to the 1998 survey we have established a greater IT emphasis, in part stimulated by e-commerce developments. Yet this is at variance with the low level of alliances reported by CEOs with information technology companies. Geographical scope appears to be driving the 3PL industry at present.

The most frequently cited problems faced by the industry are downward pressure on prices and margins, the availability of qualified personnel, and the problems of IS development. This is the same as in the previous survey. However, new problems this year are the Pan-European and regional management stresses. As 3PL companies Europeanize/globalize their operations, they begin to encounter management problems associated with mixed business cultures, management reporting structures/communications, and the management of alliance partners. The development of conjoint strategies between users and 3PL service providers seems to rely on compatible cultures.

Geographic Expansion and Alliances

The past decade has seen moves toward centralization of European (and in some industries global) logistics. Multi-nationals are changing their concepts from decentralized to centralized sourcing and distribution, and shippers are tending to rationalize their service providers in line with their network needs. This is reflected in the CEO responses to questions on the primary reason for entering new markets. The vast majority of answers focused on the need to internationalize operations, but, interestingly, many CEOs felt compelled to enter new markets because of their customers' drive for Europeanization and globalization.

While in agreement on the importance of globalization, user plans and provider strategies are not always in sync.

http://peters.ASCET.com

While North American users are focusing more on outsourcing of European and Asian logistics, providers are focusing on NAFTA, with U.S. providers consolidating their position in their own region.

The overall preferred entry strategy was direct investment and alliances with foreign companies. There was no significant difference in the entry strategy used according to region although restrictions on foreign ownership in certain parts of Asia would mitigate toward alliances with local partners.

Over two-thirds of the companies have established alliances with other providers of 3PL services primarily to increase their geographical networks and extend their portfolio of services. When compared with findings in the U.S. survey, it appears that alliances are more often by European companies. It would appear that the pace of change, with respect to shipper demands for geographical and service scope, often as part of a 3PL rationalization process, has favored alliance building. Some CEOs clearly stated that one of the significant events impacting their industry was the development of more alliances.

CEOs identified a range of factors important in making alliances work. Not surprisingly, common culture tops the list, but issues related to information technology and communications have become more important as customers demand more seamless services irrespective of the players involved.

Comparison: U.S. versus Europe

Comparisons with the North American providers revealed that European companies are more advanced in the internationalization of their operations. Half of European companies described themselves as operating worldwide (i.e., in three continents or more). European companies have quickly exploited the opportunities arising in Eastern Europe with a number of CEOs describing the region as offering significant growth. Perhaps more surprisingly, European companies have a greater presence in Asia. This is perhaps a legacy of colonial trade and the freight-forwarding origins of many of Europe's leading third-party logistics players. North American companies, by contrast, have concentrated on consolidating their position in NAFTA and developing their presence in the European market. The entry of North American providers into Europe is in its first wave and has taken place largely at the request of existing North American clients. Whether these new entrants can consolidate their longer-term position ultimately relies on their ability to attract and retain indigenous European customers.

Summary

Rationalization First, Globalization Later

Despite investment abroad, revenues for both European and North American providers are substantially weighted to their domestic markets (less than 80% of revenues for the majority of companies) with only moderate increases over the next three years. The globalization of these companies will be a slow process. As European CEOs are confident that the third-party market will remain strong, Europeanization of third-party logistics remains important, in order to provide a more complete set of services. Consolidation within Europe will continue, but for some the emphasis is already shifting toward globalization.

We can conclude that European 3PL industry restructuring is symptomatic of the drive to provide increasing geographical and service scope. This is being achieved through the glut of acquisitions, mergers, and alliances. However the slow rate at which value-added services are being taken up by shippers indicates that 3PL providers have not been successful in claiming a more prominent position in Supply Chain Management activities. Whether true Pan-European 3PL logistics providers will emerge is still questionable, but the building blocks are being put in place.

EUROPEAN CEO PERCEPTIONS OF THE THREE MOST SIGNIFICANT OPPORTUNITIES FOR 3PL COMPANIES

Opportunity	# of CEO's Listing in Top 3	1998	1996
Continued Globalization	7	18	15
Demand for 3PL Continues to Grow	6	15	-
Further Integration of Supply Chain Activities	5	13	4
Increased Operational Efficiency	7	11	-
Further Information Systems Development	5	9	7
New Markets (Eastern Europe; Asia)	4	7	-
Continued Europeanization	3	6	16
Value-added services	2	2	5

Figure 3.0 European perception of top opportunities

Setting New Supply Chain Standards: A Chemicals Industry E-Commerce Case Study

written by:
Kenneth M. Smith
Douglas A. Grimm
Michael S. Sweeney
Geon Company
http://smith.ASCET.com

To quickly gain advantage from Internet technology – and begin integrating their supply chains – some companies have enlisted e-procurement technologies to streamline the purchasing process and increase leverage with suppliers. Others have focused on providing "virtual service" via 24x7 applications that allow customer self-service. Yet neither approach offers the kind of comprehensive capabilities required to fully optimize the supply chain. Recently, the Geon Company broke new ground by using the Internet to combine Web-enabled processes and technologies with the integration and information management capabilities of its SAP system. In addition to providing substantial savings, this approach is allowing Geon to capture information about demand and then push that data downstream to its suppliers in order to improve everything from customer service, delivery, and invoicing to procurement, logistics, and manufacturing.

A Short History of Geon

The Geon Company traces its roots back to a division of the BFGoodrich Chemical Company. A scientist in search of inexpensive synthetic rubber created polyvinyl chloride (PVC) instead. The material proved to have a wide range of applications due to its low manufacturing cost, flexibility, and waterproof characteristics. In the decades since its discovery, PVC has become a basic polymer used in applications ranging from the medical to the construction industry.

One of the most difficult periods in its history began in the early 1980s when the worst economic downturn since the Great Depression hit the United States. Most of the PVC market segments were in a slump and several new competitors entered the marketplace with large amounts of new capacity. This new, low-cost, and large-scale capacity moved the PVC market into the commodity ranks. Throughout the 1980s and early 1990s, competition continued to increase while market conditions marginally improved. In 1993 the BFGoodrich Company spun off the Geon Vinyl Division into a separate legal entity, forming the Geon Company. This allowed Geon to better focus its resources on its core competencies.

The newly formed Geon Company responded by making several key strategic decisions. First, it focused internally on each of its core businesses to "fix the business" by re-engineering business and operation practices to drive the company toward operational excellence. This strategy reduced costs, increased quality, eliminated waste, and improved customer service. The stage was now set for Geon to begin transforming itself from a PVC company to a network of value-added polymer businesses focused on quality and customer service. Two critical steps in developing this network were the purchase of Synergistics Industries Ltd. and the joint venturing of its suspension resin and vinyl monomer operations with Occidental Chemical Company.

The second strategic move was to utilize information technology in a manner that supported the business process changes and locked in continuous improvement. This was accomplished by working with the different businesses and manufacturing to simplify activities, automate the appropriate processes, and then integrate these processes across the various functional groups. The core of this integration was SAP R/3, which quickly became the plat-

Kenneth M. Smith is vice president for information technology for the Geon Company.

Douglas A. Grimm is a manager in the Geon Compound Supply Chain. He is currently managing the rollout of Geon's B2B capability.

Michael S. Sweeney is an associate partner in the Andersen Consulting chemical industry practice. He is currently focused on helping chemical companies leverage their supply chains by deploying e-commerce and Enterprise Resource Planning capabilities.

Chemicals

form that enabled many of the new business changes and supply chain initiatives. This tighter integration and business-working environment has enhanced data integrity, customer on-time shipments, and reduced working capital requirements throughout the company.

These strategies have positioned the organization for growth both domestically and internationally. The Geon Company is now working toward becoming one of the leading polymer services and technology companies in the world by leveraging its current PVC, formulator, and calendaring operations and services businesses for growth. The new goal is to become a benchmark network of polymer businesses and a leader in the polymer industry.

Supply Chain Optimization

A key requirement to managing and leveraging capabilities across this network of polymer businesses was to find an effective way to integrate information across the supply chain – Geon determined that tremendous value could be created by creating an extended supply chain that linked the various businesses. This extended supply chain could be created by combining Internet-based technologies with the information management capabilities of SAP. The result was an integrated supply chain that linked Geon and Oxy Vinyls.

In 12 weeks, Geon was able to complete this link and reduce raw material inventory by eight percent. But this was just a first step. The company could also provide new value to its customers. In fact, the Internet provided a new opportunity to improve the communication and collaboration across Geon's entire network of business partners. The benefits achieved include a reduction in working capital, revenue enhancements, productivity improvements, and expense reductions. Simplifying and automating supply chain processes led to:

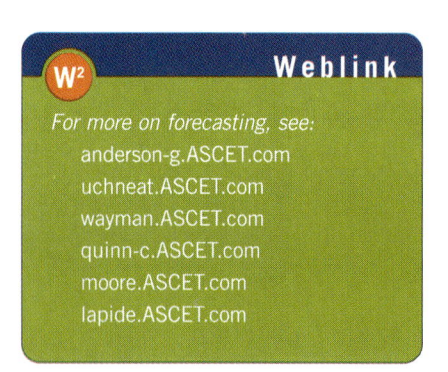

- Reduced lead times
- Decreased order handling by a factor of eight times
- Reduced data entry errors
- Increased productivity by diverting account representatives' time from fixing problems to business-enhancing activities
- Reduced logistics cost by removing the need for over 40 railcars
- Improved demand management process through sharing inventory and demand information

The new capability allowed Geon to set up direct business-to-business vendor managed inventory programs with its customers. The net result is a solution that makes the doing business with Geon easier and more profitable for its supply chain partners. The e-commerce capability also is driving new customer and supplier channels for Geon. In turn, a new set of cost drivers and activities are changing Geon's cost-to-serve model and customer segmentation strategies.

Approach

Geon worked with Andersen Consulting to design and implement its e-commerce strategy. Together, the two organizations formed a collaborative team that developed GeonB2B™ – an integrated business-to-business e-commerce platform linking Geon directly with their customers and suppliers. The solution components include:

- Extensible markup language (XML), a simplified version of standard generalized markup language (SGML) that provides a universal data interchange format among applications across the Internet
- WebMethods B2B, which provides the XML-based application integration services
- SAP BAPIs to interface data with SAP

These tools allowed the team to design and build an e-commerce solution that electronically links suppliers and customers in real-time connectivity. By letting machines communicate directly with other machines to share vital data over the Internet, Geon was able to simplify and automate numerous processes including:

- Demand planning
- Purchase and sales orders
- Changes to purchase and sales orders
- Order confirmations and acknowledgments
- Advance shipment notifications
- Invoices
- Vendor-managed inventory

For example, when Geon creates a purchase order in SAP, the purchase order passes into the supplier's system, automatically creating a sales order. Then, an order confirmation is sent to Geon with the confirmed delivery date. When the delivery is created in the supplier's system, it automatically is sent into Geon's SAP system as an advanced ship notice.

Results

The project was completed in just 12 weeks, and Geon immediately benefited in several ways:

- The company saved $2 million right away by cutting more than six million pounds of excess materials from its supply chain.
- In the system's first year, Geon expects to buy over 800 million pounds of raw materials through its new, high-value integrated direct channel.

In fact, everyone in Geon's supply chain is benefiting from the change. Favored customers can be offered loyalty-building services such as vendor-managed inventory and suppliers can forecast more accurately and therefore cut inventory. Most importantly, trading partners throughout the network of polymer businesses are saving money by being able to do business with less effort and expense on Geon's new, high-value integrated direct channel.

W² Weblink

For more on forecasting, see:
anderson-g.ASCET.com
uchneat.ASCET.com
wayman.ASCET.com
quinn-c.ASCET.com
moore.ASCET.com
lapide.ASCET.com

http://chemconnect.ASCET.com — web link

ChemConnect Provides Supply Chain Benefits Today

ChemConnect

E-commerce is here to stay and is already having a significant impact on the chemical industry. Successful e-commerce solutions include branding, transaction support, and value added services such as financial clearing, logistics support, and information services. One of the areas where e-commerce can provide significant benefits today is in the industry supply chain.

The supply chain has become an increasingly important source of value creation for the chemical industry. Between 60% and 80% of total costs are accounted for by the supply chain so that any cost savings will have a big impact on overall performance. Exchanges, such as ChemConnect's World Chemical Exchange, provide the next stage in the industry's efforts to integrate its supply chains beyond individual companies into broader supplier-to-customer networks.

ChemConnect and the World Chemical Exchange provide the only real-time window on the entire market for all types of chemicals and plastics, enabling companies to convert chemical needs, surpluses, and shortages into instant trading offers that reach a global market.

Along with real-time access to supply and demand information through the World Chemical Exchange, ChemConnect offers extensive online information resources, including a daily newswire service, a monthly newsletter, coverage of industry events, a reference library, and links to chemical journals. ChemConnect also offers My ChemConnect, a personalized home page where you can monitor the World Chemical Exchange and industry market activity.

Bringing Suppliers, Buyers, and Intermediaries Together

Every day, buyers and sellers of petrochemical, plastics and polymers, basic industrial, fine and specialty, pharmaceutical, agrochemical, and research chemicals from around the world, meet online, in real time, to conduct business. ChemConnect brings together three user communities: suppliers of chemicals and plastics, buyers who use chemicals and plastics in manufacturing operations, and intermediaries who assist clients in buying and selling chemicals and plastics.

The World Chemical Exchange and e-commerce, in general, provide a low-cost market access mechanism to enable producers to serve new customers – perhaps smaller customers or those geographically distant. It also provides a convenient meeting place for suppliers to bid on business, which generally yields a lower cost to the customer. Suppliers are able to reach a more diverse market and are able to offer more and higher quality sales information to their customers.

In addition, an e-commerce transaction can be linked into companies' ERP systems, yielding further cost reductions and improved efficiencies. As many chemical companies have invested in these large-scale systems, this further integration can be done relatively simply and easily.

About ChemConnect

Founded in 1995, ChemConnect is headquartered in San Francisco, with offices in Houston, England, and Singapore and is backed by top-tier investment firms including Goldman Sachs, Institutional Venture Partners (IVP), Weiss, Peck & Greer, CMEA Ventures, and Highland Capital Partners. Andersen Consulting, The Dow Chemical Company, Eastman Chemical Company, and Rohm & Haas are also equity investors in ChemConnect. Currently ChemConnect has 5,000 members from over 4,000 companies in 105 countries.

Contact Information

John F. Beasley
Chairman, Chief Executive Officer, and Founder

Phil Ringo
President and Chief Operating Officer

Robert E. Drury
Chief Financial Officer

Michael K. Eckstut
Senior Vice President, Business Development

Linda Stegeman
Senior Vice President, Marketing

Headquarters
44 Montgomery Street, Suite 250
San Francisco, CA 94104
Phone 415.364.3300
Toll-free 877 CHEMCON
Fax 415.646.0010

Houston Office
Three Riverway, Suite 1330
Houston, TX 77056
Phone 713.993.0373
Fax 713.993.0551

United Kingdom Office
Five Hawthorn Grove
Wilmslow Cheshire
SK9 5DE England, U.K.
Phone +44 (0) 1625.535080
Fax +44 (0) 1625.535098

Singapore Office
#15-03 Wisma Atria
435 Orchard Road
Singapore 238877
Phone +65 238.0668
Fax +65 238.0669

For more information or to become a World Chemical Exchange Member, visit the company's Web site at http://www.chemconnect.com or call 1-877-ChemCon

Categoric Software – Business Alerts System for Event-Driven Supply Chain

Contact Information

Michael Keddington
President and CEO

Anne McVey, Vice
President of Marketing

Michael Sayer
Vice President of Sales

Categoric Software Corporation
2445 Faber Place
Palo Alto, CA 94303
Phone 650.858.8182
Fax 650.858.8183
inquiry@categoric.com
www.categoric.com

Sales Offices
London
California
Virginia

Categoric Software Corporation provides proactive business event notification systems for supply chain collaboration. Categoric addresses the challenge of identifying key business events as they occur and notifying specific individuals of those events. The flagship product, Categoric Alerts, is an advanced business event-notification system that allows enterprises to streamline operations, enhance customer and partner relations, and act on business opportunities as they occur.

Categoric Alerts – Get the Right Information, to the Right Person, at the Right Time!

Categoric's Alerts facilitates collaborative planning and execution in the supply chain by alerting individuals of exceptions to business plans and rules both inside and outside corporate boundaries. Categoric Alerts identifies exceptions to business plans and rules as they occur in the supply chain, then sends the alerts to specified individuals who can act on the information – employees, partners and suppliers, and customers – via e-business media, including e-mail, pagers, cell phones, and the Web, as well as fax and EDI.

Categoric Alerts reduces safety stock levels throughout the supply chain while also reducing escalations and expedites. Since Categoric's system works on top of existing ERP and Supply Chain Management systems, companies can revamp operations without overhauling existing complex systems as well as access any data sources across the supply chain.

Categoric Alerts Transforms Businesses into Fast-Acting Enterprises

Categoric Alerts is proven

Categoric Alerts is in production use at over 40 enterprise companies in the US and Europe, including manufacturing, distribution, transportation and logistics companies, and retails.

TTSI, Carpetland International, and Rank Hovis McDougall are just a few of the global companies that have gained the power of Categoric Alerts as a SCM solution. In addition, Categoric Alerts has been licensed by other software solution providers to augment their existing products with a robust event notification system. In addition to Categoric's direct sales force, the products are also distributed by leading software companies and systems integrators.

Categoric, with its partners, delivers proven best-of-class training, professional services, and technical support with specific expertise in Alerts for supply chain planning and execution processing.

Categoric Software – The Leader in Enterprise Alerts

Since its inception in 1996, Categoric has generated attention and praise in the market. Product evaluations have resulted in exceptional reviews from respected industry analysts such as Meta Group. Bloor Research considers Categoric Alerts one of the top recent innovations, "In our view, Categoric Alerts define a new market, just as WordPerfect did for word processing and 1-2-3 did for spreadsheets. Like them, Categoric Alerts could be the next, and long-awaited, killer application."

"Although there are technologies that provide system-specific event notification, these systems are stovepipe solutions. Alerts allows people to be notified about multiple business conditions from multiple systems." – Meta Group

About Catergoric

Categoric Software Corporation is led by an experienced team of value network and industry thought leaders from Benchmarking Partners, Oracle, Centura, Remedy, Calico, TTSI, and Amdahl.

white paper

written by:

Jorge Benitez
Bruce Gordon
Andersen Consulting
http://benitez.ASCET.com

1.0 The Path Forward | 2.0 Supply Chain Innovations | 3.0 Industry Perspectives | 4.0 Making It Happen

The Race is On for Supply Chain Success

The balance of power in the chemical industry is shifting from a model in which suppliers push their product out to the marketplace to one in which customer demand for total solutions drives the chain. In reaction to this shift, the race to build new supply chain solutions is underway in the boardrooms of leading chemical companies around the globe. Fueled by the new capabilities of their information architecture and the rapidly expanding capability of the Internet, leading players are jockeying to secure the long-term loyalty of their most precious customers. In this paper, we look at the ingredients for supply chain success and how ultimately to win the race.

Fasten Your Seat Belts …

When motor racing champion Ralph Schumacher takes the wheel of his Williams Formula 1 racing car, his success depends as much on the efficiency of the supply chain that supports him as it does on the slick teamwork of his pit crew. The racing strategy requires that information, materials, and service be delivered to the point of need in split-second timing – a supply chain that squeezes every ounce of competitive advantage for the driver on race day.

In the chemical industry, the leading players have emulated the Formula 1 model by making Supply Chain Management an integral part of their winning strategies. Just as Formula 1 relies on the latest technologies, chemical companies are starting to embrace e-commerce as a means of sharpening their supply chain edge. So, if you have not yet designed your supply chain strategy, start worrying. Your customers are hard at work designing it for you.

As a collection of related supporting functions, Supply Chain Management's early origins were internally focused. Recently, however, the supply chain has matured and become more sophisticated. It has taken on an external focus, incorporating suppliers and customers in new value-sharing arrangements, with the series of traditionally separate supply chain functions integrated into a seamless whole.

Today, supply chain strategies operate on the basis of "demand-pull" rather the historical "supply-push" model. Customers no longer want just materials. They demand solutions composed of products, services, and information. Rely on old business models and practices that deliver only products to customers and you're missing two-thirds of the value that could be captured by taking a new approach.

Research by Andersen Consulting revealed that while key customers of the chemical industry are adopting supply chain strategies, the industry itself lags behind other sectors. In consumer and packaged goods, for example, supply chain initiatives outnumber chemicals 7 to 1; in electronics and high technology, 5 to 1; and in automotive, it is 4 to 1.

Experience in these sectors shows that benefits on the order of a 40% increase in sales, a 30% reduction in inventory, and a 95% increase in service performance coupled with a 25 to 50% in inventory velocity can be achieved.

Bolting in another software package is not enough to make these gains. Success comes from defining a strategy and implementing it vigorously along the supply chain.

What It Really Means

We hear a lot about developing a supply chain strategy. What does this really mean?

Supply chain strategies are designed to simultaneously lift revenue, lower cost, and improve capital utilization. Because the emphasis is on improving quality and flexibil-

Jorge Benitez is a managing partner for the Andersen Consulting organizational human performance competency unit. He is responsible for engagements at Celenese Chemicals, Huntsman Corporation, and BP Amoco Chemicals in the United States.

Bruce Gordon is an associate partner in the Andersen Consulting chemicals practice and is responsible for supply chain programs, including e-procurement. He is also a Supply Chain Management thought leader for Andersen Consulting's Chemicals Ideas Exchange and is a member of the e-commerce strategy team for the chemicals practice.

Chemicals

http://benitez.ASCET.com   179

ity while at the same time cutting overall costs, reducing complexity is the cornerstone of a competitive, effective supply chain strategy.

As the balance of power shifts from supplier to customer (witness the evolution in the automobile, consumer, and high-technology industries), the chemical industry segments closest to these businesses are being pulled into new relationships. In turn, they're discovering the potential of Supply Chain Management.

Today's challenge is to tie Supply Chain Management closely to the overall business strategy to substantially increase shareholder value.

Competitive Advantage in the New "Demand" Economy

News from chemical industry leaders is encouraging, with several embracing supply chain strategies as means of competitive differentiation. Early-stage implementations of demand-driven customer segmentation and channel strategy initiatives are forming the basis of supply chain programs that go beyond the cosmetic. A global petrochemical company, a regional polymer player, and a global specialty company are each developing cost-to-serve profiles for their customer bases. Once defined, this value-based segmentation becomes part of the fabric of daily operations and drives the development of unique service offerings, tailored to key customers. Declaring victory is premature, but early results confirm that value can be captured at multiple points in the supply chain to the benefit of all the stakeholders.

Gaining Pole Position in the E-Commerce Supply Chain

Studies by Andersen Consulting confirm the chemical industry's keen awareness of the Internet and provide a healthy debate on how to lead the field. Companies across all segments are expressing interest in low-cost channel strategies.

Global interest in e-procurement (the combination of leading practices of strategic sourcing with Web-based technologies), aimed at non-production materials, is running high in both Europe and the United States. Initial success in e-procurement suggests that savings of $3 million to $20 million per billion dollars of revenue can be achieved. Low-risk, high-return projects are emerging among leading companies in multiple segments of the chemical industry, such as diversified, specialty, and global petrochemical.

Nonetheless, many chemical companies remain stalled on the grid in a race where the prizes are substantial. To turbocharge your business, you will need to blend all the elements of e-commerce into your supply chain strategy.

The Key Elements

You've told me why a supply chain strategy is important. What are the key elements to consider?

Supply Chain Excellence

The key shift moves the supply chain from a series of related functions to an integrated process, built on the chemical industry's traditional strengths in operational excellence. The framework for supply chain success – and ultimately excellence – includes the following elements: customer

> *The key shift moves the supply chain from a series of related functions to an integrated process, built on the chemical industry's traditional strengths in operational excellence. The framework for supply chain success – and ultimately excellence – includes the following elements: customer service architecture, product portfolio management, customized logistics networks, integrated supply and demand planning, strategic sourcing, information technology enablement, and supply chain metrics.*

service architecture, product portfolio management, customized logistics networks, integrated supply and demand planning, strategic sourcing, information technology enablement, and supply chain metrics. Each company should select the elements that give them a competitive advantage.

Excellent Supply Chain Management transforms traditional transactional exchanges into supply chain partnerships, boosting revenue, improving cost efficiency and effectiveness, and significantly enhancing the use of both fixed and working capital.

Supply Chain Information Technologies

Information technology is a key enabler of future supply chain success. Recent investments in enterprise resource planning systems provide the foundation for timely and accurate transactional data. Advanced planning systems improve the speed and accuracy of decision-making and the ability to balance supply and demand in complex, extended supply chains. The ability of advanced planning systems to cope

Weblink

More on performance measurement:
lapide.ASCET.com
zimdars.ASCET.com
manheim.ASCET.com
albright.ASCET.com

For more on strategic sourcing, see:
sprague.ASCET.com
appell.ASCET.com
anderson-d.ASCET.com

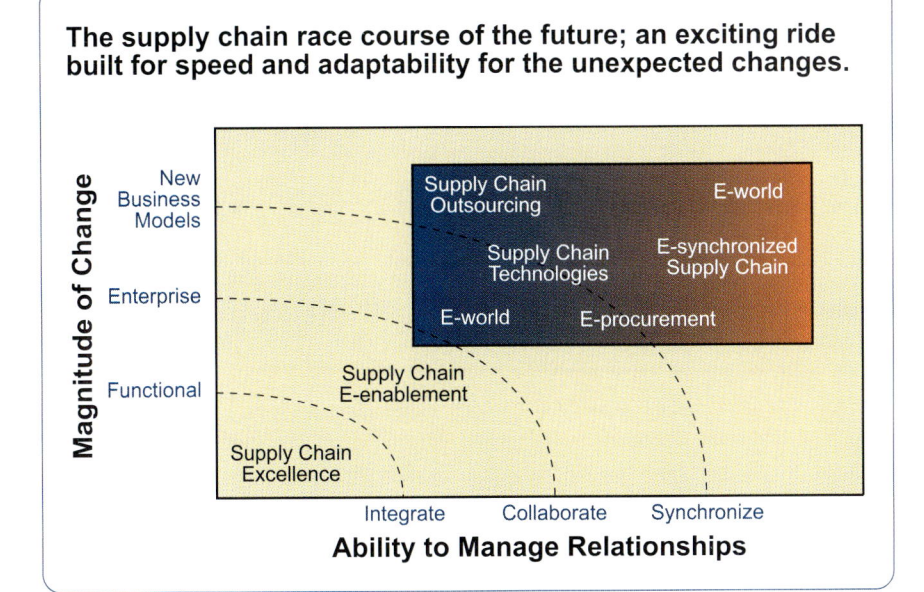

Figure 1.0 How change effects the ability to manage

The supply chain race course of the future; an exciting ride built for speed and adaptability for the unexpected changes.

Axes: Magnitude of Change (New Business Models, Enterprise, Functional) vs. Ability to Manage Relationships (Integrate, Collaborate, Synchronize). Elements shown: Supply Chain Excellence, Supply Chain E-enablement, E-world, Supply Chain Technologies, E-procurement, Supply Chain Outsourcing, E-synchronized Supply Chain, E-world.

---

with the planning needs of process industries, including the chemicals industry, is improving all the time. The best enterprise resource planning and advanced planning solutions also provide the "available-to-promise" capability that is essential to support sales via e-commerce.

E-commerce provides the opportunity to transform functional processes. The impact of e-commerce can already be seen in the procurement arena. Many e-procurement initiatives are reducing the cost of goods and services and freeing up purchasing professionals to manage qualified suppliers, negotiate better practices, and examine spending behavior. This leads to higher overall productivity. E-procurement also improves the quality of information and provides an opportunity for collaborative planning with suppliers to reduce capital needs and lower required inventory levels.

New Business Models

In addition to transforming existing supply chain processes, e-commerce has the potential to fundamentally change the way chemicals are sold and how customer demand is fulfilled via the supply chain. Already, new players are emerging in the form of virtual distributors, auctions and exchanges (for example, eChemicals, PlasticsNet, ChemConnect, ChemMatch and fobchemicals). Existing producers and distributors are also rapidly developing e-commerce capabilities; there is a new venture or alliance announcement that signals a new development in this area almost every week. This market space is incredibly dynamic and it remains to be seen who will be the ultimate winners.

Supply chain capability, in the form of physical infrastructure, operational excellence, and Supply Chain Management, is critical to the success of these new ways of doing business. Web-enabled supply chain solutions provide the opportunity to manage supply chains collaboratively and to synchronize operations. However, technology is only one part of the solution. New forms of relationships between trading partners will need to be developed and imaginative outsourcing solutions will need to be adopted to provide the necessary supply chain capability, speed, and flexibility.

A good example of an imaginative outsourcing solution is the joint venture logistics operations where the venture has access to world-class capabilities beyond the reach of the single enterprise. This reach enables the delivery of a step change in the cost of the operation, plus continuous improvement of total delivered cost.

An alternative business model is the virtual enterprise in which the Web is used as an integration tool to allow a number of companies to behave operationally as a single enterprise.

Another rapidly emerging business model is that of the Internet-enabled trading community in which a group of buyers and sellers agree to trade on a single platform such as MySAP.com or TradeMatrix.

So What Else Do I Have to Think About?

Mergers, Acquisitions and Alliances

In 1998, merger activity in the chemicals industry was estimated to be more than $100 billion and, according to an Andersen Consulting study, chemical industry alliances will account for $600 billion in revenue by 2005. In the wake of this hyper-activity, Supply Chain Management is topping boardroom agendas as a vital part of the "race-day" capabilities required for successful mergers, acquisitions, and alliances.

The boom has increased attention on Supply Chain Management as many mergers, acquisitions, and alliance deals are now announced with specific supply chain benefits baked into the value equation. This new facet in deal-making is not surprising considering that as much as 80

Converting Supply Chain Programs into Significant Business Benefits

Revenue increase: 1 to 3 percent

Supply chain cost reductions:

- Strategic sourcing of raw materials: 5 to 15%
- Strategic sourcing non-production materials: 3 to 12%
- Logistics networks: 15 to 25 %

Reduced working capital: 10 to 50%

Fixed capital impact: 10 to 15%

---

http://benitez.ASCET.com

percent of a company's expense is linked to the operations and supply chain functions that consequently offer the majority of the synergistic opportunities.

Mergers, acquisitions, and alliances provide opportunities to undertake an analysis of redundancies and synergies between two companies. Program management skills will be essential in most post-merger environments. The combination of cultural and geographical elements with the new products, customers, and suppliers defines a project whose successful completion requires huge amounts of data, strong supply chain skills, and the excess capacity to deal with the analysis and decisions of the new environment.

Growing Supply Chain Skills

The supply chain organization of the future will lose its internal focus and a re-skilled workforce will be required to operate in the new, more complex external environment. Commercial and logistical skills must be elevated to the same stature as the engineering skills that have historically been a prerequisite for career success. Creating a nimble environment, capable of initiating and sustaining change in ever-decreasing cycle time characterizes the new supply chain era.

There is no doubt that, in chemical industry boardrooms around the world, the phrase "supply chain" is gaining common currency. There is a growing recognition that the opportunities for deriving sustainable business advantages from changes to the supply chain are immense. But beware the strategists who simply re-label processes without instituting real and lasting change. The full benefits will only be achieved if the supply chain strategy is linked to the business strategy and when implementation embraces the organizational changes required to support the transformation.

External Focus and Forces

The dominant theme is that e-commerce will transform the way supply chains are formed and operated as well as the way supply chain partners interact. While the rate of change will vary by industry segment and world geography, supply chain strategy will have a profound impact on the conduct and results of the businesses that make up the chemical industry.

The leading players of the future will extend their reach way beyond existing boundaries in response to the shift in the balance of power from the supplier to the customer. The extension will occur as part of a selection process that emphasizes collaboration and synchronization among multiple layers of the networked supply chain.

There are many opportunities to begin creating this future. Fine-tuning and tightly coordinating the company's internal operations to world-class levels can be a good start. The Internet will do more to transform supply chains than can be imagined today and e-procurement is just the first of many ways in which the Internet will revolutionize supply chain activities. The potential to form supply chain partnerships through merger and alliances will grow as companies adapt their traditional business models to remain competitive. The Internet sales channels being created by pioneering chemicals companies show how the Internet will challenge the very structure of how chemicals are produced and sold. The first movers to build strong Internet and supply chain capabilities by grasping these opportunities will be the true winners.

Copyright©2000 Andersen Consulting LLP

… **white paper**

written by:
Fritz Lescher
Aspen Technology, Inc.
http://lescher.ASCET.com

Making Your Enterprise Internet-Ready: E-Business for the Process Industries

As the future of e-business in the process industries comes into focus, manufacturers are beginning to ask themselves how they can make their enterprises "Internet-ready." The answer comes down to people, plants, and business processes. Changes brought about by the Internet will force manufacturing enterprises to become more agile and more responsive. To accomplish this, process manufacturers will need to deploy integrated information systems, which allow them to view the actual capabilities of their plants in real time. Next, they will need to have business processes in place to facilitate rapid decision-making. Finally, they must optimize their extended supply chain by integrating their internal business processes with their partners' business processes.

E-Business Growth in Process Industries

Estimates of the potential for business to business (B2B) commerce are so large they can lose their meaning. Forrester Research predicts U.S. B2B trade conducted via the Internet will nearly double annually, growing from $43 billion in 1998 to $1.3 trillion in 2003. The process industries are expected to grow more quickly, approaching $500 billion by 2003. For some segments of the process industries, nearly 10% of the industry's trade could move online. Forrester predicts that in the petrochemicals industry e-business will move from its experimentation phase today to a "hypergrowth" phase in 2000 and 2001.

Internet Allows All Process Manufacturers to Differentiate

In the short term, the Internet offers all process manufacturers the attractive possibility of differentiating themselves from their competitors in a commodity market. Over the long term, e-business will impact individual segments of the process industries differently. Downstream segments such as polymers, specialty chemicals, and pharmaceuticals will see more demand for customized products and will have more opportunities to sell and market their products directly to end users. Upstream segments, such as refining, will feel the most impact from the close collaboration with business partners that e-business demands. The implications for all process manufacturers are the same, however – where you sit in the value chain will determine where you should focus your energies.

The Internet is a Tool, Not a Panacea

The e-business leaders in the process industries will not be the companies that launch the glitziest Web site or deploy the most sophisticated Internet-enabled manufacturing technology. They will be the companies that align their people and internal business processes to gain the maximum leverage from Internet technology and tap into the vast potential of e-business. Companies that ignore their own business processes and skip ahead to forging Internet links with their business partners will, in the words of Michael Hammer, simply be exposing their own poor business processes to the rest of the world. In the hyper-competitive environment of the Internet, that could be a fatal, self-inflicted wound.

This paper outlines the future of e-business in the process industries and explains what process manufacturers can and should be doing today to prepare for the e-business era. This paper does not address each and every issue manufacturers will face, nor does it focus on all of the underlying technologies. Rather, this paper sketches out the broad picture and identi-

Fritz Lescher is marketing communications manager of New Providence, New Jersey-based Aspen Technology, Inc.

Chemicals

http://lescher.ASCET.com   183

fies the major actions process manufacturers should be taking today as e-business in the process industries enters its predicted "hypergrowth" phase over the next two years. E-business has not yet caused the revolutionary change in the asset-intensive process industries that it has in information-based industries such as publishing and financial services. However, it is becoming clear that when the dust finally settles, the changes brought about by e-business will be no less dramatic in the process industries than they have been in information-based industries.

The Internet is Driving Two Fundamental Changes

The Internet – and the telecommunications revolution more broadly – are driving two fundamental changes in the way we communicate and interact: increased connectivity and increased speed. E-business is simply a ripple effect of these two changes.

Increased Connectivity

The simple technology on which the Internet is based has dramatically expanded the ability of individuals and companies to connect with each other. Whereas a customer and a supplier may only have communicated once or twice a month via phone in the past, they are increasingly likely to be directly connected to each other today.

Increased Speed

Faster communications "pipes" allow people to transfer more information more quickly. Limited bandwidth in the past restricted most business interactions to a brief fax or a terse Electronic Data Interchange (EDI) message. Today, entire databases can be transferred in seconds. And if your products can be converted into bits you can distribute them electronically, too.

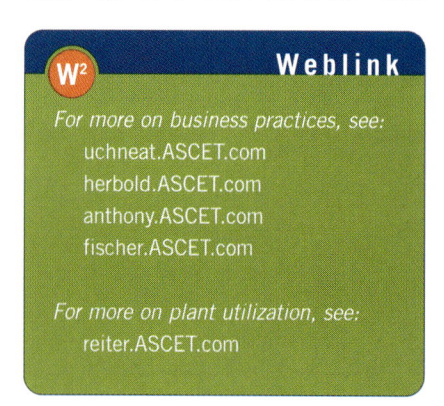

Ripple Effect

The ripple effects of the Internet will significantly impact process manufacturers.

The increased speed and connectivity, which the Internet enables, is creating a ripple effect throughout the process industries. At a high level, the Internet is forcing three major changes for process manufacturers: (1) fostering increased intimacy with business partners, (2) automating internal business processes and exposing them to the world, and (3) opening new markets, thereby creating sales opportunities as well as threats.

Increasing Intimacy with Business Partners

Continuous connectivity with customers and suppliers has created new opportunities to collaborate, share information, and provide more customized customer support. The fact that companies can communicate instantaneously is leading to expectations that they should communicate instantaneously. However, the bottleneck usually comes when they get to the "what." What information will they exchange? Will it be accurate? Will it be meaningful? This increased pace of communication with business partners is leading to higher expectations about response times. However, a company's ability to respond ultimately depends on the information they have readily available, the accuracy of that information, and the business processes that support the dissemination of that information.

Automating & Exposing Internal Business Processes

The speed and connectivity of the Internet is affecting business processes on two levels. First, it is accelerating internal business processes. Secondly, it is exposing companies' business processes to their business partners. The increased velocity of internal business processes does not necessarily constitute an improvement. More often, simply performing existing processes faster highlights the bottlenecks, problems, and inconsistencies of these processes. The increased speed thus acts as a catalyst for change. Likewise, exposing your business processes to your business partners is not good in and of itself. It is only something you want to do if your business processes are worth sharing. Otherwise, the Internet is just exposing your bad processes to the rest of the world. Anyone who has received poor customer service from the Web-based storefront of a bricks-and-mortal retailer has experienced bad business processes attached to the Internet.

Opening New Markets

Changes brought about by the Internet are altering the competitive landscape in the process industries on both the marketing and sales fronts. On the marketing front, virtually every major company now has a Web site. These Web sites provide an immediate international presence – even for small manufacturers. Manufacturers are becoming increasingly savvy about using their Web sites to differentiate their products and to "level the playing field" with respect to their larger competitors. For example, Huntsman has a Web site dedicated to its Spectar co-polymer product (www.spectar.com) while Dow has launched its second-generation Web site to support its Styrofoam and Trymer products (www.styrofoam.com). Monsanto has gone further, creating Farmsource (www.farmsource.com), a site that offers a broad array of news and information to its agrochemical end-users.

On the sales front, Internet trading exchanges are making it easier to link buyers and sellers to facilitate the sale and distribution of products in the process industries – especially for off-spec products and smaller orders. For example, LTV Corp. sold 100 tons of excess steel online in January via Metalsite Inc.'s Web site. By August, LTV had expanded its online sales to six product lines and 50,000 tons a month. A whole host of similar Internet exchanges with names like eSteel and eChemicals are being launched every month to serve specialized segments of the process industries. These exchanges will make it easier for customers

---

Weblink

For more on business practices, see:
uchneat.ASCET.com
herbold.ASCET.com
anthony.ASCET.com
fischer.ASCET.com

For more on plant utilization, see:
reiter.ASCET.com

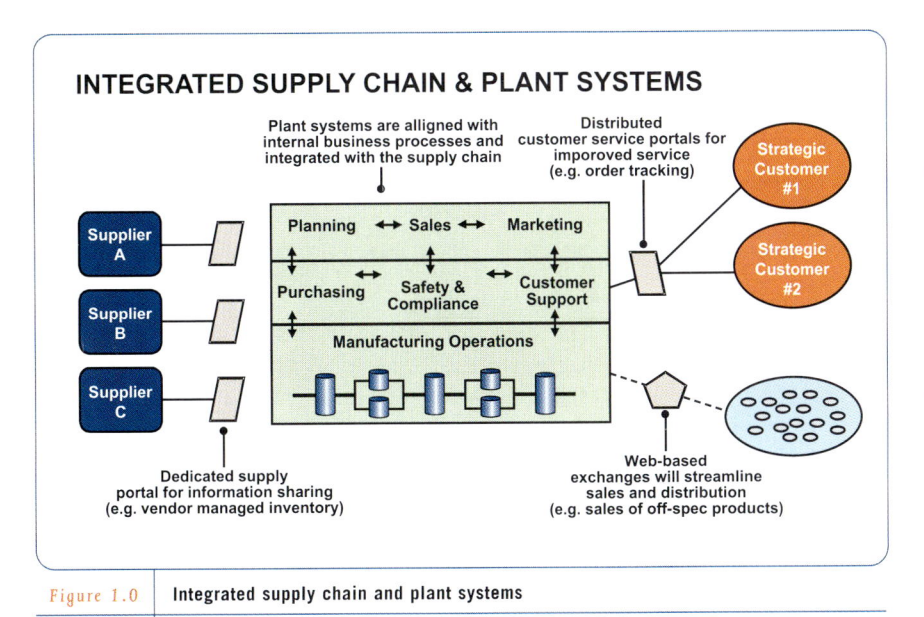

Figure 1.0 Integrated supply chain and plant systems

to compare prices. Process manufacturers that are well positioned to plug into these exchanges will benefit. Others may be left holding large inventories of unwanted products.

Process manufacturers – especially manufacturers of downstream products – are also setting up their own storefronts and in some cases attracting new customers. The specialty chemicals division of Ciba, for example, began selling its products via the Web and has since been receiving about two requests from new customers every day.

The Future

The future of e-business in the process industries is coming into focus. Most people working in the process industries are already feeling the ripple effects described above at some level, but they want more specifics. They want to know more precisely what e-business means for them and how they can prepare for it. In short, the future of e-business in the process industries is coming into focus and it looks, in many ways, like e-business in any other industry. Information is created and distributed in real time. The distance between customers and suppliers effectively shrinks and expectations rise. However, there are some important differences.

The main characteristic that sets the process industries apart from other industries is their asset-intensiveness. Process manufacturing plants are huge and costly. What's more, due to the continuous nature of most processes, product changeovers are more complex and less frequent than in discrete manufacturing facilities. Therefore product customization and improved customer service are less likely to come from make-to-order production than from improved business processes, a better and more accurate understanding of the plant's capabilities, and more accurate product planning via collaborative forecasting. These improvements will allow process manufacturers to meet their customers' rising expectations and serve their individual needs.

The e-business future for the process industries suggests that leading e-business manufacturers will know the true capabilities of their manufacturing enterprises. They will have consistent and interoperable business processes and use software and Web-based services to support those improved internal business processes. Leading manufacturers will answer their customers' demands for improved customer service by providing windows (sometimes called portals) into their operations. These windows will help integrate shared business processes such as improved product planning and collaborative forecasting.

Finally, Internet-based exchanges will streamline pricing and distribution. Commodity products will move more quickly and efficiently through the distribution network while specialized, value-added products command premium prices and become increasingly customized to end-user needs. As in other industries, e-business in the process industries entails a transfer of power from vendors to their customers. Vendors who understand and embrace this shift stand to reap significant benefits.

Business Processes Will Be Streamlined

Manufacturers will only capture the benefits of increased connectivity if they are able to collaborate more effectively with their business partners. To start with, this means that internal business processes must be streamlined and made interoperable with their business partners' processes. If a company rushes to collaborate with business partners before it has optimized its internal business processes, it is courting disaster.

Once a company has streamlined, consistent, and interoperable internal processes, it is "Internet ready." The next step is to create an extended enterprise by integrating those business processes with their business partners. Many companies have experienced the pain of integrating their internal business processes – often in conjunction with the implementation of an ERP system, such as SAP R/3™. Integrating business processes externally with business partners will be equally challenging for process manufacturers. They will need to deploy advanced software systems that facilitate and automate the integration of their business processes with partners so they can collaborate and transact B2B commerce over the Internet.

One basic example of collaboration is the use of supplier-managed inventories, where customers share information about the demand for their products so that their suppliers can ensure that there will be enough raw materials on hand to manufacture the end products. Shell is among the companies that are currently experimenting with this shared business process.

http://lescher.ASCET.com

Web-Based Services Will Support Internal Business Processes

Not all business processes involve established relationships, such as those maintained with customers, key suppliers, and distributors. A good portion of them involve infrequent or occasional interactions or one-off requests. Emerging Web-based services will play a key role in supporting many of these non-standard business processes. In particular, such Web-based services will be especially useful in cases where a business process requires obtaining multiple quotes or where information from many different sources must be brought together to solve a problem.

The most obvious example of the first case would be the business processes that a purchasing agent engages in. Here, the purchasing agent must obtain quotes from multiple suppliers and determine if the goods offered meet the company's required specifications. In the past this might have been done manually via phone and fax. Today sites like Chemdex (www.chemdex.com) claim that their services can "reduce costs and streamline enterprise procurement processes" in the life sciences industry.

In the second case, consider the challenge design engineers face today when performing a cost-benefit analysis for expanding the capacity of a particular process.

Here, the engineer needs to first research the problem and determine how other people have solved similar problems. Then the engineer needs to model the new process using process design software. This step entails several sub-steps such as obtaining information about the plant, process, and physical properties of chemicals in different states. Finally, once the engineer has designed the new process, he or she needs to obtain cost information on any new required equipment, and perhaps get quotes for selling old equipment that is no longer needed. A Web-based service that supported the business processes of a design engineer would bring all of these disparate services and information sources together so that they could be searched and utilized in minutes.

BUSINESS PROCESS INTEGRATION WITH TRADING PARTNERS
PRIVATE PROCESSES vs PUBLIC, SHARED PROCESSES

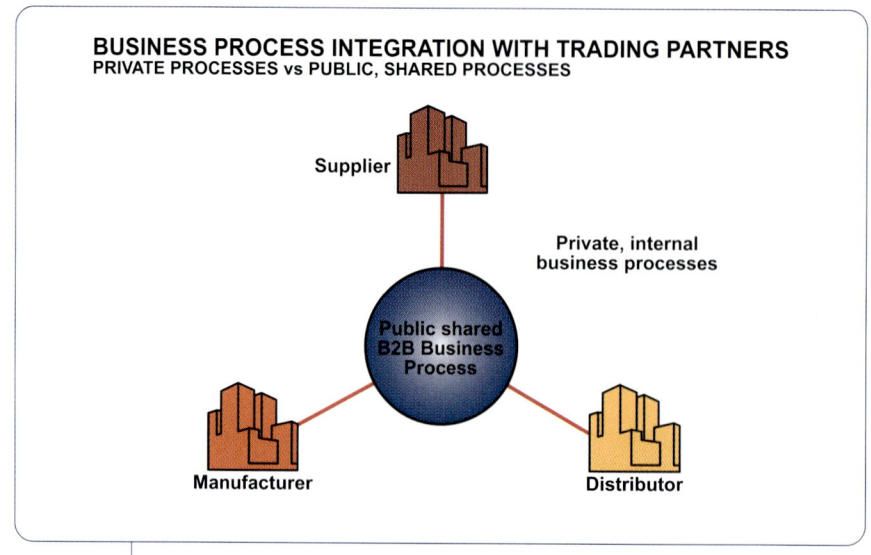

Figure 2.0 Business process integration with trading partners

Portals Will Provide "Windows" Into Your Operations

Just as computers have used the Internet to interconnect and form a "super network," companies will use the Internet to connect as well. One of the principal ways companies in the process industries will connect and collaborate is through the use of portals, or windows, into manufacturing enterprises. These portals will help to integrate inter-company business processes and streamline the extended supply chain by allowing customers to automate key business functions such as collaborative forecasting and planning.

This collaboration will increase the likelihood the right product will be made at the right time, cost, and quality and be sent to the right customer. This is especially important in the process industry since transitioning from one product to another is a complex and costly endeavor. BASF is already doing this by allowing suppliers to check current inventory and calculate forecasts based on real-time information from its IT systems. Dow has a similar arrangement with some of its business partners.

Integrated Supply Chain & Plant Systems Will Be Required to Enable E-Business

A trap manufacturers will face is creating Internet windows with nothing for their business partners to view. For collaboration to become a reality, manufacturers will need to ensure they have reliable, up-to-date information to share with their business partners. This will require integrated supply chain and plant systems that are updated in real time and model-centric – based on consistent, accurate physical and financial models of their manufacturing processes. Without this underlying technology, manufacturers will not be able to make real-time, profitable decisions about which products to make, where to make them, and when to make them.

The Internet Will Raise the Bar on Customer Service

The increased communication enabled by the Internet is raising customer expectations ever higher. This is compounded by the fact that popular Web-based retailers, such as Amazon.com, have set a high standard for customer service on the Internet. The Internet will ultimately enable and require a similar level of customer service from companies in the process industries.

There are two principle ways in which manufacturers will use the Web to improve customer service. First, they will service non-strategic customers more cost effectively. For many companies, 80% of the customers account for only 20% of revenues. The opportunity for servicing these customers more efficiently is enormous. The other way manufacturers will use the Internet is to provide exceptional customer service to their top customers – the other 20%.

Manufacturers are already creating customized Web sites that allow customers to place and track orders via the Internet. Air Products (www.airproducts.com), Condea Vista (www.condeavista.com), Eastman Chemicals (www.eastman.com), and GE Plastics (www.polymerland.com) are examples of companies that are doing this on their public Web sites today. GE goes so far as to allow users to customize polymers to their specific needs. The strategy is paying dividends. Already 15% of GE Plastics' $1 billion sales are now conducted via the Internet and Internet-routed sales are increasing at 20% per month.

Some manufacturers are also rolling out the red carpet for key customers. AlliedSignal, for example, has set up private Web pages built for its key customers so they can access individualized product data, technical and R&D information, as well as place orders, track inventory, and pay bills. Closer relationships through these types of interfaces and the streamlined business processes that support them will increasingly allow manufacturers to use exceptional customer service as a "reward" for their very best customers.

Internet Exchanges Will Streamline Distribution

Internet exchanges will help streamline the sales and distribution of the products that process manufacturers create. Burgeoning online exchanges such as eSteel, Metalsite, e-Chemicals, and Chematch are vying to make the business of trading chemical commodities more liquid and efficient. Companies like DuPont, Elf Atochem, and Huntsman have also experimented with these types of exchanges.

Internet exchanges create opportunities and challenges for manufacturers. On the positive side, they open up new market segments such as customers who want to buy small quantities and, in downstream processes, the direct-to-consumer market. In past years these segments would have been too expensive for large manufacturers to sell and serve profitably.

The online exchanges will also provide an effective outlet for off-spec products. In short, online exchanges will help grease the distribution channel for commodity chemicals and, perhaps, make pricing more transparent.

Manufacturers who use these exchanges strategically could reduce their inventory carrying costs by more efficiently offloading low-priced goods and thus freeing up their time to sell and market their differentiated, value-added products.

In short, the future of e-business in the process industries as described above is shifting power toward the consumer just as it has in other industries. This is a double-edged sword since every manufacturer is both a supplier and a customer. Process manufacturers must find ways to exploit their newly found power over their suppliers while they marshal their own resources to make themselves agile to compete in the hyper-competitive e-business era.

What Process Manufacturers Must Do to Prepare for the E-Business Era

E-business has clearly had a smaller impact on the process industries to date than it has in other industries such as personal computers and online stock trading. However, as the above examples demonstrate, the pace of change is rapidly accelerating. When the dust settles a few years from now the change will be no less dramatic than it has been in other industries.

Now that the future is coming into focus, process manufacturers are beginning to ask themselves how they can make their enterprises "Internet ready." The answer comes down to three issues: (1) people, (2) plants, and (3) business processes. Manufacturers need to understand that the Internet will impact their entire business. Before they can enter the e-business era and reap the rewards, manufacturers must ensure that their people, their plants, and their business processes are "Internet ready."

By its nature, the Internet cuts across a company's entire organization. Therefore, companies must organize their people around their key business processes to facilitate the integration of those business processes with their trading partners. Furthermore, manufacturers must prepare their people to make decisions at Internet speed. This means organizing, delegating, and equipping them with accurate, up-to-date information about their plants. Finally, process manufacturers need to know their manufacturing capabilities – especially operating constraints and product profitability – and need to ensure that their plants and extended supply chain are sufficiently agile to respond to change.

Start With an Enterprise-Wide Strategy Driven from the Top

The Internet is a bomb, not a missile. Process manufacturers need to understand that the Internet impacts their entire organization. The Internet affects business processes that cut across every functional group within an organization. From product development, to marketing, to sales, to customer service, to internal processes such as human resources, the Internet will affect how process manufacturers work and interact with their customers, suppliers, and partners.

The only way to ensure a manufacturing enterprise will be Internet ready is for e-business initiatives to be led from the top. Without executive management sponsorship, e-business initiatives will become yet another sales, IT, or marketing initiative – which improve one or two parts of the organization but fail to prepare the organization to move into the e-business era. Ask someone who has tried to lead an e-business initiative, and they will tell you that a lack of top-level management support is tantamount to failure.

Decisioning Bottleneck Information Flow

Some of the largest bottlenecks on the path towards e-business arise when companies restrict the flow of information. The increased pace of change fostered by the Internet requires faster decision-making. Decisions require information. If companies are unwilling or unable to share critical information, both internally and with business partners, they are creating bottlenecks and restricting their ability to successfully enter the e-business era.

Organize Around Business Processes

The Internet is creating extended enterprises by interconnecting suppliers, manufacturers, distributors, and customers into dynamic trading communities. However, creating extended enterprises implies business processes must be extended as well. To prepare, process manufacturers must organize themselves primarily around business processes, rather than product lines or business units. This is the way their business partners will expect to interact with them.

If manufacturers attempt to knit their disparate business processes together across multiple business units, and then haphazardly integrate those processes with their business partners, they will be setting themselves up for failure. For example, if customer service is a business process and a manufacturer is organized around five product categories, each with its own customer service organization, it will be very difficult for that manufacturer to provide the seamless, unified customer service, which customers expect.

Integrate Business Processes with Trading Partners – Not Just IT Systems

The extended enterprise that Internet and e-business pundits have been forecasting can only become a reality if enterprises integrate their business processes such that they behave like an extended enterprise. It is simply not enough just to integrate your IT system with your trading partners. The prerequisite for integrating business processes between companies is for manufacturers to align and integrate their own internal business processes.

Integrating business processes between companies will not be easy. Stories about the difficulties of ERP implementations aimed at streamlining internal business abound. Breaking down the barriers between organizations, where power and decision-making are more dispersed, may prove to be as difficult as some of the ERP implementations.

To succeed, manufacturers will need to utilize sophisticated business process automation software that facilitates inter-company business process integration. This type of software keeps internal business processes shielded from shared, external processes. An example of an internal business process is transmitting a customer order to manufacturing for execution. An example of a shared process is processing a request for quotation and purchase order for additional raw materials.

Deploy "E-Business Ready" Manufacturing Execution Systems to Ensure Agile, Responsive Plants

Your plants are out of date or incorrect data and information are useless. To make decisions at Internet speed, manufacturers must know the actual capabilities of their plants in real time so they can rapidly and profitably respond to the increasing demands of their customers. Manufacturing data must be made more meaningful and readily accessible throughout the manufacturing enterprise than it is at most process manufacturers today.

This accuracy and accessibility requires integrated, Internet-enabled manufacturing execution systems based on accurate, consistent models of the plant. Why is a model-based architecture critical? Without accurate physical and financial models of the plant it is impossible to predict how the plant will perform when producing a particular product under varying operating conditions, and thus whether or not a product can be produced profitably, on time, and to the customer's specifications.

For example, if a polymer manufacturer does not know the time to transition from one grade of polymer to another, it cannot accurately schedule the plant. This means when a customer calls to request a custom batch of polymer, the manufacturer cannot confidently determine whether it would be profitable to alter the production schedule to accommodate the customer's request or not. These kinds of decisions will have to be made in minutes or perhaps seconds in the future to remain competitive.

Once process manufacturers know the true capabilities of their plants and what their customers are demanding, they need to be certain their plants will respond. They must be certain they can push the limits of their plants while running them safely, efficiently, and predictably. Deploying truly integrated plant design, operation, and management technologies, based on accurate, consistent models is the only way for process manufacturers to ensure they are prepared for the e-business era.

Integrate Your Extended Supply Chain and Manufacturing Execution Systems

The greatest point of cost, complexity, and uncertainty in the extended supply chain of the make-centric enterprise is the plant. How can you process customer orders over the Internet, promise delivery dates in real-time, provide key manufacturing information, and know if you are making money if your extended supply chain system is not tightly integrated with your manufacturing execution system? This reality is one of the unique characteristics that set the process industries apart from other companies such as those making tennis shoes or personal computers.

http://aspen.ASCET.com — web link

Aspen eSupply Chain Suite Helps Companies Make Faster, Smarter Decisions at All Levels

The Internet is compelling manufacturers to optimize their own extended supply chains while seamlessly integrating with their customers, their suppliers, and emerging trading exchanges. In order to connect their manufacturing enterprises to the Internet, offer improved customer service, or participate in online trading exchanges, manufacturers must manage their supply chain as one of their core assets.

Competitive manufacturers can no longer afford the inherent capacity and inventory buffers that have characterized their supply chains in the past. Emerging e-supply chains require up-to-date, accessible information, the ability to collaborate with customers and suppliers, and a deep understanding of the manufacturing environment.

The Aspen eSupply Chain Suite transforms Supply Chain Management (SCM) from periodic and isolated events to an efficient enterprise-wide process that reduces delays, cuts cycle times, and increases profits. Companies can make faster, smarter decisions at all levels — from deciding where to build a new plant or when to make the next batch of product to knowing precisely when a customer's order will be shipped.

- Inside the plant gates, companies can generate accurate plans and schedules based on current market and operating conditions.
- Across the internal supply chain, companies can optimize their enterprise-wide supply chain by considering all of their plants as a unified manufacturing enterprise, including the flow of materials across multiple plants and storage facilities.
- Across the extended enterprise, manufacturers can easily link to customers, suppliers and online exchanges creating a collaborative, flexible extended enterprise

The Aspen eSupply Chain Suite combines powerful SCM solutions with flexible business-to-business collaboration solutions. AspenTech is the only company to bridge the gap between operations and finance, enabling tight business process integration between plant systems, ERP, global supply chain planning and optimization, and trading partners. You make faster, smarter decisions at all levels — from strategic planning to detailed scheduling and order promising.

Integrated Supply Chain Optimization at Phillips Chemical Company

The Plastics group in Phillips Chemical Company took a close look at its manufacturing/distribution cycle and ordered a fulfillment re-engineering project, Smart Inventory Forecast Technology (SIFT). The challenge was to have the right product at the right location at the right time to better manage its supply chain.

The software needed to achieve SIFT's goals had to include a broad range of functionality to accommodate demand forecasting, long-range planning, and production scheduling across four product lines. Phillips' technical standards and the capability to integrate with any database or ERP system was also an essential factor.

The Aspen MIMI supply chain solution from the Supply Chain Division of Aspen Technology, Inc. was chosen for the project because Aspen MIMI could address Phillips' current business requirements as well as scale to Phillips' long-term needs.

Aspen MIMI has enabled Phillips to look at old ways in a new light. For example, Phillips discovered Aspen MIMI was suggesting resin grade switches that differed from Phillips' standard. The software suggested it was economically better to accept a more costly grade switch because it produced a product that was in demand. Aspen MIMI has also sharply reduced forecasting errors. Overall, forecasting accuracy now exceeds 90%.

Fill rates have also increased — one product line has seen an increase of more than 20% in the fill rate since using Aspen MIMI.

Contact Information

Lawrence B. Evans
Founder, Chairman of the Board, and CEO

Joseph F. Boston
Founder and President

Stephen Doyle
Senior Vice President, Internet Business

Mary A. Palermo
Executive Vice President

David L. McQuillin
*Executive Vice President,
Worldwide Sales and Marketing*

David A. Mushin
Executive Vice President

**Aspen Technology, Inc.
Worldwide Headquarters**
Ten Canal Park
Cambridge, Massachusetts 02141-2200
Phone 617.949.1000
Fax 617.949.1030
info@aspentech.com

**Supply Chain
Division Headquarters**
200 South Street
New Providence, NJ 07974
Phone 908.464.8300
Fax 908.464.4134
supplychain@aspentech.com

Creating Value at Web Speed for Softgoods Companies

Essentus (formerly Richter Systems) was founded thirty years ago to serve the complex, specific business needs of footwear and apparel industries. In the past two years the company has transformed itself from a custom software integrator to a global provider of business-to-business commerce software solutions and services as well as business improvement processes that help customers derive measurable value for their brands – adding as much as 30% to 50% to the bottom line. In addition, Essentus is focused on fully leveraging the vast power of the Internet for softgoods, manufacturers, and retailers who must react at lightning speed to the frenetic marketplace and shifting trends that define the world of high fashion.

Essentus, financed by the General Atlantic Partners, has new management, improved customer care, new products for companies of all sizes, and, most importantly, a new vision. That vision is to increase returns and create value for the softgoods industry by enabling end-to-end Supply Chain Management (SCM) software and services solutions.

Value Proposition

Today, over 300 companies worldwide (including Liz Claiborne, Carrefour, Maidenform, Kentucky Textiles, Genesco, Armand Thiery, Celio, UNIONBAY, Kellwood, and The Jenna Lane Group) are using Essentus solutions to orchestrate their complex supply chains via advanced collaboration, hosted applications services, and SCM technologies. And Essentus has a track record of demonstrated success stories.

Essentus creates real business value, with a bottom-line performance impact that is measurable over time, by:
- Building a competitive advantage through systems
- Enabling fundamental organization-wide process change
- Increasing cross-functional interaction and adding new performance measures to build accountability

In addition, Essentus creates and capture value challenges by helping customers:
- Balance supply and uncertain demand
- Identify trends
- Remove supply chain bottlenecks
- Optimize inventory levels

The improved decision-making that Essentus allows is a major factor in both cost reduction and revenue growth.

Essentus' Expanding Product Line

- Essentus Supply Chain Solutions – Sourcing, demand management, and business intelligence for companies with over $50 million in sales
- Essentus Merchandising – an ideal solution for retailers looking to gain added visibility beyond the warehouse
- Essentus Express – An entry-level solution that includes sourcing, demand management, and business intelligence for companies with under $50 million in sales
- Essentus E-Business Suite – A family of business-to-business collaborative products (e-Inquire, e-Collaboration, and e-Implementation) designed to fully leverage the power of the Internet by enabling companies to link disparate and geographically dispersed business units, and to engage in real-time communication and collaboration
- Essentus Business Processing Outsourcing – Essentus' newest service offering, Essentus Business Processing Outsourcing is designed to help companies build their brands, rather than built IT organizations. With an experienced team ready to assist you, services include IT hosting, off-site application support, and off-site third-party software administration.

The Essentus Professional Services division is available for enterprise-wide implementation, training, and project planning.

Contact Information

Paul Butare
Chairman and CEO
pbutaree@essentus.com

Tom Dziersk
Vice President, Marketing and Sales
tdziersk@essentus.com

Chuck Shields
Vice President, Professional Services
cshields@essentus.com

Henri Seroux
VP & Managing Director, EMEA
hseroux@essentus.com

Essentus International Inc.
(Formerly Richter Systems)
1430 Broadway, 14th Floor
New York, NY, 10018-3308
Phone 212.391.5858
Fax 212.391.2265
www.essentus.com

written by:
Bruce Walton
Michael Princi
Andersen Consulting
http://walton.ASCET.com

From Supply Chain to Collaborative Network: Case Studies in the Food Industry

Collaboration among supply chain partners is not new. But developments in information technology and, in particular, the Internet, have created an explosion in the economic value that collaborative initiatives can deliver. But any executive contemplating such changes should be mindful that while the opportunity is energized by new economical and sophisticated methods of interaction, the true value lies in considering why, how, and with whom collaboration is carried out. As this article will show, collaboration within the framework of a traditional supply chain is not the only, or necessarily the most profitable, opportunity.

What's New in Collaboration?

Much of the value creation and hence excitement around collaboration has focused on common language standards and new information technologies that foster interaction. Collaborative Planning, Forecasting and Replenishing (CPFR), for instance, promises new efficiencies, inventory reductions, and service enhancements while point-of-sale (POS) and scan-based trading (SBT) drive the lockstep integration of the supply chain players. Although these initiatives certainly require new levels of leadership, trust, and communication, the focus remains on the optimization of information and product flow between existing nodes in a traditional supply chain, with the somewhat vertically integrated corporation at the center (see Figure 1.0). However, the more significant impact of collaboration and its supporting technologies will be to drive fundamental change in the shape of the supply chain, the number of players within it, and their individual roles as they deliver goods, services, and information to the consumer.

Considering the traditional food supply chain, it is evident that some forms of collaboration have been chipping away at the vertically integrated company for some years – namely contract manufacturing (co-packing as well) and third-party logistics. More recently, logistics and information technologies have fostered the ability to successfully obviate distributors in favor of delivering directly to retail venues (direct store delivery) and to optimize inventory management and service between any set of partners. Today, new players in both the business-to-business and business-to-consumer e-commerce arenas are offering other collaborative services to multiple links in the supply chain, including suppliers, retailers, and consumers. These aggregators, market makers, and agents offer efficient consolidation nodes for information and products, effectively showing a single face and transaction point to both the provider and user of the goods.

So what? Aren't we still just talking about the more efficient flow of information in a standard supply chain? No. In fact, we are looking at the types of relationships and efficient sharing and aggregation of knowledge that will finally allow for the realization of the promise of core competencies. It is core competency meets supply chain integration meets e-commerce. New knowledge of what makes collaborative relationships successful, in concert with information technologies, applications, and providers that make familiar knowledge management concepts a reality, are allowing organizations to more effectively partner with other companies up and down the full supply chain. The old vertically integrated company is physically disintegrating, and in its place will likely be some form of collaborative network (see Figure 2.0), in which each player can truly focus on their core competency, or competencies, and excel at them. Such a network, in which we see intra-

Michael Princi is a senior consultant in Andersen Consulting's Strategic Services competency. He has worked with clients in electronics and technology. His primary focus areas are outsourcing, procurement, and, most recently, e-procurement and B2B e-commerce solutions.

Bruce Walton is a senior manager in the Andersen Consulting Supply Chain Practice. He has worked with clients across a broad range of industries including telecommunications, food and consumer packaged goods, medical products, and electronics. His primary focus areas are manufacturing operations, demand and supply planning, inventory management, procurement, and B2B e-commerce solutions.

Consumer Goods

company optimization as well as inter-company optimization, ultimately is much more efficient than the intermediate supply chain solution that focuses on optimization of the links between the partners in the chain.

What does this mean for your company? It means you can start to take the concept of core competency more seriously. You need to map your supply chain and markets against your capabilities and seek out partners that fill your capability gaps, or with whom you can share capabilities or to whom you can transfer capabilities. What should your company turn into – a brand management shell, a specialty manufacturer, a researcher and developer of food technologies? It is not likely that a long-standing manufacturer will transform into a Web-based materials portal, or vice-versa, yet your company will look substantially different. In fact, your "company" will be a broad-based, electronically-linked network of entities with distributed capabilities, held fast by the common goal of winning consumers with high-quality products delivered flawlessly at the right price point.

Let's move from the theoretical to the real world, and illustrate some key food industry collaborative trends with case studies. Some are well-known food industry giants that are making notable strides in establishing strong partnerships and expanding their collaborative networks, while others are new players in new roles that are facilitating the type of radical changes discussed above. Their successes are encouraging, and may offer insights for you and your company, whether you find yourself within the food industry or otherwise.

Case Studies in Collaboration: Who's Making it Work?

Collaborative Planning, Forecasting, and Replenishment – Nabisco with Wegman's

A truly robust form of collaboration is occurring in the realm of Collaborative Planning, Forecasting, and Replenishing (CPFR). With this type of collaboration, a retailer and a manufacturer share forecasts via two-way interactive communication links to reduce pipeline inventory while concurrently improving service levels. Wal-Mart, Warner-Lambert, Benchmark Partners, SAP, and Manugistics started using this approach in 1995, however, it was not until recently that manufacturers and retailers enthusiastically espoused this strategy.

Nabisco, the largest cookie and cracker maker in the United States, has emerged as a leader in CPFR. In a pilot program, Nabisco and Wegman's, a Northeastern supermarket chain, shared forecast data for 22 items, mostly from the Planter's line of products, which includes Planters nuts and Corn Nuts snacks. Nabisco chose the Planters line of products due to the high degree of promotion and breadth of the categories it provides. Traditionally, these two factors create a high degree of variability and disparity in the forecasts of trading partners. The sales force at Nabisco generated a forecast and compared it with Wegman's forecast. Though this process was initially done manually, the process was automated with Manugistics software that compared the two forecasts and alerted both parties of any variance.

The program was an overall success, as category sales increased 15.5% at a time when these same categories were down 8% at other retailers. Service levels increased to 97% from 93%, and days-of-inventory was reduced by 18% or 2.5 days. Additionally, Planter's market share increased to 53.6% under this pilot.

These results demonstrate the power of CPFR. As information technology resources become available, we will see the scalability of CPFR into larger categories and across other product lines. CPFR is not a panacea, however, as transportation and distribution are still going to be critical to ensuring timely replenishment. So in concert with CPFR, Nabisco has been taking steps to ensure that this "downstream" end of the supply chain is synchronized through collaboration as well.

Collaborative Manufacturing
Pillsbury and Seneca Foods

Contract manufacturing was one of the first forms of collaboration across the supply chain. Companies seeking to increase return on assets looked closely at their operations. They identified functions outside their core competency and sought alliance partners that possessed the capability to close the performance gap. Pillsbury, one of the world's leading food companies, went through this exercise in the early 1990s. They realized that their core competency was in growing vegetables using proprietary seed technology, not in production and canning. A logical strategy for them involved outsourcing production for their Green Giant line of canned vegetables and selling off their manufacturing plants. To execute this strategy, in 1995 Pillsbury entered an arrangement with Seneca Foods, a major processor of produce that primarily cans and freezes vegetables, and transferred ownership of six canning facilities in the United States.

The success of this collaborative arrangement is demonstrated by Pillsbury's reduction of corporate assets by more than $700 million. Pillsbury reduced its cost of goods sold as a percentage of sales from 75% in 1993 to 66% in 1997. During the same period, operating margins increased from 8.3% to 13.3%. Pillsbury is expanding the benefits of this relationship beyond production into areas of product development. They are now able to get their new products to market 50% faster, capturing an entirely new stream of revenues that they were previously unable to realize.

Seneca Foods achieves some remark-

Weblink

For more on collaboration, see:
uchneat.ASCET.com
quinn-f.ASCET.com
ramanathan.ASCET.com
enslow.ASCET.com
anthony.ASCET.com
johnson.ASCET.com
anderson-g.ASCET.com
fischer.ASCET.com
moore.ASCET.com

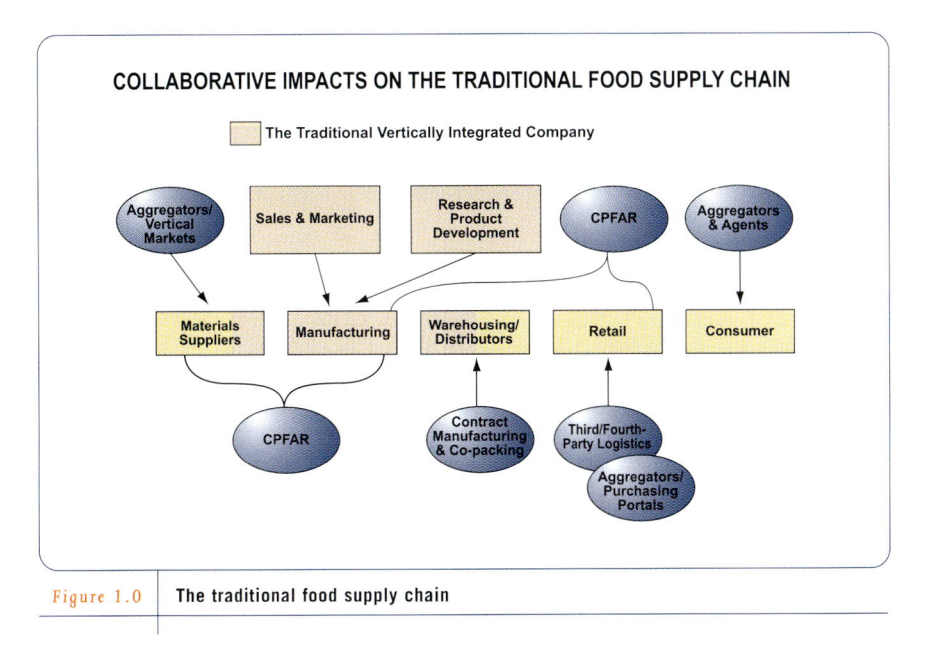

COLLABORATIVE IMPACTS ON THE TRADITIONAL FOOD SUPPLY CHAIN

Figure 1.0 — The traditional food supply chain

able benefits from this relationship also. Over half of Seneca's production volume is from its relationship with Pillsbury. This increased volume allows Seneca to allocate overhead over larger volumes and ultimately realize greater margins. Pillsbury is also sharing procurement strategies and volume discounts with Seneca.

Pillsbury currently outsources approximately 30% of its production and only owns two Green Giant production facilities. They expect to see contract manufacturing account for 40 to 50% of the company's production, based on the success it has achieved with arrangements with Seneca and other parties such as J.R. Simplot, one of the largest processors of frozen potatoes, frozen fruits, and other vegetables.

Collaborative Logistics Management
Nabisco

The proliferation of third-party logistics providers is facilitating another source of collaboration across the supply chain. The 1999 *Food Industry Transportation and Fleet Management Report* found that while more companies are outsourcing some or all of their transportation needs to third-party logistics providers, most still operate private fleets. However, Nabisco has been very aggressive in its use of third-party logistics providers; they have outsourced all of their transportation and distribution warehousing. Like Pillsbury, Nabisco took inventory of its core competencies and determined that it is not a transportation or warehousing company. Its logistics expenditures grew to six percent of total sales and it had $260 million of raw and finished material on hand, which equated to 96 days of inventory. When looking at transportation, Nabisco realized that driver costs were upwards of 54% of total transportation costs – its largest expense category. To recapture this lost value, Nabisco set a goal of six percent reduction in its total logistics spend and turned to outsourcing to achieve this reduction.

Nabisco is using technology to manage its third-party logistics providers. Through the use of distribution requirements planning tools that interface with the plant-level scheduling tools, Nabisco gains access to real-time data. Now Nabisco is able to track its third-party providers using trip recorders, routing software and many types of tracking software to capture precise information regarding inventory in transit. This tracking has led to significant gains in efficiency and utilization, while reducing required safety stocks, which translates into significant savings.

Nabisco has turned collaborative relationships into a competitive advantage. They have instituted a drop-trailer program, managed purchases in full-truckload increments, and designed mixed pallet loads that are deliverable directly to the buyers' stores – creating value for all parties involved. The third-party logistics industry will continue to grow as food industry players realize the importance of distribution to the replenishment process. However, this realization has spurred even more aggressive models that bypass the distribution center altogether.

Collaboration Between Manufacturer and Retailer (Direct Store Delivery)
Frito-Lay with Wegman's

The emergence of the direct store delivery model is intricately tied to the emergence of point-of-sale data capture. Within the supermarket channel with aggregate sales of $100 billion, nine of the top 20 categories are direct store delivery and contribute almost $50 billion of sales and provide 72% of the industry's sales growth.

The business case for direct store delivery is compelling. Under this model, the retailer gets out of the inventory management business and becomes a lessor of shelf space. If the retailer were responsible for the staging, receiving, stocking, shelf management, and order placement for the direct store delivery lines, approximately 100 hours of labor per week would be added to their responsibilities. Since the grocery industry operates on slim margins, the effects would be significant.

While both direct store delivery and warehouse suppliers claim to have the same 23% to 25% margins, the former model removes the added cost of warehousing, delivery, and merchandising. The retailer sees a final contribution margin that averages 8.6% versus a contribution margin of 5.7% for non-direct store delivery items. This difference goes right to the retailer's bottom line.

Wegman's entered into an arrangement with soft drink manufacturer Pepsi and Frito-Lay, a large snack food manufacturer, which is a testament to the power of collaboration between retailer and supplier under the direct store delivery model. Pepsi

http://walton.ASCET.com

approached Wegman's with a proposal for the Frito-Lay line and Pepsi products. The beverage category was a low-margin category that received high incidence; the salty snack category was a high margin category with only half the incidence of beverages. Pepsi proposed its "House Party" promotion which would drive up the sales of the high-margin salty snack category.

Under this arrangement, Wegman's allocated Frito-Lay prime retail floor space. Pepsi and Frito-Lay provided in-store displays, increased inventory, and increased visits by merchandisers, sometimes as many as two to three per day. The results far exceeded anyone's expectations. Transaction data showed people were buying more of each product, and buying more frequently. Wegman's saw an eight percent increase in its salty snack category and had more than $1 million in incremental sales contributing $200,000 in incremental profit. Pepsi saw a 26% increase in the sale of beverages and a 28% increase in the sale of Frito-Lay products. These results have encouraged Wegman's management to collaborate more closely with its direct store delivery suppliers, and to expand its use of the model.

Collaboration with the Consumer

Aggregators and Agents Bypass Retail – Peapod and Streamline.com

In the realm of shipping direct to the consumer, technology is enabling new players to enter the market and compete with traditional grocery stores, taking somewhere between eight to 12% market share of grocery sales. The players in this segment have to rely on collaboration with their supply chain partners to ensure that the consumer is satisfied, because while consumers may be willing to accept stock-outs in traditional stores, they will not tolerate stock-outs by the consumer direct players.

These players rely on collaboration with suppliers to ensure that daily inventory levels are adequate and deliveries are based on continuous replenishment. Peapod, an online grocery retailer founded in 1989, provides consumer direct services primarily through the use of retailers. Its

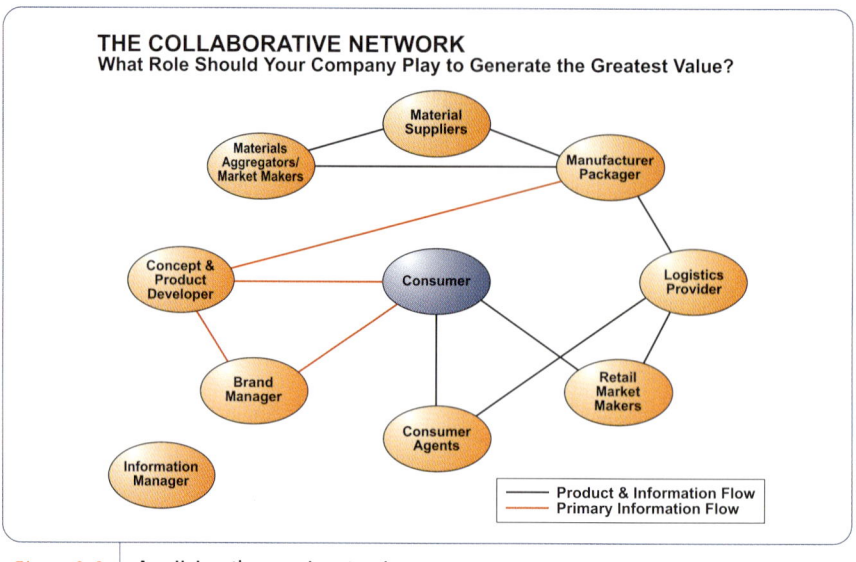

THE COLLABORATIVE NETWORK
What Role Should Your Company Play to Generate the Greatest Value?

Figure 2.0 | A collaborative supply network

strategy is not to compete with the retailers but rather become a symbiotic extension of their business. Customers place their order through a personal computer, and a personal shopper retrieves the groceries and delivers them to the customer. Peapod's revenue is derived from delivery fees and the margin they generate from a retailer discount. The retail partner benefits because Peapod adds incremental volume to their sales and shares the data captured from consumers. This method of delivery has limited scalability; as Peapod grows, it is moving to a warehouse fulfillment model. It should achieve a threefold increase in picking times and reduce the number of stock-out/substitution instances.

Streamline, a delivery, buying, and errand service, uses the warehouse fulfillment model, striking partnerships and supply relationships with large food manufacturers and distributors. Via suburban warehouses, Streamline acts as an agent to the consumer by delivering a conglomeration of basic grocery items, prepared meals, dry cleaning, film processing, video rental, and postal service/package pick-up. As with Peopod, orders are personal computer-based, though delivery is on a pre-scheduled, weekly basis. Streamline's efficiency, however, comes from its warehousing, picking, and transportation model, which is much more efficient than picking from a grocery store aisle. Its margins are enhanced by its physical location as well. Traditional retailers are spending 15% to 18% of sales on real estate located in residential areas. Warehouse fulfillment centers avoid this cost because they are located in less expensive industrial centers.

Ultimately, one can imagine an agent that gains an intimate understanding of a family's need and consumption patterns and looks to fulfill their demand at the right time at the lowest price from their marketplace of suppliers. Look to Webvan, a California-based Web grocer, as it expands a similar model on a national basis.

Collaboration Between Retailers and Manufacturers with Supplier Aggregation

Marketorder.com

The food industry is not immune to the business-to-business e-commerce excitement, even though only 35% of firms report using electronic data interchange (EDI), most of which is entirely for purchase order exchange. The emergence of procurement portals and application service providers (ASPs) specifically for buyers and sellers in the food industry demonstrates the powerful impact of technology – specifically the open standard of Internet-based e-commerce. This form of collaboration creates a breakthrough that EDI could never accomplish with its point-to-point solution and expensive infrastructure requirements. The portals and ASPs use collaborative technology to add value for both buyers and suppliers. Since direct store delivery has become the replenishment method for almost half of the items in the typical grocery store, ordering from multiple suppliers with disparate ordering systems has become a complex task. This is greatly simplified by the use of a portal or ASP that allows buyers to aggregate their orders to multiple suppliers through one common interface. The result is a significant reduction in the cost of placing orders and the elimination of costly order entry errors. The supplier shares in the benefit through reductions in their order processing costs and simplification of supply forecasting and trend analysis.

Marketorder.com, an application service provider, was formerly Marketware, a company that provided proprietary order replenishment networks for over 15 years to large industry players such as Ahold, the Netherlands-based food retailer with numerous locations in the eastern United States, and Supervalu, the largest food wholesaler in the United States. The company migrated its technology to the Web and changed its name to reflect its new robust capabilities. Through its relationships with large players such as Ahold and Supervalu, Marketorder.com is offering an application that brings together all the suppliers of a buyer under one replenishment ordering process. The retailers benefit from the application's ability to handle high volumes, reduce operating costs, and generate additional sales. Marketorder.com found that its customer base typically was spending between $15 and $20 to process an order. Marketorder.com reduces the administrative cost of procurement to roughly $2 to $3 per order. The company makes available its legacy systems to any retailer, large or small, without the retailer incurring the tremendous capital outlay of installing and maintaining the legacy system, or a comparable EDI network.

The technology that makes this possible is a Microsoft Windows CE-driven handheld device, which the retailer leases from Marketorder.com. The retailer and the suppliers reach a sourcing agreement; then, based on this agreement, Marketorder.com uploads the supplier catalogues onto the handheld device. Suppliers can request a number of promotion items for categories that are heavily promoted. Marketorder.com leases the equipment to the retailer, allowing a continual refresh as new technology and features are added to the handhelds. This precludes the retailer from investing in technology that can quickly become obsolete — another value added by Marketorder.com. The supplier benefits from the reduction in cost for capturing and processing the order, and there are almost no data entry errors. The initiative is so compelling that Supervalu is rolling out a program to establish Internet-based communication with the 1,000 or more suppliers with whom it does business in an effort to reduce the administrative cost of ordering.

Conclusions

These examples from the food industry illustrate the variety of forms that supply chain collaboration can take. The arrival of e-commerce and its empowerment of new players such as agents and aggregators have only served to add further opportunities. Each yields its own unique economic benefits; increased service levels, reduction in logistics costs, increased sales, or reduction in real estate costs are just a few examples. But the real news is the hastened demise of the vertically integrated company and the rise of a network of players each with its own strong core competencies. Any company that fails to assess strategically its own unique capabilities and stake a position in the evolving collaborative network may lose more than an opportunity to improve operations. It may lose its position in the supply chain altogether — an end game to which no one would aspire.

References

Cooke, James Aaron, "CPFR: The Countdown Begins," Logistics Management Distribution Report, November 30, 1999 No. 11, Vol. 38; Pg. 59

Andel, Tom, "Harness the Power to Own Your Customer; Supply Chain Flow", Material Handling Engineering, June 1, 1999, No. 6, Vol. 54; Pg. SCF13

Kuhn, Mary Ellen, "Teams that work; Pillsbury's Alliance Strategy," Food Processing, February 1, 1999, No. 2, Vol. 60; Pg. 19

Kuhn

Andel

Cooke, James Aaron, "Delivering Value," Logistics Management Distribution Report, November 30, 1999, No. 11, Vol. 38; Pg. 51

Wellman, David, "The Direct Approach To The Bottom Line," Supermarket Business, August 1, 1999, No. 8, Vol. 54; Pg. 15

Wellman, David, "The Direct Approach To The Bottom Line"

Wellman, David, "Direct Store Party," Supermarket Business, Sept 1, 1999, No. 8, Vol. 54; Pg. 15

Wellman, David, "Direct Store Party"

"Sense of Sell; Selling Produce through the Consumer-Direct Market," Progressive Grocer, August, 1998 No. 8, Vol. 77

Mathews, Ryan, "You Say You Want a Revolution? Grocery Industry Being Transformed Toward Consumer-Direct Marketing Models," Progressive Grocer, March, 1998, No. 3, Vol. 77; Pg. 22

Wellman, David, "The Direct Approach To The Bottom Line"

Interview with Larry Andrews form Marketorder.com

Hardgrove, Amy, "Speeding Toward Seamless Data Exchange," Grocery Headquarters, April 1, 1999, No. 4, Vol. 65; Pg. 84

Copyright© 2000 Andersen Consulting

The "e" in Uniteq

Uniteq is a leading provider of supply chain execution software and e-process applications. We focus on the consumer products industry with particular emphasis on wholesale and retail food and drug/pharmaceutical segments. Our e-process applications leverage the power of the Internet to strengthen business alliances, increasing customer satisfaction and productivity, and driving down costs.

Products

Our e-process applications are Web-architected and focus on e-procurement and e-fulfillment. Our direct e-procurement application is powerful enough to handle inventories of almost any size, up to several million items; we have the most comprehensive e-fulfillment engine that includes order management and billing functionality. We also offer a complete e-fulfillment group of applications supported by our best-of-breed warehouse management system. The applications run on multiple operating systems and platforms, and a variety of databases including DB2 and Oracle.

The e-procurement application optimizes replenishment purchases via automatic decision analysis tools and online purchase order management. It calculates rapidly changing factors such as product demand, trends, seasonality, service levels, vendor discounts, and promotional buys. It uses these factors to produce an optimum suggested order. The software is designed to allow organizations to collaborate on sales forecasts and replenishment plans with their trading partners.

The e-fulfillment engine manages the order from sourcing to pricing and invoicing, keeping order visibility online throughout the fulfillment process. Major components include: order management, invoice processing, costing and pricing, data management, and distribution center planning tools. The e-fulfillment group of applications includes our best-of-breed WMS software with Labor, Yard, Available-to-Promise, VAS, and QA modules. These systems are backed by years of implementation experience.

Direction

We believe that building collaborative alliances is the driver for moving into the next era of buyer-seller relationships and critical to truly enable an optimized supply chain. Using the Internet as a means of collaboration will not only enhance demand planning and integrated Supply Chain Management, but also leverage the particular strengths of trading partners.

We envision wholesalers forming communities (or even their own ASP), delivering value-added services to their customers and suppliers, not only offering new channels of revenue, but also highly differentiated services to attract new customers. It is simple to deploy, requiring only a browser to access the Internet. Retail chain stores can enjoy the same benefits as they seek closer collaboration with their stores and suppliers, driving profitable growth as the supply chain moves to become the supply Web.

Customers

We have been providing leading companies with software that has the qualities of flexibility, reliability and scalability that no company can do without in the age of the Internet. Our customers include: Longs Drug, Winn-Dixie, McKesson, UniChem, and Williams-Sonoma, as well as customers such as QVC and dot-com companies that require highly scalable solutions.

Contact Information

Owen Shea
President and CEO

Jeff Bailey
CFO

Bob Carlier
VP, Marketing

Uniteq Headquarters
100 Marine Parkway,
Suite 375
Redwood City, CA 94065
Phone 650.637.6700
Fax   650.637.6720
www.uniteq.com
Info@uniteq.com

Industry-Wide Internet Initiatives in Food and Consumer Packaged Goods

written by:

Duane Marvick
Roger Dik
Andersen Consulting
http://marvick.ASCET.com

The food and consumer packaged goods industry is creating a compelling new agenda that will determine the industry's winners and losers. This agenda is mandating a focus on four key areas: realizing the value of information technology, organizing around customers, converging for simplification and standardization, and focusing on assets and capabilities to reduce the total cost of serving customers and preparing for growth. This new agenda, with e-commerce at its core, is being driven by flat growth, increasingly demanding customers, a growing global retail oligopoly, and emerging technologies.

While e-commerce has contributed to the industry's need for significant change, it also is providing new ways to overcome those challenges. Low collaboration and integration costs reduce the need for high levels of costly vertical integration. Returns and market valuations are increasingly derived from intellectual property and supplier and customer relationships and less from physical assets. It is becoming simpler and more cost-effective to obtain information about suppliers, manufacturers, retailers, and consumers. And entering the food and consumer packaged goods markets has never been easier – new companies may begin competing with only virtual channels for sourcing, making, moving, promoting, selling, and servicing goods.

Transforming business models to take advantage of, and remain competitive in, the new economy is difficult for many traditional consumer products companies. Keeping up requires rapidly addressing changing supply and demand opportunities and threats within the constraints of their existing technology, processes, and organizations. In some cases, entirely new strategies and business models are required. Industry executives must ask their organizations the following strategic questions:

- What e-commerce investments will provide the greatest impact on shareholder value?
- How do we best balance risks and rewards between short-term quick hits and longer-term strategic capability improvements?
- How can we quickly and successfully leverage the new business models emerging in the marketplace?

Andersen Consulting has developed a well-defined framework to help consumer products companies approach opportunities and risks within the world of e-commerce. This Value Realization Framework (see Figure 1.0) helps assess potential opportunities to determine which strategic e-commerce initiatives will best fit the organization and to rule out those initiatives for which the risks outweigh potential benefits. Consumer products companies should view their portfolio of opportunities in a balanced way to drive both strategic advantage and shareholder value.

A number of e-commerce initiatives – including e-procurement and e-HR (electronic human resources) – can provide tangible, bottom-line benefits with relatively modest risk. Others have a somewhat higher risk profile and important, albeit less tangible, benefits. These include initiatives such as e-CRM (customer relationship management) and e-R&D (research and development). Still others have the potential for dramatic strategic advantage and business value, but also have a significantly higher risk profile. For example, some consumer products companies have launched what Andersen Consulting calls intentions-based value networks, such as Procter & Gamble's Reflect.com, or have aggressively affiliated with an inten-

Roger Dik is an associate partner with Andersen Consulting's Strategic Services Practice. His consulting activities focus on satrategy, planning, and inplementation issues of major multinational consumer products companies worldwide.

Duane L. Marvick is an associate partner in the Andersen Consulting Supply Chain Practice. With over 20 years of logistics experience, his areas of expertise include supply chain and logistics strategy, distribution network design, distribution operations management, distribution center facility design, warehouse management systems, transportation operations management, and transportation systems.

Consumer Goods

tions-based value network, such as Ralston-Purina and iVillage.com. Additionally, for companies driven by consumer marketing, the opportunities to exploit online marketing to enhance and leverage offline tactics are significant.

Furthermore, the pace of some initiatives is in large measure driven by overall industry initiatives or the ability to partner with the leading retailers that are prepared to undertake the initiative. Collaborative Planning, Forecasting, and Replenishment (CPFR) and trade exchanges are two such examples of initiatives that are firmly becoming part of the fabric of the food and consumer packaged goods industry.

Collaborative Planning, Forecasting, and Replenishment

Collaborative Planning, Forecasting, and Replenishment has a number of advantages lacking in other industry-wide initiatives. Low-cost technology (the Internet) and standard processes simplify the implementation. Companies may begin CPFR as a pilot with a single trading partner to demonstrate the value proposition. Based on a high degree of collaboration between manufacturers and retailers, CPFR provides visibility into valuable consumption data at the retail level.

Business Issues and Challenges Addressed by CPFR

Today, supply chain forecasting and replenishment processes remain sources of ineffi-

Weblink

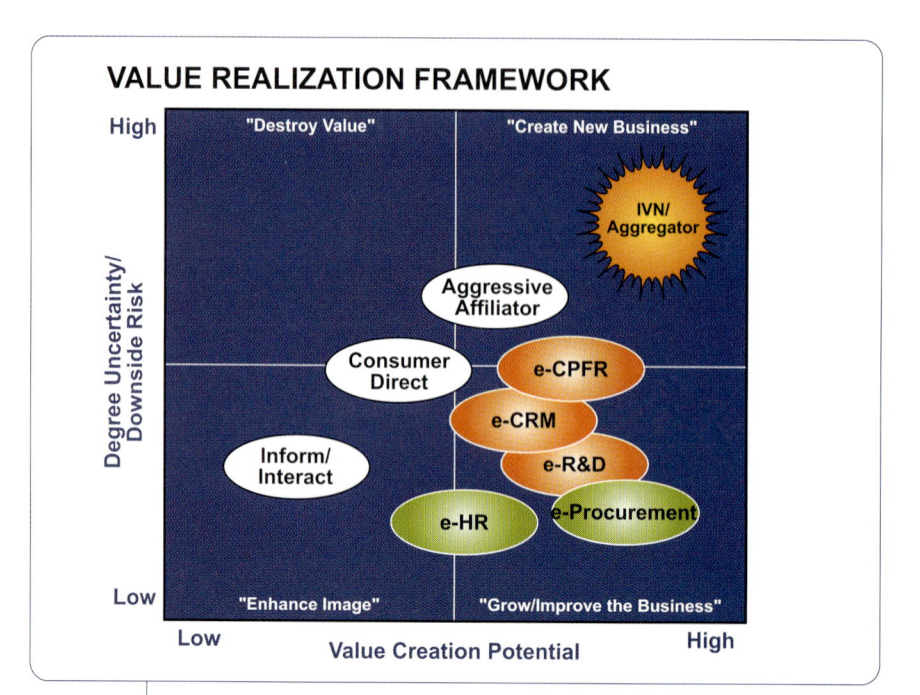

For more on bar codes, see:
zimdars.ASCET.com
hill.ASCET.com

For more on e-procurement, see:
quinn-f.ASCET.com
anderson-d.ASCET.com
cavander.ASCET.com
benitez.ASCET.com
smith-c.ASCET.com

Figure 1.0 Value realization framework

ciency. Unpredictable demand results in inaccurate demand forecasts that in turn result in production and distribution errors and expedition costs. Most companies also build excess inventories in the supply chain to address the unpredictable nature of demand. They also create cycle-time and inventory buffers to protect against variability in supply. Because of limited visibility to inventory and order information across the supply chain, fulfilling demand may frequently require expediting orders and a build-up of excessive inventory at different points along the supply chain – often called the "bullwhip effect." Lastly, planning of replenishment based on distribution center data instead of consumer data drives manufacturing to make-to-stock processes rather than make-to-order, again driving up supply chain inventories while potentially creating out-of-stocks.

Taking these inefficiencies into account, the supply chain becomes a source of significant opportunity for the food and consumer packaged goods industry to improve operations by removing inefficiencies and raising operating margins. For example, an Andersen Consulting/Coca-Cola supermarket retail study[1] revealed that 8.2% of items were out of stock, representing 6.5% of sales. Consumers refuse to buy an alternative item 3.4% of the time, which results in lost sales of 3.1% of the 6.5% lost sales, translating to $7 billion to $12 billion in lost sales dollars. Furthermore, a study by Benchmarking Partners[2] showed that retail chain sales were approximately $2.6 trillion in 1997, and the supply chain held approximately $1 trillion in inventory to support these sales. According to guidelines from the Voluntary Interindustry Commerce Standards (VICS) Association, there is potentially $150 billion to $250 billion in excess inventory in the supply chain due to forecasting and replenishment inefficiencies.

Emerging Trends in CPFR

Collaborative Planning, Forecasting, and Replenishment is based on supply chain collaboration between trading partners and focuses on a better understanding of the customer. With CPFR, trading partners determine the strategic plan for collaboration and create a single, shared forecast to replenish with 100% fill and acceptance rates. Development of sales forecasts and

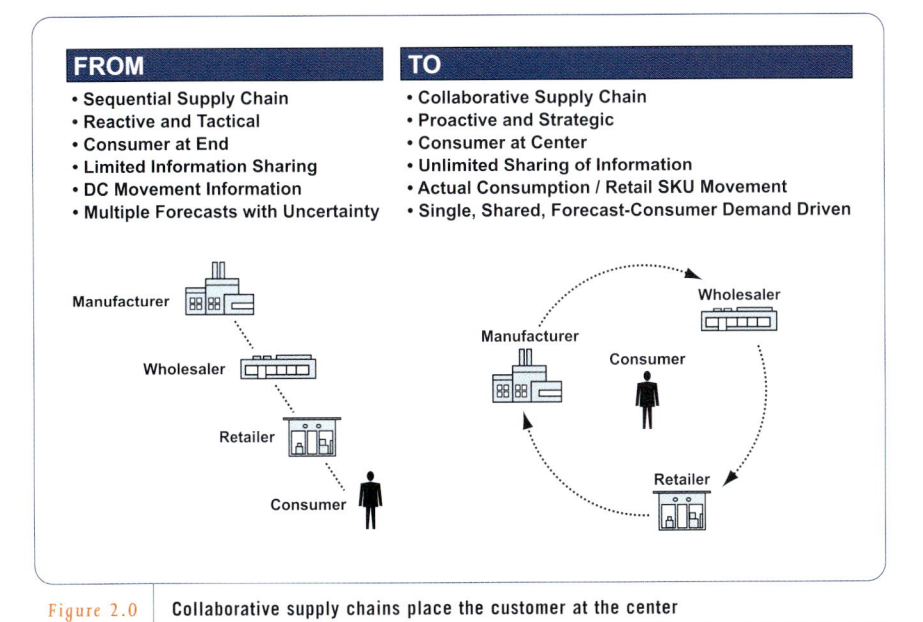

FROM
- Sequential Supply Chain
- Reactive and Tactical
- Consumer at End
- Limited Information Sharing
- DC Movement Information
- Multiple Forecasts with Uncertainty

TO
- Collaborative Supply Chain
- Proactive and Strategic
- Consumer at Center
- Unlimited Sharing of Information
- Actual Consumption / Retail SKU Movement
- Single, Shared, Forecast-Consumer Demand Driven

Figure 2.0 Collaborative supply chains place the customer at the center

order forecasts driven by consumer demand information is an iterative process. Partners continuously identify exceptions to both sales and order forecasts, make changes, and communicate revised forecasts to ensure the effective generation of orders (see Figure 2.0).

Collaborative planning and forecasting commonly takes place between manufacturers and retailers with a dependence on consumer demand. However, collaboration can take place in two additional forms. One is internally within departments, across divisions, and between geographic regions of larger companies where operations are based on a single forecast (or at least reduced iterations of the forecast). A second form of collaboration may take place between manufacturers and suppliers in what would be likened to a kind of reverse CPFR. An example of this type of collaboration is the purchase of materials based on collaborative forecasts and demand/supply information being shared between the manufacturer and its suppliers.

Internet-Enabled CPFR

Recent technological advancements in basic forecasting, demand planning, and supply planning have resulting in sophisticated CPFR software solutions. Examples of these include tools from Syncra, i2 Technologies, Manugistics, Logility, BAAN, Oracle, SAP, and PeopleSoft, to name a few.

The Internet is allowing companies to either utilize their own proprietary software or to leverage the software of others to successfully execute CPFR partnerships. Communication can take place with direct interfaces between trading partners – either both partners have CPFR software or both partners may access one partner's software on that partner's server. Additionally, both trading partners can access CPFR software hosted by an application service provider.

CPFR processes can also be customized to include specific market activity calendars, configurable alerts, plan variance thresholds, notification calendars, forecast exception criteria, and proposed resolutions. The software can also support the monitoring and measuring of results of forecast accuracy, adherence to business process rules, performance against key business measurement metrics, and actual results against critical planning and event targets.

CPFR Benefits

CPFR positively impacts and produces significant benefits for manufacturers, retailers, and consumers. Manufacturers get the benefit of visibility to promotional information from the retailer and what the retailer is projecting to order based on collaborative consumer-driven forecasts (core forecast, seasonal forecast, and promotional forecasts). Manufacturers can adjust production schedules to meet anticipated demand, thus increasing productivity, reducing costs, and improving asset utilization. Having advanced forecasted demand information allows the manufacturer to reduce inventories and avoid spoilage and obsolescence.

Retailers, in turn, can reduce inventories to save distribution center and store back-room space, thus reducing capital costs, lowering operating expenses, and improving asset utilization. Retailers also increase revenues by being in stock on promoted items and everyday items. Consumers benefit by having products in stock at the time of sale and reap the benefits of reduced product costs due to supply chain operating costs and inventory reductions.

VICS estimates that a $7 billion to $12 billion opportunity for increased sales exists for the food and consumer packaged goods industry[3]. These benefits will be realized with a single trading partner as out-of-stock situations are minimized and sales are increased; however, as the number of trading partners increases to critical mass, sales increases will peak. Reductions in distribution and production costs to expedite rush orders will be reduced since replenishment will be based on more accurate forecasts – this, plus the reduction of inventory carrying costs as cycle and safety stock buffers are reduced, represents a $150 billion to $250 billion opportunity[3] for the industry. Finally, service levels and supply chain efficiencies will improve with each new trading partner until an optimal level is achieved.

The benefit of effective collaboration is that each trading partner understands the effect of its operation on that of the other partners. An understanding of the operational drivers and uncertainties, as provided by collaboration, information exchange, monitoring, simulation, and adjustments, allows trading partners to optimize their respective operations by knowing about

http://marvick.ASCET.com

both upstream and downstream events and resulting business impacts.

CPFR Case Studies

A number of food and consumer packaged goods companies have piloted and are in the process of implementing CPFR. Some of these companies include Nabisco, Wegmans Food Markets, Wal-Mart, Warner-Lambert, Sara Lee, Heineken, Schnuck Markets, Kmart, Procter & Gamble, Goody's Family Clothing, and JC Penney. A number of these companies have reported significant results:

- Nabisco and Wegmans: During a 13-week pilot, shared common demand and supply forecasts for limited SKUs of Planters line. Results included reduced cycle times, significantly reduced inventory levels, and improved customer in-stock position. Forecast accuracy improved significantly.
- Wal-Mart and Warner-Lambert: Conducted a manual CPFR pilot by jointly developing forecasts. The companies eliminated two week's worth of inventory, halved the order cycle times, and eliminated out-of-stocks for the test product, Listerine.
- Wal-Mart and Sara Lee: Used a more sophisticated messaging system over the Internet and shared development of forecasts. According to Wal-Mart, consumer goods firms that fully collaborate achieve 97% in stock with 99% fill rates, compared with non-collaborative forms at 84% in stock and 77% fill rates.
- Heineken: Developed a Web-based solution to tie existing Heineken systems to distributors through Internet browsers to develop, update, and share forecast information. Experienced a 50% to 67% reduction in cycle time, inventory reduction from 65 to 40 days, and realized an increase in sales force productivity.

CPFR Barriers/Constraints

Developing trusting relationships between trading partners is the single biggest barrier to successful collaboration. This undoubtedly will require significant process changes and, potentially, a major cultural change within the organization. Companies must internally break down the functional silos within the organization and must learn to work with external trading partners in a give-and-take process, focused not on a win/lose but a win/win mindset. These major changes must start at the top of the organization, with company leadership internally and externally articulating the commitment to trust and sharing between trading partners. The true spirit of collaboration cannot exist if partners are not willing to share in the benefits. Therefore, metrics and key measurement criteria must be established and agreed to early on; this becomes the basis for benefits sharing in successful collaboration agreements.

CPFR Key Success Factors

Establishing trust between collaborating partners is the key to a successful, ongoing CPFR program. Trust must be earned – one trading partner at a time – so that the relationship is truly long-standing. Additionally, senior management must dedicate human and technological resources to support collaboration. Training of resources, together with development and implementation of supporting technical software, is vitally important. Furthermore, one must understand one's own core competencies or strengths and recognize those of trading partners. By leveraging and building on each other's core capabilities, partners can, together, deliver exceptional value to the end consumer and thus achieve collaborative success of the individual partners. Finally, it is important to develop your CPFR strategy, identify partners, and initially conduct CPFR pilots to test and fine-tune the execution of the strategy.

Additional lessons learned from previous piloted CPFR implementations include:

- Define a collaboration strategy and continually redefine operating strategies to increase revenues, improve service levels, and reduce operating costs.
- Create processes to focus on collaboration and proactive management of information and enhance existing processes to align with collaborative processes.
- Establish win/win relationships with trading partners, new roles, and shared objectives and measures to enable collaboration and a focus on the consumer.
- Leverage existing technology and existing industry standards to simplify CPFR implementation.
- Establish baseline value drivers, measurement systems, and benefits sharing before collaboration begins.
- Start collecting all scorecard data as early in the process as possible.
- Filter collaboration findings and decisions back into the operational systems of each of the respective partners – must act on information to achieve benefits.
- "Pre-collaboration" time is critical to address technical settings, establish standards, and confirm business practice alignment so that collaboration can be conducted effectively.
- Use an external tool from comprehensive scorecard tracking.

The key is "don't wait on the sideline" to see what others are doing. Start with a pilot, just a single trading partner, and learn as you go. Given the very effective CPFR software solutions on the market today and the ease of communications via the Internet, those that do "wait and see" will not only fail to reap the financial benefits of CPFR, but most certainly will lose their competitive position in the food and consumer packaged goods marketplace.

Trade Exchanges and UCCnet℠

The technological revolution, spurred by e-commerce and the Internet, is allowing companies today to conduct e-business through numerous Web-enabling technologies. In addition to CPFR, another extremely fast-growing method of connecting e-business trading partners is the formation of various trade exchanges, or electronic marketplaces, which bring together buyers and sellers of goods and services via the Web. Initial applications of trade exchanges have been in the area of auction/bid marketplaces whereby sellers could post products for sale out on the Web, with potential buyers bidding for these products – the result being an electronic matching of buyers/sellers and electronic consummation of the sale. The most recent use of trade exchanges is the electronic capability for companies to access purchasing software engines to procure both direct and indirect materials. Companies pay an access fee for use of the purchasing software and for access to content providers of electronic catalogs for goods and services. Arrangements can then be made for companies to pay on a per-transaction basis. Demand from the various buying companies is aggregated to create volume purchase requirements for suppliers. The procurement engine allows supplier connectivity to check specification, delivery lead-time, and pricing criteria. Supplier bidding for fulfilling aggregated purchase demand volumes, purchase order creation, and order confirmation can also occur via the trade exchange.

Trade exchanges are occurring in most industry verticals, and the benefits are numerous. Purchase demand is aggregated between trade exchange participants, allowing volume purchase discounts with suppliers. Electronic auction houses connect buyers and sellers for the purchase and sale of excess inventories, commodities, or service offerings. Companies can also take advantage of paying access and transaction fees for use of software to forego outright license purchase, integration, and implementation of software to facilitate e-business. The trade exchange can also become the conduit through which trading partners create and share forecasts and consumer demand information for e-CPFR. Trading partners can also create, share, and update item information through the trade exchange. Additional benefits are identified with each new entrant into the electronic marketplace.

UCCnet for FCPG

In the Food and Consumer Packaged Goods (FCPG) industry, an organization called UCCnet[SM] has been established to leverage both e-commerce and the Internet to conduct e-business trading on the Web. The Uniform Code Council (UCC) has been attempting to bring standards to the food industry for many years, which would allow exchanging electronic information between trading partners, primarily through EDI transactions. This initiative, part of the initial ECR program, has been slow and expensive to develop. However, the advent of Internet-based XML communications and the development of trade exchanges now allow this goal to come very close to being accomplished through the formation of UCCnet.

UCCnet Mission and Vision

The mission of UCCnet is to provide value by enabling the formation of collaborative relationships through an electronic trading community. They aim to achieve this goal by synchronizing UCC and EAN item information for all trading partners with industries served by the Uniform Code Council and by providing trading partners access to compliant business applications and services. Their trading community aims to provide an Internet-based, easily accessible trading community that forms a cost-effective, non-discriminatory, and universal platform for the synchronization of item information among trading partners. UCCnet is a technology-neutral, open, scalable, and distributed architecture that offers participants a secure, reliable mechanism for the synchronization of item content. They encourage voluntary participation of all solution providers to develop service offerings and products consistent with UCCnet's open architecture and not inhibit competition in any way.

UCCnet Scope

UCCnet is being developed as the electronic exchange for information and services through a common, open, scalable platform between B2B trading partners in over 23 industries. The open, Internet-based platform will replace EDI transactions with less expensive, more flexible electronic communications between suppliers, manufacturers, wholesalers, retailers, and third-party providers. The open architecture of UCCnet will foster open competition and development of compatible application systems and services by solution providers (hardware vendors, software vendors, and ISPs).

Users of UCCnet will pay a one-time fee to access the e-business applications and solutions contained within the core system, and will pay a tiered transaction fee for actual use based on company size, number of users, and transaction volumes.

Six key pilot companies in the food industry have been actively involved in the development of UCCnet. These food manufacturers, wholesalers, and retailers, who are represented by the Food Marketing Institute (FMI) and the Grocery Manufacturers of America (GMA), include Procter & Gamble, Ralston Purina, PepsiCo/Frito-Lay, SuperValu, Kroger, and Wegmans Food Markets.

Capability Offerings and Timetable

UCCnet plans to roll out its electronic marketplace capability offering in four phases:

> *The key is "don't wait on the sideline" to see what others are doing . . . Given the very effective CPFR software solutions on the market today and the ease of communications via the Internet, those that "wait and see" will not only fail to reap the financial benefits of CPFR, but most certainly will lose their competitive position in the food and consumer packaged goods marketplace.*

Phase 1
- Item Introduction
- Item Maintenance
- Authorization/De-Authorization
- Delisting

Phase 2
- Pricing
- Product Imaging
- P.O. Shipment Status (ASN)
- Product Movement (POS)

Phase 3
- CPFR
- Available to Order

Phase 4
- Consumer Marketing
- Auction Systems
- Advanced Logistics

The above business practices will be rolled out across numerous business processes including table loading, order generation, order processing, product shipping, product receiving, and billing/payment.

As of February 2000, UCCnet has completed its proof of concept, developed its Web site, and begun development of its core product life cycle foundational services. The organization has secured letters of intent from over 70 food manufacturers, wholesalers, and retailers with revenues of more than $400 billion per year to participate in its e-commerce offering. UCCnet plans to roll out its core item management services, including new item introduction, item search, and item maintenance, by mid 2000, first to the six key pilot companies and then to larger participant organizations.

UCCnet Benefits

UCCnet will provide an enhanced, electronic, two-way communication of data and information between trading partners and will build on the results achieved from the joint FMI and GMA study of 1998. The USC II EDI electronic communication study[4] conducted between Procter & Gamble and HEB Grocery resulted in these significant results:

- 75% reduction in invoice discrepancies and product delivery errors
- 30% improvement in quality of purchase orders
- 80% improvement in speed to shelf of new product offerings
- Improvements in retail scan accuracy
- 100% ASN accuracy between shippers and receivers
- Significantly reduce administrative costs

UCCnet will provide significant benefits for trading partners in the supply chain, and with key item management capabilities become the primary e-CPFR communication enabler between manufacturers and retailers. They will provide the foundation for enhanced, scan-based trading, available-to-order/promise, advanced logistics, auction systems, and consumer marketing capabilities.

Suppliers will gain visibility into manufacturer production requirements. Manufacturers will gain accurate information on retail/consumer sales to aid them in procurement of materials and the production of products to more predictably meet regular and promotional consumer demand and more effectively develop and introduce new products to the marketplace. Wholesalers will gain visibility into retail/consumer demand to reduce inventories and improve operating efficiencies. Retailers can access consumer information that will allow them to improve pricing, promotion, merchandising, marketing, and selling effectiveness and increase sales revenues by improving category management and increasing in-stock position. Consumers will benefit by having the right product at the right price available for purchase when they want it.

Summary

With its introduction and roll-out, initially in the food and consumer packaged goods industry, UCCnet plans to be the sole industry-developed and supported foundation for Internet-based e-commerce. UCCnet plans to be the food industry trade exchange, providing value by enabling the synchronized exchange of information and data, the formation of collaborative e-business relationships, and access to compliant business applications and services through an electronic trading community. Organizations and Internet-based technological solutions such as UCCnet will potentially change the face of business in the food industry.

Footnotes

[1] Coca-Cola Retail Council Independent Study, Retailer Operation Data, Prism Partner Store Audits, 1996

[2] Benchmarking Partners, Inc., U.S. Commerce Department Monthly Sales and Inventory Reports

[3] Voluntary Interindustry Commerce Standards (VICS) CPFR Voluntary Guidelines, 1998

[4] USCII Case Study published in ECR Best Practices document, 1998

Copyright©2000 Andersen Consulting LLP

Astra Pharmaceuticals and Zeneca Group: Post-Merger Integration for Procurement

Mergers are exciting, but once they are complete the real work begins. How do two or more businesses integrate operations, resources, staff, and practices? The integration effort anticipates the long-term success or failure of a merger. While successful integration leads to significant synergies, cost savings, and sustained growth, unsuccessful integration hurts the company, which suffers for a very long time from additional overhead, multiple policies and processes, conflicting strategies, and different cultures. For these reasons it is critical that integration efforts are carefully designed and that a cohesive and effective approach is taken to integrating all the functional areas within an organization.

One of the most disruptive and challenging events that a company can go through in its lifetime is a major merger of its businesses. Soon after the excitement and fanfare of a merger is announced (and sometimes months beforehand), the real challenge of integrating the two or more businesses begins. The integration effort is the real test of whether the merger will eventually be viewed as a success or as a failed attempt to improve the business. However, the rewards and penalties of integration can be tremendous and long lasting. For instance, companies that successfully achieve benefits from significant synergies, cost savings, and sustained growth. On the other hand, companies that have failed at integration seldom recover completely and feel the pains of carrying additional overhead, multiple policies and processes, conflicting strategies, and different cultures for a very long time.

For these reasons, it is critical that integration efforts are thought through ahead of time and that a cohesive and effective approach is taken to integrating all the functional areas within an organization. For example, since Astra Pharmaceuticals and Zeneca formally merged in 1999, the two companies have been undergoing integration efforts, and expect to complete the integration during the third quarter of 2000. The goal of the merger was to achieve synergies as well as to leverage leading practices across the two companies. In this article we lay out the approach that was taken by these two major companies in merging their procurement areas. This approach began with the organization integration as the focus and quickly migrated to process and systems integration.

As a first step in organizing the company for integration, it was important to set up a core team at the functional area level (for example, the operations core team). The core team then defined the integration program for the overall functional area which included: identification of the integration program team, including the sponsor group and task forces; development of a detailed plan for each phase of the integration program; and the development of the guiding principles for integration.

In defining the integration principles, the Astra Zeneca core team began at a general level and then developed specifics for the functional area.

General integration principles include:
- Focus on the leading practice way; not the "old" company A or company B way
- Do things 100% fast – 70% right
- Ensure quality through prioritizing issues and using rigorous fact-based analysis
- Actively reach out to people in the other company
- Pursue a cross-mix of perspectives
- Use "common" language and terminology
- Communicate, communicate, communicate
- Surface issues immediately at the source
- Support agreed upon decisions

Min Chang is a senior manager in the Andersen Consulting Supply Chain Practice. She focuses on supply chain solutions for the pharmaceuticals and high-tech industries.

David Mordia is the leader of purchasing services AstraZeneca. His expertise is in purchasing, facilities, engineering, and the pharmaceuticals industry.

Consumer Goods

Functional integration principles include:
- Focus on the customer
- Effectively balance innovation, synergy, and cost
- Set clear goals and a solid plan to achieve them
- Develop single, transparent, and objective processes
- Create teamwork and collaboration
- Provide accountability for decisions or outcomes
- Support decisions and each other

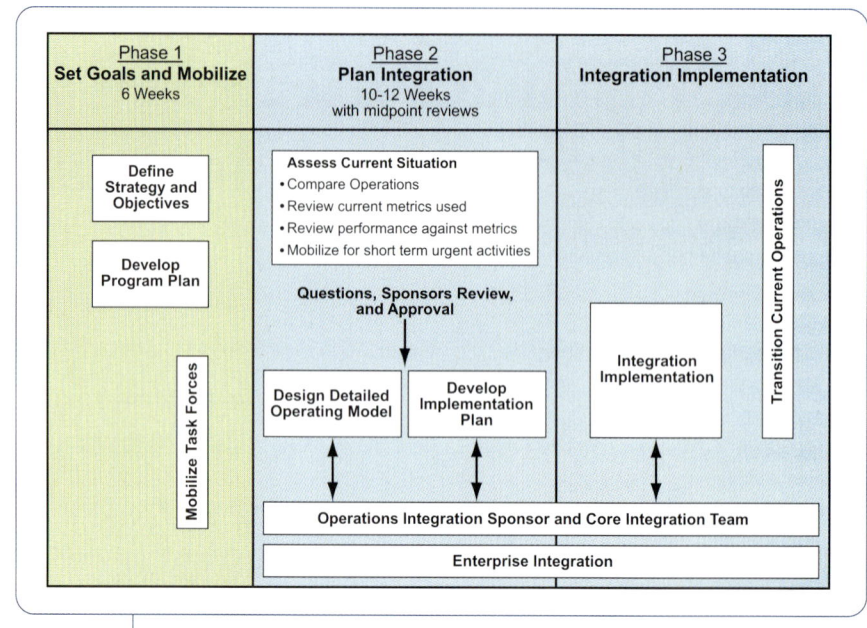

The integration approach used by the operations core team as well as the procurement task forces encompassed three phases: Phase I – Set Goals and Mobilize; Phase II – Plan Integration; Phase III – Integration Implementation. As part of Phase I, the team structure was defined and the team charter was created by the overall operations functional area and by the individual procurement task force. The charter basically helped the team fully understand the objectives of the integration effort within their functional area including the scope, deliverables, activities, and critical success factors. In addition to developing the charter, each task force also developed a detailed work plan for all phases with specific integration milestones.

Phase 1

In Phase I the procurement task force was formed with representation from procurement professionals and their customers from both former organizations. In addition, the task force further expanded the team into several workstreams to address each of the key commodity areas (including information systems, marketing, and sales). The objectives and goals of these workstreams were to complete Phase I – III of the integration effort for their respective commodity areas. Each workstream also developed its own team charters and workplans. The intent of this approach was to cascade the integration effort down into the organization and ensure involvement, contribution, and ownership from as many levels of the organization as possible and feasible.

Phase 2

During Phase II the focus lay in the assessment of the "as-is" environment as well as the development of the "to-be" organization, including a high-level process and systems design. In assessing the as-is environment for procurement, the workstreams analyzed the current organizational structures, the current resource levels (e.g., full-time equivalent performing procurement activities in both former organizations), the total spend associated with each organization, the supply base managed, the policies in place in each organization, and the systems capabilities available. The goal of the as-is assessment was to fully assess the current environment at each former organization so that the workstreams could understand the varying customer requirements and could leverage and utilize the leading practices from each former organization in the to-be design. One of the critical components of the as-is assessment was the full-time equivalent or baseline analysis. This analysis was the basis for creating the resource baseline that allowed the workstreams to fully understand and capture the procurement activity levels being performed in each former organization. In addition, this baseline eventually served as the basis from which synergies were achieved.

Once the as-is assessment was complete, the workstreams focused on the to-be design. The first step in developing the to-be integrated procurement organization was to develop the vision for the end-state. This included defining the procurement organization's customers, the value the procurement organization will be adding, how the organization will be adding the value and how it will measure success. It was critical to define the overall procurement organization vision up front since it would be the guiding principle for the subsequent design of the rest of the procurement organization.

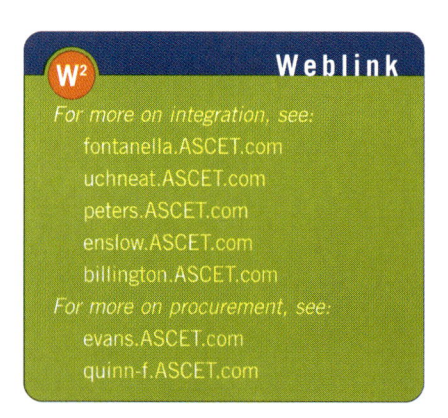

Figure 1.0 **Phases of integration**

Weblink

For more on integration, see:
fontanella.ASCET.com
uchneat.ASCET.com
peters.ASCET.com
enslow.ASCET.com
billington.ASCET.com

For more on procurement, see:
evans.ASCET.com
quinn-f.ASCET.com

Figure 2.0 Integration vision

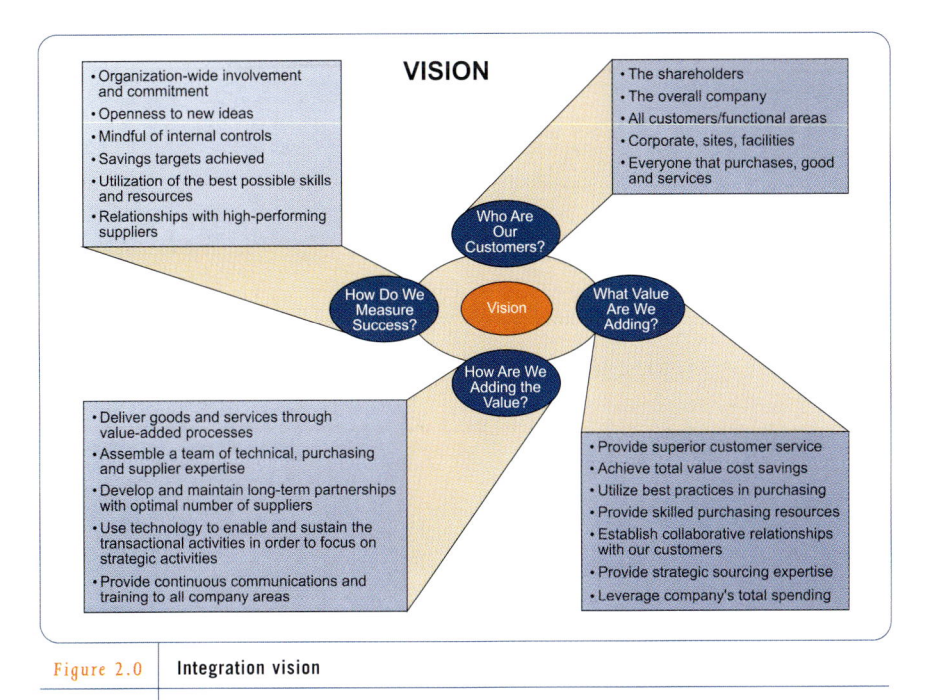

In addition to defining the end-state vision, it was critical to develop the end-state operating model as well. The end-state operating model should represent the strategy, organization, processes, and systems that the integrated organization would like to reach within a certain timeframe (usually a couple of years).

Once the vision and operating model were defined, the next step was to develop the "is" and "is not" activity list. The objective of doing this was to determine at a high level the activities that the to-be procurement organization would be involved in and the activities that the to-be procurement organization would not be involved in. A clear activity list helped focus the organization design effort as well as set the parameters in terms of the expected procurement workload.

In addition, the workstreams also developed the to-be commodity and customer lists that detailed the commodity scope that the organization would cover as well as the customer base that it will serve.

Finally with the vision, operating model, activity list, and commodity and customer scope as inputs, the workstreams drafted several straw models of potential to-be organizations. These straw models were analyzed for strengths and weaknesses and compared against the vision and end-state operating model. This approach was carried through each commodity area within the overall procurement organization; the only variation was that at the commodity level the workstreams defined the detailed commodity scope along with the customer base and critical success factors. These were inputs to developing the straw models for each major commodity area.

Once the straw models were evaluated and the eventual to-be design was chosen, job profiles were developed for each position within the organization structures. These profiles served as the basis for beginning the staffing process for the new procurement organization. Also, the final organization designs and resource count were inputs to the budget development process for the procurement organization as a whole.

Phase 3

The last activity in Phase II was to define the transition plan or implementation plan. The transition plan included the detailed implementation plan for executing the to-be organization design including the process and systems work needed to complete the transition.

The implementation approach included continuing the organization integration through staffing and resource transition planning; developing the detailed to-be processes to support the new organization; and developing the to-be systems to enable the transition. In addition to these efforts, the team also started the strategic sourcing effort with pilot commodity categories and pursued near-term integration savings with longer-term strategic sourcing savings to be achieved in later months. The implementation plans created included detailed tasks, timing, and resource requirements for the continuing organization, process, and systems transition. The next phases of work will work to execute against these plans.

Conclusion

In summary, post-merger integration in the procurement area is a challenging task, but if managed successfully, the effort can create an integrated, effective organization with streamlined processes and systems and an organization that is stronger combined than it was separate.

Copyright© 2000 Andersen Consulting LLP

Sterling Commerce – E-Business Integration Solutions for Supply Chain Optimization

Contact Information

Warner C. Blow
CEO
J. Brad Sharp
President and C.O.O.
Jim Hoyt
Vice President Technology

Sterling Commerce, Inc.

Administrative Offices
4600 Lakehurst Court
Dublin, OH 43016-2000

Phone 800.299.4041 ext. 700
(U.S. & Canada Only)*

Fax 614.793.7221

e-mail gentran_info@stercomm.com

*Inquiries outside of the U.S. and Canada may directly contact one of our global offices. Visit our Web site to find the location nearest you:

www.sterlingcommerce.com

E-business integration is no longer a future solution for businesses. It is the way business is being conducted today. It is a universal mandate to simplify and streamline business processes within the supply chain to reduce costs and improve responsiveness to customer demands. Sterling Commerce, Inc. (NYSE:SE) is the world's leading provider of e-business integration solutions. Our mission is to help companies capitalize on the extraordinary opportunities for growth and profitability brought about by the Internet and supporting technologies.

Sterling Commerce E-Business Integration solutions squarely address the most important issues companies face as they transition their supply chain processes to meet an Internet-driven economy: how to build and manage their global supply chain communities, how to better integrate their business processes within the supply chain, how to achieve greater competitiveness through new sales channels, how to improve productivity and enhance responsiveness to customers, and ultimately how to reduce costs and increase revenues and profit. We help customers meet these goals by focusing on e-sourcing, e-business communication infrastructure, e-business integration, and e-community management.

E-Sourcing

E-sourcing provides resources to help companies solve a range of business problems through managed E-business integration services and outsourcing. E-sourcing takes the burden of managing the supply chain away from the company thereby allowing the company to focus on its core competencies while still improving performance and integration across all business operations.

E-Business Communication Infrastructure

E-business communication infrastructure is a portfolio of software and services that focus specifically on the complexities of managed data delivery within the enterprise and throughout the enterprises' entire supply chain. This allows companies to exchange business information with maximum flexibility and adapt to changing business demands.

E-Business Process Integration

E-business process integration is a portfolio of software and services to integrate complex and diverse business processes, both within an enterprise and among its supply chain community e-business process integration recognizes that companies need to integrate business processes with any other business process, no matter who owns it or where it resides. In addition, e-business process integration uses multiple technologies, including the Web and Internet, to integrate an entire supply chain community effectively and efficiently.

E-Community Management

E-community management is a set of software and services used to build, manage, and service integrated supply chain communities. E-community management allows companies to open their business processes within the supply chain to a much wider community including customers, consumers, suppliers, carriers, banks, and governments.

The Role of Technology in Supply Chain Integration

The use of technology within the supply chain is not new. Market leaders in almost every industry have been using some type of technology within their supply chain for several years in order to automate and streamline their business processes. The ultimate goals of the technology are not new either. As always, enhancing the supply chain process through technology will minimize the time, money, and effort spent on non-production related activities so the company can focus on its core competencies. The end results – increased profit, enhanced market share, and increased shareholder value.

With the exploitation of the Internet, however, the results of using technology in the supply chain can be even more substantial than before. The Internet has provided a cost-effective way of extending supply chain integration technology to the outer edges of the supply chain, most notably the smaller partners, suppliers, and customers within the trading community. The Internet has also made it possible to streamline processes and transactions in real time, speeding up important processes within the supply chain and getting the product to the end-user more efficiently.

What Do You Need from Your Supply Chain Integration Solution?

Any Supply Chain Integration solution you choose should be able to incorporate a wide range of technologies and solutions to help you integrate the entire supply chain. There is no supply chain community that will require a homogeneous technology for integrating its information and business processes. Inevitably, each member of the supply chain community will require differing degrees of technology, spreading across everything from transport to integration levels.

Sterling Commerce employs a wide range of solutions in order to be a complete Supply Chain Integration solution. We recognize that companies and supply chain communities need a wide array of options at their disposal. As a matter of fact, Sterling Commerce has been the leading provider of diversified supply chain integration solutions for over 25 years, and our software and services support approximately 96% of all Fortune 500 companies.

About Sterling Commerce

Sterling Commerce is a worldwide leader in providing e-business integration solutions for the Global 5000 and their commerce communities. The company is one of 40 companies included in the Dow Jones Internet Services Index and one of 100 companies included in the *USA Today* Internet 100 Stock Index. The company provides solutions to address e-business process integration, e-community management, e-business communication infrastructure, and e-sourcing.

The Checklist: Recognizing the Complete Solution for Your Supply Chain

Before considering any Supply Chain Integration solution, make sure to consider all of the things that will be important for success. Does the solution provider…

• Provide a multitude of ways to employ the Internet and supporting technologies including XML?

• Have the most comprehensive framework for building, managing, and servicing Global 5000 supply chain communities?

• Have experience working with multiple industry groups?

• Have over 25 years of experience managing business processes within supply chains?

• Accommodate the varied transport channel requirements for the moving of business info between the supply chain community, including extensive private and Internet protocol support?

• Provide full-scale, reliable, scalable, secure business process integration both within the organization and throughout the entire supply chain?

• Provide a complete set of services including outsourcing, implementation, training and education to maximize ROI?

---

http://sterling.ASCET.com

NONSTOP Solutions: Delivering E-Replenishment to the Pharmaceuticals Industry

Contact Information

Jeff Galt
President and CEO

Homer Dunn
Chairman and Founder

Dave Flood
VP Purchasing Applications and Services

Gerard Cunningham
VP Marketing

NONSTOP Solutions Headquarters
550 California Street
San Francisco, CA 94104
Phone 415.283.1880
Fax 415.282.1899
www.nonstop.com

Products and Services

SCORE" Replenishment and Procurement Applications – hosted on-site at NONSTOP or at client's site
SCORE Collaborative Application for Manufacturers – hosted on-site at NONSTOP or at client's site

Guaranteed Results Service

Replenishment optimization, specific financial results are guaranteed based on detailed opportunity assessments
NonstopRx.com" – first e-replenishment hub for Rx industry that optimizes product, information, transaction and money flows

---

NONSTOP Solutions is the first business-to-business e-replenishment company. It offers Internet-based replenishment optimization applications and services and NonstopRx.com, a trading hub for direct, mission-critical replenishment goods in the pharmaceutical industry.

NONSTOP's Internet-based products and services optimize replenishment, information flow and transactions for core finished goods ranging from pharmaceuticals to autoparts to CDs. The result for our clients is a massive increase in free cash flow and huge reductions in operating costs. This creates large improvements in Return On Invested Capital, raising shareholder value. For example, NONSTOP optimized replenishment processes for Longs Drugs Stores resulting in a 48% decline in replenishment costs and the creation of close to $80 million in free cash flow. NONSTOP has more than 55 customers in pharmaceutical, auto parts, grocery and retail industries, and over $20 billion of inter-company transactions flowing through its suite of offerings.

NONSTOP Addresses a Value Chain Challenge

How do you ensure that customers always find what they need while simultaneously minimizing the cost of replenishing goods?

NONSTOP answers this question using the proprietary, breakthrough optimization science of Stanford Professor Hau Lee. Applying complex mathematical algorithms developed by Dr. Lee, NONSTOP optimizes across all replenishment costs – transportation, inventory carrying, handling, and purchase administration costs as well as product price variability (due to promotions, price increases, etc.) – to achieve the overall lowest cost while at the same maintaining high product availability. Other solutions attempt to lower the cost of each component cost individually, resulting in sub-optimal, much higher overall costs.

NONSTOP also optimizes the information, transaction, and money flows supporting the replenishment process. As a result, both replenishment and the business processes facilitating replenishment not only become hyper-efficient, but stay that way. This generates increased return on investment, significant freed-up working capital, and reduced operating costs, resulting in greater value for shareholders. Customers have more capital, profits, and time, which can be used to grow the company and its earnings.

Offerings

NONSTOP offers a suite of Replenishment Optimization Applications and an E-Hub

Guaranteed Results Service is the premium offering for wholesalers and retailers. Each client is assigned a dedicated NONSTOP team focused solely on delivering results. Since fees are based on meeting guaranteed financial targets, NONSTOP's goals are fully aligned with its client's.

SCORE™ replenishment and purchasing applications optimize the flow of goods between plants, distribution centers, and stores, and provides a collaborative option for manufacturers. The applications are robust, flexible, and easy to use, and can be hosted onsite at NONSTOP or at the client's site.

Buying Profit Optimization is included in both NONSTOP's Guaranteed Results Service and in SCORE applications.

NonstopRx.com, serving the pharmaceutical industry, is the first replenishment-focused e-commerce hub. In addition to wiring manufacturers, wholesalers, and retailers together, this network makes the product replenishment, contract management, marketing, and payment reconciliation processes for pharmaceutical trading partners dramatically more efficient, reducing operating costs and freeing up both capital and time. Customers access NonstopRx.com through SCORE or the Guaranteed Results Service.

Collaborative E-Commerce: Driving Productivity in 2000 and Beyond

The next major innovation in technology-enabled productivity gains is collaborative e-commerce. CPFR, the first standards-based collaborative e-commerce initiative, provides early lessons on how this trend will evolve. The development of standards prior to extensive testing and experimentation is a new approach to change; the long lead times in developing tests and necessary infrastructure to execute collaborative e-commerce prior to broad-scale implementation indicate industry adoption will take a few years. Consumers and financial markets will drive companies to adopt collaborative best practices, and within the next five years the economy will be able to shed 25% of the inventory it currently takes to support retail sales.

For the past nine years, the U.S. economy has experienced an extended business cycle, driven at least partially by productivity gains enabled by technology. The U.S. Commerce Department reports that the monthly inventory-to-sales ratio for the U.S. consumer value chain, which began the decade at 1.52, has steadily dropped to 1.33. In 1999 alone, inventory productivity improved from 1.39 to 1.33, representing $55 billion in inventory productivity improvements across the US retail value chain (see Figure 1.0).

Contributing to the economy's productivity improvements during the 1990s were technology investments in enterprise resource planning (ERP) solutions and advanced planning and scheduling (APS) solutions. Transaction processing and planning capabilities allowed companies to gain real-time control of their operations while optimizing business processes. Today, leading companies are looking to collaborative e-commerce as the next major driver of productivity improvement.

Collaborative e-commerce extends the transactional and optimization capabilities of ERP and APS solutions beyond the boundaries of the enterprise, integrating value-chain planning and transaction processing with trading partner applications across the value chain. The resulting collaborative business processes have the power to provide productivity improvements significantly greater than those achieved over the last decade.

Lessons Learned About Collaborative E-Commerce

Collaborative e-commerce is still in its infancy. The concepts can be applied to many different business processes and produce benefits across a range of industries. The process of moving from collaborative concept to industry implementation and benefits is the new challenge facing industry leaders. Collaborative Planning, Forecasting, and Replenishment (CPFR), the collaborative e-commerce initiative underway in the retail/consumer goods industry, has made significant progress in the transition from concept to implementation and provides some early lessons learned for all industries in meeting this challenge.

Standard Setting Is Done Backwards

Creating a collaborative business practice standard before testing and validating the concept leads to faster industry adoption. Learning from the painful experience in the 1980s when companies had to rationalize a large number of proprietary approaches to EDI to enable its use, the Voluntary Inter-Industry Commerce Standards (VICS) initiated the development of a standard approach to the CPFR business process before the concepts had been widely tested and validated. A central benefit to defining the industry guidelines before testing is that a standard hypothesis

---

Jim Uchneat is a research director with Benchmarking Partners, a leading e-business transformation firm dedicated to the business-to-business (B2B) marketplace. Jim leads the Collaborative Planning, Forecasting, and Replenishment (CPFR) working groups. His expertise lies in upgrading operations to best practices by linking/enabling supply chain and e-business technologies with customer-focused processes.

Prior to joining Benchmarking Partners, he was supply chain director for CVS Stores. He is part of a team of practitioners who teach an MIT course for executives and graduate students entitled "Developing the CEO Team's Value Chain Network Strategy." He can be reached at juchneat@benchmarking.com.

Consumer Goods

provides a baseline for experimentation and discussion.

The VICS community of interest that formed the CPFR guidelines for the retail/consumer goods industry also generated the network of participants that engaged in the early experimentation. The willingness of early innovators to share the results of their testing efforts and further the understanding of CPFR provided the foundation for expanded industry experimentation.

The VICS community also provided a platform for feeding the technology requirements supporting the CPFR guidelines to software companies. Based on these inputs, low-cost or free solutions evolved to support the early collaboration tests. The participation of the software companies in the standard setting process created a competitive, yet cooperative, environment. Challenges faced by the software developers were brought to the VICS community for discussion and enhancement of the CPFR guidelines. The software companies took an active role in marketing the concept of CPFR through both collective and individual market development initiatives. The result of their participation in the process has been the development of better software, more effective guidelines, and expanded industry awareness of the opportunities associated with implementing CPFR.

The VICS model for collaboration standard setting has since been followed by the high technology industry's RosettaNet initiative. In fact, RosettaNet

Weblink

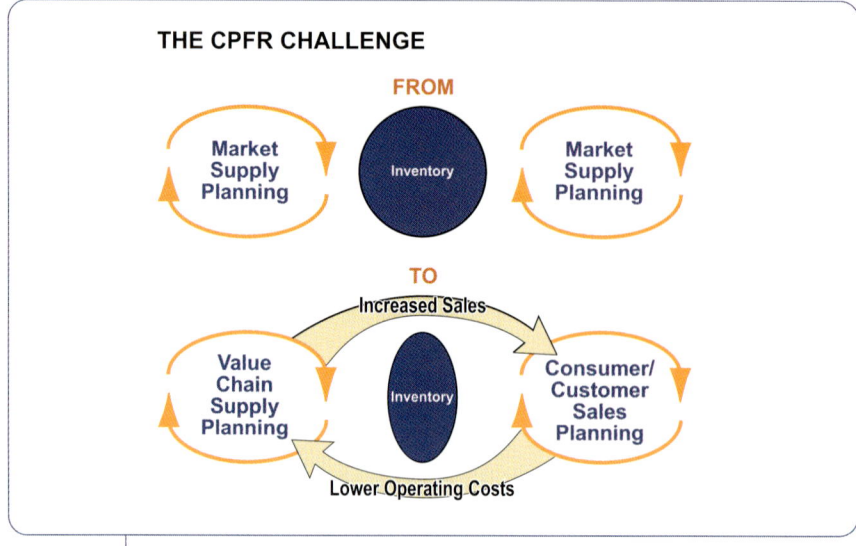

For more on ERP, see:
- hicks.ASCET.com
- herbold.ASCET.com
- anthony.ASCET.com
- martella.ASCET.com
- sprague.ASCET.com
- culotta.ASCET.com
- albright.ASCET.com

For more on the value chain, see:
- reiter.ASCET.com
- culotta.ASCET.com

Figure 1.0 Total Business Inventories/Sales Ratios (Source: U.S. Department of Commerce)

reviewed the CPFR guidelines built for the retail/consumer goods industry and later adopted them in the suite of high technology collaboration guidelines. Expect this new model of standard setting and cross-industry cooperation to become a common approach to furthering inter-enterprise collaboration.

Testing Collaborative Concepts

CPFR pilot tests proved out the benefits but did not lead to immediate expansion of the concept. More internal infrastructure development is required.

Pilot initiatives are a fairly standard approach to testing new concepts, especially those that are expected to have a significant impact on the business. When the concepts involve integration with trading partner applications, the testing becomes much more challenging. Trading partners may have different priorities for the test as well as different capabilities to support the test. The net result is that the testing process takes longer to implement and the ability to reach conclusions from the test that can be projected across the trading partner base may be limited.

The business results achieved to date by CPFR pilots vary widely but have consistently been positive. The most surprising results have been in the area of sales. While a number of pilots have seen dramatic sales growth triggered by changes in their product assortment or pricing strategies, a few trading partner pairs found they were able to significantly reduce lost sales by improving their shelf in-stock position. Since the lost sale is one of the hardest problems to measure, retailers and suppliers often overlook the opportunity.

Even the pilots that were focused on growing sales or reducing supply chain costs experienced a positive impact on inventory. In nearly all cases, the inventory improvements ranged between 15% and 35%. Most of these benefits were captured between one set of trading partners. Extending collaboration back into the supply base provides an opportunity for additional savings and further improvements in the total inventory-to-sales ratio.

The Technology

CPFR exchanges more data between trading partners requiring technology that can plan and execute each business at a lower level of detail.

Across the CPFR initiative, the most significant challenge for companies developing tests has been achieving the internal capability to support the new business practices. CPFR involves a fundamental shift from planning the business from a top-down market and brand approach to a

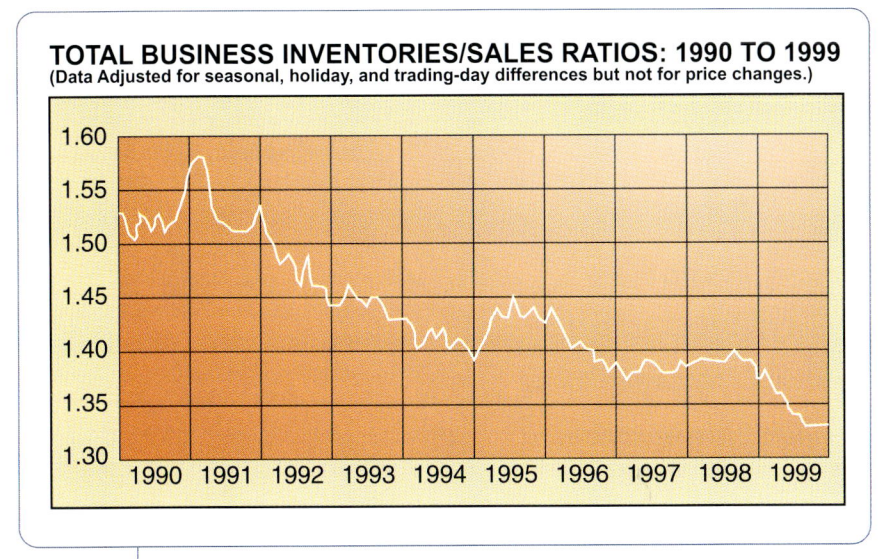

Figure 2.0   The CPFR Challenge (Source: Benchmarking Partners, Inc.)

bottom-up, customer-specific demand approach. Consumer goods companies traditionally plan demand and supply integration by deploying inventory to markets, not to specific customers. They do not integrate customer-specific demand information into supply planning until most of the costs in the supply process have already been incurred.

Retailers have a different approach to the same problem. They assume supply availability and try to manage problems by leaning on suppliers that fail to deliver. The majority of retailers do not provide forecasts, and those that do frequently find that most suppliers do not have a technology infrastructure that can make effective use of the forecast information. The result has been that both retailers and consumer goods partners testing CPFR have had to develop manual processes to support their tests. The manual processes are necessary to test the concepts, but they are not scalable and constrain the expansion of CPFR (see Figure 2.0).

The most common outcome of CPFR tests is the development of new technology infrastructure requirements to support the collaborative processes. Consumer goods companies require technology infrastructures that integrate customer-specific demand planning into market planning, available-to-promise planning capability, and make-to-order execution capability. Retailers are focusing on promotion and replenishment forecasting capabilities, as well as purchasing systems that can incorporate constrained supply information. Piloting companies have found that these technology requirements do not usually replace the ERP and APS solutions that were deployed in the 1990s. Instead, they tend to enhance existing solutions with incremental functionality. Those companies that have failed to upgrade their ERP and APS infrastructures are finding themselves further behind the curve in their ability to adopt innovative best practices in collaborative e-commerce.

Creating Collaborative E-Commerce Critical Mass

Preparing to develop CPFR critical mass takes time and an appreciation of the work required changing cultures.

CPFR tests have demonstrated that the benefits of collaboration are real – but so are the high costs of the supporting manual processes. For that reason, most companies piloting CPFR minimize the number of tests they engage in while they add the functionality that will allow them to efficiently expand collaborative operations. The early retail and CPG CPFR innovators have found that it is not uncommon to take a year or longer to develop a scalable approach to collaboration.

The early innovators of CPFR are just beginning to roll out collaborative practices across large networks of trading partners. Speed-to-implementation and ease of ongoing integration management are critical, and leaders are incorporating a fair amount of standardization into their roll-out approaches. Retailers, in particular, are under pressure to standardize their approach to collaboration because of the large number of trading partners required to establish CPFR as the core business process. A large retailer may need to bring up over 200 suppliers to achieve to critical mass. A large consumer goods company, on the other hand, may need to bring up only 10 to 15 of its largest customers to reach critical mass. As a result, CPG companies can afford more customization in their relationships.

Retailers have been leading the CPFR roll-out, creating multiple collaboration processes capable of supporting a wide range of supplier competencies. As suppliers improve their collaborative competencies, they progress through the alternatives to achieve increased benefits. This approach supports scalable trading partner training as well as the retailer's ability to manage internal process alignment with a limited number of collaborative process alternatives.

Change Management

As most people that become engaged in CPFR initiatives will attest, implementing the technology is the easy part. Change management, particularly changing a culture to be collaborative, is much more difficult. Business process roles and responsibilities, as well as performance measures, all must change. These changes take longer to successfully integrate into the company than the supporting technology. The book is still being written on how companies will overcome the change management challenges. Two large retailers offer very different approaches. One retailer is providing access to information and training about its collaboration processes, as well as incentives for business partnership improvements. The other retailer is charg-

white paper

ing suppliers for installing its CPFR capabilities and is charging a monthly fee for usage. It is too early to tell which approach will prove most effective; however, the first appears to be reflective of a collaborative culture while the other has adopted a more traditional arms-length approach to trading partner relationships.

Continued Growth

25% in inventory productivity improvement in five years is possible.

Lowering the U.S. inventory/sales ratio from 1.33 to below 1.0 while growing sales will happen. Collaborative e-commerce initiatives like CPFR will continue to drive these improvements. Trading communities in the high technology, automotive, and transportation industries also have working groups developing and testing collaborative e-commerce business practices. These industry groups are actively learning from one another through the support of the technology provider community that works across industries.

> *During the 1990s, transaction processing and planning capabilities allowed companies to gain real-time control or their operations while optimizing business processes. Today, leading companies are looking to collaborative e-commerce as the next major driver of productivity improvement.*

The speed to 1.0 will be constrained by the ability to change business practices and embrace collaborative cultures. But the pressure from consumers and the financial markets will drive this change sooner rather than later. Consumers are not going to let prices rise in an information rich environment, and the financial markets understand the power of the Internet and expect to see it incorporated into business strategies. The time to 1.0 will be less than five years with the early adopters being the early winners.

Benchmarking Partners

For additional information on Benchmarking Partners, please visit their Web site at www.benchmarking.com.

Benchmarking Partners is the leading e-business transformation firm dedicated to the business-to-business (B2B) marketplace. Since 1994, Benchmarking Partners has been the CEO team's partner focused on reinventing the business-to-business environment for the Internet economy. As the leading research-based consulting firm, Benchmarking Partners is committed to accelerating the benefits from demand/supply chain and e-business initiatives. By applying best business practices and best-in-class information technology within the enterprise and across e-commerce trading partners, Benchmarking Partners helps clients to accelerate strategic and tangible return on Internet (ROI). Our clients are leading multinational manufacturers, distributors, retailers, healthcare providers, financial service companies, and information systems solution suppliers.

Reported information and opinions reflect the most accurate information available at the time of publication and are subject to change.

For more information, contact Benchmarking Partners, One Main Street, Cambridge, MA 02142, or call us at 617-225-7800.

Copyright ©2000 Benchmarking Partners, Inc.

Third Generation E-Business and the Supply Lattice

written by:

George Moakley
Intel Corporation
http://moakley.ASCET.com

Online commerce is drawing a greater share of customers and markets. Although automated back-end systems and user-friendly Web interfaces are improving customer relationships, this is only the earliest step in an online revolution. The next step is to solve the main problem of the supply chain, which is the efficient incorporation, integration, and utilization of information provided by multiple suppliers. Supply Chain Management should give people a greater governing role in defining business rules. E-business applications will automatically integrate the information, sort it, apply the rules, and make decisions, thus automating your ability to react.

Every day companies like Amazon.com, Dell Computer, and Federal Express are winning customers and earning market share by shifting commerce online. Automated back-end systems, combined with user-friendly Web-based order interfaces, are streamlining operations and creating innovative customer relationships. But this is just the beginning of the Web revolution.

In the next generation of Internet business, companies will solve a major supply-chain problem – how to efficiently incorporate, integrate, and utilize the rich inflows of information provided by multiple suppliers. Purchase agents must still manually enter and track every product order they make. What's more, they must check with numerous supplier representatives and Web sites in order to ensure that they have the latest information about pricing and availability. Services such as e-mail notification do little to streamline operations, since these data do not integrate into customer systems.

Let me give you an example. Believe it or not, Intel now has 650,000 known suppliers of everything from chip wafers to hotel rooms. With so many, you'd think our goal would be to greatly reduce the number for easier administration and lower overhead. In fact, we're looking to e-business to expand that number by automating our supply chain. To find the best suppliers, we want our computer applications to do the tedious work of running through all the possible combinations of all those suppliers.

A staff member might consider a few scenarios that combine two or three suppliers to fill a need, but the computer can come up with a combination of say, 57, that, over the next five days and 3,000 separate purchase orders, fills our need for the best price and availability.

In most of today's e-business supply chains, the human is a processor in the system. In Supply Chain Management, he or she has to look at a series of Web screens, integrate the information, perhaps by cutting and pasting between different applications, and get back on the Web to implement the decision. Our vision for Supply Chain Management is to give people a greater governing role of defining business rules. E-business applications will automatically integrate the information, sort it, apply the rules and make the decision, thus automating your ability to react.

The Generations of E-Business

The evolution of e-business has already passed through two important generations. In the first generation, companies established a static presence on the Web, publishing HTML-based Web sites that serve as online catalogs. In the past two years, innovative companies have launched second-generation e-business programs, linking their Web front-ends with back-end order management and inventory control systems. Such deployments let the customer place and track orders directly from a company's Web site, reduc-

George Moakley, Director of Enterprise Architecture at Intel, is the lead architect for Intel's Distributed Enterprise Architecture Lab (DEAL). DEAL's charter is Intel's vision and architecture for enterprise computing and e-business solutions. Mr. Moakley started with Intel as Distributed Computing Architect for Intel's manufacturing and IT organization, defining the architecture and strategies Intel would use for its internal information systems architectures. Before joining Intel, he spent nine years managing information systems in the aerospace, retail, and mining industries.

Mr. Moakley is an Editorial Board member for Achieving Supply Chain Excellence through Technology.

Electronics & High Tech

ing transaction costs and giving customers more control over the order process.

This second generation of Internet business is largely vendor-centric, in that it centers on the ability of vendors to automate internal processes and link them to customers via the Web. By linking Web sites to back-end systems, vendors can display up-to-the-minute information about inventories, pricing, and order and shipping status. A growing universe of tools and utilities has allowed businesses to Web-enable their back-end systems, linking even complex ERP applications such as SAP and Baan to easy-to-use Web-based interfaces.

In the final phase of the e-business evolution – the third generation – vendors extend the benefits of automation to their customers. Vendors not only deliver information directly into customer systems, they facilitate transactions triggered by events communicated between computers. Companies engaged in third-generation Internet business conduct business programmatically, applying sophisticated business rules to control activities like pricing and purchasing. The result? Vendors adopt a customer-centric approach that employs automation to deliver maximum competitive value to external customers.

The Vision of the Third Generation

The benefits of third generation e-business become apparent when you look at the multi-faceted nature of business relationships. An individual may buy his or her books from a single vendor, but a manufacturer typically sources individual parts from multiple vendors in order to ensure timely delivery and competitive pricing. What's more, the manufacturer purchases thousands of different products for its various manufacturing and business operations. If every vendor presents a distinct order interface, it becomes very expensive for the customer to adapt its personnel and business systems to each case.

Third generation e-business automates that complex mesh of business relationship that can best be described as a supply lattice. Rather than manually scanning vendor Web sites for updated pricing information, for example, customers automatically receive pricing updates in formats tailored to their internal systems, and send similar data out to their customers, creating a lattice of connections rather than a linear supply "chain." Applications then act across the lattice on updated data and take actions based on business rules. Humans set the parameters of decision-making through business rules, but machines are taking the actions.

Consider a business that uses an application to monitor in-house inventory. When inventory levels for a product become low, the application sorts through possible actions to determine the most profitable course. The program draws on a continuous feed of product pricing from numerous vendors to determine the best mix of price and availability among its suppliers. The system might even split the order, taking a rush shipment of product at a higher price to fill the immediate inventory shortfall. The remainder of the order is then placed at a lower price with a vendor who can deliver product later in the week.

Another example of a third-generation supply lattice: Say a customer cancels an order for 500 widgets. With a glut of inventory, the widget manufacturer sends an event notification across the Web, computer to computer, to all its widget customers: "If you place an order with me in the next 15 minutes, I'll give you the widgets for half price." One customer receives that event and immediately issues another event to its customers: "If you will buy 500 widgets, you can have them at 25% off." One of those customers receives the event and replies, "I will buy those," and the company that got the acknowledgement sends its order to the manufacturer, buying the widgets. The whole process could take 15 minutes and occur at 3 a.m. in the morning.

With customer-side integration, then, as soon as you receive the event you can make a decision, because your automated response generates another event. Such e-business links can be the source of significant competitive advantage. Even if your widgets are more expensive, the net cost of buying from you can be cheaper if the right connections are in place. And if you and your competitors all sell widgets that contain a key ingredient from the same supplier, and the supplier changes its price, you gain an edge by being the first to inform your customers about the price change in a way they can react to.

Making Supply Lattice Connections

Of course, this kind of hands-off interaction takes loosely-coupled, flexible applications with embedded service interfaces, replacing rigid standards such as electronic data interchange (EDI). The result? Business systems interoperate, while protecting core systems from the vagaries of both customers' systems and Internet connections.

By enabling intelligent interaction and failable links among customers and vendors, third-generation applications can construct the supply lattice mentioned earlier. This complex mesh of business linkages enables a change at any one company to be communicated and reflected at all the connected companies. So a price shift at a vendor will not only be reflected among a community of customers, it will kick off a change in the way those customers interact with other vendors as they seek the best terms for their purchases.

With this supply lattice in place, the stage is set for new species of transactions. Low transaction costs can increase the granularity of transactions, enabling micro-transactions that today are too triv-

Weblink

More on customer-centric solutions:
enslow.ASCET.com
hurley.ASCET.com
uchneat.ASCET.com
wayman.ASCET.com
bruce.ASCET.com
sprague.ASCET.com
srivastava.ASCET.com

ial to conduct. A company might employ micro-transactions to fine-tune inventory levels to squeeze efficiencies out of a just-in-time (JIT) purchasing system. On the other side of the coin, long transactions will enable customers to place a tentative hold on products and services months in advance, enabling them to arbitrage among numerous sources to gain the most advantageous terms.

We can create such applications today using existing software technologies to perform broad-based data exchange. For example, component model technologies such as Microsoft's Component Object Model (COM) and Sun's Enterprise JavaBeans enable developers and corporations to craft modular solutions that link together applications and services. In the years to come, independent software vendors (ISVs) will react to the emerging market opportunity and provide a rich selection of component solutions. The result: Companies will soon be able to buy, license, or craft sophisticated component-model solutions to enable third-generation e-business deployments.

Additionally, XML technology enables broad, machine-based interaction. XML is being used by organizations such as the RosettaNet Consortium to craft an agreed-upon way to exchange information within the technology products industry. The arrival of new software integration tools from ISVs will soon make this task easier.

The result will be a new species of compound applications that embed elements of other applications. That way, customers can accept software components from vendors and integrate event-driven communications directly into their business applications. Purchase agents no longer need scan vendor Web sites to track price changes – rather, the change is pushed directly to their application via an embedded component.

Balanced Computing

Compound applications, event-driven communications, and loosely coupled business solutions put a premium on processing power. From the server to the client, every link in the supply lattice must rapidly acquire, process, and act on constant streams of data. In fact, the ability of an enterprise to compete will depend largely on the computing infrastructure and how quickly it reacts to market conditions.

Which vendor can most rapidly produce price updates based on changes to physical inventory and world markets? Which customers can best link to a wide array of suppliers and effectively arbitrage orders in order to garner best pricing and delivery? First-mover advantage will depend on a balanced distribution of computing power in the enterprise.

Intel calls this the balanced computing model. It is a new way of combining traditional compute models to meet emerging information delivery needs. Balanced computing combines existing server-centric, network-centric, and connected PC compute models to enable businesses to distribute applications and information to many diverse constituents.

The dynamic interaction enabled by these emerging solutions will have a seismic impact on business practices and expectations. Ultimately, customers will look beyond product quality, competitive pricing, and service when selecting vendors. They will seek out suppliers who make their enterprise more competitive. That means suppliers must work to integrate their internal business systems with customers in order to speed the pace of business and wring new efficiencies out of the supply lattice. An emerging class of solutions is even now arming companies with the tools they need to join the third generation of Internet business.

web link — http://pandesic.ASCET.com

Pandesic – Delivering on the Promise of E-Commerce

Contact Information

Harold Hughes
CEO and Chairman
of the Board (Founder)

Pete Wolcott
President

Ed Harley
Chief Operating Officer
(Founder)

Paul Larose
Chief Financial Officer

Pat Holmes
Chief Technology Officer

Catherine Yetts
Vice President, Customer Success

Ed Felton
Vice President, Engineering
and Operations

Employees
350 worldwide

Business-to-Business
Aggregator, Distribution, Multistore

Business-to-Consumer
Consumer Direct, E-tail, Events,
Multistore, Sports

Pandesic Sales and Services
Pandesic sells its service in the US, Europe, Latin America, and Japan through a direct sales force and, in conjunction with authorized partners. Pandesic is headquartered in Sunnyvale, CA with research and development operations in Folsom, CA.
408.616.1900

Key Technology Partners
Software and Hardware
Intel, SAP R/3, Microsoft, TaxWare, Cybercash, TanData, Citibank

E-Marketing Strategy Partners
Akamai, eGain, Flooz, LinkShare, Net Perceptions, Netcentives, and Screaming Media

Authorized Hosting Partners
Intel Online Services
Digex

The Internet Revolution is not about technology. It is about revolutionizing the way business is convened, constructed, and conducted. According to the latest figures from Forrester Research, the value of online commerce transactions will top $1 trillion by 2002. Whether you are a pure dot-com company, an existing brick-and-mortar company, or a business-to-business venture, you need to build an e-business presence that extends your market reach, radically improves customer service, supports virtual collaboration with business partners, and reaches new heights in business efficiency and productivity.

In the fast-paced world of the Internet, it is difficult to keep up with the changes of the marketplace, as well as the changes in technology. The need to have the best and newest technology is a given for companies that seek to launch a world-class business online. Most online business decision makers today, however, are finding that it is no longer the smart choice to build an e-commerce solution in-house when there are technology experts who specialize in building, training, and deploying these systems on behalf of customers.

No longer do companies need to spend $10 - $30 million on a customized solution that will take 6-12 months to implement. Instead, companies can benefit from an optimized, standard solution that can be deployed in 10-12 weeks, which includes continual software upgrades at no additional cost. Pandesic's e-business solution gives online businesses everything needed to run a successful, robust, and scalable e-business. Pandesic customers have access to an e-commerce engine that automates the entire e-business enterprise, 24x7x365 support, lifetime upgrades, the necessary hardware to run the system, and the expertise of hundreds of e-commerce specialists.

The Pandesic platform is the foundation for many diverse e-businesses, including virtual dot-com e-tailers, brick-and-mortars, product brands, business-to-business entities, and multi-store systems. For each of these businesses, Pandesic delivers the most comprehensive e-business solution by connecting the front-end Web site to the back-end processing and shipping. Pandesic customers receive the necessary support to implement and scale a seamlessly integrated e-business solution. With Pandesic's expertise, experience, and combination of world-class technologies from Intel, SAP, Microsoft, and Digex, we enable e-businesses to go to market cost-effectively and quickly on an infrastructure that can scale with growth.

Pandesic seamlessly automates the business processes that occur both before and after a purchase is made – customer acquisition, Web cataloging, order processing, pick/pack/shipping, returns processing, procurement, accounting, reporting, and more. Our automated business processes reduce expenses and increase customer satisfaction. Not only will your customers experience convenient, reliable, and secure transactions, they will also get access to real-time information on inventory, shipping status, order history, and e-mail confirmations with the click of a mouse.

Pandesic offers flexibility, profitability, and scalability. An open front-end architecture allows online businesses to flexibly customize and extend the look, feel, and functionality of their unique site. Pandesic's proven e-business processes increase profitability by improving efficiency and productivity, thus reducing manual order processing and customer service costs. Finally, with both technical and business process scalability, Pandesic can scale to match any business' rapid rate of growth.

The Pandesic E-Business Solution

Formed in 1997, Pandesic LLC was founded jointly by Intel Corporation and SAP America, Inc., a subsidiary of the German software company SAP AG®, one of the largest software companies in the world. This alliance combines Intel's vast global logistics experience and SAP's

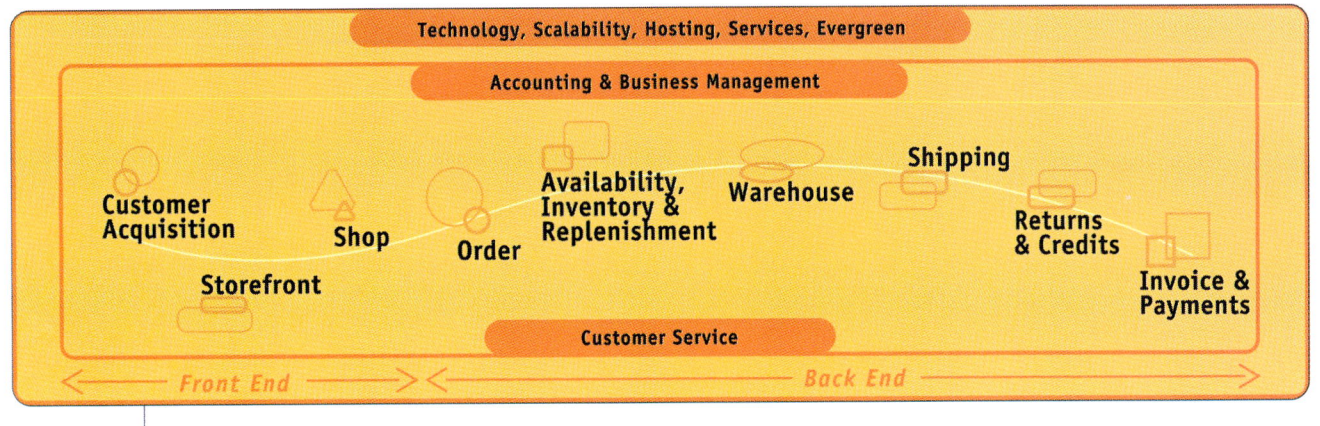

Figure 1.0 The front-end addresses customer interfaces; the back-end addresses business, warehouse, and supplier interfaces.

business process expertise with the cost-effectiveness of the Web.

The Pandesic, e-business solution is an integrated and complete solution that allows online businesses to use the Web and integrated business processes to automate the selling of goods to individuals or businesses. The Pandesic e-business solution includes software, services, and hardware. Pandesic offers online businesses a flexible and profitable e-business solution that can grow.

Benefits of the Pandesic E-Business Solution

The Front End: An Open Architecture

Businesses want total control over the design, functionality, and extensibility of their Web site, and Pandesic's "open" front end delivers this flexibility. Pandesic's front-end includes customer acquisition, storefront, and shop features. Companies can customize their unique site, develop new functionality, or extend their commerce site with other third-party applications such as a Personalization and Membership application or collaborative filtering tools.

The Back End: Proven E-Business Processes

Pandesic has standardized and automated e-business processes so that an online business does not need to develop, implement or customize their own back-end processes such as back order scheduling, printing pick-and-pack lists, and general ledger postings. By leveraging these best-practice processes, an online business can increase its profitability by lowering transaction processing costs.

Scalability for Growth: Technical and Business Process Scalability

To keep pace with business' growth, a solution must have:

- Scalable technology – electronically process growing numbers of orders
- Scalable business processes – physically process growing numbers of orders. The electronic processing of thousands of orders per day isn't enough. Pandesic's scalability helps online businesses ship those orders quickly out of a warehouse and assists in processing the hundreds of customer-service requests for returns.

The Pandesic, e-business solution's technology and business processes are designed to scale, enabling a merchant to process thousands of orders per day.

About Pandesic

Pandesic is the leading e-commerce application service provider (ASP) for the dot-com enterprise. With the Pandesic e-business solution, customers receive the control and infrastructure necessary to build and scale a successful e-business.

Pandesic provides an optimized and managed e-business solution that e-businesses utilize to drive their commerce strategies. An end-to-end e-business solution is one that provides everything needed to conduct business online including:

- A bundled best-of-breed e-business application that automates the entire life cycle of a business transaction from the customer experience through to the fulfillment of the order, including returns and credits
- Hardware
- Hosting of the e-commerce site
- Lifetime upgrades
- E-business services such as training, 24x7x365 support, ongoing maintenance, and on-call expertise in business processes and marketing.

The Pandesic E-business Solution is a standard platform "purpose built" for real-time business-to-business and business-to-consumer business.

Business-to-Business
- Aggregator
- Distribution
- Multistore

Business-to-Consumer
- Consumer Direct
- E-tail
- Events
- Multi-store
- Sports

http://pandesic.ASCET.com

Compaq's Supply Chain Strategy Weaves a Business Community Fabric

Contact Information

Frank Lanza
Director Supply Chain Management, Professional Services, Enterprise Systems and Services Group

Compaq Computer Corporation
2 Results Way
Marlborough, MA 01752
Phone 978.496.8277
Frank.Lanza@compaq.com

Compaq Computer Corporation
20555 SH 249
Houston, TX 77070
Phone 281.370.0670

Enterprise Resource Planning (ERP) systems have been established to connect, integrate, and enable all facets of the enterprise. The result is dramatically improved flow of information within an organization. Many businesses expected that their investment in ERP systems would solve the execution problems posed by e-commerce, but this has not proven to be the case. Typical implementations were built around existing business trends and practices, which meant data was kept within a single organization. But supply chain integration and e-commerce change the game. Transaction volume increases exponentially as trading partners' ERP data becomes critical to business decisions. A scalable environment must be in place to accommodate the real-time, changing needs which emerge. ERP systems become the "backbone" on which progressive supply chain capabilities are built. While ERP generates large amounts of data through the integration of functions such as ordering, processing, and manufacturing, Supply Chain Management (SCM) uses the ERP data together with iterative analysis to optimize distribution and logistics.

Managing a production environment where business never stops becomes critical. The volume of information processing increases dramatically and with unpredictable demand due to the wider access distribution. This, with the simultaneous increase in performance requirements, presents a radical change in information systems requirements. For example, imagine a distributor accessing your Web site to order some equipment. As part of the transaction they need to know if you can meet their delivery requirements. Since you build to order, the customer's purchase decision depends upon visibility into your vendor's supply chain – all on Internet time!

Supply chain has changed from a sequentially run batch program to a real-time continual assessment of inventory capabilities. Information becomes part of the product. Your ability to respond to supply chain decisions will provide competitive leadership in e-business. Can you provide your customers the information they demand? What decisions are you willing to make with inadequate data? SCM changes the relationship between trading partners and between companies and their customers. For SCM to be successful, information must be shared beyond the doors of the organization. This requires sophisticated customer relationship management. It also requires technologies such as data warehousing and e-procurement, which help customers and suppliers plan together, schedule together, and exchange goods and services. In short, the growth of the Internet and SCM enable a new e-commerce landscape which links buyers, sellers, and suppliers into a single virtual organization, or e-value chain.

The Supply Chain Management Evolution

Many manufacturing and distribution enterprises are shelving their make-to-stock push strategy for a customer-centric, make-to-order pull strategy. They have plenty of incentives. By managing the flow of raw materials to finished goods more accurately, enterprises can increase inventory turns, reduce cycle times, and improve product quality. The result is greater customer satisfaction. At the same time, the transition to "make-to-order" is more complex, with shorter product life cycles and "zero inertia," or the agility required to stop on a dime as customer changes. As supply chain processes evolve, the role of information in business changes significantly.

The issue is: Have we changed the way we manage data to fit our evolving business?

One of the initial roles of information was for administration, described as delivering to internal personnel information about business processes after the fact. A second role of information has been to become an integral part of the production processes. A key differential is time requirements, which have now become "real time." Some of the classic examples that we have seen include airline reservation systems, financial trading, factory automation, and package shipping and tracking. A third role is for information to become valued by the consumer as an integral part of the product. Information has been a key part of many products, but until recently the information was provided by "customer service" personnel. Frequently the service was difficult to obtain and service costs were expendable if necessary to meet P&L.

The Internet has shown companies that their costs decrease and customer satisfaction increases when customers can answer their own questions about issues such as delivery, arrival times, availability, product choices, and configuration. Here, the key differential is the accessibility of the information to both customers and supply chain partners. While the information is essentially the same, the shift toward providing access to the information has been significant, both in terms of market value and systems requirements. The evolving role and importance of information and the demands of speed and agility placed upon its delivery and access can be realized only with a comprehensive and integrated SCM approach. But what are other implications of the shifting role of information?

Production and Operations is the New Primary Critical Success Factor!

Historically, the development and implementation of the applications required the greatest amount of skill, and had the most business impact if done poorly. But with the complexity and the scale of information management, coupled with real-time demands on a continuous (24x7) basis, information management tasks become the most difficult with the most financial exposure. The delayed implementation of an application pales in comparison to the cost of e-commerce being "down." Maintenance now might be described as

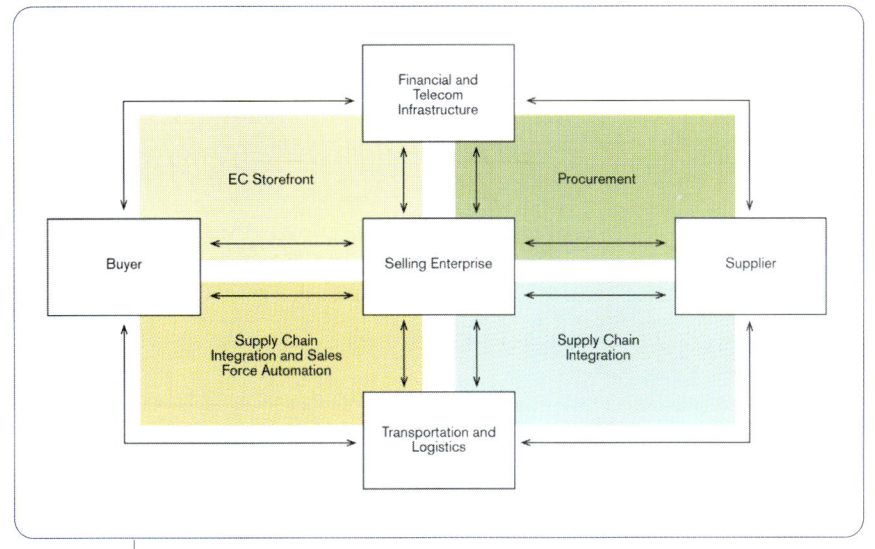

Figure 2.0 | Electronic commerce landscape linking buyers, sellers, and suppliers

having to change tires on a car while it is still being driven. In the past the focus of operations was the efficient management of multiple applications on single systems to achieve economies of scale; today's challenge is the management of single applications of massive scale and complexity on multiple systems!

In addition to availability and scale, the Internet requires many business applications to behave differently. Traditionally most "business" applications have differed significantly from "technical" applications in their systems requirements. Business applications have required greater I/O storage and sequential record "processing" from tapes and disks. Main memory processing was not demanding. On the other hand, technical applications frequently involved iterative comparisons so a relatively small amount of data was continually used for computations.

Today's supply chain applications demand both voluminous data and intense computing and modeling. Best practice supply chain decisions now include vendors' inventory in the decision process, which means an order of magnitude more data. At the same time, to assess the "best" answer to a customer's question requires multiple iterations against very large databases. Every customer decision that cannot be supported in Internet time is a missed opportunity for customer retention and sale. There is no tolerance for latency in data access. The only real way to provide that capability is to keep the data resident in main memory (or on "local" direct access disks)! Finally, an increasing number of applications are becoming customer-driven, in part because information is becoming part of the product value. Therefore operational decisions now have the dual demands of real-time decisions coupled with extraordinary data requirements, all being driven by the customer. Furthermore, while its use becomes more volatile and diverse, information integrity and security become more critical.

E-Commerce Landscape Linking Buyers, Sellers, and Suppliers

Compaq is committed to creating solutions that enable customers to maximize their supply chain effectiveness and create strategic business advantages. Our heritage of superior manageability is key to today's complex and massively scaled systems. Digital Equipment Corporation led the industry in clustering technology while Compaq had established Intelligent Manageability through Compaq Insight Manager (CIM). Compaq provides the best Web-based, heterogeneous production and operations management to the enterprise.

solution provider

web link — http://compaq.ASCET.com

Compaq's Professional Services is experienced in systems and network architecture and off-site management including diverse and competitive platforms. Compaq was the first to provide 64-bit computing recognizing that high-intensity applications require superior computing ability. Compaq offers the best choice for demanding Supply Chain Management applications. Finally, Compaq meets the challenge of often unpredictable system requirements of e-business through programs such as "Capacity on Demand" whereby customers can quickly and affordably acquire storage on massive scale.

Compaq's innovative Storage Area Network (SAN) allows customers to manage their storage resources efficiently while providing greatest access and control. Also, by powering many of the leading service providers, Compaq and its partners can deliver complete systems with infinite scale and low cost of entry. Compaq's goal is to provide the best choices for designing, building, and maintaining world-class SCM systems. By relying on strengths of manageability, performance, and scale, Compaq delivers SCM solutions that propel customers to competitive advantage. Our resources include the widest range of enterprise computing systems, from high-performance and NonStop servers to PCs and handheld computers. Compaq not only leads the industry in Intel-based solutions but also delivers the first 64-bit computing (Tru64 UNIX on Alpha) and the most complete enterprise storage solutions available. More SAP customers rely on Compaq than any other platform; Compaq ProLiant servers out-sell competitor's NT products by more than two to one for leading ERP and SCM systems.

Superior Partnerships with Application Providers

Compaq was the first to deliver SAP R/3 PAQ bundles, shaving two months off a typical R/3 installation. SAP customers voted Compaq the "Award of Excellence" three years in a row. As a development partner of i2 Technologies, and the largest customer of both i2 and Oracle's i-procurement, Compaq has established professionals skilled with the leading supply chain applications. Our e-infrastructure service architects and constructs the network and systems management for many of the largest e-business. Critical to successful implementation is the linkage between the application environment and the technology infrastructure. Compaq's supply chain integration and e-procurement practices are skilled with leading applications including i2, CommerceOne, and many others.

Compaq Solutions

Compaq is bringing supply chain benefits to enterprises as diverse as a ski resort operator in Colorado and a glue manufacturer in Ohio. For Vail Resorts, a network linking 500 POS terminals is allowing cashless transactions at retail, restaurant, and lift pass locations at four resorts. At Elmer's Products, the entire organization is now integrated, from marketing through manufacturing and, ultimately, to the customer. In addition, Compaq's e-commerce expertise empowers businesses such as Barnes & Noble and the US Postal Service to prosper on the Internet, a fundamental of today's supply chain. Our family of offerings simplifies planning, deployment, and ongoing operations, leading to fastest time to success and an increased return on investment. And, based on our proven solutions and superior partnerships, Compaq solutions enable customers to confidently extend their business.

Compaq's Strategic Alliances and Partnerships

No one goes it alone in Supply Chain Management. Proven alliances and partnerships with channel partners, application vendors, and systems integrators benefit our mutual customers. Compaq has established partnerships with leading application vendors including SAP AG, Baan, JD Edwards, i2 Technologies, Oracle Applications, PeopleSoft, Siebel, and CommerceOne. We participate with these companies and more than 170 others in Microsoft's Value Chain Initiative, an effort dedicated to enhancing supply chain efficiencies around the globe. Among Compaq's systems integration partners are the worldwide leaders in implementing ERP and Supply Chain Management solutions: Andersen Consulting, Deloitte & Touche, KPMG, and PricewaterhouseCoopers. To assist our partners and our customers, Compaq launched activeAnswers. Specifically designed to enable faster time to solutions, activeAnswers delivers tools and proven methodologies to enable customers to plan, deploy, and operate enterprise applications more rapidly and cost-effectively. If you would like an demonstration, please go to http://www.compaq.com/activeanswers.

Compaq Professional Services

Customers may also call on highly rated Compaq Professional Services for integration services. Compaq Professional Services is the only services organization with its service processes integrated globally to be able to service customers consistently. The result is that Compaq customers receive the same quality support through a single point of contact. Compaq offers services for infrastructure/technology, management/outsourcing, and customer support. For instance, Compaq can assess an overall data center as a "Healthcheck," can provide Global Helpdesk for over 1000 applications, can guarantee high availability through service agreements, and can provide complete technology asset management. Compaq Professional Services is the best choice for the rigorous management and operations demands of SCM and e-business.

Compaq is a Global Enterprise Leader

Companies adapting their business models to Internet speed and global competitiveness must shift their IT infrastructures to accommodate the changes. As a global enterprise leader, Compaq is well positioned among IT companies to lead customers through the challenges and opportunities of SCM and beyond. By anticipating the evolution to high performance, non-stop, business community computing, Compaq will deliver dependable IT solutions that leverage and transform enterprise computing into a strategic business advantage.

Savings Opportunities to the Electronics Industry: An Interview with Derek Lidow

q&a with

Derek Lidow
iSuppli
http://lidow.ASCET.com

The electronic components supply chain is costly, unreliable, inefficient, and misaligned – and it offers great opportunities for improvement. Studies show that suppliers spend approximately 10% of their revenue planning, managing, and delivering the products required to support customers. Because links in the electronic components supply chain can be unreliable, it can often be difficult to count on the products a company needs to show up on-time. iSuppli helps reduce billions of dollars in mark-ups and transaction fees by aligning, integrating, and servicing supply channels.

What are some of the key opportunities for improving the electronic components industry supply chain?

The electronic components supply chain is costly, unreliable, inefficient, and misaligned – and offers great opportunities for improvement.

Studies show that suppliers spend approximately 10% of their revenue planning, managing, and delivering the products required to support their customers. Customers spend close to the same amount managing their inbound supply chain. Put a distributor in between and that adds another 20% to the cost of goods. There are so many links in the chain, with each one adding expense, that the supply chain ends up costing the electronics industry large sums of money.

Because links in the electronic components supply chain can be unreliable, it can often be difficult to count on the products a company needs to show up on time. Supply and demand are volatile and often constrained. New and end-of-life products make the situation even harder to manage.

This $250-billion electronic components market is inefficient. Pricing is inconsistent, illogical, and hard to manage. Information is not available to determine what is a fair price to pay, or to charge, for electronic parts.

Sales channels are often misaligned with the needs of the customers and the resources of the suppliers. Today, suppliers service their customers either directly utilizing scarce and expensive resources, or indirectly, through distribution. Both of these channels adequately service certain types of customers and their needs; however, many customers and suppliers need a more efficient channel that is lower in cost and higher in visibility, perhaps without some of the service customization of today's direct channels.

What role do you see business-to-business trading networks playing in today's electronics components supply chains?

Various types of B2B marketplaces have appeared recently and play only a niche role in today's supply chains. In 1999, according to reports in *Electronic Buyers News*, less than one percent of electronic components were traded on B2B networks.

Most of these marketplaces are based upon some form of auction format and only handle portions of the transaction flow. Market-making has remained separate from e-fulfillment and cash flow management. Most marketplaces still focus on putting together customers and suppliers one at a time, which is costly and time-consuming.

In the future, new models that are better suited for transacting and optimizing high volume flow business will begin to appear. These B2B networks will bring value and functionality to customers and users that cannot be achieved with the old supply chain models based upon point-to-point contacts. Point-to-point relationships will always be valuable, but the flows of information and products are best optimized when working through a network.

Derek Lidow is the founder of iSuppli, a dot-com start-up focusing on supply chain solutions for high-volume direct materials procurement and delivery. Mr. Lidow serves on the board of directors for International Rectifier and is a member of the Leadership Council of the School of Engineering at Princeton University.

Electronics & High Tech

What is iSuppli's approach to enabling supply chain improvement opportunities?

iSuppli's business model focuses on creating efficient links between the users and suppliers of electronic components with the simultaneous flow of information, products, and cash. iSuppli substitutes a network for thousands of individual chains. The links created by iSuppli are both electronic, for exchanging information and money, and physical, for exchanging products.

iSuppli accumulates the flow demand for multiple customers and places large aggregate orders with each supplier. Supply and demand imbalances are handled immediately by world-class experts in each product area, enabling far faster and more effective resolution of issues. Suppliers only have to prepare a single large shipment, rather than many smaller ones. The large shipment is picked up and taken to a cross dock where it is broken down into customer-specific shipments that are delivered to assembly lines around the world, typically in less than 48 hours. The flow of cash is also handled by the network, according to industry standard payment terms, to ensure timely payments.

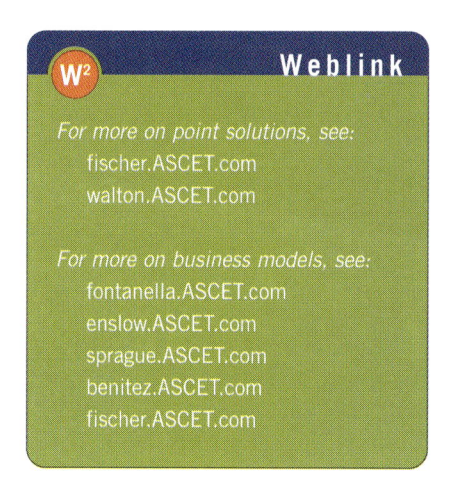

iSuppli interacts with its customers and suppliers via secure extranet sites that share accumulated supply network statistics among all the users, and provides secure and confidential access to an individual customer's or supplier's specific current and historical data.

How does iSuppli leverage technology and process simplification to provide supply chain improvements?

Technology plays a key role. Several technologies and processes have only recently been developed and have been uniquely combined to enable an extremely efficient supply network.

First, the pervasive use of the Internet by businesses has been a critical enabler, as vast amounts of supply information flow between partners. With the underlying information network in place, a supply network can be formed by providing a centralized connection node in the form of an extranet gateway.

Second, hardware and system costs have fallen to the point where the complex databases required for analyzing and presenting supply chain information can be effectively managed and scaled.

Third, global logistics networks that can reliably and cost-effectively move and track goods from just about any point in the world to any other within a few days are now possible. Short fulfillment cycle times are essential in order to create an effective supply network, because visibility diminishes rapidly with time; cost-effectiveness requires that only relevant information and required products flow in the network.

With these foundation technologies and processes in place, iSuppli has designed and implemented a system to manage such a network. The system handles the accumulation of demand and then the planning, sourcing, and flow of product within the logistics network. The system also links to the Electronic Funds Transfer network to enable "cross-docking" of cash receipts and payments.

What benefits can customers and suppliers of electronics components realize by using such models?

The benefits of iSuppli's network, where point-to-point links are created between users and their suppliers, are faster reaction times, billions of dollars in lower overall costs and reduced inventories, and greater visibility for both users and suppliers.

Since iSuppli operates with no mark-ups on any product and no flotation of any cash, it's a completely efficient supply network that saves money for both the users and the suppliers of electronic components. Users of electronic components only pay a subscription fee to use the network for specified part numbers. So utilizing iSuppli also results in the elimination of billions of dollars in mark-ups and transaction fees. Suppliers pay nothing, so they can share savings with the customers, making the supply network even more cost-effective.

Weblink

For more on point solutions, see:
fischer.ASCET.com
walton.ASCET.com

For more on business models, see:
fontanella.ASCET.com
enslow.ASCET.com
sprague.ASCET.com
benitez.ASCET.com
fischer.ASCET.com

Supply Chain Strategy: Real Options for Doing Business At Internet Speed

A fresh approach is urgently needed to deal with the changing realities of the global business environment. How can strategic thinking guide us to the approach we need to compete successfully? Why are portfolios of real options becoming a key component of supply chain strategy? And what previews of the future can we envision?

written by:
Corey Billington
André Kuper
Hewlett-Packard Company
http://billington.ASCET.com

Facing Reality

The dynamic nature of the environment faced by business managers around the world has never been more evident than in the explosive growth of the Internet. This expanding universe of opportunity allows customers to be more demanding and forces reconsideration, if not modification, of traditional business models. Some new competencies required to deliver customer value — always the primary measure of success — are missing. For example, if we gather market information, examine trends, customize our supply chains, and deliver products efficiently, we may find that our responses to the changing situation are too slow and we are late to market.

Facing reality is not easy. The challenge for managers is so urgent, however, that they may require new approaches for survival. Even successful businesses should open themselves to strategic thinking in real time. And at the heart of this challenge, the supply chains on which our future success depends may undergo a significant transformation.

In this article, we argue that strategy development for the future depends on the ability to create portfolios of options to be exercised in real time, enabling fresh options as the supply chain becomes more effective. To meet the expectations of increasingly sophisticated customers, we need a dynamic supply chain strategy that responds to complex behaviors as it senses them. As in the symbiotic responses of natural populations, each option enables further options that can be exercised according to prevailing conditions.

Why emphasize options? The complex interaction of uncertainties in a changing world makes adherence to a fixed strategy very risky. We must navigate through stormy weather. Everywhere we look, suppliers are changing their priorities and commitments, customers are acting upon regional and personal preferences, and competitors are increasing the turbulence. The expectation that we will deliver customized products and services compels us to figure out what's being demanded even as we attempt to satisfy that demand. In such fluid situations, any rigid approach is bound to fail. Optionality in the alternatives we choose is becoming an essential feature of successful approaches to the future.

Strategic Thinking

In general, supply chains are moving from vertical integration (within a single company) to multilateral integration (across many partners). The information, material, and financial flows within the network are continually redirected as demand fluctuates. Managing each of these flows has become more difficult as the situation becomes more complex, so organizations are learning a new competency — the ability to create and exercise options across the supply chain. How does this new competency work? How are options defined, evaluated, and exercised?

To begin, we can recognize optionality in business strategies that have become familiar in recent years. Here are examples of real options already in play:

Postponement

Delaying product differentiation until precise information about customer demand is known

Corey Billington is the Director of Strategic Planning and Modeling at Hewlett-Packard. His consulting teams help Hewlett-Packard divisions become more effective by improving their business processes and by strengthening their decision-making capabilities. The principles for Supply Chain Management pioneered by Corey and his team are widely used at Hewlett-Packard and have greatly benefited the company.

André Kuper is a process technology manager working in the Strategic Planning and Modeling (SPaM) team at Hewlett-Packard Company. His work focuses on accelerating the knowledge diffusion and implementation of innovations in transforming business models to incorporate the internet. He worked to help Hewlett-Packard business apply knowledge in asset management and Supply Chain Management since 1995.

Electronics & High Tech

http://billington.ASCET.com   223

gives us optionality in the manufacturing of products. From the dyeing of fabrics in the clothing industry to customized configurations of network printers, companies use postponement to manage material flows to meet unpredictable demand. We hold an option to produce only the models we need when precise demand information is available.

Dual Response

As an approach for dealing with demand variability, this manufacturing strategy achieves efficiency and responsiveness in the same supply chain. Efficiency is achieved by satisfying most of the demand with stable production in highly cost-effective locations, while responsiveness results from variable – that is, optional – production (at higher cost) much closer to the market. We hold an option to produce and ship exactly the right amount very quickly.

Multiple Sourcing

This strategy achieves "assurance of supply" through (1) procurement policies drawing from multiple sources of components or (2) product designs that allow the use of components from different sources. Like postponement and dual response, multiple sourcing makes material flows through the supply chain more efficient, though more rapid and complex information flows are required in the process. We hold an option to procure and use the lowest priced component when manufacturing the product.

Weblink

For more on strategic planning, see:
hicks.ASCET.com
sprague.ASCET.com
berger.ASCET.com
For more on integration, see:
quinn-c.ASCET.com
herbold.ASCET.com
uchneat.ASCET.com
For more on auctions, see:
fischer.ASCET.com
dobrin.ASCET.com

Spot Markets

Matching demand with supply – a classic problem in information and financial flows – is handled by switchboards for linking buyers and sellers. Otherwise, unlikely transactions become possible in this dynamic market space where spontaneous relationships occur between interested parties. We hold an option to obtain parts (or eliminate excess) at uncertain market prices that may be strikingly advantageous.

Strategies like these have shown supply chain managers that optionality has a significant impact on business success. Strategic thinking extends the notion of optionality to material, information, and financial flows. Integration of these options will be the hallmark of strategies that transform business models – especially for doing business at Internet speed. Moreover, we are learning that an excellent approach to deployment is to use optionality as a way to distribute risk. Evaluation of strategies will focus on risk profiles that change not only if, but when, particular options are exercised. The best strategists will be those for whom timing is a paramount concern.

Real Options

Business managers know instinctively that strategies require conscious choices from sets of alternatives. Most of the time, however, these alternatives are based on simple themes that emphasize realistic objectives, completeness across the set, and an assessment of the probability of success. The idea that alternatives can be selected according to the value created by optionality has only recently emerged. We are learning how to develop business strategies in which value increases with the potential to exercise options.

How can optionality become a distinguishing characteristic of future strategies? What makes an option an option? Here are some fundamentals:

Segmentation

Options are segmented so they can be exercised in parts. More value can be created when there is subtlety in the potential action.

Scalability

Options are scalable so the magnitude of their application or impact can be controlled. The action can be focused, shifted or zoomed as the opportunity changes.

Time-Sensitivity

Options are time-sensitive. They gain power from their potential to be exercised in the future, in part or all at once. The value created by an option is actually a profile of values distributed in time.

Creativity

Options can be designed to create new options. They have the "halo effect" of sources that propagate other sources as they move.

With this view, we can appreciate the instincts of the business strategist who observed, "When the future is highly unpredictable, it pays to keep lots of options open."

Optionality in Supply Chains

How can we create optionality in supply chain strategies? To survive in the turbulence of the global business environment, we clearly need more robust supply chains. One way to achieve robustness is to develop options for real-time execution as we move products to customers. With the Internet, for example, we can get better prices through multiple bids; we can sample more suppliers; we can manage partnerships; we can change the order fulfillment process on the fly. As customers become better informed, more demanding and more fickle, we respond by becoming more responsive, customer-focused, and fashionable.

As an illustration, consider the flower business. What is the potential for real options as we make business decisions? How much leeway do we have in deciding when to harvest? Should we wait for better conditions? Are buds in short supply? Are full blossoms popular? If we get caught by an early winter, will we lose the whole crop? On the one hand, we must respond to weather, soil quality, pests, and other factors. On the other, we must ready ourselves for seasonal peaks and valleys as well as for consumer preferences. Material flows – including when to harvest – are strongly influenced by information flows about supplier and consumer behavior.

In consumer electronics, the situation is similar.

Supply Side

We create structured contracts with suppliers and expect flexibility in dealing with uncertainty. We determine the range of expected demand, we order any amount within this range, and we hope not to be charged for costs that result from the uncertainty. Eventually, these costs begin to affect us, but that's acceptable within limits. Without this relationship, our supply might be disrupted.

Demand Side

We provide branded products with high service levels over a long horizon (six to 12 months) and optimize our supply chains using the best information we can get. This strategy works when uncertainty is limited (that is, we can forecast accurately). If there's a high brand premium and we get the right product, our profit opportunity may be substantial. This is especially true if customers perceive the product as desirable and are willing to wait for it; they behave like they have no other choice.

In general, people at Hewlett-Packard are good at making choices from the alternatives available. Teams responsible for purchasing or sales, for example, usually make the right decision. Unfortunately, most organizations are poor at designing situations that offer choices for selection. It's hard to envision options, particularly when we've been told to be as efficient as possible. Creating options can be both unfamiliar and expensive. In fact, many organizations aggressively limit options to ensure efficiency, striving for standardized processes even when the environment is highly uncertain.

Optionality on the Supply Side

How can we create optionality on the supply side? Instead of structured contracts based on forecasts, suppose we have the ability to create spot markets for parts. At Hewlett-Packard, we use Trading Hubs.com, a business-to-business Web site that provides the capability needed to support a dynamic procurement strategy. For components needed for manufacturing, we have the following choices:

- Make a structured contract with the supplier (as in the past) that forces the supplier to manage the demand-supply risk.
- Make a fixed contract for less than the amount we need and go to the Web site (spot market) to purchase the remainder. We accept the risk of not finding sufficient supply.
- Make a fixed contract for more than the amount we need, and go to the Web site (spot market) to sell the excess. We accept the risk of not finding sufficient demand.

We now have three strategic choices. Moreover, the ability to time the purchase or sale on the spot market provides optionality. Structured contracts are still a possibility, but the ability to create a spot market gives organizations more flexibility. Suppliers and manufacturers should jointly determine who ought to be compensated for managing the demand-supply risk. We need both knowledge and tools to create and evaluate real options like these.

Optionality on the Demand Side

Strategies that provide optionality on the demand side are also possible. Here are some examples.

Alternate Labels

We can create a second label for the product. If we have too much product, what can we do with the excess? Dye them blue, affix the new label, and sell them at a discount. This approach allows us to assume risk from suppliers and vent it through the market by taking a lower premium on the second label. If the supplier's risk reduction is more valuable than our overall margin loss, the supply chain is more competitive. A fixed quantity would be available for an uncertain period, providing a material flow option.

New Channels

HP Shopping Village, HP Kiosk, and HP Store are examples of new channels for reaching customers. We can create products from excess parts, assign special product numbers, and sell at special prices. When the supply is gone, the product disappears. This approach provides options in material flows at both ends of the supply chain, and the information flow to customers is used to exercise them. Channels like these provide options for quickly reducing inventory levels.

Auctions

On the demand side, auctions of products and office supplies allow us to reach customers in new ways. Information can be provided to attract customers who want the benefits of dynamic pricing. The more we learn, the more we can exercise options to everyone's advantage. Should we disposition more product? Should we introduce an advertising campaign? Are there ways to challenge the competition? Can we trigger additional options when conditions are favorable?

All these approaches thrive on excellent information. Resources required to gather data are well spent when we learn the value of alternatives across the supply chain. Consider, for example, the surveys by which we learn more about customer loyalty. The product and channel attributes that inspire customer loyalty are more valuable when options have been designed to reinforce them. In many situations, moreover, our attitudes toward information access are changing. Traditional strategies that keep information proprietary actually inhibit customer loyalty and limit our partnership options. Paradoxically, greater openness works to our advantage in engaging customers, managing risks, and sharing rewards across the supply chain.

Portfolio Management

In every strategic dimension, we need to consider how options fit together in a portfolio, so we can take advantage of the "portfolio effect" – the ways options create synergies and gain strength by their interaction within the portfolio. We need portfolios of supplier options, partnership options, core competencies, metrics, and other sophisticated alternatives that give us greater flexibility in the ways we can run the business.

What's the reason for talking about portfolios? A strategy that features option-

> **Little has been done in the last 20 years to more accurately project the "true" asset base of the corporation in the global marketplace. And, assets that are not measured are likely to be under-funded. Thus, a failure to understand the contribution of marketing activities to shareholder value continues to diminish the role of marketing thought in corporate strategy.**

ality in the selected alternatives offers many opportunities to manage risk. The whole purpose of portfolio management is to reduce risk where possible and manage the remaining risk. We need to find the best solution for the changing business situation — taking advantage of the options immediately available — not necessarily the optimal solution for a particular scenario.

Managers should avoid forcing efficiency through controls or standard procedures when the future is highly unpredictable. The challenge is to create options and allow people to exercise them as the world changes. Since precise planning is impossible and we have cheap, ubiquitous information, we must learn to transform information into knowledge for exercising the right alternatives from our portfolio of options.

Previews of the Future

As we look into the future, the need for risk management across the supply chain is clear — especially the need to diminish the overall risk by shifting specific risk to the partner in the best position to manage it effectively. This requires that we reach agreement on the points in the supply chain where risks can be mitigated. (This is similar to deciding where to hold inventory.) In the future, we will need portfolios of real options — on the demand as well as the supply side — for taking advantage of risk and redistributing the costs and benefits among participants. The result will be more efficient, effective, and responsive supply chain networks. A cornerstone of this approach will be mutual trust and openness, built on open agreements on which options are available, who will manage them, and how the costs and benefits will be shared among the supply chain partners.

Recent decisions at General Motors to centralize their procurement of steel — purchasing surplus from a Web-based spot market and auctioning the excess to their suppliers, subcontractors, and partners — indicate that optionality on the supply side is for real. Toyota's participation in this network has changed the landscape for steel manufacturers, who are less likely to exact premiums from smaller customers (as these will be able to exercise options with the big guys). Instead of proprietary information and dedicated relationships, as in the past, supplier-manufacturer relationships have suddenly broken open.

Situations like these are appearing in the electronics industry. IBM will manage procurement of Cisco parts, leveraging its procurement power (here proprietary information still applies). With increased shortages of strategic parts like DRAM and ASICS, however, any reliance on proprietary information may be wishful thinking. By contrast, Hewlett-Packard has found that open relationships with suppliers are a key success factor in ensuring supplier loyalty. On the supply side, optionality must be available from manufacturers without driving their suppliers out of business or endangering their assurance of supply. On the demand side, customers must be given a wide range of options. Just as consumers can buy airline tickets at flexible prices, combine orders to achieve volume discounts, and pursue comparison shopping online, supply chain partners will expect the same dynamics from their counterparts, looking for demand side optionality between business partners.

Hewlett-Packard: Enabling Nimble Supply Chains

Supply chains are constantly being re-made faster and smarter, and are serving wider circles of users who find them easier to use. Innovative solutions have been developed and hardened by the largest corporations and their suppliers, in collaboration with solution partners. Now, they can be deployed cost-effectively by the smallest companies. And the view ahead, as Hewlett-Packard sees it, gets brighter still.

Industry observers increasingly witness technology-savvy companies with nimble supply chains eating the lunch of competitors operating traditional ERP and supply chain processes. This is not to say that transitions to the new processes were necessarily straightforward or easy. Business and IT innovators have dealt with their share of hurdles, of course both internal and external. But beyond these trials, they're now realizing significant benefits, many of which provide inescapable reading in IT and trade magazines.

Collectively, the world's major industrial players have invested millions of hours and billions of dollars over the last several years to improve and integrate ERP and Supply Chain Management. Much of this activity is fueled by projections of business-to-business e-commerce growing to $7.29 trillion in 2004 (GartnerGroup) from $145 billion in 1999 and is further spurred by expectations of cutting expenses by conducting transactions over the Internet.

New Opportunities throughout the Enterprise

Hewlett-Packard Company, for one, continuously sees new opportunities in myriad businesses throughout the enterprise. Opportunities arise in traditional areas such as inventory management, distribution, and customer service, as well as encompassing newer fields like e-business and online stores that help customers access retailer location information or facilitate direct online sales.

www.shopping.hp.com, HP's Shopping Village, has seen monthly sales grow 500 percent since June 1998. During the 1999 Holiday season, the Shopping Village supported significant revenue growth across all 160 product categories offered.

Hubs: A New Fabric for the Way Business is Conducted

In bringing more business to and through the Web, significant attention is paid to speed of response, which will arguably become the primary measure of the success of businesses in serving their customers. One approach to the quest for ways to respond faster to customers is to have flexibility built into the supply chain. How important is it to have such options? Executives continually invent strategies to meet business needs, and IT must support them in an effective manner. Newer business models exercise real options to fit changing situations and create synergies throughout the enterprise. The effect creates spot markets for goods and services that, between businesses, are the essence of Trading Hubs. And the hub, of course, brings us back to the underlying and essential role of the Internet.

Hubs, trading communities, and, more recently, value collaboration networks aren't simply new versions of ERP and Supply Chain Management solutions. Nor is the Internet just a pipeline for B2B transactions. Combined, they provide an entirely new fabric for the way in which business is conducted.

Contact Information

Richard A. Hackborn
Chairman

Carleton S. "Carly" Fiorina
CEO and President

Robert P. Wayman
EVP, Finance and Administration and CFO

S.T. Jack Brigham III
SVP, Corporate Affairs and General Counsel

Duane E. Zitzner
President, Computing Systems

Hewlett-Packard Headquarters
3000 Hanover St.
Palo Alto, CA 94304
Phone 650.857.1501
Fax 650.857.7299

www.hp.com

TECSYS – Software Solutions that Fit. Perfectly. Profitably.

Contact Information

Peter Brereton
President and Chief Executive Officer

Robert Nehme
Vice President of Marketing

TECSYS Inc.
Corporate Headquarters
1840 Trans-Canada HWY
Dorval, Quebec Canada
Toll-Free 800.922.8649
Phone 514.333.0000
Fax 514.333.0109
solutions@tecsys.com
www.tecsys.com

U.S. Headquarters
8101 North High Street
Suite 160
Columbus, OH 43235
Phone 614.844.5555
Fax 614.841.3980

Products and Services

EliteSeries™ – The leading e-commerce-based distribution enterprise solution includes Executive Information System, Order Management, Warehouse Management, Electronic Commerce/EDI, Value-Added Services, Financial Management, and Project Accounting Systems.

TECSYS™ end-to-end order fulfillment solution offers the best of both worlds – e-business front-end capabilities and rich back-end distribution functionality!

Elite.eCom™ TECSYS' advanced e-business software is described by analysts as the most fully developed e-commerce solution of all the distribution-centric vendors.

EliteWorld.Net™ TECSYS' one-stop Web portal solution provides you and your trading community with single-click, browser-based access to your entire world…anytime, anywhere!

TECSYS Services™ The expanding world of TECSYS services includes e-business services, professional services, training, distance learning, help desk, and custom enhancements

---

"In Wholesale Distribution, TECSYS Inc. is off to a running start with its adoption of Internet technologies and introduction of the Elite.eCom suite. TECSYS still leads its competition with the most developed e-commerce product for this vertical market […]." supply-chain.com: *The Report on Supply Chain Management*, August 1999, AMR Research Inc.

Order Fulfillment Solutions for the Internet Age

A seismic shift in the way the planet conducts business is in full swing. At the heart of this shift sits the Internet. Business – all business – is migrating to the Net. Regardless of industry or niche, companies require a successful online strategy to survive in today's digital economy with its virtually infinite competition and sky-rocketing customer expectations.

However, with all its power, potential, and promise, e-commerce is falling dramatically short of expectations in one critical area: order fulfillment. Both click-and-mortar and pure dot-com companies are discovering that it's one thing to take online orders, and quite another to fulfill them with the precision and speed required by today's demanding customers. Industry analysts agree: TECSYS offers the most advanced Business-to-Business (B2B) e-fulfillment solution in the marketplace.

Integrated B2B E-Fulfillment Solutions

Founded in 1983, TECSYS is the sole provider of fully integrated B2B e-commerce-based order fulfillment solutions for high-volume distribution enterprises. Our commitment to deliver superior e-fulfillment solutions for both brick-and-mortar and click-and-mortar distributors has generated average annual growth of 50% and an accelerating win rate within the industry.

Given that distributors are increasingly inventory brokers as opposed to inventory managers, many are switching from the traditional Buy-Hold-Ship paradigm to a Sell-Source-Ship model where costs must be reduced to support market prices. This new e-commerce-based model is clearly shifting the industry towards fully integrated, e-business solutions like the TECSYS EliteSeries™.

A Seamlessly Synchronized Distribution Enterprise

With its zero-footprint, browser-based architecture, the TECSYS EliteSeries injects unprecedented efficiency into your distribution enterprise, focusing all your resources on the same goal: superior customer satisfaction through precise order fulfillment.

The EliteSeries allows information – the backbone of any distributor's operations – to flow seamlessly, minimizing duplication of effort across the supply chain. It enables you to streamline and synchronize your enterprise, driving costs and errors out of your business processes.

TECSYS solutions are currently delivering unrivaled order fulfillment precision to some 300 mid-sized and Fortune 1000 corporations in telecommunications, health care, consumer goods, electrical products, computers, hardware and more. Clients include: Caliber Logistics/Cardinal Health, Elkay Plastics, Robinson Knife, Shoppers Drug Mart, SP Richards/Genuine Parts Company, Sprint/North Supply, Steiner Electric, Tana/Kiwi Brands, and Uni-Sélect.

Distribution-Centric Focus

By focusing exclusively on our niche, we've developed an in-depth understanding of our customers' needs, which means we understand the trends and pressures reshaping the distribution industry better than any other vendor. It also allows us to deliver the leading price/performance solution and timely implementations in the distribution marketplace.

Creating a High-Performance Downstream Petroleum Supply Chain

Managing the downstream petroleum supply chain presents some of the most difficult challenges found in Supply Chain Management today. Maximizing the value of hydrocarbons throughout the supply chain has become the crucial key to profitable success. Maximizing this value requires that executives have the tools to decide what products, in what quantity, are manufactured, bought, sold, stored, moved, exchanged, or marketed and where these activities take place. To this end, a powerful combination of Internet collaboration and advanced planning capabilities is being rapidly pressed into action to understand demand, integrate the plan, and coordinate the commercial and operating activities. These innovations aimed at maximizing the value of inventory throughout the supply chain can provide lessons from which companies in other industries may also benefit.

The Unique World of the Petroleum Supply Chain

The downstream petroleum supply chain is unique in a number of important ways. Raw materials and products are more fungible, and, in many cases, perfectly substitutable. However, the capital assets employed to manufacture, store, and move raw materials and inventory are inflexible. There are many ways to participate in the industry, and prices are extremely volatile and reasonably transparent (though not easy to predict). In other words, there are many choices to be made at each stage along the supply chain pertaining to what, when, and where to produce, buy, or sell products.

In recent years, the supply chain has become even more challenging to manage (see Figure 1.0). Most downstream companies have reduced or eliminated excess operating inventories, making the entire industry more susceptible to disruptions in supply or demand. Environmental regulation has caused a dramatic increase in the number of products that must be segregated and managed. Nontraditional participants (for example, national oil companies or independent marketers) achieve returns on their investments through means other than refinery or fuels margins. The physical infrastructure of the industry is evolving as refining capacity is being both shut down and expanded, and new infrastructure, such as pipelines, is being built. In general, the economic fundamentals of the business continue to be poor.

Key Issues that Drive Success

To respond to these challenges, different value levers and capabilities are becoming important for managing the downstream petroleum supply chain. Because price levels are determined by large liquid markets and by local competitor behavior, there is a premium on evaluating competitors' economics and anticipating their behavior. The large number of "make versus buy" possibilities along the value chain necessitates understanding the market value and cost at each link in the supply chain. The large volatility in gross margins over the operational planning horizon requires frequent and speedy reevaluation of all alternatives.

For many industries, traditional supply chain value levers are found in transportation, inventory, and warehousing. These levers are important for the downstream petroleum supply chain as well; however, they are not as important as managing the value of the hydrocarbon itself. Consider, for example, the inventory value lever. In many industries, it is a given that a unit of inventory will be worth less

Don A. Eichmann is an associate partner in the Andersen Consulting Supply Chain Practice. Mr. Eichmann is an expert in leveraging energy supply chains to deliver exceptional value and competitive advantage. He has consulted with oil companies in North America, Asia, Europe, and South America.

tomorrow than it is today. The life cycle of a computer is so short, for instance, that prices are always declining. Thus, a one-dimensional strategy of reducing inventory is appropriate. Hydrocarbons, on the other hand, could be worth less tomorrow, or they could just as easily be worth more. Additionally, the location of the inventory can also have a major influence on its value. Therefore, managing when and where inventory is held is far more critical than just reducing the amount of inventory. In addition to complex inventory management, the multidimensional aspects of managing hydrocarbon value includes decisions about sourcing, timing of buys and sells, and distribution to various markets.

Sourcing decisions can be very dynamic if a company is operating across a geography with more than one spot market that influences price. For example, in the United States, a mid-Atlantic market could be supplied from the Gulf Coast via the Colonial pipeline or from New York Harbor via marine transport. If you were to examine a record of gasoline spot prices and transportation costs from the past few years, you would see that the optimal source point changes frequently and that the amount of money at stake is large. For example, if you were to source Baltimore from the Gulf Coast as a matter of policy, you would have made the correct decision 43% of the time and had a $.60 per barrel advantage over sourcing from New York Harbor. However, you would have made the wrong decision 57% of the time and

Weblink

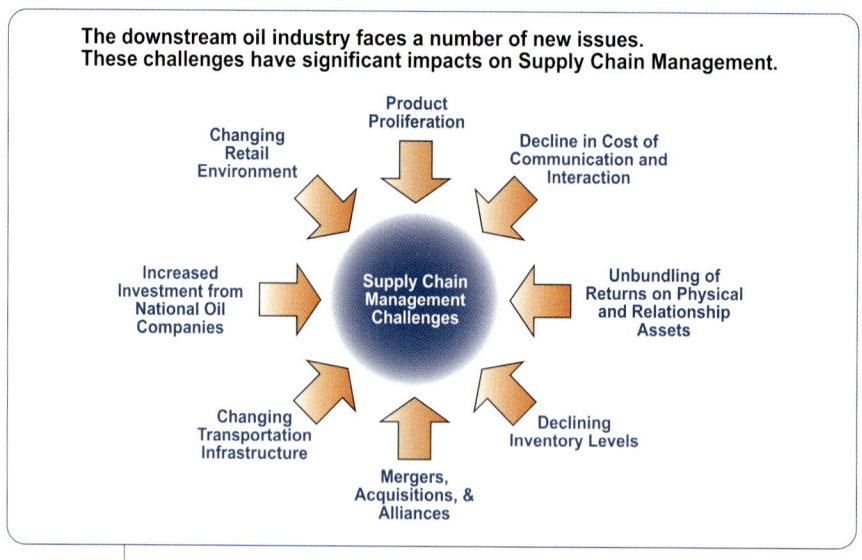

For more on upstream/downstream solutions, see:
moore.ASCET.com
lescher.ASCET.com

For more on resource planning, see:
uchneat.ASCET.com
ramanathan.ASCET.com
martella.ASCET.com

Figure 1.0 The challenge of managing supply chain in downstream oil industry

The downstream oil industry faces a number of new issues. These challenges have significant impacts on Supply Chain Management.

Supply Chain Management Challenges:
- Product Proliferation
- Decline in Cost of Communication and Interaction
- Unbundling of Returns on Physical and Relationship Assets
- Declining Inventory Levels
- Mergers, Acquisitions, & Alliances
- Changing Transportation Infrastructure
- Increased Investment from National Oil Companies
- Changing Retail Environment

had a $.69 per barrel disadvantage. Having the ability to switch sources rapidly and accurately could be worth more than $.60 per barrel on more than one-half of the barrels moving through a Baltimore terminal. However, the differing transit times between sourcing products from the Gulf Coast versus New York Harbor, along with the integrated constraints of the supply network, make it difficult to execute a strategy based on such flexibility.

Another critical decision that must dynamically be made to optimize the value created by a downstream petroleum company is the amount of discretionary volume to sell in each market. Non-discretionary businesses are those such as branded retail sales. In this type of business, pure marketing decisions dominate temporary supply optimization possibilities. For example, you would not purposely choose to run branded service stations out of product just because supply costs rose temporarily. On the other hand, discretionary business, by its definition, is business that you can choose to participate in and the degree to which to participate. Examples of this might include gasoline or distillate sales to non-branded distributors. There is a significant price volume relationship for this type of business. The lower your price (relative to competitors) the more of the market share you can attract. Of course, competi-

tors will not idly stand by while you take share away. The competitive structure of a market will determine the shape and slope of the price-volume relationship.

Theoretically, an oil company uses an understanding of these curves to determine in which markets to conduct discretionary (and to a lesser extent, non-discretionary) business. However, in practice, few companies can dynamically integrate decisions about how much to participate in Market A versus Market B or if selling to the spot market might be a better answer for a short period of time. Most companies try to forecast volumes that will be sold to discretionary customers, rather than try to understand the price/volume relationships and position products to maximize the overall margin. Of course, the margin maximizing solution cannot be found without extensive input from both supply and marketing functions within a downstream operation.

Building a Right Business Solution

What's so hard about managing the downstream petroleum supply chain? It hinges on making complex trade-offs in an environment where new market opportunities, unplanned events, and price volatility all interact through a physical system with very tight constraints (see Figure 2.0). Most

Many Factors Complicate a Downstream Company's Planning Environment.

- Refinery upsets
- Demand variability
- Transportation outage

Unplanned events → Meet non discretionary requirements

Market opportunities → Make money

- Buy/sell blend stocks
- Time pricing
- Storage plays
- Regrade product
- Alternate sourcing
- Butane Blending

Constraints
- Transportation
- Branded product demand
- Capacities
- Lead times
- Contracts

Least cost supplier — Profit maximizer

Price volatility
- Relative to crude
- Between products
- Between markets

Figure 2.0 — Market opportunities, events, and price volatility interact through a physical system with very tight constraints

---

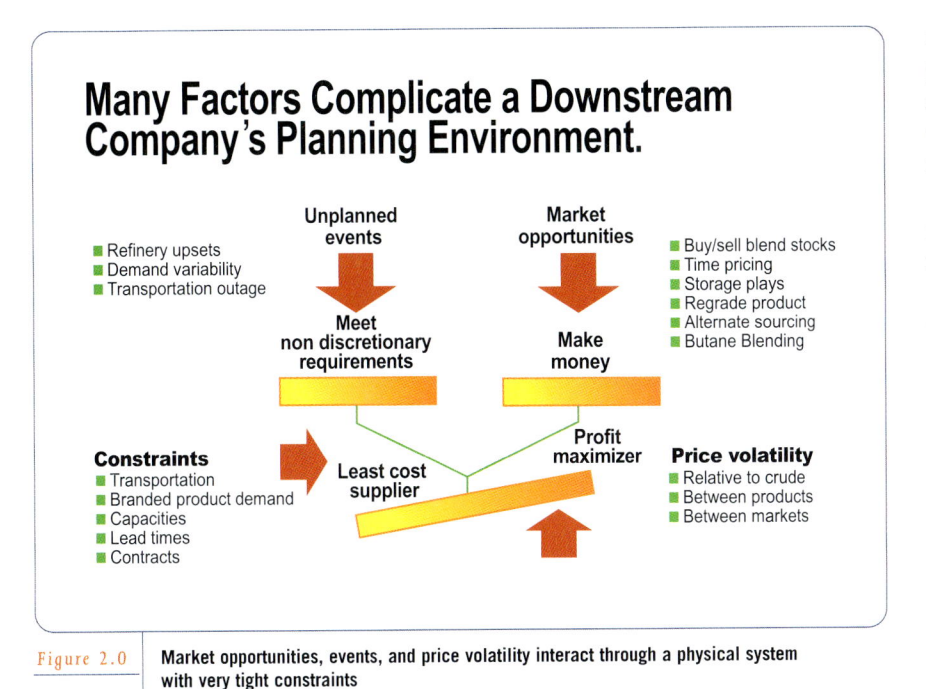

oil company executives will tell you that running the business when everything is going according to plan is straightforward. The problem is that this never happens.

To more profitably operate the downstream petroleum supply chain, an oil company must be able to make the complex decisions and change those decisions as necessary (and as feasible) when circumstances change. To do this, it is essential that an explicit planning basis be developed to encompass all of the essential planning variables. Such a planning process and engine must be used to convert the plan basis into a comprehensive, economically sound plan, and the actual results should be measured and compared to the plan for evaluation and instructive lessons (see Figure 3.0). A Web-centric planning process, supported by advanced supply chain planning and measurement tools, forms the basis for all three of these capabilities (see Figure 4.0).

The Web facility enables collaboration across the organization to gather and evaluate the plan inputs, which include both structural and temporal elements. Many of these elements are challenging (if available at all) to collect on a frequent and accurate basis. The Internet can enable rapid communication and a discussion of key elements each time one of the elements changes significantly. The Internet can even be used to set system alarms on critical elements to signal that a plan should be revised due to some unforeseen change in market or company conditions. With older technology, most petroleum companies simply haven't been able to easily access this necessary information – many companies are still faced with difficult manual procedures just to determine a company-wide inventory position in a timely enough manner to act. However, as petroleum supply chains become increasingly sophisticated, the Internet will provide an inexpensive and efficient way to integrate the supply chains of multiple oil companies. Applications for Internet trading, exchanging, and tracking are being launched and will be used by the more advanced companies shortly.

With the new technology, advanced supply chain planning software can be used to optimize the supply chain and generally to maximize profit while observing all constraints. While traditional supply chain software companies have targeted their planning tools at discrete manufacturers, their software can be used to solve the more continuous/batch supply chain problems common in the petroleum industry. Any solution must handle both discretionary and non-discretionary activities that oil companies participate in.

Another critical tool is the performance measurement system. This system must be able to compare actual results to the plan and explain to management where and why there are differences. Most supply chain performance measurement systems stop far short of this goal. They can only report the raw overall differences between plan and actual with perhaps a few variance analyses to provide some indication of what happened. A system that is integrated with the planning process and an oil company's ERP system can provide management with far more insight than can be gained from traditional approaches. In fact, the system must answer questions such as "Did the adjustments we made to capture an opportunity make us money?" Or, "How well did we mitigate the consequences of a refinery upset?" Configuring the measurement and feedback approach around a series of accounting books or "supply books" allows the segmentation of results into meaningful business insights. For example, one oil company could not easily answer these questions. At the end of a month when they closed the books, it was a surprise to them how much money the supply chain made or lost. After a rather terrible month, the CEO asked the straightforward question, "Why did we lose such a large amount of money?" After two more months, the supply chain executives admitted that they had no real idea. The firm's systems and measurements simply could not diagnose the causal factors. This company did not learn from its mistakes and consequently was resigned to committing the same or similar mistakes in the future.

The Internet can also be used to coordinate commercial and operational activities. Key elements include publishing the plan to all involved parties, monitoring actions as they are taken, and distributing the findings and learnings from the previous plan period to all involved. Actions that

http://eichmann.ASCET.com

deviate from the plan are then immediately obvious and will either trigger re-planning or management actions to correct the activity and return it to plan.

The Right Time for Change

There will certainly be resistance to implementing these ideas in most oil companies. In most companies' supply chain planning departments, there tends to be a bias toward internal activities rather than an external focus on planning. The strong measurement philosophy requires putting a stake in the ground for the plan, which may be culturally resisted. Typically, traders don't like the additional constraints and oversight. Finally there is a perception that the systems might not be up to the task.

However, there has never been a better time to implement this kind of solution. Oil companies are more ready for change than they have ever been. After a series of difficult transitions, their organizations are more accustomed to change. People are more technology-savvy and less wary of the technology required. At the same time, the information technology infrastructure is much stronger; enterprise resource planning systems and the Internet have improved data availability and quality while making collaboration less costly. Finally, the decision support technology has advanced dramatically as computing power continues to escalate and software vendors have devoted more of their resources to the process industries.

In Summary

In summary, success in the downstream petroleum supply chain requires more than driving down costs and managing absolute levels of product inventory. Making the right executive decisions requires a finely tuned understanding of the many parameters that affect hydrocarbon value. It is here that the marriage of the Internet and advanced planning capabilities can create a competitive edge. The arrival of the Internet provides an economic channel for the information gathering, collaboration, measurement, and monitoring. Now that the technological capabilities are no longer the bottleneck, industry leaders must manage the cultural upheaval that accompanies such a radical change in the operating paradigms. But the prize, a more sophisticated and accurate platform on which to make operating decisions, will put petroleum companies at a significant competitive advantage.

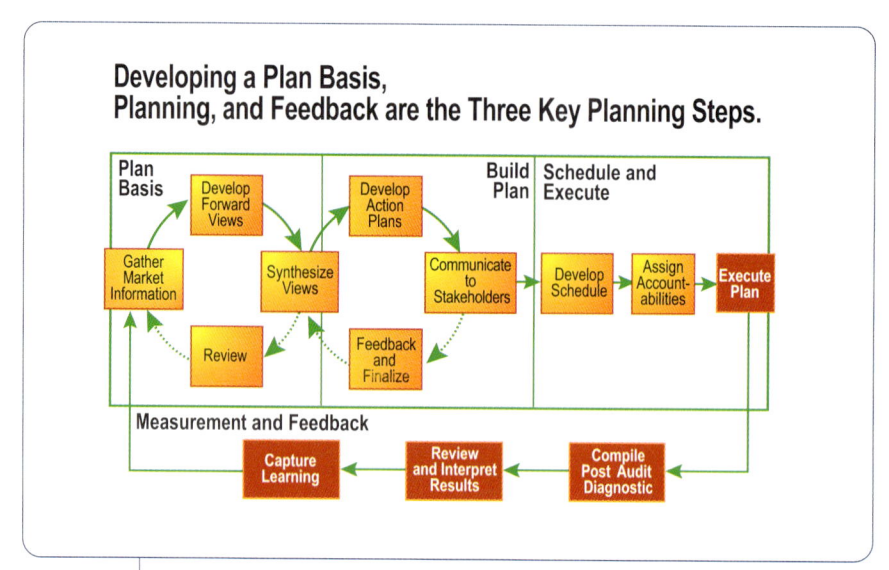

Figure 3.0 — Plan for evaluation and instructive lessons

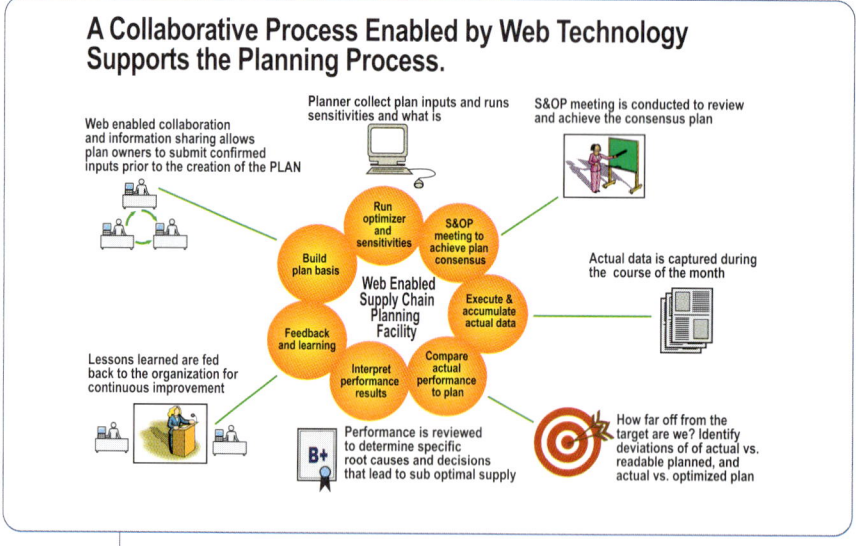

Figure 4.0 — A Web-centric planning process

Note

This discussion focuses on the products supply chain; however, most of the concepts apply to the crude supply chain as well. "Supply chain" in this context is intended as a non-organizational definition that includes many of the functions that might be located in a refining, supply, trading, or marketing organization.

Copyright©2000 Andersen Consulting LLP

E-Commerce in Energy and Natural Resources: A Dynamic, Challenging Landscape

written by:

Barry Jennings
Charles Trimarco
Andersen Consulting
http://jennings.ASCET.com

The Internet is changing the way business-to-business e-commerce is conducted across every industry. The ability to work with both customers and suppliers in the real-time world of e-commerce is crucial to a company's long-term success, especially for the energy and natural resources industries. Challenges, choices, and opportunities await these companies as they continue to focus attention on conducting the trade of goods and services and enhancing revenue over the Internet. The business-to-business e-commerce market can significantly improve the value chain for energy and natural resources companies by reducing costs, improving revenue, and lowering working capital.

It's almost impossible to pick up a newspaper, magazine, or industry periodical and not see a headline that discusses how the Internet is changing the way business is conducted across any industry. The role of business-to-business e-commerce is significant because it is creating new models that will allow real-time communication between businesses to reduce the high cost of information transfer. Relationships with customers and suppliers and the ability to change to an e-commerce environment are critical to the future success of a company. Forrester Research estimates business-to-business e-commerce will increase from $43 billion in 1998 to $1.3 trillion by 2003. The energy and natural resources industries must take full advantage of this opportunity in order to effectively compete within their respective marketplaces. This article discusses challenges, choices, and opportunities that await energy and natural resources companies as they continue to focus their attention on conducting the trade of goods and services and enhance revenue over the Internet.

Challenges

The energy industry is comprised of oil, natural gas, and petrochemical companies while the natural resources industry is made up of forest products, metals, glass, and mining companies. Both industries are experiencing business challenges that are impacting profitability. Natural resources companies are cyclical, commodity-driven, and capital-intensive in nature with minimal opportunity for differentiation. There are times when demand exceeds supply, thus driving up price and improving profitability. However, more often than not, supply exceeds demand, which creates an oversupply and drives prices down. This cyclical nature is the result of an inability to maintain a level balance between supply and demand. Another challenge facing the industry has been the inability to generate earnings above the cost of capital. Customer requirements and the capital-intensive nature of the business have made companies focus on improving productivity and reducing costs. Finally, consolidations within the industry and the desire for global versus domestic presence have presented a new set of issues. The energy industry is facing a similar situation due to crude oversupply, competition from domestic and European markets, a poor outlook from Asian markets, and an increased regulatory burden. With so many challenges facing both industries, participation in business-to-business e-commerce will be a key factor in order to sustain a competitive position.

Historically, most energy and natural resources companies have been slow to invest in new technologies that are information-related

Barry Jennings is a partner in the Andersen Consulting Supply Chain Practice. He has extensive experience in developing and implementing winning supply chain strategies. He leads supply chain activities within the energy and natural resources industry and provides expert counsel on strategic sourcing and eProcurement.

Charles Trimarco is a senior manager in the Andersen Consulting Supply Chain Practice. He focuses on developing supply chain solutions for energy and natural resources clients.

Energy

There are several accepted myths which have slowed progress, including:

- Business models offer limited opportunities
- Products can't be delivered over the Internet
- High barriers to entry eliminate "start-ups" as a competitive threat
- Industry customers are not demanding e-commerce capabilities
- Existing business models work well with e-commerce activity

In reality, energy and natural resources companies have the ability to create significant value by utilizing the capabilities of e-commerce. The business-to-business e-commerce market can significantly improve the value chain for energy and natural resources companies by reducing costs, improving revenue, and lowering working capital. New sourcing tools, sales channels, and materials recovery options have become available to companies who are looking to participate in e-commerce. Effective customer segmentation, brand image building, transaction cost reduction, and improved forecasting accuracy are additional areas in which e-commerce plays a key role. Energy and natural resources companies must understand the risks, cost reduction, and revenue opportunities that business-to-business e-commerce provides. In order to accomplish this, a company must ask several questions including:

- What do customers want to buy?
- What business should I be in?
- Who are my competitors, and how do I need to be positioned?
- What is my operating model?
- With whom should I partner/network?

Several companies are starting to consider how business-to-business e-commerce will play a role in their future. Increased competition, timely information, a reduction in costs, and meeting customer demand around the intimacy that e-commerce provides are examples of why companies must begin utilizing this capability.

Success Stories

Many traditional and new e-business companies are entering the energy and natural resources market space to provide e-commerce services. Value propositions include cost savings, one-stop shopping, product selection, and education. Utility.com, Essential.com, Energy.com, Greenmountain.com, Energyagent.com, Chem Connect, Inc., and Enermetrix.com are examples of companies pursuing opportunities in the e-economy. ChemConnect Inc. is the world's largest global Internet exchange for all chemicals and plastics. More than 4,000 member companies participate in ChemConnect's World Chemical Exchange. In addition, BP Amoco recently selected ChemConnect Inc. as its third party platform for Internet-based chemical trading. Enermetrix.com, another e-business, is a leader in Internet commerce for the energy industry. The company provides Internet technology and business process standards. Finally, Petroleum Place and its subsidiary, The Oil & Gas Asset Clearinghouse, are partnering with InfoMech to sell oil and gas properties through a Web site. InfoMech is integral to the Web auction space.

In order to succeed in the e-commerce space, energy, and natural resources companies must have an organized and well thought-out approach. Vision and direction, supplier management, demand management, organization strategy, technology strategy, and transaction strategy are the other pieces that should be part of an organization's business objectives. An effective strategy can improve productivity and reduce costs by targeting benefits in a specific market or location. In addition, the type of commodity, operating model (internal or outsourced solution), and pricing mechanism must be defined to achieve benefits:

- An effective solution will allow customers to deal directly with suppliers. This will allow a greater focus on other value-added activities within a company.
- Data collected from an internal system can be analyzed to adjust sourcing policies and process flows.
- Improved planning is also a benefit of an e-procurement strategy because integration of inter-company business processes allows for effective planning with suppliers, which reduces working capital and lowers inventory levels.

The good news is that benefits are sustainable since many of the current purchasing practices are changed. Slow manual processes, inaccurate data, and limited information on purchase orders that currently take place are eliminated. Additional improvements include easy access to data, improved purchase cycles, and lower administration costs.

A further example of an area where e-procurement can be extremely effective in reducing costs is in the area of indirect material purchasing. Non-production (MRO) purchasing is typically an area that is poorly managed by most companies. *Purchasing Magazine* estimates that $1.4 trillion is currently spent on indirect materials and services. Minimal volume leveraging, out-of-contract spending, lack of enterprise software, and non-compliance are reasons for high spending in this area. Examples of indirect goods and services include office furniture, office equipment, janitorial supplies, travel, and temporary help services. A company can experience a 5-10 percent reduction in the price of goods and services, a significant reduction in purchase and fulfillment cycles, and a 25-50 percent reduction in inventory costs through e-procurement. Suppliers also benefit from an e-procurement program that in turn helps a company negotiate better pricing. Benefits are obtained through increased volume, automated order management, and lower inventory and service costs.

An effective business-to-business e-commerce strategy enables energy and natural resource companies to significantly improve service, reduce costs, and pursue new revenue streams. Succeeding will require an e-commerce vision, coordinated efforts, preparation, and proper execution. Energy and natural resources companies that are able to take advantage of this opportunity will see a much brighter future.

written by:

Mark J. Genereaux

MSAS Supply Chain Solutions Group

http://genereaux.ASCET.com

Enabling Technology Through Outsourcing

In the mid-1990s, Mobil replaced its decentralized supply chain approach with a streamlined 3PL approach, contracting supply functions to the MSAS Supply Chain Solutions Group. In utilizing MSAS, Mobil hoped to reduce its fleet, centralize its railcar management, and increase its shipment visibility; MSAS (and its Mobil-targeted Rail Transportation Service Group) successfully achieved these goals, reduced costs, and increased productivity and efficiency as well. Current objectives for both Mobil and MSAS include customer order placement and on-time delivery in a JIT environment; the future includes increased effiency through technological and software solutions.

The Beginning of a Partnership

In 1995, Mobil Oil began an extensive process of evaluating various components of its supply chain, including its rail transportation management programs. Its goal was to assess the entire process, develop system improvements, and maximize efficiencies throughout the organization. Based upon recommendations presented to Mobil by Andersen Consulting, Mobil recognized the value of outsourcing the necessary expertise relative to rail transportation management.

Until this point, the Mobil operating model was a very decentralized approach, with each individual plant site operating its own rail program. Economies of scale and a network view of rail fleet activity were lacking. Mobil realized that developing the internal resources to accomplish the mission would take longer and would be a greater expense than acquiring the systems and the knowledge from an experienced third party logistics provider such as MSAS Global Supply Chain Solutions Group.

MSAS offered Mobil customized solutions to address its areas of need quickly, efficiently, and cost-effectively. The components of the solution included trained personnel, tested systems, customized reports, and a proven continuous improvement methodology. Additionally, MSAS's core focus of acquiring continuously improving technology and supply chain process knowledge afforded Mobil the benefit of ongoing enhancements, which were not a core competency within the Mobil organization.

Program Objectives

The relationship between the two companies group began with MSAS managing the Mobil Lubes Division fleet (approximately 1,100 cars). Specific objectives outlined within this program were to achieve three primary goals: fleet reduction, centralized railcar management, and increased shipment visibility. MSAS, utilizing QTSI's track and tracing system, helped reduce Mobil's lube fleet by approximately 150 railcars. MSAS provided centralized management of rail cars by staffing resources in a command center environment, as well as at high-volume shipping locations.

MSAS has been successful since the program's inception in reducing cost, increasing productivity, and keeping Mobil Lubes product moving efficiently through the supply chain. This success opened the door for MSAS to manage the bulk of Mobil Oil's rail movement. Through this evolution, the Rail Transportation Services Group (RTSG) was created.

Regarding rail transportation specifically, increased focus is now given to customer order placement and on-time delivery processes, including plant sourcing, order quantity, order frequency, and lead times in a JIT environment. Loading cars to maximum capacity, railcar turn-around time, scheduled ship date compliance, intransit, and on-hand inventories at destination are all reviewed daily and measured. Additionally, entirely new scopes of work have been introduced, including managing the export of product destined for South America

Mark J. Genereaux is Senior Vice President of MSAS Supply Chain Solution Group (formerly Mark VII Worldwide Logistics) headquartered in Dallas, TX. He has been with MSAS since 1993 where he has helped build the company into a leading Supply Chain Management services provider. Prior to joining Mark VII, Genereaux was with Missouri Nebraska Express (MNX), a Midwest-based full truckload carrier.

Genereaux is a graduate of the Aviation Officer Candidate School (AOCS) and was a distinguished Naval aviator. He studied at Texas Tech University where he received a BS in Geophysics.

Energy

through all transportation modes for the Chemical Products Division.

The program objectives included reduced rail transit times, decreased variability, fleet sizing analysis, rail car availability, and mode selection optimization. In addition to fleet reduction and freight management, the RTSG has moved to include program performance and on-time delivery. Over time, the objectives expanded significantly to include an end- to-end Supply Chain Management concept.

MSAS Resources

MSAS has provided Mobil with a broad scope of tools to create customized solutions. Technology-based resources such as computer networking, e-commerce capability, and state of the art software tools form the backbone. MSAS personnel offered professional logistics training and experience that, combined with a focus on identifying opportunities and improving processes over time, provided the intelligence to effectively utilize the technology tools. MSAS' financial depth and stability ensure longevity and ability to stay current with advancing technology. Additionally, MSAS provided global reach through all modes of transportation and pack types, including specialized containers like ISO tanks.

Mobil Super Distributor Center (SDC) program

An example of combining technology and transportation process management capabilities into a customized solution is the Mobil Super Distributor Center (SDC) program, which MSAS developed and operates for Mobil.

The SDC program includes optimizing inbound transportation of chemical additives from multiple supplier locations to a warehouse in Beaumont, TX, and managing the physical distribution of product from the warehouse to South America. The outbound leg includes the movement of freight inter-modally from the 31 chemical additive suppliers are located on the East Coast, with several in the South and Midwest. The outbound container shipments are transported to ports in Houston and loaded on vessels for various destinations in South America.

Key to the success of the SDC is MSAS's custom-designed Distribution Center Application (DCA), which is used for warehouse management, inventory control, and order processing. This Internet-enabled system is fully scalable for current or future programs, and features a Sequel Server back end with a Visual Basic front end. The system was designed and built exclusively for the Mobil SDC to fully interface with MSAS' transportation management application (TRACS). The DCA optimizes inbound orders by consolidating several supplier orders to achieve order efficiency.

The core of optimization in TRACS is the TRACS Load Builder. The Load Builder can accept a set of filtered orders or can be triggered to dynamically run a filter against all shippable orders. The Load Builder considers all delivery options, based on all carrier, consignee, and ship point parameters, and develops the optimum shipping plan to meet service requirements. All shipments that are run through TRACS are assigned a unique reference number that is exported to our Multi Modal Billing System. Invoices are then generated with all pertinent load information.

This powerful combination provides MSAS with the ability to manage warehousing operations and optimize the transportation of the freight. Prior to the implementation of the SDC, Mobil had neither warehousing capability nor transportation optimization capability to combine larger quantity warehouse replenishment orders into truckload shipments.

The Future

The SDC program is expected to grow, with plans underway to expand into other countries. MSAS is also developing another initiative for Mobil Chemical Products division, to implement and execute transportation of freight via truck, rail, inter-modal, and ocean vessel.

The ultimate vision for the program includes end-to-end Supply Chain Management for all Mobil products moving through the physical distribution network. A key driver is the customer's desire to optimize manufactured and purchased materials (finished and raw), transportation processes and inventory pipelines, compress order to delivery lead times, and improve on-time customer delivery. Competitive advantages of cost savings and service improvement enhance customer loyalty, market share, and profitability.

MSAS Supply Chain Solution Group operates as a non asset-based, full-scope logistics services provider. As a result, MSAS maintains no bias in the solutions created for specific customer needs. Strategic alliances and licensing agreements with top industry software creators like i2 Technologies, McHugh Software, and Insight provide internal data collection, analysis, and distribution expertise in a Citrix and SQL Server environment. EDI functionality and Internet-order entry and visibility capabilities provide the advanced technology and flexibility to design each program to meet individual needs.

This plug-and-play approach has enabled the creation of powerful networks of data collection, analysis, and exchange to create both process knowledge and tactical decision support information. The opportunities to streamline and improve processes using MSAS capabilities are clearly evidenced by the Global Optimization program underway for Mobil CPD. The ability to link customized tools together to provide end-to-end supply chain inventory management and visibility in a multi-source, multi-customer, multi-modal environment will optimize resources and assets on a global scale.

The key to the success of Mobil and other MSAS customers is to continue our commitment to providing an objective execution of integrated logistics networks. We recognize that we must provide cutting-edge, forward-thinking technology solutions to every challenge our customers face. We are also focused on continued development of strategic relationships in software solutions, and to remaining highly competitive as technological advances in the industry emerge.

Copyright©2000 *Andersen Consulting LLP*

EMI Music Creates a Hit with Supply Chain: An Interview with Mike Frey

EMI Music is the world's third largest music company with operations in more than 50 countries. EMI has hundreds of local and international artists, including some of the biggest names in the recorded music industry. The Rolling Stones, Garth Brooks, Janet Jackson, Lenny Kravitz, the Beatles, and Smashing Pumpkins are just a few of the artists on EMI's roster. The company's North American operations recently undertook the re-engineering of its supply chain to leap from having one of the industry's lowest service levels to, in the estimation of its key customers, the best. Mike Frey oversees the company's North American supply chain operations, and he recently completed a series of improvements that have transformed the way EMI serves its customers.

What operational challenges does the music industry face?

There are a number – the first is the unpredictable nature of selling music. Consumer tastes are constantly changing, and the past success of an artist's album doesn't necessarily mean that their next album will perform the same way, making it very difficult to plan. And when an album takes off, it takes off fast, and we have to be able to respond quickly. Inventory is also a huge issue. Retail floor space is expensive and retailers only want to carry enough inventory to meet consumer needs. Most of our customers are eliminating their traditional warehouses. They also want to minimize their risk of returns, and returns tend to run high in our industry. We introduce thousands of new titles each year, and most of these albums have a short life cycle – we don't want to be caught with excess inventory or returns.

In terms of distribution, our customers are putting more pressure on distributors to ship store-ready product directly to their retail stores. This means shipping product that has security tags and customer-specific price stickers to upwards of 25,000 locations. These challenges have placed a great deal of pressure on us to significantly improve our supply chain's efficiency and delivery performance.

How did you go about identifying the issues that were hampering EMI's performance?

Feedback from customers indicated that our service and delivery performance did not stack up to that of our competitors, and we set out to develop the capabilities to put us at the top. The first step was to better understand what our customers needed. We conducted a series of extensive customer interviews to identify deficiencies in our performance as well as to better understand current and future customer needs. A troubling piece of feedback was that our customers said that they usually knew when we had a hit album when EMI was out of product. This meant that our first issue was to quickly transform our ability to deliver hit product – those titles that are the best-selling albums in the market. In less than 150 days, we reduced our delivery cycle time by 60%, improved delivery performance to above 95%, and reduced our inventory levels by 45% for hit product. This did a great deal to improve our customers' confidence in our operations.

We then addressed the most critical aspect of our operations: releasing new music. New releases make up 40 to 50% of our customers' business. It is very difficult to predict how a new album is going to sell before it's available in the retail stores. And, of course, we hope every new album will become a hit. So as a solution to the

Mike Frey is the senior vice president of customer fulfillment operations for EMI Recorded Music. In addition, he is leading efforts to enable EMI to meet future digital and Internet business opportunities.

unpredictable nature of music sales, traditionally we pushed our customers to order more product than they needed up front. This practice, however, was resulting in unproductive inventory and excessive returns. Except for the cases in which an album unexpectedly takes off, our customers routinely had more product than they could sell, and in our business, unsold albums are accepted as returns. We pushed excess product on our customers up front due to our fears that if an album became a hit, we would not be able to respond fast enough to our customers' and consumers' needs.

The other major issue was with our delivery performance for catalogue music. This segment includes albums that have been in our catalogue for as long as 10-20 years. Our catalogue includes artists like Frank Sinatra, Nat King Cole and specialty genres like jazz, blues, and classical music. We had very low on-time and complete delivery performance for this segment. Our poor performance was heightened by excessive levels of inventory for product that was not selling as well.

You were fairly aggressive in your performance targets, and expected results in a short period of time. What were the elements of the new program?
The key focus of the supply chain effort was to dramatically improve our time-to-market for all categories of product (new music releases, hits, and catalogue albums). Our goal was a 75% to 80% reduction in order cycle time with a target delivery of same day for top-selling product and next-day delivery for the balance of our catalogue. We also set out to significantly reduce our costs and reduce inventory by 50%. We will use the future cost savings to fund value-added services for our customers, including store-ready product, security tags, and price stickers.

To achieve these objectives, we implemented improved demand-based planning and pull scheduling across our operations. A key differentiating strategy was to physically integrate production and distribution so that a single, cross-functional team of people are responsible for managing product from the start of production until it is received by our customers. Rather than storing our catalogue product in a remote distribution center, we developed the capability to fulfill customer orders for catalogue directly from our integrated fulfillment center in the Midwest, which is near our key customers' distribution centers. For new releases, we implemented a make-to-order model – manufacturing new releases to actual customer orders – so that product comes off the production line and is directly packed for shipment. This enabled us to cut the customer order cycle time by 60% and reduce our inventory liability by 40%. Our new abilities allow us to increase our service while reducing our inventory and costs. Finally, we renamed the combined manufacturing and distribution business "Customer Fulfillment Operations."

How have EMI's customers been responding?
Customer feedback has been outstanding. Numerous customers have rated us as their top-performing distributor. Because our strategy focused on quickly meeting our customers' critical needs, their perceptions began changing midway through the implementation effort. We've recently put our new capabilities to the test with our new D'Angelo album. Within two weeks of its release, demand was four times what we had expected. With our old model, we would have had to focus all our resources on this one album, causing our performance on other albums to suffer. Today, our quick response capability enables us to meet the enormous spikes in demand that come with having the number one album on the charts, on time, and with no impact to delivery performance.

How has EMI used technology to achieve these performance improvements?
By focusing on process simplification and dramatically reducing non-value added steps we were able to achieve these improvements with little technology investment. The Andersen Consulting team we worked with challenged the way we were making and delivering music, and they helped us develop and implement practical improvements. By looking for ways to simplify our processes, they helped us reduce our technology investments.

What technology we did leverage was focused on fulfillment automation and electronic integration with our customers to provide such capabilities as advanced shipping notification and electronic receipt. With the unpredictable nature of our product, our most effective means of improving our ability to plan is to collaborate with our retail customers. Our planning initiatives include utilizing our marketing efforts and point-of-sale purchases to identify activities that drive consumer purchases. By providing quick response capability and capturing consumer information, we can support both local and national market activity more effectively.

How are you applying the success of EMI's supply chain to emerging Internet channels?
The Internet is dramatically changing the face of the music industry, as is evident by the pending mergers of AOL and Time Warner, and EMI Music and Warner Music Group. All forms of Internet fulfillment (including ordering a physical CD, streaming music online, or downloading music directly to consumers) represent another type of supply chain that requires technology, consistent processes, planning, security, high-performance delivery, and consumer marketing. With the Internet model, roads and trucks are being substituted with high bandwidth communication networks and servers. Currently the sheer size of electronic audio and video files is limiting the number of people who download music online. Cheaper telecommunications costs and emerging compression technology will quickly minimize this barrier. Our challenge as an industry is to effectively support and leverage all current and future channels of consumer buying – and use them in new and unique ways. For example, there are growing opportunities for new and developing artists to gain exposure to consumers through the Internet and new listening devices, which ultimately generate more albums sales.

Preview Systems, Inc. – Enabling Digital Goods E-Commerce Networks

PREVIEW SYSTEMS

Digital goods consist of copyrighted products such as software, music, video, documents, and other products that can be produced, distributed, licensed, and used electronically. Typically, the large companies that dominate these industries leverage extensive and complex distribution channels for the physical distribution of digital products stored on media such as CD-ROM, DVDs, etc. While electronic distribution and licensing offers tremendous advantages over the existing physical methods, it also poses significant technical and business challenges.

Preview Systems develops and deploys an internet-based software infrastructure designed to manage efficiently all aspects of the digital supply chain, linking the producers of digital goods, such as software publishers and music labels, with any of their worldwide distribution partners.

The "Digital Supply Chain"

The "digital supply chain" has three unique characteristics. First, the supply chain can be real-time, and eliminate production and distribution delays. Second, physical inventory can be replaced by "virtual" inventory, and eliminate production and inventory costs. Third, the commerce of digital products is based on "rights", which must be protected. Electronic distribution can be enforced automatically by electronic distribution rights transmitted along the digital supply chain. Use of the digital products can be managed using digital license rights, even after delivery to the end-users, and provide more flexibility than traditional licenses.

Preview Systems licenses the infrastructure software, which consists of encryption tools, servers, databases, secure communication protocols, e-commerce integration modules, and digital rights management client modules. Typical customers include large software publishers, music labels, distributors, and resellers. The platform can also be used on an outsourcing basis from a number of application service providers. The infrastructure supports end-user interfaces in 14 languages, and is commercially available on a global basis.

Business Model

The business model of the company is based on providing a common infrastructure to all parties within the relevant industries, enabling both existing and new participants to leverage a common infrastructure. Preview Systems does not sell any digital products to end-users, and thus does not compete with those licensing its technology. Thanks to its unique business model and real-time secure networking technology, Preview Systems can link producers of digital goods to multiple competing or complementary distribution channels, maximizing the market reach and minimizing the time to market for digital products. When new products become available electronically, simultaneously via any direct and indirect channels, channel conflicts are reduced and revenues are increased. The software infrastructure is licensed based on transaction fees, and includes an annual minimum.

A Distributed, Secure, Interoperable and Scalable platform:

This infrastructure ensures that new products can be widely distributed immediately upon release, and can be licensed to end-users via multiple direct and indirect distribution channels. Distribution rights and usage rights are automatically enforced, ensuring protection of the digital content both before and after the delivery to the end-users. As commercial transactions are completed, digital products are automatically fulfilled and digital licenses are issued. For each transaction, an audit trail is created, and the sell-through information is

Contact Information

Vincent Pluvinage, Ph.D.
President and CEO

Cay Horstmann
Chief Technology Officer

Jeff Brown
VP Professional Services

Preview Systems, Inc.
1601 S. DeAnza Blvd., Suite 100
Cupertino, CA 95014
Phone 408.517.3200
Fax 408.517.3206
www.previewsystems.com

http://preview.ASCET.com

Figure 1.0 Preview's End-to-End Network Solution

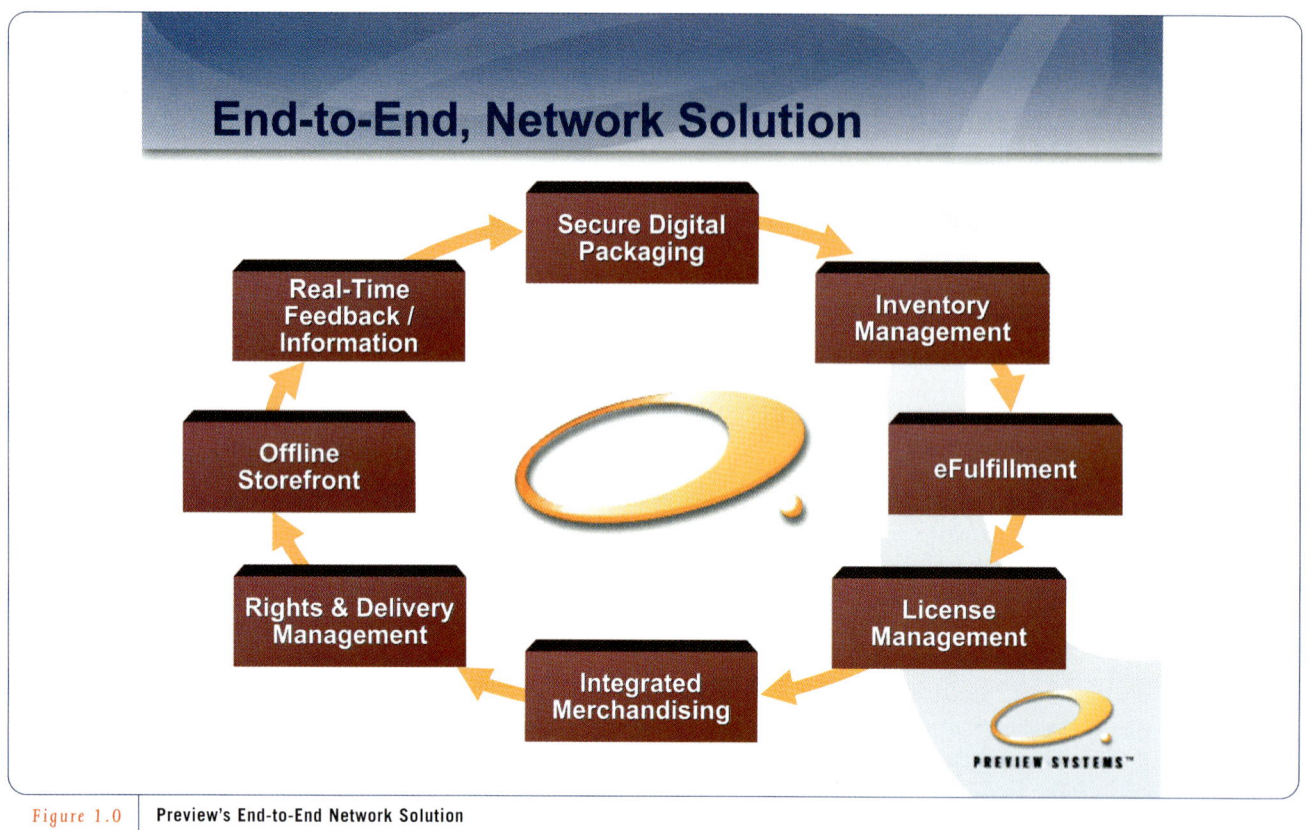

electronically transmitted in real time back to each party in the supply chain. The seamless integration and automation of secure real-time e-commerce transactions reduces logistics costs. The absence of physical production costs, shortages, or obsolete products eliminates many inventory costs.

The network infrastructure is distributed across three levels. At one end of the supply chain, digital products are encrypted and distribution rights and other commercial information are entered into a server's database. Numerous publishers can use this server to simultaneously sell directly from a Web site, while also connecting securely to servers operated by any of their distribution partners, such as distributors or service providers. Using a software module called the "gateway", such partners typically enable a large number of Web point-of-sales owned by retailers or corporate resellers. Each one can offer to license the digital products in the same Web-based shopping basket used to sell other physical goods, controlling all aspects of the purchase: pricing, branding, bundling, etc. Once the transaction is completed, the "gateway" issues the digital license and instructs the server to deliver the digital products. The products are automatically delivered to the end-user, where they can immediately be used according to the licensing rights purchased.

Preview Systems software infrastructure is designed to inter-operate with various established platforms: Windows NT and Sun Solaris operating systems; Microsoft SQL, Oracle, and Informix databases; Microsoft Site Server, Open Market, and BroadVision commerce servers, etc. The electronic distribution is also designed to leverage the Akamai worldwide network of cache servers. The platform is designed for scalability and can support a very large number of simultaneous transactions.

The Preview Systems' infrastructure is increasingly being adopted by leading companies such as Symantec, Macromedia, Ingram Micro, Buy.com, and EMI Music.

white paper

written by:

Gary Sutula
R.R. Donnelley & Sons

Greg Cudahy
Andersen Consulting

http://sutula.ASCET.com

Streamlining the Printing Supply Chain: A Capabilities-Centric Approach

From Gutenberg in the 1400s, to high-speed presses in the 20th century, and on to print-on-demand technologies as we enter the new millennium, the printing industry stands at the core of human history. Benjamin Franklin's wisdom is part of the fabric of the American experience due to his prominence as a printer; the printed press helped keep resistance movements alive in Europe during World War II. Fashion and media empires have been built, grown, and destroyed on the printed page. Yet, as the 21st century dawns, there are many who question the future of print in a digital age. How can a medium steeped in age-old traditions survive as heretofore unimagined technological changes happen with increasing rapidity?

The fact of the matter is that print is alive and well, and likely to stay so for a long time. As early as the 1980s, many forecasts were predicting reduced printing and related raw material demand (such as for paper and ink) because electronic substitution, primarily due to the advent of the personal computer (PC) and electronic data interchange (EDI), the business-to-business exchange of computerized transactional information. In fact, the opposite occurred. The explosion of information availability, combined with lower costs and individual access to personal printing capacity, dramatically increased printing activity throughout the economy. In the past year, book and magazine volumes in the North American and European economies reached record levels. Resurgent economies in Asia/Pacific and emerging markets have generated new demand and attracted new capacity. The world economy truly is built on a foundation of paper.

What is even more true, however, is that the printing and publishing strategies of the past will not be viable even in the relatively near term. Consolidation of smaller printing operations by roll-up operations such as Consolidated Graphics has begun to reduce inefficiencies in the supply market; new critical mass has been generated at the large player level, as demonstrated by the recent merger of Quebecor and World Color (now QuebecorWorld). In distribution, the number of magazine distributors in the United States has been consolidated by a whopping 80% in the past few years alone. Publishers demand lower costs and higher service, new channel players with new requirements (such as Amazon.com and BN.com) are added with increasing speed across the globe, and consumers demand greater selection, higher levels of customization, and increasing levels of service, all at a lower total delivered price.

Furthermore, there is a new distribution channel to manage. The digital pipeline is revving up. Print-on-demand technologies are expected to be a feature of book retail stores and warehouses, providing rapid turnaround even on titles that may have been out of print for decades. Books, magazine articles, newspaper stories - all can be downloaded from the World Wide Web, and emerging technologies such as NuvoMedia's RocketBook and SoftBook's Reader 250 are showing the way to a world where "e-books" become more portable and viable.

In the face of this environment of discontinuous change, the successful printing company of the 21st century must abandon the long-cherished traditions of the "printer" and move into the realm of full-scale communications company. This is a tremendous challenge, because the old-school printers must become highly efficient in the traditional printed material offerings while simultaneous-

Gary L. Sutula is Senior Vice President and Chief Information Officer at R.R. Donnelley & Sons Company. Prior to joining R. R. Donnelley, he held the same position at Transamerica Financial Services.

Greg Cudahy is a partner in the Andersen Consulting Supply Chain Practice where he serves as the firm's global supply chain lead for the media and entertainment industries. He focuses on all aspects of supply chain strategy and operations with particular emphasis on integrated planning, procurement, and fulfillment.

Media & Entertainment

ly focusing on growth, innovation, and time-to-speed in the emerging electronic media channels. One cannot succeed without the other. Traditional print will languish without direct, effective, and efficient links to the new economy; the printer has no strategic advantage in electronic media if its existing primacy in printed materials and publishing relationships is not leveraged.

At the heart of this challenge is one key fact: Supply chain excellence is paramount. The key is to balance the potentially diametrically opposed imperatives embodied by the need for a new 21st century strategy.

The Need for Greater Efficiency

Every cost in the printed material value chain, from the forest to the front door of the end consumer, must be managed to its absolute minimum, while service levels must be maintained or improved. Unnecessary variations, particularly those driven by poor communications across the supply chain, must be eliminated.

The Need for Increased Speed, Variety, Personalization and Flexibility

The velocity of change in the electronic marketplace for media content is unheralded. Users must receive their information in the desired format, via the desired channel, with the expected personalization, and in the desired "chunks". This means maximizing flexibility (the potential enemy of pure efficiency) and thinking about methods of compensation that vary greatly from the

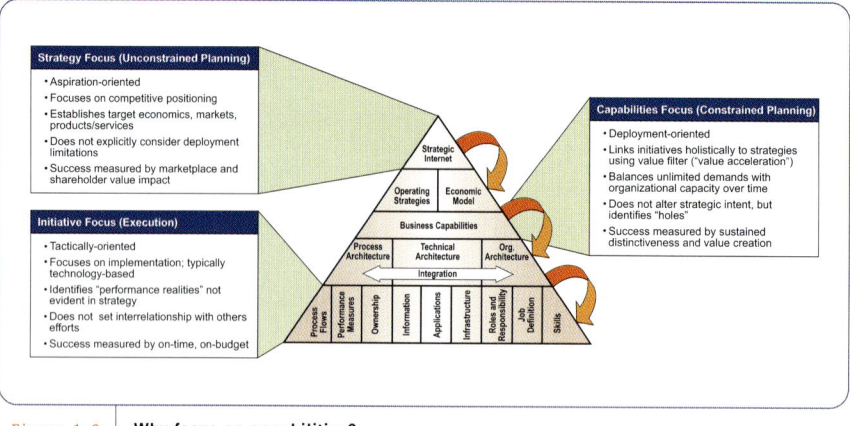

Figure 1.0 Why focus on capabilities?

---

model of payment for a finished good, which is so common today.

The good news is that technology, particularly those applications that are supply chain-oriented, can actually make these seemingly contradictory objectives work in a fashion that is highly complementary. The trick is in determining the appropriate mix and timing of technology in an environment with unlimited desires, limited resources, and seemingly endless software and hardware options.

R.R. Donnelley and the Move to the New Economy

Headquartered in Chicago, Illinois, R.R. Donnelley & Sons Company is one of the largest print-oriented communications companies in the world. Founded in 1864, it enjoys a rich history and reputation in the printing industry. Donnelley operates 55 plants, predominantly in North America, with additional operations in selected markets in Central Europe, the United Kingdom, South America, and Asia. In addition to these production operations, the company provides customer service in nearly 200 locations worldwide. 1999 global revenues of over $5.2 billion were delivered by a workforce of 35,000 employees.

As a broad-range provider of print-related media services, Donnelley sees its mission as "bringing the written word to life worldwide using traditional and emerging media." It executes this mission via five market-facing business units:

- Merchandise Media serving the consumer and B2B catalogue, advertising, retail insert, and direct mail markets
- Magazine Publishing Services serving the consumer, trade, and specialty magazine markets
- Book Publishing Services serving the trade, children's, religious, and educational book markets
- Telecommunications serving the global directory needs of telecommunications providers
- Financial Services serving the communication needs of the financial markets and health care industries

In addition to these end-market-facing entities, Donnelley also operates another highly strategic business unit, Donnelley Logistics Services (DLS). DLS provides distribution operations support for Donnelley print customers to ensure lowest total delivered cost at a high level of service, and services the needs of customers who are outside the current scope of Donnelley print operations.

Donnelley's historical business expansion has been largely evolutionary as print capacity and plants have been added via acquisition and organic growth. This capacity has been largely developed under the business unit framework mentioned previously, and each plant has been run as a profit center. Corporate functions are relatively lean, and the emphasis has been on ownership and customization at the field level.

This approach has generated strong

Weblink

For more on scheduling, see:
 lapide.ASCET.com
 uchneat.ASCET.com

For more on transportation, see:
 manheim.ASCET.com

For more on optimization, see:
 enslow.ASCET.com
 prince.ASCET.com
 hicks.ASCET.com
 hurley.ASCET.com

CAPABILITIES FRAMEWORK

Capability	Description
New Offering Development	Identify, develop, and deploy new products and services faster than any company in the industry.
Value-Added Selling	Move from being a purely responsive printer to a proactive provider of media solutions with creative pricing.
Media-Independent Services	Lead the industry in the management and delivery of content (physical or electronic) and services using a totally web-enabled architecture.
Maximized Customer Value	Add greater customer value through improved segmentation of customer needs and targeted offerings.
Unified Supply Chain Network	Operate the Donnelley network as an integrated asset and fully interface with customers and suppliers.
Reliable Planning and Scheduling	Optimize operational performance "within the four walls" of existing print operations in a uniform, reliable fashion.

- Growth-Oriented
- Efficiency-and Growth-Oriented
- Efficiency-Oriented

Figure 2.0 **Why focus on capabilities?**

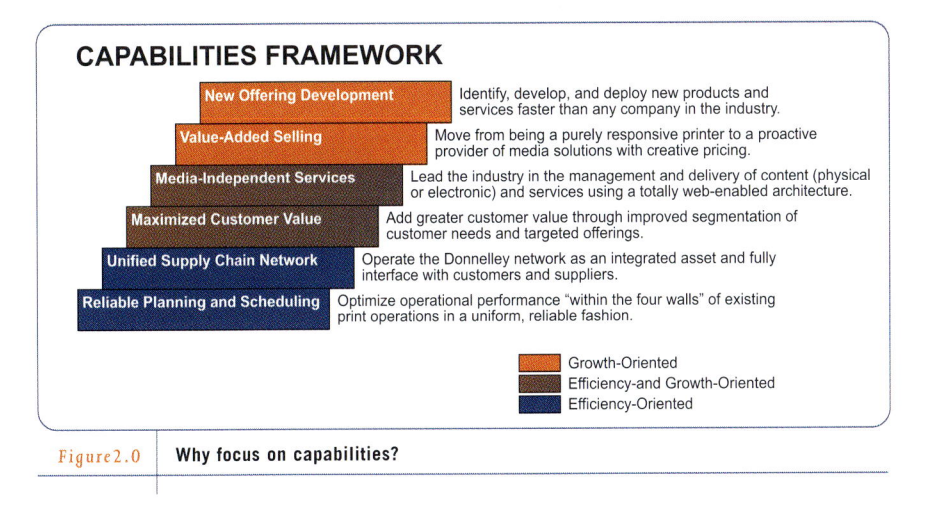

customer relationships, a reputation for high quality, and a deeply ingrained, plant-oriented corporate culture, not to mention solid economic returns. Yet as Donnelley, and the printing industry in general, move into the new millennium, this approach has also left the company with a host of challenges that are more apparent in the increasingly competitive communications arena:

- **System Proliferation:** Plant-specific solutions have resulted in hundreds of applications and little commonality from location to location, increasing the cost of rolling out and maintaining systems.
- **Customer Integration:** Close ties between customers and individual plants have created relationships that are strong and effective, but customization (and associated inefficiencies) remains the rule, not the exception.
- **Enterprise Management:** Custom processes and systems from plant to plant, along with limited standardization of metrics, have constrained the ability to manage the system as one integrated set of assets, leaving room for further improvements in asset productivity.
- **Electronic Interfaces:** While Donnelley has taken an industry-leading position in terms of electronic manipulation and production/distribution of content, there is still room to grow into a world-class digital asset management provider.

Addressing these challenges in a fast, efficient, and effective manner will determine whether or not Donnelley emerges as the dominant print-oriented media provider of the coming decade.

Capabilities: Faster, Better, Cheaper

To ensure success in this challenge, in spring 1999 Donnelley launched a program to establish its technology priorities to achieve its world-class goals. Entitled "Information Technology for Strategic Advantage" (ITSA), the program was the first enterprise-wide undertaking in the history of the company to examine technology needs and their fit with strategic objectives. The effort included all business units, all geographies (with initial focus on the United States), and strong corporate participation.

Early on, it became very clear that the traditional "strategy drives technology drives development drives implementation" approach to enacting business change was too antiquated and failed to address the interdependent nature of strategy and technology in today's economy. The conduct of strategy development and technology planning must be simultaneous, with constant iterations as the business moves forward.

To achieve these objectives, the team adopted a distinctive capabilities framework to guide the effort. The capabilities framework is a methodology which ensures that only technology that enables the handful of strategic imperatives for a company is implemented, and that such capabilities are deployed in "wave" fashion that allows for maximum net benefit to the company (see Figure 1.0).

A given technology component rarely generates a business case purely on its own; other technologies, process changes, and organizational improvements must be orchestrated to truly deliver change and business results. On the flip side, when a technology is implemented, it usually provides benefit to more than one single strategic initiative. The capabilities construct enables a company to think about how all of these interdependencies are interwoven, and to focus its resources on those areas that are synergistic and deliver the greatest business value over a given time-period. This process required the team to identify the critical capabilities for Donnelley in the coming years against a handful of key criteria.

The initial activities involved cataloging all of the existing applications across business units (well over a thousand), ongoing technology-related initiatives (over 200 developmental and hundreds of maintenance/enhancement-related), and the strategic objectives of each business unit. Most importantly, the team began collecting strategic plans and business benefits expected to be attained by each business unit over a three- to five-year horizon.

With these facts in hand, the team conducted an exercise in cross-referencing strategic plans (and related business benefit targets) to information technology initiatives (either ongoing or in the works). Using a metric called linked EBIT – earnings before interest and taxes – each strategic effort was analyzed to confirm or deny whether the appropriate technology was existing or planned to support the business benefits targeted. Likewise, technology initiatives were evaluated to validate their fit with the stated strategies of Donnelley and its business units. The linked EBIT metric allowed the team to calculate what impact, if any, individual initiatives had toward achieving business results, and to identify where technology shortcomings

http://sutula.ASCET.com

were likely to constrain the projected business benefits.

The results were revealing. The connection between strategic imperatives, economic objectives, and technology initiatives was unclear and/or tenuous in many cases. Cross-business unit leverage of common processes and technologies to support differing business unit- and plant-specific needs was less than optimal. While the information technology and operations personnel involved in business and technology change were working feverishly and producing quality results, the list of initiatives (viewed for the first time from a total enterprise perspective) was longer than could likely be completed in a reasonable period even with double or triple the resources. Prioritization was based on factors that varied dramatically from group to group within the company.

The results of this assessment, combined with a cross-business unit analysis of business value and commonality of need, enabled the team to establish the critical capabilities on which Donnelley should focus its developmental efforts over the coming years. Economic impact was evaluated by not only looking at the typical business case factors (revenue enhancement, cost containment, and asset productivity), but also by examining the tremendous value produced by leveraging the rollout of a capability in an enterprise-wide fashion (better, faster, cheaper).

Using a capabilities framework to reprioritize its activities (see Figure 2.0), Donnelley was able to achieve consensus across executives at both the corporate and business unit levels – critical to making large-scale transformational change happen. In addition, ongoing and planned work was reprioritized and nearly 90 initiatives were either eliminated or deferred, freeing financial and human resources to focus on the truly strategic capabilities. Finally, an integrated program management office featuring integrated information technology, operations, and finance participation was chartered and given the authority and accountability for ensuring that current and future development initiatives are in sync with enterprise capability priorities.

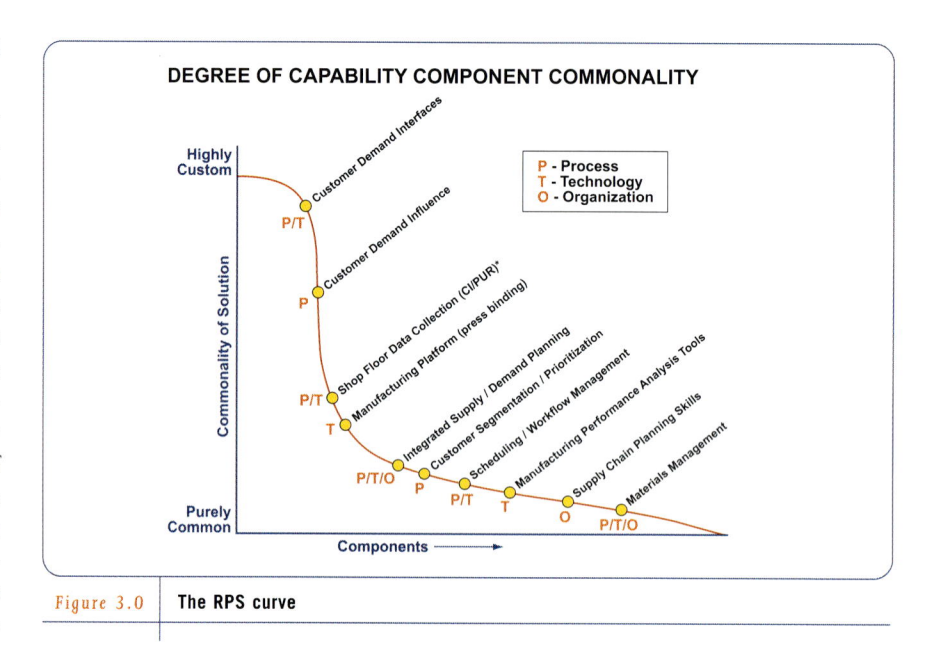

Figure 3.0 **The RPS curve**

Reliable Planning and Scheduling: Flawlessly Executing The Basics

At the heart of the Reliable Planning and Scheduling (RPS) capability is the need to provide a relatively frictionless process for executing basic supply and demand planning activities at the plant level. It is the foundation upon which not only improved efficiency will be built (directly and in support of other capabilities such as Unified Supply Chain Network), but a key requirement to enable more growth-oriented capabilities, such as media-independent services.

To achieve the targeted results in the committed timeframes, Donnelley must execute rapidly, efficiently, and with a high level of quality. This means that certain new cultural norms must be adopted. Strategy development must be quicker and more flexible with greater allowances for course corrections during rollout. Process and system development must be executed with much greater emphasis on commonality of core components and customization only to the extent that it is rewarded by improved business results. Capability and application deployment must be released in "waves" which rely heavily on pilots and seeding the organization with new skills and best practice demonstrations.

The challenge in any organization with even a short history of firmly established operational and cultural experiences (much less one with a long history) is that everything seems unique enough to require customization, whether it be technology, business processes, or relationships. In the case of RPS at Donnelley, closer examination suggested that only a few critical components (be they process, technology, or organization) required high levels of customization, and these were predominantly in the areas closer to the customer interface. This left a set of core components that could be developed in a much more customized fashion. The conceptual curve below illustrates the relative need for customization in each major area of RPS (see Figure 3.0).

As Donnelley rolls out the first wave of RPS, there are three primary applications that will form the basis of the technology to be deployed: plant-level planning and scheduling, roll-level inventory, and transportation management. In 2000, Donnelley will design and pilot each of these technologies with accelerated deployment across the enterprise, anticipated to begin by mid- to late-year.

Plant-Level Planning and Scheduling

Obviously, Donnelley currently executes well in this area; it's at the core of the company's success. However, the wide varia-

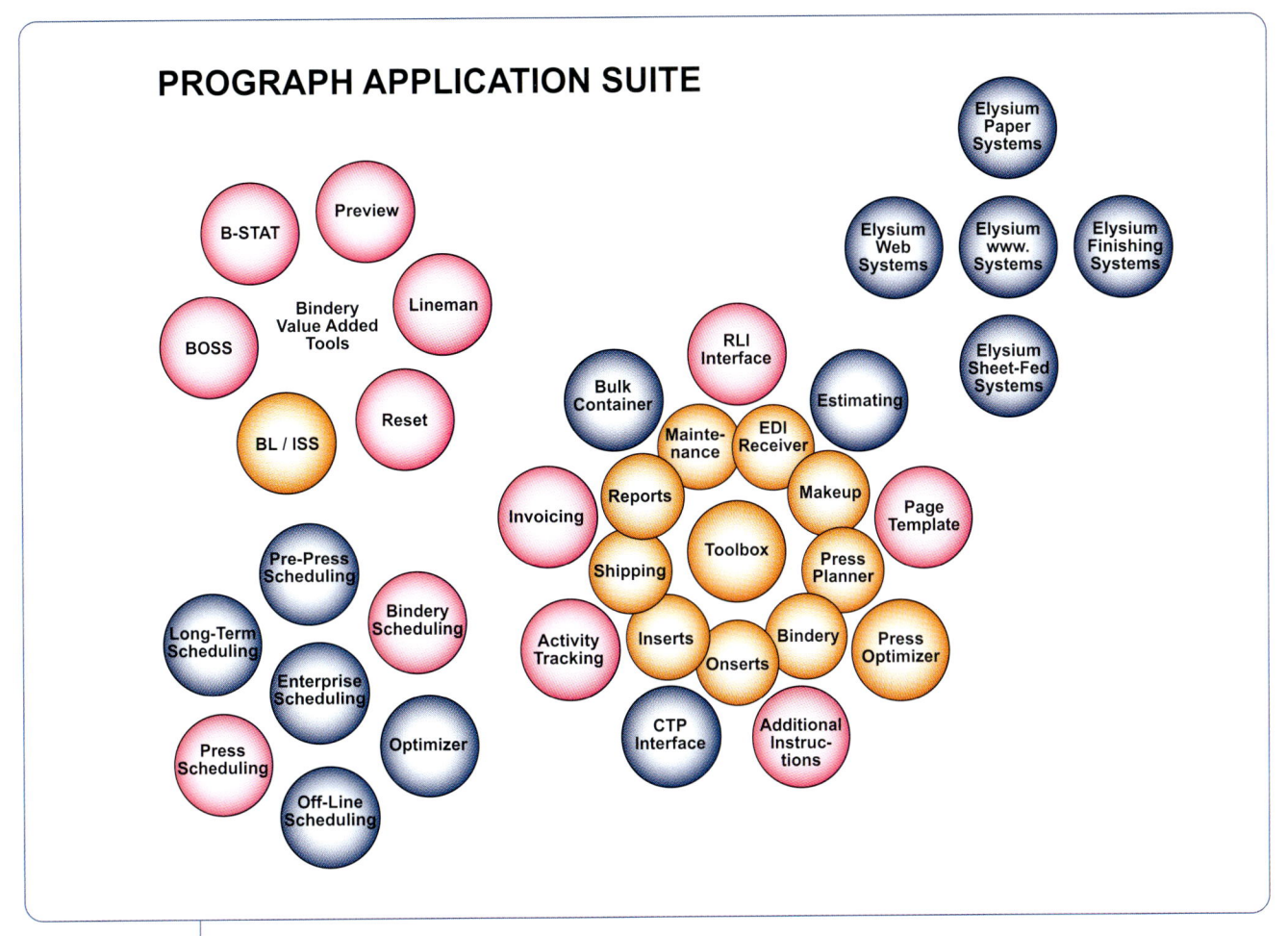

PROGRAPH APPLICATION SUITE

Figure 4.0   Prograph Application Suite

tion in approach across the 55 plants, combined with the dramatic improvement in technology options in the market, suggests the need for a new, improved approach to RPS "within the four walls" of Donnelley's plant network. One of the packaged solutions which Donnelley is investigating for adoption across the company is Prograph, which has already had demonstrated success within several Donnelley plants.

Founded in 1986, Prograph's mission is to provide innovative, personal computer-based custom software and management solutions for the printing and publishing industries. Headquartered in Pittsburgh, the company is a leader in this particular software vertical. Other large customers include QuebecorWorld, Brown Printing, Perry Judd's, AARP, Computerworld, Inc., Rodale Press, and Time Inc.

Prograph's applications provide packaged solutions specific to the printing environment, one with a very complex make-to-order process. Specifications for some printing jobs are very intricate, with trim size, varying signature lengths, paper stock, and complex binding with geographic and demographic versions. Prograph captures the specifications of the job and can readily accept EDI transactions from the customer to reduce information entry. Prograph systems also handle the complicated problem of supply chain planning in a make-to-order environment such as magazine printing, where each time the product is made, the product is different and there are frequently multiple versions. Elysium systems will collect data on the press regarding counts, waste, quality, and so on (see Figure 4.0).

Several Donnelley plants have been using Prograph systems for customer service and scheduling for a number of years, while other plants have independently begun researching these tools. Prograph's Toolbox module can also provide customer information management functionality. The scheduling suite can meet many of the distribution requirements planning, demand planning, master planning, and workflow/scheduling requirements. Finally, the Elysium shop floor systems can fulfill the shop floor data collection need. Current development and deployment activities related to Prograph will be coordinated across Donnelley under the ITSA umbrella.

Roll-Level Inventory

In the printing industry, paper inventory is one of the largest cost components and one of the most significant quality issues from both a product and service perspective.

http://sutula.ASCET.com   245

Paper stock is sourced from a variety of suppliers, in a variety of grades, colors, and brightness, and may frequently be provided and owned by the publisher. The complexity can be quite daunting, particularly when integrated with the planning and scheduling functions. There are a number of software providers in the marketplace that address this topic, and one of the primary candidates Donnelley is investigating for enterprise-wide use is AbitRol®.

EDIWISE is a wholly owned division of Abitibi-Consolidated Inc, a large paper making company. Their flagship product, AbitRol®, is the cornerstone of a paper management system designed to enable printing facilities, such as newspapers, to manage the flow of paper product through their operations, from placing orders to handling shipping manifests, via the electronic exchange of information with their paper supplier(s). AbitRol® is currently used by over 160 pressrooms and commercial printers across North America, South America, and Europe.

As with Prograph, different plants, business units, and groups within Donnelley have been working independently toward a paper management solution. Recent efforts by corporate information technology to integrate these efforts under the ITSA program and implement a complete end-to-end paper management solution across all plants have united these individual projects. An end-to-end solution for Donnelley would include: inventory management and tracking, consumption, waste management, EDI, and the ability to integrate bar code scanners. Additionally, key to the objective of more reliable planning and scheduling is the ability to collect paper quality information directly off the press and to exchange this information with paper suppliers to improve materials performance. AbitRol® is expected to meet most of Donnelley's needs for paper management.

Transportation Management

While transportation management does not technically meet the "inside the four walls" descriptor, it is an integral component of satisfying customer needs under the reliable planning and scheduling umbrella. Superior performance is absolutely critical, particularly in time-sensitive printed material categories such as magazines and consumer catalogues. From a software perspective, this is a very crowded field. Donnelley has elected to pilot i2 Technologies' RHYTHM Transportation Optimizer as part of RPS.

i2 was founded in 1988 on the principle that manufacturing planning could not only be executed faster, but based on the real business goals and conditions of the enterprise. Since then, i2 has consistently developed new intelligent planning technologies for every phase of producing, delivering and selling goods and services, including solutions that support intelligent e-business and e-commerce.

Donnelley's complex distribution network requires simultaneous optimization of inbound transportation to printing plants, outbound direct to selected customers and/or their distribution centers, and transit through the DLS network of consolidation facilities that flew into various postal delivery insertion points (such as bulk mail centers, sectional center facilities, and destination delivery units). This means that Donnelley must interface not only with a variety of suppliers, customers, and third-party transport providers, but, extensively with the U.S. Postal Service as the largest private postal customer. i2's Rhythm module is being piloted to establish its ability to operate in this complex environment.

Donnelley's first step is to model its environment within Rhythm Transportation Optimizer as a "proof-of-concept" within. Donnelly plans to integrate i2 with its custom-developed, legacy Freight Management System (FMS). FMS will still be used to plan and manage the transportation, with extracts being fed to i2 for optimization, then loaded back into FMS for execution. Under the RPS umbrella, this will complete the cycle of end-to-end planning integration within Donnelley.

Deploying Change

The degree of change embodied in Donnelley's IT for Strategic Advantage program and associated distinctive capabilities is truly massive. However, in order to maintain its industry-leading position, and to accelerate its move into the e-commerce space, Donnelley must execute successfully against these strategic objectives in a fashion and speed that is unprecedented in the traditional media industry. This means that the ability to balance enterprise solutions with high levels of customer-focused flexibility will be key. Superior supply chain performance, be it physical or electronic, is at the heart of this change, and the capabilities construct will ensure that Donnelley is successful in applying its financial and human capital in a manner that maximizes the business results of becoming a full-scale communications company.

Promises Kept – The Challenge of E-Fulfillment

The advent of the Internet has led to a revolution in how goods are sold to consumers; it is heralding a world where information flows freely and consumers have the ultimate power in selecting their purchases. While presenting and selling products is relatively straightforward on the Internet, product delivery is, as the link between the virtual world and its actual counterpart, the Achilles' heel of e-commerce. Success in Internet retailing depends on effective fulfillment of customers' needs and expectations. This success requires well-run operations and a facility for making service promises that can be met, and then delivering on those promises.

The Importance of E-Fulfillment

The rise of the Internet as a channel for selling products to consumers and businesses is now one of history's most rapid revolutions in business. It has captured the world's attention. It heralds a new world order where information flows freely and consumers have increasing power to choose what they will buy, from whom they wll buy it, and most importantly, how their demand will be met.

Much of the attention during this rise has been on new marketing capabilities enabled by the Internet – its ability to captivate a market and generate demand. Web sites, banner ads, portals – indeed much of the new vocabulary that has surrounded the rise of this medium – are words that have been newly coined to describe the phenomenon. One of the biggest impacts of the Internet is to transform products that are traditionally purchased in physical stores into seemingly virtual products that can be obtained on demand, at the point of use, and even be priced on a per-use basis.

Despite this focus on the virtual world, a huge portion of Internet commerce still revolves around presenting, selling, and then delivering physical products to consumers and businesses. Delivery of the product – "e-fulfillment" as Andersen Consulting has come to call it – is the essential link between the virtual and physical worlds. It is the point of convergence. It has also proven to be the Achilles heel of many, if not most, businesses that attempt to utilize the Internet channel to reach their customers. Andersen Consulting refers to these businesses as "e-tailers."

Challenge of E-Fulfillment

Why is e-fulfillment so difficult? After all, catalog and mail order businesses have been delivering products on demand to consumers and businesses for more than 100 years. What's different about this new way of doing business?

In many ways, e-fulfillment is the same as catalogue or mail order fulfillment, and it would be easy to mistake one for the other on a first look at the operations supporting them. However, some subtle aspects of e-fulfillment make it so challenging that even the most experienced operators have difficulty with delivery execution.

First, customers expect a level of performance, speed, and precision for e-fulfillment that is significantly beyond their performance expectations for more traditional businesses. Compounding the affect of high expectations, Internet technologies make it possible for customers to access vast amounts of information, and customers expect ready access to the status of their orders. Every step, or misstep, is visible to the customer, often as the process is occurring. This visibility places a tremendous premium on e-tailers being both reliable and fast during each phase of their operations.

Finally, in the world of the Web, everything

Robert E. Mann is an associate partner in the Andersen Consulting Supply Chain Practice. He has spent the last 18 years helping retailers and direct marketers with their supply chain and operations challenges. He now leads the e-fulfillment practice.

Retail

http://mann.ASCET.com 247

is dynamic. This is potentially true of the products and services offered to customers. It is quite literally possible for an e-tailer to change its entire offering in a matter of minutes, which from a marketing perspective is a distinct advantage. However, this advantage can wreak havoc on carefully designed fulfillment processes, material handling systems, and warehouse buildings. These physical processes suffer from the limitations of physical matter which, unlike a Web site, cannot change instantly to accommodate a new offering.

Getting all aspects of e-fulfillment right is clearly an important key to success in Internet commerce. It will affect how likely customers are to buy from you, and most importantly, it will affect a substantial portion of the costs of the business. It may even be argued that effective e-fulfillment is the differentiation needed for e-tailers to make a profit.

Consumer Expectations and E-Fulfillment Performance

Most e-tailers seem to be principally concerned with capturing customers – profits can come later. To understand how e-fulfillment contributes to that goal, it is crucial to understand what consumers want when they shop on the Web.

Prior to the 1999 holiday season, Andersen Consulting conducted a thorough study of experienced Internet buyers in order to determine their plans for holiday gift buying. The results of the study have important implications for the development of capabilities that e-tailers need to possess, and for how they should be organized to achieve those capabilities.

Demographics of Shoppers

The typical Internet shopper is likely to be a relatively young male, with more than a high-school education and with children at home. The typical Internet shopper is also likely to be experienced with the Internet and has been online for two or more years. According to the most conventional measures, this profile of shopper appears to comprise an ideal target market.

Propensity to Shop

Importantly, over half of the shoppers in the survey often or always make comparisons between the Web, retail stores, and catalogues to find what they need. Even though they religiously comparison shop, online purchasing does not yet capture a substantial portion of the attention of these buyers. In fact, less than half of them actually buy online more than once a month, which is much less frequent than their purchases through conventional shopping channels. These facts support the notion that there is a tremendous market potential for e-commerce retailers who can provide service that is as easy and reliable as store-based retailers. It also supports the conclusion there is a big gap between what consumers value and the service perceptions they have about Internet shopping. So what exactly *do* they value?

Important Values and Concerns

Consumers perceive convenience and price as values available to shoppers on the Web. These values have been effectively communicated and delivered by e-tailers. This fact, supported by another Andersen Consulting holiday study of e-tailers' ordering and fulfillment performance, showed that it typically takes 11 to 14 minutes to place an order on the Internet, almost certainly less time than a store visit would take. This isn't the problem then. What other aspects of confidence are missing?

Repeatedly, studies have shown that consumer confidence in a business is almost entirely determined by the degree to which promises of performance are kept. Andersen Consulting believes that there is little confidence among consumers that e-tailers can make and keep high quality fulfillment performance promises. The earlier Andersen Consulting study also identified four specific barriers to consumer acceptance that are directly related to fulfillment performance: returns, shipping and handling costs, lack of online customer service, and difficulty accepting deliveries. In addition to fulfillment performance reliability, these factors need to be priority issues for e-tailers.

One example of how consumer confidence is undermined is the finding that orders attempted could not even be placed 26 percent of the time – for a variety of reasons having to do with Web site issues or network performance. While this doesn't relate to fulfillment, it certainly does create a lack of confidence among consumers. Essentially, more than one-quarter of the time, customers who were ready to buy were locked out of the store. How long would a store-based retailer last under these conditions?

Consumers want to know that an e-tailer has the product they want, and can deliver it in a timely manner. Less than half (45%) of all e-tailers studied could tell a customer whether the product desired was in stock. Even worse, fewer – less than 40% – could give even a range of delivery dates for an order. Compounding these factors, almost a third of the e-tailers didn't confirm customer orders via e-mail and only 20 percent of them sent any sort of shipment confirmation. Having these kinds of services goes a long way in developing confidence among consumers.

Interestingly, recent M.I.T. research has seemingly refuted one of the central beliefs of e-commerce retail sales – that the Internet creates a "frictionless" environment. First, price differentials across the Internet – the difference between highest and lowest prices for a particular product – are actually greater on the Internet than they are for a typical brick-and-mortar retail market. Despite the fact that these price differentials are theoretically more visible on the Web, some com-

Weblink

For more on ERP, see:
hicks.ASCET.com
herbold.ASCET.com
anthony.ASCET.com
martella.ASCET.com
sprague.ASCET.com
culotta.ASCET.com
albright.ASCET.com

For more on the value chain, see:
reiter.ASCET.com
culotta.ASCET.com
berger.ASCET.com

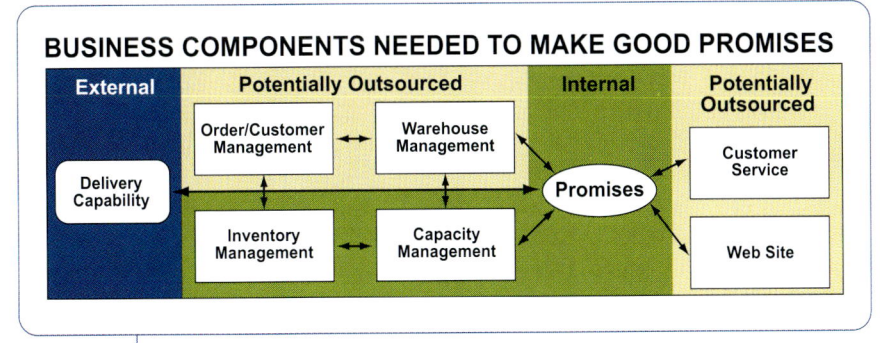

BUSINESS COMPONENTS NEEDED TO MAKE GOOD PROMISES

External	Potentially Outsourced	Internal	Potentially Outsourced
Delivery Capability	Order/Customer Management ↔ Warehouse Management	Promises	Customer Service
	Inventory Management ↔ Capacity Management		Web Site

Figure 1.0 — Business components needed to make good promises.

panies are able to charge substantially more than others are. Second, consumers have a greater tendency to stay with a preferred site that has served them well, despite price savings available on other sites. In fact, it appears that consumers will pay as much as a 10% price premium for the best performance. This value of higher performance far outstrips its cost. Furthermore, it suggests that the market will reward those e-tailers that succeed in making and keeping performance promises with both higher customer loyalty and higher prices.

Speed alone is not sufficient to create increased consumer confidence. Although there seems to be a natural tendency to expect higher speed from an electronic medium, this expectation does not seem to translate into things like shipping lead times. Consumers seem to be quite happy to accept the speeds that are commonly delivered by e-commerce companies. What they are not prepared to accept is a promise that is not kept. In other words, it is quite acceptable to offer a standard service level of five to seven days for delivery. It is not acceptable to then miss that offer by even a single day. Whatever is promised must be delivered – without fail!

Making Good Promises

What does it take to make and keep e-tail promises? Fundamentally, seven activities must be integrated in order to make service promises that have the potential to be kept by the organization. These include activities such as delivery capability, order management, inventory management, capacity management, and customer service (see Figure 1.0). Within each of these activities, there are both technology and process obstacles to effective integration. Furthermore, each activity must be closely tied to the others, in a web of synchronization, so that before a promise is made to a customer, a complete picture of the organization's operational capabilities are viewed. This goal is particularly challenging for e-fulfillment because such integration often involves external parties, like parcel delivery companies, and potentially a complex web of third-party service providers handling everything from Web site operations to telemarketing and fulfillment center operations. Integrating e-fulfillment activities is challenging enough for a company trying to do it all internally. However, when such a business model includes third-party service providers and other supply chain participants, it can become almost overwhelming. Luckily, advancements are being made that will make this integration easier over time.

Information Needs

Making good promises requires the exchange of large quantities of information. Consider the example of a customer placing a single order on a Web site. The customer first wants to know that the product is available. This requires that the e-tailer have a connection between its inventory management systems and its Web site that is 100% up-to-date and real-time. Then, the customer wants to know when the product will arrive. This requires the e-tailer to have a way of assessing available fulfillment and delivery capacity compared to accumulated demand in prior orders. Again, the comparison must be done dynamically and immediately. If the desired arrival date cannot be met with the e-tailer's standard delivery service, the customer may want a recommendation about the best way to get their product. Finally, the customer wants confirmation of payment acceptance, package tracking information, and other transactional information that will allow them to assess that the service promise made by the e-tailer is satisfied. A large number of interconnections and a great deal of information must be employed to present these answers to the customer.

One way integration will become easier is by the use of data interchange standards at a business process level. The Internet standard for this is XML, which allows information to be "tagged" in a meaningful way so that recipients can interpret and incorporate it into their own business needs. Traditional electronic data interchange (EDI) protocols that rely on periodic, batch exchanges of information are simply too slow to support most e-fulfillment activities. Data dictionaries, which define the meaning of the various types of information that can be exchanged in XML, have been created for only some of the industries that need them. The availability of such standards will improve as projects such as RosettaNet demonstrate more and more of the power of this level of business interconnection. However, XML interchanges will still likely be built one by one with trading partners. Andersen Consulting expects major application providers to increasingly incorporate this type of technology in their products, making it easier to create these customized connections.

The company Electron Economy typifies another route to tight integration of these activities, which is very specific to eFulfillment and the supply chain. Electron Economy seeks to create a standard interconnection model through a clearinghouse approach. By providing translation and physical interconnection services between service partners, they hope to make it simple for their customers to not

http://mann.ASCET.com 249

only create tight integration, but also to change their partners very rapidly as conditions dictate. For example, the clearinghouse will have pre-established connections with several fulfillment operations providers. A client company e-tailer will then be able to connect to the clearinghouse and access any or all of the already-connected fulfillment services. So far, this capability has been demonstrated only in a limited way. Ultimately, the extended network approach may give rise to closely cooperating groups of companies that can provide wide-ranging functional and geographic services, perhaps targeted to particular vertical e-tailing markets.

Process Needs

More than information is needed to make and keep good promises to customers: execution reliability is essential to actually making it happen. Consistency in execution is also needed, requiring consistent measurements that are relevant to the types of promises being made. Again, this can be very challenging when an e-tailer partners with other organizations for their e-fulfillment. For things to work well and reliably, each organization must measure things like process lead-time, quality, and productivity so that all participants work to the same performance goals that are directed toward the ultimate objective of customer service.

Capacity flexibility is another aspect of the process that is extremely important for effective e-fulfillment. During the 1999 holiday season, almost every e-tailer was troubled by demand that exceeded most predictions, which was many times the typical demand on fulfillment capacity. It is important to be able to recognize capacity issues in making promises to customers, but it is also important to be able to flex capacity upward by large amounts when demand dictates it. Otherwise, an e-tailer runs the risk of not being able to keep the promises it makes to its customers — and will take too long to fulfill orders in the desired timeframe.

Labor flexibility, which is a growing challenge due to low unemployment, is one way to provide flexible capacity. This approach places a premium on very disciplined training, supported by technology, to enable the quick integration of new employees into the process — employees who may only be with the e-tailer for a few weeks. Point-of-need training is a feature that is increasingly being incorporated into e-fulfillment models.

Capacity flexibility is also being achieved by creating a network of service providers that can take on a portion of the volume as demand rises. Obviously, this approach compounds integration challenges and raises the importance of the technology solutions discussed earlier.

Conclusion

Success at Internet retailing depends on effective fulfillment of customers' needs and expectations. This success requires well-run operations and a facility for making service promises that can be met, and then delivering on those promises. A complex network of information and process interconnections is required — something that has been difficult for many companies to achieve. As e-tailers increasingly turn their sights toward profits — not just sales — being able to do this continually and efficiently will be essential. Otherwise, customers will gravitate to those businesses that are best able to make and keep their promises, reliably and at a fair price.

Copyright©2000 Andersen Consulting LLP

Internet Fulfillment: The Next Supply Chain Frontier

written by: Beth Enslow
Descartes Systems Group
http://enslow.ASCET.com

The advent of Internet commerce has made it possible to buy and sell goods in near-real time with increasing levels of visibility and personalization of the order process. Business customers and consumers now expect this same speed, visibility, and personalization in the fulfillment process. To drive process efficiencies and meet customers' rising service expectations, companies must turn their logistics operations into high-speed, e-business fulfillment networks by leveraging key converging technologies. Companies that successfully master this transition will be able to create new business models and revenue streams around their e-fulfillment activities. Companies that stumble will lose preferred provider status because they will be unable to keep up with changing fulfillment models and customer requirements.

Logistics Follows Trade

Throughout history, logistics has followed trade – once you sell it, you have to get it there. Centuries ago, traders began selling Asian spices and silk in European markets, and logistics experts followed by building robust trade lanes connecting the continents. Similarly, we have now seen the rise of "Internet trade," with an explosion of online procurement applications, electronic marketplaces, and Web storefronts. Internet trade has led to a radical reduction in front-end order-taking times and the creation of new trade-oriented business models, such as those of Priceline.com, Dell Computer, and Amazon. However, e-commerce trade applications have also revealed fundamental weaknesses in traditional logistics models.

Throughout the 20th century, most companies were able to hide behind fulfillment inefficiencies because of elongated order cycle times and multiple inventory buffers. As we enter the 21st century, marketing, selling, and order placement can now take place in seconds over the Internet. This radical compression of trade processes has not been matched by an equivalent compression in processes across the fulfillment network (see Figure 1.0). Relevant fulfillment information is often hours, days, or weeks old by the time it is passed from one enterprise system to the next – and often electronic information is not available at all. At best, this leads to inefficient re-keying of information, further elongating information cycle times, and introducing data errors. At worst, relevant information is never shared, resulting in massive operations inefficiencies and poor customer service levels. The physical movement of goods is fundamentally constrained by this data latency, lack of connectivity, and lack of information visibility. In turn, this has led companies to create time and inventory buffers to protect themselves from uncertainty and variability in the fulfillment process. To solve this velocity discontinuity, what is needed are new fulfillment processes based on the notion of "Internet logistics."

Why Are Traditional Fulfillment Models Failing?

As customers become used to operating at "Web speed" in front-end processes, they are becoming increasingly impatient with poorly synchronized, long lead-time fulfillment processes that provide little flexibility and even less visibility. They are seeking fulfillment partners that can operate in "Internet time," characterized by agile, high-velocity processes.

Indeed, evidence is mounting that it is the ability to profitably meet continually changing

Beth Enslow is Vice President, Strategic Initiatives, for Descartes Systems Group, a leading provider of e-commerce fulfillment software and solutions. Prior to joining Descartes, Ms. Enslow spent five years at GartnerGroup, most recently as Research Director of GartnerGroup's Integrated Logistics Strategies Service, running its supply chain and logistics advisory practice on a global basis. Ms. Enslow has also worked for a number of other research and consulting organizations where she specialized in e-business and Supply Chain Management strategies and technology. She holds a mechanical engineering degree from Cornell University.

Retail

commitments made to customers over the Web that will separate the winners from the "wannabes" in the Internet economy. Anyone can post a product catalog on the Web; very few organizations can create personalized delivery experiences that optimize the flow of goods and information throughout the customer fulfillment network (see Figure 2.0).

The analog world now has to conform to the higher bar of the digital world. This means that enterprises must decrease their reaction times. Event-driven responsiveness and dynamic optimization are the price of admission to the digital economy. Rather than reacting to changes in customer demand and in internal and external fulfillment capabilities in weeks or months, companies must design fulfillment networks that can reconfigure processes, relationships, and roles in days, hours, and even minutes.

To create high-speed fulfillment networks, companies must first understand some of the structural barriers to fulfillment agility. One of the most significant constraints is the lack of real-time connectivity among trading partners. The need to increase agility to meet more dynamic customer demand requires shortening the time-to-plan horizon and lowering safety stock. This means that most companies must move rapidly to real-time information sharing. Without real-time information about what is happening across the complete fulfillment network (not only within the company), order fulfillment in the Internet trade environment becomes costly and difficult.

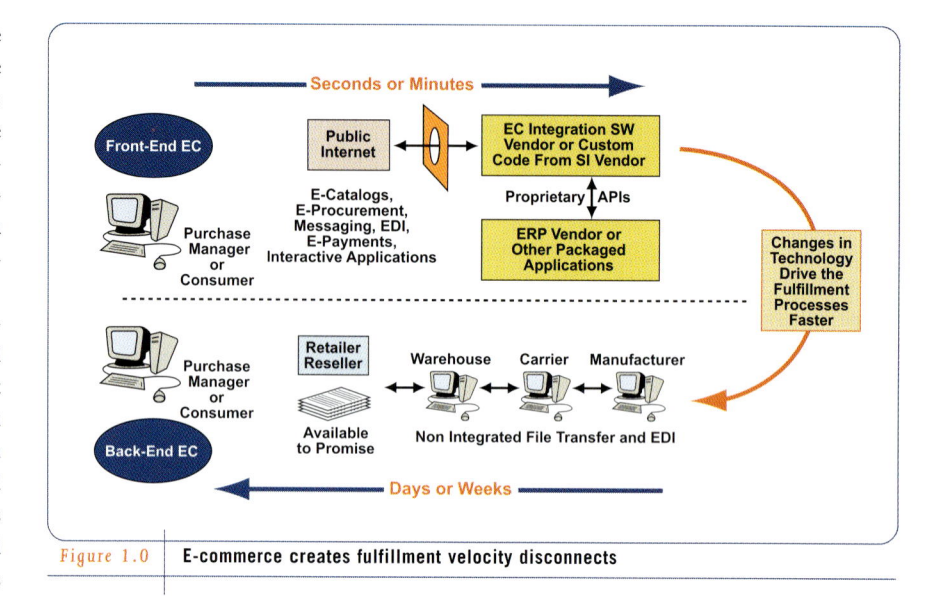

Today, the primary means of systems integration internally and across the fulfillment community has been on a point-to-point basis (particularly bilateral file copying and batch EDI), with many interfaces hard-coded (see Figure 3.0). Operating in the traditional application spaghetti environment not only results in long fulfillment cycle times and bloated inventory levels, it also means that changing trading partners or applications or adopting new business models is often prohibitively expensive and time-consuming.

In a world that increasingly values agility, traditional integration architectures and fulfillment systems are a handicap. Increasingly, enterprises are discovering that:

- The majority of information needed to manage high-speed fulfillment processes resides outside the enterprise.
- External data are often in formats and semantics that cannot be understood by internal applications.
- External data are often incomplete and dated by the time they are received.

Trading partners' business processes are difficult to understand and thus difficult to dynamically re-engineer relationships with because there is no shared meaning, data context, or common set of design principles.

These connectivity challenges are exacerbated by the fact that traditional fulfillment systems are transaction-oriented systems based on a monolithic data model focused on the enterprise. These traditional fulfillment systems:

- Lack the flexibility and compartmentalization necessary to integrate and interoperate in a high-speed fulfillment network.
- Lack the ability to make sense of process flows and events from a multiple-enterprise context.
- Lack the ability to provide visibility of the movement of goods and information across the fulfillment community, with user-defined, exception-based alerting.
- Are unable to provide personalized views of relevant information.
- Are unable to optimize processes in the context of the fulfillment community vs. a single enterprise.
- Are not built for dynamic business-to-business (B2B) collaboration, with concurrent decision dialogues.

Creating High-Speed E-Fulfillment Networks

The shift to the e-business economy is requiring enterprises to adopt new B2B

Figure 1.0 | **E-commerce creates fulfillment velocity disconnects**

Weblink

For more on fulfillment, see:
bruce.ASCET.com
fischer.ASCET.com
anderson-d.ASCET.com

For more on 3PLs, see:
prince.ASCET.com
peters.ASCET.com

For more on logistics, see:
prince.ASCET.com
hicks.ASCET.com
moore.ASCET.com

integration and knowledge-sharing strategies. These strategies require changes in processes and in supporting information technology. Every new client solution configuration, every new acquisition, and every new partner puts added stress on the integration capabilities of those business systems that have formerly been focused on optimizing the internal management of assets. Companies must embrace a new spectrum of B2B technologies and logistics models that are architected to be deployed across a constituency of trading partners, allowing them to cooperate and collaborate. A company's pool of assets, along with the assets and systems of its fulfillment partners, must be able to be configured into numerous, unique client-oriented logistics solutions. These tailored fulfillment solutions must be able to be rapidly reconfigured in response to new and changing product and service demands of different clients.

These high-speed, e-business fulfillment networks require a new IT architecture that:

- Captures, integrates, analyzes, and presents information residing in applications and information stores beyond the enterprise's boundaries, including wireless and mobile devices
- Masters issues of syntax and semantics in a distributed computing environment that often involves complex, hard-to-predefine business processes and information flow
- Is designed for zero-latency information transfer, so as soon as information is captured by the system, it is made immediately available to any other system (or user) that needs to know about the information
- Is event-based and workflow-enabled, interoperating based on external events (e.g., point-of-sale information that automatically triggers a shipment release, or proof of delivery that triggers an invoice payment)
- Contains real-time alert capabilities between companies and their trading partners
- Can be configured uniquely for each trading partner's point of view

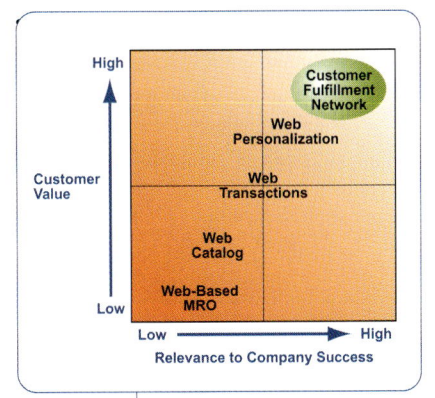

Figure 2.0 E-fulfillment is critical to customer satisfaction and market differentiation.

found in the distributed logistics environment, which are much more dynamic and complex than those found in most manufacturing processes

- Enables a company and fulfillment community to deploy different and changing e-business models by channel, product, and customer vs. forcing the organization into a rigid enterprise data model or process

High-speed e-fulfillment systems must be designed to integrate with external systems from the inside out rather than from the outside in. They must be built to accommodate, rather than exclude, external data, processes, or applications. And they must be designed to provide transparency of data and events to authorized participants throughout the fulfillment network, solving the issues of connectivity and visibility (see Figure 4.0).

E-fulfillment networks enable a company to:

- Quickly grasp control of the supply chain beyond "the four walls" of the business
- Improve inbound and outbound inventory visibility and thereby reduce inventory obsolescence and cycle times
- Increase outsourcing capability and leverage core competencies
- Gain a better view on performance within the business and throughout the fulfillment network
- Manage more fluid business relationships and higher velocity data and product flow
- Streamline distribution and remove fulfillment bottlenecks and redundant processes
- Achieve high-velocity, tightly synchronized business processes that can flexibly adapt to changing business conditions and objectives
- Develop personalized service capabilities and offerings for customers

Converging Technologies Enable Fulfillment at Web Speed

Creative destruction, the term coined by Harvard economist Joseph Schumpeter, is the continuous process by which emerging technologies push out the old. Creative destruction is rapidly occurring in the fulfillment world. The convergence of Internet technology, mobile and wireless devices, and dynamic optimization techniques is enabling dramatic restructuring of logistics processes. This convergence presents logistics professionals and business managers with an opportunity to create new businesses and revenue streams around redefined fulfillment processes.

Among the technologies that will redefine how fulfillment systems are managed are: 1) connectivity architecture, 2) supply chain visibility technology, and 3) dynamic optimization technology. These technologies enable organizations to build high-performance customer fulfillment networks, solving both inbound and outbound material flow visibility and real-time decision support issues.

Connectivity

To manage real-time supply chains, companies require an e-fulfillment network architecture that includes real-time source data collection and advanced B2B integration. Collecting data at point of capture and funneling it via a zero-latency messaging architecture to interested systems and users throughout the supply chain ensures a high level of data quality and timeliness. This makes planning and transactional applications more effective through more timely and higher-quality information flow.

http://enslow.ASCET.com   253

Increasingly, source data collection will originate from wireless devices that capture execution data in real time through the use of RFID tags, bar code scanners, GPS, Web forms, and wireless telemetry.

Advanced B2B integration solves the problems of heterogeneous syntax and semantics, and eliminates the need for point-to-point connections by using many-to-many message brokering techniques. This lets companies rapidly integrate disparate systems across trading partner boundaries, enabling more fluid business relationships. This makes it easy to plug and unplug trading partners and systems as business scenarios change.

Advanced B2B integration also supports channel-wide business processes while still supporting each trading partner's unique point of view. It supports information flow through the enterprise, between enterprises, and to individual users, allowing the synchronization of planning, scheduling, and execution processes using data from different systems and sources.

Most importantly, enterprises should realize that advanced B2B integration is not just about gluing systems together; it is about adding intelligence to the messaging environment. It is about creating new services, new revenue streams, and new efficiency opportunities based on the context of the information flowing through the systems. As the need to share resources and collaborate with partners becomes the foundation of process alignment and channel integration strategies, information interoperability will become the cornerstone of logistics strategies.

Visibility

Supply chain visibility technology involves the real-time monitoring and exception-based alerting of the movement of goods and information across a supply chain, including both inbound and outbound activity (see Figure 5.0). It lets fulfillment organizations gain tighter control and real-time understanding of supply chain activities beyond the four walls of the business. In many regards, it acts as a command and control system for the customer fulfillment network, enabling the monitoring and control of third-party activities like supplier lead times and carrier performance.

Providing real-time visibility of the movement of goods and information across the fulfillment network greatly enhances the network participants' confidence in the system. This directly translates into less "just in case" inventory and time buffers. Unlike reporting systems that tell you what's wrong long after you can do anything about it, supply chain visibility systems enable companies to proactively respond to fulfillment problems before they impact the end customer. This real-time service failure avoidance leads to customer service improvements through increased delivery reliability and timeliness. Moreover, enterprises can also use this visibility to spot opportunities for cost or time savings, such as merge in transit and cross docking, or to deploy delayed allocation and other advanced logistics strategies.

Because of the vast quantities of data surrounding the fulfillment process (some companies process millions of line items a day), it is crucial that the individual user be able to personalize the visibility experience and see only relevant information. A warehouse manager may want visibility of everything that will show up on the dock tomorrow morning so receiving and put-away can be optimized. A production scheduler may want to receive alerts only for supplies that are going to be late according to the production plan so that rescheduling or alternate sourcing can be done to insure that customer commitments will still be met. A customer service representative may want to receive alerts of all shipments that are going to be late to an important customer. A transportation manager may want to receive a carrier performance scorecard every Friday, with the ability to drill down to issues like lead-time variability by lane. A field installation worker may want to know when all goods are going to arrive at the customer location so that installation can be timed to coincide. This personalization of exception-based fulfillment information is what adds context and value to what otherwise would be just streams of transactional and planning data. From an interenterprise systems and scalability perspective, it is also important that the user can do the configuration and management of this personalization experience and does not have to rely on a database administrator to get a new view of fulfillment data.

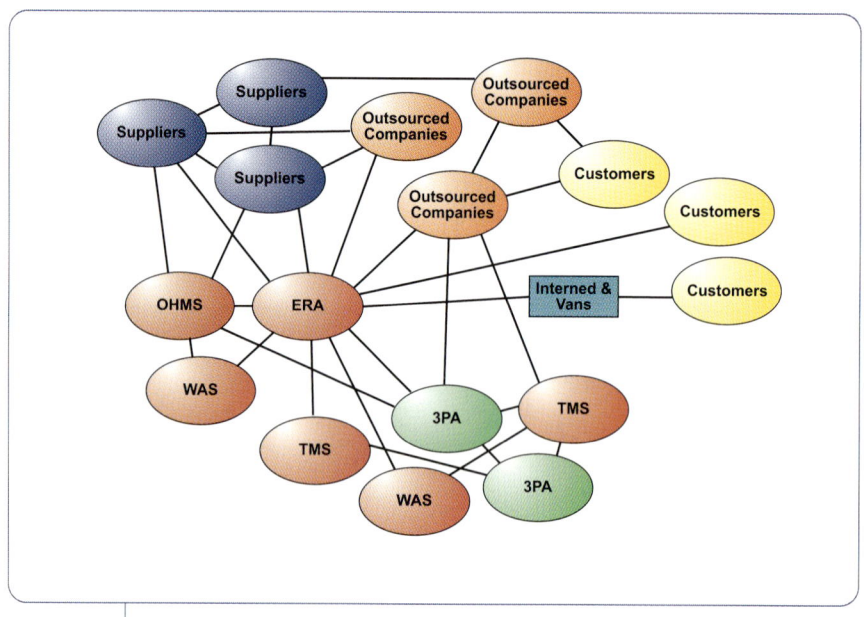

Figure 3.0 | Traditional fulfillment architecture: Application Spaghetti

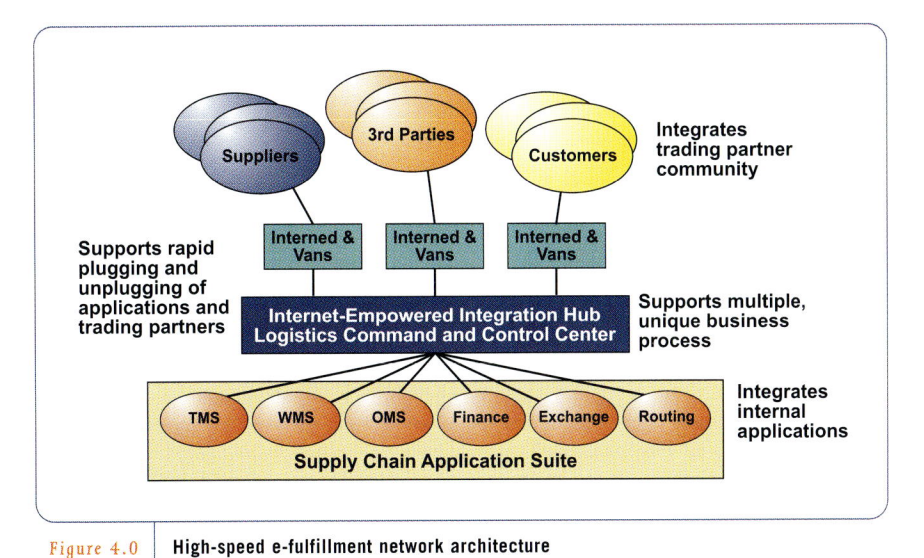

Figure 4.0 High-speed e-fulfillment network architecture

The data and performance information gathered by the supply chain visibility system also enables the fulfillment network to implement statistical process control and total quality management processes. For instance, statistically measuring on-time performance and lead time variability by product, carrier, and lane enables an organization to systematically search out and eliminate the bottlenecks, redundancies, and inefficiencies in the fulfillment network.

Dynamic Optimization

As fulfillment cycles compress in response to the radically shortened order cycle times of Web commerce, planning cycles will compress as well. In a world where marketing the product, taking the order, making or sourcing the product, and shipping the product may happen in the same day, there is an increasing need for optimization technologies designed for short-time-to-plan horizons. Fulfillment organizations must begin to adopt systems that can re-plan, re-sequence, and reprioritize in real time. If a truck is delayed, a high-speed fulfillment network cannot afford to wait until the next hour or day to re-route it; new plans must be produced in seconds or minutes. While linear programming and other techniques are appropriate for long time-to-plan horizons, techniques of dynamic optimization must be applied for short time-to-plan problems.

Creating New Businesses and Revenue Streams through E-Fulfillment

While a high-speed e-fulfillment network reduces inventory levels and operational inefficiencies, it is its ability to support completely new business models and create new revenue streams that is truly noteworthy. Following are examples of how companies can create innovative e-fulfillment strategies.

Home Delivery: Conquering the Last Mile

The exponential increase in Internet commerce is fueling interest in servicing consumers directly. As consumers increasingly use the Internet for online shopping, the delivery of goods and related services into consumer homes is increasing dramatically. Home delivery of groceries, "mobile concierge" services, and big-box items, such as furniture, electronics, and major appliances pose different logistical challenges from Web orders delivered to the home via small parcel. The former are items that may require special handling, installation, or other services associated with the delivery, or may require the customer's presence at the time of delivery.

Webvan, Peapod, Shoplink, and other leading Web home delivery companies have discovered that personalizing the delivery experience, increasing customer convenience, and ensuring delivery profitability are key to conquering "the last mile of the supply chain": delivery of goods and services into the consumer's home. Accomplishing this requires software that enables:

Fast, On-Time Delivery with Delivery Status Reporting (Visibility)

Customers expect goods and services to be delivered quickly and when promised; a disappointed customer will be less likely to place an order again. This requires the ability to accurately predict and execute on-time deliveries to the consumer's home or alternate pick-up location (e.g., their office). Customers want to know the status of their delivery. If the order cannot be delivered when originally promised, then they want a new estimated time of arrival. Meeting these requirements requires dynamic route optimization software with accurate driving distances, times and directions (not crow fly estimates), as well as a forward predictability functionality so that the consequences of a late delivery or a traffic jam can be determined for later orders and new ETAs or reoptimized schedules can be generated.

Customer Self-Scheduling (Dynamic Optimization)

Major motivators driving online shopping are convenience and control, so it is not surprising that consumers wish convenience and control over the delivery issue as well. In addition to providing rapid turnaround of orders and on-time deliveries within narrow delivery windows, consumer direct and home delivery companies will need to offer the shopper the opportunity to "self-schedule" delivery or service via the Web or a store kiosk – without the intervention of the seller. This requires a transition from traditional batch resource-centric scheduling (which only cared about optimizing driver and vehicle utilization from the enterprise's view) to a new generation of dynamic routing software that provides customer-centric scheduling. Customer-centric scheduling gives the consumer the ability to choose a delivery or service appointment time win-

http://enslow.ASCET.com   255

dow from a set of options, but the optimizer will only present the options that will produce efficient and productive route schedules. Real-time optimization capabilities let the system continually optimize delivery window choices as new orders are placed. Personalizing the delivery experience is proving to be a powerful way to build brand. Webvan, for instance, has built its brand around creating a customer delivery experience that allows users to select from multiple 30-minute delivery windows.

Mobile and Wireless Devices (Connectivity)

Mobile and wireless devices act as source data collection devices by reporting delivery status, collecting consumer information in the home, scanning totes and other delivery packages, and so on. This information can be used for a variety of productivity-enhancing purposes, including re-optimizing schedules, re-routing vehicles in real-time, and improving driving and service time estimates. These devices are also important as a receiving device for information – such as receiving new delivery instructions with new driving directions, or receiving repair or installation instructions.

Customer-centric delivery is only possible when supported by the proper technology. Many couriers today fail to make a profit on residential deliveries because they have not implemented supporting technology. Profitable home delivery requires real-time optimization of routes and supply chain visibility of inventory and orders. When combined with solutions for mobile and wireless communications and the ability to let customers self-schedule deliveries, home delivery suddenly becomes a viable proposition for Web and traditional retailers, manufacturers, distributors, and logistics providers.

Virtual Logistics Providers: Managing Complex Logistics Flows at Web Speed

A new breed of non-asset-based logistics providers are using B2B integration technology, supply chain visibility, and dynamic optimization to restructure traditional fulfillment channels. For example, Virtual Supply Logistics, a new logistics service provider, is creating a whole business around using these technologies to reinvent the fulfillment process of white and brown goods in the Asia-Pacific region. Specifically, it is leveraging these technologies to streamline the order fulfillment process in national retail chains in Australia and New Zealand, including industry leaders Harvey Norman and Vox Retailing. VSL will use B2B integration technology to integrate the retailers to white and brown good suppliers and to a virtual network of third-party delivery and installation agents throughout the Asia-Pacific region. This will enable home delivery directly from the supplier facilities, bypassing multiple nodes in the traditional fulfillment network, allowing dramatic cost reductions from the current process.

By using supply chain visibility technology to gain real-time visibility of the movement of goods and information across the entire fulfillment network, VSL can synchronize its partners' disparate systems and activities over a neutral information network. This will enable shipment directly from suppliers' warehouses to consumers' homes, with third-party service and installation workers coordinated to arrive at consumers' homes when the goods arrive, reducing the cost of delivery, decreasing damage rates, and increasing service levels.

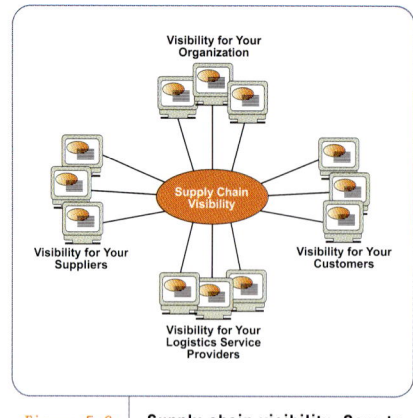

Figure 5.0 **Supply chain visibility: Core to e-fulfillment networks**

3PLs of the Future: IT Becomes the Competitive Weapon

Shippers are no longer looking to their logistics service providers simply to move goods and cut transportation costs. They also expect their providers to help them improve their supply chain processes and increase their revenue. Leading providers in the next five years will help their customers succeed with mass customization and Web commerce initiatives, and the management of multiple customer universes. This requires not just moving boxes but analyzing and redesigning supply chain structures and flows to increase their customers' supply chain agility and velocity.

Most third-party logistics providers (3PLs) are constrained from effectively managing their client base because they lack a real-time command and control system that supports multiple parties and business models. A number of Web fulfillment accounts keep passing from 3PL to 3PL because the logistics service providers do not have a high-speed information architecture to enable physical fulfillment activities to operate at Web speed.

The vast majority of 3PLs buy one IT system at a time to serve individual customers. The end result is a jumble of systems that prevent visibility across the customer base, and thus prevent leverage and economies of scale. To co-mingle loads, share capacity and labor, maximize continuous moves, and deliver time-definite service, providers must deploy B2B integration, supply chain visibility and dynamic optimization architecture, and tools and methods across all customers and extend those systems to customers to create multiclient networked systems. Logistics providers like Conway, Exel, and TNT are deploying e-fulfillment network architecture and visibility solutions that serve as a real-time command and control system across their multiple clients' fulfillment networks. This enables them to provide new levels of service and efficiency for their customers that were not attainable with previous generations of fulfillment technology. In effect, they are competing as much on their information infrastructure as on their physical infrastructure.

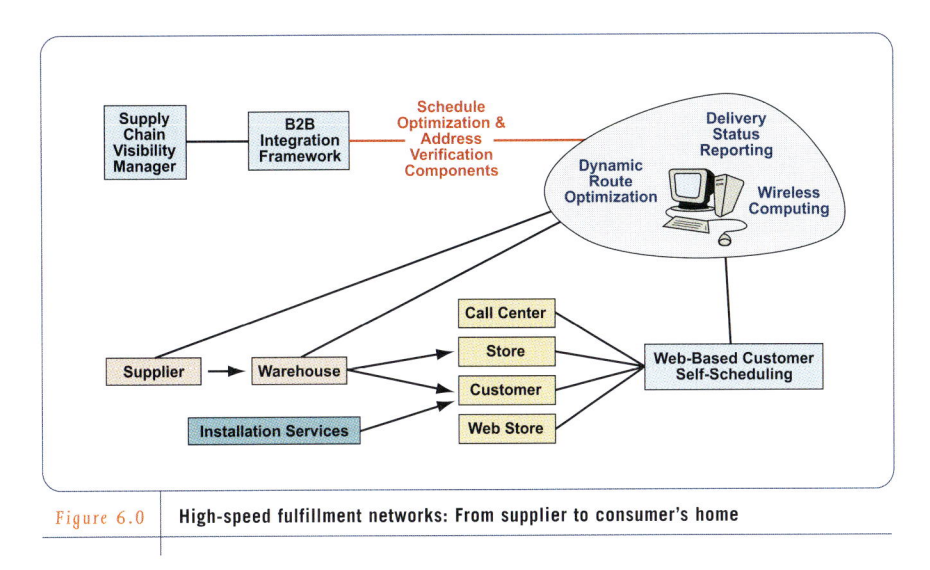

Figure 6.0 High-speed fulfillment networks: From supplier to consumer's home

workers. More than 500 Ericsson employees around the world now use the e-fulfillment system to track orders, proactively manage delivery exceptions, and monitor delivery lead-times and performance. Combined with organizational changes and tighter supplier oversight, this real-time connectivity significantly enhanced delivery performance and customer service levels and contributed to a 72% reduction in lead times and order-to-cash cycles.

Conclusion
The rapid adoption of Internet trade methods is driving equivalent innovation in Internet fulfillment methods. Enterprises now have the ability with e-fulfillment technology to reinvent fulfillment processes and relationships, creating brand new businesses and revenue streams, and reshaping entire industries. Key to success will be embracing technology that enables connectivity, visibility, and dynamic optimization across the fulfillment network. These technologies help slash transaction and interaction costs and let companies redefine the customer value proposition around the delivery experience.

Descartes' E-Fulfillment Software and Solutions
Descartes specializes in creating software solutions for e-fulfillment operations around the world. Descartes' B2B integration, supply chain visibility, and dynamic fulfillment optimization technology enable companies to create high-performance customer fulfillment networks – aka DeliveryNets™. These solutions empower organizations to deliver reliable, responsive customer service in a profitable manner and to create innovative new products and services. Descartes products are used today by more than 850 companies in 35 vertical industries and 50 countries worldwide. Customers include Webvan, Peapod, Shoplink, Virtual Supply Logistics, Rentway, and Ericsson.

Portals and Exchanges: Providing Fulfillment Information Services
Innovators will use e-fulfillment technology to create logistics portals and transportation exchanges, providing value-added information and business process outsourcing services in addition to providing simple access to a variety of transportation-related applications. These systems will enable more fluid business relationships and higher velocity data and product flow, reducing the need for data to pass in and out of every ERP system (typically by batch file or paper), as the goods and services flow throughout the supply chain. E-fulfillment systems let the marketplace manager leverage technology and processes across multiple customers, creating network effects. These network effects can include group buying power for lower transportation rates, the ability to dynamically balance demand across the transportation community, and the ability to communicate seamlessly with other community members.

While some logistics portals and transportation exchanges will be developed by start-up organizations, many others will be built by established organizations seeking to develop new services and revenue streams. Rentway, Canada's largest fleet leasor, for instance, has created a Web-based fulfillment information service for its customers. Customers can access the hosted Web service to obtain optimized local fleet routes on a pay-by-use basis. Key to the success of these portals and exchanges will be their ability to deploy an information architecture that can support the diversity of trading partners and their evolving business models.

High-Performance Manufacturing: Managing Global Fulfillment Networks
Global manufacturers and other organizations that must manage distributed logistics operations are deploying high-speed e-fulfillment systems to gain significant operational improvement and customer service enhancements. Ericsson, a global telecommunications system manufacturer, was unable to provide customers with timely delivery information because it had no visibility of the movement of goods inbound or outbound. Ericsson deployed an e-fulfillment network architecture and supply chain visibility system to connect and reconcile the disparate data semantics of hundreds of air carriers, freight forwarders, trucking companies, warehousing facilities, and field service

http://enslow.ASCET.com

Descartes Systems Group – A Leader in E-Fulfillment Software Solutions

Contact Information

Peter Schwartz
CEO
Art Mesher
Executive Vice President,
Corporate Strategy and
Business Development
Willem Galle
Executive Vice President
of Products & Technology
Pierre Donaldson
Executive Vice President
of Worldwide Operations

Products:
Descartes offers e-fulfillment
software solutions

Services:
Descartes offers application
hosting options for many
of its products.

The Descartes
Systems Group, Inc.
120 Randall Drive
Waterloo, Ontario
N2V 1C6, Canada
Phone 519.746.8110
Fax 519.747.0082
info@descartes.com
www.descartes.com

Descartes is the global leader in e-fulfillment software and hosted application services. Our Internet logistics software enables companies to reinvent logistics flows, creating high-speed, high-performance fulfillment networks – aka DeliveryNets™. Descartes is a publicly traded company (NASDAQ:DSGX) (TSE:DSG), with offices and customers around the world.

Our DeliveryNet solutions provide organizations with world-class transactional, visibility, and optimization technology to radically improve their fulfillment operations in today's high-speed Internet economy. DeliveryNet software and hosted applications are available for businesses that need to manage and optimize physical product movement (both inbound and outbound) or monitor outsourced fulfillment processes. These businesses include manufacturers, transportation carriers, third-party logistics companies, home delivery operations, field service organizations – and new market aggregators such as e-marketplaces, vertical portals, and transportation exchanges.

Descartes solutions are used today by more than 850 customers in over 35 verticals and 50 countries worldwide. Our customer base consists of blue chip, Fortune 1000 companies and start-up operations and dot-coms, including Coca-Cola, DeliverEtoday, Emery, Exel Logistics, Ericsson, Foster's, Nabisco, KNGT, Pepsi-Cola, Sun Microsystems, TNT, Virtual Supply Logistics, Webvan, and many others.

Global Logistics Network

Unlike traditional tools vendors or software providers, Descartes also provides an Internet-based Global Logistics Network. This network connects participants in the fulfillment community in a real-time, seamless information network. By leveraging the common ecosystem, participants can gain significant network effects, including:

- Lowering transportation costs through real-time supply/demand balancing and volume aggregation
- Enabling co-mingling and merge in transit to lower logistics costs and improve customer satisfaction
- Improving capacity utilization across global, intermodal networks
- Gaining instant capacity and load visibility across public, semi-private, and private sections of the ecosystem on an authorized basis
- Increasing fulfillment speed and reliability to end customers via collaborative logistics activities
- Giving participants a single point of connection to all other community members
- Accelerating the building of new fulfillment marketplaces and exchanges
- Accelerating selling into new markets and geographies; accelerating sourcing from new markets and geographies

What Makes a DeliveryNet Special?

Descartes DeliveryNets are proven, reliable, and highly scalable software solutions built on advanced Internet-based technology. Our solutions enable companies to achieve radical efficiencies in logistics processes and to deploy new e-fulfillment marketplace and exchange services.

Descartes is the only e-fulfillment software provider that combines core competencies in real-time business-to-business integration, supply chain visibility, and dynamic fulfillment optimization and execution technology. We

Figure 1.0 — Peter Schwartz, Descartes' Chief Executive Officer

believe these are the essential ingredients for running high-speed supply chains in a profitable manner.

Based on Descartes' e-fulfillment messaging and integration framework, called e-Frame, Descartes' DeliveryNet solutions let users dynamically manage and optimize the delivery of goods, services, and information through their entire value network – from their suppliers' suppliers to their customers' customers.

You can choose a portfolio to meet your e-fulfillment needs or create your own DeliveryNet.

Transportation & Logistics

DeliveryNet.LOG, for logistics providers, is the industry's only Web-based solution that combines real-time inventory visibility, wireless and mobile communications, transportation routing and scheduling optimization, and warehouse optimization, allowing logistics service providers to configure multiple customers' supply chain scenarios in one logical computing environment. This dramatically reduces the time it takes to bring on new customers, lowers operating costs, and lets the logistics service provider take advantage of network effects across its customer base.

DeliveryNet.LOG is a proven solution that runs on e-Frame, Descartes' highly scalable, multi-client open framework that lets logistics service providers integrate and manage a plug-and-play portfolio of applications, including third-party warehouse management systems, order management systems, transportation management systems, and supply chain planning systems. This lets logistics service providers gain more value from their existing applications and significantly reduces the cost of implementing new applications in the future. e-Frame also connects to external systems at customer or trading partner locations, creating a seamless information network to complement a logistics providers' physical network. This includes the ability to seamlessly bridge international trading partners.

Portals, Exchanges & E-Marketplaces

DeliveryNet.PORTAL enables customers to create new e-fulfillment businesses and revenue streams. Third-party logistics providers, transportation exchanges, e-fulfillment operations, vertical portals, and e-marketplaces can use DeliveryNet.PORTAL hosted application services to:

- Connect their community in a real-time messaging environment
- Streamline and optimize their customers' logistics activities
- Offer their customers value-added e-fulfillment services.

Descartes' growing Global Logistics Network also enables these organizations to connect new customers, tap into new markets and rapidly create new e-fulfillment service bundles, capturing time-to-market advantages. Special pricing for market aggregators allows these organizations to accelerate their customer value proposition without huge up-front investments.

Home Delivery & Consumer Direct

As the industry leader in serving delivery-sensitive operations, Descartes has more experience in optimizing routes and creating high-performance fulfillment networks than any other organization. Descartes has designed DeliveryNet.HOME to enable home delivery operations to create innovative service and delivery offerings for consumers while optimizing

http://descartes.ASCET.com

resource utilization.

DeliveryNet.HOME is the only home delivery solution that has the accuracy and precision in its data-collection and optimization techniques to allow users to guarantee delivery windows as narrow as 30 minutes. Only DeliveryNet.HOME offers Web-based self-scheduling for customers with advanced yield management optimization for the delivery operation. And only DeliveryNet.HOME offers home delivery operations an integration and messaging backbone – e-Frame – that can be used to integrate and manage internal and external fulfillment processes, connecting internal systems and integrating with suppliers, retailers, transportation carriers, third-party logistics providers, and third-party delivery agents.

Manufacturers

DeliveryNet.MFG is a proven solution that is unmatched in functionality, reliability, and scalability. It is the only solution on the market helping manufacturers manage millions of transactions a month across a global supply network, providing real-time integration and global visibility of product and information movement. DeliveryNet.MFG has been helping manufacturers achieve high-speed, highly reliable fulfillment processes for years using Internet-based technology. DeliveryNet.MFG does not require systems replacement; rather, it complements manufacturers' existing investments in ERP and supply chain planning technology by managing the dynamic logistics processes outside the four walls of the enterprise.

DeliveryNet.MFG is offered in a hosted environment to increase the speed of implementation and reduce upfront hardware and software investments. The hosted environment also enables manufacturers to benefit from the cost-saving opportunities associated with participating in Descartes' Global Logistics Network. Descartes' global presence ensures that implementations can be supported on a worldwide basis.

Field Service Management

DeliveryNet.FSM is the first solution that combines street-level route optimization with skilled worker scheduling, customer self-scheduling, inter-enterprise integration, and real-time inventory visibility. Serving as a real-time command-and-control system, DeliveryNet.FSM enables precise service and delivery scheduling, high-velocity service fulfillment, and increased asset utilization. Its optimization and visibility applications can be seamlessly integrated with customer relationship management systems. Built with a highly scalable, inter-enterprise architecture, DeliveryNet.FSM can support a global, multichannel field service or assembly operation or be scaled for a regional operation supporting a handful of routes.

Direct Store Delivery

DeliveryNet.DSD is a comprehensive solution for direct store delivery operations, supporting their need to manage the order process outside the four walls of the business. Features like dynamic geo-coding, dynamic routing and scheduling, route optimization, load optimization, merchandizing, off-truck sales, pre-sales, full route reconciliation, full unit accountability, promotional pricing, returns/empties management, vending, and DSD order management set DeliveryNet.DSD apart from any competitive offering. Route design and service policy optimization are intrinsic to the system architecture, enabling analysis of sales, profitability, service policy, delivery performance, and customer retention by route.

Built with a highly scalable e-business architecture, DeliveryNet.DSD supports large, complex distribution models and DSD companies in merger and acquisition mode, and scales down to meet the needs of local and regional DSD businesses.

E-Transport Software and Exchange Solutions

E-Transport, a division of Descartes, is a leading provider of Internet-based logistics software and exchange solutions for the multimodal transportation market, including deep expertise in ocean transport. E-Transport has a blue chip customer base which includes global leaders in transportation such as Maersk Sea-Land, K-Line, Hanjin Shipping Company Limited, Hyundai Merchant Marine and P&O Nedlloyd. E-Transport's pricing database is used by over 80% of the largest global ocean carriers and provides hosted software solutions to more than 1,000 shippers, carriers, logistics service providers and other intermediaries.

For more information on E-Transport, please read the E-Transport profile in this directory.

For more information on all of Descartes's solutions, please call 1-800-419-8495 or email info@descartes.com. www.descartes.com.

http://etransport.ASCET.com

E-Transport – Logistics Software and Exchange Solutions for Multimodal Transportation

E-Transport, a division of Descartes Systems Group, is a leading provider of Internet-based logistics software and exchange solutions for the multimodal transportation market, with extensive expertise in ocean transportation. E-Transport has a blue chip customer base that includes global leaders in transportation such as K-Line, Maersk Sea-Land, Hanjin Shipping Company Limited, Hyundai Merchant Marine, and P&O Nedlloyd. Its solutions are targeted at Business-to-Business shippers, receivers, carriers, freight forwarders, third-party logistics providers, e-marketplaces, vertical portals, and transportation exchanges. E-Transport's pricing database is used by over 80% of the largest global ocean carriers and provides hosted software solutions to more than 1,000 shippers, carriers, logistics service providers, and other intermediaries.

E-Tranport's hosted offerings

Logistics Contracts Management

E-Tranport's logistics contracts management automates the complex negotiation and price management of international transportation, a situation that has escalated because of the 1999 U.S. Ocean Shipping Reform Act. It allows cross-enterprise collaboration in creation of transportation service contracts.

Industry-Standard, Vendor-Neutral Rate Clearinghouse

E-Tranport offers an industry-standard, vendor-neutral rate clearinghouse that is used by shippers, carriers, and aggregators to rapidly calculate total bottom-line ocean freight costs.

For example, 16 of the top 20 ocean carriers in the world use E-Transport's hosted rate management software solution to offer rating services on their Web sites to their customers.

Real-Time Activity Monitoring and Notification with Performance Reporting

E-Tranport provides real-time activity monitoring and notification with performance reporting provides visibility throughout the transportation supply chain. It enables real-time problem identification and better tracking and management of fulfillment operations.

Cross-Enterprise Workflow Tools for International Freight Documentation and Processes

E-Tranport's cross-enterprise workflow tools for international freight documentation and processes seamlessly integrate shipment information across enterprises and complement existing enterprise-computing systems. They reduces shippers' and third party logistics transaction processing costs by up to $100 per transaction.

Participants can use E-Transport's solutions to optimize and streamline their own supply chains, as well as building their own marketplaces and exchanges on top of the network.

For More Information about E-Transport

For more information how E-Transport and Descartes can improve the way you look at logistics management and enhance your supply chain visibility, come to our Web sites or call us.

Contact Information

Robert M. Ryan
Chairman and Chief Executive Officer

Edward J. Ryan
Vice President, Sales and Marketing

Donald Stewart
Director, Business Development

E-Transport Headquarters
(Subsidiary of Descartes Systems Group)
200 Hightower Blvd.
Pittsburgh, PA 15205-1135
Toll Free 800.394.0020
Phone 412.788.2466
Fax 412.490.3599

www.etransport.com
sales@etransport.com

World Locations
Miami
New Jersey
San Francisco
London
Shanghai

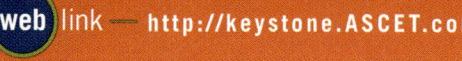

Keystone Internet Services – Providing Full-Service E-Commerce Solutions

Contact Information

Frank DiMaria
Sr. Vice President,
Sales & Marketing
201-272-3225
fdimaria@keystoneinternet.com

Todd Schenke
Marketing & Sales Coordinator
201-272-3265
tschenke@keystoneinternet.com

Keystone Internet Services
1500 Harbor Blvd.
Weehawken, NJ 07087
800.669.3535
www.keystoneinternet.com

Keystone Internet Services (KIS) is a recognized leader in providing full-service quality solutions to the e-commerce world. KIS provides clients with innovative logistics solutions, integrated marketing, merchandising, inventory control, and e-care/customer services that are enabled by our proprietary information technology platforms and total quality management processes. The KIS team continues to drive unprecedented growth and exceptional levels of return on capital by building solutions for customers that make them the best in their business.

Overview of Products and Services

A 50-year heritage has given KIS the advantage over others that do direct consumer order fulfillment. KIS has seen many changes over the years, ranging from technological advances in warehouse operations to the influence of e-commerce on retailers, manufacturers, and business-to-business. And Keystone has been in the midst of it all, constantly refining and enhancing their services.

E-Care/Customer Service is a direct link between you and your customer. KIS offers real-time order processing, and is ready to manage your Web and/or telephone orders 24x7 at over 1000 call stations. KIS call centers easily handle over 10,000 calls per hour and quickly and efficiently respond to e-mail inquiries. State of the art technology features Automated Interactive Response Services as well as Chat Management. But technology is not their only strong aspect – KIS representatives take over 80 hours of training and are frequently monitored for quality assurance; all so that you have peace of mind knowing your customers are being handled by professional, courteous, and well-trained associates.

KIS fulfillment programs offer an infrastructure that processes over 11 million packages a year. Your merchandise will be stored in environmentally controlled warehouses measuring over 1.2 million square feet. KIS state of the art technology allows for up to the minute inventory status and control, and ensures high quality standards. KIS picks, packs, and ships precious porcelain and fine apparel to large pieces of furniture. Specialized packing and assembly, kitting, and returns are no problem.

KIS also offers companies that want the security of maintaining their current inventory channel, but still want to launch an e-commerce solution, an innovative tool to help penetrate both channels. Warehouse-Within-Warehouse allows Keystone to run a "mini-warehouse" in your DC, which gets the product to your customers more quickly and economically. KIS can also work with your deconsolidators and "cross doc" retail distribution operators to build an integrated supply chain solution for your e-commerce channel. And this won't compromise your inventory planning! Warehouse-Within-Store is another solution that calls for Keystone's IT systems to manage Web orders, and pick orders from local store networks where the orders originate – using KIS personal "shoppers." This ensures better transit time for customers, current inventory channels are not disrupted, and walk-in returns are likely to come back to where they were picked.

Web site design, hosting, and maintenance is the hub of their customized services program. Your current site can become e-commerce-enabled or KIS can start from scratch to get your business on the Internet. KIS also offers customized warehouse scenarios including embroidering logos and initials on a variety of fabrics, laser etching that will engrave almost any surface, and KIS can even imprint designs on golf balls and tees!

Thus, KIS connects the e-world with the real world through plug-and-play solutions, using pioneered and proven systems for data warehousing and data marketing, as well as maintaining alliances with partners who drive Web traffic while providing complex trading networks.

Evolving E-Business:
Not the New Thing, Just the Next Thing

written by:
David Cavander
Dechert-Hampe & Company
http://cavendar.ASCET.com

Over the past decade, manufacturers and retailers have worked together in ECR, Category Management, Continuous Replenishment, and Focused Account Teams with the goal of dramatic cost savings. Trading relationships today are evolving to higher levels of collaboration, communication, and connectivity. The new goal is marketing effectiveness and consumer loyalty. E-business is accelerating the transformation by breaking down the barriers of time and space between manufacturers, retailers, and consumers. Attention has shifted to top-line growth and an emerging focus on collaborative one-to-one marketing. Manufacturers and retailers are now seeking to jointly develop consumer-driven marketing programs that are retail-centered and brand-focused.

Global Connectivity

Historically, large cities arose to facilitate trading. Similarly, large Internet communities today have arisen to facilitate social and commercial interaction. In North America, over 60% of households own a personal computer and most are connected to the Internet. Use of the Internet and the World Wide Web are growing "biologically." Usage is doubling every 100 days and is projected to be "invisible" within three years, which means that it will be as available globally as electricity, telephones, and VCRs.

In many industries and categories, Internet-based players now offer consumers dramatically new levels of customization and personalization in information and transactions. Dell Computer sells over $10 billion worth of machines via the Internet internationally. Traditional "on-land" retailers are going "online." As one very recent example, Wal-Mart just announced a strategic alliance with AOL as AOL acquired Time-Warner, the world's leading content provider.

Business Evolution

Most retailers and manufacturers today are Web-enabled in some form or another. So far these efforts have been directed toward providing information and access to consumers. The real economic power of the Internet is its ability to deliver cost savings. Many time-consuming and administrative business tasks can now be accomplished automatically within and across diverse computer systems and platforms. The order of magnitude of cost savings is in the range of 200-to-one or more.

E-Commerce Defined

E-commerce has two key components, the more obvious involving all aspects of business-to-consumer interaction. Typically, these activities are managed by the same traditional business entities that manage the offline interaction – marketing departments, advertising agencies, promotion agencies, direct marketing agencies, and Web developers.

The second and not-so-obvious component of e-commerce includes the whole area of business-to-business and trading partner activities, both on land and online. In the retail environment, these areas are typically managed by the purchasing function, and in the manufacturing environment these activities have been traditionally managed by the sales function.

B2C (Business-to-Consumer)

Traditional "push" and "pull" marketing methods over the past several centuries have largely involved one-way communications from the marketer to the consumer. In contrast, the Internet offers marketers a new capability for two-way communication and the ability to respond dynamically with "individual" consumers, provided consumers grant permission

David Cavander is a research analyst at Dechert-Hampe & Company in Mission Viejo, California.

Retail

for two-way interaction.

Relative to the Internet, consumers "opt in" to any given community or service in a market space of virtually unlimited choice. The Internet is an environment of "abundance," where the only real scarce component is human attention. As a consequence, Internet marketing really involves "membership" management.

And consumer membership is driven by factors such as attraction, community-building, and value-added content.

Many evolving Internet marketers are focused first on building relationships with consumers and only harvest revenue as a late step in the process. Since two-way interaction now matters more as a requirement for consumer involvement, traditional marketers will also need to increase their focus on relationship marketing.

B2B (Business-to-Business)

In today's marketplace, trading partner activities are simultaneously "going global" and becoming more consolidated. Over the past decade, both retailers and manufacturers have placed a sharp focus on cost savings throughout the supply chain. In many instances, these efforts have led to a range of mergers and acquisitions. For a typical retailer, 30 to 50 top vendors now generate the majority of volume and profit; conversely, for the typical CPG manufacturer, a short list of 20 to 30 top retailers generates over 80% of volume and profit.

In addition, manufacturers have accomplished dramatic changes in their supply chains. Categories that had involved miles of conveyor belts have been transformed into cellular manufacturing and global sourcing. Business units and divisions that operated autonomously have been consolidated with a common infrastructure.

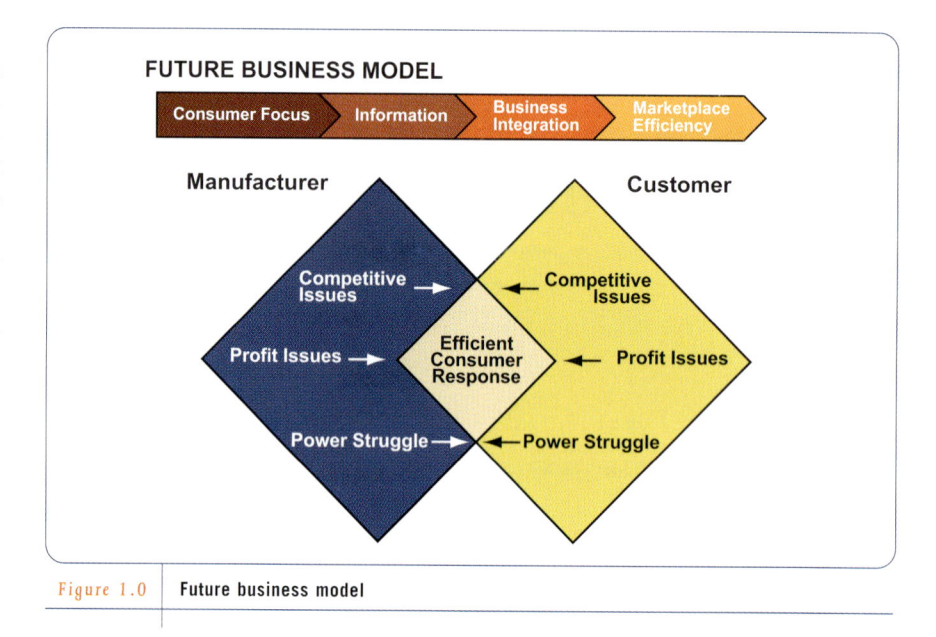

While costs today are still a critical factor, manufacturers are now concerned with product innovation, non-price-value added, and less complexity, and have begun compensating their advertising agencies using results based formulas. Also in the past 12 months or so, top retailers are re-addressing the issue of "growing the top line."

Go-to-Market Synergies

Physical location, which had always been a point of differentiation for the traditional retailer, is now both less and more critical. The less critical part is that consumers are now more willing and able to shop online, which may result in fewer in-store visits. The more critical part is that when consumers do visit a store, they will expect a higher level point-of-purchase "experience" while there.

The Internet has eroded the retailer's traditional sources of competitive advantage. For the retailer the implications of "Web-involved" lifestyles include:

- Higher consumer expectations
- More points of relative competition
- A narrower spectrum of unique value-added and differentiation
- A changing role for "brick-and-mortar" retailing

Manufacturers now compete with retailers and simultaneously have an increasing need for improved collaboration and business alignment. The implications of "e-lifestyles" for the manufacturer are:

- The mediums for the brand message are becoming even more fragmented.
- The importance of the physical store as a marketing medium increases.
- The integration of data for operational use is critical (causals, household panel, point-of-sale off-take, frequent shopper, relationship marketing).

The bottom line is that successful collaborative marketing is based on delivering brand relevance and richness as desired and perceived by consumers.

E-Construction

There are two key factors that drive overall success for both the B2C area and B2B activities. First, key aspects of consumer and customer loyalty are established through efforts at attraction, content, non-price value-added, and less complexity.

Figure 1.0 Future business model

Weblink

For more on ECR, see:
  hill.ASCET.com

For more on CPFR, see:
  lapide.ASCET.com
  uchneat.ASCET.com
  quinn-f.ASCET.com
  anthony.ASCET.com
  culotta.ASCET.com
  anderson-g.ASCET.com

WEB-ENABLED TRADING - HUB AND SPOKE

Snack Distributors, Wholesaler, Snack Distributors, Beer Distributors, Retail Warehouse → Hub ← Manufacturer, Broker, Store (Front, Back), Bakery, Soft Drink Bottler

Figure 2.0   Web-enabled trading

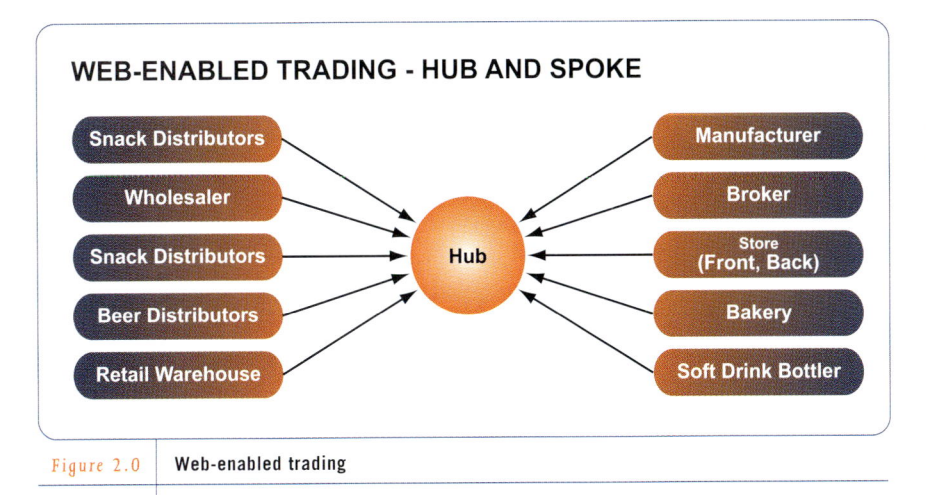

Second, the "behind the scenes" operations must truly deliver on the brand promise. This new, extended CPG enterprise achieves higher productivity through open connectivity, wide breadth and depth of communications, and collaborative strategies and operations.

ECR industry studies depicted traditional manufacturer and retailer trading relationships using a "bow-tie" analogy where business functions were isolated islands of activity. With the natural progression of business and trading practices in response to connectivity, consumer focus, and globalization, this working paradigm has evolved to the "diamond" analogy, where business functions now work continuously together on alliance teams. With e-construction, the "diamond" becomes even more "fluid."

E-construction involves optimizing the collective best assets of trading partners including brands, marketing resources, store formats, merchandising best practices, category management knowledge, promotional vehicles, sales force, brokers, planning tools, and more.

The first task is to "de-construct" the framework and workloads that previously held these assets together. Secondly, trading partners utilize new, Web-enabled tools to take away the barriers of time, space, and information. Thirdly, trading partners "re-construct" the extended enterprise for consumer deliverables that are better aligned with an "e-oriented" and "e-paced" marketplace.

The "bow tie" and ECR involved efficient replenishment, efficient merchandising, promotion, and administration. With e-construction, these functions are evolving and extending into the seven B2B building blocks of the "diamond":

- E-analytics
- E-procurement
- Global, collaborative marketing
- E-launch
- Web-enabled trading
- E-content asset management
- Online agents and robots

E-Analytics

Leading "brick-and-mortar" retailers have to work hard to create and deliver a unique in-store experience through store formats that are tailored to neighborhood conditions. Almost universally, retailers have a high need for market and consumer-profiling information that would allow even more detailed "tuning."

With Web-enabled information, services and online shopping, retailers and manufacturers are now working together to fully integrate online shopping data, loyalty program data, household panel data, point-of-sale off-take data (by store and item), and marketing mix information.

As a result, there is a new level of "operational intelligence" being delivered by advanced data mining and data visualization and predictive models of consumer response. For example, online retailers can now identify unrealized purchase potential by comparing a single consumer's behavior to patterns of similar individuals. As another example, Microstrategy Inc., a provider of retail decision support systems, has grown to over $200 million in profitable, annual revenues.

E-Procurement

Outside of the CPG marketplace, a number of industries have established global, Web-enabled "smart" supply chains. Leaders in these areas include Cisco, Dell, Boeing, Ford, Microsoft, Chevron, Honda, and others.

These companies often operate in a build-to-order (BTO) mode with ultra-low in-process inventories. For just-in-time re-supply, smart systems instantly pass final customer demand requirements to preferred or alliance materials and component vendors located around the world.

Leading providers of Web-enabled procurement systems include i2 ($400 million), Commerce One, Broadvision, and Ariba.

P&G is currently developing the "ultimate supply chain" for real-time, Web-enabled operations. Their vision is to integrate their entire forward- and backward-facing extra-nets. Their IT spending includes global collaborative technology, Web-enabled supply chain, data standards, and data warehousing.

Another P&G e-initiative is Reflect.com, a $50 million B2C partnership for beauty care. Reflect.com will sell personalized products exclusively over the Internet. Here P&G is creating a new brand in one of the richest consumer products categories – as well as cutting traditional retailers out of the pipeline. Fulfillment for these product is direct to households.

Global, Collaborative Marketing

Recognizing that the consumer now expects a high level of "personalization," both retailers and manufacturers need to demonstrate the "how-have-you-heard-me" and "show-me-why-this-is-for-me" aspects of marketing. Retailers are aware that manufacturers often have a broader

http://cavander.ASCET.com

and deeper knowledge and understanding of consumer motivation, in addition to highly recognized and valuable brands to offer. Conversely, manufacturers appreciate that top retailers generate significant store traffic and consumer trust through their own marketing.

Saatchi & Saatchi has recently formed a collaborative marketing division. They fully embrace the potential of the retail store as a marketing medium and view collaborative marketing between manufacturer and retailer as necessary, strategic, and long-term in nature.

To ensure and support its global customer development strategy, P&G has established market development organizations (MDOs), which are responsible for combining the plans of P&G's seven global business units into a single integrated program on a customer-specific basis including marketing strategy, customer development, and external relations.

In addition, global retailers such as Wal-Mart, Carrefour, Ahold, Metro, and Costco have recently begun to request global strategic and operational support from their vendors. Ahold recently conducted a global promotion across 4,000 stores in 17 countries to 30 million consumers.

To ensure repeat in-store visits, traditional retailers will need to increase their focus on building consumer loyalty. Consequently, Best Buy and Wal-Mart are already working closely with top suppliers to establish a Web presence and directly link online and on-land marketing activities.

Ralston Purina has been developing successful collaborative relationship marketing programs with consumers and retailers since 1990; Ralston Purina and iVillage recently announced a major content initiative tailored for women who own pets. Purina overlaps its own database with that of a grocery partner, such as Safeway. Matching households receive direct marketing incentives to visit the grocery partner's local store to purchase Purina O.N.E. Purina's O.N.E. product manager has stated that one of the most valuable uses of the database has been an improved understanding of how to target all of the communication vehicles used to market the brand. In addition, the relationship marketing has dramatically reduced the cost of consumer retention.

E-Launch

Typically, a new product launch is preceded by several years and upwards of $30 million in efforts that include strategic consumer research, consumer segmentation, competitive positioning, product design optimization, advertising development, test marketing, recipe re-formulation, factory scale-up, and more.

Recently, Microsoft and Best Buy announced a strategic alliance to develop and launch new Microsoft products within the Best Buy on-land and online franchise.

With the development of Shoplink.com, Homegrocer.com, Webvan.com, Wal-Mart.com, Petsmart.com, and others, there is now a significant capability to introduce new products without having to first fill the pipeline with finished goods inventory and to better focus trial and repeat marketing incentives.

As a further illustration of marketing synergies to be gained, Whiskas Pouches was launched on-air with a powerful link to its Web site for direct requests from consumers for samples as well as PC downloading of a streaming video commercial.

Web-Enabled Trading

Productivity studies have consistently shown that for CPG manufacturers using direct or broker sales and merchandising forces, 35% to 60% of working labor is applied to the paperwork associated with orders, invoices, deductions, and trade funds administration. Several ECR initiatives have sought to address improved transaction efficiency between trading partners. Examples include EDI, UCS II, invoice accuracy, collaborative planning and forecasting (CPFR), and efficient promotion.

Several new industry consortiums have been developed a range of Web-enabled standards. These include RosettaNet, UCCNet, and Microsoft BizTalk. These new Web standards address all of the core electronic data interchange and electronic funds transfer functions as well as utilize improved Web and database capabilities.

In the past 12 to 24 months, several progressive industry players have conducted two "scan-based trading" pilots. One of the key enablers of scan-based trading is synchronization of item/SKU and pricing information between trading partners.

For DSD distributors, concepts such as scan-based trading offer the potential of a 30% improvement in route productivity resulting from reduced back-door receiving activities.

The Phillip Morris Masters Program and the P&G "go live" formulas are examples of programs that are less complex and more automated.

In the U.K., Sainsbury has worked with Nestlé to run promotions using a new Internet-based information sharing and collaboration system. Sainsbury provides this system at no cost to over 3,000 vendors. The system allows all of Sainsbury's suppliers to work with buyers in planning, executing, and managing promotions. At any given point in time, their store system is conducting over 4,000 promotional activities or events.

In the U.S., viaLink offers a Web-based service for item catalogs and pricing synchronization. Early adopters of viaLink's central (and extra-net) hub include Kraft USA, Coors, Certified

> **E-business is not the new thing, it's the next thing. It's the natural progression of business and trading practices that strive for consumer loyalty, customer satisfaction, competitive advantage, and sustainable growth and profitability.**

FUTURE VISION: THE SMART SUPPLY CHAIN

Leaders have a Smart Supply Chain - extending their supply chain network in both directions with customers and suppliers. The results:

- Enhance ROA by improving materials/asset turns and managing down costs; customers have a 25% more efficient ordering process.
- Receive more than 90% of its product orders via the Internet.
- Reduced new product time to volume by three months, enhancing revenues by more that $200 million annually.
- Created a scalable system that enabled savings of $20 million annually through reduction in freight costs, revenue generation and reduced inventory.
- Improved accurate ordering and forecasting, which helped to increase customer satisfaction by 25%, while reducing the use of customer service reps.

Figure 3.0   Two Models for Getting Started

Grocers, and Ahold. In addition, a number of wholesalers and distributors, including McLane and Fleming, now offer Web-based information services to their retail base.

Content Asset Management

As stated previously, most of the consumer products marketplace's Web and e-commerce development has been focused on the business-to-consumer or "front-of-screen" activities.

Even the more established consumer shopping sites have not yet addressed the opportunity for Web-enabled business-to-business activities with their vendors.

Online grocers like ShopLink obtain item information and packaging graphics by either downloading this information manually from vendor sites, or through traditional delivery of materials by the vendor sales representatives. Due to time factors and other conditions, online retailers have needed to undertake their own photography of vendor brands in order to populate their online shopping catalog.

Interestingly, innovative and highly progressive on-land retailers such as HEB and Ahold are currently developing self-service and self-loading systems to be required of their vendors.

A typical CPG manufacturer creating advertising slicks, product packaging photography, promotional materials, and merchandising materials has annual digital media spending in the range of one to three percent of total gross sales volume. For a billion-dollar CPG brand, these go-to-market digital assets represent an investment of $10 million to $30 million annually.

Current Internet technology already exists to provide easy-to-implement, rapid development, integrated, and inexpensive solutions to manage these assets. "Content" databases, standards, and "push" communications can now fully automate the wide deployment and delivery of digital audio, images, video, and multi-media from manufacturers to retailers.

Infomediaries, Robots, and Agents

Internet technology takes away the barriers of time and space on many levels – individual-to-individual, member-to-group, group-to-group, B2C, B2B, headquarters-to-associate, headquarters-to-store, and others.

Any "cell" or "system" can instantly and simultaneously interact with any other element in the network. This interaction can involve potentially sensitive information (e.g., credit and credit card information) and significant online search time and effort.

For today's CPG marketplace, brokers are key intermediaries in the deal, the order, and the merchandising. Travel, automobile retailing, mortgage loans, and insurance are examples of industries that are currently being revolutionized by new kinds of online agents and robots. With the Internet, key functions such as price setting, coordinating exchange, arbitrage, and market making could now be accomplished globally and automatically.

In several states (e.g., Massachusetts and California), there have been a number of legislative efforts aimed at protecting consumer privacy for e-mail addresses and related information.

One area of public concern involves the integration of point-of-sale, media, shopper loyalty, household panel, and online information (and behavior). A common feature of many community and content sites is a voluntary "opt-in" step where individuals authorize in advance subsequent one-to-one communications as well as behind-the-scenes information sharing. Info-mediaries, who "know all about the consumer" and act as their exclusive agent when dealing with retailers or manufacturers, will be created. These agents will keep private information about individuals.

On-land retailers such as Petsmart and Wal-Mart are now offering a broad array of online services targeted at their unique shopper base. For Wal-Mart, these services include personal shopping aids, travel, a real estate company, an online pharmacy, prescription plans for employers, Chase Mastercard, and more.

http://cavander.ASCET.com

solution provider

web link — http://datamax.ASCET.com

Designing and Manufacturing Thermal Printers for the Bar Code Industry

DATAMAX

Contact Information

Marvin A. Davis
CEO

Willard (Bill) Nix
Senior VP Sales and Marketing

Bill Bouverie
Senior VP Engineering

Robert Wohlers
Chief Technical Officer

Datamax World Headquarters
4501 Parkway Commerce Boulevard
Orlando, FL 32808
Phone 407.578.8007
Fax 407.578.8377

Datamax International
Herbert House
Elizabeth Way, Pinnacles
Harlow, Essex CM19 5FE UK
Phone 44.1279.772200
Fax 44.1279.424448

Datamax designs and manufactures one of the bar code industry's broadest lines of thermal printers, offering printers in all segments of the thermal bar code printer market. The company also markets a range of portable, desktop, and online bar code symbology verifiers. Datamax continues to be one of the world's leading manufacturers of thermal bar code printers in terms of product volume shipped and installations worldwide.

The Datamax Home/Office Solution

The DMX E-3202™ is the first printer in Datamax's new entry level or E-Class™ product line. This direct thermal label and receipt printer is designed for a wide variety of on-demand printing applications meeting both POS receipt and coupon printing requirements, and low volume label printing requirements.

With a footprint of less than 6 inches and weight of less than 1.5 pounds, the E-3202 is suitable for all PC-based small office/home office labeling requirements. The unit produces high-quality 203 dpi text and graphic images at a print speed of 2 ips and supports a media width of 3.34" with an image area of up to 3.14" wide.

The Datamax Enterprise Applications Solution

Datamax offers the DMX I-4206 as the first in a new class of printer products targeted at the industrial 4-inch thermal printing market for such applications as ERP, Material Requirements Planning, Warehouse Management System, distribution, and manufacturing. Utilizing a 66mhz microprocessor and a 32-bit bus capable of print speeds up to 6" per second, the DMX-I-4206 is one of the fastest first label throughput printers available.

Some of the printer's optional features include a field installable thermal transfer mechanism and internal rewind, peel and present mechanism, on-demand present sensor, and external rewind that supports a full 8" OD supply roll. To comply with ever-growing network requirements, a Micro Print Server allows multiple users on various platforms to share the same printer through Novell NetWare, UNIX, Windows® NT, LAN Manager, Apple Talk and DEC.

The Datamax Solution for Heavy-Duty Applications

The new DMX-W-6308™ features tough all-metal construction designed to withstand adverse work environments, making it ideal for heavy-duty applications in the automotive, chemical, transportation, distribution, and paper-processing industries. The printer is manufactured with a powerful 32-bit 90-MHz Motorola Coldfire™ processor and 16 MB of standard memory, resulting in accelerated first-label throughput of variable-data printing. The unit prints a 6-inch-wide image area at 8 inches per second on a maximum media width of 7".

The DMX-W-6308 is equipped with an adjustable-contrast LCD front-panel display that provides total printer configurability and feature accessibility. The multi-language LCD can be used to configure options such as a rewinder, cutter, or peel-and-present sensor.

The High-Performance Datamax Solution

Datamax has introduced the DMX-ST-3210 direct thermal printer. Manufactured as a breakthrough product, specifically for use in the ticketing industry as a high performance, value-priced printer, the ST-3210 redefines on-demand printing price and performance criteria for industry specific applications.

've # Automatic Identification and Data Collection: Scanning Into the Future

written by:

John M. Hill
Cypress Associates

Brett Cameron
Datamax Corporation

http://hill.ASCET.com

The success of Supply Chain Management (SCM) as a vehicle for improved productivity and improved return on investments often overshadows the fundamental components that make SCM a reality. One of these components is the bar code. For the benefit of the newcomer, this paper briefly outlines what Supply Chain Management is, how the Automatic Identification and Data Collection (AIDC) industry and bar coding affect SCM, and how SCM systems can benefit from the bar code application technologies of today and tomorrow.

Supply Chain Management

Supply Chain Management is defined generally as a process-oriented, integrated approach to procuring, producing, and delivering products and services to customers. SCM has a broad scope that includes sub-suppliers, suppliers, internal operations, trade customers, retail customers, and end-users. SCM covers the management of material, information, and funds flow. Simply stated, SCM is the science of moving or processing "something" to "somewhere." It is fueling the rebirth of the Industrial Age by reducing costs, improving service, enhancing revenues, and empowering both the providers and users of products and services.

The advancements in manufacturing, transportation, and the development of computer and communication technologies ("the information technology revolution") have, without a doubt, aided in the development and explosive growth of SCM in today's economy. Some of these advances have been born out of the Automatic Identification and Data Collection (AIDC) industry. Commonly known as the "bar code" market, the AIDC industry has been at the forefront of both the bar code and bar code data capture development; it has dramatically improved the amount of data transferred and the success at which it is accurately collected. Bringing portability, standardization, and validation to the data that drives the SCM world has been the single task of the AIDC industry. What is done with that data — how it is collected, processed, communicated, stored, or otherwise manipulated — determines its value as computers and networks come to be regarded as technology tools for enterprise coordination.

What is AIDC?

AIDC is Automatic Identification and Data Collection. All code-reading systems share the following features:

First, there is a product, part, component, package, pallet, tote box, barrel, etc. Accurate identification of this item, while moving into or through production, warehousing, or the distribution pipeline, will contribute to higher throughput, lower labor costs, more efficient handling, increased security, more accurate audit trails, or some combination of them all.

Next, a label, tag or coding device is affixed to the item so that it can be automatically read to identify what the item is, where it came from, where or to whom it's going, or whatever else might be needed by the user.

And then an automatic or hand-held bar code reader, optical character reader, magnetic stripe reader, vision system, or radio frequency interrogator will read the code, validate it, and convert the content into system-meaningful control and information output.

Finally, the code reader transmits the output to networked PC's, mini-computers, relays, solenoids, microprocessors, programmable controllers, diverters, counters, video displays, horns, bells, whistles, etc....for data manipulation or communication.

John M. Hill of Cypress Associates, Supply Chain System Solutions, is a member of the board of directors at Datamax Corporation.

Brett Cameron is director of product marketing at Datamax Corporation.

Electronics & High Tech

http://hill.ASCET.com   269

Why Automatic Identification?

Today, JIT, Quick Response, Efficient Consumer Response (ECR), and contemporary SCM systems all address the productivity challenges that businesses have faced for years.

Most firms recognize that control of raw material, semi-finished, and finished goods inventories from receipt through processing to shipment and sale is fundamental to improved productivity. Tighter stock control leads to faster order turnaround, improved resource utilization, lower inventory investment, and reduced costs.

Further, a simple reduction in time per unit produced may well be counter-productive without enhancement of the discipline and control that guard the integrity of receiving, processing, assembly, packaging, storage, shipping, and transportation operations.

The best decision-making is executed on the basis of feedback on events while, not after, they occur. It follows, then, that to achieve greater productivity, contemporary systems must provide discipline and control that is based not only upon plans and performance goals, but also upon the dynamics of the actual operation. These are not new concepts. Their mastery, however, has become critical to survival.

Automatic identification systems have emerged during the past 30 years as the major source of real-time feedback. They allow businesses to monitor operations, manage resources, and flag anomalies before they impact throughput and launch the JIT and Quick Response programs, which have been so important to growing market share and the bottom line.

Technologies for Automatic Identification

Included under the automatic identification umbrella are the following technologies:

- Bar Code
- Optical Character Recognition
- Radio Frequency Identification (RFID)
- Machine Vision
- Magnetic Stripe
- Smart Cards
- Touch Memory
- Voice Data Entry
- Radio Frequency Data Communications (RFDC)

Worldwide automatic identification sales have grown from about $1 billion in 1986 and are expected to reach $10 billion in 2000. Although the lion's share of the market belongs to bar code, other technologies have gained acceptance in those applications where they provide the better solution. Users generally find that the technologies are more complementary than competitive.

Coding for Automatic Identification Systems

Codes, code media, and coding devices are the key to and the Achilles' heel of automatic identification systems. Prospective users should take the time to familiarize themselves with the alternatives – and carefully evaluate them in the light of their specific application requirements. Coding for identification systems consists of the following five major elements:

- Code Content – The characteristics and amount of data to be encoded as well as the symbology or coding algorithm
- Code Medium – The materials to be used to fabricate the code or coding device
- Code Generation – The method of fabrication
- Code Verification – The technique(s) used to check the quality and readability of the code
- Code Application – How the code is affixed to the item

The size and format of the code will depend not only upon content but also upon available coding area, the nature and speed of product flow, and the type of reading equipment to be used.

Medium selection, generation technique, and application method will depend upon the intended uses and the environment in which the code will be expected to perform. Assessment of the myriad of options available must be thorough, as the one selected can well determine the success or failure of the entire SCM process.

The Bar Code

The Technology
Early bar code scanners used a white light source or helium-neon laser, rotating mirrors, and sensors to locate, read, and decode miniature patterns with high data content anywhere within a field of view then as much as two feet high by two feet deep. Sweeping through this field at rates of up to 360 times per second, scanners took several looks at each code as it passed and compared and validated them prior to providing an output. Given proper code design, the devices accommodated wide variations in code alignment and orientation. Their capabilities represented a major breakthrough in automatic data capture.

Background
In 1933, initial patents covering the use of optical sensors for package sortation were issued in Switzerland. On October 20, 1949, Norman Woodland and Bernard Silver filed a U.S. patent application, disclosing the first bar code symbology as well as an optical scanner that could read intelligent codes on the fly.

Until the mid-1960s, the primary focus of identification technology was in the area of direct machine control – from conveyor line sortation to automatic bobbin replenishment in textile mills. Early systems

---

Weblink

For more on procurement, see:
  evans.ASCET.com
  quinn-f.ASCET.com
  herbold.ASCET.com
  fischer.ASCET.com
  culotta.ASCET.com

For more on data management, see:
  ramanathan.ASCET.com
  srivastava.ASCET.com
  manheim.ASCET.com
  johnson.ASCET.com

used photo-electrics and retro-reflective inks and tape arranged in machine-readable formats or patterns. The systems were invariably justified on the basis of labor cost reduction.

In the 1960s, railroads around the world evaluated optical code readers for automatic rail car identification and the grocery industry launched its program for automating supermarket checkout.

Although labor savings were cited as the basis for justification of investment, the pioneers saw significant additional potential in the real-time information provided by these systems that identified items-in-process with unique multi-digit serial numbers. The main thrust of the rail industry program was improved utilization of the existing rail car fleet through better, more timely visibility of car location. That of the grocery industry was tighter control of inventories, stock replenishment, and check stand security.

In 1969, Volkswagen installed the first white-light moving beam scanner to identify and count components moving along an overhead conveyor line. In 1971, Buick Motor Division of General Motors installed the world's first industrial laser scanning system to count transmissions as they moved from production to shipping on a power and free conveyor.

Within two years, pioneers at Kimberly Clark, Scott Paper, General Trading, Kroger, and a number of other consumer products companies had implemented scanning systems to control the flow and sortation of finished products to shipping. In every case, labor cost reduction was used for purchase justification. The real payoff, however, came from improved visibility, accuracy, discipline, and control of line operations.

Automatic Identification Manufacturers (AIM) & Bar Code Standards

In 1971, a group of five companies including Computer Identics, Identicon, MEKontrol, 3M, and the Electronics Corporation of America met in Pittsburgh with executives of the Material Handling Institute, Inc. (MHI). Their objective was to examine the possibility of forming a trade group to legitimize and promote the use of identification technology for tracking and controlling product movement in manufacturing and distribution. Chartered in 1972 as the Automatic Identification Manufacturers (AIM) product section of MHI, the group's first roster included nine companies with estimated total identification product sales of less than $25 million. An independent, global trade association today, AIM lists over 170 member companies with annual sales projected to reach $10 billion by the year 2000.

Although the AIM umbrella covers the range of identification technologies available, there is little doubt about the significant impact of its efforts on the dramatic growth of the bar code market segment.

In spite of early successes in the automotive industry and consumer products warehousing industry, growth during the 1970s was slow. A primary constraint on growth was suppliers' reluctance to collaborate on code or symbol standards for non-point-of-sale applications, and user concern that a premature purchase might leave them with a non-standard, unsupported solution. In the material-handling sector, conveyor and storage system suppliers were generally reluctant to sponsor bar code implementation unless specifically requested by the client. The situation began to change a few years later with pressure for symbology standardization from the government and consumer product manufacturers.

In conjunction with inter-industry Federation of Automated Coding Technologies (FACT), the Uniform Code Council (UCC), and other organizations, AIM has developed standards for manufacturer identification programs, symbology specifications, symbol and equipment testing, academic curricula, and related seminars and conferences.

Today, formal standards have been promulgated by the United States Department of Defense, the American National Standards Institute (ANSI), and such industry organizations as the Automotive Industry Action Group (AIAG), the Health Industry Business Communications Council, the Telecommunications Industry Forum, and a host of other trade and professional groups worldwide.

Primary symbologies for which standards have been developed include:

- Universal Product Code (UPC)/ European Article Number (EAN): The numeric-only, linear symbols developed for grocery supermarket point-of-sale applications in 1973 and now widely used in a variety of other retail markets. UPC/EAN are fixed-length codes suitable for unique manufacturer and item identification only. They are not often used in the manufacturing or warehouse environment.
- Interleaved 2-of-5 Code: A compact, numeric-only, linear symbology used in a number of applications where alpha character encoding is not required; e.g., the current standard for grocery shipping container ID (SCC-14).
- Code 39: An alphanumeric, linear symbology adopted by a wide number of

> **Automatic identification systems have emerged during the past thirty years as the major source of real-time feedback. They allow businesses to monitor operations, manage resources, and flag anomalies before they impact throughput, and launch the JIT and Quick Response programs, which have been so important to growing market share and the bottom line.**

http://hill.ASCET.com

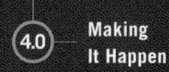

industry and government organizations for item and shipping package and container identification.

- Code 128: The linear symbology of choice for Quick Response and Efficient Consumer Response (ECR), Code 128 provides the architecture for high-density encoding of the full 128-character ASCII set, variable length fields, elaborate character-by-character, and full symbol integrity checking. It provides the highest numeric-only data density for a linear symbol. UCC/EAN-128 was adopted in 1989 in the U.S. by the Uniform Code Council (UCC) and internationally by EAN International (European Article Number Association) for serialized shipping container identification (SSCC-18).
- Two-Dimensional Stacked and Matrix Symbologies: Two dimensional symbols emerged during the late 1980s as a result of improvements in scanning technology and requirements in some sectors for encoding large amounts of data in relatively small areas.

Two-dimensional stacked symbology, PDF-417, has the capability of encoding up to 2,000 characters in four square inches, the equivalent of the entire Gettysburg Address. Two-dimensional codes allow companies to add quality assurance, traceability, and reliability to the manufacturing and distribution process. The benefits of 2-D symbologies include more data capacity and improved error correction. 2-D symbologies represent tomorrow's technology in practice today.

The AIDC industry is constantly developing new and better ways of improving total Supply Chain Management; for example controlling processes through a manufacturing line to effective warehouse and inventory management, and then tracking the movement of goods in the distribution and delivery chain, right into the retail store and beyond. Primary areas of focus for AIDC development include manufacturing (WIP, product ID, location), goods receiving, inventory control, warehouse management, shipping, finished goods or packing, distribution (finished goods, pick/putaway), and transportation (compliance labeling, electronic data interchange).

SCM and AIDC Tomorrow:
Radio Frequency Identification (RFID)

The future of AIDC will represent unprecedented growth of SCM opportunities. The AIDC industry is taking the current technology of radio frequency identification (RFID) and expanding its breadth and scope to improve the total supply chain and information transportation marketplace.

RFID is an automatic identification technology which complements scanned 1-D and 2-D bar codes, while extending the applicability of data capture and computing products. RFID tags carry data that can be modified using radio frequency technology. In essence, each tag carries an electronic memory. This feature fits into SCM where information is to be exchanged, modified, or collected without reference to a common database. The ability to write/validate and print on demand, under the guidance of the International Standards Organization (ISO) concerning the standardization of RFID for "Item Identification," has opened a floodgate of opportunities and applications for variable on-demand RFID labeling.

SCM is a fundamental component in the business community and our daily lives. Technology, automation, and competition will continue to improve the SCM process. To that end, the Automatic Identification and Data Collection market will continue to improve on its current technologies while developing new and exciting products that will propel the SCM process forward. The AIDC industry will continue to encourage clients to implement new and improved SCM processes, and will aid in successfully providing what all businesses desire – customer satisfaction.

Fasturn – Transforming Apparel Industry Transactions for Buyers and Sellers

Contact Information

Dr. Frank Litvack
CEO and Co-Founder

Marilyn Tam
Chief Operating Officer and President

Owen Tucker
Vice President, Supply Chain

Janet Fox
Vice President of Global Markets

Marti Umphrey
Director of Global Marketing
Phone 310.407.2604
Fax 310.407.6990

Fasturn, Inc. Headquarters
2029 Century Park East,
Suite 1401
Los Angeles, CA 90067
Phone 877.Fasturn
Fax 310.407.2689
info@fasturn.com
www.fasturn.com

Fasturn transforms the way buyers and sellers in the $100 billion apparel industry meet and manage their transactions. Currently, widely disbursed marketplaces make it difficult for all but the most efficient apparel companies to effectively access the best suppliers and manage transactions. Moreover, in today's fast-moving fashion industry, quickly changing trends put great pressure on companies to increase the efficiency of their procurement and sales operations. With Fasturn, buyers and sellers in the global apparel marketplaces connect, finding the tools, services, and information that they need to optimize the potential of their business. Fasturn users enjoy lower prices, improved quality, shorter transaction cycles, and a rich information exchange.

Buying and Selling

Fasturn provides industry-specific tools to facilitate any sourcing or sales need. A sophisticated procurement engine empowers Fasturn users to source goods from qualified facilities located around the world. In addition, Fasturn offers a wholesale e-marketplace where sellers can display their goods in password-protected virtual showrooms and offer fixed-price sales or auctions.

Transaction Management

Fasturn is the first online trading community to incorporate the advantages of Supply Chain Management (SCM) technology with a powerful procurement and e-commerce platform. Fasturn facilitates management of the buying process by alerting users to problems at the earliest possible moment in the procurement process, giving the user an opportunity to react and assess timely solutions to the problem. The clear advantage of using Fasturn is the avoidance of unpleasant surprises, more efficient management of transactions, and the reduction of transaction cycle time and process costs.

Transaction Support

The services and information offered by Fasturn include up-to-date quota information, inspection and quality control services, logistics support, customs clearance, credit verification, online payment and collection processing, and transaction risk insurance.

Who is Behind Fasturn?

The Fasturn team includes an experienced group of industry and business professionals located in Los Angeles, New York, and Seoul, Korea. Fasturn maintains affiliated offices in all major commerce centers such as Asia and Latin America. Major partners include i2 Technologies for its SCM technology, CIT, and Finova for factoring and finance matters, Expeditors International, Robert Krieger International, and Carmichael International for logistics and customs clearance support, Scient for assistance in development of e-commerce strategy, and The SGS Group for factory inspection and certification.

A Case Study – VF Corporation Meets IT Integration Needs with NEON's MQSeries Integrator

Contact Information

George F. (Rick) Adam, Jr.
Chairman & CEO

Pat J. Fortune
President & COO

Harold A. Piskiel
Executive Vice President & CTO

Robert I. Theis
Executive Vice President & CMO

New Era of Networks, Inc. Headquarters

6550 Greenwood Plaza Blvd.

Englewood, CO 80111

Toll Free 800.815.NEON (6366)

Phone 303.694.3933

Fax 303.694.3885

www.neonsoft.com

Products and Services

e-Business Application Integration (e-AI)

NEON e-Biz Integrator™ -
The integration backbone for the extended enterprise.

NEON e-Biz 2000™ -
An integration server for small to medium enterprises.

VF Corp, Greensboro, NC

The next time you're at a department store trying on jeans or browsing through the lingerie department, chances are you will encounter products manufactured by VF Corporation. For over 100 years, Greensboro, NC-based VF Corp. has ranked among the largest apparel makers in the world, although its identity is hidden largely behind the high-profile brand names it manufactures and sells. These include such well-known labels as Wrangler, Lee, and Rustler jeans; Bolero, Lou, Siltix, Vassarette, and Vanity Fair intimate apparel; JanSport daypacks; Jantzen swimsuits; and Red Kap occupational clothing and uniforms, to name just a few.

The Challenge

With current revenue approaching $6 billion per year, and a goal to hit $7 billion by 2001, VF Corp. is spearheading sales through its consumerization initiative, a drive to focus its key business processes on identifying and fulfilling consumer needs. For example, the company wants to be able to predict precisely what brand, color, and quantities of jeans to supply retail stores in each geographic area at various times of the year.

Achieving this level of supply chain planning has meant completely reengineering its operations. Lead by CEO Mackey McDonald, VF Corp. launched an aggressive program of across-the-board restructuring, consolidating 14 separate divisions into five "coalitions": Jeanswear (including workwear), Intimates, Playwear, Knitwear, and International Operations and Marketing. Previously, each division operated as an autonomous entity, with its own sales and marketing operations, financial systems, and IT infrastructure. Now the entities of the coalitions needed to work together.

John Davis, then a divisional CIO and now Vice President, Business Systems-Supply Chain, was part of a task force chartered with implementing common IT systems for the company. "We faced a huge integration challenge combining 14 disparate operating environments into one common set of IT systems," Davis relates. "Shared information services was a crucial part of the corporate consolidation. It was only after we entered the planning stage, however, that we realized what a huge task we had laid out for ourselves."

In 1996, after an exhaustive examination of best practices both internal and external, VF Corp. had refined its business processes and decided to buy best-of-breed software packages to implement them. The company chose SAP R/3 ERP software as its core transaction system. Other software packages included Logility for forecasting and demand planning, i2 Technologies' Rhythm for supply chain planning and scheduling, data mining tools from SAS Institute, and Gerber PDM for apparel product development, specification, and merchandising. "We bought a lot of packages which increased the magnitude of the integration challenge," Davis recalled. SAP R/3 includes many pre-integrated functions, but it still needed to be customized to handle the uniqueness of the apparel industry. In addition, VF Corp. had numerous homegrown systems, which it wanted to retain and enhance.

The integration team quickly realized that traditional file transfer protocols, which require point-to-point interfaces, would be woefully inadequate for these complex integration challenges. "It would have been impossible to manage this level of integration with the types of point-to-point interfaces we used in the past," Davis recalls. "Even if we could overcome the initial development challenges, it would be too costly to maintain and inherently unreliable. We needed a more flexible application integration solution."

The Applications Solution Strategy

Davis consulted his colleagues within the manufacturing industry, as well as experts such as GartnerGroup, for enlightenment. Gartner analyst Roy Schulte confirmed Davis' hunches, asserting that a typical large enterprise devotes 35% to 45% of its programming efforts to developing and maintaining programs whose only purpose is to transfer information among systems. Davis thought even these percentages were low. "Knowing that we were going to be moving a lot more data between different systems than your average company, we were probably looking at around 60% of programming time dedicated exclusively to routing and formatting messages between applications running on different databases," he said.

To help with the physical intricacies of creating system to system interfaces, VF Corp. purchased IBM's MQSeries® in 1997, a year before it planned to roll out its new information systems. MQSeries provides "any-to-any" connectivity on more than 35 computing platforms. However, it doesn't give developers an automated method for routing, transforming, and formatting messages between systems. "We were sort of stuck," recalled Davis. "Some of our programmers wouldn't use MQSeries, and preferred to develop integration routines manually."

To augment MQSeries, IBM consultants recommended that Davis look at MQSeries Integrator, a product jointly developed and marketed by IBM and New Era of Networks (NEON). MQSeries Integrator, an enterprise application integration engine, is made up of MQSeries, NEONRules, and NEONFormatter. Using NEONRules and NEONFormatter, MQSeries Integrator provides intelligent, rules-based message routing, content transformation, and formatting across multiple computing platforms and operating systems.

VF Corp. evaluated another application integration product as well, but opted for the NEON technology due to its comprehensive capabilities and the tight relationship between NEON and IBM. Davis was also impressed with the scalability of MQSeries Integrator. "If we have to upgrade systems, we shouldn't have to change our existing applications or interfaces," he explains. "Everything is done through a central hub concept. This reduces the complexity enormously, and eliminates a point-to-point interface architecture."

To further the automation process, VF Corp. also purchased NEONadapter for R/3, an adjunct set of format conversion libraries that act as the data interface between SAP and other applications in the enterprise. NEONadapter automatically loads IDoc definitions into the NEON Formatter repository by analyzing the SAP R/3 IDoc metadata, thus eliminating the need to recode non-SAP applications to under-stand the SAP message protocol. At last, Davis and his team were ready to forge ahead. Programmer resistance melted, as automation, ease of use, and reliability made "doing things the old way" far too tedious to even consider anymore. "The arithmetic is pretty simple," beamed Davis. "MQSeries Integrator allows us to avoid having to manually program disparate systems and applications for routing and formatting, while NEONadapter eliminates the need for manually constructed IDOC definitions for R/3."

Getting it Together

Consultants from NEON worked with VF Corp. to develop a proof-of-concept in October 1998. Once they had established a re-usable development architecture, they began the task of integrating the Jeanswear coalition systems just one month later. These systems contained 35 interfaces, 27 of which have been targeted for integration via MQSeries Integrator. In addition, MQSeries Integrator is being used to integrate legacy applications with the new Jeanswear systems. "We're moving along rapidly," Davis reported. Learning MQSeries and MQSeries Integrator proved to be both fast and easy. "Our programmers picked it up very quick-

Figure 1.0 — Rick Adam, Jr., NEON Chairman and CEO

ly," Davis continued. Eighteen programmers and analysts attended a NEON training class, and three of them became power users on the Jeanswear integration project. "They knocked out these interfaces in short order." Today, with the main data integration issues solved, Davis had nothing but praise for MQSeries Integrator. "MQSeries Integrator gives us the ability to reconcile different platforms, applications, and data formats, and to translate messages from different protocols, different programming languages, all of that. It's a huge time saver, and it provides the widest possible coverage. Whether it's UNIX, Windows NT, or OS/390, it doesn't matter."

In closing, Davis issues a word of advice for other large organizations facing similar enterprise integration projects. "Lots of organizations get mired in the complexity of point-to-point interfaces," Davis says. "The more packages and systems you have, the larger the effort and the greater the complexity. That's where NEON's application integration products are a lifesaver."

With the success of the Jeanswear coalition project, VF Corp. is actively working on integrating their other four groups. With NEON, they can meet their IT integration needs now and in the future. This positions VF Corp to accomplish its consumerization initiative and remain a leader in a highly competitive market.

Copyright © 2000 New Era of Networks, Inc.

4.0 Making It Happen

Tools and Techniques to Advance Supply Chain Performance

The previous sections have examined how technology can be leveraged to enable innovative supply chain solutions and the significant value that can be achieved through re-invention of the supply chain. Reaching the milestone of improved performance, however, requires knowledge of not only where to go, but how to get there – how to make it happen.

The process of realizing change has many fronts, including understanding where to start and how to scale fast, how to identify where the opportunities lie, how to affect change within the organization, how to realign processes such as product development, manufacturing, procurement, or planning, and how to measure the supply chain for continuous improvement.

This final section discusses the techniques and methodologies available to assist a company in making an Internet-enable supply chain a reality. From an innovative training approach that draws on flight simulation techniques, to ways to achieve rapid results from an e-procurement initiative and online performance measurement tools, our contributors provide insight on both how to get started and how to maximize the value of your supply chain initiatives once they are underway.

Our contributors provide insight on both how to get started and how to maximize the value of your supply chain initiatives once they are underway.

white paper

written by:

Kevin Kavanaugh
Ocean Spray Cranberries, Inc.

Paul Matthews
Andersen Consulting
http://kavanaugh.ASCET.com

Maximizing Supply Chain Value

Very few executives would disagree that supply chains are undergoing a radical transformation. They will almost certainly be able to point to significant initiatives in their own supply chain. But are they the right initiatives? Are they capturing the strategic benefits that supply chains can deliver or are they strictly cost-focused? This article details the stages that most companies go through as they elevate Supply Chain Management to drive strategic competitive advantage.

In the past, companies urged their operations functions to add value through cost-containment initiatives. While the approaches may differ in the end, each of the Supply Chain Management tools of the 1980s and 1990s, including material resource planning, just-in-time production, kanban, continuous improvement, time-to-market, and total quality management focused on traditional issues of cost control and improving operating performance. These approaches are too narrowly focused to maximize supply chain value or drive corporate value. Yesterday's view of the supply chain as a cost center no longer works.

Competitive advantage, e-commerce, product proliferation, diverse sources of supply, and increasing customer requirements are exerting pressure on existing supply chain models. A company must understand how to unleash the underutilized strategic value tied up within the supply chain. The role of the supply chain in the organization needs to be redefined to maximize a company's value.

As an example, a manufacturer of graphic arts printing plates had been going through a period of significant change. Having once commanded a large market share and strong profits, sales began to erode. In an effort to retain market share, the company pursued a strategy of lowering price. This tact resulted in decreased margins and associated lower profitability. To combat the decreased margins, more than 100 supply chain cost reduction efforts were initiated.

While these short-term, tactical solutions helped the printing plates manufacturer to reduce costs and maintain margins, they failed to address the company's core problem – reduced demand for the company's primary product, printing plates for silver halide-based film. With the rise of new print processing technologies (primarily, digital and computer imaging technology), printing plates were no longer required to create the desired images/pictures.

The graphic arts printing plate manufacturer had defined the role of the supply chain as reactive and focused on reducing costs. Ultimately, the existing assets and infrastructure for graphics arts printing plates did not enable movement into the new, changing market. The strategic value of the supply chain was not maximized.

The New Role of Supply Chain

Supply chain impacts on a company are numerous and substantial. Supply chain costs can equal one-half, or more, of a company's revenues, while completing the demand generation-fulfillment cycle by linking a company and its products and services with customers. The supply chain enables a company to manufacture products at target cost levels, ensuring the right goods are received by the right customers in the right quantities at the right time.

Given a supply chain's integral role in executing a company's business strategy, it can do more than successfully fulfill demand generation needs. The role of the supply chain can be defined in five stages (see Figure 1.0). At the lowest levels of strategic value contribution, supply chain is purely execution focused – management develops plans to increase supply chain efficiency and cost performance. At higher levels, it is demanded that the supply chain demonstrate strategic value to the organization. The supply chain involves containment of operating costs, effective

Kevin M. Kavanaugh is vice president of operations for Ocean Spray. In this role, he is responsible for procurement, manufacturing, logistics, demand planning, and customer service. Kevin joined Ocean Spray in 1982 and has held a variety of management positions in finance, operations, and marketing.

Paul Matthews is a managing partner in the Andersen Consulting Supply Chain Practice, responsible for Integrated Materials & Manufacturing. The majority of his work has focused on developing and implementing manufacturing and operations strategies. His clients have included Fortune 100 companies in healthcare, industrial and consumer products, automotive, and the transportation industry.

http://kavanaugh.ASCET.com

deployment of capital, risk management, and even revenue generation.

It should be noted that while each stage has distinct attributes and properties, the stages are not mutually exclusive. For example, within a company's overall supply chain, procurement may exhibit traits of an Efficient Reactive Supplier while manufacturing and logistics more closely resemble an Efficient Proactive Supplier. Additionally, a given function within the supply chain may also display more properties of multiple stages. In the aforementioned graphic arts printing plates manufacturer example, manufacturing's processes and personnel characteristics may be those of an Efficient Proactive Supplier, but it may invest in capital projects as a Reactive Supplier would.

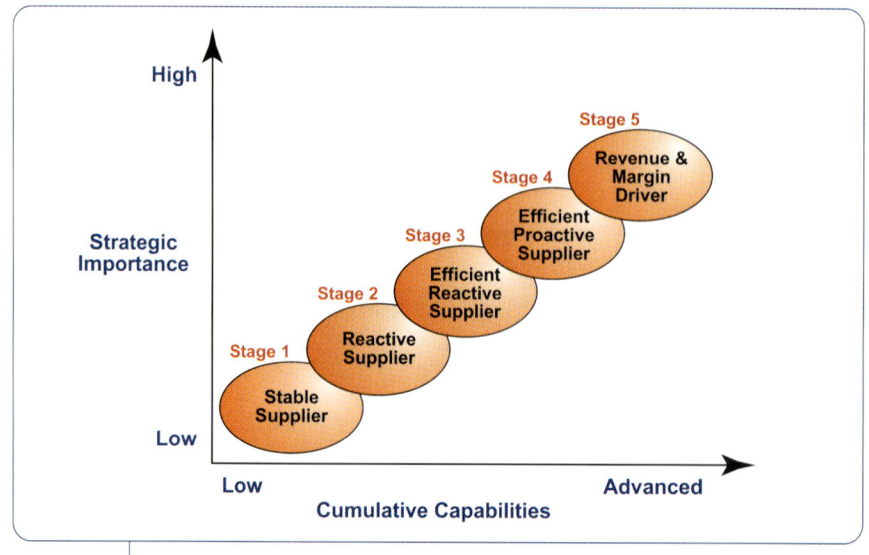

Figure 1.0 — The Role of Supply Chain

Stable Supplier – Stage 1

The least strategic stage of a supply chain is that of the Stable Supplier. The low level of strategic importance at this stage has as much to do with the external environment in which the company operates as it does with the relationship between supply chain and other company functions. Stable companies exist in mature, slow-to-change industries, such as table salt manufacturers, where supply and demand are in equilibrium. With predictable supply and demand, minimal forecasting is needed. The supply chain knows, with a good deal of certainty, how much product to produce each period. This predictability eliminates the need for the supply chain to be reactive to demand changes, as occurs in the next stage.

The process discipline, personnel skills, and technology emphases are all designed for long runs with few line changes. The production process is an excellent example of scale production. Costs are kept low, not because processes are regularly re-engineered, but rather because the predictability of demand allows for minimal intrusion of management decisions and changes. Capital assets are dedicated to specific tasks. Overhead and management levels can be held to a minimum since there is little risk of sudden market changes that will require immediate strategic changes.

Reactive Supplier – Stage 2

As a Reactive Supplier, expectations of the supply chain's role in the overall company strategy is still minimal. The supply chain typically acts to fulfill demand by responding to and supporting the company's sales and marketing strategies. The position of Reactive Supplier is very unstable – while service may be high, it is at any cost. Unless a firm excels substantially in other functional areas (for example, demand generation, production innovation, etc.) or other value disciplines (for example, product leadership and customer intimacy), it is extremely difficult for a company to survive for the long term as a Reactive Supplier.

The supply chain is viewed by other functions and views itself as a cost center. Although the supply chain may make efforts to control costs, often these efforts fail or fall short of their stated goals. Functional silos predominate and frequently seek to maximize their own efficiency, often at the expense of the entire supply chain system. Management tends to view workers as "replaceable assets" with little money or time invested in further developing the skills of operations people. Little attention is spent on acquiring competitive technology or capital assets, or modifying existing technology to support the latest sales and marketing needs. The mantra of many is to ensure throughput continues at any cost.

Efficient Reactive Supplier – Stage 3

In the move from Reactive Supplier to Efficient Reactive Supplier, the supply chain and the rest of the company still view the supply chain's contributions to the firm's competitive position as minimal, or at best, moderate. The supply chain's role is still one of fulfilling demand, not one of influencing demand. However, the supply chain now fulfills demand by acting as an efficient, integrated unit not as individual fiefdoms – it is an integrated supply chain with low costs and excellent customer service.

An internally integrated supply chain process seeks to work in concert to reduce the total delivered cost of finished goods. No longer does manufacturing seek to maximize its own efficiencies at the detriment of logistics or procurement. Line managers, foremen, supervisors, etc., understand and have performance measures showing them how their actions affect upstream and downstream processes. They take actions that are directed to reducing the total delivered cost of finished goods.

The role of technology also changes with Efficient Reactive Suppliers. Many companies become fixated on the management concepts of improved operating efficiencies – often with little regard to the capital management side of costs. In their efforts to reduce total delivered costs, many firms view the acquisition of technology as the supply chain's top priority. Companies

SUMMARY OF THE ROLE OF THE SUPPLY CHAIN

	Strategic Impact	Process Focus	Personnel Roles	Capital Spending
Stable Supplier	Minimal	Long runs; few changeovers	Little autonomy	Dedicated assets
Reactive Supplier	Minimal	Minimize functional costs	Workers are replaceable assets	Equipment modification
Efficient Reactive Supplier	Minimal – Moderate	Integrate supply chain activities and minimize supply side costs	Integrated supply chain managers; replaceable workers	Production equipment
Efficient Proactive Supplier	Moderate – High	Integrate supply chain activities and minimize supply side costs	Integrated supply chain managers make demand suggestions; Line workers provide suggestions	Information technology to enhance integration
Revenue and Margin Driver	High	Integrate supply and demand chain activities across companies and partners	Managers integrated with trading partners	Information technology to enhance integration cross-company

Figure 2.0 Summary of The Role of the Supply Chain

invest in new equipment and automate with the desire to reduce labor costs and improve capacity and throughput.

Efficient Proactive Supplier – Stage 4

A significant transformation occurs when Efficient Reactive Suppliers become Efficient Proactive Suppliers. The most noticeable difference is in the relationship structure between the integrated supply chain and the sales and marketing organizations. The supply chain now proactively makes recommendations to other corporate groups regarding how a new product design or a new raw material substitute may further reduce supply chain costs or complexity. The supply chain fully understands the areas in which it can make a substantial impact, and sales and marketing consider the supply chain an equal partner. The company expects the supply chain to regularly step forward and demand changes to such items as design specifications if such changes will lead to even greater efficiencies.

The integrated processes within the supply chain are in many ways similar to those found in Efficient Reactive Suppliers. However, now supply chain groups actively pursue demand generation by suggesting product design or service changes to further enhance the efficiency of the supply chain. Further, supply chain groups understand how their actions impact not only upstream and downstream supply chain activities, but also how demand generation decisions influence the supply chain's actions.

Efficient Proactive Suppliers invest in new technology, where appropriate. Often this technology takes the form of integrated information systems to permit once disparate groups such as sales, procurement, manufacturing, and logistics to view the same information and share ideas at the same time.

Revenue and Margin Driver Suppliers – Stage 5

Revenue and Margin Driver Suppliers take actions that go much further than improving supply chain efficiencies, reactively or proactively. They fully integrate the demand generation and fulfillment sides on an inter-company basis, achieving true supply chain-wide integration. For the first time in the supply chain's evolution, the supply chain is expected to actively contribute to not only the execution of, but also to the development of a company's overall corporate strategy. Senior level strategic direction setting meetings now include active upfront input from the supply chain. Today's build-to-order personal computer supply chains are examples of revenue and margin drivers.

The supply chain uses its interactions with external parties to help develop new strategies. Enterprise resource planning investments are leveraged though two-way, real-time data linkages with customers, suppliers, and alliance partners. A true "pull" demand signal travels seamlessly across organizations. Business agreements are developed with partners with a total profit objective. Forecasting, planning and replenishment processes are fully integrated across companies with clear material visibility, continuous replenishment, and coordinated product design efforts. Technological knowledge and advances are shared with partners. Measurements involve total inter-company supply chain revenue, cost, asset return, and profitability.

Most technology emphasis is on information systems. The ability to access same-time information and transfer it to customers, suppliers, and alliance partners is invaluable. Often such investments, whether direct or in the form of agreements with third parties to provide such capabilities, provide greater revenue or margin levels.

Summary

For many companies, supply chain value can be maximized by elevating the supply chain to greater strategic importance (see Figure 2.0). Supply chains must transition from a cost-focus to value-focus perspective. Company leaders must recognize the imperative to make this paradigm shift happen in their organization. Yet a change of mind-set is insufficient; it must be backed by actions and initiatives that change the way the supply chain operates. The organizations, infrastructure, processes, and systems must be put in place to integrate not only internal supply chain functions, but integrate with customers, competitors, and alliance partners. Focusing capability development efforts to build these strategic linkages may mean reviewing old viewpoints but will ultimately drive the greatest returns from a supply chain change program.

http://kavanaugh.ASCET.com

Optimizing the E-Business Supply Chain with Cognos Enterprise Business Intelligence

Contact Information

Ron Zambonini
President and CEO

Terry Hall
Chief Operating Officer

Donnie Moore
Chief Financial Officer

Cognos Incorporated, World Headquarters – Canada

3755 Riverside Drive
P.O. Box 9707, Station T
Ottawa, ON
Canada
K1G 4K9
Phone 613.738.1440
Fax 613.738.0002

Cognos Corporation, World Headquarters – US

67 South Bedford Street
Burlington, MA 01803-5164
Toll Free 800.426.4667
Phone 781.229.6600
Fax 781.229.9844

To find out more about how Autozone, Sutter Health, and other organizations worldwide are achieving e-business success with Cognos EBI, visit www.cognos.com

---

Supply Chain Management (SCM) systems have revolutionized how businesses plan, implement, and understand their manufacturing, distribution, and customer processes. The advent of e-business has seen these processes accelerate to Internet-speed. To keep pace, organizations rely more than ever on the fast exchange of information along the supply chain. While SCM systems contain a backbone of data about transactions, Enterprise Business Intelligence (EBI) provides the means to evaluate supply chain performance. Moreover, EBI lets companies view the entire supply chain process from one end to the other and understand how it impacts other parts of the enterprise.

Improving Business Processes

As transaction-oriented applications, SCM systems generate vast amounts of data that offer valuable insights on key supply chain indicators – supplier on-time performance, inventory levels, capacity, and so on. While this information helps organizations better understand and manage processes, SCM's strategic value escalates when SCM data is viewed in combination with data about related processes from other functional areas in the enterprise, such as finance, operations planning, and human resources.

Coordinating SCM with other enterprise data can yield answers to more strategic questions:

- What is the impact on labor and capacity of this proposed rush order?
- How will this engineering change impact inventory levels?
- What shortages should be addressed first?
- How will cash flow be affected by switching suppliers?

EBI is the enabling infrastructure that lets people quickly gain a clear understanding of how SCM decisions and outcomes impact other key areas of the enterprise. For instance, Cognos EBI at AutoZone enables vendors to view and analyze their inventory data so they can identify trends and proactively take measures to meet needs in specific locations or fulfill seasonal demand.

Improving Relationships With Suppliers

EBI enables organizations to analyze and assess the performance of both traditional and e-business supplier relationships. It also facilitates the sharing of information with suppliers, partners, customers, and others in the supply chain. In this way, organizations collaborate more effectively. For example, EBI gained from internal and supplier data enabled Sutter Health to negotiate better supply acquisition terms that create price parity across its affiliates and saved $17 million over three years.

With Cognos EBI, companies gain a complete view of their supply chain and its impact on other areas of the enterprise. Together, EBI and SCM form the foundation for continuous improvement of supply chain processes and information-driven relationships in an e-business world.

About Cognos

With over one million seats in thousands of companies worldwide, Cognos is the leading vendor of EBI solutions. By delivering information to everyone across the supply chain and giving them powerful ways to analyze it, EBI from Cognos lets people coordinate decision-making and improve business performance.

Leaders of the Web.com: Accelerating the Transition to the Web-Based World

Successful multinationals are finding that their proven methodologies for developing and implementing corporate strategy leave them lead-footed when confronting the scale and pace of change in the Web-based world. Andrew Berger of Andersen Consulting describes how exploiting the experience of acknowledged leaders in e-commerce will enable successful companies to take a fast track – but nevertheless low-risk route – to a fully e-synchronized supply chain.

Very few executives in major multinational companies still deny that the Internet and the World Wide Web are going to have – indeed are already having – a profound impact on their companies and the competitive environment in which they operate.

Media and stock market attention has been focused on the emergence of a few Internet "pure plays" whose market capitalization has been driven to previously unimagined levels, often in companies with largely non-existent sales and profits. Meanwhile, a few sophisticated global multinationals in such areas as computers and communications have been less ostentatiously, but arguably more imaginatively, implementing new business models that combine the excellence of their conventional operations with innovation in the application of the Web to virtually every aspect of the supply chain. As a result, companies such as Dell Computers, Cisco Systems and Sun Microsystems have been able to grow by 25% per year, to operate on a global scale without taking on excessive levels of people and assets, and to achieve levels of profitability 20% or more than their nearest competitors.

A superficial analysis of the short history of the Web might suggest that the success of Internet pure plays such as Amazon.com and AOL has been achieved by radically changing the economics of the value chain and thus sucking value out of the conventional multinationals. On closer inspection it is clear, however, that it is the financial markets out of which the value has been sucked, while the impact on the value chain has been confined almost exclusively to the handling of orders and customer relationships. In other words, it is fair to say that, thus far, most companies who have achieved a measure of "e-success" have done so by focusing on the easy bits. The much more difficult problems relating to the less glamorous but nonetheless fundamental aspects of the value chain including, notably, e-fulfillment, have been largely neglected, as those who never received their Christmas orders may well testify.

In contrast to such companies as Amazon.com and AOL, sophisticated multinationals like Dell and Cisco may not currently enjoy quite the multiples of market capitalization over revenues and earnings of the Internet pure plays, but they have clearly demonstrated that it is in the supply chain that the true value of the Web revolution is to be found. Indeed, it is no exaggeration to suggest that the implementation of full e-synchronization has the potential to release at least $100 million of value from the supply chain of the average Fortune 1000 multinational. As the Web revolution reaches what might be called "the end of the beginning," to borrow a phrase from Winston Churchill, the challenge for conventional multinationals is how to move at Web speed in order to unlock that value.

The fact that some Internet pure plays have found that the more conventional aspects of their businesses have proven rather more difficult to manage than they had anticipated is certainly no justification for complacency on the part of more traditional companies. Such organizations urgently need develop an e-commerce strategy based on their own strengths in terms

Andrew Berger is an Andersen Consulting partner with global leadership responsibilities for New Business Models in the Andersen Consulting Supply Chain Practice. He works primarily in the electronics and high-tech industries. He is deeply involved in the creation and execution of new business models enabled by the latest Web technologies and globalization of organizations and their supply chains.

of their operational excellence, their traditional relationships, and their own distinctive assets and capabilities. This strategy will need to recognize the overwhelming and urgent need for the organization to make a breakthrough into the world of the Web. Failure to do so will lead to increasing vulnerability to attack, not only from traditional competitors who may have moved more rapidly to implement e-commerce solutions, but also from new collaborative ventures bringing together the capabilities of, for example, leading Internet pure plays and sophisticated multinationals. The potential of such "e-invaders" to disrupt markets can be judged from the tremors sent through the entertainment and media world by the merger of AOL and Time-Warner. Moreover, the success of the ChemConnect, a Web-based chemical exchange, whose alliance partners include Andersen Consulting, Dow Chemical, and Rohm & Haas, (plus the recent announcement of a joint venture between Shell and CommerceOne), suggest that no market will be immune to such "e-invasions."

Nor will failure to move fast enough to develop and implement an e-commerce strategy be reflected solely in short-term financial or competitive setbacks. It is already clear that e-commerce generates its own virtuous circle. As the Web-based world grows, capital and talent will seek out companies with a valid value proposition within that world. Their success will lead to further growth across the board

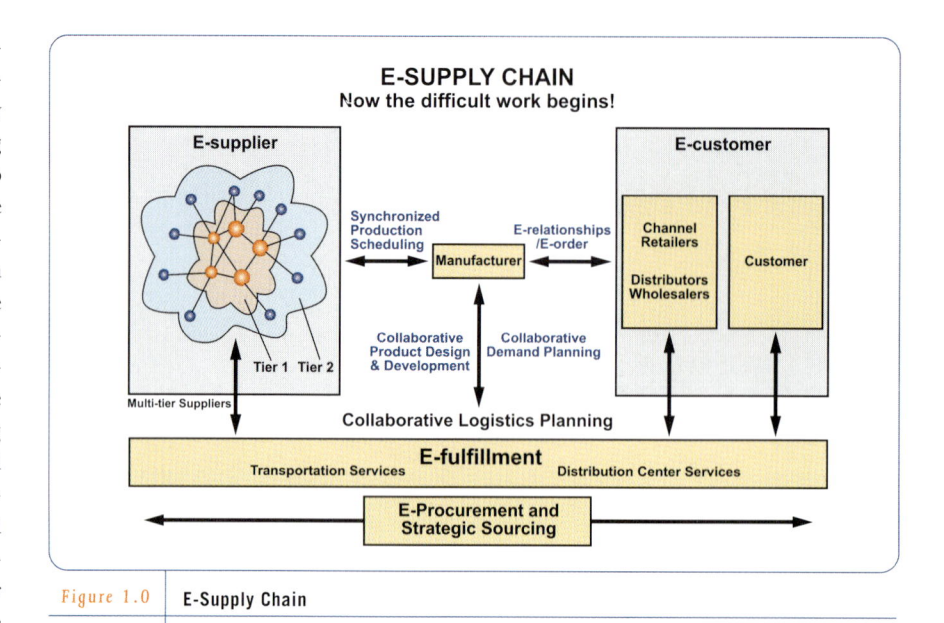

Figure 1.0   **E-Supply Chain**

and in turn to a reinforcement of the pattern. Conversely, companies unable to put forward such a value proposition will find themselves progressively starved of capital, talent, and markets and quality partners.

The problem for the conventional multinational, faced with the challenge of the Web, is that its traditional, carefully honed methodologies for strategy development and implementation – originally designed to ensure that no stone is left unturned, no eventuality left uncovered, and no deficiency in capability left unresolved – are simply too slow and too cumbersome for the Web-based world. Quite simply, by the time the strategy has been developed and implemented, the problem it addresses will have changed, and faster competitors will have already stolen the proposition. The Web has not so much moved the goal posts as created a whole new game. Even well-managed and successful businesses risk finding themselves playing a game that no longer exists, making assumptions that are no longer valid, and accepting constraints that no longer apply.

The solution to this problem is, from the outset, to emulate and adopt Web-based behavior. Companies that succeed in the Web-based world accept that they cannot do everything themselves. Instead, they identify those areas and capabilities in which they excel and look to others to provide the same level of excellence in all other required capabilities. Thus, the key to shortening the time-scale for developing Web-based expertise is to maintain the excellence of one's own operations while avoiding reinventing the wheel by finding partners whose wheels already demonstrate proven excellence.

Leaders of the Web.com

To that end, Andersen Consulting, itself recognizing that it does not have a monopoly of Web-based expertise, has teamed with Oracle and Sun Microsystems in an initiative dubbed "Leaders of the Web.com." This initiative is designed to move organizations rapidly from basic awareness of new ideas to the achievement of demonstrable returns from their Web investment in a time-scale commensurate with the pace of change in the Web-based world.

The three organizations'[1] credentials for offering such a proposition are well known: Sun is a leading provider of Web-server hardware, Oracle a leading provider of Internet database and related software, and Andersen Consulting a leading provider of Internet services with, at last count, Internet related revenues more than 10% ahead of its nearest rival. The Leaders of the Web.com approach is to move conventional multinationals into the Web-based world using a simple, but radical notion: "Think

Weblink

For more on scalability, see:
  bruce.ASCET.com
  anderson-d.ASCET.com
  billington.ASCET.com

For more on strategic planning, see:
  hicks.ASCET.com
  manheim.ASCET.com
  lapide.ASCET.com

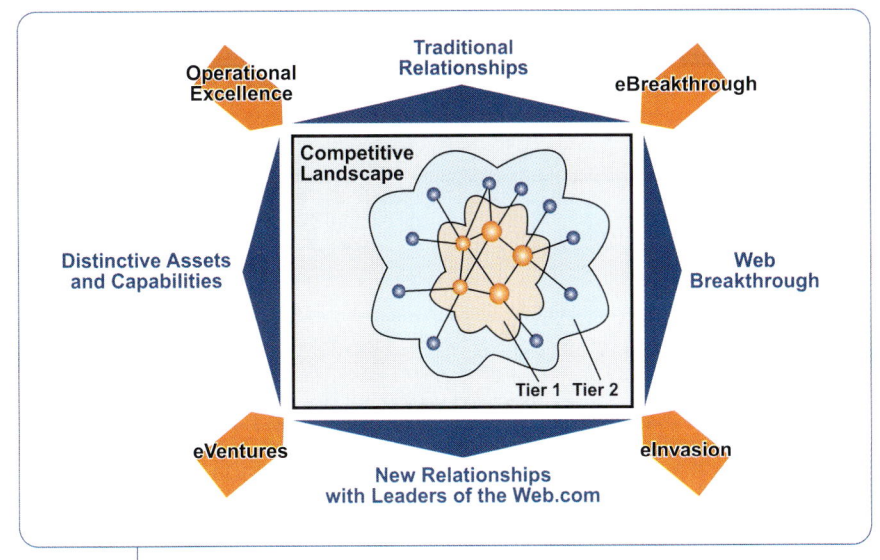

Figure 2.0 New models for e-commerce strategies

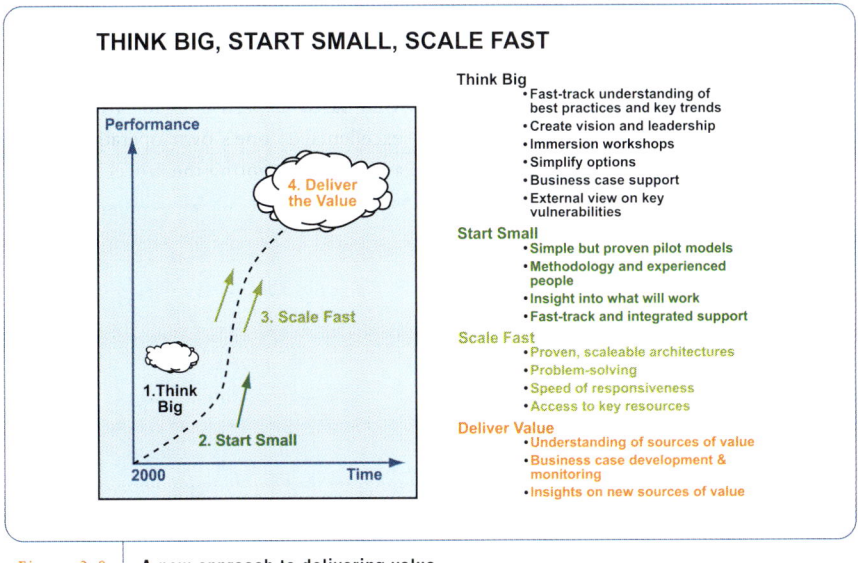

THINK BIG, START SMALL, SCALE FAST

Think Big
- Fast-track understanding of best practices and key trends
- Create vision and leadership
- Immersion workshops
- Simplify options
- Business case support
- External view on key vulnerabilities

Start Small
- Simple but proven pilot models
- Methodology and experienced people
- Insight into what will work
- Fast-track and integrated support

Scale Fast
- Proven, scaleable architectures
- Problem-solving
- Speed of responsiveness
- Access to key resources

Deliver Value
- Understanding of sources of value
- Business case development & monitoring
- Insights on new sources of value

Figure 3.0 A new approach to delivering value

big, start small, scale fast."

Thinking big means accepting from the outset that the ultimate aim is, within a relatively short time-scale, a complete transformation of the organization's entire value chain. Aiming for anything less not only forfeits the larger share of the value proposition but drastically reduces the opportunity to build partnerships with other Web leaders, while rendering the organization's market position progressively more vulnerable to predatory e-invaders.

Starting small recognizes that, while the scale of the ultimate objective must be kept in mind at all times, the most immediate requirement is to gain experience and to prove fundamental methodologies at a scale where the risk of failure can be minimized and its consequences can be tolerated.

Subsequent success then depends on the ability to scale fast. Successful pilot projects can easily generate complacency about subsequent full-scale implementation. Indeed the Web-based world already is littered with horror stories of implementations that have failed to scale satisfactorily, exposing companies to ridicule from their customers, and immediate and permanent punishment in the financial markets. Ultimate success is not about being the "first mover" but about being "first to scale the right thing."

Underpinning the Leaders of the Web.com approach is the recognition that conventional methodologies for planning and implementing strategic change cannot deliver within Internet time-scales. In particular, the standard approach to developing awareness and understanding at the outset of a project – typically a six-to-12 month process involving discussion with a wide range of individuals and organizations – is too time-consuming, cumbersome, and obsessed with completeness to provide a basis for a successful corporate e-commerce initiative.

The Leaders of the Web.com approach bypasses much of this initial effort by allowing the organization to tap directly into the experience of the leaders themselves, and to collaborate with them on a fast-track focused awareness and understanding process. Such an approach ensures that the organization embarks on its strategic change with a coherent view of the aims and objectives, and a common language in which to develop and define its strategy.

Acceptance from the outset that it is "blindingly obvious" that immediate action is essential to the long-term survival of the company will, of itself, obviate the need for much of the work that traditionally would precede strategic change of the scale envisioned. Equally important is to switch the traditional focus on detail, completeness, and accuracy to a willingness to trade completeness against speed. Indeed recognizing the true value of time to market in the e-world involves accepting that a 70% complete solution within the restricted time-scale is acceptable while a 100% solution outside it is useless.

The accelerated and focused approach goes much further than simply fast tracking the initial learning process, important though that is. Leaders of the Web.com pro-

http://berger.ASCET.com

vides support for both the mobilization phase and the development of a Silicon Valley-style e-commerce strategy that defines both the organization's current capabilities and its future requirements. Based on the premise that the most important and valuable learnings will come from real experience, it then provides for the selection and fast-track execution, with expert support, of a suitable pilot project. During that execution period, learnings from the pilot can be incorporated in an iterative manner into the parallel development of the corporate strategy. As a result, by the end of the 90-day pilot execution phase, not only will plans be in place for the scaling and roll out of the pilot itself, but the future technical architecture and complete corporate e-strategy of the organization will be in place. That, in turn, ensures that as the scaling and roll out of the pilot proceeds, the organization is in a position to develop its full e-commerce blueprint. With blueprint in hand, the organization can plan the roll out of the full spectrum of Internet applications, again incorporating learnings from the pilot scaling and roll-out as it proceeds. As a result, the organization will be in a position to proceed to full roll-out of its complete e-commerce strategy, based on an already proven methodology and technical architecture, in the shortest possible time from the original inception of the project.

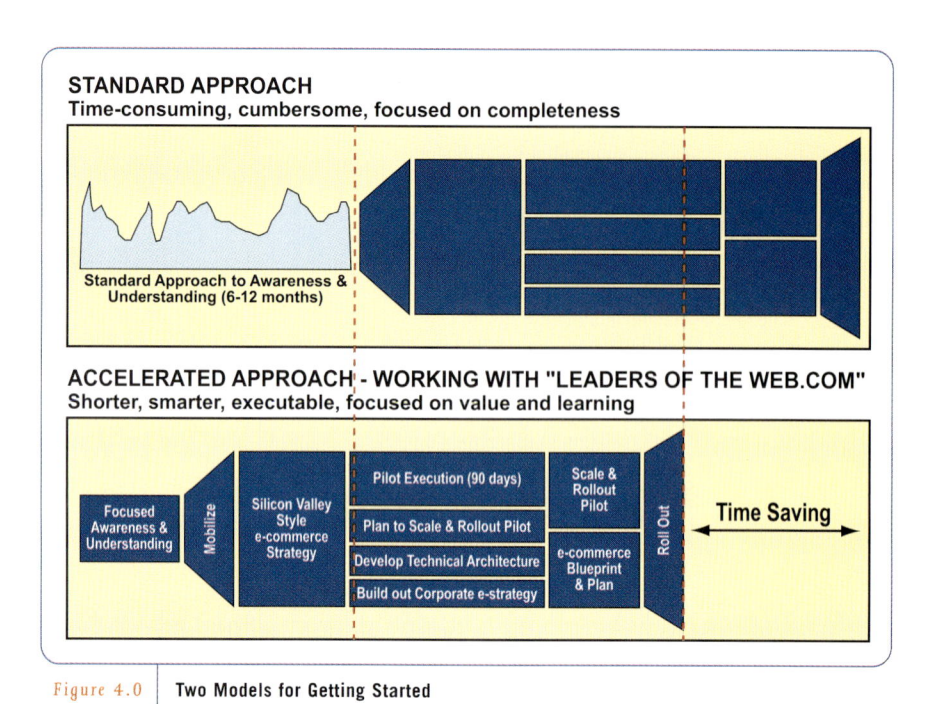

Clearly, Leaders of the Web.com will not suit every organization. Indeed, many multinationals, particularly those closely related to the computer and communications industries, already are well advanced in their journey to the Web-enabled world. However, there is no doubt that many well-established and successful multinationals will face real pain as they reassess their value chains and prepare to transition to the new e-commerce reality. To them, Leaders of the Web.com offers a fast track into the world of e-commerce that minimizes the risks inherent in major strategic change of this scale while recognizing that there is no competitive advantage in being a fast follower.

Figure 4.0 | Two Models for Getting Started

Copyright©2000 Andersen Consulting LLP

What About Measuring Supply Chain Performance?

written by:

Larry Lapide
AMR Research
http://lapide.ASCET.com

Most consultants' recipes for affecting business change and behavior in an organization use ingredients for measuring ongoing performance. Many feel that continuous improvement in an organization relies on "measuring, measuring, and measuring again." Once a company's road map for change is laid out, it can develop a set of performance metrics or key performance indicators (KPIs) to ensure that it knows when it is meeting its objectives. Such organizations should choose a limited number of metrics and align executive to management-level measures; we offer suggestions for setting performance targets or internal or external benchmarks, and include advice on how to start measuring supply chain performance.

The current interest in performance measurements has led to a variety of supporting adages or cliches in the industry, such as:

- "Anything measured improves."
- "What you measure is what you get."
- "Anything measured gets done."
- "You can't manage what you do not measure."

These are not new business ideas, but there are a few new twists. Using measurements to support manufacturing operations has its roots back to the late 19th and early 20th centuries with ideas espoused by Frederick W. Taylor, the father of applying scientific methods to running business. His ideas for time and motion studies of operations were successfully used to scientifically manage production lines and warehouse operations. These ideas, however, led to exaggerated business processes that transitioned into "running a business by the stopwatch" with employers treating human employees as if they were highly reliable, predictable machines to be monitored and controlled. Over time, the workplace's view of performance measurement became more humane and these exaggerated types of monitor and control methods fell out of favor, replaced by a focus on measuring a business' performance rather than that of the individual.

Throughout the last decade, companies have expended significant amounts of time and effort to re-engineer their supply chains through business process change and technology focused on implementing integrated Supply Chain Management (SCM) principles. While substantial financial and human resources have been spent on doing this, there has been little sign of realized benefits. While consultants are recommending supply chain measurement, they generally lack formal approaches to it. In addition, while SCM software providers are selling solutions that enable companies to drastically improve their supply chain performance, these same vendors do not adequately provide tools needed to measure these improvements. In this report, AMR Research discusses supply chain performance measurement and the results of research conducted to address the following questions:

- Why is performance measurement important?
- What general approaches are available to measure supply chains?
- What advice can be followed when selecting performance measures?
- What methods are available for setting performance targets?
- What are application vendors doing to support supply chain performance measurement?
- How should a company get started?

Why Is Performance Measurement Important?

Measurement is important, as it affects behavior that impacts supply chain performance. As such,

Larry Lapide is VP and Service Director for Supply Chain Strategies at AMR Research. Larry has over 25 years of business experience including over 12 years in the consulting industry and 10 years in the high-tech industry. He focuses on business practices and technologies enabling efficient supply chain operations. His primary areas of expertise are in demand planning and forecasting, inventory and distribution planning, and production planning and scheduling.

Larry was formerly an associate partner in Andersen Consulting's Logistics Strategy Practice where he served manufacturing and retailing clients across a diverse set of industry segments, including high-tech, telecommunications, consumer products, and industrial products.

performance measurement provides the means by which a company can assess whether its supply chain has improved or degraded. The importance of using measures to help ensure that a supply chain is performing well can be illustrated by the following anecdotal story:

Tom is driving on a long trip in a car that has a broken speedometer and a broken gas gauge. He has been traveling for several hours, keeping track of the time and looking at his odometer to determine how fast he is going. He is sure that he has been obeying the speed limits – when he is stopped by a patrolman and given a speeding ticket. Slowing down, he drives for two more hours keeping track of the time and his odometer, but once again is stopped by a patrolman and given another speeding ticket. During the remainder of the trip Tom slows down to a speed that he now believes will avoid getting another speeding ticket. He drives for one more hour when the car stops all of a sudden. He ran out of gas!

Not a very good trip for Tom, primarily because he was missing some very important key measurement devices in his car – the speedometer and the gas gauge. Unlike Tom, most people would be extremely reluctant to drive this car. In a similar way, however, there are many companies that run their supply chains without a good set of measurements in place. Like Tom, the only way they are able to find out if they are meeting their supply chain goals is after the fact, by diagnosing poor financial results, or when they lose an important customer – events similar to Tom's speeding tickets.

Weblink

For more on performance indicators:
  reiter.ASCET.com
For more on VMIs, see:
  anthony.ASCET.com
  moore.ASCET.com
For more on value added, see:
  peters.ASCET.com
  srivastava.ASCET.com
For more on forecasting, see:
  wayman.ASCET.com
  quinn-c.ASCET.com

There are several lessons on the importance of measuring supply chain performance to be learned from this story:

- Measurements are important to directly controlling behavior and indirectly to performance – the speedometer reading impacts how hard or soft Tom pushes on the gas pedal.
- A few key measurements will go a long way toward keeping a company on track towards achieving its supply chain improvement objectives – like those on a speedometer and a gas gauge.
- Seemingly relevant, but cumbersome, measurements are of little use, and are possibly a hindrance, in helping to improve supply chain performance – like the odometer in the car.
- Picking the wrong measures and leaving out important ones could lead to supply chain performance degradation – like running out of gas.
- Driving a supply chain based only on after-the-fact measures, like losing an important customer or having poor financial performance is not very effective – the way getting speeding tickets and running out of gas is an expensive way to drive a car.

What General Approaches Are Available To Measure Supply Chains?

Traditionally, companies have tracked performance based largely on financial accounting principles, many which date back to the ancient Egyptians and Phoenicians. Financial accounting measures are certainly important in assessing whether or not operational changes are improving the financial health of an enterprise, but insufficient to measure supply chain performance for the following reasons:

- The measures tend to be historically oriented and not focused on providing a forward-looking perspective.
- The measures do not relate to important strategic, non-financial performance, like customer service/loyalty and product quality.
- The measures do not directly tie to operational effectiveness and efficiency.

In response to some of these deficiencies in traditional accounting methods for measuring supply chain performance, a variety of measurement approaches have been developed, including the following:

- The Balanced Scorecard
- The Supply Chain Council's SCOR Model
- The Logistics Scoreboard
- Activity-Based Costing (ABC)
- Economic Value Analysis (EVA)
- Balanced Scorecards

The Balanced Scorecard recommends the use of executive information systems (EIS) that track a limited number of balanced metrics that are closely aligned to strategic objectives. The approach was initially developed by Robert S. Kaplan and David P. Norton and was discussed in an article, titled "The Balanced Scorecard – Measures That Drive Performance," published in the *Harvard Business Review*, January-February 1992. While not specifically developed for supply chain performance measurement, Balanced Scorecard principles provide excellent guidance to follow when doing it. The approach would recommend that a small number of balanced supply chain measures be tracked based on four perspectives:

- Financial perspective (e.g., cost of manufacturing and cost of warehousing)
- Customer perspective (e.g., on-time delivery and order fill rate)
- Internal business perspective (e.g., manufacturing adherence-to-plan and forecast errors)
- Innovative and learning perspective (e.g., APICS-certified employees and new product development cycle time)

An industry has grown around the Balanced Scorecard approach with a variety of firms that provide consulting and solutions for implementing performance measurement, such as:

- Renaissance Worldwide, Inc. (Newton, MA) got its start doing this Balanced Scorecard consulting and grew to be one of the 30 largest consulting firms.
- Gentia Software Inc. (Boston, MA) markets a software application, Gentia's Renaissance Balanced Scorecard that

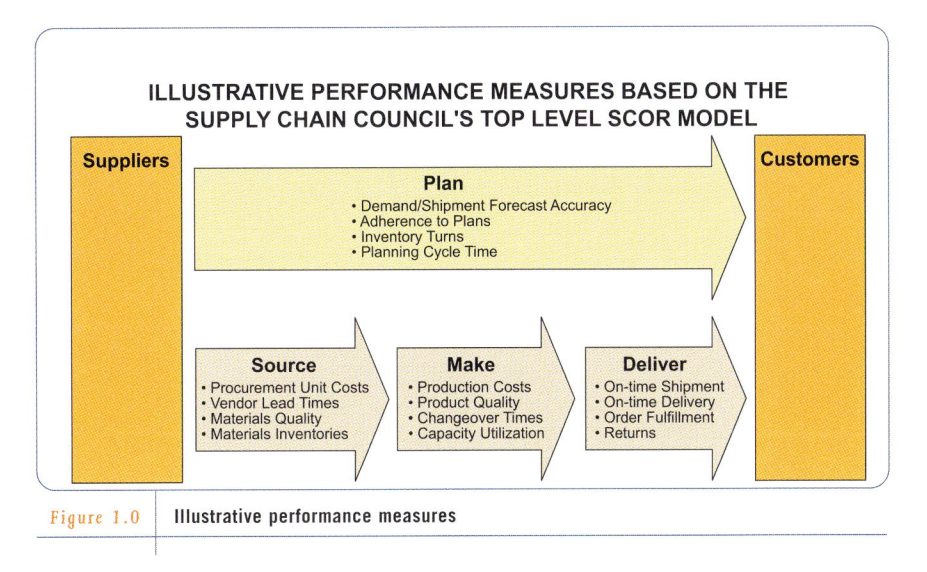

ILLUSTRATIVE PERFORMANCE MEASURES BASED ON THE SUPPLY CHAIN COUNCIL'S TOP LEVEL SCOR MODEL

Suppliers → Plan (Demand/Shipment Forecast Accuracy, Adherence to Plans, Inventory Turns, Planning Cycle Time) → Customers

- Source: Procurement Unit Costs, Vendor Lead Times, Materials Quality, Materials Inventories
- Make: Production Costs, Product Quality, Changeover Times, Capacity Utilization
- Deliver: On-time Shipment, On-time Delivery, Order Fulfillment, Returns

Figure 1.0 Illustrative performance measures

incorporates Renaissance Worldwide's performance measurement approach.
- Corvu Corp. (Edina, MI) sells a Balanced Scorecard System software application that provides interactive scorecard functionality.

Supply Chain Council's SCOR Model

The Supply Chain Council's SCOR Model provides guidance on the types of metrics one might use to get a balanced approach towards measuring the performance of one's overall supply chain. The SCOR Model approach advocates a set of supply chain performance measures comprised of a combination of:

- Cycle time metrics (e.g., production cycle time and cash-to-cash cycle)
- Cost metrics (e.g., cost per shipment and cost per warehouse pick)
- Service/quality metrics (on-time shipments and defective products)
- Asset metrics (e.g., inventories)

In contrast to the Balanced Scorecard, which is focused on executive enterprise-level measurement, the SCOR Model approach directly addresses the needs of supply chain management with balanced measurements. Figure 1.0 depicts an illustrative set of supply chain measures balanced among the SCOR Model's top-level processes.

The Logistics Scoreboard

Another approach to measuring supply chain performance was developed by Logistics Resources International Inc. (Atlanta, GA), a consulting firm specializing primarily in the logistical (i.e., warehousing and transportation) aspects of a supply chain. The company recommends the use of an integrated set of performance measures falling into the following general categories:

- Logistics financial performance measures (e.g., expenses and return on assets)
- Logistics productivity measures (e.g., orders shipped per hour and transport container utilization)
- Logistics quality measures (e.g., inventory accuracy and shipment damage)
- Logistics cycle time measures (e.g., in-transit time and order entry time)

Logistics Resources sells a spreadsheet-based, educational tool called The Logistics Scoreboard that companies can use to pilot their supply chain performance measurement processes and to customize for ongoing use. The tool and a monograph (Logistics Performance, Cost, and Value Measures that documents the tool and its use) are distributed by The Penton Institute (Cleveland, OH). In contrast to the other approaches discussed, The Logistics Scoreboard is prescriptive and actually recommends the use of a specific set of supply chain performance measures. These measures, however, are skewed toward logistics, having limited focus on measuring the production and procurement activities within a supply chain.

Activity Based Costing

The Activity-Based Costing (ABC) approach was developed to overcome some of the shortcomings of traditional accounting methods in tying financial measures to operational performance. The method involves breaking down activities into individual tasks or cost drivers, while estimating the resources (i.e., time and costs) needed for each one. Costs are then allocated based on these cost drivers rather than on traditional cost-accounting methods, such as allocating overhead either equally or based on less-relevant cost drivers. This approach allows one to better assess the true productivity and costs of a supply chain process. For example, use of the ABC method can allow companies to more accurately assess the total cost of servicing a specific customer or the cost of marketing a specific product. ABC analysis does not replace traditional financial accounting, but provides a better understanding of supply chain performance by looking at the same numbers in a different way.

ABC methods are useful in conjunction with the measurement approaches already discussed as their use allows one to more accurately measure supply chain process/task productivity and costs by aligning the metrics closer to actual labor, material, and equipment usage.

Economic Value-Added

One of the criticisms of traditional accounting is that it focuses on short-term financial results like profits and revenues, providing little insight into the success of an enterprise towards generating long-term value to its shareholders – thus, relatively unrelated to the long-term prosperity of a company. For example, a company can report many profitable quarters, while simultaneously disenfranchising its customer base by not applying adequate resources towards product quality or new product innovation.

To correct this deficiency in traditional methods, some financial analysts advocate estimating a company's return on capital or economic value-added. These are based on the premise that shareholder value is increased when a company earns more than its cost of capital. One such

http://lapide.ASCET.com

measure, EVA, developed by Stern, Stewart & Co., attempts to quantify value created by an enterprise, basing it on operating profits in excess of capital employed (through debt and equity financing). Some companies are starting to use measures like EVA within their executive evaluations. Similarly, these types of metrics can be used to measure an enterprise's value-added contributions within a supply chain. However, while useful for assessing higher-level executive contributions and long-term shareholder value, economic-value-added metrics are less useful for measuring detailed supply chain performance. They can be used, however, as the supply chain metrics within an executive-level performance scorecard, and can be included in the measures recommended as part of The Logistics Scoreboard approach.

What Advice Can Be Followed When Selecting Measures?

While the approaches described above provide guidance for supply chain measurement, they provide less help in assessing specific metrics to be used. In this regard, a key driving principle, as espoused by the Balanced Scorecard, is that measures should be aligned to strategic objectives. Supply chain strategy, however, differs for every company and depends upon its current competencies and strategic direction. Companies, for example, can generally fall into the following developmental stages that will dictate the types of measures and the degrees to which they will need to focus:

- Functional Excellence – a stage in which a company needs to develop excellence within each of its operating units such as the manufacturing, customer service, or logistics departments. Metrics for a company in this stage will need to focus on individual functional departments.

- Enterprise-Wide Integration – a stage in which a company needs to develop excellence in its cross-functional processes rather than within its individual functional departments. Metrics for a company in this stage will need to focus on cross-functional processes.

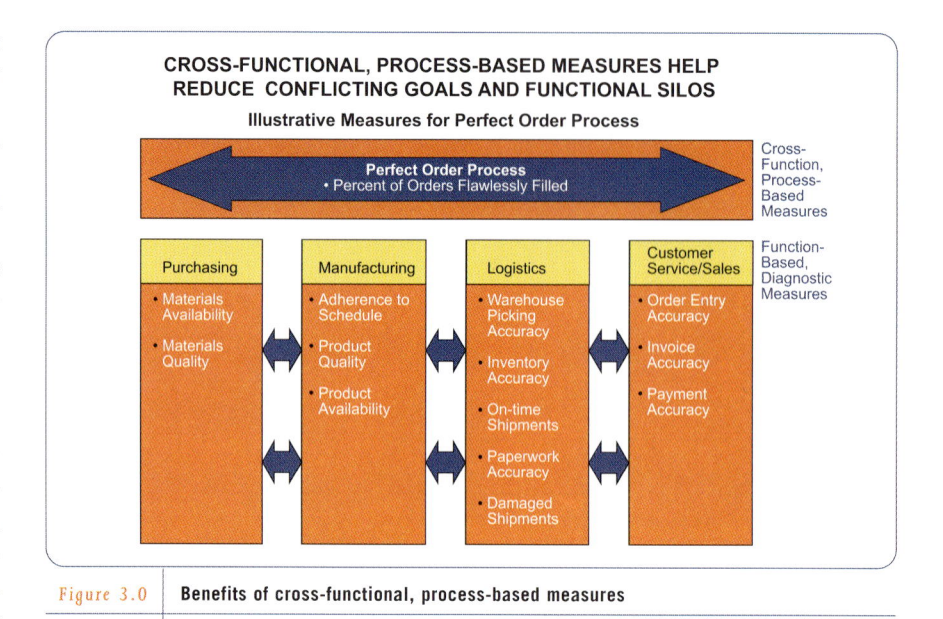

Figure 3.0 Benefits of cross-functional, process-based measures

- Extended Enterprise Integration – a stage in which a company needs to develop excellence in inter-enterprise processes. Metrics for a company in this stage will focus on external and cross-enterprise metrics.

Historically most companies have focused their performance measurement on achieving functional excellence. With the advent of Supply Chain Management (SCM) principles aimed at integrating their supply chains, many have objectives to increase their degree of enterprise-wide integration and extended enterprise integration. In order to achieve these types of objectives, their performance measurement systems will need to align to them. Advice for these supply chain measurement systems falls into five areas that include:

- Function-based measures
- Process-based measures
- Cross-enterprise measures
- Number of measures to be used
- Alignment of executive to management-level measures

A set of measures developed by a leading consumer products manufacturer is also discussed, providing an illustration of the type that might be selected.

Do Not Focus Only On Function-Based Measures

A major problem encountered with most performance measurement systems is that they are functionally focused. Within these systems, each functional area measures its performance in its own terms, with individuals evaluated based on their ability to meet objectives consistent with their department's performance measures. Individuals working under these measurement systems tend to drive operations toward improving their own area's performance, frequently at the expense of the performance of other functional areas. When each functional area sets its performance measures in isolation from those of others, it often leads to functional silos and conflicting organizational goals.

Figure 2.0 depicts a typical set of function-based supply chain-related performance measures used by many manufacturers. These types of measures used in isolation of each other tend to create conflicting goals among functional areas as follows:

- Customer Service and Sales – In these functional areas, employees are measured by their ability to maintain customer service levels. Measured in this context only, these employees tend to drive operations toward satisfying potentially smaller-sized customer orders and carrying high levels of finished goods inventories by

LIST OF POSSIBLE SUPPLY CHAIN MEASURES

Customer Service Measures	Process, Cross-Functional Measures	Extended Enterprise Measures
Order Fill Rate Line Item Fill Rate Quantity Fill Rate Backorders/stockouts Customer satisfaction % Resolution on first customer call Customer returns Order track and trace performance Customer disputes Order entry accuracy Order entry times	Forecast accuracy Percent perfect orders New product time-to-market New product time-to-first make Planning process cycle time Schedule changes	Total landed cost Point of consumption product availability Total supply chain inventory Retail shelf display Channel inventories EDI transactions Percent of demand/supply on VMI/CRP Percent of customers sharing forecasts Percent of suppliers getting shared forecast Supplier inventories Internet activity to suppliers/customers Percent automated tendering
Purchasing Related Measures	**Manufacturing Related Measures**	**Logistic Related Measures**
Material inventories Supplier delivery performance Material/component quality Material stockouts Unit purchase costs Material acquisition costs Expediting activities	Product quality WIP inventories Adherence-to-schedule Yields Cost per unit produced Setups/Changeovers Setup/Changeover costs Unplanned stockroom issues Bill-of-materials accuracy Routing accuracy Plant space utilization Line breakdowns Plant utilization Warranty costs Source-to-make cycle time Percent scrap/rework Material usage variance Overtime usage Production cycle time Manufacturing productivity Master schedule stability	Finished goods inventory turns Finished goods inventory days of supply On-time delivery Lines picked/hour Damaged shipments Inventory accuracy Pick accuracy Logistics cost Shipment accuracy On-time shipment Delivery times Warehouse space utilization End-of-life inventory Obsolete inventory Inventory shrinkage Cost of carrying inventory Documentation accuracy Transportation costs Warehousing costs Container utilization Truck cube utilization In-transit inventories Premium freight charges Warehouse receipts
Administration/Financial Measures	**Marketing Related Measures**	**Other Measures**
Cash flow Income Revenues Return on capital employed Cash-to-cash cycle Return on investment Revenue per employee Invoice errors Return on assets	Market share Percent of sales from new products Time-to-market Percent of products representing 80% of sales Repeat versus new customer sales	APICS trained personnel Patents awarded Employee turnover Number of employee suggestions

Figure 3.0 Possible supply chain measures

stocking inventories in multiple locations close to customers to shorten cycle times
- Logistics – In this functional area, employees are measured by transportation and warehousing costs, and inventory levels. Measured in this context only, Logistics personnel tend to keep inventories low and batch customer orders to ensure that trucks are shipped full and picking operations are minimized. On the inbound side, these employees will want to receive full truckloads at their warehouse docks to minimize receiving costs, usually at the expense of increased inventories.
- Manufacturing – In this functional area, employees are measured in terms of manufacturing productivity. Measured in this context only, they want to make longer production runs that result in higher levels of finished goods inventories. In a make-to-order manufacturing environment there will be a tendency to consolidate customer orders into longer production runs, making them less responsive to dynamic customer demands.
- Purchasing – In this functional area, employees are typically measured by materials costs and supplier delivery performance. Measured in this context only, buyers will purchase in large quantities to get volume discounts and use more suppliers for each item to ensure a low price. This behavior results in purchasing excess, potentially low quality, raw materials.

It is apparent from the behavior described above that use of only function-based measures could drive employees toward changing functional performance in entirely different directions. These types of measures alone have reinforced functional silos, reducing the effectiveness of many supply chains and fostering arms-length transactions among departments, leading to processes that are slow to respond. In addition, performance improvement initiatives get focused on a single objective that frequently runs counter to increasing the efficiency of the total supply chain. For example, an initiative focused on reducing transportation costs focuses on filling up outbound trucks. While this seems benign, it may not be best from a total supply chain perspective when customer orders are held up to fill up a truck, or if customers are forced to order in greater quantities.

Include Process-Based Measures to Improve Enterprise-Wide Performance

To help integrate their supply chains, companies are starting to break down the functional silos by organizing around cross-functional processes. This is done by either creating departments responsible for an overall process or creating cross-functional teams that drive an overall process, such as:
- Order fulfillment (e.g., order-to-cash)
- New product development/introduction (e.g., concept-to-first sale or production batch)
- Total cycle time (e.g., materials purchase to customer payment or cash-to-cash)

To support these organizational changes, companies are supplementing function-based measures with some process-based performance measures. While this approach does not advocate the total elimination of function-based measures, it places focus on the performance of an overall process, using these measures as diagnostic information to assess what is affecting overall performance.

For example, the perfect order concept measures the percent of customer orders that are flawlessly fulfilled. This metric is one that measures the effectiveness of the order fulfillment process, crossing the boundaries of functional departments. Under this measurement system, a failure during any step in the process or in any functional department, such as an item shortage on an order line or a wrong invoice, can result in a failure to meet the overall objective of flawlessly fulfilling an order. In addition to measuring the overall perfect order process, diagnostic measures for each task in the fulfillment process would need to be used.

Figure 3.0 depicts a set of order fulfillment measures based on a perfect order process concept. It illustrates the hierarchical relationship of process-based measures with their diagnostic function-based measures. The cross-functional, process-based measures provide visibility to strategic aspects of supply chain performance, while the func-

PERFECT ORDER PROCESS TASK RELATED MEASURES

Task Related Measure	Description
Product availability	Product available to satisfy all order lines
Order entry accuracy	Order entered correctly in lines and in quantities
Warehouse picking accuracy	All items picked in correct quantities (e.g., in make-to-stock environment)
Production accuracy	All items produced in correct quantities and quality (e.g., in make-to-order or assemble to order)
On-time product shipment	All items shipped to customer on time
On-time product delivery	All products delivered to customer on time
Product quality	All products delivered are not defective or damaged
Paperwork accuracy	All documentation is accurate, including advanced shipping notices (ASNs) and bills of lading
Customer inquiry service	All queries on order status handled with courtesy and responsiveness
Invoice accuracy	Order correctly billed (e.g., for pricing and terms & conditions)
Payment accuracy	Payment correctly recorded

Figure 4.0   Perfect order process task-related measures

tion-based measures are more diagnostic in nature, useful for pinpointing problem areas.

Include Cross-Enterprise Measures To Improve Extended Enterprise Performance

The cross-functional process approach to measuring supply chains is applicable for inter- as well as intra-enterprise processes. For example, many would agree that the two most important bottom-line measures of overall supply chain performance relate to:

- The availability of the right products at the point of consumption
- The total landed cost to get the products to the point of consumption (including all material, manufacturing, transportation, warehousing, and inventorying costs along the supply chain)

While these are the penultimate of supply chain measures, it is rare for one organization to control its whole supply chain's performance. Supply chains are typically comprised of many value-adding trading partners that control the portions in which they transact business. While this might be the case, SCM principles dictate that significant benefits can accrue when integrated inter-enterprise processes are in place, to synchronize and optimize the supply chain. These inter-enterprise processes should also be measured to help ensure that they are effective.

To ensure the effectiveness of cross-enterprise processes, a company should measure performance of parts of their supply chain that lie outside their own enterprise. This leads to the question of "Should you measure what is not within the domain of your enterprise or what you cannot control?" Some more specific questions relating this issue are:

- Is a manufacturer responsible for the fact that its products have poor availability on the retail shelf?
- Is a shipper responsible for the freight operations of downstream customers that pay for their own transportation or pick up products at the shipper's location?
- Is an upstream component parts supplier responsible for the fact that a manufacturer's order could not be produced due to lack of the supplier's part?
- Is a manufacturer responsible for on-time delivery to the customer after it has tendered a shipment to a transportation carrier?

Most people would answer "no" to most of these questions, stating that it is useless to measure anything on which you have little or no control. In situations, however, where performance directly or indirectly impacts the availability or cost of products at the point of consumption, the answer should be "yes" to all of these questions.

As an illustration, take the case of a leading toy manufacturer's sales executive who hired people to visit a sample of some of his customer's retail stores shortly after the end of the Christmas holiday season. He had pictures taken of the shelves to assess the availability of his product following the Christmas rush. The pictures showed that in many cases the state of the shelves was a mess, with most items in disarray and most products out of stock – sure to impact the manufacturer's post-holiday sales! This executive, who took the position that his company needed to share some of the responsibility for this, started initiatives to correct it. He implemented programs that were aimed at working more closely with customers on joint store-level planning and in-store merchandising. The strategy paid off resulting in better product availability on his customer's store shelves.

The lesson to be learned from this illustration is that at times it does makes sense to measure what you cannot control, as you may uncover a deficiency in your supply chain's performance. Once found, initiatives can be developed to address the problem and the performance measures can be used as the "call to action." These initiatives usually involve some form of program aimed at taking some level of control of upstream or downstream supply chain activities – extending beyond one's enterprise. Some manufacturers have been implementing SCM programs to extend their control. These programs and their associated performance measures include:

- Vendor Managed Inventory (VMI) programs: customer sales, in-stock availability, and inventory turns
- Continuous Replenishment Programs (CRP): customer sales, in-stock availabil-

ity, and inventory turns
- Quick Response initiatives: customer sales, in-stock availability, and inventory turns
- Forecast-sharing programs: forecast accuracy, order fill rates, and inventory turns
- Production scheduling sharing programs: adherence to schedule and order cycle time
- Category Management programs: customer category sales and in-stock availability

As more companies implement SCM programs, they will be placing greater emphasis on cross-enterprise processes, extending beyond their enterprise. This will lead to the need to implement performance measurement systems that include some external measures, including some for processes that lie outside of a company's domain of control.

Choose A Limited Number of Metrics

A major challenge for many companies when developing a supply chain performance measurement process is limiting the number of measures. Most companies are involved in complex business operations that span across multiple business divisions and geographical boundaries, involving a multitude of sub-processes, tasks, and organizational departments. Wanting to measure everything, there is a tendency to measure too much. The number of measures needs to be limited to ensure that the process is not too cumbersome to administer. One strategy-consulting firm recommends that their clients limit the number of measures to be tracked in each area to between three and five, helping to ensure that the measurement process is not unwieldy.

Align Executive to Management-Level Measures

To ensure that a reasonable number of metrics is defined, an organizing framework is required to select only those that are most important. A key-enabling concept taken from the Balanced Scorecard approach is to focus the measurement process on managing the business, not monitoring and controlling it. Measures should be aligned to supply chain performance objectives to be achieved, not to whether employees are adhering to managerial practices and directions. In this way supply chain performance, not actions, are measured.

To establish a rational set of performance measures, one needs to start with an understanding of the strategic supply chain objectives of a company's executive team. For example, to what degree is the company trying to achieve functional, enterprise-wide integration and extended enterprise integration excellence? Once understood, a limited and balanced set of measures that directly aligns to these strategic objectives needs to be developed. These become the executive level measures used to provide the executive team with indicators as to whether or not their supply chain is performing according to their strategic intent. This set should include a balance of cause and effect type metrics helping executives determine when a particular process area needs to be improved.

In addition to executives, management personnel also need performance measures to help ensure that their supply chain activities are performing well. These measures will be more detailed, tracking both tactical and operational types of activities. To ensure that the executive and management teams are not driving the organization in different directions, the management-level measures need to be aligned with the executive-level measures. Figure 4.0 graphically depicts the relationship and contrasting nature of executive and managerial measures. Using the lower level measures, managers can gauge how well they are doing relative to the overall strategic goals set in place by the executive team. In addition, the lower-level metrics enable executives to drill-down into the more diagnostic metrics, detecting where corrective actions are needed.

An Illustrative Set of Supply Chain Performance Measures

A number of leading-edge companies are beginning to implement supply chain performance measurement systems, some calling them scorecards, while others call them dashboards or cockpits.

While the metrics shown are largely executive-level in nature, this company has plans to break out each of the metrics into more detailed managerial levels. This set of measures provides a good illustration of a balanced set of measures that might be selected to support a manufacturer's supply chain performance measurement process.

What Methods Are Available For Setting Performance Targets?

An important issue in performance measurement is how a company can use measures to gauge its supply chain's performance. To do this effectively, a target for each measure needs to be established, providing the framework for determining the answer to three questions that arise when evaluating a performance metric:

- Has the metric improved from the last time it was reviewed?
- By how much?
- How close is the metric to where it should be?

In order for this evaluation to be meaningful, however, the direction of improvement needs to be established. Should the metric have gone up or gone down? Frequently, in looking at productivity-related metrics an increase represents an improvement; similarly, for cost-related metrics a decrease represents an improvement. This is not always the case! For example, an increase in manufacturing productivity and a decrease in cost would normally be considered an improvement. It would not be an improvement if it caused degradation in customer service performance.

In a way similar to picking a set of balanced metrics, performance targets need to be jointly, not individually, developed. To achieve objectives some metrics may need to increase and others may need to decrease. Each metric in the set has to be viewed in conjunction with the others to determine its proper target. For example, in a situation where a company is trying to achieve same day delivery, delivery times should decrease, while warehouse handling and transportation costs might actually increase.

Thus, while there a variety of ways

in which to set performance targets, they should always be jointly set in the context of strategic objectives. Generally, there are four methods that can be used to set performance targets, described in detail below:

- Historically based targets
- External benchmarks
- Internal benchmarks
- Theoretical targets

Historically Based Targets

Historically based target setting is the most frequently used among all the methods. In using this method, performance targets are based on historical baseline levels. For example, a company having an historical order fill rate of 90% might set a performance target at 95%, trying to improve by five percentage points. This method is the most frequently used because it is the easiest to implement. Once the baseline metrics are established, the same procedures and systems that were used to establish the baseline numbers can also be used on an ongoing basis to measure changes in the metrics.

External Benchmarks

Using external benchmarks to help set performance targets is currently popular, but difficult to use in practice. In general, benchmarking has been in the business limelight for almost ten years, with companies looking outside their operations for best practices and performance comparisons. This method relies on collecting information on performance metrics of companies internal and external to one's industry. A few organizations have collected some benchmarking data in a formal way, including:

- Herbert W. Davis and Company (Fort Lee, NJ) is a small consulting firm that has been conducting logistics cost and service surveys for over 20 years, including its most recent survey that is comprised of information on around 300 North American manufacturer, distributor, and retailer companies. (Davis uses the results to support its consulting business.)
- Pittiglio, Rabin, Todd &McGrath (PTRM) (Weston, MA) conducts a supply chain a benchmarking study, its Integrated Supply-Chain Benchmarking Study. The last published study, fourth in the series, included information on about 225 worldwide participants. (The company uses the results to support its consulting business.)
- The Demand Activated Manufacturing Architecture (DAMA) project, a part of the American Textile Partnership, has collected benchmark data on the performance companies, mostly in the 'soft goods' industries. This data was obtained from Kurt Salmon Associates, Inc. (Atlanta, GA) and The Garr Consulting Group, a division of Deloitte & Touche, Inc. (New York, NY), and The Logistics Institute of the Georgia Institute of Technology.

Once external benchmarking metrics are collected, a company's internal metrics are generated and a gap analysis is done – typically looking at the best-in-class within their own industry as well as external to it. This is followed by more analysis to assess the degree to which the company can achieve these performance levels, including what business practice changes are necessary to close the gaps.

While appealing, the external benchmarking method has a major shortcoming to it as to which set of companies are comparable. A substantial amount of analysis is required to ensure that external benchmarks are meaningful, especially when using data from companies that operate within different business environments (e.g., differing products or sales channels). This makes the use of external benchmarks difficult, since comparable external benchmarks may not be available or too controversial. On the other hand, external benchmarks, especially from one's competitors, may be extremely important towards keeping an organization's supply chain competitive.

Internal Benchmarks

Performance target setting using internal benchmarks is a common approach, since it requires only internal measures. Within this method, comparable functional departments, processes, and facilities within a company are measured in the same way. For example, there may be a set of metrics in use for all warehousing facilities, another set for all manufacturing plants, and another set for all customer service departments. Similar to the external benchmarking approach, "best-in-class" functional organizations are identified and their benchmark metrics are used as the basis for establishing performance targets for other functional organizations.

In contrast to external benchmarking, internal benchmarking data is easier to collect. The method is less controversial when comparing business operations since internal organizations usually operate in similar business environments. While this internal benchmarking method is easier to implement, it too has some serious drawbacks to it. The major one involves stretching the organization to achieve better performance. That is, using a "best-in-class" internal organization to set targets may limit the company's performance relative to its competitors.

Theoretical Targets

The use of theoretical target setting is a relatively new method advocated by some consultants. Under this method a company conducts an analysis to theoretically determine how its supply chain performance could be improved. It would then implement the business changes necessary to achieve these improvements and put a set of performance targets in place based on estimates made during the analysis.

In particular, one consultant, Paul Bender of Bender Consulting/SynQuest, Inc. (Atlanta, GA), advocates the use of supply chain optimization to help set theoretical performance targets. Using his approach, a company would first undergo an analysis to determine how it should optimize supply chain performance. It would then use the estimates made during the analysis to set its performance targets. For example, a company might determine that in order for it to maximize its long-term profits, it should increase on-time order due-date performance, while increasing its manufacturing costs and decreasing its air freight charges. The company would

ILLUSTRATIVE SET OF BALANCED METRICS DEVELOPED BY A CPG MANUFACTURER

Supply Chain Measure	Corresponding Metric
Customer Service	Order fill rate Line item fill rate Dollar fill rate Cycle time components and variability On-time delivery Backorder duration Perfect order fill rate Customer satisfaction survey results
Asset Management	Inventory days of supply Inventory accuracy Inventory turns Cash-to-cash cycle time
Forecast Accuracy	Orders versus forecasts Shipments versus forecast
Costs	Various costs
Value-Added	Economic value added
Manufacturing Measures (MRPII) • Customer Service • Sales Plan - family product level • Detailed Sales Forecast • Production Plan • DRP Replenishment Performance • Master Schedule Performance • Master Schedule Stability • Manufacturing Performance • Supplier Performance • Materials Inventory Accuracy • Bill of Materials Accuracy • Routings	% Complete shipments on-time Actual sales versus plan Actual sales versus plan Actual production versus plan Warehouse receipts versus orders % Items completed % Schedule changes Actual production versus schedule Actual receipts versus scheduled Accurate records versus counted Accurate bills versus audited Accurate processes versus audited

Figure 5.0 Balanced metrics developed by a CPG manufacturer

then use the results of the analysis to increase its performance targets for manufacturing costs and on-time order due-date performance, while appropriately decreasing the target on its airfreight charges.

While conducting an optimization analysis is an intuitively appealing method for determining performance targets, it is not always the easiest to do. Another alternate approach involves the use of supply chain simulation analysis that includes conducting what-if studies on initiatives to improve performance. The results of these studies could then be used to set theoretical targets. For example, a "what-if" study might be conducted to assess inventory reductions that might accrue from statistical safety stock setting. The study's estimated reductions would be used to reset performance targets for inventory turns.

Setting performance targets on a theoretical basis is most useful for insuring that a balanced set of metrics is developed. Often, only by doing a thorough analysis can one assess how an initiative would impact various aspects within a supply chain.

In practice, a combination of the four performance target-setting methods described above should be used. No one method is practical for determining targets since one cannot always get a full set of comparable benchmarking information or conduct the extensive analyses needed to develop a full set of theoretical performance targets.

What Are Application Vendors Doing To Support Supply Chain Performance Measurement?

Application vendors are faced with a challenge when trying to provide supply chain performance measurement functionality within their software products. Users often wish to include metrics relating to information not residing within the vendor's application database. (Figure 5.0 shows the potential sources from which a supply chain performance measurement system may have to draw data). This is especially the case when measuring the performance of cross-functional and inter-enterprise processes, which involve drawing information about any functional department within a company, or about customer/supplier activities. Also, most advanced planning and scheduling (APS) applications focus on the future, rarely concerned with what went on in the past (except relative to measuring forecast errors). While Enterprise Resource Planning (ERP) vendors that offer SCM functionality have more of the necessary data within their product suites, they have not focused on supply chain-related performance measurement. Until recently they have focused most of their historical reporting functionality on providing transactional auditing, tracing, and tracking.

Given the interest shown in supply chain performance measurement, substantially driven by business consultants, vendors have started to consider supplementing their product suites by offering enhanced supply chain performance reporting capabilities.

Traditional SCM Vendors Provide Reporting On A Limited Number of Metrics

Traditionally SCM application vendors have focused their development efforts on enabling planning, scheduling, and execution, targeted toward supporting decision-making, not tracking historical performance. Some SCM vendors have functionality to report historical supply chain performance focused around either functional or planning-related metrics. For example, SynQuest provides standard reporting on a variety of metrics such as forecast error, inventory turns, and order completeness, while also allowing users to define related metrics within each of its function-based modules. Similarly, Manugistics (Rockville, MD) provides standard reporting functionality on forecasting performance and on-time delivery, as well as some general purpose capabilities to report on user-defined metrics such as order fulfillment, factory

http://lapide.ASCET.com

floor conformance, warehouse space utilization, and promotional effectiveness.

In contrast to these two vendors, i2 Technologies (Irving, TX) provides a solution, RHYTHM Reporter, which is enabled by incorporating OLAP technology from Arbor Software's (Ann Arbor, MI) Essbase product. The solution allows users to create reports on information contained within the Supply Chain Planner application and includes a variety of standard reports focused on master planning, profit optimization, and demand fulfillment. Similar to i2, Logility (Atlanta, GA) provides some reporting capability by incorporating OLAP technology from Cognos (Ottawa, Canada). Logility provides standard interfaces into Cognos' solution to support users doing customized analysis. Logility also provides standard reporting capabilities within its functional modules that can report on a variety of measures such as forecast error, assembly line utilization, late orders, and warehouse receipts.

Similar to i2 and Logility, AMR Research expects that other SCM vendors will start to provide OLAP-based solutions to allow their customers to track additional supply chain performance measures. For example, webPLAN (Ottawa, Canada), formerly called Enterprise Planning Solutions, is developing a product, onPLAN, which will provide users with a KPI business report card. The product, which was released in 1998, imbeds OLAP technology from InterNetivity, Inc. (Ottawa, Canada) that enables numeric and graphical reporting, and the drilling down and slicing and dicing of data.

There are two new noteworthy SCM vendors that focus exclusively on performance measurement. One is VIT (Palo Alto, CA), which offers the SeeChain software application suite that consists of five modules: Demand Accuracy, Raw Materials, Production Performance, Finished Goods, and Fulfillment. The vendor has a unique graphical user interface that allows users to drill down from higher, aggregated measures to lower detailed measures, enabling them to easily diagnose non-performing supply chain elements. This vendor comes the closest to offering an application that enables users to view their overall supply chain, limited only by data that can be drawn by a company into a single database structure the company provides. Another SCM vendor that provides unique performance measurement functionality is Maxager Technology (San Rafael, CA). The company specializes in an application that reports on historical product-level profitability and production performance. The vendor provides users with shop floor data collection applications and uses constraint-based costing methods to assess product level production performance. Similar to other SCM solutions, the application provides refined estimates of manufacturing performance representing only a portion of the overall supply chain performance measures needed.

ERP Vendors Offering SCM Functionality Are Starting to Address Supply Chain Performance Measurement

Some ERP vendors also offering SCM functionality have put more focus on historical performance measurement than the SCM vendors; having specialized in providing solutions focused more on transactional history. While these vendors have built some OLAP-based performance reporting functionality into their product suites, they are still a long way from fully meeting the needs of supply chain performance measurement.

SAP (Walldorf, Germany) has been offering a logistics-related performance-reporting product, its Logistics Information System (LIS). This R/3-based application allows a user to assemble information from a range of R/3 modules and provides functionality to analyze the data in a number of ways, including in tables and graphs. As part of its new Advanced Planner and Optimizer (APO) product initiative, the company is planning to provide users with functionality that measures a set of pre-defined supply chain KPIs within its Supply Chain Cockpit product. The company has also recently laid out ambitious plans to develop more general-purpose functionality under its Business Intelligence initiative, announced at SAPPHIRE '98. In addition,

TYPICAL FUNCTION-BASED MEASUREMENTS AND RELATED GOALS

	PURCHASING	MANUFACTURING	LOGISTICS	CUSTOMER SERVICE/SALES
Measures	• Supplier Performance • Cost Per Unit Purchased	• Set-ups and changeover Times • Plant Utilization • Waste and Scrap	• Inventory Turns • Transportation Costs • Warehouse Productivity	• Customer Satisfaction • Customer Order Cycle Time
Goals	• Multiple Supplies (potential varying quality) • Large Purchase Orders • Increased Materials Inventories	• Long runs • Increased Finished Goods • Decreased Materials Inventories • Bulk Customer Orders • Product Quality	• Decrease Finished Goods Inventories • Centralized Stocking Locations • Bulk Customer Orders	• Increased Inventories • Multiple Stocking Locations Close to Customers • JIT Customer Orders

Figure 6.0 Function-based measurements and related goals

SAP recently purchased a minority share in ABC Technologies, Inc. (Beaverton, OR), a leading player in activity-based costing and management solutions. ABC Technologies will integrate its functionality into R/3 to enable general-purpose performance measurement based on the ABC approach. This functionality will also be applicable to measuring supply chain performance.

Oracle (Redwood Shores, CA), a database vendor that has always provided some performance measurement functionality, has plans to expand it. Similar to SAP, it will offer ABC costing functionality, having recently purchased PriceWaterhouse-Coopers LLP's (New York, NY) activity-based costing, budgeting, and management software, ACTIVA. While more general purpose in nature, some of the ABC functionality should be applicable to measuring supply chain performance.

PeopleSoft (Pleasanton, CA) is also adding general-purpose performance measurement that will be applicable to supply chain measurement. The vendor is currently working with on an initiative to provide a solution based on the Balanced Scorecard and ABC approaches.

How Should A Company Get Started?

Based on our research, we have concluded that there is no one recommended approach or set of measures to be used to measure one's supply chain performance. While espousing the importance of measuring supply chain performance, leading consultants have no definitive set of metrics to recommend. All agree, however, that approaches such as the Balanced Scorecard, the SCOR Model, The Logistics Scoreboard, and others discussed herein, provide excellent guidance when developing a supply chain performance measurement system. In addition, although the software vendors we polled enable a limited range of supply chain performance measures, they are improving and planning to add more functionality to their product sets. Over time, we expect vendors to offer more complete packaged applications for supply chain performance measurement.

All this should not dissuade users, however, from starting to measure their supply chain's performance in the context of assessing the success of initiatives aimed at achieving strategic objectives. It is too important! With substantial resources – dollars and people – being applied towards implementing various supply chain programs, users should measure performance to insure desired change happens.

For those users just getting started, implementing supply chain performance measurement should not be done all at once. For example, one could start by first implementing executive-level scorecard measures in a manual fashion. This could then be followed up with more automation, through the use of database tools and the addition of managerial-level metrics. As application vendors develop more capabilities in the area of performance measurement further automation of the process can be implemented over time.

Based on the research done for this report, we would recommend the following steps be taken when implementing supply chain performance improvement and measurement:

- Have executives articulate the strategic supply chain vision and company objectives, including the degree of focus to be placed on achieving functional, enterprise-wide integration and extended enterprise integration excellence. For example, the functional excellence portion of the vision might be that "we will reduce our manufacturing costs over the next two years" and related objectives would be to reduce manufacturing operating and material costs.
- Define executive level measures for each objective for their scorecard. The total number of measures used should be limited to up to 20 or so. For example, these might be metrics such as material cost per pound purchased and operating manufacturing cost per unit produced.
- Establish managerial level objectives and measures that align to the executive level ones. These should be more tactical and operational, providing diagnostic information on whether executive objectives are being met. Breaking down the higher-level measures typically does this. For example, these might be measures for a particular plant's cost per ton purchased for a specific class of material.
- Identify supply chain initiatives that specifically address the executive and managerial performance improvement objectives. For example, this might include a core supplier program reducing the number of material suppliers to ones with the lowest cost, meeting quality standards.
- Establish targets for all metrics defined, using a combination of historical performance, external/internal benchmarks, and theoretical estimates (often obtained from operational quantitative analysis of the supply chain initiatives). A timeline for achieving the targets needs to be established for each metric, consistent with the schedules developed for the supply chain initiatives. For example, while a program might be expected to ultimately reduce material costs by 3%, targets for its first year of implementation might be only 1%, with an additional 2% improvement the next year.
- Implement new initiatives in concert with a formal measurement system to keep track of performance improvement over time, using a combination of whatever technology makes sense; be it based on spreadsheets, database products or a vendor's suite of packaged applications.

While these steps are useful for getting started, ongoing supply chain performance measurement requires that the steps be revisited on a routine basis, as objectives change and new programs and initiatives are undertaken. Keeping the measurement process aligned to supply chain objectives and activities will provide the information needed to drive your supply chain's performance, helping to ensure that resources are appropriately applied and desired strategic change is happening.

Robocom's RIMS is Essential for Warehouse Management

Contact Information

Irwin Balaban
Chairman

David Dinin
President and CEO

Lawrence B. Klein
EVP, Worldwide

C. Kenneth Morrelly
SVP

Elizabeth A. Burke
VP, Finance, CFO, and Treasurer

Robocom Sytems International Headquarters
511 Ocean Avenue
Massapequa, NY 11758
Toll-Free 800.795.5100
Phone 516.795.5100
Fax 516.795.6933
sales@robocom.com

Robocom Clients Include

Food
Unilever
Golden Circle
AgrocomMaxser
Van Den Bergh

Medical
C.R. Bard
Roche
Ethicon
Arrow International

Petro-Chemical
Exxon
Mobil
Amoco
Aeroquip
Textron/Flexalloy
Copeland
Crown Lift Truck
Modine Manufacturing
TBC
JCB Service
Harada

Robocom's RIMS Warehouse Management System (WMS) is an essential part of today's warehouse-improving the flow of critical information and optimizing the use of all warehouse assets. RIMS operates on multiple platforms and has database capabilities to seamlessly support internet transactions on internet time.

Unparalleled customer satisfaction and warehouse efficiencies are achieved through the application of RIMS directed at changing the value of information and inventory by balancing supply chain with market demand.

RIMS is Reliable

Today, over 90% of our clients utilize RIMS without modifications. Since RIMS is implemented as a standard product, a 16-week implementation cycle provides a rapid time to benefit and a timely return on investment. RIMS provides standard warehouse functionality that addresses most industries with a specific concentration in these industries: government, automotive/aerospace, food manufacturers, consumer goods, petro-chemical, and medical/pharmaceutical.

Focused on the development of RIMS, continuing research and development assures Robocom's customers that their investment will continue profitable operation through periodic product upgrades. Robocom has an extensive network of distributors and integration partners around the world that specialize in the implementation of RIMS.

RIMS is Cost-Effective

RIMS, a fourth-generation WMS, automates your warehouse, allowing greater customer service, a rapid return on investment, immediate cost savings, and improved overall efficiencies. Users of RIMS benefit from increased labor productivity, throughput enhancement, and cost reduction with a 16-week implementation time, RIMS is an exciting information technology management tool that turns vast amounts of warehouse data into information and then into knowledge about your warehouse, distribution, or supply chain process. Certified interfaces to various host and legacy systems including QAD, SAP, and Baan.

Platforms Supported by RIMS
- Windows NT, UNIX, or Linux
- Character or GUI Client
- Databases Supported: Progress, Oracle, and any ODBC-compliant database.
- HP, IBM, Digital UNIX platforms, and NT servers

Warehouse Management Functionality
- Receiving
- Putaway
- Picking
- Shipping
- Cycle Counting
- Rewarehousing
- Labor Planning
- Volume Optimization
- Reverse Logistics
- Quality Control
- Assembly Kitting
- Production Module
- Government Property

TrackingRobocom/RIMS experience comes from installation in 90 of the most complex interactive environments. This means we have "probably seen it before" and can assist you in suggestions for the re-engineering of your process. The below installed base demonstrates unparalleled flexibility and breadth, continual process refinements, and leads to faster WMS implementation.

Q&A with

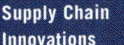

Paul Albright
SeeCommerce
http://albright.ASCET.com

Business Velocity through E-Supply Chain Excellence

The editors asked Paul Albright, President and CEO of SeeCommerce (formerly VIT) how supply chain visibility and performance measurement can be used to derive significant business value from existing technology investments. He discusses how SeeCommerce's SeeChain applications help companies diagnose problems and pinpoint opportunities, which result in improved supplier performance, lower carried inventory costs, and, ultimately, competitive advantage.

Why should senior executives explore supply chain visibility and performance measurement?

We need only to look back at Christmas 1999 to understand the significance of a high-performance supply chain. For dot-coms and brick-and-mortar manufacturers alike, fulfillment problems devastated bottom lines – and valuations. Manufacturers realized, the hard way, that understanding the performance of their supply chains was far more important to their success than a glitzy Web presence.

Now that the manufacturing world is embracing an e-business model, executives realize that running an extended supply chain without performance visibility is like trying to fly an airplane by looking at the fuel gauge. Key decision-makers need a transparent, real-time view of the supply chain so they can proactively take advantage of changing conditions and avert disasters before they happen. In today's competitive environment, business managers simply can't afford to wait weeks – or months – for the information they need. They need to see how their manufacturing initiatives are performing real-time, so their employees and partners can immediately collaborate to make faster, better decisions across the global supply chain.

How is SeeCommerce helping companies leverage their existing technology investments to exceed their supply chain performance goals?

Our Internet applications deliver new value for companies' past investments in ERP (enterprise resource planning) and manufacturing systems by providing immediate views of supply chain information on demand. Each user actually sees data in business context so he or she can take action with confidence. Our customers consider SeeChain essential for competitive advantage, allowing them to see, investigate, and take action on supply chain problems in real time through the Web.

Our applications represent a new era for software – technology that provides business managers, which are 95% of the users – with information they understand and need to do their daily jobs better. It's summarized so users see transparent views of their requested data on the fly – why should they care if it comes from SAP, i2, Manugistics, or some other system? Because it's all via the Internet, we supercharge their organizations in weeks, not months, so users gain a rapid return on investment.

What do you see in the future for supply chain technology? What new collaborative technology is on the horizon?

We believe that the next wave in supply chain technology will be Supplier Relationship Management (SRM). The world has come to understand the value of CRM (customer relationship management) and ORM (operating resources management). SRM presents a new level of business effectiveness.

The driving premise behind SRM is that you're only as good to your customers as your suppliers are to you. A leading industry analyst reported that there is a trillion dollars of inefficiency left in the supply chain, much of which is supplier-related. With the rise of e-commerce and online procurement, the business-to-business world must embrace a whole new type of

Paul Albright is President and CEO of SeeCommerce. Prior to joining SeeCommerce, Mr. Albright was Senior Vice President of Worldwide Marketing and Channels for Informatica. During his tenure as Senior Vice President, Informatica became the established leader in data mart, analytical applications, distributed computing, and Internet technologies.

white paper

supplier relationship. In order to take full advantage of direct supplier and independent trading exchanges, businesses need a dynamic supplier collaboration system to evaluate and improve myriad supplier relationships.

To help our customers collaborate with their suppliers, we recently introduced SeeChain Supplier. It's designed to help major manufacturers and distributors greatly improve suppliers' performance and collaboration. Measuring supplier services based on various metrics, including timeliness of order fulfillment and downstream quality of goods, SeeChain Supplier aggregates and analyzes supplier performance data from existing transaction systems and presents it daily via the Web.

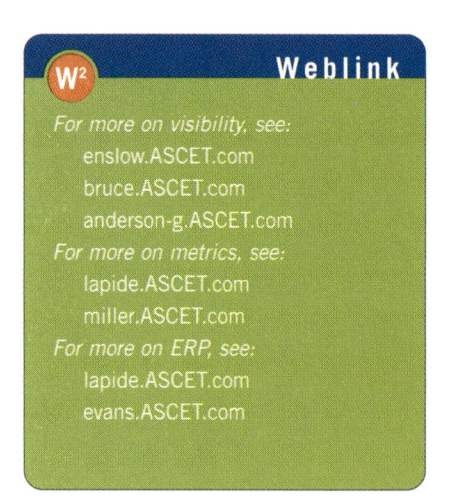

Several of our customers have had supplier-rating systems for years, but they were typically reactive, not proactive. They report that SeeChain Supplier significantly enhances their ability to collaborate with thousands of suppliers, which they expect to result in up to a 15% improvement in supplier performance. Since performance, in turn, affects cost savings, parts availability, and customer satisfaction, they should see a definite bottom-line impact from using the SeeChain Supplier application.

What types of companies can best benefit from this technology?

Companies from a wide variety of industries can benefit from supply chain visibility and performance measurement software, including high-tech and packaged-goods manufacturing, pharmaceuticals, automotive, and retail.

Typically, we work with Global 1000 companies that wish to leverage the Web to gain competitive advantage by enhancing the performance of their supply chain operations. They've usually made significant investments in ERP and operational systems, and they have chosen us to provide intuitive, secure access to their information. As a result, hundreds of decision-makers can make better decisions faster.

Why is SeeCommerce is in a position to help major manufacturers and distributors realize bottom-line benefits?

With first-to-market standing, strong analyst support and A-list financial backing, SeeCommerce is well positioned to be a valuable, stable partner for our clients. By delivering real bottom-line impact, we've secured multi-billion dollar, market-leading Global 1000 companies as customers, some of whom have been in production and gaining measurable business value from our products since Q4 of 1998.

While some niche players offer pieces of our solution, no one can provide the breadth of domain expertise we hold in supply chain and Web technology. With every implementation we gain even broader expertise, which, in turn, we fold into the product. This allows our customers – as well as us – to get further and further ahead of any potential competitive threat.

W² Weblink

For more on visibility, see:
enslow.ASCET.com
bruce.ASCET.com
anderson-g.ASCET.com

For more on metrics, see:
lapide.ASCET.com
miller.ASCET.com

For more on ERP, see:
lapide.ASCET.com
evans.ASCET.com

Assessing the Value in Your Supply Chain: An Interview with Jeffrey Miller

Jeffrey Miller, an associate partner in the Andersen Consulting Supply Chain Practice, is a leader in value chain performance and the development of new business models. As leadership sponsor for Andersen Consulting's diagnostic approach to identifying supply chain value, he focuses on helping clients identify and link their supply chain core capabilities to business and financial outcomes. We spoke with Jeffrey about the complexities of identifying actionable supply chain improvement opportunities that deliver sustainable improvement in a company's performance.

What do you see as the key issues that companies face in addressing supply chain performance improvements?

There are many challenges that a company faces when seeking to improve supply chain performance. The supply chain is a particularly complex system that offers numerous opportunities for enhanced performance. But, to make the right improvements, appropriate supply chain performance metrics must be chosen. Determining which metrics to collect and then how to interpret them requires a clear connection between the measured process and its contribution to revenue, cost, and capital performance. The difficulty is that there is often a gap between supply chain operational measures and the financial outcomes a company is trying to achieve. To make significant progress, you have to have the supply chain operational side connected to the financial side. For example, if I am an assembler of computers, continuity of supply will likely be one of my most important supply chain performance goals. I must understand my suppliers' capabilities to respond to surges in my demand and connect these capabilities to my financial outcomes. Performance targets are built around these metrics. So the question becomes "How do I determine the contribution each of my core supply chain operations make toward my business and financial goals?" This is a different question, for example, than simply asking, "How can logistics improvement contribute to cost minimization?"

How does Andersen Consulting assist their clients with this issue?

Traditional methods of measuring supply chain performance through purely functional metrics (which are often financially oriented) are no longer sufficient to meet the business goals of our clients. Our clients need to capture critical quantitative performance data across (and between) functions, as well as qualitative insight into supplier and partner relationships.

To address this need, we developed the Supply Chain Value Assessment, or SCVA. SCVA is a framework that connects the operating performance metrics of specific supply chain processes to the desired financial outcomes against which the business measures itself. We built a framework around these performance and financial linkages, supported by a set of Internet-based tools and technologies that enable our client and consulting teams to define and implement the proper metrics. New kinds of metrics which reside at the "seams" between processes are key to helping our clients identify the right areas of their supply chain upon which to focus their improvement efforts.

What is the SCVA framework?

In the SCVA, we use qualitative and quantitative techniques to measure progress toward achievement of desired business outcomes. The SCVA helps build the value proposition for making a change to supply chain structure or operation. It determines the value of changing what we do –

Jeffrey Miller, an associate partner in the Andersen Consulting Supply Chain Practice, is a leader in value chain performance and the development of new business models. As partner sponsor for Andersen Consulting's diagnostic approach to identifying supply chain value, he focuses on helping clients link their supply chain operations to business or financial outcomes. We spoke with him about the difficult nature of identifying actionable supply chain improvement opportunities that deliver sustainable change to a company's performance.

http://miller.ASCET.com 301

white paper

the value of closing a performance gap. The SCVA framework finds the weak areas in supply chain operations and connects the value of improvement to revenue lift and cost reduction opportunities.

SCVA applies several tools and methods to collect, analyze, and report data. These three core activities contain embedded Andersen Consulting knowledge of leading supply chain practices and business performance equations. The entire SCVA resides as an Internet-based collaborative business application. In this way, geographically dispersed groups may all contribute to the analysis and supply chain value proposition efforts.

Naturally, what makes this framework effective is the supply chain practitioners' knowledge — that of our clients coupled with our own experience and expertise. Cross-functional experience is vital to interpreting the information collected and calculated through SCVA, since it builds the value propositions for directing your actions to the opportunities with greatest potential value.

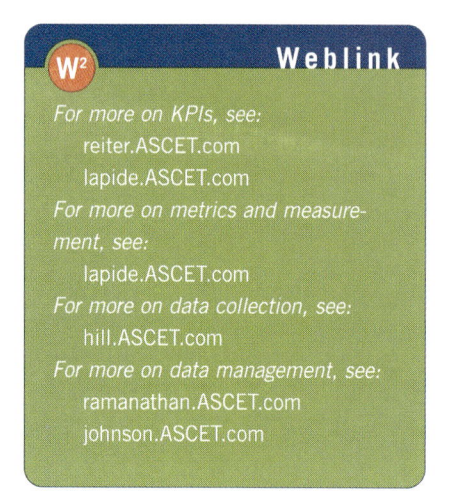

Weblink

For more on KPIs, see:
  reiter.ASCET.com
  lapide.ASCET.com

For more on metrics and measurement, see:
  lapide.ASCET.com

For more on data collection, see:
  hill.ASCET.com

For more on data management, see:
  ramanathan.ASCET.com
  johnson.ASCET.com

Can you describe the SCVA process?

To begin, we meet with our client — and depending on the scope of the endeavor, their key business partners — to identify initial data to be collected based on our joint initial assessment of supply chain performance and opportunities. Benchmark reference data are used here. Simultaneously, we conduct a series of interviews with key executives, customers, and suppliers to collect qualitative data. For example, a questionnaire might present the client's planning leader with a statement such as "I share lead times for critical materials with my suppliers on a timeline that supports their ability to meet my needs." The client respondent checks off whether he strongly agrees, agrees, disagrees, etc. Similarly, the client's suppliers are presented with the statement "My customer shares with me the lead times and identifies critical materials to support my ability to meet his need," and again, checks the box which best represents his perception, from strongly disagree to strongly agree.

The results are often surprising to clients. With significant frequency, there is a very large disconnect between the perceptions of the client and the perceptions of their supplier. This perception gap regarding the operating performance of the other party must be addressed before a substantive conversation can be had about advancing the capabilities and responsiveness of the supply chain. Often, such business partners believe that they are each contributing the information that the other side needs, when in fact our interviews often reveal the opposite is true. These relationship and perception issues must be closed before attacking the factual performance issues. Following this initial qualitative work, we'll decide on the specific operating data to be collected in support of the analysis and business case. We collect factual performance data to support the calculation of key performance indicators (KPIs). These KPIs often reside in the "white space" between functions of particular interest. In addition, we ask specifically for source metric data. We then use the toolset to calculate the KPIs directly through the framework, rather than requesting the KPI value itself. In this way, we assure that the KPI is calculated the same way each time.

What is the value that a diagnostic of this nature delivers?

Supply Chain Value Assessment is more than a diagnostic, it is a framework for building fact-based value propositions to change supply chain structures and operations. For clients who have institutionalized SCVA, it has become a new, fact-based "currency of conversation" between the client and trading partner on supply chain performance. Fact-based discussions on supply chain performance and the supporting metric data, results and interpretations also help to mitigate the risk of failure since the approaches and data inputs have been agreed to by key process stakeholders. Finally, by conducting SCVA across stakeholder groups, the sustainability of change programs is enhanced. Systems of metrics are tied to financial outcomes, and continuously guide improvement programs across disciplines. Speed to benefit, risk mitigation, and sustainability — these are the three leading goals for any supply chain transformation or performance improvement program, and SCVA is the performance management engine which supports each one.

Copyright©2000 Andersen Consulting LLP

Are All of Your Trading Partners "Worth It" to You?

It is no longer sufficient for your organization to simply be lean, agile, and efficient. Your entire supply chain must also perform like you do. If some of your trading partner suppliers and customers are excessive high-maintenance to you, then they erode profit margins. Who are they, and how much do they drag down margins? How does one properly measure customer and supplier profitability? How does one de-select or "fire" a customer or a supplier? To be competitive, a company must know its sources of profit and understand its cost structure.

All Customers and Suppliers are Not Created Equal

If two customers purchased from your company the exact same mix of products and services at the exact same prices during the exact same time period, would they be equally profitable? Of course not. Some customers behave like saints and others like sinners. Some customers place standard orders with no fuss, while others demand non-standard everything. Some customers buy your product or service and you hardly hear from them, while others you always hear from — and it is usually to change their delivery requirements, inquire about and expedite their order, or return or exchange their goods. In some cases, just the geographic territory the customer resides in makes the difference.

Employees often wonder if the bothersome or remote customer is worth it. What they are really asking is this: If we added up the costs of our time, effort, interruptions, and disruptions attributed to those kinds of customers, in addition to the costs of the products and base services that that customer drew on, did we make any profit? That is a good question. How do we know? How do we know the level of profitability of any or all of our customers? Most organizations do not. Since organizations are continuously pursuing prospects, they might want to know how profitable they will be relative to each other or to our existing customers.

Employees can ask a similar question about the inbound costs from their suppliers. Are some suppliers so much more difficult to work with that they ultimately drag down the organization's profits?

If all of these "extra" costs are passed on to customers by ultimately increasing prices to the end-consumer, what is the risk that our entire supply chain has finally pushed the consumer to switch to a substitute or a competitor's product, or postpone their purchase altogether? That means lost sales to everyone. It is no longer sufficient for your organization alone to be lean, agile, and efficient. Your entire supply chain must also perform efficiently.

The Pursuit of Truth About Profits

Why would you want to know answers for what your employees are asking? Possibly to answer more direct questions about your customers and suppliers, such as:

- Do we push for volume or for margin with a specific customer?
- Are there ways to improve profitability by altering the way we package, sell, deliver, or generally service a customer?
- Does the customer's sales volume justify the discounts, rebates, or promotion structure we provide that customer?
- Can we realize benefits from changing strategies by influencing our customers to alter their behavior to buy differently (and more profitably) from us?
- Can we shift work to or from our suppliers based on who is more capable?

---

written by:

Gary Cokins
ABC Technologies, Inc.
http://cokins.ASCET.com

Gary Cokins is the Director of Industry Relations for ABC Technologies, Inc., a leading provider of activity-based information software. He is an internationally recognized expert, speaker, and author on advanced cost management and performance improvement systems.

Gary is chairperson of a CAM-I Special Interest Group defining the design rules for ABC models, which will support the eventual introduction ABC standards and conceivably certification.

Mr. Cokins is a member of Journal of Cost Management Editorial Advisory Board. He is an instructor for the Institute of Industrial Engineers (IIE), National Association of Purchasing Management (NAPM), and the American Society for Quality (ASQ).

To be competitive, a company must know its sources of profit and understand its cost structure. A competitive company must also ultimately translate its strategies into actions. For outright unprofitable customers, you would want to explore the possible options of raising prices, or surcharging them for the extra work. You may want to reduce the causes of your extra work for them, streamline your delivery process so it costs you less to serve them, or finally alter their behavior so that those customers place fewer demands on your organization.

In Peter Francese's book, *Marketing Know-How*, he posed key questions around a customer/marketing model that basically instructs marketers to "follow the money!" Francese starts by asking what kinds of customers are loyal and profitable – and what kinds are only marginally profitable, or, worse yet, are losing you money. The good news is there is now a cost measurement methodology called activity-based cost management (ABC/M) that can economically and accurately trace the consumption of your organization's resource costs to those types and kinds of channels and customer segments who place varying demands on you. Determining your "costs-to-serve" customers is logical with ABC/M. ABC/M also traces the consumption on you by varying supplier behavior; high maintenance suppliers erode your margins as well.

Figure 1.0 shows the framework for how ABC/M traces, segments, and re-assigns costs based on the cause-and-effect demands triggered by customers and their orders. ABC/M refers to these triggers as "activity drivers." When the cost of processing a customer's orders is subtracted from the sales for those orders, you can know historically whether you made or lost money. You will also know whether or not an accepted price quote for a future customer order will be profitable or not.

Employee Denial, Guilt, and Resistance to Change

Here is an ironic question. Why would some people not want to have access to customer profitability data? Some

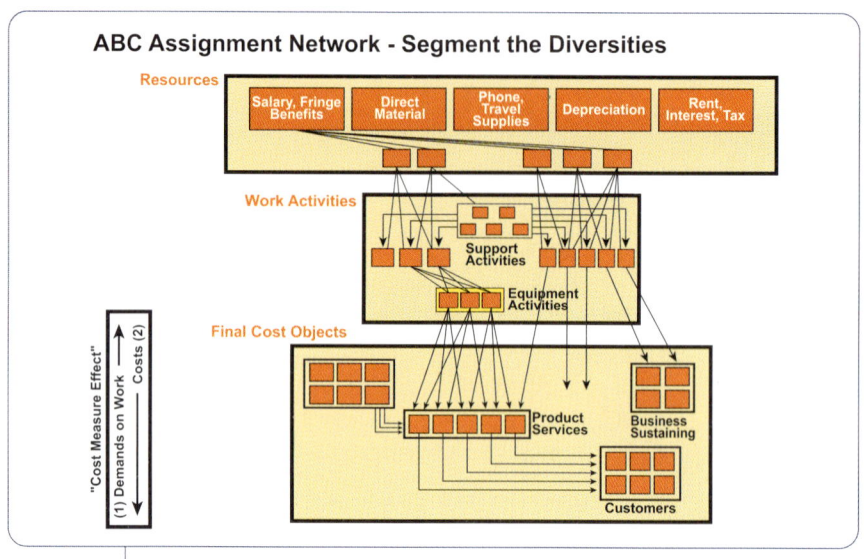

Figure 1.0 — The ABC/M framework

employees intuitively suspect the truth – that there are losers – but these employees will likely presume that their companies would never want to "drop" those customers; they also perceive that those customers still provide sales volume that somehow "covers the overhead." But all the product costs, base service costs, and unrecognized extra costs may not be fully recovered by the sales prices!

In other situations, some employees are evaluated or incented with commissions that are based on sales volumes, so they don't place as much importance on costs and profits – only on sales volume. Some employees believe that on average there is very little that distinguishes any differences between customers, so they basically view customers as clones of each other. Some employees may think that those customers who create extra demands on work through their unwelcome expedites, frequent small orders, slow-bill collection follow-up, difficult or distant access, and the like, those high-maintenance customers should be subsidized by effort-free customers. These employees are not disloyal – they need education on how profits are generated, and a change of mindset.

The issue here is not only determining the profit contribution of customers, including "accurate" costs for the products

they buy, but also understanding the elements of customer-specific work that comprise the entire costs to serve each of them. Your suppliers can be similarly viewed; those who cause you extra work are ultimately dragging down the profit margin from your customers. It is no longer acceptable not to have a rational system of assigning so-called non-traceable costs to their sources of origin – whether those sources be suppliers, products, or customers.

Finally, your advanced suppliers may very well be examining you this same way. Are you a high maintenance customer to them? Might they be considering "firing" you because you are not worth it to them?

Beneath the Iceberg: Unrealized Profits

What is the reality of profits and losses? When companies take the time to define and measure their in-house work activities and directly associate them to the bigger and smaller consumers of their work, the obvious occurs. In addition to the products and base-services provided to customers, there are big users, small users, and those in between other portions of your workload. But since pricing is usually determined (and quoted) based on average-based standards, those customer-driven imbalances are rarely reflected in the pricing. High-maintenance and low-

304 Achieving Supply Chain Excellence Through Technology

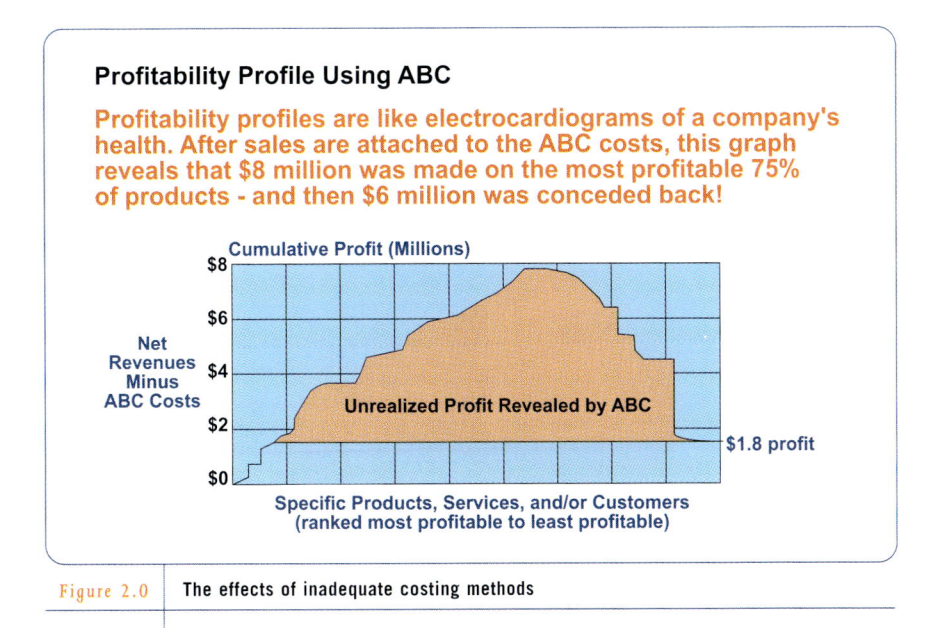

> **Profitability Profile Using ABC**
>
> Profitability profiles are like electrocardiograms of a company's health. After sales are attached to the ABC costs, this graph reveals that $8 million was made on the most profitable 75% of products - and then $6 million was conceded back!
>
> *Cumulative Profit (Millions)*
> Net Revenues Minus ABC Costs
> Unrealized Profit Revealed by ABC
> $1.8 profit
> Specific Products, Services, and/or Customers
> (ranked most profitable to least profitable)

Figure 2.0   The effects of inadequate costing methods

maintenance customers are equally priced and reported as equally profitable; this is not accurate.

When the inequities are replaced with true consumption measures of the "costs-to-serve" customers, the companies who have performed this analysis realize that they make a high profit on the winners but simultaneously give back a great deal of unrealized profit on the losers. Both the profits and losses are usually big numbers. The company only banks the net difference. That is the "bottom-line" profit number that senior management sees. Although not empirically tested, experiences with these measures show that the total amount of the profits, excluding any losses, usually exceeds 200% of the resulting reported net profit – and greater than 10 times has even been measured!

Figure 2.0 illustrates how unrealized profits can be hidden by inadequate costing methods. The accountants are not properly assigning the expenditures based on cause and effect. The graph shows each product's cost and net of sales, and reveals the profit of each product and service line. The products are rank-sorted left-to-right by the most to the least profit margin rate. The very last data point equals the firm's total net profit, as reported in their profit and loss statement. For this organization, total revenues were $20 million with total costs $18 million to net at $2 million; but the graph reveals the mix of that $2 million. The last data point "foots-and-ties" as the total reported profit, but gives no visibility to the parts.

How can this be happening? How can such unrealized profits be so offset by the unprofitable products and customers? The major reason is that no one sees it. Some people intuitively believe it, but they can't prove it. In many organizations, the managers refer to their cost accounting system as "a bunch of fictitious lies – that we all agree to."

Traditional financial reporting in no way reveals the separate profit and losses for several reasons. First, it examines and reports department level expenses but not the work efforts within a department. Secondly, the non-direct product and non-base-service costs are only allocated (which is a dirty word to ABC/M) to products or base services; these costs are rarely isolated and directly charged to specific customer segments causing these costs. In financial accounting terms, the costs for selling, advertising, marketing, logistics, warehousing, and distribution are immediately charged to the "time period" in which they occur. Consequently the accountants are not tasked to trace the costs to channels or customer segments. Today's selling, merchandising, and distribution costs are sizable –

it now costs more for General Motors to sell cars than to make them!

As evidence, a high-tech semiconductor manufacturer performed ABC/M and discovered they were making roughly 90% of their profits from 10% of their customers. That alone is not unusual, but they were losing money on half of their customers. Upon discovering this, the manufacturer explained to some of its unprofitable customers how they could alter their own behavior to lessen the workload on the manufacturer so that a fair profit could be attained. The remaining unprofitable customers were "fired" – they were asked to take their business elsewhere, as there was little hope the sales would cover their costs. This manufacturer's sales levels then predictably dipped, but profits tripled. The lesson is the "quality of profit" associated with sales volume and product mix; there should be a focus on the customer contribution margin devoid of simplistic cost allocations similar to the current focus of cost accounting on product profit margins.

Structural Deficiencies with Traditional Financial Accounting

The fact is behavior of customers and suppliers themselves are the source of a much greater amount of work-creation than most people imagine. For wholesalers and distributors, one can argue that customers cause almost all of the work. But even once that is understood, traditional accounting systems are ill-equipped to trace the costs. What is needed is to accumulate the costs of the various support work activities for the order-fulfillment work, and then to reassign this order-fulfillment work into the product and customers who cause work to happen in varying amounts – and in proportion to their use. Traditional financial accounting systems are structurally unable to accomplish this.

Why? Traditional accounting only reports employee-related salary and fringe benefit costs – which reveal no insights to the content of work performed by employees – and that workload may be controllable. Traditional accounting also groups

http://cokins.ASCET.com

ABC is a Cost Re-Assignment Network

In complex, support-intensive organizations, there can be a substantial chain of support activities prior to, and upstream from, the work activities that eventually trace into the final cost objects. These chains result in activity-to-activity assignments, and they rely on intermediate activity drivers in the same way that final cost objects rely on activity drivers to re-assign costs into them based on their diversity and variation.

The direct costing of indirect costs is no longer an insurmountable problem, given the entry of computerized ABC software that evolved in the early 1990s. ABC/M allows for assigning intermediate direct costs to a local process output or to an internal customer or required component material that is causing the demand for that work. That is, the design of the ABC cost flowing assignment network no longer has to "hit the wall" from limited spreadsheet software and its restricted columns-to-rows math. The new generation of ABC/M software is arterial in design. Eventually, via this cost assignment and tracing network, ABC/M re-assigns 100% of the costs into the final products, service lines, customers, and business sustaining costs.

Let's review the cost assignment network in Figure 1.0, beginning where customers (or beneficiary receivers) initiate the demands on work that ultimately require resources to be consumed.

Starting at the bottom module, all organizations have customers that behave as final cost objects; this existence ultimately creates the need for a cost structure in the first place. For example, customers purchase varying quantities or amounts of the organization's products or service lines. As noted earlier, in some unique cases,

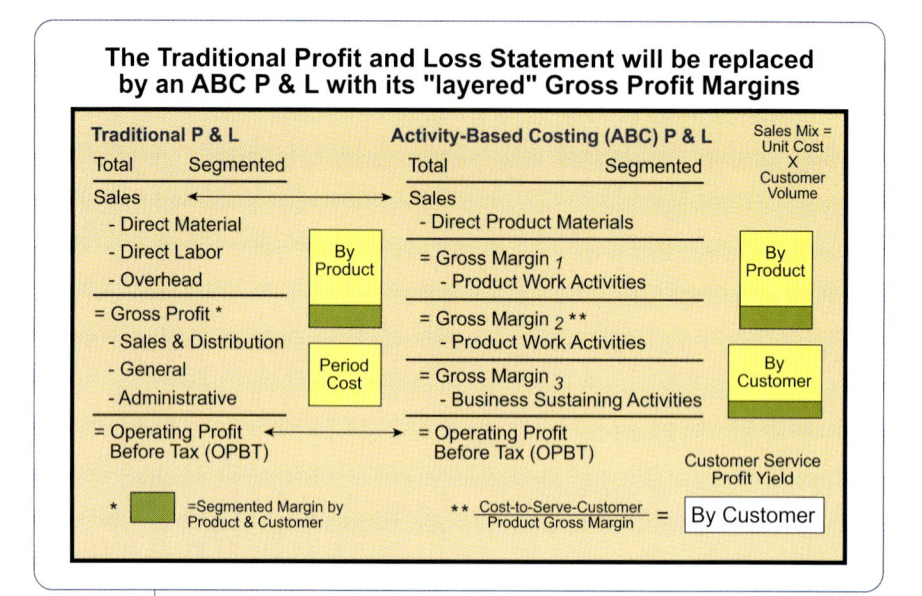

The Traditional Profit and Loss Statement will be replaced by an ABC P & L with its "layered" Gross Profit Margins

Figure 3.0   ABC P&L margin layers

costs according to the hierarchical and vertical appearance of the organization chart, denying any view of the true end-to-end business processes that start and finish with customers. Business processes are unaware of artificial organizational boundaries.

In contrast, ABC/M flexibly defines and measures costs at the level of work activities, regardless of function. Revisit Figure 1.0. The unique work activity costs caused by one's suppliers, such as processing their purchase orders or negotiating deals, are burdened by those products that are purchased. The National Association of Purchasing Management (NAPM) refers to this as the "total cost of ownership (TCO);" this means the invoice price of the purchase does not reflect the entire cost of procuring that product. Just think about the differences between technically sophisticated suppliers who use EDI and bar-coding and archaic suppliers who use error-causing faxes. Which type of supplier causes more of your workload and costs – apart from the direct material purchase cost? Suppliers cause you different workloads independent of volume.

Calculating costs with ABC/M then allows re-assembly and assignment-tracing for all the work activity costs to reflect how each customer, channel and market segment consume the costs to get served.

With activity-based costing, the traditional profit and loss statement changes and becomes like the layers of an onion-skin. Figure 3.0 contrasts the traditional P&L with an ABC P&L. It shows a simple report revealing varying margin layers. The left side of the figure shows what most managers see today. Only the products are costed (and the product overhead costs are themselves frequently mis-allocated to the products). The right side ABC P&L shows that first, exclusively product-related margins can be viewed, and without the misleading distortions from overhead cost mis-allocations (traditional overhead cost allocations apply volume-based factors without correlation, and not use-based activity drivers that possess cause-and-effect relationships). Then, as customers consume (i.e., purchase) their unique quantities of the mix of products, where some products may be stand-alone profitable and some not at the product level, then the "cost-to-serve" customer-related costs are combined to calculate the next profit contribution margin layer.

ABC/M Contribution Layering

A true ABC/M system operates as a re-assignment system. Let's revisit Figure 1.0. Figure 1.0 reveals how the costs flow

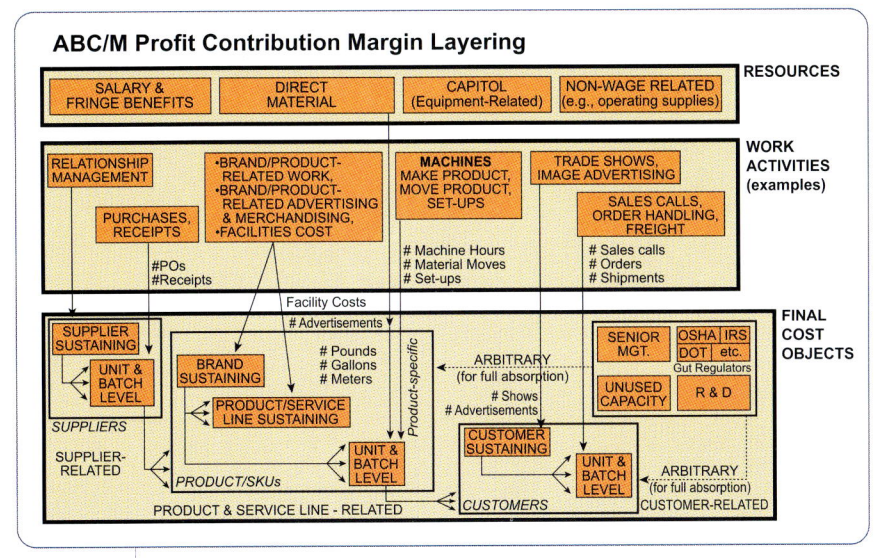

Figure 4.0   ABC/M Profit Contribution Margin Layering

through the cost assignment network.

One of the insights gained from ABC/M is an understanding of how final cost objects, such as suppliers, products, channels, and customers, vary with the work-related activities that they consume. Some activities, such as opening a new customer's account or placing a product into a box, vary directly with each specific supplier, customer or product (i.e., cost object) processed or serviced. These are called unit-level costs. Workloads vary directly with each unit of output.

There are other activities, such as changing over machine settings in order to make different products, for which the time or work effort varies independently of the batch size (i.e., the quantity of the machine run volume). These kinds of work activities vary directly with each event when the machine is re-set. Another example, customer-related, is where the length of time processing a customer invoice is independent of the price of the invoice. These are referred to as batch-level costs.

Both unit-level and batch-level costs can be attributed to specific suppliers, products, or customers without debate since the products or customers are the final cost objects causing and consuming the work. There is a third higher level activity cost type referred to as "sustaining" costs. Sustaining costs can be applied to the business as a whole, or to customers, products, or suppliers.

Figure 4.0 expands on the ABC/M cost assignment network's final cost object module. It displays two layers of "nested" consumption sequence of costs. A metaphor for this consumption sequence is the predator food chain from the animal kingdom, where large mammals eat smaller mammals who eat plants. The final-final cost object, which in this figure is the customer, ultimately consumes all of the costs, except for the business sustaining costs.

Within each of the major final cost object categories (suppliers, product/service line, and customers), they each have their own "sustaining costs" which are assignable to their end-product or end-customer. However, when tracing these "sustaining costs," they can not apply a measurable quantity volume as applied by the batch-level and unit-level activity costs. For example, a branding program may benefit a select group of products, for which those products can be specified, but how much of the branding cost to each product? These "product sustaining costs" can be traced using some "shared" basis, such as sales unit-volume or spread evenly, even though there is no cause-and-effect.

In short, sustaining costs can be assigned to products or to customers using what may appear as the old flaws of cost different suppliers create differing demands on work for similar products, so the suppliers may also be segmented to reflect their variation. Note that the supplier's total product or service line costs, although they may be identically priced as those of an alternative supplier, would now reflect different costs reflecting the varying ease or difficulty working with that supplier.

It is in this final cost object module where diversity is most apparent and into which all upstream activity costs flow.

Next, skipping past the middle module (i.e., activity costs) and moving up to the top module, the traditional general ledger expense balances are displayed. The cost assignment diagram in Figure 1.0 only reveals assignment paths from the payroll-related costs; but paths for the non-payroll expenses, such as supplies and operating expenses, exist for any organization. These paths are simply not shown to reduce the complexity of Figure 1.0, but all of the non-payroll related resource costs also flow through the cost assignment network. Payroll-related costs are very important to ABC because they are the more controllable expenses. The activities performed by workers who use those resource costs "drag" along and consume many of the other non-payroll resource costs such as supplies. (Figure 1.0 traces the ledger expense balances into a "staging" account of work groups, which in turn are re-assigned to the work activity costs using resource drivers, such as timesheets.)

The most important ABC module is arguably the middle one – the activity module. This module is not only where the work activity costs are initially costed, but then they are further re-assigned to the supplier, product, service line, channel, customer or

http://cokins.ASCET.com   307

business sustaining final cost objects – those objects that collectively create demands on the organization's work. Unfortunately, for many organizations, after they have expended the effort to define their work activities and calculate their activity costs, they stop. Activity costs are actually the starting point of both ABC and ABM, not the end!

Business Sustaining Costs

Business sustaining costs are those costs not caused by products or customer service needs. The consumption of these costs can not be logically traced to products or customers. One example is the accounting department closing the books each month. How can we measure which product caused more or less of that work? We can't.

Another example is lawn maintenance. Which customers or products cause the grass to grow? These kinds of activity cost can not be directly charged to a customer, product or service in any equitable way; there is simply no "use-based" causality originating from the product or customer. The need to recover these costs via pricing or funding is eventually required, but that is not the issue here; the issue is fairly charging cost objects when no causal relationship exists.

Business sustaining costs (or organization sustaining for governments and not-for-profit organizations) can eventually be "fully absorbed" into products or customers, but such a cost allocation is arbitrary. There is no cause-and-effect relationship between a business sustaining cost object and the other final cost objects. When these costs are assigned into final cost objects, organizations often refer to them as a "management tax" representing a cost of doing business apart from the

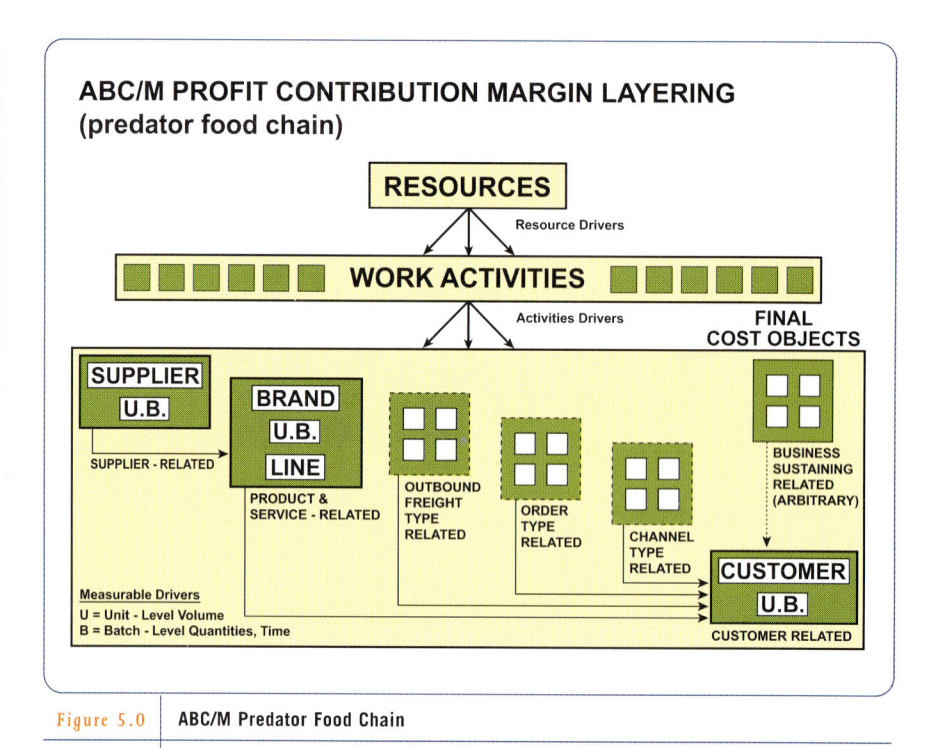

ABC/M PROFIT CONTRIBUTION MARGIN LAYERING
(predator food chain)

Figure 5.0 ABC/M Predator Food Chain

allocations. They capture the diversity of mix segments and isolate the sustaining costs to the type of final cost objects that cause the activity costs, usually to a subgroup within that final cost object.

Additional Final Cost Object Types

In effect, what ABC/M does is reflect how the variation and diversity of cost objects segment activity costs and resource costs. If there are substantial costs and sufficient diversity in another type of cost object, for example, the type of customer order (standard, special, adjusted, international, etc.), then the "order type" can qualify as its own separate and visible final cost object. Another example might be type of freight-haul trip, such as truck, marine, or rail, or as less-than-truck load (LTL) versus full truck load. This type of receiving final cost object would serve as an intermediate repository to capture diversity of the type of work output. After activity costs are traced to these final cost objects, then those costs are re-traced to the customers based on the mix of order-types consumed by each customer. Hence, "all customers are not created equal." ABC/M equitably traced

all the costs based on unique usage.

Figure 5.0 displays three potential cost object types that could be isolated and assigned to an intermediate destination for activity cost accumulation prior to being re-assigned to customers.

Note that without being isolated, these activity costs would have been directly assigned to customers from the same activity costs. But by isolating them, via a two-step cost assignment method, the activity costs are initially grouped the way they match the workload, and then the customer is shown to be "purchasing" the output. The second of the cost assignments is referred to using ABC/M lingo as cost object drivers (the term "activity driver" is no longer applicable as the work activity already accumulated in the final cost object.)

For advanced ABC/M users, they may wish to view product profitability including customer costs (e.g., to determine and print prices in their price list catalog). Today's advanced ABC/M software allows multidimensional views of various combinations of cost objects. A two-way bi-directional linkage replaces the sequence of the predator food chain. Other dimensions can

ABC/M CUSTOMER PROFIT & LOSS STATEMENT
CUSTOMER: XYZ CORPORATION (CUSTOMER #1270)

SALES	$$$	Margin $ (Sales - Costs)	Margin (% of Sales)
Product-Related			
Supplier-Related Costs	$ xxx	$ xxx	98%
Direct Material	$ xxx	$ xxx	50%
Brand Sustaining	$ xxx	$ xxx	48%
Product Sustaining	$ xxx	$ xxx	46%
Unit-Batch	$ xxx	$ xxx	30%
Distribution-Related			
Outbound Freight Type*	$ xxx	$ xxx	28%
Order Type*	$ xxx	$ xxx	26%
Channel Type*	$ xxx	$ xxx	24%
Customer-Related			
Customer-Sustaining	$ xxx	$ xxx	22%
Unit-Batch*	$ xxx	$ xxx	10%
Business-Sustaining	$ xxx		8%
			8% Operating Profit
Capital Charge (inventories, receivables)	$ xxx	$ xxx	2%
			6% Economic Profit (for EVA)

* Activity Cost Driver Assignments use measurable quantity volume of Activity Output (Other Activity Assignments trace based on informed (subjective) %s)

** Capitol charges can also be directly charged as imputed interest to products & cust.

Figure 6.0   3-D ABC/M Profit Contribution Cube

include geographical sales territories, store locations, or specific salespeople.

The ABC/M Customer Profit and Loss Statement

As costs flow from one final cost object to another final cost object, each flow will consume the unique mix of the upstream cost object. In simpler terms, an individual customer's total costs (apart from its direct costs-to-serve) are inclusive of only the product quantities and mix that he or she purchased. Furthermore, each product incurred its own activity costs with a cause-and-effect relationship, not with an arbitrary indirect cost allocation.

Figure 6.0 reveals the "layering" of costs similar to Figure 3.0, but in the shape of a 3-D cube. The costs for each successive step along the "predator food chain of costs" are inclusive of only the unique mix of costs that were purchased or consumed. ABC/M's "drivers" always provide the assignment bridge into the next successive level that consumes the upstream costs.

Figure 7.0 is an example of an individual customer profitability statement. Using ABC/M, there can now be a valid P&L statement for each customer, as well as logical segments or groupings of customers. There can be a tremendous amount of detail below each of these reports. For example, the individual products and service lines purchased can be examined as they are a mix of high and low margin on their own. Within each product or service line, the user can further drill down to examine the content and cost of the work activities and materials ("the bill of costs") for each product and service line. ABC/M users refer to this data mining and navigating as "multi-dimensional reporting;" they use "online analytical processing (OLAP)" tools for viewing the output of the ABC/M calculation engine. This is powerful information. The sum of all of the customer profit and loss statements for this type of report will add to the entire business' enterprise-wide profit (or loss). That is, it reconciles with the company's official books – the bottom line.

Revelations From the New Cost Data

Note that back in Figure 3.0 the three margin levels do not include any "business sustaining expenses," the company internal tax, which were not caused by suppliers, products, base-services or customers. It is true that these expenses must some way be eventually recovered in total via pricing to be overall profitable, but an ABC/M profit and loss statement reveals that they do not necessarily have to be recovered by all products and services.

Examples of final cost objects that comprise business sustaining cost objects may include: senior management (at individual levels, such as corporate, division, and local) or government regulatory agencies (such as environmental, departments of transportation, occupational safety, or tax authorities). In effect, these organizations, via their policies and compliance requirements, or via their informal desires such as briefings or forecasts, place demands on work activities that are not caused by or attributable to specific products or customers.

Other categories of expenses that may be included as business sustaining costs are idle capacity costs or research and development (R&D). R&D costs might be optionally assigned so that the timing of the recognition of expenses is reasonably matched with revenue recognition for sales of the products or service lines. However, remember that ABC is managerial accounting, not regulated financial reporting, so strict rules of accounting principles (GAAP) need not be followed, but can be borrowed.

products and by all customers.

This revelation can give progressive and innovative companies tremendous flexibility to price low for emerging products and for targeted new customer prospects, and to price higher with more loyal and secure customers less likely to switch to competitors. However, if too often or too many prices are set slightly above the "marginal costs," as time passes where products are phased out and customers depart, then the profit structure risks being slowly replaced without enough sales recovering the business sustaining costs. So this practice must be carefully managed. For example, low prices to capture new customers will need to be gradually increased over time.

The ratios of the "costs-to-serve-cus-

http://cokins.ASCET.com   309

tomers" to the product mix margin are revealing when compared on a customer-by-customer basis (or by segment or channel). A traditional belief that large volume customers produce proportionately large profits may be dispelled. Companies using ABC often discover that if given an extra hundred dollars to "serve" a customer, it would return a relatively higher profit contribution from mid-size or smaller customers.

Migrating Customers to Higher Profitability

Figure 8.0 provides a two-axis view of customers with regards to the "composite margin" of what each purchases (reflecting net prices to them) and their "cost-to-serve." Each quadrant of the matrix shows a different type of customer. Figure 8.0 debunks the myth that companies with the highest sales must also generate the highest profits. This is not necessarily true!

Figure 9.0 shows various customers as points of an intersection of Figure 8.0's matrix. The objective is to make all customers more profitable – represented by driving them to the upper-left corner. This can be accomplished by: (1) managing their "cost-to-serve" to a lower level, (2) reducing their services, or (3) raising prices or shifting the customers purchase mix toward richer, higher-margin products and service lines. (Note that migrating customers to the upper-left corner is equivalent to moving individual data points from right to left in Figure 2.0.)

Knowing where customers are located on the matrix requires ABC/M data.

Intra- Versus Inter-Organizational Costing

Supply Chain Management is forcing all participants in the value chain to want to know what the costs and profit margins are for the all of their upstream and downstream trading partners. Many hold the misconception that the only view for this information would be a cumulative time-flow chart starting with Mother Earth's minerals and resources and ending at the retail store's shelf. Figure 10.0 shows the problem. Each trading partner cannot see the true costs up to their point in the chain; they are blocked

ABC/M CUSTOMER PROFIT & LOSS STATEMENT
CUSTOMER: XYZ CORPORATION (CUSTOMER #1270)

SALES	$$$	Margin $ (Sales - Costs)	Margin (% of Sales)
Product-Related			
Supplier-Related Costs	$ xxx	$ xxx	98%
Direct Material	$ xxx	$ xxx	50%
Brand Sustaining	$ xxx	$ xxx	48%
Product Sustaining	$ xxx	$ xxx	46%
Unit-Batch	$ xxx	$ xxx	30%
Distribution-Related			
Outbound Freight Type*	$ xxx	$ xxx	28%
Order Type*	$ xxx	$ xxx	26%
Channel Type*	$ xxx	$ xxx	24%
Customer-Related			
Customer-Sustaining	$ xxx	$ xxx	22%
Unit-Batch*	$ xxx	$ xxx	10%
Business-Sustaining	$ xxx	$ xxx	8%
			8% Operating Profit
Capital Charge** (inventories, receivables)	$ xxx	$ xxx	2%
			6% Economic Profit (for EVA)

* Activity Cost Driver Assignments use measurable quantity volume of Activity Output (Other Activity Assignments trace based on informed (subjective) %s)
** Capitol charges can also be directly charged as imputed interest to products & cust.

Figure 7.0   ABC/M Customer P&L Statement

ABC/M CUSTOMER PROFITABILITY MATRIX
Customers with high sales volume are not necessarily highly profitable. Customer profitability levels depend on whether the net revenues recover the customer-specific cost-to-serve.

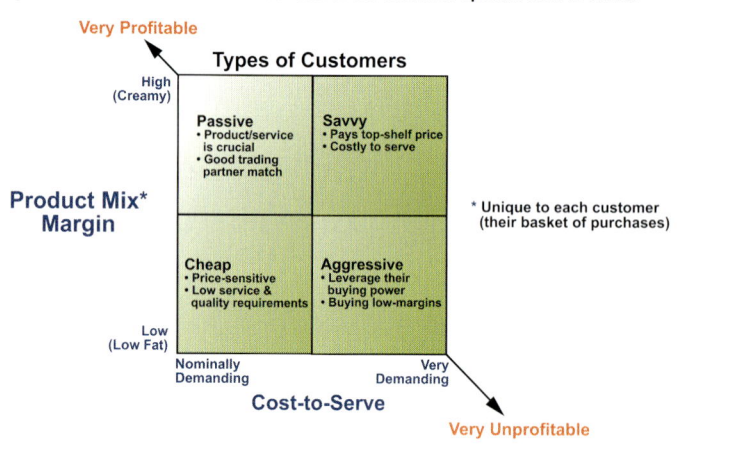

Very Profitable

Types of Customers

High (Creamy)

Passive
- Product/service is crucial
- Good trading partner match

Savvy
- Pays top-shelf price
- Costly to serve

Product Mix* Margin

* Unique to each customer (their basket of purchases)

Cheap
- Price-sensitive
- Low service & quality requirements

Aggressive
- Leverage their buying power
- Buying low-margins

Low (Low Fat)

Nominally Demanding   Very Demanding

Cost-to-Serve

Very Unprofitable

Figure 8.0   ABC/M Customer Profitability Matrix

and shielded not only by their direct supplier's price, but also the "cost shields" of their supplier's suppliers.

If one of the suppliers in a supply chain is benefiting from obscenely high profits, how do any of the trading partners know? Let's imagine a change where that particular supplier reduced its price, and that price reduction passed through the chain to the end-consumer. This would sales raise volume for every partner in the entire value chain. In fact, the lower-tier supplier's prof-

its might incrementally become relatively higher than before because of that price reduction – and that is certainly true for every other trading partner.

In order for the entire supply chain to effectively perform margin management, it must be able to have some form of "open book" visibility to the supplier's product-specific costs. Today, each buyer can already see the invoice or catalogue-listed price of their suppliers' products as well as those of their suppliers' suppliers – but no one can

ABC/M CUSTOMER PROFITABILITY MATRIX
Knowing where channels or customers are located requires knowing their true costs via ABC.

With the facts, customers than be migrated toward higher profitability by: (1) managing the service costs, (2) reducing their services, (3) renegotiating prices and or shifting their purchase mix to richer products

Figure 9.0 — ABC/M Customer Profitability Matrix

INTER-ORGANIZATIONAL COST AND PROFIT BLINDNESS

The only way that buyers and sellers along the Supply Chain can meaningfully discuss opportunities, is if each trading partner has activity-based cost management (ABC/M).

Figure 10.0 — Migrating Customers to Higher Profitability

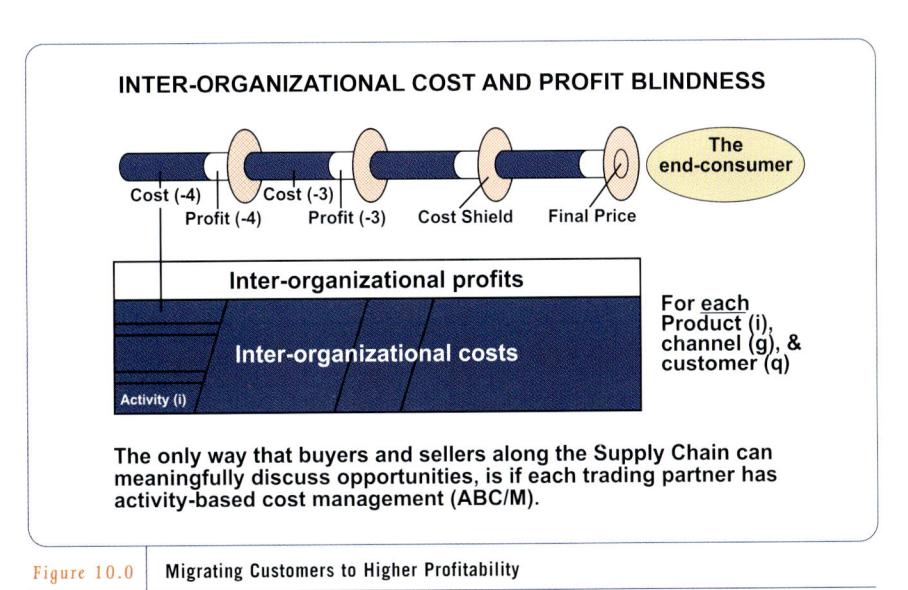

see the profit margins specific to each product and to each customer!

The only way to have view of these costs will be through open-book collaboration and trust. And since the only relevant costs to a buyer are those specific products and services that he or she is procuring, then each supplier requires a strong cost system. This means that each supplier needs a reasonably accurate cost assignment system with "bill of activity" cost visibility. The visibility of work activity costs – segmented by product, by service, and by customer – enables mutual and intelligent discussions among the trading partners as to where to remove waste and redundancies or to shift functional skills and tasks amongst the participants in the value chain. The sad truth is, many of the trading partners have archaic and poor product cost allocation practices and no repeatable or reliable cost assignment methods for distribution, sales, and customer management.

With most suppliers, Newton's Third Law of Cost Accounting applies: "For every freeloader, there is an equal and opposite sucker." That is, even if suppliers disclose their specific product and service costs, from which profit margins can be derived, the calculated costs are likely to be bogus, or at least have uncertain error. This means that all the suppliers' products are probably over- and under-costed. Until the supply chain applies some forms of activity-based methods for absorption and direct costing, then the supply chain participants will be weakened from making insufficiently informed decisions. Inter-organizational costing will remain a dream.

Beware the Learning Organization

As progressive organizations – and some may be your competitors and your suppliers – gain proficiency and mastery with the business intelligence provided by ABC/M, they can be formidable. What those companies are recognizing is that each individual customer affects the profitability of their brand products, base services, and market segments. The effect is due to the customer's purchasing habits, delivery location, discount/rebate structures, or other diverse ways it places demands on its suppliers. When equipped with ABC/M's superior data, your competitors can "cherry-pick" the premium-profit customers, strategically price for new product entry, and even send "false signals" with price quotes deliberately set at levels to lose the business so that their competitors will not suspect they have a far more accurate quoting engine.

Future competitive differentiation will be based on the speed rate at which organizations learn, not just the amount they learn. Your organization should understand and master ABC/M as the route to understanding your customer profitability, and your trading partners should not be blind to where they make or lose money.

Having the visibility to all of this cost and margin data is a beginning. People must act and make decisions with this data. But in the land of the blind, the one-eyed man is king.

http://cokins.ASCET.com

webPLAN – E-Business and the CEO's Imperative

Contact Information

Michael G. Ker
President and Chief Executive Officer

R. Duncan Klett
*Chairman of the Board and
Vice President of Supply Chain Research*

David R. Haskins
*Vice President of Development
and Professional Services*

Darryl M. Praill
Vice President of Marketing

Randy J. Sexton
Vice President of Sales

Michelle S. Van Tol
Chief Financial Officer

webPLAN Headquarters
350 Palladium Drive
Kanata, Ontario
K2V 1A8
Phone 613.592.5780
Fax 613.592.0584

Customer loyalty in an e-business world can be measured in nanoseconds. You have to provide compelling reasons for them to buy from you, every time, because a world of alternative vendors is only a mouse click away. It's a given that your products must be of the highest quality at competitive prices. You need to offer your customer more. Much more. Only a Web-intrinsic business model provides that. An integrated Web solution adds velocity to all stages of the manufacturing process. It can give customers visibility into manufacturing operations, right through to suppliers. And visibility is only half the equation. Customers need to collaborate on plans and schedules, in real time, over the Web.

Today most companies are still learning how to enable collaboration and reshape their corporate cultures to embrace change. It is an urgent matter. The early adopters will experience immediate, rapid growth. The laggards will not survive.

Collaborative E-Supply Chain Optimization with webPLAN CeO

webPLAN's solution to the e-business imperative is collaborative e-supply chain optimization – webPLAN CeO. It integrates supply chain management, product lifecycle management, and CRM for both enterprise and strategic planning and tactical execution. The virtual cornerstones of the e-business model are self-service, visibility, collaboration, optimization, and Web-intrinsic nature.

Once adopted, the webPLAN CeO model will continue to evolve. Industry exchanges, open to any suppliers that service a common vertical market, will seamlessly integrate, further increasing velocity and profitability. Through these trading exchanges, different communities will be able to collaborate on supply and demand needs, manufacturers will be able to locate the materials they need, when they need them, and better service their customers. All parties will enjoy the benefits of increased top-line growth, and bottom-line profitability.

Visionary Solutions

webPLAN has two distinct solution sets that deliver a complete e-business advantage to manufacturers.

webPLAN eSupply-Chain™ facilitates true omni-directional collaboration using the Web. It is much more than simply publishing static HTML versions of ERP data. With webPLAN eSupply-Chain, customers can configure and place orders online, suppliers are instantly alerted to demand, and the manufacturer has developed an optimized plan and schedule in record time. The only client technology required to join the community is a standard browser.

webPLAN APS™ facilitates collaboration between an unlimited number of users within the factory. webPLAN APS integrates with any existing enterprise systems, storing the data in memory to permit a virtually unlimited number of what-if scenarios, and provide instant understanding of the impact of changes. And webPLAN APS is pragmatic – fast to implement, easy to use, and with ROI in its first quarter of use.

Glass House Manufacturing

webPLAN enables manufacturers, their customers, and suppliers to collaborate and transact business in real time, within secure Internet communities. It's a solution that combines customer service and order management with manufacturing and supplier fulfillment. It provides all trading partners with visibility into the process. Visibility is knowledge, knowledge is power, and power is what you need to win.

Like all journeys, the decision to implement an e-business model requires a first step. Keep in mind that vision must be backed up with Web-centric product, and the product must be Web-intrinsic. If it isn't, it's simply a legacy system. Act now. Today's e-business adopters are already in a rapid growth phase. Time is short.

E-Business and the Supply Chain: Is It Simply supply-chain.com?

E-business is changing the Industrial Age models of customer acquisition, procurement, pricing, and customer satisfaction as well as how we measure the performance of a corporation. Focus on the customer is all-important. Customers want to buy products anytime, anywhere – cheaply and quickly – and fulfillment processes must be structured to meet the demanding requirements. The effect of e-business on the total supply chain is no less spectacular. Already the successes of Fortune 500 and smaller companies committed to a Web model offer irrefutable proof that e-business spikes the performance curve on the buy side and the sell side. This paper will discuss the changes being driven by e-business, and it will examine the technologies that will make your company successful.

Forget everything you know about the Supply Chain Execution (SCE) game, because the Internet has changed all the rules, from servicing customers to licensing and installing applications.

An Overview

Often, when logistics managers receive their report cards for performance, many need to repeat their courses. Cass Information Systems (St. Louis, MO), in its annual survey of U.S. Logistics, reported that spending was stuck at 10.6% of Gross Domestic Product (GDP) for the third straight year. Zero productivity growth is not good news.

And things will not be getting easier. The industry is in the midst of a revolution, and Web technology is the firebrand stirring up the masses. We can now order anything from home – from computers and flowers to vacations on faraway tropical islands. The Internet is a merger of content and commerce. We can shop, compare competitive offerings, review data sheets, get pricing, and even order all in one session. The Internet takes inefficient channels and makes them efficient, thus reducing the trivial activities we take for granted. So what does it all have to do with logistics?

The efficiencies the Internet offers consumers are not going unnoticed by corporations constantly looking to grow market share and reduce cost. Somewhere in your company, people are gathered right now to design an e-business strategy. The strategy may be driven by a senior manager at the request of a forward-thinking CEO seeking to replicate performance gains he has seen in other companies. Perhaps it's a tiger team assembled to respond to a competitive threat.

Either way, customer service will define it. Your company must be able to commit product availability, price, and delivery date at time of order entry to the customer. If the product is not immediately available to ship, your company must know when it will be available and allocate it to the customer through a Capable-to-Promise (CTP) transaction. Performance has to be close to flawless, because supplier-switching costs for your customer on the Internet are next to zero.

It doesn't matter if you have a vertically integrated company, owning everything from raw materials to finished goods, or a company depending on service providers and contract manufacturers for execution. Nor does it matter whether the product is built to order or built to inventory. Distribution channels will change. You will have to ship directly to customers rather than send bulk orders to distributors. You may even find it more efficient to ship directly from a supplier's dock to the end-customer. The e-business model requires that all members of the supply chain act as a part of one seamless fulfillment process.

John Fontanella is the research director for AMR Research's supply chain execution group. He has over 20 years of business experience in logistics, manufacturing, and marketing in both the high-tech and third-party logistics industries.

So now we have our marching orders: Increase logistics productivity while radically transforming the supply chain. Impossible tasks? You don't really have a choice, since your competitor will be doing the same. Besides, the two goals are compatible. As in e-commerce, the trivial is eliminated and channels are made more efficient, adding up to less cost and better customer service.

E-Business is Different

The Internet is not a channel – it's a medium, on par with a mall store or catalogue. Consider e-business anything less, and you greatly underestimate the Internet's commercial potential. Like other media, the Internet is developing operating norms unique to its style of buying and selling. Some are established; others are still forming. Internet commerce makes the customer the center of all e-business activities. The customer can view, compare, and price competing products in one session. Smart search engines look for best-fit, lowest-cost products. Auctions and exchanges make the concept of list price obsolete by determining what the market is willing to pay for goods and services in real time. The result is a fully informed customer armed with multiple choices with which to make the buying decision.

Few companies want to compete on price alone, yet the Internet is forcing businesses to do so. The only way to stop the slide into a constant price war is to stand out in other ways. The speed, accuracy, and completeness with which orders

Weblink

For more on XML, see:
dobrin.ASCET.com
herbold.ASCET.com
anthony.ASCET.com
culotta.ASCET.com

For more on VANs, see:
culotta.ASCET.com

For more on supply chain velocity, see:
enslow.ASCET.com
bruce.ASCET.com
benitez.ASCET.com

MANAGEMENT STYLES AND GOAL DIVERGE

Focus Area	Industrial Age Supply Chain	Web-Based Supply Chain
Scope of supply Chain Management	Multiple Processes	Multiple Enterprises
Supply Chain Process Behavior	Predictable Consistent	Ad Hoc Experimentation Channel Disruption
Competitive Advantage	Physical Assets Cost	Speed and Knowledge
Planning	Staff Manager and Analysis Clear Delineation with Execution	Entire Trading Community Simultaneous Planning and Execution
Work Environment	Command and Control Dumbed-Down Job Responsibilities Leave Personality at Home	Decentralized Authority Deal with Ambiguity Bring Personality to Work
Assets	Physical	Process Knowledge
Cycles of Change	Months and Years	Days and Weeks
Internet Utilization	Channel	Medium
Supply Chain Focus	Cost and Asset Utilization	Customer

Figure 1.0 Management styles and Goals Diverge (Source: AMR Research, 1999)

are filled and delivered is the sustaining differentiator. To build a supply chain capable of operating at such high levels of performance and efficiency demands a revamping of how we think and operate.

The Industrial Age supply chain was asset-based, relatively customer-insensitive, and slow to acclimate to new business conditions (see Table 1.0). The Web-based supply chain is a responsive, fluid environment that transforms as rapidly as e-business models change. Rather than managing multiple processes in an enterprise, multiple enterprises are managed with one collaborative process. Flexibility will no longer be sacrificed for consistency. In fact, experimentation is required to find the new, successful models. How fast an organization can adapt to new environments dictates how successful it will be. Management styles change, too. People have to be self-starters, working in only roughly defined jobs with little structure. It's a prerequisite for fast action. Planning will no longer be the province of a few senior managers. The entire trading community will participate for its survival and prosperity. Change will happen quickly, and if unsuccessful, the organization will change again.

The characteristics of our supply chain are becoming less defined and much more variable (see Table 2.0). A greater demand will pop up for international shipments since the Internet is a global medium. Excellence in fulfillment operations becomes a critical issue as competition heats up, and they will require the integration of the entire inter-enterprise supply chain. As a result, customer service expectations will be very high, much greater than they are today. The customer retention rate will be a direct reflection of how well fulfillment is executed. Orders will demand instant turnaround, and the rate at which they come will vary widely. Order size will range from very small to very large and more frequent, and units of measure will range from individual units to cases and pallets. Promotions will happen at a much higher frequency as companies go into online, real-time price wars. Disintermediation will take its toll on operations. Absent are the shock-absorbing channel partners that buffer us from an erratic market, so tightly controlled processes like returns management, revenue management, and customer settlement will change greatly.

Evolution of a Web Fulfillment Process

Defining Web-based systems is controversial and there is no one right answer. However, one point is clear: Systems built

Figure 2.0 Internet presence established (Source: AMR Research, 1999)

Diagram: INTERNET PRESENCE ESTABLISHED — Customer Web Browser → Pull View Data → Enterprise ⊘ Supply Chain Partners
- Product and Service Information
- Order, Inventory, and Transportation Status

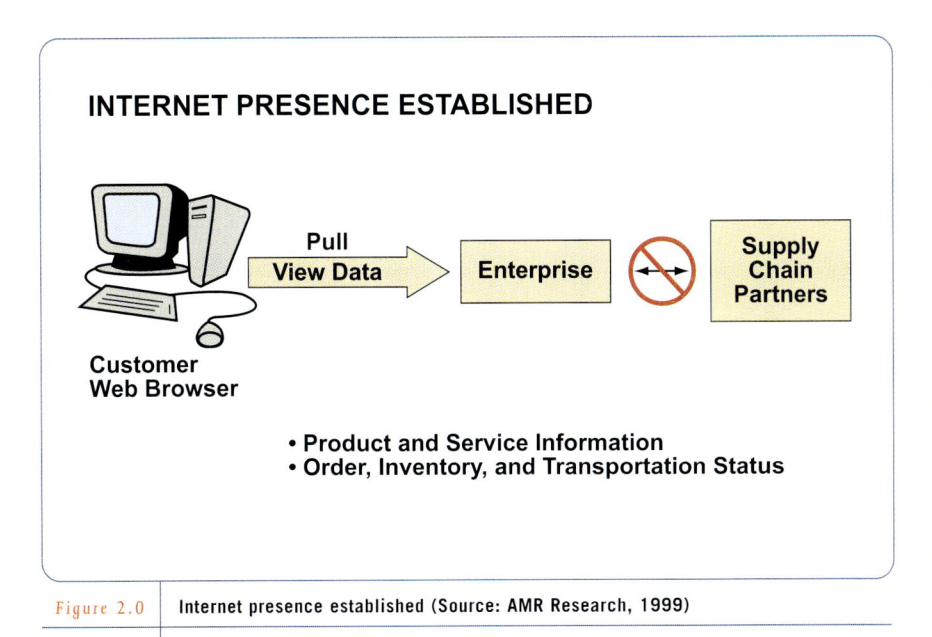

using Web technologies offer significant advantages over the green-screened UNIX systems common with SCE vendors today. Navigation is vastly improved, application integration is simplified, and with component architectures, benefit realization should be much quicker with less complex system installs. Reductions in the cost of ownership should come, as functionality is more centralized on servers. Web-based technologies are generally regarded as superior. The real question becomes, "What is my migration path and what vendors should I be looking at?"

Stage One: Internet Presence Is Established

Four levels of system evolution exist for the Web-based supply chain. The vast majority of today's users are in the first stage – Internet Presence Established – while a growing percentage are moving to the second – Commerce Is Initiated. As trading partner integration grows toward collaborative execution, performance is greatly enhanced. The third stage – Demand-Centered E-Business – represents a very real target for the near term. The fourth – Demand Web Fulfillment – is a conceptualized view of how Web-based systems will work together across companies and enterprises, given current technology direction.

Most companies start on the Internet at this stage. Establishing an Internet presence is a one-way flow of information, generally providing product and service information to customer inquiries; its value comes from informing the customer. Users can access order, inventory, or transportation status. Third Party Logistics (3PL) has made it a common service offering. Companies afraid of channel cannibalization caused by selling directly on the Internet are often frozen here. SCE vendors extended their applications out to the Web to satisfy the demand for the capability.

Stage Two: Commerce Is Initiated

Buying and selling on the Web begins at the second stage. Customers can place orders directly on the merchant's commerce server, configure them, authorize payment, and be notified of expected delivery dates. SCE systems figure prominently, providing inventory information, transportation routing and scheduling, and order management to the customer-facing applications. The fulfillment process is from the Industrial Age, and service failures are frequent. Systems are not integrated inside a company, duplicate data entry is common, and no collaborative execution processes exist between partners.

Stage Three: Demand-Centered E-Business

Customers buy from your company for one of three reasons: convenience, price, or scarcity. Combine two or more reasons and you provide even greater value to the customer and profits for yourself. How well you deliver to customer expectations dictates how successful you will be. Execution becomes critical, and collaborative execution between supply chain partners is essential. Acting as the demand center, your company coordinates and makes sure the entire supply chain is focused on serving the customer. An information backbone connects the community. You have full visibility to supply chain inventories, purchase order status, transportation status, and alert and workflow processes. Information is also pushed to the customer as opposed to the pull-only model in the first two stages.

Stage Four: Demand Web Fulfillment

Supply Chain Management (SCM) moves from art to science. The fourth stage is a conceptualized vision, but at least we can discuss a totally integrated supply chain, confident that technology will be able to support the scalability, breadth of functions, and communications required for such an aggressive undertaking. Completely event-driven, information and data flow both ways throughout the entire trading community. Systems automatically optimize for disruptions in supply and demand, with rules built to manage fulfillment and automation of business decisions between systems and enterprises.

Web-Enabled Versus Web-Based SCE Systems: There Is a Difference

As the benefits of e-business became apparent, SCE software vendors rushed to adapt their applications to the Internet. The quickest way was to make their applications accessible by browser, a process most often called Web-enabled (see Figure 5.0). It made green-screen UNIX systems accessible to suppliers, customers, and service providers, and provided them much of the same functionality as internal users. Advantages for the vendors include quick, low-cost development. Users now had the ability to make their supply chain much more scalable, allowing partners without the capability to integrate electronically to access the user system directly. Web-enabled was a satisfactory response to the initial e-business rush, and, for many situations, it still remains one. Its limitations, however, far outweigh its benefits if compared with more sophisticated technology. (Figure 6.0.)

Web-based SCE systems, designed to take advantage of the latest technology, are the result of protracted, expensive development efforts by vendors. To build the applications, vendors often spend 30% to 50% of annual revenue over two to three years on research and development. The transition to Web-based systems represents a huge gamble for vendors, particularly if they are publicly traded. As expected, earnings slide, as does share price. For the vendor, Web-based systems represent a true commitment to Web technologies, moving the user into an entirely different set of supply chain capabilities.

Web-based systems are not your current applications with a browser interface slapped on them (see Figure 5.0). They have Graphical User Interfaces (GUIs) with all of the navigation functions typical of today's Internet browsers. The bulk of the accessed application remains on the server, so the difficulties of connecting a Wide-Area Network (WAN) diminish. They are either totally or partially built with components that allow implementation of the application in stages, and they make the task of modifying much more straightforward. Web-based applications are configurable by the user and come with workflow and alert mechanisms to manage the process by exception. The systems are built to be self-teaching, with screens that are very intuitive and customized for a particular use. Such features become valuable as you bring partners onto the system. The systems are built to scale with the increase of transaction volume as you connect to your supply chain and customers. Most significantly, Web-based systems are designed to support the newer communication standards like Extensible Markup Language (XML), which makes integration much more efficient than through flat-file or EDI transactions. Web-based systems are required in order to evolve the fulfillment process deep into the third stage.

Web-based systems do not negate the extensive commitment your company has made in EDI. In fact, EDI will remain a very significant part of the overall strategy to wire up the supply chain. The standard data definitions and transactions developed will continue to be a mainstay in inter-company communications. Transport mechanisms may vary in the future, and as companies become more comfortable with security and data integrity issues, EDI transaction will be transmitted over the Internet instead of via the expensive Value-Added Networks (VANs) in place today. The transactions will also be much more flexible. Rather than drive industry standards to describe very specific activities, as EDI was forced to do in the past, Web technologies allow a trading community to use the standards to describe and communicate virtually any activity occurring in its fulfillment process.

SCE Principles to Follow

Four principles should guide you as you design your supply chain systems strategy to meet e-business requirements. How quickly your company can reinvent itself around the new drivers of e-business dictates its future success.

Total connectivity with the trading community is the end game. Metcalfe's Law that the value of a network grows exponentially as nodes are added applies to the supply chain, too. For the first time, technology allows companies to electronically connect with every trading partner and service provider in the community cheaply and quickly. Traditional EDI implementations could only enlist 20% of them, which is not enough. E-business is all about managing multiple enterprises with one process, real-time, and online.

Velocity is the yardstick for performance. It's not just a matter of doing things well; it's how quickly you can do things well. When things don't go well, it becomes a matter of how fast you can adjust with a new prototype process and how ready you are to change again if it fails. The new dot-com companies talk about implementing complex SCE systems in weeks, not months. Don't forget: Internet years last only 90 days, so you have to accelerate change four-fold to be competitive.

Flexibility equals opportunity. No one can predict what the sustainable buy-and-sell models on the Internet will be, but we know one thing – they will be different than today. Systems and processes have to be ready to support new methods of sourcing raw material, purchasing services, responding to customer inquiries, and making final delivery. Trading exchanges, auctions, and the aggregation of products from multiple manufacturers will all be typical models of commerce in the future. Today's structured business models of limited suppliers, fixed distribution channels, and fulfillment processes optimized for efficiency will be archaic. Your systems can't be the gate to change; they should be the causal factor.

Service sets companies apart from the competition. Are you spending millions building a Web site to attract customers? In the early stages of e-business, customer acquisition is the single most important measurement of success. Almost any company is capable of building customer-facing applications to educate, inform, and induce customers toward a purchase. Unfortunately, very few companies consistently perform to the customer's expectations of delivery and service once the purchase is made. Building a fulfillment process capable of reaching such high-performance standards takes time, money, and commitment. Customers see through the techno-glitz of the Web site. They will be

COMMERCE IS INITIATED

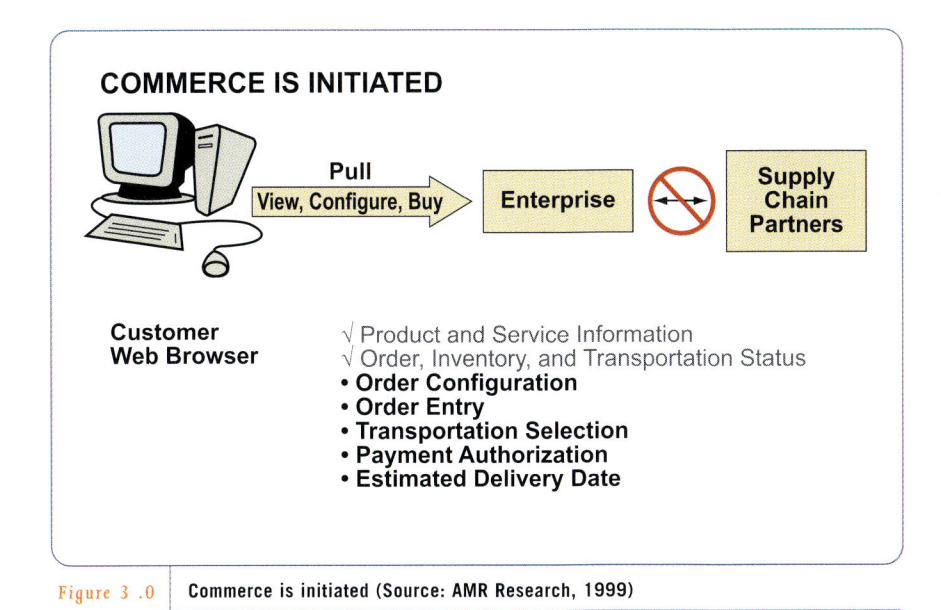

Pull: View, Configure, Buy → Enterprise ⊗ Supply Chain Partners

Customer Web Browser
√ Product and Service Information
√ Order, Inventory, and Transportation Status
• Order Configuration
• Order Entry
• Transportation Selection
• Payment Authorization
• Estimated Delivery Date

Figure 3.0 | Commerce is initiated (Source: AMR Research, 1999)

repeat customers when the entire transaction is carried through to their satisfaction.

So how do you think you will do in the world of e-business? Enterprise application software vendors are asking the same question.

Supply Chain Execution: Everyone Is Getting into the Act

Meeting customer service expectations on the selling side of the Internet and reaping some of the efficiencies on the Internet's buy side are seen as tremendous growth opportunities for traditional SCE software vendors. However, they won't have the field to themselves. Competition is heating up. Startup companies with the latest in technology and strong domain knowledge are attacking perennial sore spots of the supply chain. Supply chain planning companies such as Manugistics, Inc. (Rockville, MD) and i2 Technologies, Inc. (Irving, TX) announced comprehensive product offerings that transcend the traditional concept of planning. Manugistics is rolling out e-Chain to support supply chain communities and trading exchanges on the Internet. e-Chain Communities lets users collaborate with trading partners by sharing secure information about their supply chains. e-Chain Fulfillment gives users the ability to translate sell-side requirements into supply-side needs to ensure accurate promise dates based on inventories, manufacturing and transportation capability, and material supply. This product will also allow a manufacturer to extend ATP functionality to its customers. Virtual Service Provider enables 3PL providers and distributors to share information, such as track-trace data, with their customers and suppliers over the Internet.

Not to be outdone, i2 Technologies introduced Intelligent e-business products and services under its RHYTHM eCustomer Suite umbrella. They are built on the acquisition of SMART Technologies, Inc. (Austin, TX) and a Scandinavian-based configurator application vendor. The suite includes four products: eCommerce, eCare, eChannel, and eConfigure. They enable users to create personalized Web sites for upselling and cross-selling, with configuration checking, order status, and order tracking.

ERP software vendors are also in the hunt. SAP AG (Walldorf, Germany), J.D. Edwards & Company (Denver, CO), Oracle Corporation (Redwood Shores, CA), PeopleSoft, Inc. (Pleasanton, CA), and Baan Company N.V. (Barneveld, the Netherlands) are all extending their applications out to the Internet. New products coming online are built with a component architecture, and information backbones are being put in place to connect them with outside suppliers, service providers, and customers.

QAD, Inc. (Carpinteria, CA), the mid-market company with aggressive plans to move into the top tier of ERP software vendors, just released MFG/PRO version 9.0. It's a Web-based product situated well with current and potential users. Also, QAD's On/Q suite, in beta with six customers from the Food and Beverage and Consumer Packaged Goods (CPG) markets, provides full Web-based supply chain management and order fulfillment capability, including complex order processing, commodities management, contract management, pricing, promotional planning and management, route scheduling, and ATP.

In Wholesale Distribution, TECSYS, Inc. (Dorval, PA) is off to a running start with its adoption of Internet technologies and introduction of the ELITE.eCOM suite. TECSYS still leads its competition with the most developed e-commerce product for the vertical, but it'll have to fight to maintain the position. Daly.commerce's (Providence, RI) commerce@work is fast approaching as a contender for the top spot.

Mission Number One: Wiring up the Supply Chain

The war over who will provide the information backbone of the extended enterprise will be waged in the next year. ERP, SCE, and SCM software vendors, new start-ups, and interlopers will all be contenders, coming from far outside the supply chain arena, anxious to prospect for new sources of wealth. The stakes are considerable. The winners become the hub of activity for their customers' supply chain, set the de facto standard for the network, and have a platform from which to create a whole new generation of supply chain tools to manage the intercompany supply chain.

A seamless supply chain gives compa-

http://fontanella.ASCET.com   317

nies the ability to move swiftly and decisively, eliminate the mundane and repetitive, and execute with precision. The approach is different than integration attempts of the past, in which the objective was to connect individual processes between trading partners, such as EDI transaction sets for purchasing or shipment status. "Seamless" implies that multiple enterprises making up a trading community are managed with one process to produce one outcome: a satisfied customer.

The Supply Chain Integration Hub

Enterprise application integration software developed specifically for the supply chain is designed for a number of purposes:
- To electronically connect trading partners with a user's enterprise system(s)
- To let the user transmit information electronically or via a browser
- To allow companies to use the Internet to keep communication costs low
- To be capable of capturing, interpreting, and translating data from a dizzying array of global sources
- To populate the customer's systems on demand
- To guide partner systems to the appropriate data source

Products differ in both breadth and scope. Some focus on transportation, others order management, and several want to be all-encompassing by managing the flow of data through the full range of supply chain information requirements. What makes supply chain application integration software unique is the tools and applications layered on top of the brokering software itself, making it truly worthwhile.

The roots of The Descartes Systems Group, Inc. (Waterloo, ON) are in direct store delivery and route sales. The company, with its Energy product family, has become expert at managing both long-standing or purely opportunistic trading relationships, similar to what Internet exchanges are becoming. Descartes believes worldwide distribution networks operate in a similar fashion. Following the acquisition of Calixon N.V. (Rotterdam, the Netherlands) in 1998, Descartes introduced Energy DeliveryNet.com, an intelligent message-brokering product suite designed to allow user companies to sell to whom they want, when they want, and where they want. The suite is also designed to support permanent or casual business relationships and virtually any type of messaging, from EDI to XML transaction sets. Energy DeliveryNet.com's product suite includes a global visibility manager, which tracks purchase orders, containers, and individual components from manufacturers to delivery points worldwide. Its operating system acts as a transaction backbone, allowing event-driven assembly of products and collaborative execution. The company also introduced the Energy DeliveryNet.com Mobile Business Optimizer (MBO), which electronically connects shippers, carriers, customers, and delivery vehicles via the Internet. Based on the real-time status of the delivery truck, MBO recalculates delivery schedules and triggers alerts to trading partners and customers. With the introduction of MBO, Descartes is changing the way home delivery is conceived and managed, and home delivery will become a hot topic during the coming year.

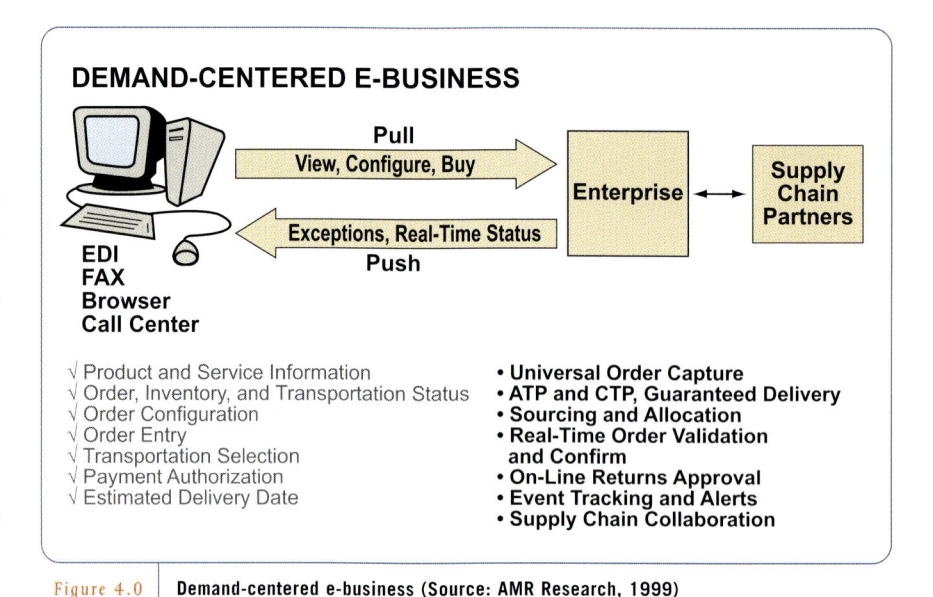

Like the other software applications in the group, Energy DeliveryNet.com is available as a hosted service. Descartes also offers the Trading Partner Connectors Service, a relatively unique service that allows trading partners to set up and test EDI message exchange. The company offers a set of tools designed to configure and monitor its operating system. Energy DeliveryNet.com is installed in the telecommunications, 3PL, wholesale distribution, and high-tech industries.

Optum, Inc. (White Plains, NY) has introduced SCE Response Center, integrating its WMS and TMS products to its suite of supply chain execution products. SCE Response Center's strength is its ability to allocate and reserve orders against in-transit inventories. It monitors the location and movement of inventory from the manufacturing shop floor to the ultimate destination, and it invokes procedures, such as cross-docking or expedited shipment, to meet aggressive delivery dates based on order urgency and quantity. Its goal is to maintain continuous inventory movement by deploying inventory according to the latest demand information. SCE Response Center seeks the most efficient flow and creates distribution paths specific to products. Products can have dedicated distribution hubs or a hierarchical distribution scheme, moving from factory to central and regional distribution centers and on to the customer. SCE Response Center is rules-based, so supply chains can

Figure 4.0   Demand-centered e-business (Source: AMR Research, 1999)

be customized to meet product or customer requirements. It also manages the balancing of inventories within a distribution network to meet minimum stocking requirements or to prepare for anticipated surges in demand.

Orders can also be sourced using SCE Response Center, which factors in real-time inventory information, requested delivery date, and the associated delivery costs for the various alternatives. The system is also capable of monitoring and allocating in-transit inventory.

SCE Response Center's installed base includes a large electronics distributor, a manufacturer of communications equipment, and a television home-shopping retailer.

Baker Street Technologies, Inc. (Richmond Hills, ON) concentrates on high-tech distributors in the PC channel. InterTrac acts as an activity hub for order fulfillment, tracking the life cycle of every customer order, including all supplier activity, on a single screen. Updates are real-time, and information is viewed via a browser. The company uses workflow technologies, giving the product event-tracking and issue alerts for exception management. The system gives real-time visibility into selected business documents such as purchase orders, sales orders, and invoices. It also provides user-customizable management reporting, performs profitability analysis, and has modeling capability to determine true cost and profitability. The service is Web-hosted, with full user support.

Celarix, Inc. (Boston, MA), with its i-suite, responded to retailers' need for supply chain visibility. i-suite's first installation, with a large international retailer, went live in July. i-suite is rules-based and does tracking of events through the entire pipeline. Alert capability is built in to notify user organizations of shipment disruptions and service failures. It also has a decision-support module for performance measurement and process diagnostics. Optimization tools, freight payment support, and a total landed cost module are scheduled to be introduced in the third quarter of this year. It is Web-hosted and installation is quick, if the first customer is any indication. Retek Information Systems (Minneapolis, MN) is also providing visibility to inbound shipments with its Pathway product, but the product is intended to support Retek's retail fulfillment applications rather than to be marketed as a stand-alone product.

Viewlocity, Inc. (Atlanta, GA) is one of the more intriguing companies in the market. Formerly known as the EAI vendor Frontac AMT International (Stockholm, Sweden), the company has experience working with large integration products within corporations. Viewlocity is no stranger to the Logistics market; the company estimates that 80% of its work is done in this area.

AMTrix, Viewlocity's flagship product, is designed to connect trading communities together. Like the Energy product family, it is meant to quickly integrate companies to take advantage of opportunistic, ad hoc relationships. It allows users to enter and monitor business rules, and it pushes alerts to appropriate personnel. Given the strong base the company has in logistics, it seems well positioned to layer on additional SCE applications.

Manugistics and i2 Technologies are also in the race to provide intelligent message-brokering for the supply chain. Planning and execution no longer have a clear dividing line in the supply chain. Hooking Advanced Planning and Scheduling (APS) functionality up with the execution processes creates new opportunities for the vendors. i2's Internet Fulfillment Server lets users integrate back-end supply chain planning and visibility to support Web-based, multivendor promises of delivery dates, incorporating merge-in-transits, auctions, and profit-optimized price quoting based on lead times. Manugistics announced Open Application Integration (OAI) as the preferred method to integrate with its applications.

Flexibility Requires Nimble SCE Applications

Flexibility in supply chain execution means that the applications must change and adapt as quickly as the business around them. Warehouse management systems have to be able to give real-time stock status to the commerce server, reconfigure for frequent promotional changes, efficiently handle different units of measure simultaneously, and be able to manage the returns process inevitable in e-business. Transportation management systems need to route and schedule shipments in any mode, pass transportation costs to the customer, and perform real-time optimization as business conditions change. Order management systems allocate, price, and promise delivery to the customer. ITL systems edit and check incoming orders for compliance to government regulations as well as financial and trading terms. Systems built to support specific verticals, such as Wholesale Distribution, should have multiple functions bundled together with a Web front-end for customer ordering and supplier management. All of the systems involved in executing e-business should be able to scale to high levels of transactions, be quick to implement, and, in many cases, offer the application as a service in a Web-hosted environment.

E-Business Is Forcing Change for WMS Vendors

E-business requirements are forcing major changes for WMS vendors in functionality, fit, feel, and architecture. Conforming to the new operating norms is not a trivial task for any vendor in the space. Most started development of Web-based systems, and the results are beginning to appear.

Catalyst International, Inc. (Milwaukee, WI) got ahead of the e-business curve two years ago by starting development of a Web-deployable front-end. Introduced with Catalyst WMS Release 8.0 in 1999, this capability lets the user view the application through a browser, giving it the look and feel of a Web page. Benefits include the following:

- User training is much quicker.
- Navigation is based on common Web practices, simple compared to the green screens of the old UNIX versions.
- It's cheaper and easier to deploy because the architecture is server-centric.
- It's able to communicate in multiple data

formats for easier integration with Integration Hubs and other SCE systems.

Catalyst is already reaping the rewards of being first in the marketplace, being chosen by several large Internet retailers. Internet retail is a major source of incremental growth for WMS vendors, as mainstream store-based retailers spin off Internet business units with separate systems and infrastructure.

Users are starting to look for integrated execution suites to serve as fulfillment engines for e-business, particularly a new breed of 3PL startups wanting to support e-commerce merchants. Companies such as FlowZone Logistics, Inc. (Beaverton, OR) provide total fulfillment services to Internet retailers, ranging from inventory management and warehousing to transportation and status inquiries. Like their Internet customers, the 3PL companies are looking for SCE systems that are quick to implement, can scale to a large number of transactions, operate in real time, and support all of the data needs required by the commerce server front end. An integrated suite means they can quickly deliver the necessary functionality. WMS vendor HK Systems, Inc. (Milwaukee, WI) is positioned well to serve the market. It has WMS and TMS functionality as well as a billing module for third-party services. The company also introduced Order@dvantage, a sell-side order management module capable of capturing and processing orders on the Internet. While not as broad a footprint, Provia Software, Inc. (Grand Rapids, MI) offers WMS third-party billing via its acquisition of Logistics Concepts, Inc. (Grand Rapids, MI) and offers TMS through a relationship with Pinnacle Distribution Concepts, LLC (Knoxville, TN). HK Systems and Provia Software provide packaged applications, which is significant since system implementation is counted in weeks, not months.

EXE Technologies, Inc. (Dallas, TX), the top revenue generator in WMS, announced in June the integration of Exceed with Microsoft Corporation's (Redmond, WA) Site Server, Commerce Edition. This integration confirmed EXE's intention to lead in e-commerce order fulfillment. It also followed with a joint announcement with i2 about collaboration. The company announced EXEconnect to support the integration of its products with third-party applications, Web interfaces, and data warehouses. EXE is also using EXEconnect to integrate the components within its own suite of products.

Optum's WMS offering, the SCE Demand Center, is user-configurable, so the application can be altered to meet changing business requirements, particularly when used in conjunction with the SCE Configurator. Optum also agreed to jointly market and sell its full SCE series with AnswerThink Consulting Group (Miami, FL) for an integrated e-business supply chain system.

Yantra Corporation (Acton, MA) bills its products as the e-business fulfillment engine, and its technical platform suggests it should be very effective. The company provides an integrated product that includes warehousing, transportation management, and yard management. The system has a component-based architecture and is one of the most sophisticated technical offerings within the SCE systems space. Designed to handle high levels of transactions, the system is also highly configurable. Industries it serves include apparel, electronics, CPG, automotive parts distribution, and 3PL. Yantra was recently selected as the fulfillment piece of a large national retailer's new e-commerce business.

ASN Enabler is a new module added to Manhattan Associates, Inc.'s (Atlanta, GA) PkMS WMS. Installed on a supplier's Windows-based PC, it lets the supplier send Advanced Shipping Notices (ASNs) via the Internet and generates the necessary shipping labels and manifests. Integrated into PkMS, ASN Enabler electronically updates the system of incoming shipments. Many suppliers don't have the resources to implement a similar function using EDI, making it a cost-effective way to raise connectivity rates with suppliers and the performance of the supply chain. The company is also introducing Vantage Point, a logistics alert module that uses push technology to notify internal and external entities of exceptions in the pipeline. Manhattan's strong relationship with UPS Worldwide Logistics (Atlanta, GA), which targets e-business customers, led to it being selected as the 3PL's WMS of choice. Given its roots in retail, PkMS can scale from very small to very large orders, and it will continue to be attractive to companies entering e-commerce.

McHugh Software International (Waukesha, WI) changed its WMS to be server-centric. It also implemented message-brokering technology, called McHugh Open Component Architecture (MOCA), which will expose its application to others in the supply chain for data retrieval and processing. A premier high-tech company chose McHugh in July of 1999 because of McHugh's component architecture.

Renaissance Software, Inc. (Lake Success, NY) staked its future on converting to Web-based technology with the e-WMSSCM part of its e-series SCM suite. The gamble turned out to be successful. E-WMSSCM was built from the ground up using Sun Microsystems, Inc.'s (Palo Alto, CA) JAVA. Functionality includes location and productivity management, inventory control, pick planning, and transportation. It is worth a look for mid-market companies.

Integrated Order Fulfillment for E-Business

Industri-Matematik International Corp. (IMI – Stockholm, Sweden) offers the widest scope of integrated order fulfillment functionality in the SCE software market. Already a major force in the North American CPG industry, IMI leaped on the Internet with Vivaldi, the successor of its System ESS. The company added warehouse management to its core functionality of order and purchasing management and, with its purchase of Astea International, Inc. (Horsham, PA), a Customer Relationship Management (CRM) module. Through Vivaldi, IMI is also offering intelligent messaging tools to coordinate, monitor, and measure the physical movement of goods across the supply chain. E-business is a natural fit for

DEMAND WEB FULFILLMENT

Internet Presence Established

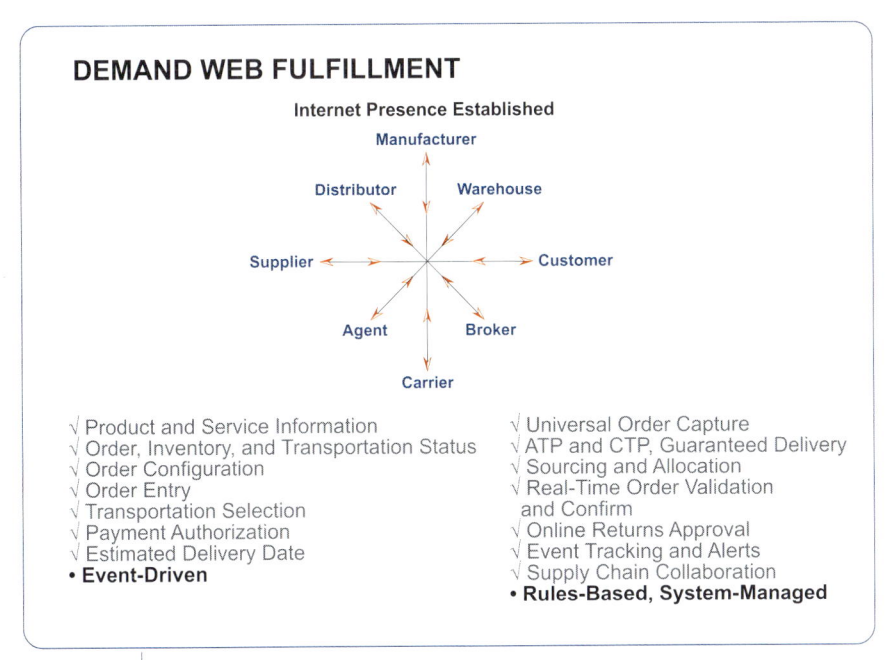

Manufacturer — Distributor — Warehouse — Supplier — Customer — Agent — Broker — Carrier

√ Product and Service Information
√ Order, Inventory, and Transportation Status
√ Order Configuration
√ Order Entry
√ Transportation Selection
√ Payment Authorization
√ Estimated Delivery Date
• Event-Driven

√ Universal Order Capture
√ ATP and CTP, Guaranteed Delivery
√ Sourcing and Allocation
√ Real-Time Order Validation and Confirm
√ Online Returns Approval
√ Event Tracking and Alerts
√ Supply Chain Collaboration
• Rules-Based, System-Managed

Figure 5.0 Demand Web Fulfillment (Source: AMR Research, 1999)

IMI. The vendor has best-of-breed pricing and promotion functionality and is turning the core system into components, allowing it to complement rather than compete against resident ERP systems.

TMS Vendors Want To Be Part of the E-Business System

TMS vendors have always been dependent on inter-enterprise communications, and now the Internet is opening up all sorts of opportunities. Transportation management is important for e-business. As in other forms of commerce, it is a significant portion of cost. At the time of order entry, the customer has to be given transportation alternatives, pricing, and expected delivery dates to complete a successful transaction. As exceptions occur while product is in route, transportation management systems should provide optimized recovery plans that will allow the shipper to meet the committed delivery date, or at the very least notify the customer of a change in shipping arrangements. Transportation exchanges are becoming integral parts in the process of purchasing services, and users should expect TMS vendors to provide software to manage the process.

No one wants to own much inventory in e-business, and if they have to, they don't want to own it for very long. TMS should help identify and plan opportunities to streamline transportation, employing such tactics as drop-shipping, merge-in-transit, and cross-docking. Their input to SCM, OMS, and WMS is critical for inventory allocations, developing ATP dates, and workflow.

CAPS Logistics, Inc., A Baan Company (Atlanta, GA) recently introduced BIDPRO and RoutePro Replenisher. BIDPRO is designed to reduce the complexity of analyzing carrier quotes for transportation services, searching for the lowest cost alternatives to meet the company's service objectives. RoutePro Replenisher optimizes delivery routes for inventory replenishment. Being a Baan company, CAPS will also take advantage of the ERP vendors' architecture and strategy to adapt its applications to the Internet.

Other major TMS software vendors, such as Optum and i2, integrated their products into suites that make transportation considerations a component of decision-making. Web-based startups are also rushing to market, and they are going to give established TMS vendors fits in the marketplace. Focused on managing execution, all are Web-hosted. TransView Corporation's (Minneapolis, MN) e-Logistics product suite books and tracks international and domestic shipments, and its e-Exchange creates trading markets for shippers and service providers looking and selling logistics services. It can be used for structured contracts as well as spot deals, and can provide visibility of carrier capacity over time. With e-Payment, e-Logistics also offers freight payment and settlement of logistics service charges, supporting a trend AMR Research views as the bringing the function back in-house. Pinnacle Distribution Concepts, with its FreightLogic application, and InVantage, Inc. (Taylor, MI), with its eShip, manage transportation for Truckload (TL) and Less-Than-Truckload (LTL) requirements and are adding functionality to manage multi-modal shipments.

With the expected rush of small package shipments caused by selling direct to the end-consumer, TanData Corporation (Tulsa, OK) and Kewill Logistics, Inc. (North Billerica, MA) provide shipment management tools to route, price, label, manifest, ship, and track parcel shipments, online and in real time. The applications are generally transparent to the user, and most will likely find them built into their WMS and TMS or commerce servers. TanData has created partnerships for its Progistics product with Commerce One, Inc. (Walnut Creek, CA) and INTERSHOP Communications, Inc. (San Francisco, CA). United Parcel Service of America, Inc. (UPS, Atlanta, GA) has a minority investment in the company. Kewill, with its Clippership product, supports all major small package carriers and is the underlying technology of RPS, Inc.'s (Pittsburgh, PA) QuickShip and Multiship service offerings.

ITL Software Vendors: A Big Part of the E-Business Mix

Don't ignore international trade logistics when designing your e-business strategy. Global markets, either for buying or selling, are almost synonymous with doing business on the Internet. You need automation to make ITL efficient. Sourcing products or components from overseas? What is

http://fontanella.ASCET.com 321

white paper

the true door-to-door cost of your decision? If you are shipping orders to international customers, the orders must be audited at point-of-entry for regulatory compliance and financial and trade terms. Customers will also want to know their true costs including freight, duties, taxes, and service charges, all of which are too complicated to figure manually.

RockPort Trade Systems, Inc. (Gloucester, MA) targets retailers and 3PLs involved in sourcing and transporting products from offshore. The company's product, RockBlocks, is already workflow-enabled, and the company plans to extend the application out to the Web by the end of the year. It plans to introduce RockPortal, a customer-centric extranet allowing users to link over the Internet with trading and service partners. It also will be rolling out GoRockWorld, a trading exchange for banks, freight-forwarders, agents, and manufacturers.

In the third quarter of this year, NextLinx Corporation (Silver Spring, MD) will introduce Velocity, its Web-enabled, three-tier architecture. International Software Marketing, Inc. (Brookfield, WI) added order processing functionality to its Web-ready WT/3 to process international shipments. The product has been implemented at a major CPG manufacturer. Vastera, Inc. (Dulles, VA) has been offering a Web-enabled product, its EMS-2000 GLOBAL PASSPORT, since 1997. With SMARTeCOMMERCE, which the user can configure, the company is moving to the next level, building in messaging architecture that allows bi-directional communication. Vastera will also be offering Web-hosted services through partners or as part of an overall ERP strategy.

Syntra Technologies (New York, NY) made its core application, Global Logistics System (GLS), available as a Web-hosted service, calling it GLS.com. Functionality is being made available in stages, with compliance for order management being the first offering. The firm has already signed its first Internet-based high-tech customer. The company is also announcing its long-rumored Global Commerce Management, which will add several modules, such as TLC and merge-in-transit, to the base GLS system.

Capstan Systems, Inc. (San Francisco, CA) is the newest vendor in the field. Offering a fully Web-based ITL application with an XML data structure, the product also has collaborative planning and execution features as well as an innovative, self-service methodology called Dynamic Deployment. Dynamic Deployment takes a potential user through a five-step process, beginning with construction of a value proposition and finishing with a prototype system configured to user requirements.

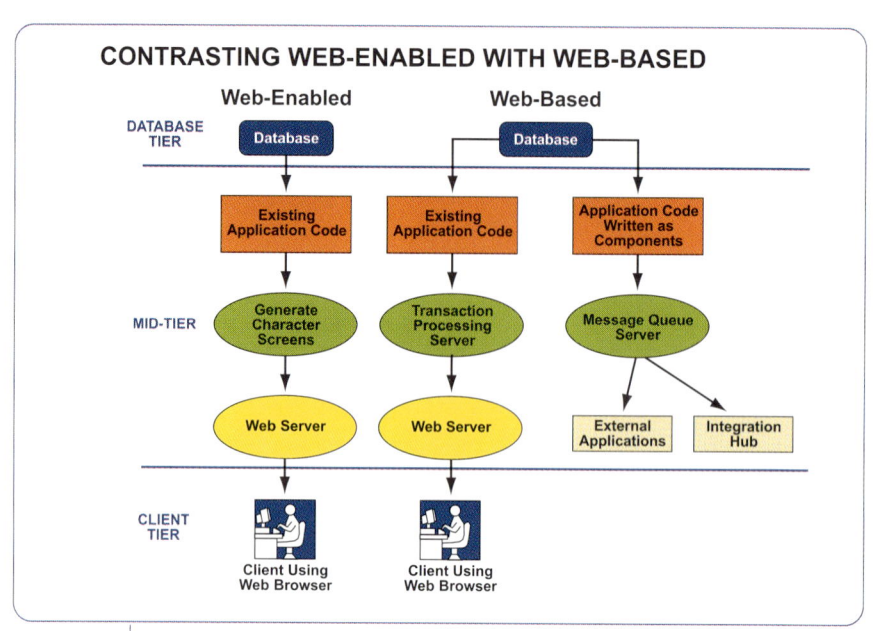

Figure 6.0 Contrasting Web-Enabled with Web-Based (Source: AMR Research, 1999)

322 Achieving Supply Chain Excellence Through Technology

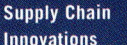

The Value of New Planning Systems: An Interview with Narendra Mulani

The key issue for businesses no matter what they offer is the need for planning. The advent of the Internet has not altered this fact, or planning itself, but it has accelerated the process. Narendra Mulani, an associate partner in Andersen Consulting's Supply Chain Practice, is a leader in supply chain planning technology and performance. We spoke with him about the importance of supply chain planning in today's business environment and the steps companies can take to more rapidly achieve performance benefits from their planning processes and tools.

What is the importance of planning to supply chain performance, and how has e-commerce influenced its importance?

The key issue – regardless of whether you provide raw materials or you make finished goods to stock or make finished goods and configure them to order – is that you still need to plan. If you make to stock, you need to plan how much you're going to sell, when and where. If you configure to order, you still need to know how much, when and where so that you can position the materials and have the right capacity available to meet demand. And finally, if you are a provider of raw materials, you essentially need to plan in order to understand when your raw materials need to be positioned and where they need to be positioned for finished goods production.

You know, 10 years ago, the real feeling was that if you got the forecast right you did a good job, and everybody was focused on that. Today, no one tries to get the forecast right. You try to get a consensus on demand right, and you make sure that you've got the flexibility in your supply chain and you have the tight cycle times in your planning cycles so that when demand signals change you can reverberate that through your extended supply chain. So planning is as much about anticipating demand as it is about the flexibility and velocity by which you take the demand signal and pass it through the system.

The advent of the Internet has not fundamentally changed the process. It has accelerated the process and brought some tremendous new options to how you plan, but you're still providing the same finished goods to the same customers. You now just have much more speed. The customer now expects much more flexibility and a much more immediate way of their demand being fulfilled.

What are the biggest challenges facing companies when implementing planning solutions?

Well, the e-commerce revolution and globalization are doing two things. They're changing your channels and simultaneously changing the profiles of your suppliers. Which means the supply chain isn't static. Supply chains are very dynamic and they're dynamic either because customers are pulling demand differently or the economics of manufacturing and distribution are changing on you. And therefore, for you to remain cost competitive you have to change your supply chain. So the real dynamic here is that if your channel mix changes or your supply chain changes, you have to be flexible enough to change your planning processes and structures to reflect that in time. Rigid planning systems have been deadly in terms of their negative effect on manufacturers that were considered advanced in the early 1990s. They were advanced but they set their planning systems in concrete and they forgot about them, so when the market changed, they had a great deal of difficulty responding to the changes. And, it took them a long time to recover. In fact, some of them still haven't figured out that what they did was set planning processes in place that are sensitive to neither changes in the market nor their own supply chain.

The first hurdle you're going to have to

Narendra Mulani, an associate partner in the Andersen Consulting Supply Chain Practice, is a leader in value supply chain planning technology and performance and the development of new business models. We spoke with him about the importance of supply chain planning in today's business environment and the steps companies can take to more rapidly achieve performance benefits from their planning processes and tools.

q&a

overcome in terms of introducing a new planning system is defining your leverage – either in terms of meeting customer demand or reducing cost in your system. If you're starting from scratch or you're reengineering your planning system, focus on your major points of leverage. Understand what they are and build the business capability to be able to affect that leverage. I'll give you a simple example: personal computer manufacturers. Although direct-to-consumer shipping is the current wave, 70% of all personal computers bought by households still sell through retail stores. Manufacturers carry the cost of the depreciation on that personal computer while it's sitting on the shelf. So for a personal computer manufacturer, their leverage is simple – the less shelf inventory that exists in the channel for their computers, the higher their return can be. That's one of the largest points of leverage. So once you understand your leverage, build the planning capabilities that allow you to sustain that leverage. Start at the leverage point and work back from there. Otherwise, this can be very intimidating and you diffuse your dollars in a way that will not give you the return you should get.

We find the value in the white space. We find the metrics that tell you things that aren't obvious because you only see through the lens of your own organizations. SCVA doesn't lay claim to being the only way to do that but it puts a structure around highlighting those unique features.

What approaches can companies take to more rapidly achieve the benefits of these planning systems?
Again, I'll give you a historical perspective. Ten years ago, there was very little application software available. So a lot of it was custom developed and we would go through a very traditional development cycle – getting user requirements, performing the detailed design, developing the code, testing it and getting user acceptance. Two things have changed. The first is that applications are now available. The second is that the speed with which the supply chain changes, and therefore the speed with which you have to deploy, is fundamentally different. To be able to affect the marketplace, you've got 5 to 6 months to design, prototype, and implement. What we have done at Andersen Consulting is reflect that in how we build planning systems with clients. A planning system is fundamentally different from a transaction system. It's only effective if you use it. It's a decision support system and the value it provides is only the value that you as a business user see in it. So essentially we have built a set of very flexible but "bulletproof" methodologies that emphasize user acceptance in terms of making sure that the user owns the solution at the end of the development.

There are three things that we emphasize when we partner with a client to implement a new system. One is the emphasis on user acceptance. So from conception to delivery there's a natural tendency for the client to say, "Yes, I've owned it all along. It's been my baby even though you built it for me." The second thing we emphasize is the ability to prototype – we build the system in front of our clients, and create the processes and systems in front of our clients. The third emphasis is the use of what we call business scenarios to affect this change. It's the combination of our technology skills and business development that enable our clients to build new planning capabilities.

Could you elaborate upon the types of different scenarios? Are they out-of-the-box? Are they customized?
Again it depends on the maturity of the organization. The normal method for building business scenarios is to begin by talking with the expert leaders on the client team. We bring in knowledge of traditional scenarios from similar environments to spark the conversation – it could be order fulfillment or aggregating a demand plan or supplier signals or what have you. The important thing about scenarios is that they are owned by the business user and reflect all elements of business integration. Does the scenario achieve the operating strategy that the client is looking for? Does it accurately reflect the business process that's going to take place? What is the technology needed to support the process? And finally, is the client organizationally aligned to achieve the desired results of that business process? Does the organization have the skills in place? A business scenario is the combination of these different elements from a live business situation. Our whole development process is based on prototyping these live business situations. Therefore, a natural outcome of the prototyping process is that the business users will believe and accept ownership of the entire business solution.

Can you cite examples where this approach has really made a difference? Generally, we have used this approach in industries that have tremendous change occuring right now. For example, the personal computer manufacturing industry. We have used the approach to implement new flexible planning systems to support retail markets, as well as for cellular providers. If anybody's business is changing both from the supply side as well as the demand side, it's the cellular industry. We have been very effective in helping clients in these industries create new planning capabilities in both the upstream and downstream portions of their businesses.

I think what's important about this approach is that it consistently delivers against the benefit case. It enables clients to achieve results faster because there is no lag between the build-up of the planning capability and its deployment to the field.

What final thoughts would you leave a company preparing to introduce a new planning system?
It begins and ends with the business operations people. If they're not involved, don't bother with the initiative. The second is that if you leave out any one of those elements of business integration, you are destined to fail. It's not a matter of whether you will fail, it's a matter of when. The third point is leverage. If you are creating this capability in a silo that doesn't let you affect the overall business scenario, then your ability to achieve business value is at very high risk. Do you have the right sponsorship? Do you have the right skills? Are you going to affect all sides of business integration?

Copyright©2000 Andersen Consulting LLP

A Quick Start to E-Procurement Savings: An Interview with Charles Findlay

When improving their supply chain, businesses too often limit themselves to solving problems or supplying quick fixes. While this sort of incremental change is fine, it restricts itself to just that – incremental change. Companies that wish to implement large-scale improvements need to rethink a wide variety of factors that impact their supply chain: procurement, fulfillment, cost-cutting, and embracing the Web. By changing methods and implementing change from the highest levels on down, companies can stretch their savings targets and rapidly implement improvements; the key to this is "thinking big, starting small, and scaling fast."

What value can clients expect by transforming their procurement methods?

Many of our client organizations are aggressively working to stretch savings targets of 20% or more. You can not just pull those kind of cuts out of thin air. Significant savings on this scale need radical change and the quickest and simplest starting point is a major rethink of procurement activity. Supply chain costs often account for 75% of a typical company's operating budget. By changing the way they buy, leaders in this field have been able to achieve savings of 10–30% per billion spent on indirect goods and services. Benefits frequently fall into a number of categories. They include reducing price paid by consolidating purchases across an entire enterprise with suppliers who can deliver with the lowest total cost of ownership, reducing the cost of buying by streamlining processes to enable business users to self-service their own demand, buying less and better by proactively influencing business buyers to buy what they need from preferred suppliers, managing suppliers better through real-time feedback provided from information automatically generated as a byproduct of day-to-day transactions and finally growing revenue by then offering procurement with complementary service offerings to potentially increase profitability and effectiveness.

Companies are not willing to invest in lengthy implementations – particularly with rapidly evolving technologies. How do you address this need for speed?

Past experience has shown that it can take up to six months to implement just the first phase of a new e-procurement solution, and full roll-out can last between 12 and 18 months. This time period simply does not comply with the rapid speed at which our clients' marketplaces are changing, or indeed with the ideals of CEOs and financial directors!

To address this need, Andersen Consulting has developed a rapid implementation methodology for the implementation of Ariba e-commerce solutions. It catapults organizations forward, drawing on experience from previous engagements to implement Web-enabled e-procurement solutions. We work with our clients for about 100 days to complete an initial, limited-scale implementation that may generate early benefits and serve as a foundation for rapidly deploying the full solution across the organization. In parallel, the organization can prepare for the full roll-out by developing the business case and implementation plans.

Charles Findlay is a partner in the Andersen Consulting Supply Chain Practice, responsible for the Northern European region. He also sponsors Andersen Consulting's e-procurement work across Europe. His expertise is the development of supply chain strategies across a number of industries, with an emphasis on the impact of e-commerce on supply chains.

Do clients use the methodology to kick-start operations in their entirety, or is it more of a step-by-step implementation?

Our approach is very much a first stage implementation. It provides some early benefits which help later in the full global roll-out business case and satisfy the client's finance directors who initially invest in the program. These early benefits are essential to gaining the full support of the client's senior management team. It is then from this building-block foundation that a rapid deployment of the solution across the organization can take place. We describe this as "thinking big, starting small, and then scaling fast." So the initial 100 days of implementation concentrates on client sites within one country. Selecting one or two of the most efficient and streamlined client sites we select 50-100 sympathetic and progressive end-users. Selection of the end-users is a critical step in the process. We like to have a combination of straightforward and complex customers who are also comfortable embracing new methods. This initial implementation is also limited to 3-5 suppliers, which maximizes the usage of a few catalogs by selected users, enabling some benefits at even these early stages.

What happens during the 100 days?

The Andersen Consulting approach addresses critical path implementation issues such as integration with enterprise resource planning systems, automated approvals and work-flows, punch-out capabilities, purchase card integration, content catalog integration, and connectivity to vendor and supplier networks. There are three phases in the program. The first, analysis and design, includes a supplier summit, conference room pilot, and communication and awareness planning to prepare the client organization. During the installation and configuration phase, software is installed, user interfaces are configured, and business rules are developed. Integration to existing legacy systems is included only where this is practical, in terms of technical, application, and process considerations, in the time available. If it is not included, an alternative prototype linkage is developed to demonstrate this critical element of any final plans. The final phase, build-out and deployment, includes legacy system integration as required, supplier integration and catalogue development, and product acceptance testing.

A key element of this approach is that it provides a benchmark to support the calculation of business benefits and costs for the full-scale implementation. We may also assess other opportunities, such as the need to rationalize the supplier base.

Such a program must take up a great deal of time and resources. What resources are required to support an such an initiative?

The Andersen Consulting rapid implementation methodology is designed to place minimal demand on internal and external resources. While the size of the team will obviously vary depending on an organization's size and total spend, the average team in our implementations include between 10 and 15 full time equivalents consisting of client procurement professionals, vendor support personnel, and Andersen Consulting e-procurement specialists. It is essential that we arrive at a balanced resource team that fits with the clients requirements. As with the end-user selection, resource selection needs to be of the highest caliber.

Is there a final message you would give clients thinking of finding out more about e-procurement?

Yes. Too often supply chain initiatives start out simply as "problem solvers" or "quick hits." While there is nothing wrong with this approach, it does lead to small-scale improvements. Meanwhile, building the business case for large-scale improvements can take months. How do you get the speed and the impact at the same time? With our approach, you not only get a rapid foundation implementation which will ultimately result in large long term savings, you also get additional business benefits before the implementation stage is complete. This paves the way for a larger more aggressive roll-out program. Re-think procurement, safely embrace the Web, and dramatically cut costs at the same time.

Copyright©2000 Andersen Consulting LLP

Increasing Manufacturing Responsiveness in the E-Economy: An Interview with Paul Wimer

Businesses must take a proactive role in seeing what they must do in order to compete in the Internet world. They must find out where the market is going, how their products fit, what demand will be, how much flexibility they have, what their readiness is, and so on. We spoke with Paul Wimer, an associate partner in the Andersen Consulting Supply Chain Practice, about these issues. He is a leader in the area of manufacturing strategy and operations.

What are the key drivers or mega trends in today's e-environment?

The pervasive accessibility to the Internet has given consumers, manufacturers, distributors, and suppliers infinite visibility and vast information resources, enabling and requiring manufacturers to more quickly and more accurately respond to changes in the marketplace. The global presence of the Internet means that manufacturers are serving more markets than ever before, a situation helped by lowered export and import tariffs and duties. In addition, manufacturers now have access to an expanded base of suppliers, which stimulates competition and provides the ready opportunities to form new and more flexible alliances in the supply chain process. Another dramatic trend spawned by the Internet is the increased demand for custom-configured products. With increasing frequency, consumers are in search of goods that are tailored to their own specifications. Examples of this range from computers to appliances and include a wide array of soft goods, clothing, home furnishings, and recreational products. This phenomenon challenges manufacturers to hone their build-to-order capabilities while meeting increasingly rapid order cycle times and maintaining or increasing profitability.

How has the Internet impacted consumer behavior and what has this meant to manufacturers?

Customers are increasingly using the Internet to make purchases formerly made in brick-and-mortar stores, or through the telephone centers of traditional mail order catalogue houses. The flexibility and freedom of the Internet are beginning to supplant these traditional purchasing channels as they come to be regarded as time-consuming and somewhat cumbersome. The buying public is now looking for overnight or two-day delivery on orders placed via the Web. Whether it's a stock order or a custom-configured product, they have demonstrated an appetite for Mach speed. And they are finding it on the Internet.

This change in demand profile has rather profound implications for manufacturers in the way they manage new product development, supply chain resources, production processes, and inventory control. In this custom-oriented environment, all supply chain participants are impacted. The creation of modular designs that leverage common subassemblies have become more critical to meeting short manufacturing cycles and achieving optimal flexibility. The trick is in being able to

---

Paul Wimer is an associate partner in the Andersen Consulting Supply Chain Practice. He is a leader in the area of manufacturing strategy and operations. He is also an expert on configure-to-order manufacturing processes, which are key capabilities in the e-economy.

effectively realign manufacturing processes. Manufacturers must find a way to align their supply chain partners with a common set of goals and metrics to ensure that all the elements of the supply network are focused on flexibility, speed, and cost. Almost daily, they need to react to shorter manufacturing turnaround and changes in product specifications.

What approaches can companies take to become more responsive in this environment?
There are four fundamental approaches that a manufacturer can take to become more responsive to these Internet-driven changes. The extent to which a company pursues these options is a function of the market in which they compete, their existing capability, and the capacity to change to new manufacturing models. Consequently, you may find that taking only one step is sufficient in meeting the needs of your particular market environment.

At the first level, manufacturers must change the way they plan their inventories. They must develop a distinct inventory profile that accommodates short-cycle demands and coincides with rapidly changing consumer preferences and requests for customized products. This requires the manufacturer to build in as much flexibility as possible in terms of inventory of production goods, scheduling of assembly processes, warehousing of finished goods, and delivery of product to the marketplace. There are, of course, limits as to how much manufacturing flexibility is viable, cost-efficient and profitable. There reaches a point at which manufacturers must limit the availability of product choices. It then becomes the marketing department's mission to steer the customer to available products while at the same time giving the impression that there is a greater range of product than actually exists.

A second technique is to postpone final assembly. This requires developing a product line that can be custom-configured very rapidly. Core products are pre-assembled up to the point of customization and finished quickly at the eleventh hour, either at the factory or at a distribution center. In order to achieve this result, the product line must minimize the differences between individual items, and the assembly processes must be readily adaptable to short-notice changes in demand. In many instances, such as with white goods (appliances, for example), products may need to be redesigned in order to shorten the manufacturing cycle. Quick-fix cosmetic treatments – such as color changes and optional features – serve to create quasi build-to-order products.

The third level addresses the flexibility of the actual manufacturing plant. This is a pseudo build-to-order environment. The aim is to reduce manufacturing cycle times, while also increasing the frequency with which products are produced. Manufacturing more frequently will align your production lines more closely to actual customer sales, allowing you to reduce inventory stocks and increase your flexibility to fill orders. You must also evaluate what actions you can take to cycle through the high-running products or low-running products on a more frequent basis. So, for example, instead of having a week-long production run of a given model, you can swing in and out to produce a small amount of each type. You thereby produce an inventory level of finished stock that is commensurate with the actual daily demand. This, however, can be a challenge because every time you change over your manufacturing lines, you are likely to incur additional costs. But if you can take advantage of this flexibility by capturing additional market share or by charging a markup for the faster service, then the more frequent changeovers can be justified.

Finally, certain products might be suitable for a true build-to-order or job shop environment. In such cases, manufacturers may develop new production environments that allow flexible assembly and production on small or large scales. On the small scale, this might translate into a highly flexible and configurable line that can produce small quantities. For example, take high-end custom kitchen ranges: the demand for these items might translate to comparatively small quantities, and buyers in search of highly custom products are typically not startled by high price tags. The manufacturer, in this case, though facing an inflated cost of production, is able to enjoy substantially higher margins and capture additional market share by producing truly unique products based on actual customer orders. Alternatively, in some industries, the switch to configure- or build-to-order may require the complete redesign of a company's manufacturing process — switching equipment designed for low variability but high volumes to highly flexible equipment that allows reduced batch sizes to be manufactured economically. Like auto manufacturers who have mastered the operation of producing several different models on the same production line, many other industries are being forced to consider similar moves.

What steps should an executive take when deciding how far to travel down this build-to-order path?
Number one is trying to get a better estimate of what percentage of your demand is actually going to follow this path. Rather than giving your organization the blanket challenge of supporting Internet orders better, and assuming that a majority of your production will end up being "order today, deliver tomorrow," understand what an Internet-enabled or custom order looks like, what percentage of volume will actually be of these types of products, and what specific products within your product line will fit these characteristics.

W²   Weblink

For more on manufacturing, see:
ramanathan.ASCET.com
For more on BTO capabilities, see:
culotta.ASCET.com
For more on inventory, see:
uchneat.ASCET.com
quinn-f.ASCET.com
zimdars.ASCET.com
wayman.ASCET.com
anthony.ASCET.com
johnson.ASCET.com

Also, gauging what your competitors are doing is critical to defining what offerings they may have in the marketplace that you will have to match. Understanding what your competitors are considering may allow you to beat them to the punch by developing capabilities that will be difficult or costly to replicate. Another consideration is product uniqueness. The closer a producer gets to a one-of-a-kind product offering, the more likely it will be able to maintain or increase market share. Last, a thoughtful and realistic assessment of individual manufacturing strengths and weaknesses should be a critical component of deciding what products would be most attractive to the multiple demands being generated by consumers and what steps you may take to improve flexibility.

Andersen Consulting has developed a wide array of supply chain metrics and techniques for assessing the flexibility of a supply chain. We have also developed proprietary methodologies for answering many of the mission-critical questions we have mentioned previously, like:

- Where is the market going?
- What products will best fit the Internet purchasing process?
- How much of your total demand will originate from an Internet interface?
- What production and/or product flexibility do you have?
- What is your build-to-order readiness?
- How configuration-friendly are your product designs and product design processes?
- How flexible are your suppliers to support your build-to-order capabilities?
- What capabilities can easily be built around existing facilities?
- What capabilities can be outsourced to speed response to Internet demands?

Do you have any final, broad-brush advice for manufacturing executives?

Most importantly, go out and investigate what changes need to be made in order to compete more effectively in the Internet environment. Do not expect to master the Internet overnight. A quick assessment of your capabilities must be made and, once completed, a quick pilot of your best alternatives should be conducted. Take careful, well-studied steps before completely overhauling the way you manufacture. Pay close attention to the supply chain functions of distribution and transportation. They become critical elements in responding to the Internet customer's demand for immediate gratification. Also, strive for a creative use of existing assets. Though speed is important, rushing into a sudden change of product design, venue, or operating philosophy may result in actually degrading your overall capability. Plan and execute more frequently, particularly before attempting to restructure the manufacturing process. Successful changes are those that are well researched, well crafted, and well executed.

Copyright© 2000 Andersen Consulting LLP

PurchaseSoft E-Procurement Solutions

Contact Information

Barry Doctor
Marketing Manager

PurchaseSoft, Inc. Headquartes
7301 Ohms Lane, Suite 320
Minneapolis, MN 55439
Phone 612.941.1500
Toll Free 800.818.6545
Fax 612.941.0066
www.purchasesoft.com
info@purchasesoft.com

PurchaseSoft, Inc. offers software solutions that allow mid-sized and large enterprises to deploy strategic Internet- and intranet-based e-commerce activities throughout the organization. The company, well known for its strategic e-procurement solutions based on state-of-the-art Java™ and HTML technology, is expanding its reach into the broader e-commerce space.

PurchaseSmart™ is the company's Java-based, Web-enabled product for companies needing an end-to-end purchasing solution. Clients are able to deploy this solution simply and quickly to virtually an unlimited number of requisitioners throughout their organization. Anyone on the corporate network with access to an Internet browser can request items for purchase by easily creating their own requisition. A request for quotation can be simply e-mailed from the system and all necessary authorizations can be obtained online. Specific workflow processes can be easily adapted to the needs of individual clients. This product has been built using state-of-the-art Java-based technology from SilverStream Software, Inc. (NASDAQ: SSSW) and has been designed to be flexible to meet client's growing needs. PurchaseSmart is easy to install and implement.

Business-to-Business Online Auctions

An optional auction format allows clients to more fully participate in e-commerce by maximizing the value of their unnecessary items through open market forces, a growing trend in business. According to Forrester Research Inc., sales from business-to-business (B2B) online auctions last year generated $8.7 billion. The Cambridge, Massachusetts-based market research company predicts explosive growth within the next three years, estimating that sales will top $52 billion by 2002. If Forrester's predictions are accurate, B2B online auctions may well change the way that businesses operate in the future. Buyers in the market for excess or obsolete inventory at a reduced price should consider the benefits of an online auction.

Businesses that successfully implement electronic trading systems can realize savings in time and operational costs. Those who have succeeded have been able to cut process costs by up to 70%, and achieve up to a 300% return on investment. They are realizing big savings in processing each order – more than $70 for each – and are significantly reducing the time needed to complete a purchase requisition cycle – up to 70% according to research conducted by the Aberdeen Group of Boston. Online orders are processed more quickly and efficiently. Accuracy is maintained by automating that eliminates room for human error.

About PurchaseSoft

PurchaseSoft, Inc. is an industry leader in B2B e-commerce software solutions, focusing on strategic procurement, intelligent sourcing, and providing key reporting/analyses of a client's procurement activities. The PurchaseSoft family of solutions covers the procurement process from requisition to receipt, linking buyers, suppliers, and management through electronic cataloging, authorization workflow, Web quotations, auctioning, and asset tracking. As a result, PurchaseSoft offers medium and large-sized businesses strategic e-commerce intelligence that helps them to significantly reduce costs and increase productivity through their e-procurement and sales processes to drive more profit to the bottom line.

Performance Simulation: Developing Your People to Build a World Class Supply Chain

Senior executives are increasingly aware of the fact that the best market strategies and technologies ultimately depend upon human performance – on how well the workforce executes. Attending to this component of any change effort can significantly accelerate the benefits and sustain the business results derived from the most significant investments. Performance simulation provides a simulated environment in which individuals have the opportunity to practice making critical business decisions in a risk-free environment. The hands-on and rapid learning pace of the simulator accelerates their time to competency and ultimately maximizes the value the business can capture. This article describes how these cutting-edge techniques can significantly improve employee performance.

Consider the global financial services company that realized more than $100 million annually by avoiding unfavorable deals and making sound financial underwriting decisions. Or an industry leader in engines for general aviation aircraft and space propulsion systems who realized $400 million to 500 million in annual additions to net income by improving the quality and speed of decision-making by top managers and knowledge workers.

Understanding Performance Simulation

Like flight simulators that allow pilots to practice flying without risking damage to themselves or their planes, performance simulation provides a simulated business environment in which to test the impact of critical business decisions, and gives individuals the opportunity to practice making these decisions in a risk-free environment. The effectiveness of performance simulation derives from a number of carefully developed characteristics. Employees are provided with:

- A virtual environment that looks and feels like their workplace
- Opportunities to make decisions and experience the consequences – they learn by doing
- Real goals to motivate the learner to complete the tasks and activities
- Realistic outcomes dependent upon specific actions and strategies
- The freedom to make mistakes within a private and safe environment, which is essential to real learning
- The ability to take charge of their own learning and proceed at their own pace
- Expert advice provided through real-life stories
- Personalized coaching and feedback

These characteristics combine to generate a rich learning environment that provides employees with the support and guidance they need to fulfill realistic workplace goals. Individual measurements provide the feedback to motivate employees to continue practicing until the desired level of performance is achieved.

Improving Job Performance

Before considering the success of such a new educational approach, it is first necessary to assess the success of existing forms of training. A recent Andersen Consulting study highlighted four problems with traditional training approaches:

- Organizations fail to evaluate the impact of training.
- Training programs are frequently devised and implemented in a piecemeal, non-strategic manner.

Judith A. Stimson is an associate partner in the Andersen Consulting Supply Chain Practice. She worked for Procter & Gamble in supply chain positions of increasing responsibility for over 12 years prior to consulting for nine years. She has authored two books, Supplier Selection and Supplier Partnerships, trademarked the Executive Imprint Model, and is CIRM, CPIM, and CPM certified.

- Corporate and technological changes are driving a sustained growth in training activity.
- Poor quality training is worse than no training.

Whereas traditional teaching is governed by an instructor and geared toward remembering facts, an effective learning process should be controlled by participants and focused on applying knowledge, skill, and judgment. With the content shaped by the context rather than disassociated from it, performance simulation is driven by outcomes and goals, and it relies on demonstrated performance as the confirmation of competence. In short, what is needed is the business equivalent of a flight simulation.

When compared to traditional forms of training, performance simulation significantly improves knowledge and skill retention (see Figure 1.0). For example, in terms of retention, performance simulation's 75% retention rate outperforms all forms of training except "teaching others," which has a 90% retention rate. Other forms of training have significantly lower retention rates: lecture, 5%; reading, 10%; audio/video, 20%; computer-based training, 30%; and discussion group, 50%.

In addition to improving retention, performance simulation also increases job performance. Employees at four Andersen Consulting clients experienced an average retention score increase from approximately 40% after traditional training to 65% after performance simulation, which had a significant impact on their job performance.

In many cases, even a small but measurable improvement in job performance can offer significant business benefits. A clear example is the global soft drink company that realized more than a 10% increase in their customer satisfaction survey results, a result of improved employee behaviors and interactions with customers. In such situations the initial capital cost of performance simulation development is quickly repaid through improved business performance and reduced cost of training delivery.

Applying Performance Simulation

Performance simulation is so versatile it may be applied to a wide variety of working environments to teach employees of all skill levels how to make better business decisions. Environments in which simulators can bring benefit are grouped into three broad categories: (1) low complexity/high volume, (2) medium complexity/medium volume, and (3) high complexity/low volume.

A low-complexity/high-volume situation is defined as having large numbers of employees who perform relatively simple tasks. This environment often requires an enormous training expenditure. Consider a U.S. fast food chain with an annual turnover of 30,000 employees and average retention of just two weeks: three days of those two weeks were spent in training. With a computer-based performance simulation that resembles a computer game in which customers are served as they enter a simulated fast food restaurant, time to competency was reduced from three days to two hours.

In medium-complexity/medium-volume situations, customer service representatives in industry sectors like utilities and telecommunications require rapid and effective training to handle inquiries about new products. In the case

---

An Andersen Consulting Study

An Andersen Consulting study completed in June of 1997 analyzed the training operations of more than 100 large companies in the U.K. and provided four key findings:

Organizations Fail to Evaluate the Impact of Training
Despite increasing expenditures on training, there is little evidence that the value of this investment and its effect on human performance is being systemically measured. Nearly one-quarter of firms surveyed conducted no formal measurement, relying instead on vague assessments of the relationship between individual performance and corporate benefits. As long as training programs are assessed on the basis of input rather than outcomes, they have little chance of achieving their full benefit in terms of using resources efficiently, motivating staff or maximizing business success.

Training Programs are Frequently Devised and Implemented in a Piecemeal, Non-Strategic Manner
In 60% of the companies surveyed, the task of identifying training needs was normally left to the line managers, with the human resources or personnel director becoming involved in only 27% of the organizations. While local managers are best positioned to assess short-term performance needs, this should be complemented with training driven through close alignment with organizational strategies.

Corporate and Technological Changes Are Driving a Sustained Growth in Training Activity
Approximately 61% of the organizations that took part in the survey predicted an annual increase of five percent in training budgets. The main reason given for increasing training expenditures was to ensure that employees could keep pace with sophisticated new technology, such as computer software, specialist tools, and enterprise resource planning systems.

Poor Quality Training Is Worse Than No Training
Experience suggests that when training and development fail to match participants' expectations, the effects are likely to be de-motivating, and, therefore, potentially harmful to the organizations they represent.

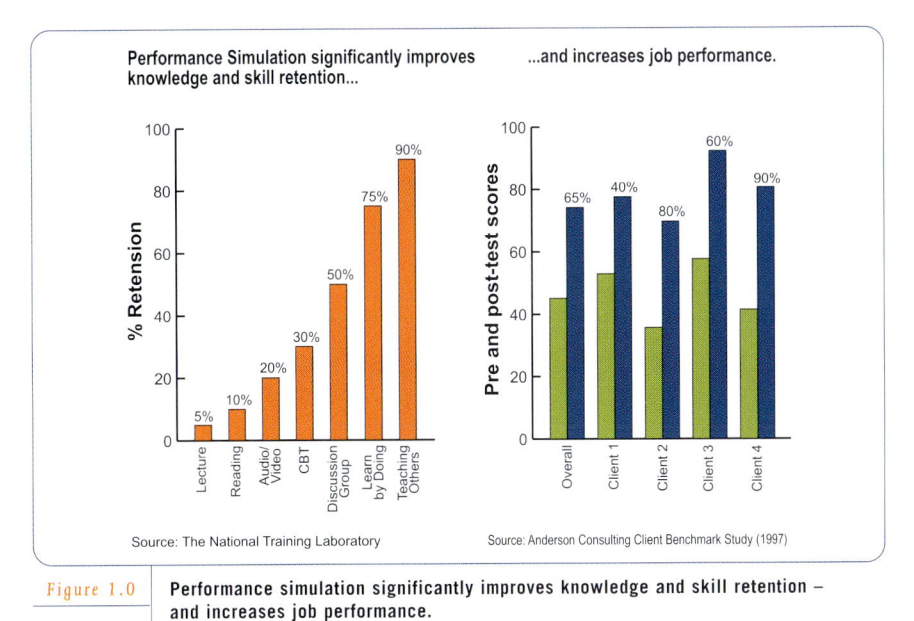

Figure 1.0 Performance simulation significantly improves knowledge and skill retention – and increases job performance.

Performance Simulation significantly improves knowledge and skill retention... (Source: The National Training Laboratory)
- Lecture: 5%
- Reading: 10%
- Audio/Video: 20%
- CBT: 30%
- Discussion Group: 50%
- Learn by Doing: 75%
- Teaching Others: 90%

...and increases job performance. (Source: Anderson Consulting Client Benchmark Study (1997))
- Overall: 65% / 40%
- Client 1: 80%
- Client 2: (pre/post)
- Client 3: 60%
- Client 4: 90%

of one large U.S. telecom company, these customer service representatives would normally spend up to two days a month off-site learning about new products. This enforced absence was reflected in declining customer service ratings. With an intranet-based performance simulation program that employees could access through their computers to simulate the inquiries they were likely to receive from customers, 1,500 customer service representatives were able to be trained on-site and be updated continually about new products. This improvement was reflected in customer service ratings.

A high complexity/low volume situation is defined as an environment in which key individuals' decisions could have a major impact on the organization. This is often the case with employees in the financial services industry. While individuals who work in areas with seemingly unlimited risks, such as trading, have often been regarded as having intuitive gifts, this notion has become increasingly challenged as a result of highly publicized cases such as that of derivatives equities traders' activities that resulted in unfavorable consequences. Companies are beginning to recognize that although intuition may play a role, improved decision-making can in fact be taught.

In the case of one leading financial institution, Andersen Consulting devised a program to improve risk management by creating a simulated environment in which employees could develop their skills without monetary loss or legal repercussions in the event of failure. Employees using this performance simulation are presented with a complex but realistic business goal, and they use real-life inputs to complete the task. They are able to interact with people and objects found in their everyday working lives. Support systems are built into the simulation to offer guidelines as they perform a series of tasks designed to achieve their desired goal.

Each performance simulation is created and customized to meet a particular company's needs. There are three phases to building a performance simulation: conceptual design, development, and implementation. The conceptual design phase generally takes six to eight weeks and results in a conceptual design report, a business case, a development plan, and a prototype. A conceptual design report contains the simulation objectives, prerequisites, tasks, topics, story line, and technology specifications and requirements. During this phase, subject matter experts are interviewed, war stories are gathered, desired behaviors are identified, and key messages are developed. The development phase takes four to eight months and results in detailed design specifications, pilot results, a tested performance simulation application, and a rollout plan. How long the implementation phase takes depends on the scope and specifics of the organization.

The Impact on Supply Chain Management

In today's supply chain environment, costs typically account for greater than 50% of revenue, percent cost of goods sold improvements more than double percent operating income increases, and 50% of savings is dependent on human performance. In addition, as many as 60% of supply chain initiatives are not implemented as planned because the people and organizational aspects of the initiative are ignored. Improved forms of training warrant companies' increased attention.

Supply chain planning is one area that can significantly benefit from improved decision-making capabilities. The success of any planning initiative depends upon the decision-makers' ability to harness the full power of the planning tools to make better business decisions. Examples of supply chain areas where this is important are forecasting demand, capacity analysis, inventory management, schedule sequencing, labor planning, material planning, load building, and route optimization.

Performance simulation can help an organization to optimize its supply chain by improving the performance of those individuals who manage these planning

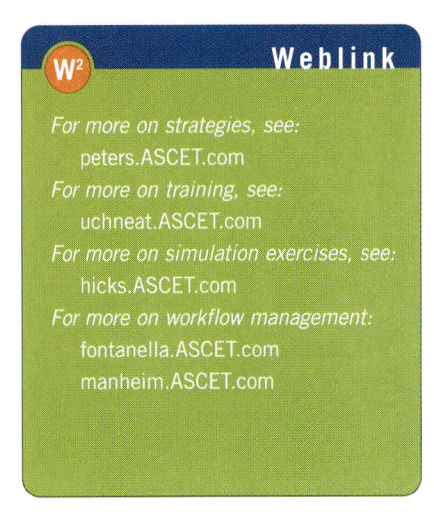

Weblink

For more on strategies, see:
  peters.ASCET.com
For more on training, see:
  uchneat.ASCET.com
For more on simulation exercises, see:
  hicks.ASCET.com
For more on workflow management:
  fontanella.ASCET.com
  manheim.ASCET.com

http://stimson.ASCET.com

areas. The following example powerfully illustrates how the rich learning environment can rapidly build expertise.

Supply Chain Planning Performance Simulation

An Andersen Consulting supply chain planning performance simulation kicks off with an introductory video by the CEO or other senior executive, highlighting the benefits this experience brings to both the learner and the company. Providing such a consistent message engages and excites the learner by providing reinforcement from a high-level executive.

Two segments typically follow the introduction: (1) Build Knowledge, and (2) Simulate Optimization. In the Build Knowledge segment, learners build a base-level understanding of supply chains, demand, master, production, and transportation planning, and, importantly, the interdependencies of these topics. Access to practice exercises, stories, a glossary, and the completion of a final test are among the many ways in which the learner is able to improve the retention of the new subject matter.

In the Simulate Optimization segment, learners enter a simulated supply chain environment in which to test the impact of critical business decisions in a specific area. An example of the inventory management area page is shown in Figure 2.0. The screen includes the following:

- A timeline that depicts the learner's progress
- An inventory dashboard that shows the metrics the learner is being measured against and the target ranges
- An inbox that provides product overviews, flash memos, guidance from key stakeholders
- Information on forecasted demand
- Actual orders
- Frozen schedules
- A worksheet to schedule receipts and plan order releases for future periods

The learner can now practice making inventory management decisions in a risk-free environment. The hands-on and rapid learning pace of the simulator accelerates their time to competency.

A typical inventory management simulation might be as follows: the learner begins by checking a memo with inventory targets for one of the products that requires inventory management decisions. The student has learned that the lead-time is two weeks, safety stock is 100, and the order quantity is 50 and will need to factor this into his or her thinking. The learner can then gather important information such as actual orders or feedback from various people, even suppliers. As would happen on the job, other parties have perspectives and insights into the learner's work, and provide guidance that is consistent with the desired vision, culture, and behaviors of the organization. Here, the learner gets a suggestion from her operations manager to review the inventory concepts to gather more information.

After reviewing these concepts, the learner feels ready to continue with the task. On the worksheet, the forecasted demand and actual orders for each period are provided and on-hand inventory is calculated. The learner is accountable to enter scheduled receipts and planned-order releases. The learner needs to keep the information from the inventory targets memo in mind, as well as the metrics shown on the dashboard. After the learner enters scheduled receipts and planned-order releases, the inputs are processed and evaluated. A large demand model runs in the background and determines the impact of the learner's actions on the on-hand inventory and dashboard metrics. In the beginning, the learners usually do well in some areas and not well in others. This process continues from planning period to planning period.

In planning period three, feedback from a teammate advises the learner to take action because safety stock fell below target levels and actual orders differed from forecasted demand, which potentially could result in a shortage. The type of feedback a learner receives will vary depending on her experience and inputs.

After the learner considers this input, she moves up the second set of releases and receipts by two weeks because inventory fell below safety stock. The demand model once again evaluates the impact of the learner's actions on the on-hand inventory and dashboard metrics. Note that this description of a typical experience gives an illusion of a linear sequence; in an actual simulation this is not the case. In this game-like environment, the learner "wins" if she reaches and maintains the target levels for the four metrics over a specific period of time (usually one year). If the learner "loses," she will have to start from the beginning again. Given the number of periods and items the learner has to enter, it is virtually impossible for the learner to "cheat" her way through the simulation. Other supply chain planning area simulations work much the same way. For example, when forecasting demand, a learner is provided with "last year this month," "promotion," and "point-of-sale data/actuals" information. She must consider this information and forecast the demand. As the learner forecasts demand, the demand model once again runs behind the scenes and the impact the learner's actions had on inventory accuracy is reflected. The emphasis in this particular simulation is on taking the trade and promotion calendar plans (for example, advertising, direct mail samples, end-of-aisle displays, coupons, customer volume discounts, consumer mail-in rebates, etc.) into account. The learner repeats this process until he or she has mastered forecasting demand over the specified periods.

Conclusion

The explosion of innovations in supply chain technologies and the arrival of the Internet is creating incredible opportunities for the companies who master them to build significant competitive advantage and shareholder value. But with this opportunity comes a difficult challenge. The complexity and speed of acclimation required to stay ahead can stretch the ability of the workforce to learn the necessary skills and understand new ideas. At best, this limitation can mean reduced returns on investments; at worst it can cause complete failure. Under these circumstances, it is clear that performance simulation has a key role to play in the most crucial supply chain change programs.

Copyright©2000 Andersen Consulting LLP

The E-Supply Chain Reaches Asian Shores

written by:
John L. Gattorna
Andersen Consulting
http://gattorna.ASCET.com

East Asian economies are recovering – at varying speeds – from the 1997 meltdown that did so much to slow their progress. This recovery finds them well suited to take advantage of the changes that have taken place in the Internet economy over the last several years. Despite ongoing problems with infrastructure, Asian companies have changed priorities and are ready to improve their operational excellence. Asian companies are now planning to enter new markets, cut costs, expand production, invest in information technology, and re-engineer their processes; Asia is now poised to take advantage of the rapidly evolving supply chain.

Beyond the Financial Crisis

The storm has passed and a sense of economic certainty is returning. Conditions are improving although they vary country by country across the region. In sharp contrast to the pessimism that existed over the last few years, particularly among indigenous Asian-owned companies, there is a new air of optimism. Multinational companies in the region, many of which took advantage of the crisis to transform their businesses, are in good shape to grab the opportunities that surely will present as the recovery continues.

Based on forecasts of GDP growth, China and Taiwan look particularly well positioned to take off. The outlook for the Philippines, Singapore, and Japan is less certain, while Thailand, South Korea, Indonesia, and Malaysia very likely have a few rough years ahead. It is interesting to note that the pace of reform in Singapore already outstrips what is required for success, but in countries such as Thailand, Indonesia, and Japan, the pace of reform has fallen well behind. If this trend continues, the disparity in performance at the country level across Asia will increase further.

Based on Andersen Consulting's research, the level of economic development suggests the key areas of supply chain focus in the different markets across Asia will be different for emerging versus more developed countries (see Figure 1.0).

Regional supply chain designs will also be influenced by a number of situational market and external factors. Emerging markets may be challenged by poor infrastructure and a high degree of government involvement while more developed markets may have modern distribution channels, some of which may be e-commerce-driven, and both intense competition and demanding customers. (See Figure 2.0).

Supply chain evolution may be charted as beginning with functional and process planning. Once achieved, a company may begin integrating its supply and demand planning. The next step is to begin industry-level collaboration using Internet-enabled technology. Finally, advanced companies will be able to develop third-party enterprises (see Figure 3.0). Even as the evolution of Supply Chain Management is changing the way business is conducted in Asia, many leading companies are only somewhere between the process planning and integrated supply and demand planning stage of the evolution curve.

Top Five Operational Strategies

The top five operational strategies, according to Andersen Consulting's survey of June 1999, indicate that companies in Asia are greatly optimistic about the future. As a consequence, they are pursuing more positive strategies. For instance in 1998, the top five operational strategies of Asian companies were:

- Cut costs
- Postpone investments
- Rationalize infrastructure
- Restructure portfolios
- Restructure debt

By mid-1999, the stated top five operational strategies of Asian companies were:

John L. Gattorna is the managing partner of the Australia/New Zealand Supply Chain Practice of Andersen Consulting. He has more than 20 years experience in international consulting for multinational corporations in the United States, South America, South Africa, Western and Eastern Europe, the Middle East, and the Asia Pacific.

He has an international reputation in the fields of logistics strategy, distribution channels strategy, and business planning in the automotive, consumer products, industrial products, and financial services industries.

He has written several books on supply chain including the international best seller "Strategic Supply Chain Alignment: Best Practices in Supply Chain Management."

- Enter new markets
- Continue to cut costs
- Invest in information technology
- Reengineer processes

So while the overall market growth rate has declined significantly, there has been a relatively sudden shift toward regionalization, and a corresponding increased emphasis on more effective supply chains, underpinned by improved processes and new technology. This trend is likely to continue, thus allowing renewed focus and energy on initiatives that will bring large benefits to top-performing organizations, fast.

From Supply Chain Theory to Reality

Up until just a few years ago, supply chain management was more theory than fact, even in the more advanced Western countries. Then two things happened to make supply chain thinking a reality. First, the coming of the Internet provided a low-cost medium for all parties in the supply chain to communicate. Then, the emergence of new user-friendly software provided the long-sought integration, both within companies, and more importantly between companies in the supply chain.

Suddenly, the basis for competition changed from the single company level to supply chain versus supply chain. Coincidentally, new capabilities became important in addition to those already taken for granted. For example, the new era in supply chain management requires companies to select and manage new alliances;

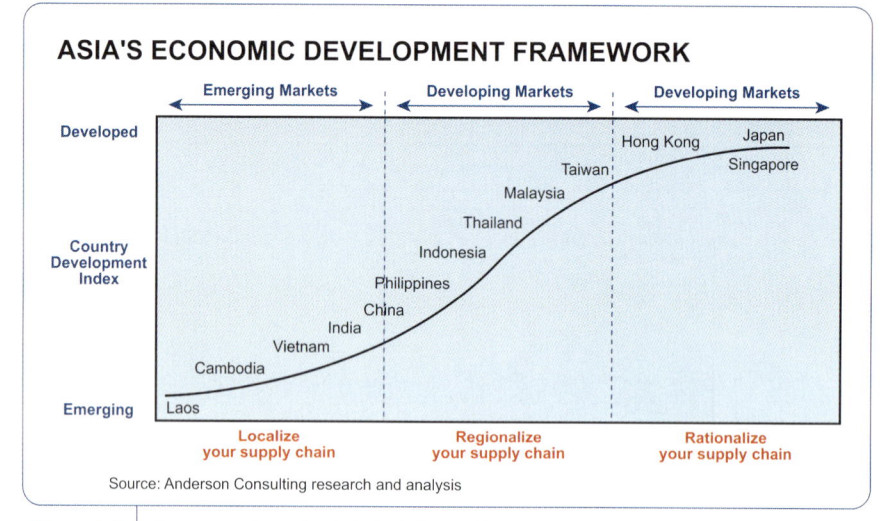

Weblink

For more on e-fulfillment, see:
lidow.ASCET.com
mann.ASCET.com
enslow.ASCET.com

For more on 3PL, see:
fontanella.ASCET.com
prince.ASCET.com
peters.ASCET.com
enslow.ASCET.com

ASIA'S ECONOMIC DEVELOPMENT FRAMEWORK

Figure 1.0 — Key areas of supply chain in Asian markets

take client relationship management to new levels; and be very familiar with all the enabling technologies required to drive a responsive supply chain, both upstream and downstream from manufacturing.

Asian companies have the benefit of being close followers in this rapid evolutionary process – and in some cases already are part of world-class global supply chains like the electronics and high-tech industries. Indeed, the new directions being taken by local and multinational companies highlight the true potential of superior Supply Chain Management. For local companies, these initiatives include:

- Consolidating competitive assets and building local market position
- Adopting a regional mind-set, if not a regional position
- Developing partnerships to acquire new capabilities, particularly in relation to technology adoption and new organizational arrangements
- Strengthening supply chain links with key customers and suppliers

For multinational companies, these initiatives include:

- Expanding market position while competitors stand by
- Developing a flexible regional stance to enable a rapid response to changing local conditions
- Using superior research and development and technology capabilities to develop new products and markets

Leveraging the position of local players to access new customers and distribution networks

Impact of E-Commerce on the Supply Chain

Electronic commerce is coming to Asia - ready or not - presenting both problems and opportunities. In terms of readiness, Singapore, with its superior information technology infrastructure, government support, and cultural disposition, is perhaps the most receptive to e-commerce. Led by countries such as Singapore, Asia will be drawn into the global economy at a much faster rate than previously thought possible. Other factors also influence receptiveness, including affordability of access, labor, macroeconomic environment, cultural predisposition, and the degree to which the government acts as a facilitator.

In many ways, e-commerce could be the catalyst that re-ignites the Asian economic miracle by delivering increased customer and shareholder value. Customer value will come in the form of market efficiencies whereby the new technologies available for reaching new customers

SUPPLY CHAIN COMPLEXITIES
Regional supply chain design will be influenced by a number of situational, market and external factors.

	Emerging Markets	Developing Markets	Developing Markets
Key Characteristics for supply chain management (Developed → Emerging)	• Poor infrastructure and distribution • High degree of government involvement • Difficulty in managing third party logistics providers	• Mix of traditional and modern distribution channels • More demanding customers • Difficulty to access sophisticated supply chain practices	• Modern distribution channels, some eCommerce driven • Intense competition • Demanding consumers

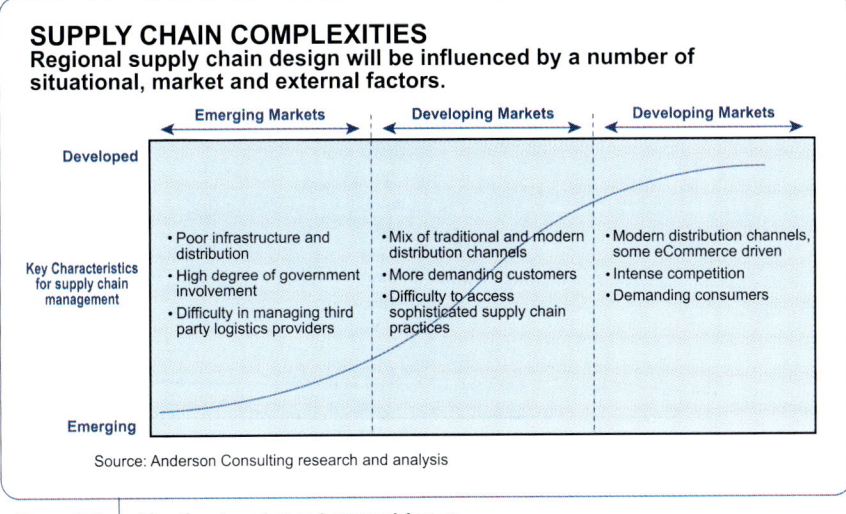

Source: Anderson Consulting research and analysis

Figure 2.0 — Situational market and external factors

through new channels will also increase customers' abilities to compare prices and features. On the other hand, market expansion will come via lower cost and easier accessibility of many goods and services that will increase demand.

It is also true that technology strategies for new business capabilities that contribute to revenue growth often lead to significant cost reduction, although technology strategies for cost reduction will not necessarily lead to new capabilities or revenue growth. One thing is certain: traditional ways of doing business and traditional commercial arrangements with channel intermediaries will disappear over time and will be replaced by arrangements founded on value creation. This will be as much the case in Asia as anywhere else. However, it can be predicted that the uptake of genuine supply chain management in Asian companies will be accelerated as a direct result of e-commerce, and the collaborative planning enabled via the Internet.

From E-Commerce to E-Fulfillment

While e-commerce provides a way of accelerating the interaction with customers at the front end, the same cannot be said for the physical fulfillment processes that generally have failed to keep pace with the electronic component of the order cycle. As such, the challenges facing companies in meeting customers' expectations in the new world are immense, and in parts of Asia where infrastructure is poor, the task is nearly impossible in the short to medium term.

The magnitude of the e-fulfillment challenge in Asia is evident when one compares what is going on in more accessible operating environments such as the Unites States. A late 1999 Andersen Consulting study of e-commerce Web site performance in the United States produced some shocking findings. In the study, 25 Andersen Consulting employees bought 480 gifts from 100 different Web sites to test "e-tailer" (electronic retailer) preparedness. They found that one-quarter of the sites accessed either crashed or were inaccessible, with successful order submission taking nearly twice as long in the morning as in the evening after business hours – a possible sign of mass on-the-job online shopping. The study compared the Web sites of traditional brick-and-mortar companies with those of pure e-tailers, and tested customer service, length of tenure to complete an order, and inventory tracking.

However, the good news is that because the discrepancies between the virtual and physical realities in the supply chain are so great, innovation will be a necessity rather than an option. There is no single right way to do e-fulfillment. Instead, companies will have to develop a model that suits them best. Andersen Consulting sees four direct-to-consumer and two store-based models emerging:

Direct-to-consumer models
- Integrated fulfillment – building e-fulfillment capability into an existing bulk distribution center.
- Dedicated fulfillment – via a purposely-built "green field" operation.
- Outsourced fulfillment – is often faster to set up so is attractive to e-tailers. Many small package carriers and some mail order companies offer some e-fulfillment service capability.
- Drop-ship fulfillment – delegates fulfillment of customer orders to suppliers.

Store-based models
- Store fulfillment – typically by supermarkets, involves fulfilling an electronic order by picking from regular retail shelves for separate, dedicated delivery and provides an opportunity to trial e-commerce.
- Flow-through fulfillment – involves shipping product either to an affiliated store for local delivery or to a designated location for subsequent customer pick-up.

Going beyond the above models, it is likely to see innovative organizational arrangements involving joint ventures between several parties, each bringing unique capabilities to the new organization. For example, the various forms of Fourth Party Logistics™ organization designs defined by Andersen Consulting have the objective of increasing scale, reducing the unit cost of final distribution, and undergoing continuous improvement to the point that a quantum increase in corporate performance is achieved. These various organization forms are especially relevant in an e-fulfillment world, and are already being considered by leading companies in Asia

The Challenge of True Transformation

In many businesses in Asia, a fundamental shift is necessary, away from the operating models that have served their purpose. It is

http://gattorna.ASCET.com

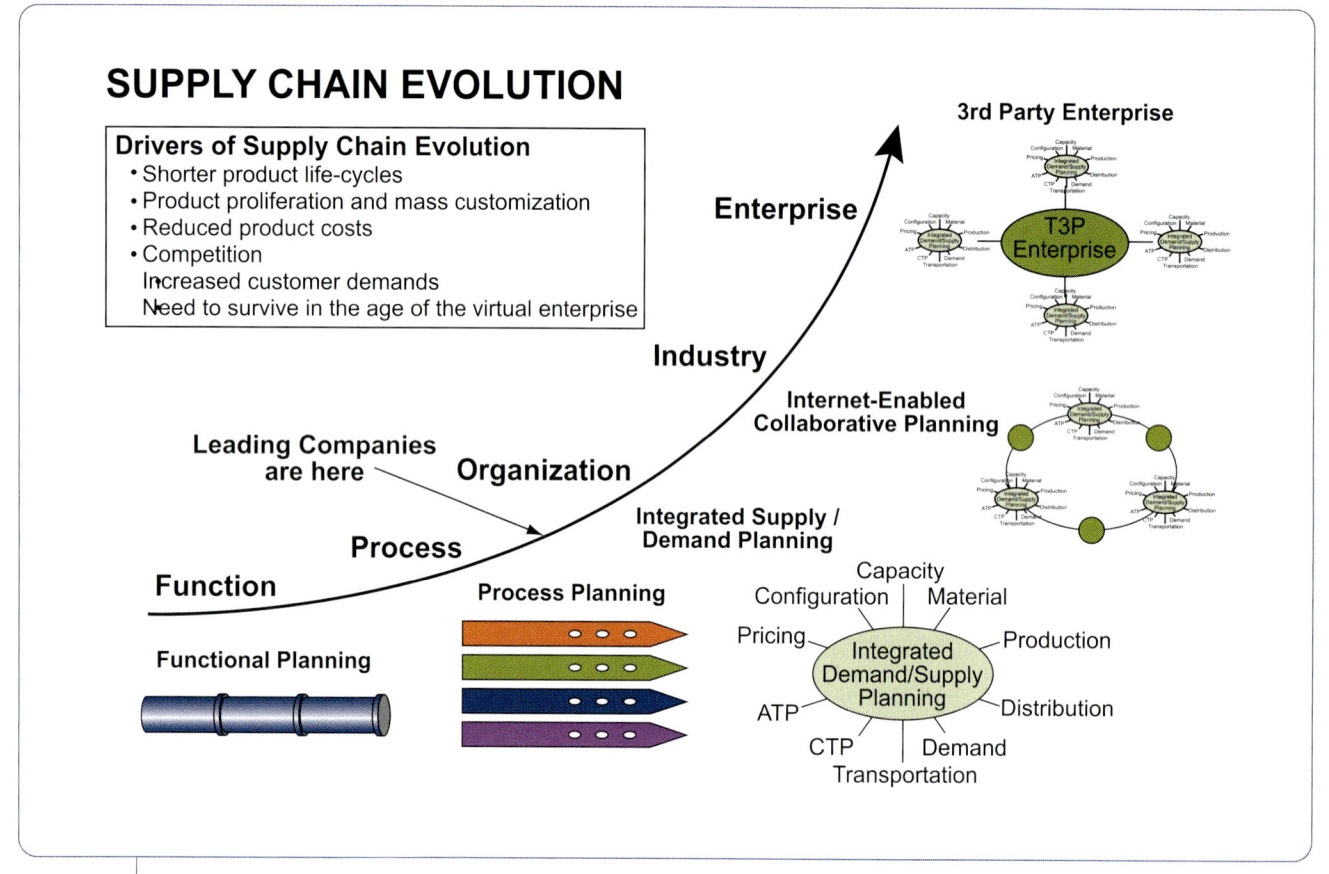

SUPPLY CHAIN EVOLUTION

Drivers of Supply Chain Evolution
- Shorter product life-cycles
- Product proliferation and mass customization
- Reduced product costs
- Competition
  Increased customer demands
  Need to survive in the age of the virtual enterprise

Figure 3.0 — Supply chain evolution

---

to be hoped that Asian management, faced with some real choices as the region emerges from crisis, will opt for innovation and creativity rather than convention and risk aversion. A window of opportunity exists for the first few years of the new millennium to use technology to drive change and transform organizations that take this approach. This means discarding thoughts of simply replacing legacy systems with new systems with similar functionality and only minimal process re-engineering. It means embracing a model that requires fundamental reengineering of the organization's processes, aligned to the chosen strategy. If this approach is adopted, benefits, such as a revenue uplift in the range of five to 10% may be expected, as well as a reduction in cost of goods sold of three to five percent, overhead reduction of three to five percent and inventory reduction of 25 to 50%. This level of improvement will have a dramatic positive value creation impact on the business that will flow through to shareholders.

However, to achieve this type of transformation companies will need to work on a number of vital areas as follows:

- Segment customers based on the service needs of distinct groups, and adapt the supply chain to serve these segments profitably. At the most sophisticated end, conjoint analysis can be used to segment customers based on "buying behaviors," and network models can be used to calculate the cost-to-serve of each segment under varying scenarios.
- Strategic sourcing analyses should be undertaken, followed by the installation of e-procurement software to sustain the savings identified, on an ongoing basis.
- Supply chain planning technology should be implemented — it is the critical link between supply chain strategy and supply chain operations. Software is now available in modular form, covering supply planning, demand planning, and forecasting, finite capacity planning (in the case of manufacturing), production scheduling, distribution planning, and delivery scheduling.

To help in this evolution, third-party logistics providers are working hard to better meet the expectations of the market through the development and provision of new innovative logistics services that go well beyond the traditional transport and warehousing services of the past. Indeed, in some cases third party logistics providers are transforming themselves into Fourth-Party Logistics Providers™ in order to ensure the appropriate capabilities are brought to bear. It could be said that the first decade of the new millennium is the "decade of capabilities," in Asia and across the world, wherever supply chain performance is taken seriously.

Electronics and High-Tech Industries – The Benchmark of Superior Supply Chain Practices

A decade ago – even five years ago – if one were to ask which industry set the benchmark for performance in logistics and supply chain practice, the answer would invariably have been the fast-moving consumer goods industry. This is no longer the case. Many consumer goods companies seemed to lose their way in recent years, seemingly distracted by Y2K issues and correspondingly long periods of systems replacement effort.

High-tech companies such as Nokia, Ericsson, Compaq, Texas Istruments, Gateway, Acer, and Samsung, typically with significant Asian operations, worked to fundamentally re-engineer the way they go to market, and succeeded. So Asian companies looking for role models need look no further than the high-tech companies operating in their own region.

Elsewhere in the world, chemicals companies also have been successful in adopting e-commerce practices to drive their supply chains, but this trend is not yet evident in Asia.

Finally, based on Andersen Consulting's work in the region, several third party logistics providers (all modes) also have been working hard to upgrade their market offerings. In particular, express logistics companies are poised to play an increasing role in delivering e-commerce solutions. Indeed, they are likely to erode the business of more traditional surface transportation companies quite significantly. The demand for definite, reliable movement of goods is increasing rapidly.

Reverse logistics is also a new and growing section of logistics, as customers seek the option of returning goods for repair or exchange. The e-commerce way of doing business online will only accelerate this trend. Since so much merchandise is sourced from Asia in the first place, reverse logistics activity is likely to be very substantial in the region.

The trend of outsourcing logistics solutions in Asia is being led by companies such as Netcell360, the first Pan-Asian provider of total Internet based e-commerce outsourcing solutions. They have formed an alliance with United Parcel Service (and UPS has taken an equity position in Netcell 360), which will provide the logistics capability and global coverage. More of these types of alliance agreements are expected to develop in Asia over the next few years.

So, e-commerce already is substantially influencing business in Asia. However, poor infrastructure and the need for more encouragement remain the two biggest challenges to growing the Internet phenomenon in Asia.

Governments across Asia have committed to promote e-business, but little has been done to ensure that Pan-Asian bandwidth can grow accordingly when e-business becomes mainstream within the next few years.

A Final Word

Asian companies are very much in the first wave of development, seeking operational excellence through improvement in individual elements of the supply chain. The challenge for the more advanced companies is to ratchet up to a whole new level of performance – the second wave – on the back of e-commerce and new organizational combinations, such as e-procurement, e-fulfillment, and shared services that ultimately will lead to the much sought-after Internet-enabled supply chain.

In this regard, the lessons learned – both positive and negative – from experiences elsewhere in the world should be invaluable in accelerating Asian companies toward new levels of competitiveness in the global marketplace.

Copyright©2000 *Andersen Consulting LLP*

Web-Centric Supply Chain Manufacturing Solutions from Datasweep

Contact Information

Vladimir Preysman
CEO/President

Kevin Chao
VP Engineering

Matt Holleran
VP Marketing

Steve Volm
VP Sales

Datasweep, Inc.
55 Almaden Blvd, Suite 600
San Jose, CA 95113
Phone 408.350.7300
Fax 408.275.0225
info@datasweep.com
www.datasweep.com

Datasweep's Advantage is a suite of Web-centric supply chain manufacturing solutions that help manufacturing companies build customized products correctly and track production information throughout the extended manufacturing enterprise. Advantage gives customers, OEMs, and suppliers real-time visibility via a Web browser into unit-level production status and performance metrics on delivery, cycle time, and quality. The Web browser interface also allows for quick and easy changes to design configurations and process flows that can be implemented immediately.

Datasweep provides Web-centric solutions for the full range of production environments from build-to-stock to build-to-order, from vertically integrated to completely outsourced. No other solution offers this level of accuracy, granularity, and efficiency for collecting and using data from manufacturing operations.

Key benefits of the Advantage suite include:

- **E-Business Backend:** Datasweep streamlines communication between customers, OEMs, and suppliers by providing online, real-time order status via a Web browser. Since 30% of all customer service calls are for order status and change orders, substantial savings in sales and customer service time and expense are realized by providing this information online.
- **Visibility:** Real-time manufacturing performance monitoring across lines and plants throughout the supply chain is visible via a Dashboard on an HTML homepage. Real-time alerting features notify the user of out-of-bounds key performance indicators. Drill-down capabilities within the Dashboard provide instantaneous detailed reports from the manufacturing floor.
- **Tracking:** Only Datasweep provides unit-level tracking of "as-built" and "where-used" information including serial numbers, lots, quality tests, operator, machine, and more.
- **Speed:** Advantage provides online, real-time visibility into manufacturing status, enabling quick response to order changes, reducing lead times, and improving on-time delivery.
- **Flexibility:** Electronic travelers give manufacturing engineers the tools and flexibility to quickly revise new products, updating, and storing the as-built information for future use.
- **Collaboration:** Collaboration becomes a multi-way, real-time exchange of information between manufacturer and the extended supply chain via a Web browser.
- **Product Lifecycle Management:** Deep unit-level traceability combined with complex analysis tools deliver data to make informed decisions on product lifecycle and product line lifecycle management.
- **Business Operations Management:** Data on cycle time, cost, and quality from each supply chain partner aids cost-benefit comparisons and management of the extended supply chain.
- **Fast Return on Investment:** Manufacturers realize substantial operational cost savings including cycle time reduction, quality improvement, inventory reduction, and administrative cost savings.
- **Visibility:** Manufacturing performance is monitored across lines and plants throughout the supply chain via a Dashboard. This desktop view immediately alerts the user when key performance limits are crossed.

The company's senior management and developers recognized the need to fill the Web-centric unit-level data gap. Having developed the leading earlier generations of manufacturing execution software, they built the Advantage system by incorporating the most advanced Internet and Web technologies, proven platforms, and powerful database design. Advantage represents their most current thinking about supply chain manufacturing solutions.

Netfish Technologies – Orchestrating Business Process Integration

Netfish Technologies is a leading provider of XML-based, business-to-business (B2B) e-commerce products and solutions that integrate business processes between trading partners or across entire trading communities. The Netfish XDI™ system is the industry's first B2B integration solution that automates complex business processes, such as materials planning and forecasting, resulting in more efficient operations and greatly reduced operating costs.

Netfish customers such as Cisco Systems, MicronPC.com, and the Government's General Services Administration (GSA) are able to save millions of dollars per year by automating procurement, distribution, logistics, and catalogue operations with their business partners. To fully automate and improve these business processes, Netfish provides a seamless solution for integrating business applications and data between companies over the Internet. The Netfish XDI system combines a complete set of application adapters, a robust XML messaging and communication infrastructure, and a powerful workflow and process management engine to create collaborative workflows between organizations and automate cross-enterprise business transactions.

Netfish, however, does not lock users into a particular B2B communication model. Netfish XDI is designed to be a company's all-in-one B2B solution, enabling process integration with both XML-capable partners, as well as EDI-oriented partners. The XDI sysetm creates a single hub within an organization for all types of transactions and workflows. Other solutions require an all-or-nothing approach to XML or other process integration model, limiting trading partner integration.

The Netfish XDI system supports all major B2B industry standards, such as RosettaNet, the BizTalk Framework, commerce XML (cXML), CommerceNet's eCo, and major EDI standards in XML, so it can communicate with any other open B2B XML solution. Common or proprietary software is never needed at either end.

The Netfish system includes the XDI Server, XDI Client and the XDI Developer suite. The XDI Server orchestrates business processes with a multitude of suppliers running the lightweight XDI Client, or other B2B/EDI software. Electronic documents are routed to each trading partner's site for approval, notification, or to update business data in the partner's business system. The Netfish XDI Developer suite converts business documents and data into XML for transacting with business partners.

The Netfish system is a 100% Java™ application, designed for extensibility, scalability, fault-tolerance, and mission-critical failover in a high-volume B2B transaction environment. These benefits translate into a more tightly integrated and automated value-chain, dramatically improving efficiency and reducing operating costs in vital business functions.

Contact Information

Ravi Iyer
CEO

E. Casey Roche
Vice President, Channels

Gene Eubanks
Vice President, Sales

610.205.2915

Netfish Technologies, Corporate Headquarters

2350 Mission College Blvd. #650

Santa Clara, CA 9505

Toll Free 877.NET-FISH

Phone 408.350.9500

Fax 408.350.9501

www.netfish.com

B2E – Leading the E-Economy through Strategic E-Sourcing

Contact Information

Orville Bailey
Co-Founder
President and CEO

Richard Waugh
Co-Founder
Vice President of Marketing

Ronald Holtz
Chief Executive Officer

Andrew McCasker
Vice President of Engineering

Amy Cutlip Cohen
Vice President of Product Management

Shirish Pareek
Vice President of Business Development

B2Emarkets Headquarters
3202 Tower Oaks Blvd
Suite 100
Rockville, MD 20852

Phone 301.230.2236

www.b2emarkets.com

Businesses across the globe are on the brink of a revolutionary, space age opportunity to re-tool their purchasing environments and establish new best practices in Supply Chain Management. In quantum leaps, the Internet – a landmark product of the twentieth century – has evolved as the technological stage on which imagination and enterprise form a creative partnership to advance education, entertainment, communication, commerce, and industry to a sky-high level of functionality and profitability. Leaders of every persuasion log on to this expedient and economical superhighway to command attention, develop and penetrate target markets, and deliver profit.

Now, buyers and suppliers are positioned as the front-line patrons of a breakthrough concept that quickly and easily identifies and channels manufacturing product and service components through a heavily trafficked supply chain. This new era of procurement practices has the combined effect of:

- Expanding the marketplace
- Nurturing competition
- Simplifying supply chain navigation
- Facilitating the sourcing process
- Reducing costs
- Maximizing profits

Industries like the automotive industry embrace a vast network of corporate giants and massive manufacturing bases that rely on complex supply chains. These characteristics readily qualify the automotive industry as the initial target for the multiple benefits of a comprehensive, state-of-the-art cyber-market.

With seasoned experience in developing and providing e-commerce solutions supporting procurement practices for internationally recognized manufacturing companies, a forward-thinking group of supply chain professionals created and introduced the concept of Strategic e-Sourcing Management (SSM). This strategic and far-reaching approach to procurement is a direct response to emerging needs and opportunities. Its implementation is through a dedicated, hosted software solution coupled with business consulting and support services and enabling subscribing buyer organizations to achieve a rapid ROI without impacting internal information technology infrastructures or resources. Suppliers of goods and services simply register at the site at no cost. SSM promotes the strategic application of best-practice sourcing processes, e-commerce technologies, and decision support tools to identify lowest-total-cost trading partners while establishing streamlined supply chain communication links.

The SSM solution, exclusively from B2Emarkets, Inc. (Business to Electronic Markets), provides a private trading community where buyers are able to negotiate and collaborate directly with preferred strategic suppliers. Outside links are also available, which means that buyers have the option to seek alternative potential suppliers, increase trade competition, and develop new sources. B2Emarkets brings the power of strategic negotiations right to the desktop, allowing large organizations to benefit tremendously from electronic negotiations through online sourcing.

While the e-procurement marketplace currently provides solutions that concentrate largely on back-end order management and fulfillment processes through order and track functionality, the SSM solution is uniquely positioned to address the higher value, more strategic source function on the front end of the process.

SSM brings these dominant features to the procurement table:

- Accumulated best practice sourcing expertise delivered to the buyer's desktop
- Enterprise-wide sharing of historical RFX and supplier pricing information

- Dynamic total cost RFX creation/analysis for production and non-production buys
- Flexible e-negotiation (reverse auction and private bid) functionality to achieve the lowest total cost
- Integration with Internet Trading Exchanges (ITE), auction engines, ERP and ORM systems

The Strategic e-Sourcing Management system is a singular solution with a software application that seamlessly blends content, commerce, and community to deliver prototypical and scalable customer benefits.

CONTENT coaches users through the four steps of the proven "Fact-Based Negotiations" (FBN) process.

COMMERCE enables users to quickly analyze and implement process improvements, qualify sources, prepare and electronically distribute Requests for Quote (RFQ), gather and analyze business and market data, negotiate market prices, and promote supply chain collaboration.

COMMUNITY creates Internet-based supplier databases – or "e-communities" – that can be utilized to manage private trading communities and selectively integrate third-party communities to develop new sources.

The SSM solution complements and works in tandem with other e-procurement exchanges. It extends the reach of the procuring enterprise, enabling buying organizations to leverage the emerging Internet exchange "e-economy" through the structured SSM process.

Another feature of SSM is that procurement users will benefit through an interface module to research new sources and deliver RFQs to targeted commodity market exchanges. Buying organizations will be able to institutionalize the best-practice, FBN strategic sourcing process to leverage corporate purchasing power by pooling volume on negotiated contracts and capturing and sharing corporate knowledge generated through the SSM solution. Additionally, a "Bill of Collaborators" module provides for instant and consistent communications across multiple e-community supply chain relationships, which enhances buyer/supplier and supplier/supplier collaboration and reduces the complexity of supply chain coordination.

The SSM solution guides the user, step by step, through the entire process of identifying sources and negotiating contracts from the initial phase of selecting the best supplier – all from a desktop platform. Additionally, the user will have access to all data from prior sourcing searches, ensuring no time is wasted re-entering information. Another benefit is enterprise-wide access to best-practice template RFQs or other related documents to simplify and streamline enterprise-sourcing activities.

www.B2Emarkets.com

The SSM solution is uniquely positioned as an enterprise-class strategic sourcing solution. As of this writing, B2Emarkets, Inc. is poised to launch the SSM product during the first quarter of 2000. B2E's focus on the e-sourcing component of procurement is a key point of differentiation from currently available e-procurement tools, which have limited their processes to facilitating purchasing transactions. The life cycle of traditional purchasing order management includes the functions of requisitioning, ordering, receiving, and paying. B2Emarkets' e-sourcing component extends that functionality by:

- Developing a sourcing strategy
- Creating and distributing RFQs
- Negotiating and executing purchase contracts

The e-sourcing process is supported by Fact-Based Negotiation methodologies:

- Process support
- Recommended actions
- Data gathering support
- Analysis insight
- Conclusion documentation

The e-community component provides an environment where trading partners are electronically enabled to locate and communicate with each other. It includes an e-Collaborate function that provides:

- A database of users and suppliers
- A Bill of Collaborators module for supply chain visibility and instant and consistent communications
- A business locator to categorize goods and services
- A business storefront to showcase individual suppliers

Buyers using SSM to procure goods and services will have access to information on not only their preferred suppliers but can also access third-party sites to research new sources.

Dedicated to virtually every aspect of the procurement process, B2Emarkets' SSM solution provides the most sophisticated, full-service strategic sourcing system in the developing e-economy. It is where supply chain leaders strike the best deals and put orders for goods and services into motion. It is the Harvard for RFX management – the desktop tool for assessing supplier capabilities, conducting secure, private, or open market negotiations, efficiently analyzing competitive bids, and awarding business based on true market prices. Its value-added features encourage an exchange of strategic best practices, share trends and analyses, and facilitate industry-wide communications. The B2E solution increases user efficiency through a template-driven, easy-to-use interface that guides the procurement professional through the entire sourcing process, significantly reducing acquisition cycle time and complexity. Far from the boutique approach of its predecessors, B2Emarkets' SSM solution is truly a comprehensive, expert system for supply chain management specialists.

The SSM solution uses industry standards such as Extensible Markup Language (XML) and deploys technology components such as the BEA WebLogics application and Oracle database. The WebLogics Application server is leveraged in the e-sourcing architecture to facilitate the use of Java Server pages to enhance systems performance, scalability, and availability. Moreover, the Remote Method Invocation (RMI) pooling functionality greatly reduces the socket utilization during RMI calls, which dramatically improves application performance.

Glossary of Acronyms

3PL	Third-Party Logistics
4PL	Fourth-Party Logistics (Andersen Consulting)
ABC	Activity-Based Costing
ABC-M	Activity-Based Cost Management
ACM	Advanced Customer Management
AIDC	Automatic Identification and Data Collection
AIM	Automatic Identification Manufacturing
APS	Advanced Planning and Scheduling
ASICS	Application-Specific Integrated Circuits
ASN	Advanced Shipping Notice
B2B	Business-to-Business
B2C	Business-to-Consumer
BOM	Bill of Materials
BPM	Best Practice Management
CORBA	Common Object Request Broker Architecture
CPFR	Collaborative Planning, Forecasting and Replenishment
CPG	Consumer Packaged Goods
CRM	Customer Relationship Management
CRP	Continuous Replenishment Programs
CTP	Capable to Promise
DRAM	Dynamic Random Access Memory
ECR	Efficient Consumer Response
EDI	Electronic Data Interchange
E-HR	Electronic Human Resources
EPS	Earnings Per Share
ERP	Enterprise Resource Planning
EVA	Economic Value Analysis
FBN	Fact-Based Negotiation
FCPG	Food and Consumer Packaged Goods
FMS	Freight Management Systems
GUI	Graphical User Interface
IES	Inter-Enterprise Solutions
ISV	Industrial Software Vendors
ITE	Internet Trading Association
JIT	Just In Time

KPI	Key Performance Indicators
LLS	Lead Logistics Supplier
LTL	Less Than Truckload
MRO	Maintenance Repair and Operations
NAPM	National Association of Purchasing Management
OBI	Open Buying on the Internet
OLAP	Online Analytical Processing
OMG	Object Management Group
ORM	Operating Resource Management
PLM	Product Life Cycle Management
POS	Point Of Sale
RFID	Radio Frequency Identification
RFQ	Request for Quote
RFX	Refrigerated Food Express
RMI	Remote Method Invocation
ROACE	Return On Average Capital Employed
RPS	Reliable Planning and Scheduling
SBT	Scan-Based Training
SCE	Supply Chain Execution
SCM	Supply Chain Management
SCVA	Supply Chain Value Assessment
SKU	Stock Keeping Units
SRM	Supplier Relationship Management
SSM	Strategic E-Sourcing Management
TCO	Total Cost of Ownership
TL	Truck Load
TMS	Transportation Management Systems
UCC	Uniform Code Council
VAN	Value-Added Networks
VICS	Voluntary Interindustry Commerce Standard
VMI	Vendor-Managed Inventory
VPN	Virtual Private Networks
WAN	Wide Area Network
WMS	Warehouse Management Systems
XML	Extensible Markup Language

http://acronyms.ASCET.com

Index

Author/Company	Project URL	Page Number
Agile Software	http://agile.ASCET.com	144
Albright, Paul	http://albright.ASCET.com	299
Anderson, David L.	http://anderson-d.ASCET.com	15
Anderson, Gordon	http://anderson-g.ASCET.com	101
Anthony, Tom	http://anthony.ASCET.com	41
Appell, Kyle	http://appell.ASCET.com	83
Aspect Development	http://aspect.ASCET.com	57
Aspen Technology	http://aspen.ASCET.com	189
B2Emarkets	http://b2e.ASCET.com	342
Benitez, Jorge	http://benitez.ASCET.com	179
Berger, Andrew	http://berger.ASCET.com	283
Billington, Corey	http://billington.ASCET.com	223
Bradley, Peter	http://quinn-f.ASCET.com	77
Brousseau, Christopher	http://appell.ASCET.com	83
Calico Commerce	http://calico.ASCET.com	170
Cameron, Brett	http://hill.ASCET.com	269
Categoric	http://categoric.ASCET.com	178
Cavander, David	http://cavander.ASCET.com	263
Chang, Min	http://chang.ASCET.com	203
ChemConnect	http://chemconnect.ASCET.com	177
Cognos	http://cognos.ASCET.com	282
Cokins, Gary	http://cokins.ASCET.com	303
Commerce One	http://commerceone.ASCET.com	128
Compaq	http://compaq.ASCET.com	218
Concentus	http://concentus.ASCET.com	119
Cudahy, Greg	http://sutula.ASCET.com	241
Culotta, Ted	http://culotta.ASCET.com	139
Datamax	http://datamax.ASCET.com	268
Datasweep	http://datasweep.ASCET.com	340
Descartes	http://descartes.ASCET.com	258
Dik, Roger	http://marvick.ASCET.com	197
Dobrin, David	http://dobrin.ASCET.com	95
DuBose, David S.	http://hurley.ASCET.com	167
Eichmann, Don	http://eichmann.ASCET.com	229
Enslow, Beth	http://enslow.ASCET.com	251
Essentus	http://essentus.ASCET.com	190
E-Transport	http://etransport.ASCET.com	261
Evans, Bob	http://evans.ASCET.com	55
Fasturn	http://fasturn.ASCET.com	273
Findlay, Charles	http://findlay.ASCET.com	325

Author/Company	Project URL	Page Number
Fischer, Dave	http://fischer.ASCET.com	133
Fitzgerald, Kevin R.	http://quinn-f.ASCET.com	77
Fontanella, John	http://fontanella.ASCET.com	313
Fourth Shift	http://fourthshift.ASCET.com	161
Frey, Mike	http://frey.ASCET.com	237
Gattorna, John	http://gattorna.ASCET.com	335
Genereaux, Mark	http://genereaux.ASCET.com	235
Gordon, Bruce	http://benitez.ASCET.com	179
Grimm, Douglas A.	http://smith.ASCET.com	175
Herbold, Bob	http://herbold.ASCET.com	21
Hewlett-Packard	http://hp.ASCET.com	227
Hicks, Donald A.	http://hicks.ASCET.com	147
Hill, John M.	http://hill.ASCET.com	269
Hurley, Mark A.	http://hurley.ASCET.com	167
i2 Technologies	http://i2technologies.ASCET.com	151
Industri-Matematik International	http://imi.ASCET.com	143
Informix	http://informix.ASCET.com	130
Intrepa	http://intrepa.ASCET.com	162
Iron Mountain	http://ironmountain.ASCET.com	100
Jennings, Barry	http://jennings.ASCET.com	233
Johnson, Eric	http://johnson.ASCET.com	37
Kavanaugh, Kevin	http://kavanaugh.ASCET.com	279
Keystone Internet Services	http://keystone.ASCET.com	261
Kinsella, Bret	http://sprague.ASCET.com	61
Kuper, André	http://billington.ASCET.com	223
Lapide, Larry	http://lapide.ASCET.com	287
Lawson Software	http://lawson.ASCET.com	116
Lee, Dr. Hau	http://anderson-d.ASCET.com	15
Lescher, Fritz	http://lescher.ASCET.com	183
Lidow, Derek	http://lidow.ASCET.com	221
Logility	http://logility.ASCET.com	146
Mann, Robert	http://mann.ASCET.com	247
Manugistics	http://manugistics.ASCET.com	48
Martella, Ben	http://martella.ASCET.com	109
Marvick, Duane	http://marvick.ASCET.com	197
Matthews, Paul	http://kavanaugh.ASCET.com	279
Miller, Jeff	http://miller.ASCET.com	301
Moai	http://moai.ASCET.com	92
Moakley, George	http://moakley.ASCET.com	213
Moore, Peter	http://moore.ASCET.com	69
Mordia, David	http://chang.ASCET.com	203
Mulani, Narendra	http://mulani.ASCET.com	323
NEON (New Era of Networks)	http://neon.ASCET.com	274

Author/Company	Project URL	Page Number
Netfish	http://netfish.ASCET.com	341
NONSTOP Solutions	http://nonstop.ASCET.com	208
Optum	http://optum.ASCET.com	94
Pandesic	http://pandesic.ASCET.com	216
PeopleSoft	http://peoplesoft.ASCET.com	45
Peregrine Systems	http://peregrine.ASCET.com	24
Peters, Melvyn	http://peters.ASCET.com	171
Preview Systems	http://preview.ASCET.com	239
Prince, Ted	http://prince.ASCET.com	163
Princi, Michael	http://walton.ASCET.com	191
Prologis	http://prologis.ASCET.com	81
PurchaseSoft	http://purchasesoft.ASCET.com	330
Quinn, Chad	http://quinn-c.ASCET.com	51
Quinn, Francis	http://quinn-f.ASCET.com	77
Ramanathan, Jay	http://ramanathan.ASCET.com	117
Reiter, Steve	http://reiter.ASCET.com	121
Retek, Inc.	http://retek.ASCET.com	31
Robocom	http://robocom.ASCET.com	298
SAP America	http://sap.ASCET.com	106
Smith, Kenneth M.	http://smith.ASCET.com	175
Sprague, Christopher	http://sprague.ASCET.com	61
Sterling Commerce	http://sterling.ASCET.com	206
Stimson, Judith	http://stimson.ASCET.com	331
Sutula, Gary	http://sutula.ASCET.com	241
Sweeney, Michael S.	http://smith.ASCET.com	175
TECSYS, Inc.	http://tecsys.ASCET.com	228
Teklogix	http://teklogix.ASCET.com	74
Tibco	http://tibco.ASCET.com	76
Trimarco, Charles	http://jennings.ASCET.com	233
Trimmer, Jeff	http://trimmer.ASCET.com	157
Uchneat, Jim	http://uchneat.ASCET.com	209
Uniteq	http://uniteq.ASCET.com	196
Verano	http://verano.ASCET.com	114
viaLink	http://vialink.ASCET.com	58
Viewlocity	http://viewlocity.ASCET.com	98
Walker	http://walker.ASCET.com	68
Walton, Bruce	http://walton.ASCET.com	191
Wayman, Bob	http://wayman.ASCET.com	27
webPLAN	http://webplan.ASCET.com	312
Wimer, Paul	http://wimer.ASCET.com	327
Zimdars, Leroy	http://zimdars.ASCET.com	159

ASCET Solutions Matrix

Company	Description	Company URL	Page Number
Agile Software	Agile Anywhere™ product suite allows supply chain partners to form virtual manufacturing networks for product introduction, manufacture, and change. Agile Buyer™ enables online procurement of direct materials, demand aggregation, and automated Web-based RFQ processes.	www.agilesoft.com	144
Aspect Development	Aspect Development, Inc. is the leading global provider of business-to-business e-commerce solutions for inbound supply and collaboration, for the enterprise and its trading partners.	www.aspectdv.com	57
Aspen Technology	Aspen Technology, Inc. is the leading supplier of integrated software and solutions that enable process manufacturers to automate and optimize their plants and extended supply chains.	www.aspentech.com	189
Calico Commerce	Calico provides sell-side e-commerce software that enables direct sales over the Internet.	www.calico.com	170
Categoric	Categoric Software Corporation provides proactive business event notification systems for supply chain collaboration by addressing the challenge of identifying key business events as they occur and notifying specific individuals of those events.	www.categoric.com	178
ChemConnect	ChemConnect is one of the Internet's leading global electronic marketplaces for chemicals and plastics. Manufacturers, buyers, and intermediaries around the world use ChemConnect's World Chemical Exchange to find trading partners, negotiate pricing, and complete transactions online.	www.chemconnect.com	177
Cognos	Understand how you can gain a complete view of your supply chain and share information with your suppliers with Cognos Enterprise Business Intelligence.	www.cognos.com	282
Commerce One	Commerce One is the leader in global e-commerce solutions for business. Through its products, portals, and services, Commerce One creates access to worldwide markets, allowing anyone to buy from anyone, anytime, anywhere.	www.commerceone.com	128
Compaq	Compaq Computer Corporation leads customers through the challenges and opportunities of SCM and beyond by delivering dependable IT solutions that leverage and transform enterprise computing into a strategic business advantage.	www.compaq.com/services	218
Concentus	Concentus Technology Corporation delivers process-driven B2B solutions that speed to market any e-business strategy.	www.concentus-tech.com	119
Datamax	Datamax designs and manufactures one of the bar code industry's broadest lines of thermal printers, offering printers in each of the low, mid, and high performance and specialty segments of the thermal bar code printer market.	www.datamaxcorp.com	268
Datasweep	Datasweep provides Web-centric solutions for the full range of production environments from build-to-stock to build-to-order, from vertically integrated to completely outsourced.	www.datasweep.com	340
Descartes Systems	Descartes is the global leader in e-fulfillment software and hosted application services, providing solutions that enable companies to re-invent logistics flows, creating high-speed, high-performance fulfillment networks.	www.descartes.com	258
Essentus	Essentus, formerly Richter Systems, delivers business-to-business commerce software solutions and business improvement processes designed to create value for retailers and manufacturers in the softgoods supply chain.	www.essentus.com	190
E-Transport	E-Transport is the leader in e-commerce and software solutions for handling back-office operations in the freight transportation industry. We link manufacturers, suppliers, intermediaries, and cargo carriers in a single, integrated exchange called the E-Transport Marketplace.	www.etransport.com	261
Fasturn	Fasturn will be the first online trading community to incorporate the clear advantage of Supply Chain Management technology. This technology converts the often complex and opaque procurement chain into a private glass pipeline, where every order has real-time online tracking.	www.fasturn.com	273
Fourth Shift	Fourth Shift designs, develops, markets, and supports fully integrated e-business enterprise applications for global manufacturing, distribution, customer relationship, and financial management. Fourth Shift provides integrated services creating unique solutions for business issues.	www.fourthshift.com	161
Hewlett-Packard	HP is further strengthening the infrastructure through e-services that enable dynamic interaction of assets available on the Internet.	www.hp.com	223
Industri-Matematik International	Industri-Matematik International provides advanced Supply Chain Management solutions that enable companies to manage the complex logistics and service challenges in pull-driven business environments.	www.im.se	143
Informix	Informix specializes in advanced information management technologies that promote Web-optimized infrastructure that delivers highly scalable transaction processing, personalized content management, integrated business intelligence, full multimedia capabilities, and complete-commerce solutions.	www.informix.com	130
Intrepa	Intrepa is a leading provider of supply chain applications focused on delivering warehouse, transportation, and labor management applications.	www.intrepa.com	162
Iron Mountain	Iron Mountain is global leader in records and information management services.	www.ironmountain.com	100
i2	i2, the world's leading Marketplace Service Provider, deploys B2B and B2C electronic marketplaces.	www.i2.com	151

Company	Description	Company URL	Page Number
Keystone Fulfillment	Keystone Internet Services is the recognized leader in providing full-service quality solutions to the e-commerce world, providing innovative logistics solutions, integrated marketing, merchandising, inventory control, and e-care/customer services.	www.keystoneinternet.com	262
Lawson Software	Lawson Software is a leading provider of Self-Evident Applications™ (SEA) for e-business and offers role-based Web solutions for financials, human resources, procurement, supply chain, and performance management.	www.lawson.com	116
Logility	The leading supplier of business-to-business collaborative value chain solutions via the Internet, Logility is a driving force in transforming the way companies conduct business.	www.logility.com	146
Manugistics	Manugistics Group, Inc. is the leading provider of e-business solutions that enable intelligent decisions across trading networks.	www.manugistics.com	48
Moai	Moai is the leading provider of negotiated e-commerce solutions addressing the needs of global 2000 and net market-maker customers.	www.moai.com	92
Netfish	Netfish provides an XML-based B2B solution to integrate business processes across corporate boundaries.	www.netfish.com	341
NEON	New Era of Networks, Inc. (NEON) develops and markets e-business integration software that integrate legacy, ERP, client/server, and Internet applications, in real-time, for the extended business enterprise.	www.neonsoft.com	274
NONSTOP Solutions	NONSTOP Solutions is the first business-to-business electronic replenishment company. Their Internet-based products and services optimize replenishment transactions for core finished goods for the pharmaceutical, auto parts, grocery, and retail industries.	www.nonstop.com	208
Optum	Optum is a leading provider of configurable end-to-end fulfillment solutions for traditional and e-commerce companies that combine robust products with consulting services to bring clients the comprehensive fulfillment solution they need.	www.optum.com	94
Pandesic	Pandesic seamlessly automates the business processes that occur both before and after a purchase is made – customer acquisition, Web cataloging, order processing, pick/pack/shipping, returns processing, procurement, accounting, reporting, and more.	www.pandesic.com	216
PeopleSoft	PeopleSoft Supply Chain Management leverages Internet technologies to break down traditional barriers between manufacturers, distributors, retailers, and the consumer.	www.peoplesoft.com	45
Peregrine Systems	Peregrine Systems is the leading provider of Employee Self Service and e-Infrastructure Management solutions that help ensure the reliability, productivity, and cost-effectiveness of organizational infrastructure.	www.peregrine.com	24
Preview Systems	Preview Systems develops and markets an e-commerce infrastructure solution that enables networks to electronically distribute and license digital goods.	www.previewsystems.com	239
Prologis	ProLogis is the largest global owner and operator of integrated distribution facilities and services with over 1.7 million square feet of facilities owned and operating throughout North America and Europe.	www.prologis.com	81
PurchaseSoft	PurchaseSoft B2B e-commerce solutions help reap fast ROI and achieve operational efficiencies.	www.purchasesoft.com	330
Retek, Inc.	retail.com solutions, powered by Retek, are designed to improve core retail processes – from assortment development and merchandise planning to sourcing, purchasing, P.O. tracking, store openings, and promotions – by linking retailers and trading partners together through the Web.	www.retek.com	31
Robocom	Robocom's RIMS warehouse management system is an essential part of today's warehouse, improving the flow of critical information and optimizing the use of all warehouse assets.	www.robocom.com	298
SAP America	As the market leader of inter-enterprise software solutions, SAP™ delivers mySAP.com™. mySAP.com provides an open collaborative business environment of personalized solutions on demand. This enables companies of all sizes and industries to fully engage their employees, customers, and partners.	www.sap.com	106
Sterling Commerce	Sterling Commerce is a worldwide leader in providing e-business integration solutions for the Global 5000 and their commerce communities, including solutions to address E-Business Process Integration, E-Community Management, E-Business Communications Infrastructure, and E-Sourcing.	www.sterlingcommerce.com	206
TECSYS, Inc.	TECSYS is the sole provider of fully integrated business-to-business e-commerce-based order fulfillment solutions for high-volume distribution enterprises.	www.tecsys.com	228
Teklogix	Teklogix is a global provider of real-time data collection and communications solutions that facilitate the flow of critical, real-time information for supply chain and logistics management.	www.teklogix.com	74
TIBCO	TIBCO Software Inc. is a leading provider of real-time infrastructure software for the Internet and enterprise that enables business to dynamically link internal operations, business partners, and customer channels.	www.tibco.com	76
Uniteq	Uniteq is a leading provider of supply chain execution software and e-process applications, focusing on the consumer products industry with particular emphasis on wholesale and retail food and drug/pharmaceutical segments.	www.uniteq.com	196
Verano	Verano's Iluminar™ Supply Chain Portal suite enables businesses to realize competitive advantage by synchronizing the activities of suppliers and other partners over the Internet.	www.verano.com	114
viaLink	viaLink enables trading partners to exchange product, price & promotion data through an Internet-based, synchronized database.	www.vialink.com	58
Viewlocity	Viewlocity products and services enable customers to obtain a higher return on assets (ROA) through increased visibility and synchronization across extended supply chain operations.	www.viewlocity.com	98
Walker	Walker's e-business solutions for the enterprise are utilized by Fortune 1000 organizations in industries including banking and financial services, retail, transportation, and utilities.	www.walker.com	68
webPLAN	webPLAN is the only complete, end-to-end, high-velocity e-business platform for manufacturers. Its web applications transform your supply chain into a strategic weapon. webPLAN creates a secure Internet community where manufacturers, suppliers and customers can conduct business in real-time.	www.webplan.com	312